One-Stop Internet Resources

Log on to ca.hss.glencoe.com

ONLINE STUDY TOOLS

- Study Central
- Chapter Overviews
- ePuzzles and Games
- Self-Check Quizzes
- Vocabulary e-Flashcards
- Multi-Language Glossaries

ONLINE RESEARCH

- Student Web Activities
- Web Resources
- Current Events
- State Resources
- Beyond the Textbook Features

FOR TEACHERS

- Teacher Forum
- Web Activity Lesson Plans

**Also Featuring a Complete Interactive Student Edition*

Discovering Our Past

The American Journey

To World War I

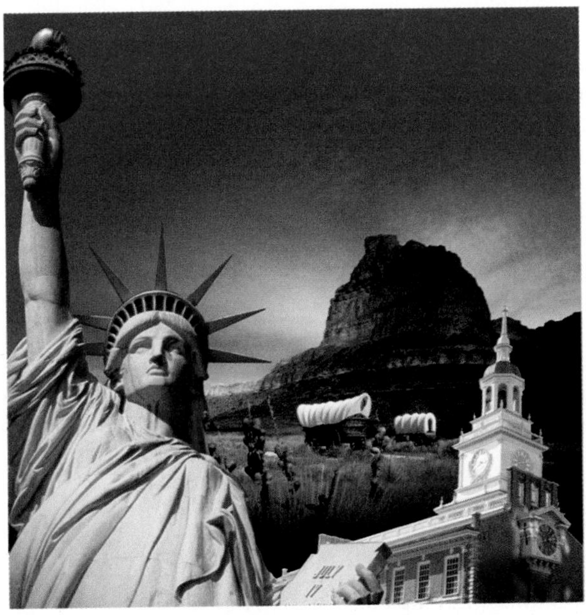

Joyce Appleby, Ph.D. ■ Alan Brinkley, Ph.D. ■ Albert S. Broussard, Ph.D.
James M. McPherson, Ph.D. ■ Donald A. Ritchie, Ph.D.

NATIONAL GEOGRAPHIC

McGraw Hill Glencoe

New York, New York Columbus, Ohio Chicago, Illinois Peoria, Illinois Woodland Hills, California

Authors

Joyce Appleby, Ph.D. is Professor of History at UCLA. Dr. Appleby's published works include *Inheriting the Revolution: The First Generation of Americans; Capitalism and a New Social Order: The Jeffersonian Vision of the 1790s;* and *Ideology and Economic Thought in Seventeenth-Century England,* which won the Berkshire Prize. She served as president of both the Organization of American Historians and the American Historical Association, and chaired the Council of the Institute of Early American History and Culture at Williamsburg. Dr. Appleby has been elected to the American Philosophical Society and the American Academy of Arts and Sciences, and is a Corresponding Fellow of the British Academy.

Alan Brinkley, Ph.D., is University Provost and Allan Nevins Professor of History at Columbia University. His published works include *Voices of Protest: Huey Long, Father Coughlin, and the Great Depression,* which won the 1983 National Book Award; *The End of Reform: New Deal Liberalism in Recession and War; The Unfinished Nation: A Concise History of the American People;* and *Liberalism and its Discontents.* He received the Levenson Memorial Teaching Prize at Harvard University.

Albert S. Broussard, Ph.D., is Professor of history at Texas A&M University. Before joining the Texas A&M faculty, Dr. Broussard was Assistant Professor of History and Director of the African American Studies Program at Southern Methodist University. Among his publications are the books *Black San Francisco: The Struggle for Racial Equality in the West, 1900–1954* and *African American Odyssey: The Stewarts, 1853–1963*. Dr. Broussard has also served as president of the Oral History Association, has chaired the nominating committee of the Organization of American Historians, was the Texas A&M University Distinguished Lecturer for 1999–2000, and received a distinguished teaching award from the College of Liberal Arts.

About the Cover: The images on the cover are: the Statue of Liberty, covered wagons beneath Eagle Rock at the Scotts Bluff National Monument in Nebraska, and Independence Hall in Philadelphia.

James M. McPherson, Ph.D. is George Henry Davis Professor Emeritus of American History at Princeton University. Dr. McPherson is the author of 13 books about the Civil War era. These include *Battle Cry of Freedom: The Civil War Era,* for which he won the Pulitzer Prize in 1989, and *For Cause and Comrades: Why Men Fought in the Civil War,* for which he won the 1998 Lincoln Prize. He is a member of many professional historical associations, including the Civil War Preservation Trust.

Donald A. Ritchie, Ph.D., is Associate Historian of the United States Senate Historical Office. Dr. Ritchie received his doctorate in American history from the University of Maryland after service in the U.S. Marine Corps. He has taught American history at various levels, from high school to university. He edited the Executive Sessions of the Senate Permanent Subcommittee on Investigations (the McCarthy hearings) and is the author of several books, including *Doing Oral History; Reporting From Washington: The History of the Washington Press Corps;* and *Press Gallery: Congress and the Washington Correspondents*, which received the Organization of American Historians Richard W. Leopold Prize. Dr. Ritchie has served as president of the Oral History Association and as a council member of the American Historical Association.

The National Geographic Society, founded in 1888 for the increase and diffusion of geographic knowledge, is the world's largest nonprofit scientific and educational organization. Since its earliest days, the Society has used sophisticated communication technologies, from color photography to holography, to convey knowledge to a worldwide membership. The School Publishing Division supports the Society's mission by developing innovative educational programs—ranging from traditional print materials to multimedia programs including CD-ROMs, videodiscs, and software. "National Geographic Geography & History," featured in each unit of this textbook, was designed and developed by the National Geographic Society's School Publishing Division.

Glencoe

The McGraw·Hill Companies

Send all inquiries to:
Glencoe/McGraw-Hill, 8787 Orion Place, Columbus, Ohio 43240–4027

ISBN 0-07-869386-1 (Student Edition)
Printed in the United States of America.
5 6 7 8 027/043 12 11 10 09 08 07

Contributing Authors, Consultants, & Reviewers

Contributing Authors

Stephen F. Cunha, Ph.D.
Professor of Geography
Director, California Geographic Alliance
Humboldt State University
Arcata, California

Douglas Fisher, Ph.D.
Professor
San Diego State University
San Diego, California

Nancy Frey, Ph.D.
Assistant Professor
San Diego State University
San Diego, California

Robin C. Scarcella, Ph.D.
Professor and Director
Academic English/ESL
University of California, Irvine
Irvine, California

Emily M. Schell, Ed.D.
Visiting Professor, San Diego State University
Social Studies Education Director
SDSU City Heights Educational Collaborative
San Diego, California

David Vigilante
Associate Director
National Center for History in the Schools
San Diego, California

Ruben Zepeda II, Ed.D.
Adviser, Instructional Support Services
Los Angeles Unified School District
Los Angeles, California

Academic Consultants

Richard G. Boehm, Ph.D.
Professor of Geography
Southwest Texas State University
San Marcos, Texas

Margo J. Byerly, Ph.D.
Assistant Professor of Social Studies Methods
Ball State University
Muncie, Indiana

Maureen D. Danner
Project CRISS
National Training Consultant
Kalispell, Montana

Frank de Varona
Visiting Associate Professor
Department of Curriculum and Instruction
Florida International University
Miami, Florida

Barbara S. Lindemann, Ph.D.
Professor of History and Ethnic Studies
History Department Chair
Santa Barbara City College
Santa Barbara, California

William E. Nelson, Jr., Ph.D.
Research Professor of Black Studies and Professor of Political Science
The Ohio State University
Columbus, Ohio

Bernard Reich, Ph.D.
Professor of Political Science and International Affairs
George Washington University
Washington, D.C.

Donald A. Ritchie, Ph.D.
Associate Historian of the United States Senate Historical Office
Washington, D.C.

Carol M. Santa, Ph.D.
Director of Education
Montana Academy
CRISS Project Developer
Kalispell, Montana

Elmer Whitcraft
Project CRISS Master Trainer
Kalispell, Montana

FOLDABLES **Dinah Zike**
Educational Consultant
Dinah-Might Activities, Inc.
San Antonio, Texas

Reading Consultants

Maureen D. Danner
Project CRISS
National Training Consultant
Kalispell, Montana

ReLeah Cossett Lent
Florida Literacy and Reading Excellence Project Coordinator
University of Central Florida
Orlando, Florida

Steve Qunell
Social Studies Instructor
Montana Academy
Kalispell, Montana

Carol M. Santa, Ph.D.
CRISS: Project Developer
Director of Education
Montana Academy
Kalispell, Montana

Bonnie Valdes
Project CRISS, Master Trainer
Largo, Florida

Teacher Reviewers

Tabitha Barry
Diegueño Middle School
Encinitas, California

Patrick Bernhardt
John Muir Middle School
San Jose, California

Jennifer Dunlap
Vail Ranch Middle School
Temecula, California

Rob Gaudette
Dale Junior High School
Anaheim, California

Tiffany Gretton
C.A. Jacobs Intermediate
Dixon, California

Brent E. Heath, Ph.D.
De Anza Middle School
Ontario, California

Wayne Osako
Haskell Middle School
Cerritos, California

Andrew Wagoner
Coalinga Middle School
Coalinga, California

California Advisory Board

Helen Ligh
Social Studies and Language Arts Teacher
Macy Intermediate
Montebello Unified School District
Monterey Park, CA

Barbara S. Lindemann, Ph.D.
Professor of History and Ethnic Studies
History Department Chair
Santa Barbara City College
Santa Barbara, CA

Reynaldo Antonio Macías
World History Teacher
Mark Twain Middle School
Los Angeles Unified School District
Los Angeles, CA

Jennifer Metherd
Program Coordinator
Tehama County Department of Education
Red Bluff, CA

Derrick K. Neal
Social Studies Department Chair
Patrick Henry Middle School
Los Angeles Unified School District
Los Angeles, CA

Robin C. Scarcella, Ph.D.
Professor and Director
Academic English/ESL
University of California, Irvine
Irvine, CA

Emily M. Schell, Ed.D.
Visiting Professor, San Diego State University
Social Studies Education Director
SDSU City Heights Educational Collaborative
San Diego, CA

Dale Steiner, Ph.D.
Professor of History
California State University, Chico
Chico, CA

Roy Sunada
Social Studies Teacher/AP Coordinator
Marshall Fundamental Secondary School
Pasadena Unified School District
Pasadena, CA

David Vigilante
Associate Director
National Center for History in the Schools
San Diego, CA

Ruben Zepeda II, Ed.D.
Adviser, Instructional Support Services
Los Angeles Unified School District
Los Angeles, CA

Contents

▼ The Golden Gate Bridge

Revolutionary War drum and fife ▶

Preparing the Declaration of Independence ▼

Contents

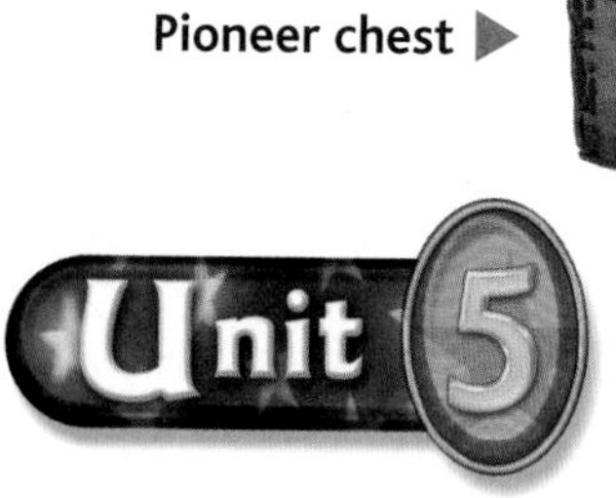

Pioneer chest

Civil War cannon

Appendix

1912 Model T Ford ▲

Features

Analyzing Primary Sources

Biography

TECHNOLOGY & History

◀ Abigail Adams

Frederick Douglass ▶

America's Literature

Why It Matters

Features

History Makers

TIME Notebook

▼ Molly Pitcher at the Battle of Monmouth

More About...

The Way It Was

Linking Past & Present

You Decide . . .

▼ Immigrant children learn American ways in the classroom.

SkillBuilder Handbook

Connecting to the Constitution

NATIONAL GEOGRAPHIC Geography & History

What If...

Maps, Charts, and Graphs

Maps

NATIONAL GEOGRAPHIC Reference Atlas Maps

NATIONAL GEOGRAPHIC Geography Handbook

Tools of the Historian

Unit 1

Unit 2

Unit 3

Unit 4

Unit 5

Unit 6

Charts and Graphs

The Federal System

National Government	National & State Governments	State Governments
Enumerated Powers	**Concurrent Powers**	**Reserved Powers**
• Regulate trade	• Enforce the laws	• Regulate trade within the state
• Coin money	• Establish courts	• Establish local government systems
• Provide an army and navy	• Collect taxes	• Conduct elections
• Conduct foreign affairs	• Borrow money	• Establish public school systems
• Set up federal courts	• Provide for the general welfare	

Primary Source Quotes

Chapter 1

Chapter 2

Chapter 3

Chapter 4

Chapter 5

Primary Source Quotes

Chapter 6

Chapter 7

Chapter 8

CHAPTER 9

CHAPTER 10

CHAPTER 11

Primary Source Quotes

Chapter 12

William Lloyd Garrison. "For Immediate Action." In *The Annals of America, V5, 1821–1832, Steps Toward Equalitarianism.* (Chicago: Encyclopaedia Britannica, Inc., 1968). 562

"Swing Low, Sweet Chariot." In *A Collection of 25 Selected Famous Negro Spirituals.* Ed. Hugo Frey. (Miami, Fla.: Warner Bros., 1999). 563

Mrs. Eugene McLean. *The Women's War in the South.* Ed. Chalres G. Waugh and Martin H. Greenberg. (Nashville: Cumberland House, 1999). 563

Chapter 13

Captain D. P. Conyngham. In *A Civil War Treasury of Tales, Legends and Folklore.* Ed. B.A. Botkin. (New York: Random House, 1960). 571

William T. Sherman. http://library.thinkquest.org/3055/netscape/people/sherman.html 575

Mary Ward. In *Voices of the Civil War.* Richard Wheeler. (New York: Thomas Y. Crowell Company, 1976). 577

Samuel J. English. Letter to his mother, July 1861. http://www.eyewitnesstohistory.com/pfbullrun.htm 577

Ulysses Grant. In *Voices of the Civil War.* Richard Wheeler. (New York: Thomas Y. Crowell Company, 1976). 579

Joseph Hooker. From The Eyewitness to the Battle of Antietam. http://www.nps.gov/anti/eyewitness.htm 582

Harold Keith. *Rifles for Watie.* (New York: Thomas Y. Crowell Company, 1957). 584

Abraham Lincoln. From *Lincoln.* David Herbert Donald. (New York: Simon & Schuster, 1995). 592

Abraham Lincoln. Letter to Horace Greeley, August 22, 1862. *Letters of a Nation: A Collection of Extraordinary American Letters.* Ed. Andrew Carroll. (New York: Kodansha International, 1997). 593

Abraham Lincoln. Cabinet Meeting: September 22, 1862. In *Diary and Correspondence of Salmon P. Chase.* Salmon P. Chase. (New York: Da Capo Press, 1971). 594

Emancipation Proclamation, January 1, 1863. From the National Archives and Records Administration. http://www.ourdocuments.gov/
Select: 100 Milestone Documents 594

Mary Chesnut's Civil War. Ed. C. Vann Woodward. (New Haven: Yale University Press, 1981). 599

Abraham Lincoln. Letter to Erastus Corning and Others, June 1863. *Abraham Lincoln Papers at the Library of Congress.* Transcribed and Annotated by the Lincoln Studies Center, Knox College. Galesburg, Illinois. http://memory.loc.gov/
Search: Lincoln to Corning 600

Clara Barton. Letter to her father, 1861. In *Angel of the Battlefield: the Life of Clara Barton.* (New York: Harper, 1956). 601

Reactions from The Harrisburg Patriot and the Chicago Tribune. Cornell University Library. http://rmc.library.cornell.edu/gettysburg/
Select: Ideas are always more than battles 607

Abraham Lincoln. Second Inaugural Address, March 4, 1865. In *Inaugural Addresses of the Presidents of the United States from George Washington 1789 to George Bush 1989.* Bicentennial Edition. (Washington, D.C.: United States Government Printing Office, 1989). 610

Robert E. Lee. As quoted in *Voices of the Civil War.* Richard Wheeler. (New York: Thomas Y. Crowell, 1976). 610

Theodore Upson. *With Sherman to the sea; the Civil War letters, diaries & reminiscences of Theodore F. Upson.* (Bloomington: Indiana University Press, 1958). 616

Dolly Lunt Burge. *A Woman's Wartime Journal.* From the Academic Affairs Library, University of North Carolina at Chapel Hill, 1996. http://docsouth.unc.edu/
Search: Dolly Sumner Lunt 616

John Greenleaf Whittier. "Barbara Frietchie." From *Complete Poetical Works,* Cambridge Edition. (Boston: 1894). In *Annals of America,* V9. (Chicago: Encyclopedia Britannica, Inc., 1976). 617

Chapter 14

Mary Chesnut. *A Diary from Dixie.* (Gramercy, 1997). . . 625

Thaddeus Stevens. Speech to Congress, December 1865. http://history.furman.edu/~benson/hst41/blue/stevens1.htm 625

Charlotte Forten. From *Life on the Sea Islands.* http://www.pbs.org/onlyateacher/charlotte.html . . . 627

Andrew Jackson. http://www.senate.gov/artandhistory/history/resources/pdf/andrew_johnson.pdf 628

Charles Sumner. "For Conviction." In *The Annals of America,* V10, *1866–1883, Reconstruction and Industrialization.* (Chicago: Encyclopaedia Britannica, 1976). 633

State Convention of the Colored People of South Carolina. *Proceedings of the Colored People's Convention of the State of South Carolina, Held in Zion Church, Charleston, November, 1865.* (Charleston: South Carolina Leader Office, 1865). http://historymatters.gmu.edu/
Search: Charleston's Zion Church 636

Frederick Douglass. *Narrative of the Life of Frederick Douglass. An American Slave.* (Boston: Anti-Slavery Office, 1845). From the Academic Affairs Library, University of North Carolina at Chapel Hill, 1999. http://docsouth.unc.edu/
Search: Douglass Narrative 637

Primary Source Quotes

Chapter 15

Chapter 16

Chapter 17

Documents of American History

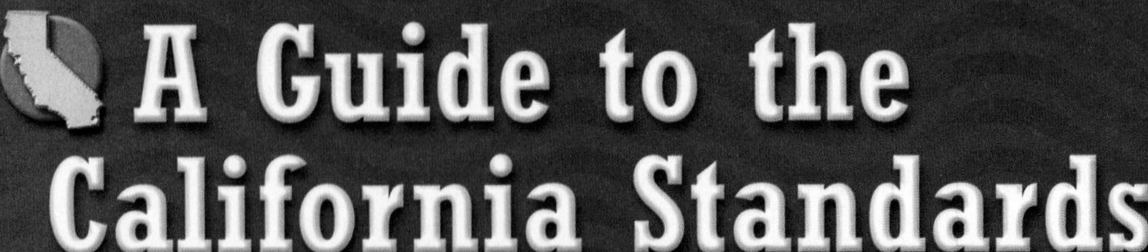

For Students and Their Families

California state capitol, Sacramento

What are the California History–Social Science Content Standards?

The California Department of Education has developed content standards for every course at every grade level. These standards can be found on the California Department of Education website. The History–Social Science Content Standards for grade 8 are designed to measure a student's knowledge of American history between the founding of our nation and World War I. The content of *Discovering Our Past: The American Journey to World War I* matches these standards.

Why should students be aware of these standards?

In grade 8, students will be tested on what they learn in grades 6 and 7 world history courses and in their United States history course in grade 8.

This Guide Contains:

Historical and Social Sciences Analysis Skills

To help you learn and understand content standards for any course you take, it is important to master the following skills. These skills focus on critical thinking, analysis, and research and will be represented like this: CA HR1.

Chronological and Spatial Thinking

CS1. Students explain how major events are related to one another in time.

CS2. Students construct various time lines of key events, people, and periods of the historical era they are studying.

CS3. Students use a variety of maps and documents to identify physical and cultural features of neighborhoods, cities, states, and countries and to explain the historical migration of people, expansion and disintegration of empires, and the growth of economic systems.

Research, Evidence, and Point of View

HR1. Students frame questions that can be answered by historical study and research.

HR2. Students distinguish fact from opinion in historical narratives and stories.

HR3. Students distinguish relevant from irrelevant information, essential from incidental information, and verifiable from unverifiable information in historical narratives and stories.

HR4. Students assess the credibility of primary and secondary sources and draw sound conclusions from them.

HR5. Students detect the different historical points of view on historical events and determine the context in which the historical statements were made (the questions asked, sources used, author's perspectives).

Historical Interpretation

HI1. Students explain the central issues and problems from the past, placing people and events in a matrix of time and place.

HI2. Students understand and distinguish cause, effect, sequence, and correlation in historical events, including the long- and short-term causal relations.

HI3. Students explain the sources of historical continuity and how the combination of ideas and events explains the emergence of new patterns.

HI4. Students recognize the role of chance, oversight, and error in history.

HI5. Students recognize that interpretations of history are subject to change as new information is uncovered.

HI6. Students interpret basic indicators of economic performance and conduct cost-benefit analyses of economic and political issues.

These content standards describe what History–Social Science Standards you should master when you complete this course.

United States History and Geography: Growth and Conflict

Main Standard US8.1 Students understand the major events preceding the founding of the nation and relate their significance to the development of American constitutional democracy.

Supporting Standard US8.1.1 Describe the relationship between the moral and political ideas of the Great Awakening and the development of revolutionary fervor.

Supporting Standard US8.1.2 Analyze the philosophy of government expressed in the Declaration of Independence, with an emphasis on government as a means of securing individual rights (e.g., key phrases such as "all men are created equal, that they are endowed by their Creator with certain unalienable Rights").

Supporting Standard US8.1.3 Analyze how the American Revolution affected other nations, especially France.

Supporting Standard US8.1.4 Describe the nation's blend of civic republicanism, classical liberal principles, and English parliamentary traditions.

▼ Windmills

Main Standard US8.2 Students analyze the political principles underlying the U.S. Constitution and compare the enumerated and implied powers of the federal government.

Supporting Standard US8.2.1 Discuss the significance of the Magna Carta, the English Bill of Rights, and the Mayflower Compact.

Supporting Standard US8.2.2 Analyze the Articles of Confederation and the Constitution and the success of each in implementing the ideals of the Declaration of Independence.

Supporting Standard US8.2.3 Evaluate the major debates that occurred during the development of the Constitution and their ultimate resolutions in such areas as shared power among institutions, divided state-federal power, slavery, the rights of individuals and states (later addressed by the addition of the Bill of Rights), and the status of American Indian nations under the commerce clause.

Supporting Standard US8.2.4 Describe the political philosophy underpinning the Constitution as specified in the *Federalist Papers* (authored by James Madison, Alexander Hamilton, and John Jay) and the role of such leaders as Madison, George Washington, Roger Sherman, Gouverneur Morris, and James Wilson in the writing and ratification of the Constitution.

Supporting Standard US8.2.5 Understand the significance of Jefferson's Statute for Religious Freedom as a forerunner of the First Amendment and the origins, purpose, and differing views of the founding fathers on the issue of separation of church and state.

Supporting Standard US8.2.6 Enumerate the powers of government set forth in the Constitution and the fundamental liberties ensured by the Bill of Rights.

Supporting Standard US8.2.7 Describe the principles of federalism, dual sovereignty, separation of powers, checks and balances, the nature and purpose of majority rule, and the ways in which the American idea of constitutionalism preserves individual rights.

Main Standard US8.3 Students understand the foundation of the American political system and the ways in which citizens participate in it.

Supporting Standard US8.3.1 Analyze the principles and concepts codified in state constitutions between 1777 and 1781 that created the context out of which American political institutions and ideas developed.

Supporting Standard US8.3.2 Explain how the ordinances of 1785 and 1787 privatized national resources and transferred federally owned lands into private holdings, townships, and states.

Supporting Standard US8.3.3 Enumerate the advantages of a common market among the states as foreseen in and protected by the Constitution's clauses on interstate commerce, common coinage, and full-faith and credit.

Supporting Standard US8.3.4 Understand how the conflicts between Thomas Jefferson and Alexander Hamilton resulted in the emergence of two political parties (e.g., view of foreign policy, Alien and Sedition Acts, economic policy, National Bank, funding and assumption of the revolutionary debt).

Supporting Standard US8.3.5 Know the significance of the domestic resistance movements and ways in which the central government responded to such movements (e.g., Shays' Rebellion, the Whiskey Rebellion).

Supporting Standard US8.3.6 Describe the basic law-making process and how the Constitution provides numerous opportunities for citizens to participate in the political process and to monitor and influence government (e.g., function of elections, political parties, interest groups).

Supporting Standard US8.3.7 Understand the functions and responsibilities of a free press.

Main Standard US8.4 Students analyze the aspirations and ideals of the people of the new nation.

Supporting Standard US8.4.1 Describe the country's physical landscapes, political divisions, and territorial expansion during the terms of the first four presidents.

Supporting Standard US8.4.2 Explain the policy significance of famous speeches (e.g., Washington's Farewell Address, Jefferson's 1801 Inaugural Address, John Q. Adams' Fourth of July 1821 Address).

Supporting Standard US8.4.3 Analyze the rise of capitalism and the economic problems and conflicts that accompanied it (e.g., Jackson's opposition to the National Bank; early decisions of the U.S. Supreme Court that reinforced the sanctity of contracts and a capitalist economic system of the law).

Supporting Standard US8.4.4 Discuss daily life, including traditions in art, music and literature, of early national American (e.g., through writings by Washington Irving, James Fenimore Cooper).

Main Standard US8.5 Students analyze U.S. foreign policy in the early Republic.

Supporting Standard US8.5.1 Understand the political and economic causes and consequences of the War of 1812 and know the major battles, leaders and events that led to a final peace.

Supporting Standard US8.5.2 Know the changing boundaries of the United States and describe the relationships the country had with its neighbors (current Mexico and Canada) and Europe, including the influence of the Monroe Doctrine, and how those relationships influenced westward expansion and the Mexican-American War.

Supporting Standard US8.5.3 Outline the major treaties with American Indian nations during the administrations of the first four presidents and the varying outcomes of those treaties.

Main Standard US8.6 Students analyze the divergent paths of the American people from 1800 to the mid-1800s and the challenges they faced, with emphasis on the Northeast.

Supporting Standard US8.6.1 Discuss the influence of industrialization and technological developments on the region, including human modification of the landscape and how physical geography shaped human actions (e.g., growth of cities, deforestation, farming, mineral extraction).

Supporting Standard US8.6.2 Outline the physical obstacles to and the economic and political factors involved in building a network of roads, canals, and railroads (e.g., Henry Clay's American System).

Supporting Standard US8.6.3 List the reasons for the wave of immigration from Northern Europe to the United States and describe the growth in the number, size, and spatial arrangements of cities (e.g., Irish immigrants and the Great Irish Famine).

Supporting Standard US8.6.4 Study the lives of black Americans who gained freedom in the North and founded schools and churches to advance their rights and communities.

Supporting Standard US8.6.5 Trace the development of the American education system from its earliest roots, including the roles of religious and private schools and Horace Mann's campaign for free public education and its assimilating role in American culture.

Supporting Standard US8.6.6 Examine the women's suffrage movement (e.g., biographies, writings, and speeches of Elizabeth Cady Stanton, Margaret Fuller, Lucretia Mott, Susan B. Anthony).

Supporting Standard US8.6.7 Identify common themes in American art as well as transcendentalism and individualism (e.g., writings about and by Ralph Waldo Emerson, Henry David Thoreau, Herman Melville, Louisa May Alcott, Nathaniel Hawthorne, Henry Wadsworth Longfellow).

▼ White sand dunes, Eureka Valley Dunes, CA

Main Standard US8.7 Students analyze the divergent paths of the American people in the South from 1800 to the mid-1800s and the challenges they faced.

Supporting Standard US8.7.1 Describe the development of the agrarian economy in the South, identify the locations of the cotton-producing states, and discuss the significance of cotton and the cotton gin.

Supporting Standard US8.7.2 Trace the origins and development of slavery; its effects on black Americans and on the region's political, social, religious, economic, and cultural development; and identify the strategies that were tried to both overturn and preserve it (e.g., through the writings and historical documents on Nat Turner, Denmark Vesey).

Supporting Standard US8.7.3 Examine the characteristics of white southern society and how the physical environment influenced events and conditions prior to the Civil War.

Supporting Standard US8.7.4 Compare the lives of and opportunities for free blacks in the North with those of free blacks in the South.

Golden Gate Bridge

Main Standard US8.8 Students analyze the divergent paths of the American people in the West from 1800 to the mid-1800s and the challenges they faced.

Supporting Standard US8.8.1 Discuss the election of Andrew Jackson as president in 1828, the importance of Jacksonian democracy, and his actions as president (e.g., the spoils system, veto of the National Bank, policy of Indian removal, opposition to the Supreme Court).

Supporting Standard US8.8.2 Describe the purpose, challenges, and economic incentives associated with westward expansion, including the concept of Manifest Destiny (e.g., the Lewis and Clark expedition, accounts of the removal of Indians, the Cherokees' "Trail of Tears," settlement of the Great Plains) and the territorial acquisitions that spanned numerous decades.

Supporting Standard US8.8.3 Describe the role of pioneer women and the new status that western women achieved (e.g., Laura Ingalls Wilder, Annie Bidwell; slave women gaining freedom in the West; Wyoming granting suffrage to women in 1869).

Supporting Standard US8.8.4 Examine the importance of the great rivers and the struggle over water rights.

Supporting Standard US8.8.5 Discuss Mexican settlements and their locations, cultural traditions, attitudes toward slavery, land-grant system, and economies.

Supporting Standard US8.8.6 Describe the Texas War for Independence and the Mexican-American War, including territorial settlements, the aftermath of the wars, and the effects the wars had on the lives of Americans including Mexican Americans today.

Main Standard US8.9 Students analyze the early and steady attempts to abolish slavery and to realize the ideals of the Declaration of Independence.

Supporting Standard US8.9.1 Describe the leaders of the movement (e.g., John Quincy Adams and his proposed constitutional amendment, John Brown and the armed resistance, Harriet Tubman and the Underground Railroad, Benjamin Franklin, Theodore Weld, William Lloyd Garrison, Frederick Douglass).

Supporting Standard US8.9.2 Discuss the abolition of slavery in early state constitutions.

Supporting Standard US8.9.3 Describe the significance of the Northwest Ordinance in education and in the banning of slavery in new states north of the Ohio River.

Supporting Standard US8.9.4 Discuss the importance of the slavery issue as raised by the annexation of Texas and California's admission to the union as a free state under the Compromise of 1850.

Supporting Standard US8.9.5 Analyze the significance of the States' Rights Doctrine, the Missouri Compromise (1820), the Wilmot Proviso (1846), the Compromise of 1850, Henry Clay's role in the Missouri Compromise and the Compromise of 1850, the Kansas-Nebraska Act (1854), the *Dred Scott* v. *Sandford* decision (1857), and the Lincoln-Douglas debates (1858).

Supporting Standard US8.9.6 Describe the lives of free blacks and the laws that limited their freedom and economic opportunities.

Main Standard US8.10 **Students analyze the multiple causes, key events, and complex consequences of the Civil War.**

Supporting Standard US8.10.1 Compare the conflicting interpretations of state and federal authority as emphasized in the speeches and writings of statesmen such as Daniel Webster and John C. Calhoun.

Supporting Standard US8.10.2 Trace the boundaries constituting the North and the South, the geographical differences between the two regions, and the differences between agrarians and industrialists.

Supporting Standard US8.10.3 Identify the constitutional issues posed by the doctrine of nullification and secession and the earliest origins of that doctrine.

Supporting Standard US8.10.4 Discuss Abraham Lincoln's presidency and his significant writings and speeches and their relationship to the Declaration of Independence, such as his "House Divided" speech (1858), Gettysburg Address (1863), Emancipation Proclamation (1863), and inaugural addresses (1861 and 1865).

Supporting Standard US8.10.5 Study the views and lives of leaders (e.g., Ulysses S. Grant, Jefferson Davis, Robert E. Lee) and soldiers on both sides of the war, including those of black soldiers and regiments.

Supporting Standard US8.10.6 Describe critical developments and events in the war, including the major battles, geographical advantages and obstacles, technological advances, and General Lee's surrender at Appomattox.

Supporting Standard US8.10.7 Explain how the war affected combatants, civilians, the physical environment and future warfare.

Main Standard US8.11 **Students analyze the character and lasting consequences of Reconstruction.**

Supporting Standard US8.11.1 List the original aims of Reconstruction and describe its effects on the political and social structures of different regions.

Supporting Standard US8.11.2 Identify the push-pull factors in the movement of former slaves to the cities in the North and to the West and their differing experiences in those regions (e.g. the experiences of the Buffalo Soldiers).

Supporting Standard US8.11.3 Understand the effects of the Freedmen's Bureau and the restrictions placed on the rights and opportunities of freedmen, including racial segregation and "Jim Crow" laws.

Supporting Standard US8.11.4 Trace the rise of the Ku Klux Klan and describe the Klan's effects.

Supporting Standard US8.11.5 Understand the Thirteenth, Fourteenth, and Fifteenth Amendments to the Constitution and analyze their connection to Reconstruction.

Main Standard US8.12 Students analyze the transformation of the American economy and the changing social and political conditions in the United States in response to the Industrial Revolution.

Supporting Standard US8.12.1 Trace patterns of agricultural and industrial development as they relate to climate, use of natural resources, markets, and trade and locate such development on a map.

Supporting Standard US8.12.2 Identify the reasons for the development of federal Indian policy and the wars with American Indians and their relationship to agricultural development and industrialization.

Supporting Standard US8.12.3 Explain how states and the federal government encouraged business expansion through tariffs, banking, land grants, and subsidies.

Supporting Standard US8.12.4 Discuss entrepreneurs, industrialists, and bankers in politics, commerce, and industry (e.g., Andrew Carnegie, John D. Rockefeller, Leland Stanford).

Supporting Standard US8.12.5 Examine the location and effects of urbanization, renewed immigration, and industrialization (e.g., the effects on social fabric of cities, wealth and economic opportunity, the conservation movement).

Supporting Standard US8.12.6 Discuss child labor, working conditions, and laissez-faire policies toward big business and examine the labor movement, including its leaders (e.g., Samuel Gompers), its demand for collective bargaining, and its strikes and protests over labor conditions.

Supporting Standard US8.12.7 Identify the sources of large-scale immigration and the contributions of immigrants to the building of cities and the economy; explain the ways in which new social and economic patterns encouraged assimilation of newcomers into the mainstream amidst growing cultural diversity; and discuss the new wave of nativism.

Supporting Standard US8.12.8 Identify the characteristics and impact of Grangerism and Populism.

Supporting Standard US8.12.9 Name the significant inventors and their inventions and identify how they improved the quality of life (e.g., Thomas Edison, Alexander Graham Bell, Orville and Wilbur Wright).

A street in San Francisco

English–Language Arts Standards

Reading

English–Language Arts Standards are addressed throughout this book in reading and writing skills and activities. Items that relate to an English–Language Arts Standard will be represented like this: CA 8RW1.0 .

8RW1.0 Word Analysis, Fluency, and Systematic Vocabulary Development

Vocabulary and Concept Development

8RW1.1 Analyze idioms, analogies, metaphors, and similes to infer the literal and figurative meanings of phrases.

8RW1.2 Understand the most important points in the history of English language and use common word origins to determine the historical influences on English word meanings.

8RW1.3 Use word meanings within the appropriate context and show ability to verify those meanings by definition, restatement, example, comparison, or contrast.

8RC2.0 Reading Comprehension (Focus on Informational Materials)

Structural Features of Informational Materials

8RC2.1 Compare and contrast the features and elements of consumer materials to gain meaning from documents (e.g., warranties, contracts, product information, instruction manuals).

8RC2.2 Analyze text that uses proposition and support patterns.

Comprehension and Analysis of Grade-Level-Appropriate Text

8RC2.3 Find similarities and differences between texts in the treatment, scope, or organization of ideas.

8RC2.4 Compare the original text to a summary to determine whether the summary accurately captures the main ideas, includes critical details, and conveys the underlying meaning.

8RC2.5 Understand and explain the use of a complex mechanical device by following technical directions.

8RC2.6 Use information from a variety of consumer, workplace, and public documents to explain a situation or decision and to solve a problem.

Expository Critique

8RC2.7 Evaluate the unity, coherence, logic, internal consistency, and structural patterns of text.

California farmland

8RL3.0 Literary Response and Analysis

Structural Features of Literature

8RL3.1 Determine and articulate the relationship between the purposes and characteristics of different forms of poetry (e.g., ballad, lyric, couplet, epic, elegy, ode, sonnet).

Narrative Analysis of Grade-Level-Appropriate Text

8RL3.2 Evaluate the structural elements of the plot (e.g., subplots, parallel episodes, climax), the plot's development, and the way in which conflicts are (or are not) addressed and resolved.

8RL3.3 Compare and contrast motivations and reactions of literary characters from different historical eras confronting similar situations or conflicts.

8RL3.4 Analyze the relevance of the setting (e.g., place, time, customs) to the mood, tone, and meaning of the text.

8RL3.5 Identify and analyze recurring themes (e.g., good versus evil) across traditional and contemporary works.

8RL3.6 Identify significant literary devices (e.g., metaphor, symbolism, dialect, irony) that define a writer's style and use those elements to interpret the work.

Literary Criticism

8RL3.7 Analyze a work of literature, showing how it reflects the heritage, traditions, attitudes, and beliefs of its author. (Biographical approach)

Writing

8WS1.0 Writing Strategies

Organization and Focus

8WS1.1 Create compositions that establish a controlling impression, have a coherent thesis, and end with a clear and well-supported conclusion.

8WS1.2 Establish coherence within and among paragraphs through effective transitions, parallel structures, and similar writing techniques.

8WS1.3 Support theses or conclusions with analogies, paraphrases, quotations, opinions from authorities, comparisons, and similar devices.

Research and Technology

8WS1.4 Plan and conduct multiple-step information searches by using computer networks and modems.

8WS1.5 Achieve an effective balance between researched information and original ideas.

Evaluation and Revision

8WS1.6 Revise writing for word choice; appropriate organization; consistent point of view; and transitions between paragraphs, passages, and ideas.

8WA2.0 Writing Applications (Genres and Their Characteristics)

8WA2.1 Write biographies, autobiographies, short stories, or narratives:

a. Relate a clear, coherent incident, event, or situation by using well-chosen details.

b. Reveal the significance of, or the writer's attitude about, the subject.

c. Employ narrative and descriptive strategies (e.g., relevant dialogue, specific action, physical description, background description, comparison or contrast of characters).

8WA2.2 Write responses to literature:

a. Exhibit careful reading and insight in their interpretations.

b. Connect the student's own responses to the writer's techniques and to specific textual references.

c. Draw supported inferences about the effects of a literary work on its audience.

d. Support judgments through references to the text, other works, other authors, or to personal knowledge.

8WA2.3 Write research reports:

a. Define a thesis.

b. Record important ideas, concepts, and direct quotations from significant information sources and paraphrase and summarize all perspectives on the topic, as appropriate.

c. Use a variety of primary and secondary sources and distinguish the nature and value of each.

d. Organize and display information on charts, maps, and graphs.

8WA2.4 Write persuasive compositions:

a. Include a well-defined thesis (i.e., one that makes a clear and knowledgeable judgment).

b. Present detailed evidence, examples, and reasoning to support arguments, differentiating between facts and opinion.

c. Provide details, reasons, and examples, arranging them effectively by anticipating and answering reader concerns and counterarguments.

8WA2.5 Write documents related to career development, including simple business letters and job applications:

a. Present information purposefully and succinctly and meet the needs of the intended audience.

b. Follow the conventional format for the type of document (e.g., letter of inquiry, memorandum).

8WA2.6 Write technical documents:

a. Identify the sequence of activities needed to design a system, operate a tool, or explain the bylaws of an organization.

b. Include all the factors and variables that need to be considered.

c. Use formatting techniques (e.g., headings, differing fonts) to aid comprehension.

Written and Oral English Language Conventions

8WC1.0 Written and Oral English Language Conventions

Sentence Structure

8WC1.1 Use correct and varied sentence types and sentence openings to present a lively and effective personal style.

8WC1.2 Identify and use parallelism, including similar grammatical forms, in all written discourse to present items in a series and items juxtaposed for emphasis.

8WC1.3 Use subordination, coordination, apposition, and other devices to indicate clearly the relationship between ideas.

Grammar

8WC1.4 Edit written manuscripts to ensure that correct grammar is used.

Punctuation and Capitalization

8WC1.5 Use correct punctuation and capitalization.

Spelling

8WC1.6 Use correct spelling conventions.

Listening and Speaking

8LS1.0 Listening and Speaking Strategies

Comprehension

8LS1.1 Analyze oral interpretations of literature, including language choice and delivery, and the effect of the interpretations on the listener.

8LS1.2 Paraphrase a speaker's purpose and point of view and ask relevant questions concerning the speaker's content, delivery, and purpose.

Organization and Delivery of Oral Communication

8LS1.3 Organize information to achieve particular purposes by matching the message, vocabulary, voice modulation, expression, and tone to the audience and purpose.

8LS1.4 Prepare a speech outline based upon a chosen pattern of organization, which generally includes an introduction; transitions, previews, and summaries; a logically developed body; and an effective conclusion.

8LS1.5 Use precise language, action verbs, sensory details, appropriate and colorful modifiers, and the active rather than the passive voice in ways that enliven oral presentations.

8LS1.6 Use appropriate grammar, word choice, enunciation, and pace during formal presentations.

8LS1.7 Use audience feedback (e.g., verbal and nonverbal cues):

a. Reconsider and modify the organizational structure or plan.

b. Rearrange words and sentences to clarify the meaning.

Analysis and Evaluation of Oral and Media Communications

8LS1.8 Evaluate the credibility of a speaker (e.g., hidden agendas, slanted or biased material).

8LS1.9 Interpret and evaluate the various ways in which visual image makers (e.g., graphic artists, illustrators, news photographers) communicate information and affect impressions and opinions.

8SA2.0 Speaking Applications (Genres and Their Characteristics)

8SA2.1 Deliver narrative presentations (e.g., biographical, autobiographical):

- **a.** Relate a clear, coherent incident, event, or situation by using well-chosen details.
- **b.** Reveal the significance of, and the subject's attitude about, the incident, event, or situation.
- **c.** Employ narrative and descriptive strategies (e.g., relevant dialogue, specific action, physical description, background description, comparison or contrast of characters).

8SA2.2 Deliver oral responses to literature:

- **a.** Interpret a reading and provide insight.
- **b.** Connect the students' own responses to the writer's techniques and to specific textual references.
- **c.** Draw supported inferences about the effects of a literary work on its audience.
- **d.** Support judgments through references to the text, other works, other authors, or personal knowledge.

California poppies, state flower

8SA2.3 Deliver research presentations:

- **a.** Define a thesis.
- **b.** Record important ideas, concepts, and direct quotations from significant information sources and paraphrase and summarize all relevant perspectives on the topic, as appropriate.
- **c.** Use a variety of primary and secondary sources and distinguish the nature and value of each.
- **d.** Organize and record information on charts, maps, and graphs.

8SA2.4 Deliver persuasive presentations:

- **a.** Include a well-defined thesis (i.e., one that makes a clear and knowledgeable judgment).
- **b.** Differentiate fact from opinion and support arguments with detailed evidence, examples, and reasoning.
- **c.** Anticipate and answer listener concerns and counterarguments effectively through the inclusion and arrangement of details, reasons, examples, and other elements.
- **d.** Maintain a reasonable tone.

8SA2.5 Recite poems (of four to six stanzas), sections of speeches, or dramatic soliloquies, using voice modulation, tone, and gestures expressively to enhance the meaning.

English–Language Arts Content Standards for Grade 8	Student Edition Pages
8WA2.2	111, 147, 512, 589, 619, 735
8WA2.3	111, 317, 441, 559, 589, 671, 701, 735, 756, 771
8WA2.4	107, 124, 163, 185, 207, 243, 245, 297, 301, 333, 369, 371, 387, 431, 457, 465, 517, 547, 563, 619, 697, 701, 711, 763, 771
8WA2.5	233, 284, 461, 603
8WA2.6	331
8WC1.0 Written and Oral English Language Conventions	
8WC1.1	297
8LS1.0 Listening and Speaking Strategies	333
8LS1.3	201, 289, 655
8LS1.4	245
8LS1.9	747, 789

To Students and Their Families,

Welcome to eighth-grade American history. You will begin your journey with early modern European history and its impact on the Western Hemisphere. Then you will continue with the founding of the United States and its history until 1914.

Take a few moments each day to review what you learned in sixth and seventh grades about world history. By reviewing what you already know, you will gain a better understanding of what you are about to learn. A sample review question is provided for each day of the school week until you have reviewed all the standards for sixth and seventh grades. Try to answer one question each day. **If you want to look back at what you learned in sixth and seventh grade, visit the Online California Standards Review and Practice at ca.hss.glencoe.com.**

WEEK 1

Content Standard WH6.1 Students describe what is known through archaeological studies of the early physical and cultural development of humankind from the Paleolithic era to the agricultural revolution.

Directions: *Select the best answer for each of the following questions.*

MONDAY WH6.1.1

1 The Paleolithic people were able to survive because they learned how to use

A rocks.
B fire.
C water.
D caves.

TUESDAY WH6.1.1

2 One of the most important technologies used by the Paleolithic people was

A tools.
B language.
C art.
D religion.

WEDNESDAY WH6.1.2

3 What are two well-known Neolithic communities?

A Europe and China
B Mexico and Egypt
C Jericho and Çatal Hüyük
D Babylon and Uruk

THURSDAY WH6.1.3

4 What revolutionary change took place during the Neolithic Age?

A building simple shelters
B hunting
C farming
D toolmaking

FRIDAY

5 Because of specialization during the Neolithic Age, people could

A hunt.
B farm.
C set up villages.
D have clothes made of cloth.

Answers are on page CA43.

WEEK 2

Content Standard WH6.2 Students analyze the geographic, political, economic, religious, and social structures of the early civilizations of Mesopotamia, Egypt, and Kush.

Directions: *Select the best answer for each of the following questions.*

MONDAY WH6.2.1

1 Mesopotamia, the cradle of civilization, lay between the

A Nile River and Red Sea.
B Rhine and Rhone rivers.
C Tigris and Euphrates rivers.
D Nile and Niger rivers.

TUESDAY WH6.2.2

2 Using artificial means of bringing water to crops is called

A adulation.
B irrigation.
C initiation.
D inflation.

WEDNESDAY WH6.2.6

3 What did Egyptians trade for in the eastern Mediterranean?

A wheat
B paper
C tools
D wood

THURSDAY WH6.2.7

4 This ruler avoided military conquests and expanded Egypt's economy.

A Hatshepsut
B Nefertiti
C Thutmose III
D Ramses II

FRIDAY WH6.2.8 Read the passage below and answer the question.

We [the Kushite officials] have come to you, O Amon-Re that you might give to us a [new] lord . . . That beneficent office [helpful task] is in your hands—may you give it to your son whom you love!

—*Anonymous*, "The Selection of Aspalta as King of Kush," c. 600 B.C.

5 Both Kushites and Egyptians believed that their rulers were

A ordinary people.
B related to the gods.
C dependent on voters.
D open to criticism.

Answers are on page CA43.

WEEK 3

Content Standard WH6.3 Students analyze the geographic, political, economic, religious, and social structures of the Ancient Hebrews.

Directions: *Select the best answer for each of the following questions.*

MONDAY WH6.3.1

1 Judaism is based on monotheism, or the belief in

A one natural law.
B one God.
C one true faith.
D many gods.

TUESDAY WH6.3.2

2 Which Israelite code of laws shaped the moral laws of many peoples?

A the Code of Hammurabi
B the Sermon on the Mount
C the Ten Commandments
D the Twelve Tables

WEDNESDAY WH6.3.3

3 The Israelites believed they were descended from this man.

A Jacob
B Moses
C Abraham
D Joshua

THURSDAY WH6.3.4

4 The Exodus is the name given to

A the exile of the Jews in Babylon.
B the Israelites' escape from slavery in Egypt.
C Abraham's journey from Mesopotamia to Canaan.
D David's escape from King Saul's soldiers.

FRIDAY WH6.3.5

Read the passage below and answer the question.

One is permitted to remove debris on the Sabbath in order to save a life or to act for the benefit of the community; and we may assemble in the synagogue on the Sabbath to conduct public business.

—*The Talmud for Today,* Rabbi Alexander Feinsilver, trans. and ed.

5 What feature of Jewish life does the Talmud show helped Jews to survive dispersal and persecution?

A religious rituals
B harvest festivals
C a class of priests
D religious laws

Answers are on page CA43.

WEEK 4

Content Standard WH6.4 Students analyze the geographic, political, economic, religious, and social structures of the early civilization of Ancient Greece.

Directions: *Select the best answer for each of the following questions.*

MONDAY WH6.4.4

1 Through mythology, the Greek people expressed their

A religious beliefs.
B love of poetry.
C love of sport.
D political beliefs.

TUESDAY WH6.4.5

2 The Persian king Darius's power depended on his

A nobles.
B tax collectors.
C army.
D chief of police.

WEDNESDAY WH6.4.6

3 The people of Athens prized education, while the people of Sparta valued

A the arts.
B military skills.
C science.
D trade with foreigners.

THURSDAY WH6.4.7

4 A legacy of Alexander the Great was the

A spread of Greek culture to southwest Asia.
B spread of Christianity.
C conquest of Italy and Spain.
D rebuilding of Sparta.

FRIDAY WH6.4.2

Read the passage below and answer the question.

Our constitution is called a democracy because power is in the hands not of a minority but of the whole people. . . . [W]hen it is a question of putting one person before another in positions of public responsibility, what counts is not membership of a particular class, but the actual ability which the man possesses.

—Pericles as recorded by Thucydides, *History of the Peloponnesian War*

5 According to Pericles's Funeral Oration, what standard did the Greeks use to decide who should hold public office?

A royal blood
B ability
C wealth
D class

Answers are on page CA43.

WEEK 5

Content Standard WH6.5 Students analyze the geographic, political, economic, religious, and social structures of the early civilizations of India.

Directions: *Select the best answer for each of the following questions.*

MONDAY WH6.5.1

1 India's earliest civilizations developed

A between the Tigris and Euphrates rivers.

B along the coasts of Southeast Asia.

C in the Indus River valley.

D on the Deccan plateau.

TUESDAY WH6.5.4

2 In early India's social system, the Kshatriyas class contained these people.

A untouchables

B priests

C common people

D warriors

WEDNESDAY WH6.5.5

3 The Buddha believed that the only way to find truth was by

A giving up family and home.

B renouncing all desires.

C praying five times a day.

D worshipping in temples.

THURSDAY WH6.5.6

4 The Indian ruler who became Buddhist, renounced war, and worked for his people's welfare was

A Asoka.

B Sarawati.

C Lakshmi.

D Babur.

FRIDAY WH6.5.7

Read the passage below and answer the question.

Thou grievest where no grief should be! . . .

All, that doth live, lives always! . . .

....

The soul that with a strong and constant calm
Takes sorrow and takes joy indifferently,
Lives in the life undying!

—*Bhagavadgita*, Sir Edwin Arnold, trans.

5 What does Krishna believe about life after death?

A There is no life after death.

B Souls pass through many lives to unite with the universal spirit.

C Souls survive and are later joined to their bodies in heaven.

D Souls pass to a dark underworld of suffering.

Answers are on page CA43.

WEEK 6

Content Standard WH6.6 Students analyze the geographic, political, economic, religious, and social structures of the early civilizations of China.

Directions: *Select the best answer for each of the following questions.*

MONDAY WH6.6.4

1 Confucius believed that peace would come to society if people

A lived in harmony with nature.

B turned to a very strong ruler for protection.

C gave up all concerns about the world.

D put the needs of family and community above personal needs.

TUESDAY WH6.6.6

2 To select the most talented people for government jobs, Han Wudi used

A a council of nobles to make appointments.

B civil service exams.

C educators who named government officials.

D a lottery system.

WEDNESDAY WH6.6.7

3 The Silk Road was significant because it

A brought China into contact with many other civilizations.

B replaced a sea route to Southeast Asia.

C helped link northern and southern parts of China.

D helped Chinese armies conquer the Himalayas.

THURSDAY WH6.6.8

4 What groups brought Buddhism to China?

A merchants and teachers

B warriors and priests

C scientists and prophets

D untouchables and laborers

FRIDAY WH6.6.3

Read the passage below and answer the question.

The sage experiences [life] without abstraction [being separated from it],
And accomplishes without action;
He accepts the ebb and flow of things,
Nurtures them, but does not own them,
And lives, but does not dwell.

—Laozi, *Dao De Jing*

5 According to Laozi, how should a wise person approach the events of life?

A with energy

B with resistance

C with acceptance

D with self-assertion

Answers are on page CA43.

WEEK 7

Content Standard WH6.7 Students analyze the geographic, political, economic, religious, and social structures during the development of Rome.

Directions: *Select the best answer for each of the following questions.*

MONDAY WH6.7.2

1 The ruling class and top officials of the Roman Republic were the

A Etruscans.
B plebeians.
C patricians.
D consuls.

TUESDAY WH6.7.4

2 Julius Caesar helped end the Roman Republic by

A declaring himself dictator for life.
B becoming part of the First Triumvirate.
C conquering territory for Rome.
D defeating Pompey's forces.

WEDNESDAY WH6.7.6

3 What was one reason why Christianity spread?

A Constantine denied religious freedom to people in the empire.
B Roman peace and order allowed people to travel in safety.
C The teachings of Christianity were all new to most Romans.
D Romans expected everyone to honor the emperor as a god.

THURSDAY WH6.7.8

4 One of Rome's most significant influences on the world is its

A invention of paper.
B creation of democracy.
C establishment of the Silk Road.
D system of law.

FRIDAY WH6.7.1

Read the passage below and answer the question.

Therefore, when I saw that a nefarious [evil] war was waged against the republic, I thought that no delay ought to be interposed to our pursuit of Marcus Antonius; and I gave my vote that we ought to pursue with war that most audacious [bold] man, who . . . was at this moment attacking a general of the Roman people.

—Cicero, "The Sixth Oration of M.T. Cicero Against Marcus Antonius"

5 In giving this speech about the struggle between Octavian and Antony (Marcus Antonius), Cicero was showing that he

A supported talks to end the fighting.
B wanted to help Rome's poor.
C was a defender of Rome's republican institutions.
D supported Rome becoming a monarchy.

Answers are on page CA43.

WEEK 8

Content Standard WH7.1 Students analyze the causes and effects of the vast expansion and ultimate disintegration of the Roman Empire.

Directions: *Select the best answer for each of the following questions.*

MONDAY WH7.1.1

1 Which of the following is an example of a lasting Roman contribution?

- **A** the invention of paper
- **B** the idea everyone is equal under the law
- **C** the founding of Christianity
- **D** direct democracy

TUESDAY WH7.1.2

2 Which best describes the size of the Roman Empire at its greatest?

- **A** Italy and North Africa
- **B** southern Europe and India
- **C** lands around the Mediterranean
- **D** southern Britain, southern Europe, Asia Minor, and North Africa

WEDNESDAY WH7.1.3

3 Constantine moved the Roman capital to Constantinople because

- **A** it lay on an easily defended site and was at a crossroads for trade.
- **B** the Visigoths had captured Rome.
- **C** Greeks made up the largest group in the empire.
- **D** Persians were trying to overrun the eastern border of the empire.

THURSDAY WH7.1.3

4 How did the Eastern Orthodox and Roman Catholic churches view church-state relations?

- **A** The emperor and the pope only had power in spiritual matters.
- **B** The emperor and the pope should not interfere in political matters.
- **C** Only the emperor had control over material matters.
- **D** The pope often quarreled with kings over political matters while Byzantine church officials respected their emperor's wishes.

FRIDAY WH7.1.1

Use the passage below to answer the question.

Didius Julianus . . . made bids to the soldiers for the rule over the Romans. For, just as if it had been in some market or auction room, both the city and its entire Empire were auctioned off. The sellers were the ones who had slain their emperor, and the would-be buyers were Sulpicianus and Julianus.

—*Aspects of Western Civilization*, vol. 1, edited by Perry M. Rogers

5 According to the quote what was one weakness of the Roman Empire?

- **A** attacks from barbarians
- **B** spread of disease
- **C** growth of corruption
- **D** too many slaves

Answers are on page CA43.

WEEK 9

Content Standard WH7.2 Students analyze the geographic, political, economic, religious, and social structures of the civilizations of Islam in the Middle Ages.

Directions: *Select the best answer for each of the following questions.*

MONDAY WH7.2.1

1 What covers most of the Arabian Peninsula?

A mountains
B grassy plains
C desert
D swamp

TUESDAY WH7.2.2

2 What belief do Judaism, Christianity, and Islam have in common?

A A prophet is the son of God.
B There is one God.
C Lying is the greatest wrong.
D Stealing is sometimes allowed.

WEDNESDAY WH7.2.4

3 As the Arab Empire spread,

A Muslims began to believe that Muhammad was a god.
B many conquered peoples converted to Islam and learned Arabic.
C Muslims forced people to become Muslims.
D many Muslims became Catholics.

THURSDAY WH7.2.6

4 Which of the following was a Muslim contribution to learning?

A the philosophy of Stoicism
B the invention of the arch
C the use of aqueducts
D the discovery that blood moves to and from the heart

FRIDAY WH7.2.3

Read the passage below and answer the question.

Serve no other gods besides Allah, lest you incur disgrace and ruin. Your Lord has enjoined [ordered] you to worship none but Him and to show kindness to your parents. . . .
Give to the near of kin [relatives] their due, and also to the destitute and to the wayfarers. Do not squander your substance wastefully, . . .
Keep your promises; you are accountable for all that you promise.
Give full measure, when you measure, and weigh with even scales.

—*The Koran,* N.J. Dawood, trans.

5 Which sentence best describes the contents of the Qu'ran?

A It states a Muslim's responsibilities toward Allah and other people.
B It tells how Muslims should behave in business.
C It explains which countries Muslims should conquer.
D It describes Muhammad's hopes for the people of Arabia.

Answers are on page CA43.

WEEK 10

Content Standard WH7.3 Students analyze the geographic, political, economic, religious, and social structures of the civilizations of China in the Middle Ages.

Directions: *Select the best answer for each of the following questions.*

MONDAY WH7.3.1

1 Buddhism became an important religion in China because

A Buddhism brought peace and comfort in a time of war and famine.
B monks and nuns did not marry.
C missionaries brought it to China.
D the emperors converted people to it.

TUESDAY WH7.3.2

2 Why did farming improve during the Tang dynasty?

A The country was at war.
B The civil system was restored.
C Farmers began to grow tea.
D Farmers developed better kinds of rice.

WEDNESDAY WH7.3.5

3 What did woodblock printing lead to?

A the making of copper coins
B the assessment of taxes
C the introduction of paper money
D the decline of the Chinese economy

THURSDAY WH7.3.6

4 The civil service exam created the scholar-official class because

A men who passed it could appoint relatives to government jobs.
B only men who passed the exam could become government officials.
C the emperor personally chose all the men who would take the test.
D sons could inherit government jobs.

FRIDAY WH7.3.4

Read the passage below and answer the question.

Of late we have dispatched missions to announce our Mandate to foreign nations and during their journeys over the oceans they have been favored with the blessing of Thy beneficent [Buddha's generous] protection. They have escaped disaster or misfortune, . . .

[W]e bestow offerings in recompense [thanks], . . . before the Lord Buddha, . . . of gold and silver.

—Louise Levathes, *When China Ruled the Seas*

5 What indicates if these journeys were important to the Chinese?

A not important because there were no disasters
B not important because Buddha did not pay attention to the journeys
C important because they went to foreign nations
D important because the Chinese are giving gifts of thanks to Buddha

Answers are on page CA43.

WEEK 11

Content Standard WH7.4 Students analyze the geographic, political, economic, religious, and social structures of the sub-Saharan civilizations of Ghana and Mali in Medieval Africa.

Directions: *Select the best answer for each of the following questions.*

MONDAY WH7.4.2

1 The rainforest kingdoms had

A surplus foods that they traded for salt.

B gold that they traded for salt.

C salt that they traded for gold.

D copper and leather goods that they traded for gold.

TUESDAY WH7.4.3

2 Why did some West Africans change from a traditional religion to Islam?

A Muhammad converted them.

B Arab armies forced them to change.

C Being followers of Islam helped them trade with Muslim Arabs.

D Sundiata forced his people to convert to Islam.

WEDNESDAY WH7.4.4

3 Why was there increased use of the Arabic language in West Africa?

A Cordoba was a center of Muslim culture.

B The Bantu gradually settled most of Africa.

C The Spanish extended their control to North and West Africa.

D Arabs traded with the kingdoms of West Africa.

THURSDAY WH7.4.5

4 In West Africa, children were often educated

A in large local schools.

B through oral stories and proverbs.

C by the government.

D after paying a large fee.

FRIDAY WH7.4.1

Read the passage below and answer the question.

The king [of Ghana] exacts the right of one dinar *of gold on each donkey-load of salt that enters his country, and two* dinars *of gold on each load of salt that goes out. A load of copper carries a duty of five* mitqals *and a load of merchandise ten* mitquals.

—Abdullah Abu-Ubayd al Bekri, "Ghana in 1067"

5 According to al Bekri, what is a source of wealth for Ghana?

A a large number of salt and copper mines in the country

B the donkeys that are raised in Ghana

C the taxes charge on goods entering and leaving the country

D the king's gold mines

Answers are on page CA43.

WEEK 12

Content Standard WH7.5 Students analyze the geographic, political, economic, religious, and social structures of the civilizations of Medieval Japan.

Directions: *Select the best answer for each of the following questions.*

MONDAY WH7.5.1

1 Which of the following came to Japan by way of China?

- **A** the model for a shogun style of government
- **B** the religion of Shinto
- **C** tanka and haiku poetry
- **D** a writing system

TUESDAY WH7.5.2

2 What was the goal of Prince Shotoku's reforms?

- **A** to create a strong central government
- **B** to make Japan the strongest country in the area
- **C** to defeat the Chinese
- **D** to divide Japan into a series of provinces

WEDNESDAY WH7.5.5

3 *The Tale of the Genji*

- **A** recounts the adventures of a Japanese sailor.
- **B** may be the world's first novel.
- **C** is a series of Noh plays.
- **D** contains instructions for how to write poetry.

THURSDAY WH7.5.6

4 A military society developed in twelfth century Japan because

- **A** the Mongols defeated the Japanese.
- **B** the emperor needed an army to attack China.
- **C** the most powerful families were trying to gain more land by fighting each other.
- **D** Buddhism honored a military way of life.

FRIDAY WH7.5.3

Read the passage below and answer the question.

It is further good fortune if . . . [a servant] had wisdom and talent and can use them appropriately. But even a person who is good for nothing . . . will be a reliable retainer [servant] if only he has the determination to think earnestly of [respect and admire] his master. Having only wisdom and talent is the lowest tier [level] of usefulness.

—Yamamoto Tsunetomo, *Hagakure: The Book of the Samurai*

5 According to this excerpt, what should a master most look for in a samurai?

- **A** wisdom that offers good advice
- **B** respect and admiration
- **C** talent in all military things
- **D** willingness to die for his master

Answers are on page CA43.

WEEK 13

Content Standard WH7.6 Students analyze the geographic, political, economic, religious, and social structures of the civilizations of Medieval Europe.

Directions: *Select the best answer for each of the following questions.*

MONDAY WH7.6.3

1 Under feudalism, whose responsibility was it to keep roads repaired and enforce the laws?

- **A** kings
- **B** nobles
- **C** serfs
- **D** priests

TUESDAY WH7.6.4

2 What was the disagreement between Pope Gregory VII and King Henry IV, the Holy Roman Emperor, about?

- **A** the boundaries of the Holy Roman Empire
- **B** the appointment of bishops
- **C** the role of monasteries
- **D** the selection of the next pope

WEDNESDAY WH7.6.5

3 What helped establish the idea that the power of government should be limited?

- **A** the Crusades
- **B** the system of feudalism
- **C** the Battle of Hastings
- **D** the Magna Carta

THURSDAY WH7.6.6

4 Which of the following was a cause of the Crusades?

- **A** the desire to free the Holy Land from the Muslim Turks
- **B** the Inquisition in Spain
- **C** the Muslim conquest of Spain
- **D** the need for trade with China

FRIDAY WH7.6.7

Read the passage below and answer the question.

After the . . . pestilence [disease] many buildings of all sizes in every city fell into total ruin for want of habitants. Likewise, many villages and hamlets were deserted, with no house remaining in them, because everyone who had lived there was dead, and indeed many of these villages were never inhabited again. In the following winter there was such a lack of workers in all areas of activity that it was thought that there had hardly ever been such a shortage before; . . .

—Historian Henry Knighton, c. 1388 in *King Death* by Colin Pratt

5 According to the excerpt, how did the Black Death affect population?

- **A** No workers were needed during the winter.
- **B** There was a shortage of housing.
- **C** All the people who had lived in some villages were dead.
- **D** Inhabitants in different cities destroyed their buildings.

Answers are on page CA43.

WEEK 14

Content Standard WH7.7 Students compare and contrast the geographic, political, economic, religious, and social structures of the Meso-American and Andean civilizations.

Directions: *Select the best answer for each of the following questions.*

MONDAY WH7.7.1

1 Which of the following was used to unite the Inca Empire?

- **A** A system of writing was developed.
- **B** Only government officials were allowed to speak Quechua.
- **C** A network of roads was established.
- **D** Horse-drawn wagons carried goods to different markets.

TUESDAY WH7.7.2

2 Like the Spartans, the Aztec

- **A** believed in human sacrifice.
- **B** celebrated the life and death of a soldier.
- **C** thought that art and poetry were important.
- **D** prized agricultural skills.

WEDNESDAY WH7.7.3

3 How did the Spanish defeat the Aztec?

- **A** The Spanish used horses and guns and were helped by an epidemic.
- **B** The Spanish had a large army of Spanish soldiers.
- **C** The Spanish used bows and arrows.
- **D** The Spanish had better ships.

THURSDAY WH7.7.5

4 Which of the following was a Mayan accomplishment?

- **A** the invention of the gun
- **B** a city built in a desert
- **C** the conquest of Mexico
- **D** the development of a 365-day calendar for planting and harvesting crops

FRIDAY WH7.7.4

Read the passage below and answer the question.

[W]e shall vanquish [conquer] them all,
we shall make them our captives,
and thus our city shall be established.
Mexico Tenochtitlan:
where the eagle screeches,
where he spreads his wings,
where the eagle feeds,
where the fish fly,
and where the serpent is torn apart.

—*The Cronica Mexicayotl* in *A Scattering of Jades,* edited by T.J. Knab

5 What is the writer describing in this excerpt?

- **A** where the Aztec set up a safe place for particular animals
- **B** how the Aztec knew where to set up their capital
- **C** where the Aztec went to hunt for food
- **D** how the Aztec thought they should act in all battles

Answers are on page CA43.

WEEK 15

Content Standard WH7.8 Students analyze the origins, accomplishments, and geographic diffusion of the Renaissance.

Directions: *Select the best answer for each of the following questions.*

MONDAY WH7.8.1

1 Interest in the Romans and Greeks led to humanism because

- **A** Europeans began to think people could make the world better.
- **B** people became more interested in heaven than in life in this world.
- **C** the Black Death became a threat.
- **D** people began to write in the vernacular.

TUESDAY WH7.8.2

2 Why was Florence important in the early days of the Renaissance?

- **A** It had conquered most of the other Italian city-states.
- **B** It controlled trade with the Byzantine and Ottoman empires.
- **C** It was the first wealthy Italian city.
- **D** It had been the capital of the Roman Empire.

WEDNESDAY WH7.8.3

3 After the Silk Road reopened,

- **A** the Mongols came to power.
- **B** Italians could sell spices to the Arabs.
- **C** demand for European wool fell.
- **D** the price of silk fell and the European demand for it increased.

THURSDAY WH7.8.4

4 The invention of the printing press

- **A** encouraged new artistic methods, such as perspective and shadow.
- **B** was based on Greek technology.
- **C** spread humanist ideas.
- **D** discouraged interest in the Bible.

FRIDAY WH7.8.5

Examine the statue below. Answer the question.

David by Michelangelo

5 In this statue Michelangelo shows

- **A** the new Renaissance knowledge of human anatomy.
- **B** the Renaissance interest in Roman, Greek, and Jewish history.
- **C** the ability to use perspective.
- **D** the symbolism of medieval artists.

Answers are on page CA43.

WEEK 16

Content Standard WH7.9 Students analyze the historical developments of the Reformation.

Directions: *Select the best answer for each of the following questions.*

MONDAY WH7.9.3

1 The Calvinist practice of congregations choosing their own leaders supported the democratic idea that

A there should be one state-supported religion.

B people should elect their political leaders.

C the king should select all colonial governors.

D government should have three separate branches.

TUESDAY WH7.9.5

2 Which of the following were part of the Counter-Reformation?

A strict rules for the behavior of priests and bishops

B seminaries closing

C an end to the Inquisition

D the disbanding of the Jesuits

WEDNESDAY WH7.9.6

3 European missionaries spread Catholicism to

A Australia

B the Middle East

C the Philippine Islands

D Spain

THURSDAY WH7.9.7

4 In 1492, whom did King Ferdinand and Queen Isabella order to become Catholic or leave Spain?

A Martin Luther

B the Jesuits

C Jews and Muslims

D John Calvin

FRIDAY WH7.9.2

Read the passage below and answer the question.

Those preachers of indulgences are in error, who say that by the pope's indulgences a man is freed from every penalty, and saved; . . .
It must needs be, therefore, that that greater part of the people are deceived by that indiscriminate and high sounding promise of release from penalty.

—Martin Luther, "Disputation of Doctor Martin Luther on the Power and Efficacy of Indulgences" (Ninety-Five Theses)

5 According to the quote, what does Luther think of indulgences?

A They will not help a person avoid punishment.

B The pope should sell more of them.

C They help people get into heaven.

D The pope should give them away.

Answers are on page CA43.

Practice It!

Next comes an easy-to-follow **practice** activity for the reading skill.

2 Practice It!

Look at the two quotes below. Each has a different opinion about "the people." On a separate sheet of paper, restate each opinion in your own words. Discuss your conclusions with a partner.

> "The people are turbulent [disorderly] and changing. . . . They seldom judge or determine right."
>
> —*Alexander Hamilton, Federalist, page 292*

Read to Write

Write a paragraph describing a person or event about which you feel very strongly. Now try to write a paragraph about the same person or event without including any personal opinion.

▲ Alexander Hamilton

> "I am not among those who fear the people. They, and not the rich, are our dependence [what we depend on] for continued freedom."
>
> —*Thomas Jefferson, Republican, page 293*

▲ Thomas Jefferson

3 Apply It!

Look for examples of bias in comments made by key figures described in the text.

CHAPTER 5 • The Federalist Era 277

Read to Write

Writing about what you read will help you remember the event.

Reading Skills Handbook

Located on pages 14–23 is a handbook that is full of good **reading strategies** to help you read your text. You can look back at this at any time as you read.

Reading for a Reason

Why are you reading that paperback mystery? What do you hope to get from your American history textbook? And are you going to read either of these books in the same way that you read a restaurant menu? The point is, you read for different reasons. The reason you are reading something helps you decide on the reading strategies you use with a text. In other words, how you read will depend on why you are reading.

Knowing Your Reason for Reading

In school and in life, you will have many reasons for reading, and those reasons will lead you to a wide range of materials:

- **To learn and understand new information,** you might read news magazines, textbooks, news on the Internet, books about your favorite pastime, encyclopedia articles, primary and secondary sources for a school report, instructions on how to use a calling card, or directions for a standardized test.
- **To find specific information,** you might look at the sports section for the score of last night's game, a notice on where to register for a field trip, weather reports, bank statements, or television listings.
- **To be entertained,** you might read your favorite magazine, e-mails or letters from friends, the Sunday comics, or even novels, short stories, plays, or poems!

Adjusting How Fast You Read

How quickly or how carefully you should read a text depends on your purpose for reading it. Because there are many reasons and ways to read, think about your purpose and choose the strategy that works best. Try out these strategies:

- **Scanning** means quickly running your eyes over the material, looking for key words or phrases that point to the information you are looking for. Scan when you need to find a particular piece or type of information. For example, you might scan a newspaper for movie show times.
- **Skimming** means quickly reading a piece of writing to find its main idea or to get a general overview of it. For example, you might skim the sports section of the daily newspaper to find out how your favorite teams are doing. Or you might skim a chapter in your textbook to prepare for a test.
- **Careful reading** involves reading very slowly and paying close attention with a purpose in mind. Read carefully when you are learning new concepts, following complicated directions, or preparing to explain information to someone else.

CHECKING YOUR UNDERSTANDING

If you were working on a research paper on the American Revolution, how would you adjust the speed at which you were reading for each of the following cases?

1. You have just found a 1,200-page work that covers the entire colonial and revolutionary era of the British colonies in North America.
2. You have discovered an article in a leading history magazine that supports every point that you are trying to make.

Reading Skills Handbook 17

Reading Skills Handbook

Apply It!

Here is an opportunity to **apply** what you have learned.

Sections

A section is a division, or part, of a chapter. The first page of the section, the Section Opener, helps you set a purpose for reading.

Looking Back, Looking Ahead

Read the **connection** between what you already know and what you are about to read.

Content Vocabulary

This list points out important social studies **terms** and their pronunciation.

Academic Vocabulary

This list names other **words** you might not know that will come up in your reading.

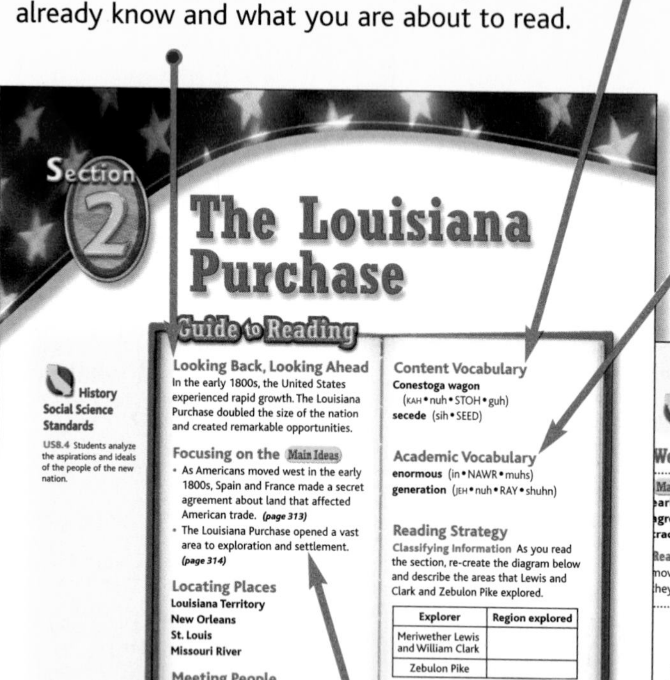

Section 2

The Louisiana Purchase

Guide to Reading

History Social Science Standards

US8.4 Students analyze the aspirations and ideals of the people of the new nation.

Looking Back, Looking Ahead
In the early 1800s, the United States experienced rapid growth. The Louisiana Purchase doubled the size of the nation and created remarkable opportunities.

Focusing on the Main Ideas
- As Americans moved west in the early 1800s, Spain and France made a secret agreement about land that affected American trade. *(page 313)*
- The Louisiana Purchase opened a vast area to exploration and settlement. *(page 314)*

Locating Places
Louisiana Territory
New Orleans
St. Louis
Missouri River

Meeting People
Meriwether Lewis
William Clark
Sacagawea (SA • kuh • juh • WEE • uh)
Zebulon Pike

Content Vocabulary
Conestoga wagon (KAH • nuh • STOH • guh)
secede (sih • SEED)

Academic Vocabulary
enormous (in • NAWR • muhs)
generation (JEH • nuh • RAY • shuhn)

Reading Strategy
Classifying Information As you read the section, re-create the diagram below and describe the areas that Lewis and Clark and Zebulon Pike explored.

Explorer	Region explored
Meriwether Lewis and William Clark	
Zebulon Pike	

NATIONAL GEOGRAPHIC Who & When?

1804 · 1805 · 1806 · 1807

Oct. 1803 Senate ratifies Louisiana Purchase treaty

May 1804 Lewis and Clark begin expedition

Sep. 1806 Lewis and Clark return to St. Louis

Nov. 1806 Zebulon Pike reaches Pikes Peak

312 CHAPTER 6 • The Age of Jefferson

US8.4.1 Describe the country's physical landscapes, political divisions, and territorial expansion during the terms of the first four presidents.

Western Territory

Main Idea As Americans moved west in the early 1800s, Spain and France made a secret agreement about land that affected American trade.

Reading Connection What challenges come with moving? Read to learn what the pioneers faced as they went west.

An American Story

Why did Americans risk everything they had to travel west? An English visitor, Harriet Martineau, observed:

> "The pride and delight of Americans is in their quantity of land. . . . The possession of land is the aim of all action . . . and the cure for all social evils. . . . If a man is disappointed in politics or love, he goes and buys land."
>
> —from *Society in America*

Moving West During the early 1800s, more and more Americans moved west in search of land and adventure. These pioneers headed over the mountains into Kentucky and Tennessee and the less settled areas of the Northwest Territory. Most of these pioneers were farmers. They made a long and exhausting journey over the Appalachian Mountains.

Settlers loaded their household goods into **Conestoga wagons** (KAH • nuh • STOH • guh), sturdy vehicles topped with white canvas. For these westward-bound pioneers, two vital possessions were a rifle for protection and hunting and an ax to hack their way through the dense forests.

In 1800 the territory of the United States extended only as far west as the Mississippi River. The area to the west of the river—known as the **Louisiana Territory**—belonged to Spain. It was an **enormous** area of land, extending south to the city of **New Orleans** and west to the Rocky Mountains. Its northern boundaries remained undefined.

Many pioneers established farms along rivers that fed into the upper Mississippi River. The Spanish allowed Americans to sail on the lower Mississippi and trade in New Orleans. For the western farmers, this right was vital. The goods they sent downriver were unloaded in New Orleans and sent by ship to markets on the East Coast.

The French Threat In 1802 the Spanish suddenly changed their policy. They refused to allow American goods to move into or past New Orleans. That same year, President Jefferson learned that Spain and France had made a secret agreement that transferred the Louisiana Territory to France. Jefferson was alarmed. He thought French control would jeopardize American trade on the Mississippi River. He authorized Robert Livingston, the new minister to France, to negotiate for the purchase of New Orleans and other French territory.

Revolt in Santo Domingo The leader of France, Napoleon Bonaparte (nuh • POHL • yuhn BOH • nuh • PAHRT), hoped to use Santo Domingo as a Caribbean naval base from which he could control an American empire. However, a revolt in Santo Domingo ended Bonaparte's dream of a Western empire.

Inspired by the ideas of the French Revolution, enslaved Africans and other laborers in Santo Domingo rebelled against the island's plantation owners. After fierce and bitter fighting, the rebels, led by Toussaint-Louverture (TOO • SA LOO • vuhr • TYUR), declared the colony an independent republic. Toussaint set up an independent government.

In 1802 Napoleon sent troops to regain control. The French captured Toussaint but could not regain control of the island. By 1804 the French were driven out of Santo Domingo and the country regained its original name of Haiti.

Reading Check **Explain** Why was the Mississippi River important to western farmers?

CHAPTER 6 • The Age of Jefferson 313

Focusing on the Main Ideas

Preview the **main ideas** of each section which are repeated in the reading.

An American Story

Read about **real-life** Americans and what they thought and did.

Pike's Expedition Even before Lewis and Clark returned, Jefferson sent others to explore the wilderness. Lieutenant **Zebulon Pike** led two expeditions between 1805 and 1807, traveling through the upper Mississippi River valley and into the region that is now the state of Colorado. In Colorado, Pike found a snow-capped mountain he called Grand Peak. Today this mountain is known as Pikes Peak. Pike's account of his expeditions gave Americans their first detailed description of the Great Plains and the Rocky Mountains.

Federalists Plan to Secede Many Federalists opposed the Louisiana Purchase. They feared that the states carved out of the new territory would become Republican, reducing the Federalists' power. A group of Federalists in Massachusetts plotted to **secede** (sih • SEED)—withdraw—from the United States. They wanted New England to form a separate "Northern Confederacy." The plotters realized that to have any chance of success, the Northern Confederacy would have to include New York as well as New England.

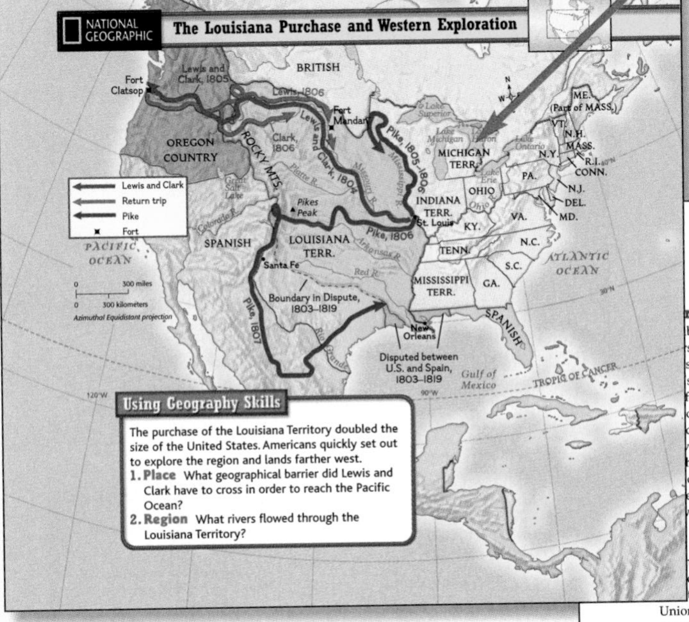

Using Geography Skills

The purchase of the Louisiana Territory doubled the size of the United States. Americans quickly set out to explore the region and lands farther west.

1. **Place** What geographical barrier did Lewis and Clark have to cross in order to reach the Pacific Ocean?
2. **Region** What rivers flowed through the Louisiana Territory?

Map

Maps help you learn how **geography and history** are related.

ralists Support Burr In 1804 the blican caucus nominated Thomas son for a second term as president. son and the Republicans, in doubt about s loyalty to the party, did not nominate for another term as vice president. Instead, chose George Clinton of New York. Burr decided to run for governor of New York. Federalists supported Burr as they were hing for a powerful ally in New York who d support their plan for the Northern ederacy. Alexander Hamilton, however, his weight against Burr's election.

and Hamilton Alexander Hamilton never trusted Aaron Burr. Now Hamilton concerned about rumors that Burr had tly agreed to lead New York out of the Union. Hamilton called Burr "a danger... man." When Burr... election for governor, he blamed Hamilton and challenged him to a duel. In July 1804, the two men—armed with pistols—met in Weehawken, New Jersey. Hamilton hated dueling and pledged not to shoot at his rival. Burr, however, did fire and aimed to hit Hamilton. Seriously wounded, Hamilton died the next day. Burr fled to avoid arrest on the charge of murder.

The Northern Confederacy Fails With Burr on the run and with almost no support in the New England states, the plans for the Northern Confederacy failed. The results of the election of 1804 showed how thoroughly the Federalists had been discredited. Jefferson and Clinton captured 162 electoral votes to 14 for the Federalist candidates Charles Pinckney and Rufus King.

Reading Check **Summarize** Why did France sell the Louisiana Territory to the United States?

Reading Check

This is a **self-check** question to see if you understand the main ideas.

History Online
Study Central Need help understanding the Louisiana Purchase and its exploration? Visit ca.hss.glencoe.com and click on Study Central.

Section 2 Review

Reading Summary

Review the Main Ideas

- American settlers in the West depended on the use of the lower Mississippi River and the port of New Orleans to trade their farm products. That control was threatened when France gained control of the Louisiana Territory.
- After the purchase of Louisiana from the French, President Jefferson sent Lewis and Clark and others to explore the new territory.

What Did You Learn?

1. Which European countries controlled the Louisiana Territory until 1800?
2. Name the famous Native American woman who Lewis and Clark met along their journey.

Critical Thinking

3. **Organizing Information** Create a diagram like the one below that lists the benefits of acquiring the Louisiana Territory. CA HR5

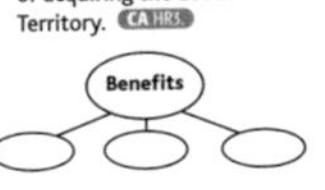

4. **The Big Ideas** Why was the French port of New Orleans important to the United States? CA CS2
5. **Cause and Effect** How could the Lewis and Clark expedition prepare people who wanted to move west? Write a paragraph describing your conclusions. CA HI2
6. **Analysis** **Assess** What was the relationship between the Louisiana Purchase and political power? How did Jefferson's political opponents react? Write an essay explaining your assessment. CA CS1 CA 8WA2.3

CHAPTER 6 • The Age of Jefferson 317

Study Central

Here you can receive **help** with homework.

Section Review

Here you can **review** the main topics and answer questions about what you have read.

California Standards

The California Historical and Social Science Analysis Skills and English–Language Arts **standards** that are covered are shown here.

Chapter Assessment

These pages offer you a chance to check how much you remember after reading the chapter.

Review Content Vocabulary

Content vocabulary is reviewed here.

Review the Main Ideas

Revisit the **Main Ideas** found in your reading.

Read to Write

You are reminded about the chapter **Big Ideas** here.

Review Content Vocabulary

1. Use the following terms to write a paragraph about the new U.S. government:

cabinet | implied powers
caucus | states' rights

Review the Main Ideas

Section 1 • The First President

2. Why did Hamilton want national taxes? Why did some oppose the taxes?
3. What was the importance of the Judiciary Act of 1789?

Section 2 • Early Challenges

4. What caused farmers in western Pennsylvania to revolt during the Whiskey Rebellion?
5. What was the significance of the Battle of Fallen Timbers?

Section 3 • The First Political Parties

6. According to Hamilton, what are implied powers?
7. What actions by France led to an undeclared war with the United States?

Critical Thinking

8. **Evaluate** Refer to the grievances listed in the Declaration of Independence. How were these grievances addressed in the Bill of Rights? CA CS1
9. **Analyze** What did President Washington say in his Farewell Address about political parties and foreign policy? CA HR1
10. **Compare and Contrast** In a brief essay, compare the positions of the Federalists and Democratic-Republicans on the national bank. CA HR5

Geography Skills

Using this map, answer the following questions about the election of 1796. CA CS3

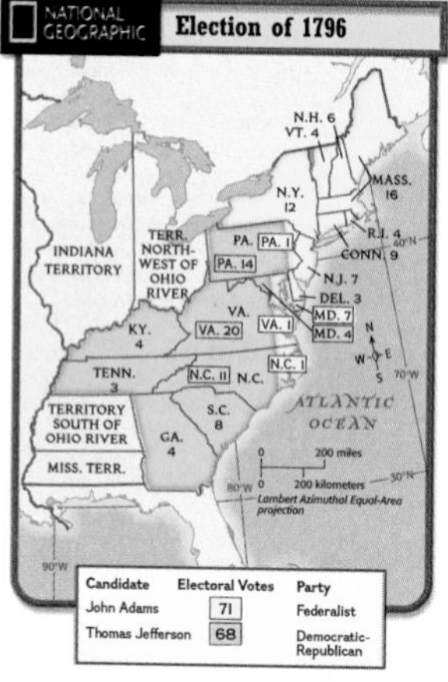

Candidate	Electoral Votes	Party
John Adams	71	Federalist
Thomas Jefferson	68	Democratic-Republican

11. **Identify** How many states did John Adams win? How many did Thomas Jefferson win?
12. **Evaluate** What was the total electoral vote count for each man? What was the election result?
13. **Region** What was the distribution of votes by state? What pattern do you see?

300 CHAPTER 5 • The Federalist Era

History Online
Self-Check Quiz Visit ca.hss.glencoe.com to prepare for the Chapter 5 test.

Read to Write

14. **The Big Ideas Government and Democracy** Political ideas and major events shape how people form governments. Select an event from this chapter. Write an essay describing how people and ideas affected government through that event. CA 8WS1.1
15. **Using Your FOLDABLES** Review the "American firsts" that you listed in your foldable. Using numbers, rank each first from the most important to the least important. Explain the reasons for your highest and lowest rankings. CA HR1

Using Academic Vocabulary

16. Read the following sentence and then write the meaning of the underlined word.
The new federal government was interested in increasing revenue in order to pay off its debts.

Building Citizenship

17. **Research** Work in groups of four to discuss and develop answers to these questions:
- How does the Bill of Rights reflect the principle of limited government?
- What are two individual rights protected in the Bill of Rights?
- Why would it be necessary to change the Constitution? CA 8RC2.0

Reviewing Skills

18. **Recognizing Bias** Imagine that you were living in the United States in 1798. Write an editorial to your newspaper that demonstrates bias about your view as to whether the Alien and Sedition Acts violated the U.S. Constitution. Use details from the text and chart about the Alien and Sedition Acts on page 295. CA 8WA2.4

19. **Sequencing** Create a time line that lists key events in President Adams's dispute with France. Write a paragraph analyzing President Adams's handling of this dispute. CA CS2

Standards Practice

Select the best answer for each of the following questions.

20 Thomas Jefferson and Alexander Hamilton served as members of Washington's

A congress.
B judiciary.
C cabinet.
D military.

21 Which amendment of the Bill of Rights protects the rights of the states?

A First Amendment
B Fifth Amendment
C Sixth Amendment
D Tenth Amendment

22 The XYZ Affair dealt with problems between the United States and

A France.
B Spain.
C Great Britain.
D Canada.

23 Hamilton proposed a national tax on imports, or a(n)

A bond.
B impressment.
C caucus.
D tariff.

CHAPTER 5 • The Federalist Era 301

Using Academic Vocabulary

Academic vocabulary is reviewed here.

Review Arrows

Look for the Review arrows that tell you are **reviewing** material you have learned before.

Standards Practice

Here you get a chance to practice questions related to the **standards**.

California Standards

A Guide to the California Standards appears on pages CA1-CA14 of your textbook. This guide lists all the History–Social Science Standards for grade 8. They are covered in your textbook. In addition, the guide includes the Historical and Social Sciences Analysis Skills and the English-Language Arts Standards, which are addressed throughout the textbook.

For Students and Their Families

Here is an explanation of what is contained in the **Guide to the California Standards.**

Analysis Skills

Here is a list of standards that relate to **thinking and research skills.** You can develop these skills in your history class.

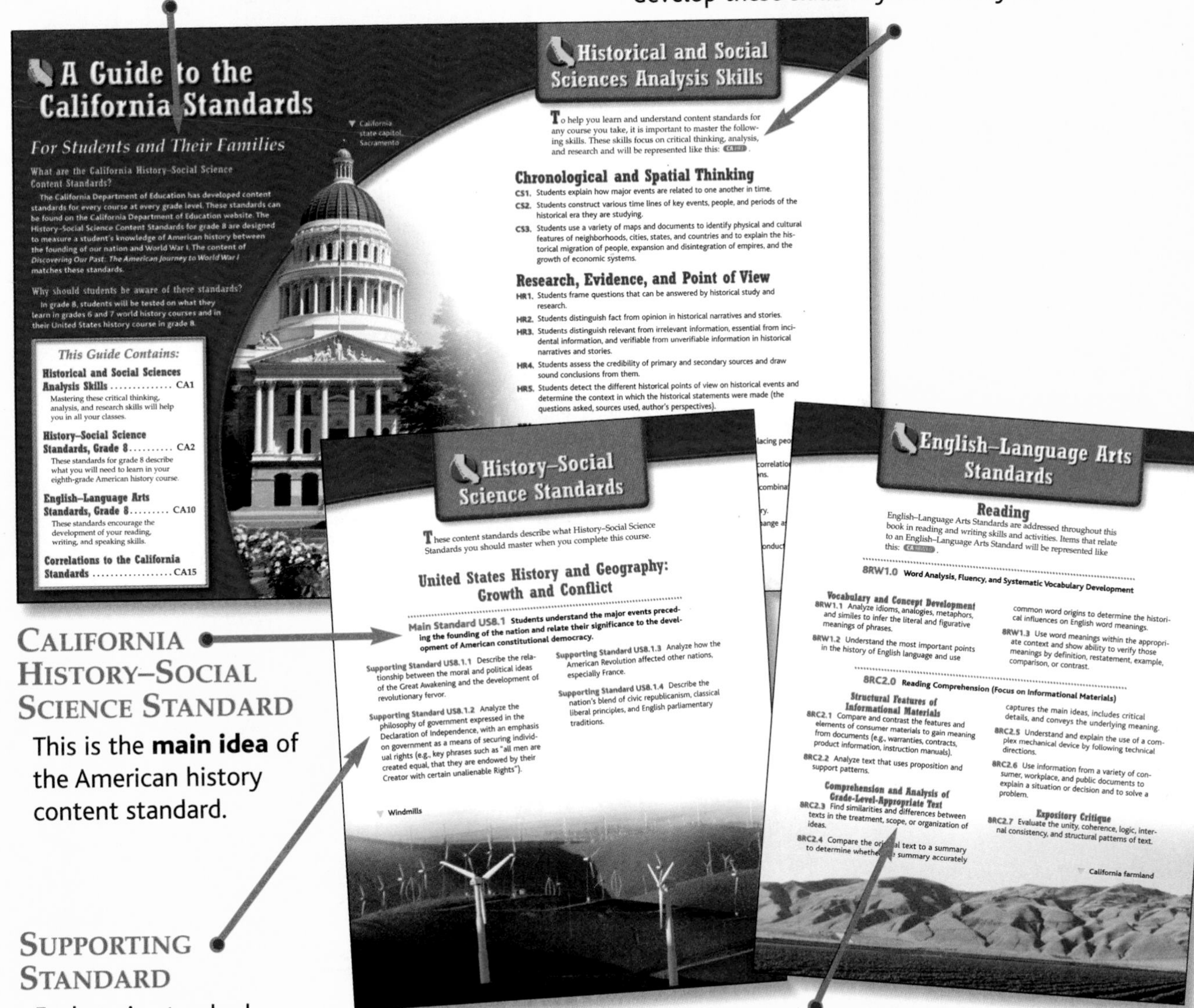

A Guide to the California Standards

For Students and Their Families

What are the California History–Social Science Content Standards?

The California Department of Education has developed content standards for every course at every grade level. These standards can be found on the California Department of Education website. The History–Social Science Content Standards for grade 8 are designed to measure a student's knowledge of American history between the founding of our nation and World War I. The content of *Discovering Our Past: The American Journey to World War I* matches these standards.

Why should students be aware of these standards?

In grade 8, students will be tested on what they learn in grades 6 and 7 world history courses and in their United States history course in grade 8.

▼ California state capitol, Sacramento

This Guide Contains:

Historical and Social Sciences Analysis Skills

To help you learn and understand content standards for any course you take, it is important to master the following skills. These skills focus on critical thinking, analysis, and research and will be represented like this: CA HR1.

Chronological and Spatial Thinking

CS1. Students explain how major events are related to one another in time.
CS2. Students construct various time lines of key events, people, and periods of the historical era they are studying.
CS3. Students use a variety of maps and documents to identify physical and cultural features of neighborhoods, cities, states, and countries and to explain the historical migration of people, expansion and disintegration of empires, and the growth of economic systems.

Research, Evidence, and Point of View

HR1. Students frame questions that can be answered by historical study and research.
HR2. Students distinguish fact from opinion in historical narratives and stories.
HR3. Students distinguish relevant from irrelevant information, essential from incidental information, and verifiable from unverifiable information in historical narratives and stories.
HR4. Students assess the credibility of primary and secondary sources and draw sound conclusions from them.
HR5. Students detect the different historical points of view on historical events and determine the context in which the historical statements were made (the questions asked, sources used, author's perspectives).

History–Social Science Standards

These content standards describe what History–Social Science Standards you should master when you complete this course.

United States History and Geography: Growth and Conflict

Main Standard US8.1 Students understand the major events preceding the founding of the nation and relate their significance to the development of American constitutional democracy.

Supporting Standard US8.1.1 Describe the relationship between the moral and political ideas of the Great Awakening and the development of revolutionary fervor.

Supporting Standard US8.1.2 Analyze the philosophy of government expressed in the Declaration of Independence, with an emphasis on government as a means of securing individual rights (e.g., key phrases such as "all men are created equal, that they are endowed by their Creator with certain unalienable Rights").

Supporting Standard US8.1.3 Analyze how the American Revolution affected other nations, especially France.

Supporting Standard US8.1.4 Describe the nation's blend of civic republicanism, classical liberal principles, and English parliamentary traditions.

▼ Windmills

English–Language Arts Standards

Reading

English–Language Arts Standards are addressed throughout this book in reading and writing skills and activities. Items that relate to an English–Language Arts Standard will be represented like this: CA 8RW1.0.

8RW1.0 Word Analysis, Fluency, and Systematic Vocabulary Development

Vocabulary and Concept Development

8RW1.1 Analyze idioms, analogies, metaphors, and similes to infer the literal and figurative meanings of phrases.

8RW1.2 Understand the most important points in the history of English language and use common word origins to determine the historical influences on English word meanings.

8RW1.3 Use word meanings within the appropriate context and show ability to verify those meanings by definition, restatement, example, comparison, or contrast.

8RC2.0 Reading Comprehension (Focus on Informational Materials)

Structural Features of Informational Materials

8RC2.1 Compare and contrast the features and elements of consumer materials to gain meaning from documents (e.g., warranties, contracts, product information, instruction manuals).

8RC2.2 Analyze text that uses proposition and support patterns.

Comprehension and Analysis of Grade-Level-Appropriate Text

8RC2.3 Find similarities and differences between texts in the treatment, scope, or organization of ideas.

8RC2.4 Compare the original text to a summary to determine whether the summary accurately captures the main ideas, includes critical details, and conveys the underlying meaning.

8RC2.5 Understand and explain the use of a complex mechanical device by following technical directions.

8RC2.6 Use information from a variety of consumer, workplace, and public documents to explain a situation or decision and to solve a problem.

Expository Critique

8RC2.7 Evaluate the unity, coherence, logic, internal consistency, and structural patterns of text.

▼ California farmland

California History–Social Science Standard

This is the **main idea** of the American history content standard.

Supporting Standard

Each main standard has **more specific** supporting standards.

California English–Language Arts Standards

These **standards** are for reading, writing, written and oral English language conventions, and listening and speaking. Each **main standard** has one or more **supporting standards.**

Previewing Your Textbook

California Content Standards

The **standards** covered on a page will be listed at the top of that page.

California Content Standards

You will also find **standards** listed in the side column at the beginning of each section.

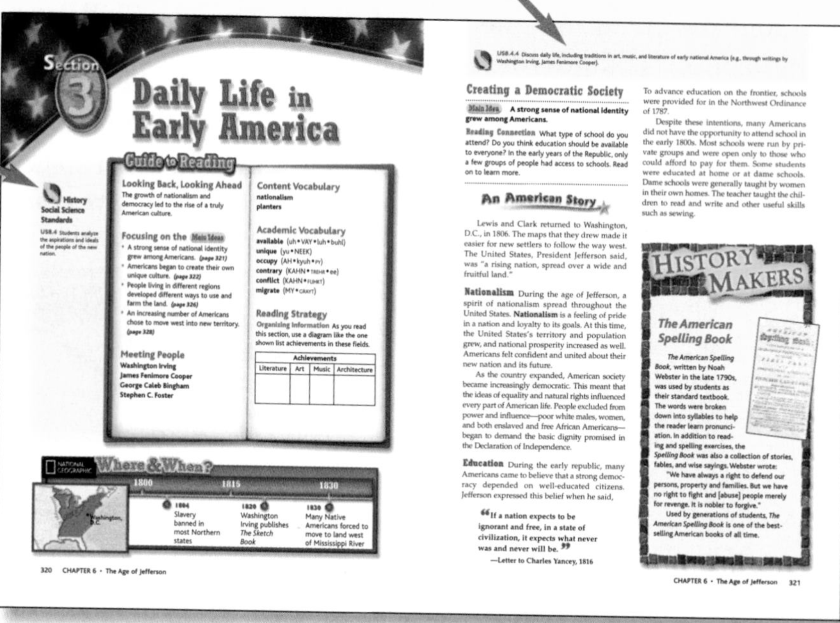

Tools of the Historian

Here is an explanation of how to use the Historical and Social Sciences Analysis Skill for **chronology.**

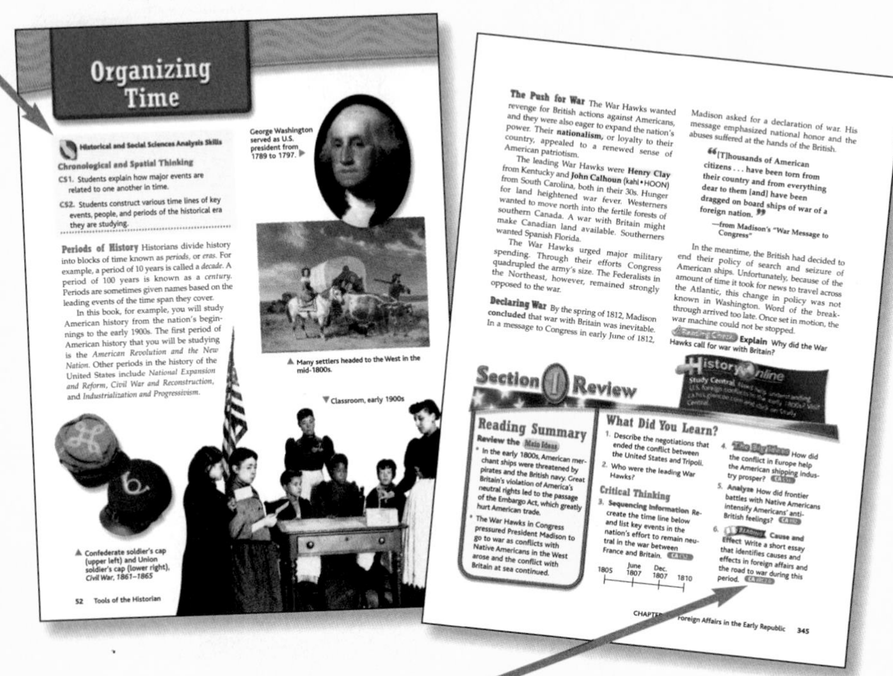

California Standards

The California History–Social Science and English–Language Arts **standards** that are covered are shown here.

California Standards Handbook

This handbook is found on pages 862–884. It gives you another chance to practice your understanding of the **eighth-grade content standards.**

Main Standard

The chart shows the **main standard** of the American history standards.

Where Can I Find It?

Here is more information about the **standard.** The explanations tell **where** in your text this standard and its supporting standards are covered.

Supporting Standards

The chart also lists the **supporting standards** for the main standards.

California Standards Handbook

US8.4

What Is the Standard?	Where Can I Find It?
US8.4 Students analyze the aspirations and ideals of the people of the new nation.	**Chapters 5 and 6** cover the early years of the Republic. New policies were developed and the United States grew in size, while daily life reflected uniquely American qualities. Additional information can be found in **Chapter 10.**
US8.4.1 Describe the country's physical landscapes, political divisions, and territorial expansion during the terms of the first four presidents.	**Chapter 5, Section 3** Political parties developed and influenced national policy. (Review pages 291–297.) **Chapter 6, Sections 2 and 3** America's [illegible]scape encouraged settlement, agri[illegible], and industry, while the Louisiana [illegible]ase extended the territory of the Uni[illegible]tates westward to the Rocky Moun[illegible]. (Review pages 313–317, 326–327.)
US8.4.2 Explain the policy significance of famous speeches (e.g., Washington's Farewell Address, Jefferson's 1801 Inaugural Address, John Q. Adams' Fourth of July 1821 Address).	**Chapter 5, Section 2 and Chapter 6, Section 1** Through important speeches, leaders, including Washington, Jefferson, and John Quincy Adams, influenced views on foreign policy and the power of the federal government. (Review pages 289, 307, and 331.)
US8.4.3 Analyze the rise of capitalism and the economic problems and conflicts that accompanied it (e.g., Jackson's opposition to the National Bank; early decisions of the U.S. Supreme Court that reinforced the sanctity of contracts and a capitalist economic system of law).	**Chapters 6, Section 1 and Chapter 10, Section 3** While the Supreme Court had ruled in favor of the National Bank, as well as other measures in support of a capitalist economic system, some politicians, such as Andrew Jackson, fought against the Bank. (Review pages 310–311, 459–460.)
US8.4.4 Discuss daily life, including traditions in art, music, and literature, of early national America (e.g., through writings by Washington Irving, James Fenimore Cooper).	**Chapter 6, Section 3** In the early Republic, daily life for Americans varied by region, and Americans began to develop their own forms of literature, music, and architecture. (Review pages 321–329.)

Standards Practice

1 What river pro[illegible]ded the eastern boundary of the Louisiana Purchase?

A Missouri River
B Columbia River
C Mississippi River
D Rio Grande River

868 California Standards Handbook

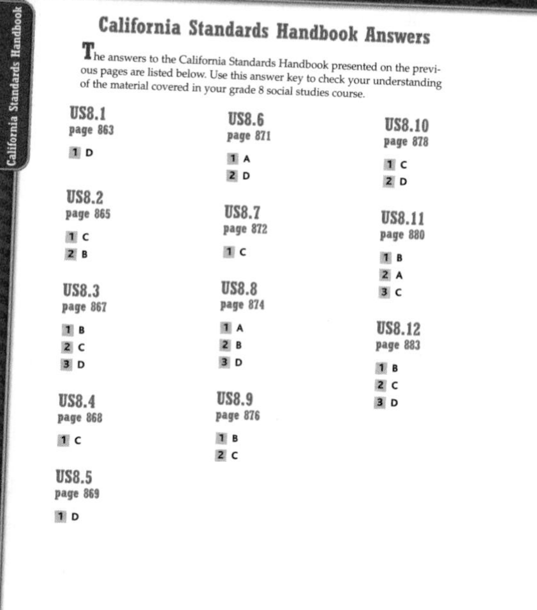
California Standards Handbook

California Standards Handbook Answers

The answers to the California Standards Handbook presented on the previous pages are listed below. Use this answer key to check your understanding of the material covered in your grade 8 social studies course.

US8.1 page 863
1 D

US8.2 page 865
1 C
2 B

US8.3 page 867
1 B
2 C
3 D

US8.4 page 868
1 C

US8.5 page 869
1 D

US8.6 page 871
1 A
2 D

US8.7 page 872
1 C

US8.8 page 874
1 A
2 B
3 D

US8.9 page 876
1 B
2 C

US8.10 page 878
1 C
2 D

US8.11 page 880
1 B
2 A
3 C

US8.12 page 883
1 B
2 C
3 D

884 California Standards Handbook

Standards Practice

Practice questions are written in the same way that you will see them on the standards assessment.

Answers to the Standards Handbook

An **answer key** allows you to check your answers.

Special Features

Special features supply more information about topics in a chapter or unit. They help history come alive.

America's Literature

The literature selection is connected to people or events in the chapter.

Before You Read

Get an idea of what the literature selection is about **before** you start reading.

Vocabulary Preview

Here are words and terms that may be new to you.

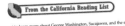

America's Literature

Crossing the Panther's Path

By Elizabeth Alder

Before You Read

The Scene: This part of the book is set at Grouseland, Governor Harrison's home in Vincennes, Indiana.

The Characters: Tecumseh is a leader of the Shawnee. His translator is Billy Caldwell, a teenager whose parents are Native American and white. William Henry Harrison is governor of the Indiana Territory. Shabonee is Native American and a follower of Tecumseh.

The Plot: Billy wants to help Native Americans regain the Ohio River valley. He believes Tecumseh can unite the tribes and accomplish this goal. In this part of the story, Tecumseh meets with Harrison. He wants to try to change Harrison's plans to help white... over more Native American lands.

Vocabulary Preview

adversary: person who supports a different side of an opinion or disagreement; enemy

disdain: a feeling that someone or something is below one's notice; contempt

dismay: confusion about how to deal with a situation

emphatically: in a forceful way

haughty: blatantly proud and scornful

wrath: great anger that is caused by something unjust

Have you ever wanted someone t... to your side of a disagreement? In t... excerpt, Tecumseh explains Native... American views about the ownersh... land. In return, Tecumseh learns fir... what Harrison thinks of Native Ame...

annuities be explained further. These were gifts of goods or money, Billy explained. Part of the annuities were paid in the form of alcohol. "It disgusts me to see the Americans use their cheap tricks against the Indian nations," Tecumseh said when Billy finished. "You have no right to ply[19] the chiefs with whiskey until they are befuddled. It is forbidden by the Greenville Treaty. You must blame yourself as the cause of trouble between us and the tribes who sold the land to you." Tecumseh argued fiercely. "I want the present boundary line to continue. Should you cross it, I assure you it will be productive of bad consequences."

Tecumseh nodded for Billy to begin translating his words, while he watched Harrison's face to read any signs that might cross his features. He was answered only by Harrison's stony expression. Billy ended the talks as Tecumseh instructed him. "Governor Harrison," he said, "Chief Tecumseh desires that this disagreement be placed before the Great Chief of the Long Knives."

Harrison coolly agreed. "Yes, I will send word of your position to President Madison; however, I can assure you that the President will protect with the sword what he considers fairly bought."

"I do not wish to make war upon the United States," Tecumseh said emphatically. "I wish only that illegal purchases of Indian lands cease. Your stance forces us to ally ourselves with the British. Tell your President what is in my heart that he may know my intentions."

"I will tell the President what you have said," Harrison answered. "But I say there is not the least probability that he will accede[20] to your terms."

"As your Great Chief is to determine the matter, I hope the Great Spirit will put enough sense in his head to induce him to direct you to give up this land."

Tecumseh put his hand on the stone head of the tomahawk that jutted from his belt. The muscles in his jaw tightened. He seemed resigned to the knowledge that none of his arguments would turn the hearts of the Americans. He looked to the east. He knew that the American President lived many days' travel toward the rising sun. He had heard that Madison was a small man, undistinguished as a public speaker, who had never commanded soldiers in a battle. This seemed puzzling, for it was strength and eloquence and prowess[21] in combat that marked a man for greatness among the Indian nations.

[19] **ply:** to keep supplying something to
[20] **accede:** to give in to a request
[21] **prowess:** skill and courage

Responding to the Literature

1. What did Tecumseh compare selling land to? Why?
2. What kept a war from starting at this meeting?
3. **Analyze** In the first three paragraphs, how do Tecumseh and Harrison each try to show that he is more powerful?
4. **Explain** What are the literal and figurative meanings of this phrase: "The President will protect with the sword what he considers fairly bought"?
5. **Read to Write** Compare the information on pages 341–342 with this selection. How did the author use both fact and imagination to write this story? Include examples to support your conclusions. List other people or events in the story that you could verify as being real or imaginary.

351

Reading On Your Own...

From the California Reading List

Do you want to learn more about George Washington, Sacajawea, and the early years of the United States? You might be interested in the following books.

Biography

Founding Father: Rediscovering George Washington by Richard Brookhiser explores Washington as a person, a soldier, and a political leader. He explains why Washington was so important in forming the future of the United States. ***The content of this book is related to*** *History–Social Studies Standard US8.2.*

Nonfiction

Old Ironsides: Americans Build a Fighting Ship by David Weitzman invites readers to see how this great warship was built. As readers follow John Aylwin, a young worker on the ship, they learn what it took to make "Old Ironsides." ***The content of this book is related to*** *History–Social Studies Standard US8.5.*

Historical Fiction

Carry On, Mr. Bowditch by Jean L. Latham tells the amazing tale of Nathaniel Bowditch. Although he had very little education, he mastered sea navigation during his voyages around the world. His book *American Practical Navigator* was used with few changes into the 1900s. ***The content of this book is related to*** *History–Social Studies Standard US8.6.*

Historical Fiction

Sacajawea: The Story of Bird Woman and the Lewis and Clark Expedition by Joseph Bruchac has Sacajawea and Clark taking turns describing events. The story also includes parts of the explorers' journals and Shoshone tales. ***The content of this book is related to*** *History–Social Studies Standard US8.4.*

352

Responding to the Literature

The questions help you check your understanding of the story. The **writing** activity asks you to analyze the reading.

Biography

Read more about important **people** and what they achieved.

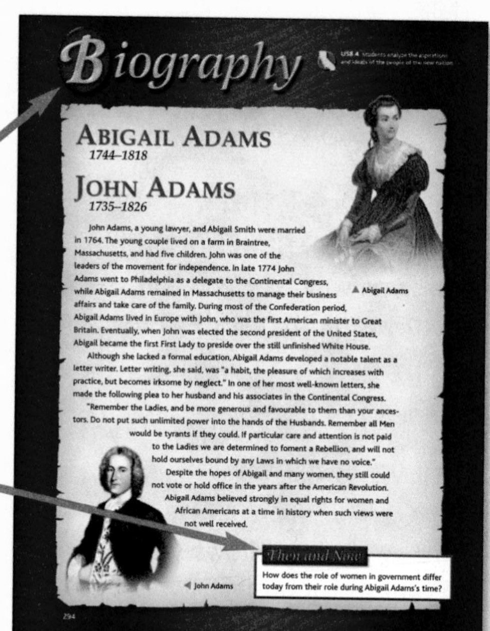

Biography

ABIGAIL ADAMS
1744–1818

JOHN ADAMS
1735–1826

John Adams, a young lawyer, and Abigail Smith were married in 1764. The young couple lived on a farm in Braintree, Massachusetts, and had five children. John was one of the leaders of the movement for independence. In late 1774 John Adams went to Philadelphia as a delegate to the Continental Congress, while Abigail Adams remained in Massachusetts to manage their business affairs and take care of the family. During most of the Confederation period, Abigail Adams lived in Europe with John, who was the first American minister to Great Britain. Eventually, when John was elected the second president of the United States, Abigail became the first First Lady to preside over the still unfinished White House.

Although she lacked a formal education, Abigail Adams developed a notable talent as a letter writer. Letter writing, she said, was "a habit, the pleasure of which increases with practice, but becomes irksome by neglect." In one of her most well-known letters, she made the following plea to her husband and his associates in the Continental Congress.

"Remember the Ladies, and be more generous and favourable to them than your ancestors. Do not put such unlimited power into the hands of the Husbands. Remember all Men would be tyrants if they could. If particular care and attention is not paid to the Ladies we are determined to foment a Rebellion, and will not hold ourselves bound by any Laws in which we have no voice."

Despite the hopes of Abigail and many women, they still could not vote or hold office in the years after the American Revolution. Abigail Adams believed strongly in equal rights for women and African Americans at a time in history when such views were not well received.

▲ Abigail Adams

◄ John Adams

Then and Now

How does the role of women in government differ today from their role during Abigail Adams's time?

294

Reading On Your Own . . .

These books are suggested readings about topics in the unit.

Then and Now

In the writing activity, you **compare** a similar situation in the past and the present.

Connecting to the Constitution

Here you will learn about how the **Constitution** has been able to respond to challenges that the Framers never imagined.

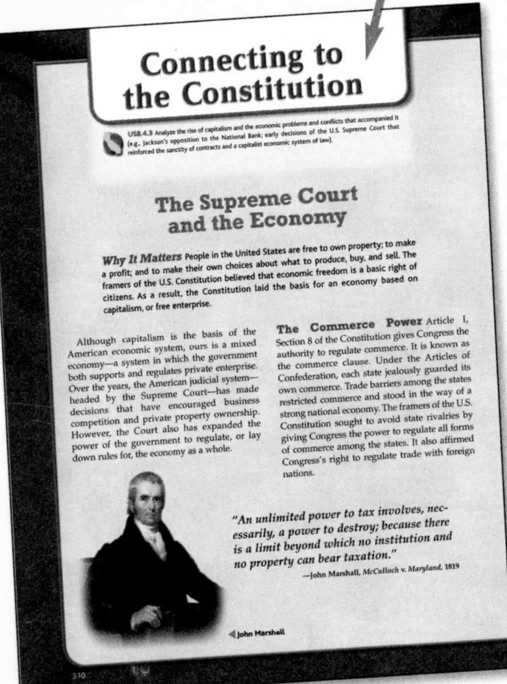

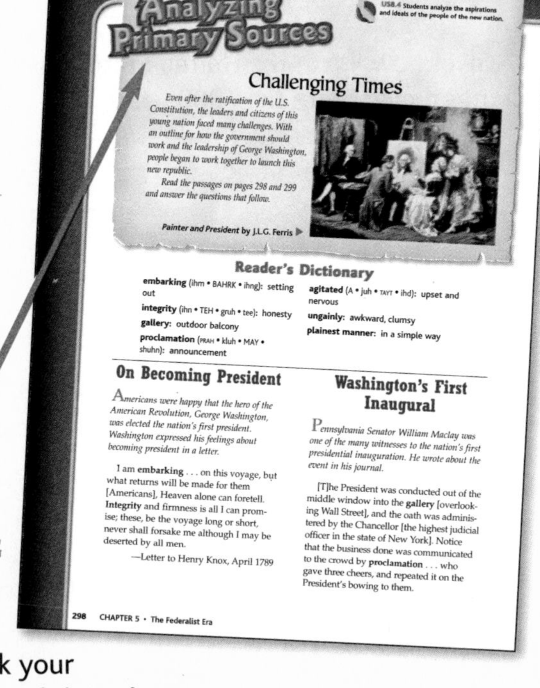

Analyzing Primary Sources

You will check your understanding of the **primary sources** and **write** a response to one or more of them.

You Decide . . .

Imagine that you can give your **opinion** when two opposing views are presented.

You Be the Historian

Give your **opinion** on the issue.

History Makers

Learn how people, decisions, objects, and events **changed history.**

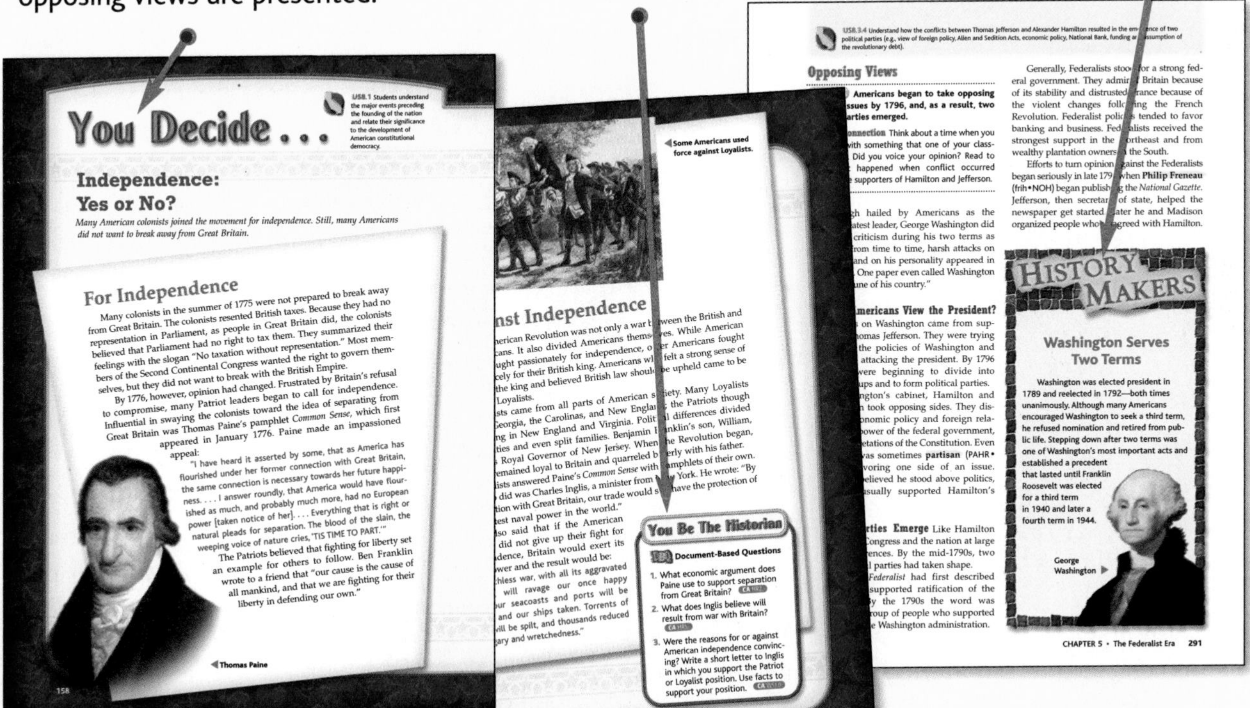

The Way It Was

Discover how life in the United States has **changed** over more than 200 years.

Why It Matters

Learn how particular events **influenced** the future.

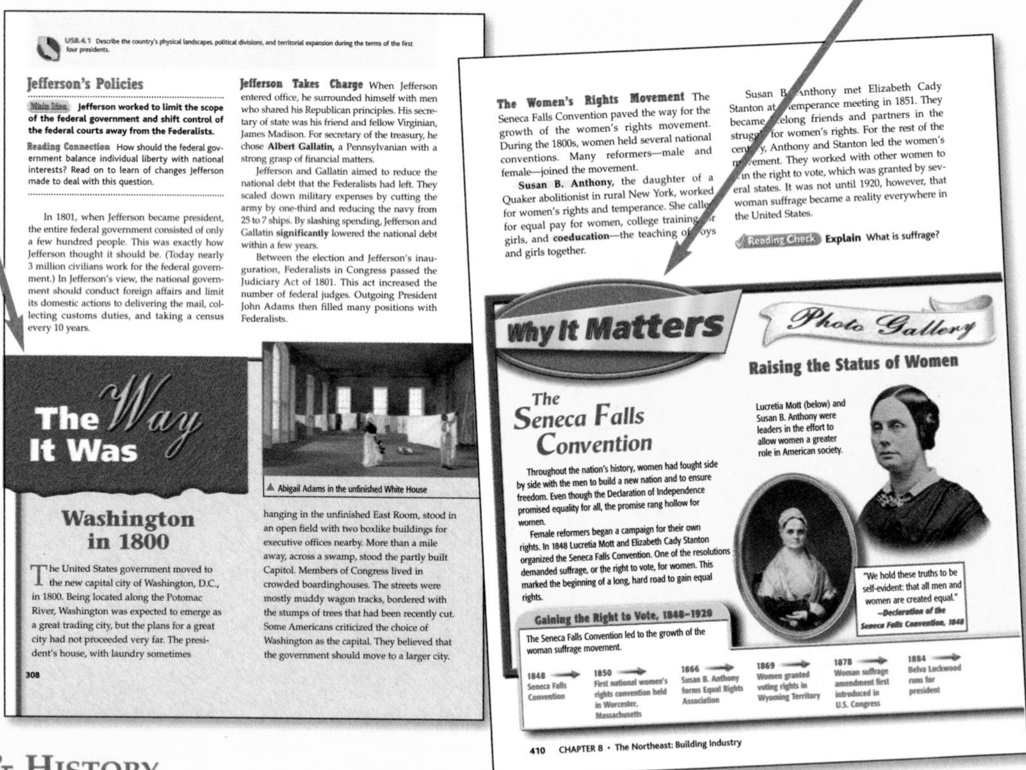

Geography & History

Find out how **geography** has affected people and people have affected the environment.

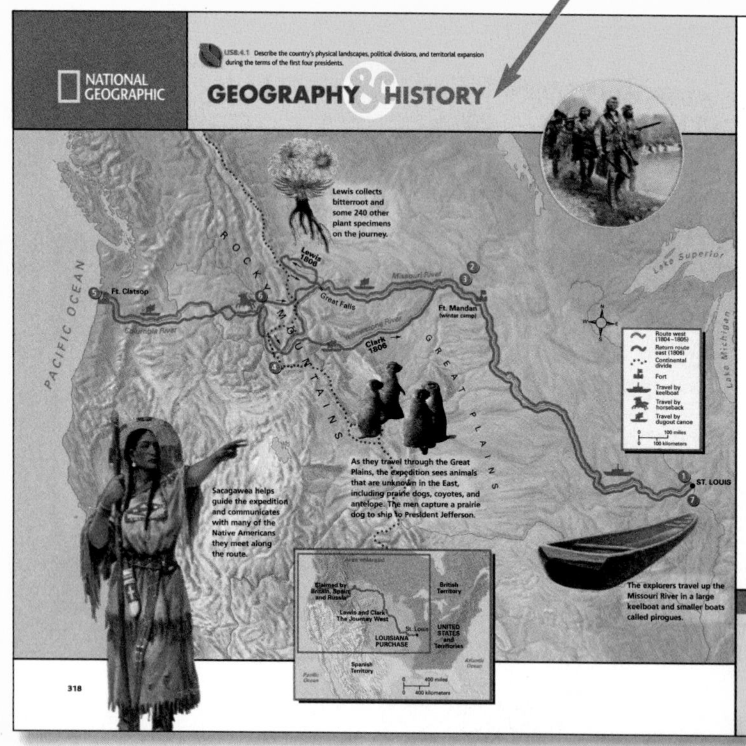

Learning from Geography

Evaluate in **writing** the impact of geography on people and events.

Scavenger Hunt

Discovering Our Past: The American Journey to World War I contains a wealth of information. The trick is to know where to look to access all the information in the book.

If you run through this scavenger hunt exercise with your teacher or parents, you will see how the textbook is organized, and how to get the most out of your reading and study time. Let's get started!

1. How many units and how many chapters are in this book?
2. What is the title of Chapter 4, Section 3?
3. You want to quickly find all the maps in the book on the Civil War. Where are they listed?
4. What time period does Chapter 7, Section 2 cover?
5. In Chapter 4, what will the *Foldables* activity help you do?
6. What reading skill will you practice in Chapter 1?
7. What are the Big, or most important, Ideas in Chapter 2? Where can you find this information?
8. There are six Web sites in Chapter 5. The first one previews the chapter. What do the other five sites do? How are some sites similar?
9. A primary source is a document or other testimony, dating from the same period as an event. In what part of chapters 1–17 can you always find primary sources?
10. Where, in the back of the book, can you quickly find the meaning of Content Vocabulary words, such as *confederation*? What is a confederation?

READING TO LEARN

This handbook focuses on skills and strategies that can help you understand the words you read. The strategies you use to understand whole texts depend on the kind of text you are reading. In other words, you do not read a textbook the way you read a novel. You read a textbook mainly for information; you read a novel for the story and the characters. To get the most out of your reading, you need to choose the right strategy to fit the reason you are reading. This handbook can help you learn about the following reading strategies:

- **how to identify new words and build your vocabulary;**
- **how to adjust the way you read to fit your reason for reading;**
- **how to use specific reading strategies to better understand what you read;**
- **how to use critical thinking strategies to think more deeply about what you read; and**
- **how to understand text structures to identify an author's ideas.**

TABLE OF CONTENTS

Problem and Solution

How did scientists overcome the difficulty of getting a person to the moon? How will I brush my teeth when I have forgotten my toothpaste? These questions may be very different in importance, but they have one thing in common: Each identifies a problem and asks how to solve it. *Problems and solutions* are part of what makes life interesting. Problems and solutions also occur in fiction and nonfiction writing.

Signal words and phrases: *how, help, problem, obstruction, difficulty, need, attempt, have to, must*

Sequence

Take a look at three common forms of sequencing, the order in which thoughts are arranged.

- **Chronological order** refers to the order in which events take place. First, you wake up; next, you have breakfast; then, you go to school. Those events do not make much sense in any other order.
  Signal words: *first, next, then, later, finally*

- **Spatial order** tells you the order in which to look at objects. For example, consider this description of an ice-cream sundae: *At the bottom of the dish are two scoops of vanilla. The scoops are covered with fudge and topped with whipped cream and a cherry.* Your eyes follow the sundae from the bottom to the top. Spatial order is important in descriptive writing because it helps you as a reader to see an image the way the author does.
  Signal words: *above, below, behind, next to*

- **Order of importance** is going from most important to least important or the other way around. For example, a typical news article has a most important to least important structure.
  Signal words: *principal, central, important, fundamental*

CHECKING YOUR UNDERSTANDING

Read the following paragraph and answer the questions about the selection's text structure below.

The Huntington City Council recently approved an increase in the city sales tax. Recognizing the need to balance the city's budget, the council president Matt Smith noted that the council had no choice. The vote ended more than a year of preparing voters for the bad news. First, the council notified citizens that there would be a public discussion last April. Then, the council issued public statements that the vote would take place in November. Finally, the council approved the increase last week even though many residents opposed it. On one hand, the increase will increase revenues. On the other hand, more taxes could lead to fewer shoppers in the city's struggling retail stores.

1. **How does the writer use comparison and contrast text structure?**
2. **How does the writer use problem and solution text structure?**
3. **What signal words show that the writer is setting the chronological order of events?**

REFERENCE ATLAS

ATLAS KEY

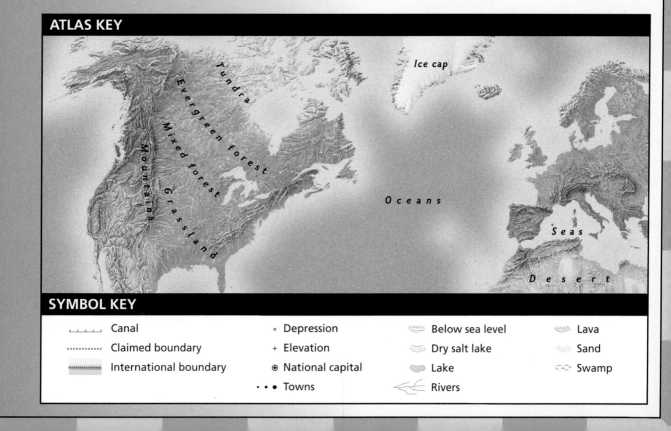

Tundra
Evergreen forest
Mixed forest
Mountains
Grassland
Ice cap
Oceans
Seas
Desert

SYMBOL KEY

Canal	Depression	Below sea level	Lava
Claimed boundary	Elevation	Dry salt lake	Sand
International boundary	National capital	Lake	Swamp
	Towns	Rivers	

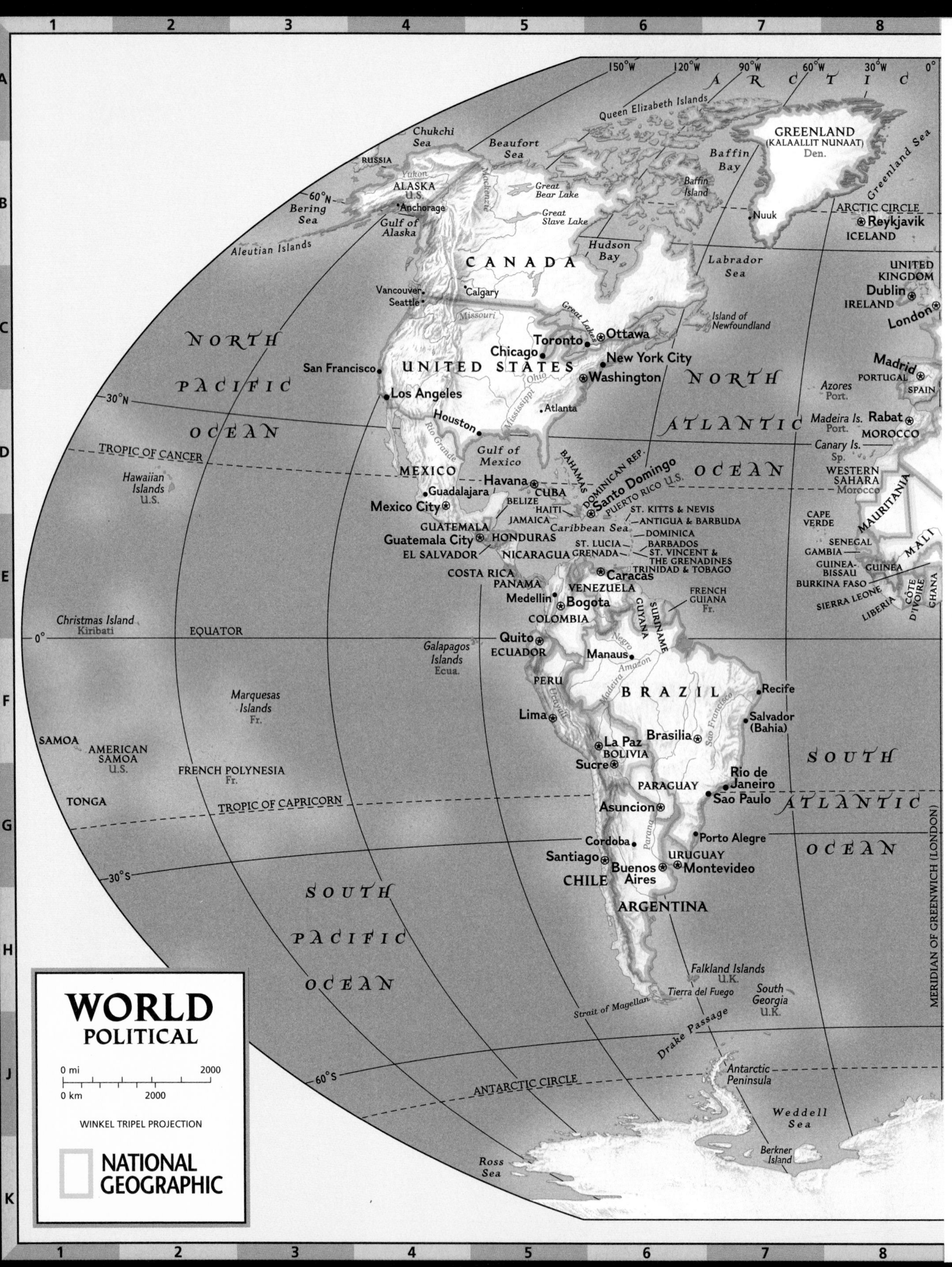

WORLD
POLITICAL
0 mi
2000
0 km
2000
WINKEL TRIPEL PROJECTION
NATIONAL GEOGRAPHIC
1
2
3
4
5
6
7
8
A
B
C
D
E
F
G
H
J
K
150°W
120°W
90°W
60°W
30°W
0°
ARCTIC
Queen Elizabeth Islands
GREENLAND
(KALAALLIT NUNAAT)
Den.
Greenland Sea
Chukchi Sea
Beaufort Sea
Baffin Bay
Baffin Island
RUSSIA
Yukon
ALASKA
U.S.
Mackenzie
Great Bear Lake
60°N
Bering Sea
Anchorage
Great Slave Lake
Nuuk
ARCTIC CIRCLE
Reykjavik
ICELAND
Gulf of Alaska
Aleutian Islands
Hudson Bay
CANADA
Labrador Sea
UNITED KINGDOM
Dublin
IRELAND
London
Vancouver
Calgary
Seattle
Missouri
Great Lakes
Island of Newfoundland
NORTH PACIFIC OCEAN
Toronto
Ottawa
Chicago
New York City
San Francisco
UNITED STATES
Ohio
Washington
NORTH ATLANTIC OCEAN
Madrid
PORTUGAL
Azores
Port.
SPAIN
30°N
Los Angeles
Mississippi
Atlanta
Houston
Rio Grande
Madeira Is.
Port.
Rabat
MOROCCO
Gulf of Mexico
Canary Is.
Sp.
TROPIC OF CANCER
BAHAMAS
DOMINICAN REP.
MEXICO
Santo Domingo
WESTERN SAHARA
Morocco
Hawaiian Islands
U.S.
Havana
CUBA
PUERTO RICO U.S.
Guadalajara
BELIZE
MAURITANIA
Mexico City
HAITI
JAMAICA
ST. KITTS & NEVIS
ANTIGUA & BARBUDA
CAPE VERDE
GUATEMALA
Caribbean Sea
DOMINICA
Guatemala City
HONDURAS
ST. LUCIA
BARBADOS
SENEGAL
MALI
EL SALVADOR
NICARAGUA
GRENADA
ST. VINCENT & THE GRENADINES
GAMBIA
TRINIDAD & TOBAGO
GUINEA-BISSAU
GUINEA
COSTA RICA
Caracas
PANAMA
VENEZUELA
FRENCH GUIANA
Fr.
BURKINA FASO
SIERRA LEONE
LIBERIA
CÔTE D'IVOIRE
GHANA
Medellin
Bogota
GUYANA
SURINAME
Christmas Island
Kiribati
COLOMBIA
0°
EQUATOR
Quito
Negro
Galapagos Islands
Ecua.
ECUADOR
Manaus
Amazon
PERU
Madeira
BRAZIL
Recife
Marquesas Islands
Fr.
Ucayali
Sao Francisco
Lima
Salvador (Bahia)
SAMOA
La Paz
Brasilia
AMERICAN SAMOA
U.S.
BOLIVIA
SOUTH ATLANTIC OCEAN
Sucre
FRENCH POLYNESIA
Fr.
Rio de Janeiro
PARAGUAY
TONGA
Sao Paulo
TROPIC OF CAPRICORN
Asuncion
Parana
Porto Alegre
Cordoba
Santiago
URUGUAY
Buenos Aires
Montevideo
30°S
CHILE
ARGENTINA
SOUTH PACIFIC OCEAN
MERIDIAN OF GREENWICH (LONDON)
Falkland Islands
U.K.
South Georgia
U.K.
Tierra del Fuego
Strait of Magellan
Drake Passage
60°S
Antarctic Peninsula
ANTARCTIC CIRCLE
Weddell Sea
Ross Sea
Berkner Island

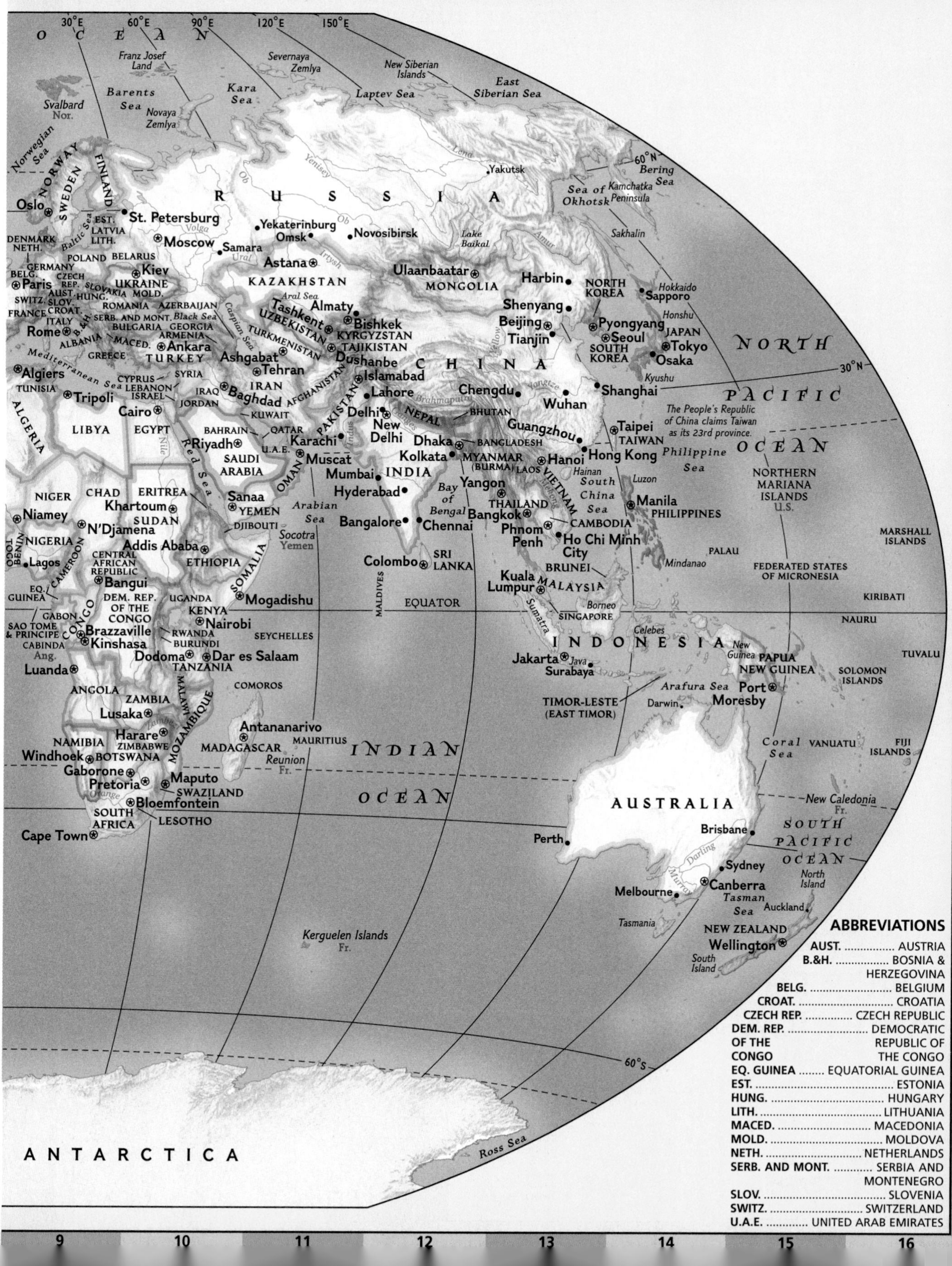
9
10
11
12
13
14
15
16
30°E
60°E
90°E
120°E
150°E
OCEAN
Franz Josef Land
Severnaya Zemlya
New Siberian Islands
Svalbard
Nor.
Barents Sea
Kara Sea
Laptev Sea
East Siberian Sea
Novaya Zemlya
Norwegian Sea
NORWAY
SWEDEN
FINLAND
Lena
Yenisey
60°N
Bering Sea
Yakutsk
Sea of Okhotsk
Kamchatka Peninsula
Ob
RUSSIA
Oslo
St. Petersburg
EST.
LATVIA
LITH.
Baltic Sea
Volga
Yekaterinburg
Omsk
Novosibirsk
Lake Baikal
Amur
Sakhalin
DENMARK
NETH.
Moscow
Samara
Ural
Irtysh
POLAND
BELARUS
GERMANY
BELG.
Paris
CZECH REP.
SLOVAKIA
Kiev
UKRAINE
MOLD.
Astana
KAZAKHSTAN
Ulaanbaatar
MONGOLIA
Harbin
NORTH KOREA
Hokkaido
Sapporo
SWITZ.
AUST.
HUNG.
SLOV.
CROAT.
ROMANIA
AZERBAIJAN
Aral Sea
Almaty
Shenyang
Honshu
FRANCE
ITALY
B.&H.
SERB. AND MONT.
Black Sea
Tashkent
UZBEKISTAN
Bishkek
KYRGYZSTAN
Beijing
Tianjin
Pyongyang
Seoul
JAPAN
Rome
BULGARIA
GEORGIA
ARMENIA
Caspian Sea
TURKMENISTAN
TAJIKISTAN
Yellow
SOUTH KOREA
Tokyo
Osaka
NORTH
ALBANIA
MACED.
Ankara
Ashgabat
Dushanbe
CHINA
Kyushu
GREECE
TURKEY
Mediterranean Sea
Algiers
Tehran
Islamabad
30°N
CYPRUS
SYRIA
LEBANON
IRAN
AFGHANISTAN
Chengdu
Yangtze
Shanghai
PACIFIC
TUNISIA
Tripoli
ISRAEL
IRAQ
Baghdad
JORDAN
PAKISTAN
Lahore
Brahmaputra
Wuhan
The People's Republic of China claims Taiwan as its 23rd province.
ALGERIA
Cairo
KUWAIT
Delhi
New Delhi
NEPAL
BHUTAN
Taipei
TAIWAN
LIBYA
EGYPT
BAHRAIN
QATAR
Ganges
Guangzhou
Nile
Riyadh
Karachi
Indus
Dhaka
BANGLADESH
Hong Kong
Philippine Sea
OCEAN
U.A.E.
Muscat
Kolkata
MYANMAR (BURMA)
Hanoi
LAOS
Red Sea
SAUDI ARABIA
OMAN
Mumbai
INDIA
Hainan
Luzon
NORTHERN MARIANA ISLANDS
U.S.
Hyderabad
Bay of Bengal
Yangon
VIETNAM
South China Sea
Mekong
NIGER
CHAD
ERITREA
Khartoum
Sanaa
YEMEN
Arabian Sea
THAILAND
Manila
PHILIPPINES
Niamey
SUDAN
Bangalore
Chennai
Bangkok
CAMBODIA
N'Djamena
DJIBOUTI
Socotra
Yemen
Phnom Penh
Ho Chi Minh City
MARSHALL ISLANDS
BENIN
TOGO
NIGERIA
Addis Ababa
CAMEROON
ETHIOPIA
SOMALIA
SRI LANKA
PALAU
Lagos
CENTRAL AFRICAN REPUBLIC
Colombo
BRUNEI
Mindanao
FEDERATED STATES OF MICRONESIA
Bangui
MALDIVES
Kuala Lumpur
MALAYSIA
EQ. GUINEA
DEM. REP. OF THE CONGO
UGANDA
Mogadishu
EQUATOR
Borneo
KIRIBATI
GABON
CONGO
KENYA
Nairobi
Sumatra
SINGAPORE
NAURU
SAO TOME & PRINCIPE
Brazzaville
RWANDA
SEYCHELLES
Celebes
CABINDA
Ang.
Kinshasa
BURUNDI
INDONESIA
New Guinea
PAPUA NEW GUINEA
TUVALU
Dodoma
Dar es Salaam
Jakarta
Java
Luanda
TANZANIA
Surabaya
SOLOMON ISLANDS
MALAWI
COMOROS
Arafura Sea
Port Moresby
ANGOLA
ZAMBIA
TIMOR-LESTE (EAST TIMOR)
Darwin
Lusaka
MOZAMBIQUE
Zambezi
Antananarivo
Harare
MAURITIUS
NAMIBIA
ZIMBABWE
INDIAN
Coral Sea
VANUATU
FIJI ISLANDS
Windhoek
BOTSWANA
MADAGASCAR
Reunion
Fr.
Gaborone
Pretoria
Maputo
SWAZILAND
OCEAN
Orange
Bloemfontein
AUSTRALIA
New Caledonia
Fr.
SOUTH AFRICA
LESOTHO
SOUTH PACIFIC OCEAN
Cape Town
Perth
Brisbane
Darling
Sydney
North Island
Murray
Canberra
Melbourne
Tasman Sea
Auckland
Tasmania
Kerguelen Islands
Fr.
NEW ZEALAND
Wellington
South Island
60°S
Ross Sea
ANTARCTICA
ABBREVIATIONS
AUST. .... AUSTRIA
B.&H. .... BOSNIA & HERZEGOVINA
BELG. .... BELGIUM
CROAT. .... CROATIA
CZECH REP. .... CZECH REPUBLIC
DEM. REP. OF THE CONGO .... DEMOCRATIC REPUBLIC OF THE CONGO
EQ. GUINEA .... EQUATORIAL GUINEA
EST. .... ESTONIA
HUNG. .... HUNGARY
LITH. .... LITHUANIA
MACED. .... MACEDONIA
MOLD. .... MOLDOVA
NETH. .... NETHERLANDS
SERB. AND MONT. .... SERBIA AND MONTENEGRO
SLOV. .... SLOVENIA
SWITZ. .... SWITZERLAND
U.A.E. .... UNITED ARAB EMIRATES
9
10
11
12
13
14
15
16

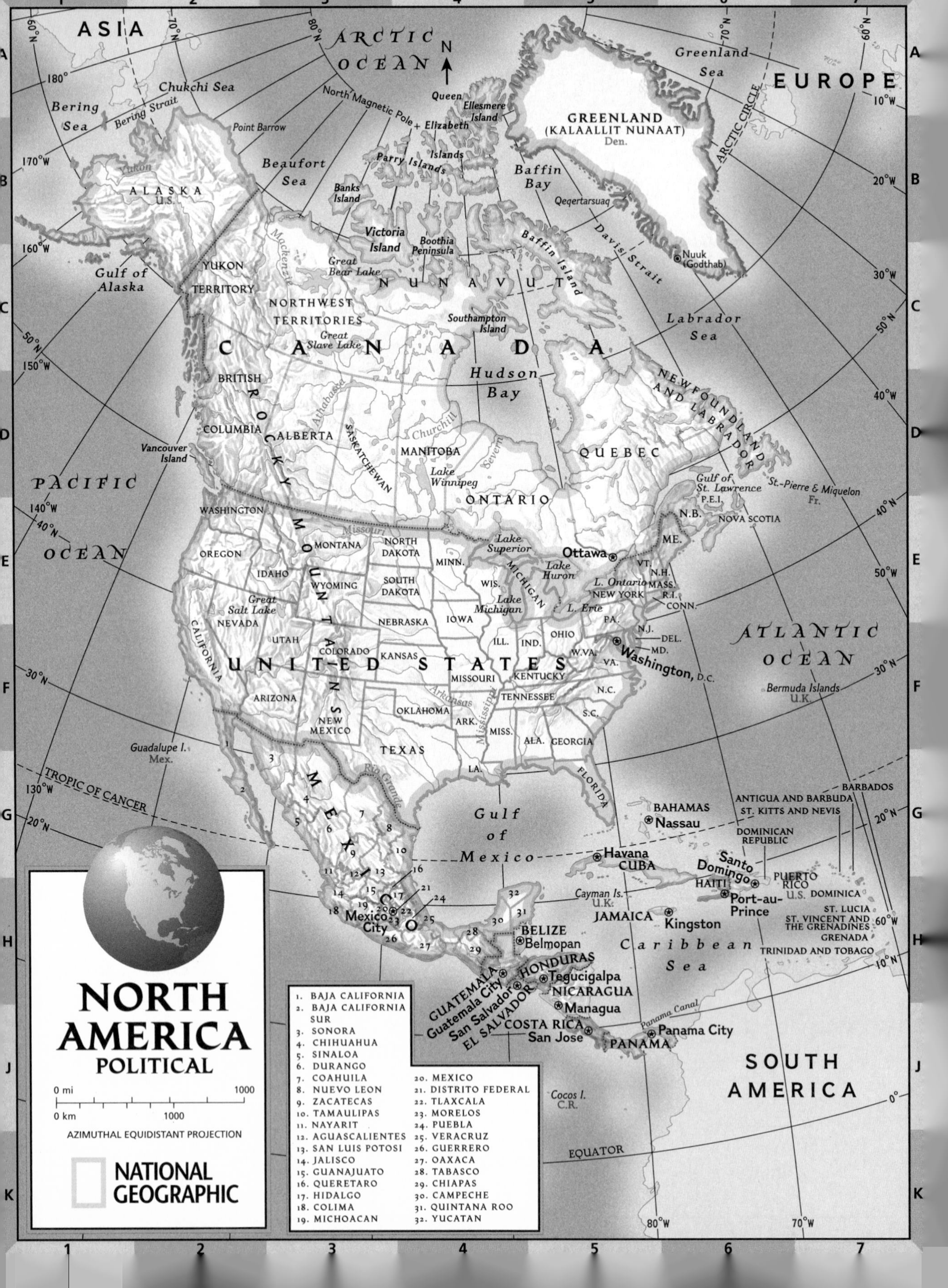
NORTH AMERICA
POLITICAL
0 mi 1000
0 km 1000
AZIMUTHAL EQUIDISTANT PROJECTION
NATIONAL GEOGRAPHIC
ASIA
ARCTIC OCEAN
EUROPE
PACIFIC OCEAN
ATLANTIC OCEAN
SOUTH AMERICA
GREENLAND (KALAALLIT NUNAAT) Den.
CANADA
UNITED STATES
MEXICO
ALASKA U.S.
YUKON TERRITORY
NORTHWEST TERRITORIES
NUNAVUT
BRITISH COLUMBIA
ALBERTA
SASKATCHEWAN
MANITOBA
ONTARIO
QUEBEC
NEWFOUNDLAND AND LABRADOR
ROCKY MOUNTAINS
Ottawa
Washington, D.C.
Gulf of Mexico
Hudson Bay
Caribbean Sea
BAHAMAS
Nassau
CUBA
Havana
JAMAICA
Kingston
HAITI
Port-au-Prince
DOMINICAN REPUBLIC
Santo Domingo
PUERTO RICO U.S.
BELIZE
Belmopan
GUATEMALA
Guatemala City
HONDURAS
Tegucigalpa
EL SALVADOR
San Salvador
NICARAGUA
Managua
COSTA RICA
San Jose
PANAMA
Panama City
Mexico City
ANTIGUA AND BARBUDA
ST. KITTS AND NEVIS
BARBADOS
DOMINICA
ST. LUCIA
ST. VINCENT AND THE GRENADINES
GRENADA
TRINIDAD AND TOBAGO
Bermuda Islands U.K.
St.-Pierre & Miquelon Fr.
Cayman Is. U.K.
Cocos I. C.R.
Guadalupe I. Mex.
TROPIC OF CANCER
ARCTIC CIRCLE
EQUATOR
1. BAJA CALIFORNIA
2. BAJA CALIFORNIA SUR
3. SONORA
4. CHIHUAHUA
5. SINALOA
6. DURANGO
7. COAHUILA
8. NUEVO LEON
9. ZACATECAS
10. TAMAULIPAS
11. NAYARIT
12. AGUASCALIENTES
13. SAN LUIS POTOSI
14. JALISCO
15. GUANAJUATO
16. QUERETARO
17. HIDALGO
18. COLIMA
19. MICHOACAN
20. MEXICO
21. DISTRITO FEDERAL
22. TLAXCALA
23. MORELOS
24. PUEBLA
25. VERACRUZ
26. GUERRERO
27. OAXACA
28. TABASCO
29. CHIAPAS
30. CAMPECHE
31. QUINTANA ROO
32. YUCATAN

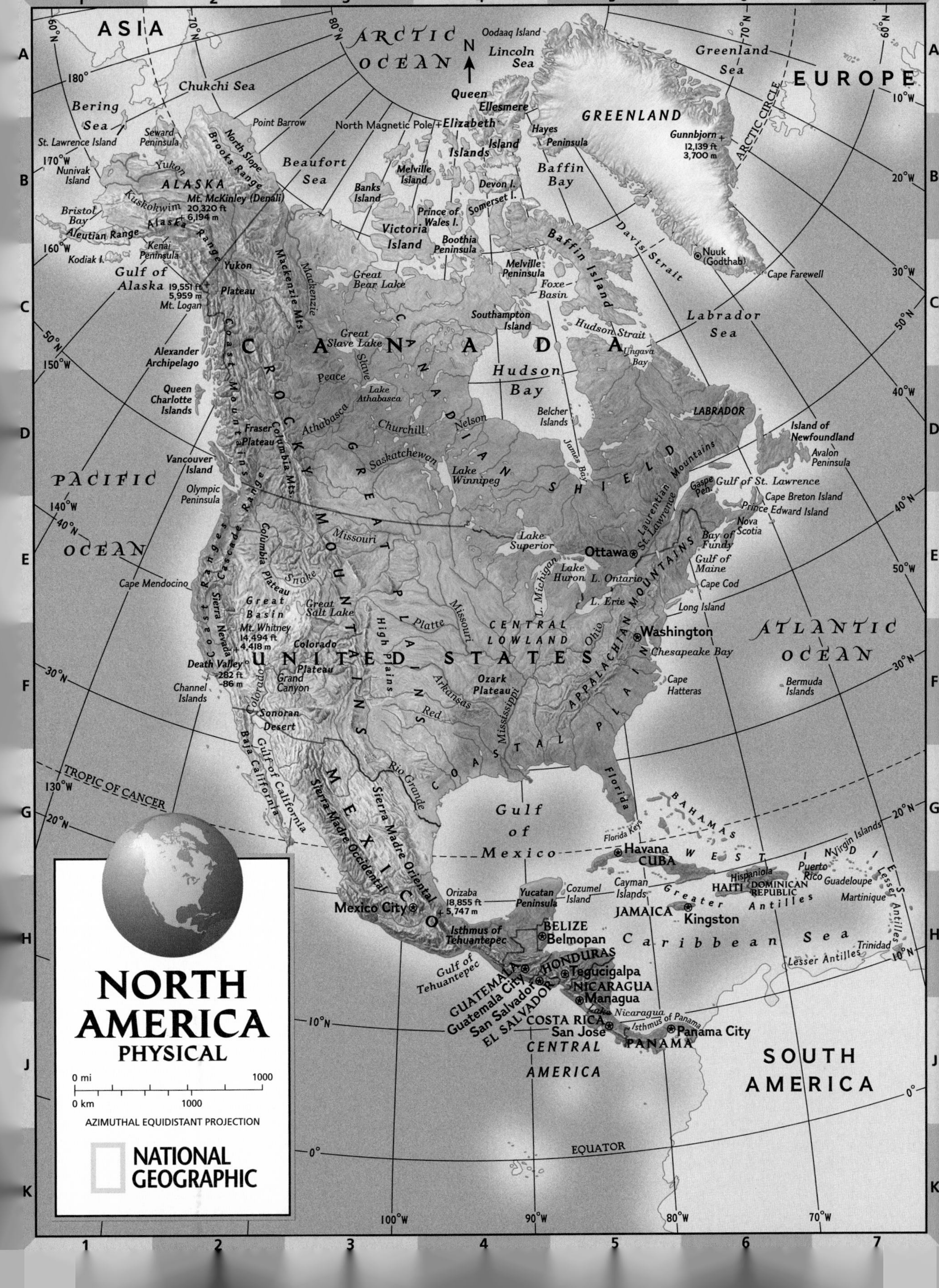

NORTH AMERICA
PHYSICAL
0 mi 1000
0 km 1000
AZIMUTHAL EQUIDISTANT PROJECTION
NATIONAL GEOGRAPHIC
ASIA
ARCTIC OCEAN
EUROPE
GREENLAND
CANADA
UNITED STATES
MEXICO
PACIFIC OCEAN
ATLANTIC OCEAN
Gulf of Mexico
Caribbean Sea
SOUTH AMERICA
CENTRAL AMERICA
ROCKY MOUNTAINS
GREAT PLAINS
CANADIAN SHIELD
APPALACHIAN MOUNTAINS
COASTAL PLAIN
CENTRAL LOWLAND
WEST INDIES
Hudson Bay
Baffin Bay
Labrador Sea
Greenland Sea
Lincoln Sea
Beaufort Sea
Chukchi Sea
Bering Sea
Gulf of Alaska
ALASKA
Mt. McKinley (Denali) 20,320 ft 6,194 m
Mt. Logan 19,551 ft 5,959 m
Mt. Whitney 14,494 ft 4,418 m
Death Valley -282 ft -86 m
Orizaba 18,855 ft 5,747 m
Gunnbjorn 12,139 ft 3,700 m
Ottawa
Washington
Mexico City
Havana
CUBA
JAMAICA
Kingston
HAITI
DOMINICAN REPUBLIC
BELIZE
Belmopan
GUATEMALA
Guatemala City
EL SALVADOR
San Salvador
HONDURAS
Tegucigalpa
NICARAGUA
Managua
COSTA RICA
San Jose
PANAMA
Panama City
Nuuk (Godthab)
TROPIC OF CANCER
ARCTIC CIRCLE
EQUATOR

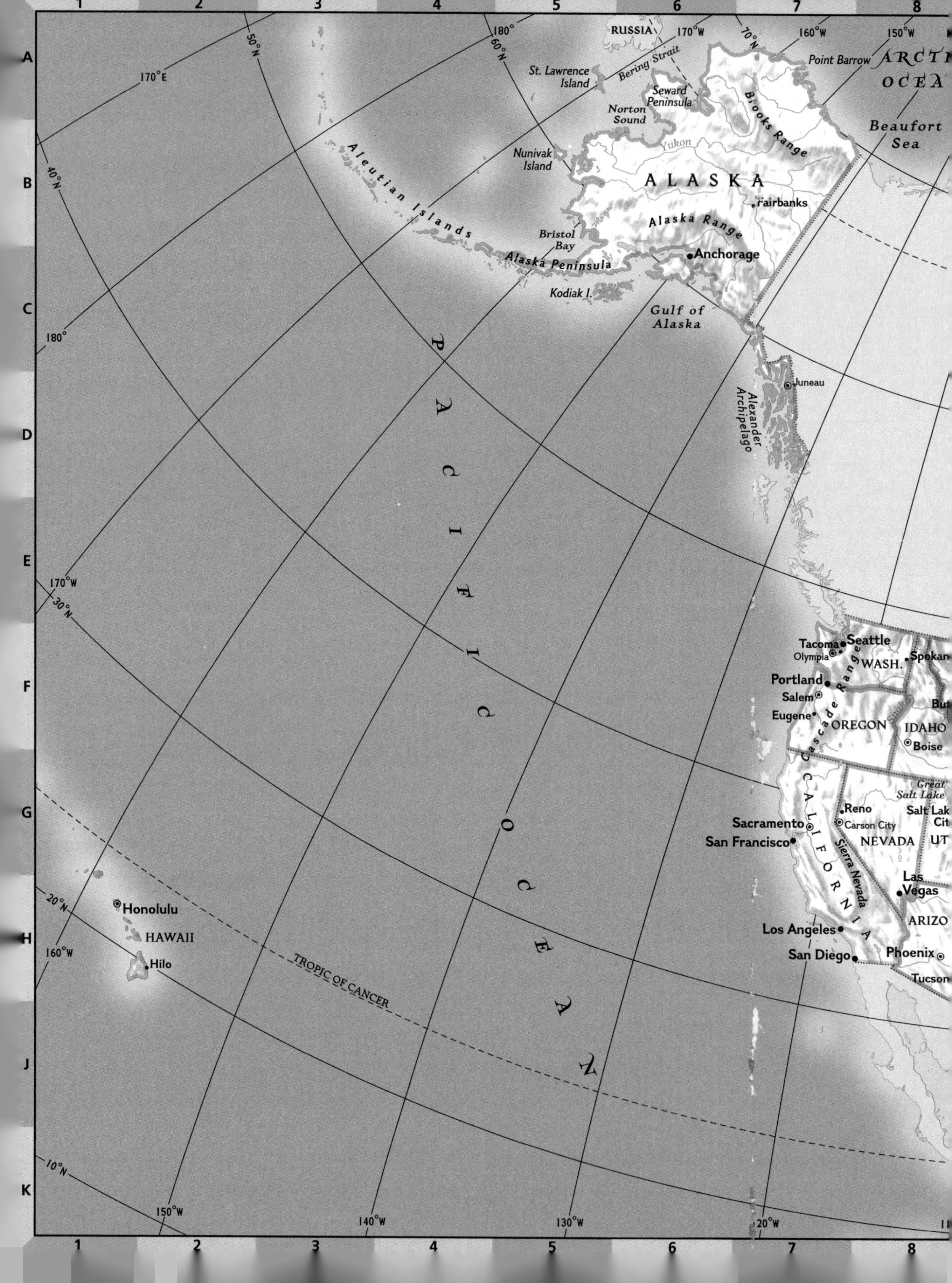
RUSSIA
St. Lawrence Island
Bering Strait
Seward Peninsula
Norton Sound
Point Barrow
ARCTIC OCEAN
Beaufort Sea
Brooks Range
Yukon
Nunivak Island
Aleutian Islands
ALASKA
Fairbanks
Alaska Range
Bristol Bay
Anchorage
Alaska Peninsula
Kodiak I.
Gulf of Alaska
Juneau
Alexander Archipelago
PACIFIC OCEAN
Tacoma
Seattle
Olympia
WASH.
Spokane
Portland
Salem
Eugene
Cascade Range
OREGON
IDAHO
Boise
Great Salt Lake
Salt Lake City
Reno
Carson City
Sacramento
San Francisco
NEVADA
CALIFORNIA
Sierra Nevada
Las Vegas
ARIZONA
Los Angeles
San Diego
Phoenix
Tucson
Honolulu
HAWAII
Hilo
TROPIC OF CANCER
180°
170°W
160°W
150°W
170°E
70°N
60°N
50°N
40°N
30°N
20°N
10°N
140°W
130°W
120°W

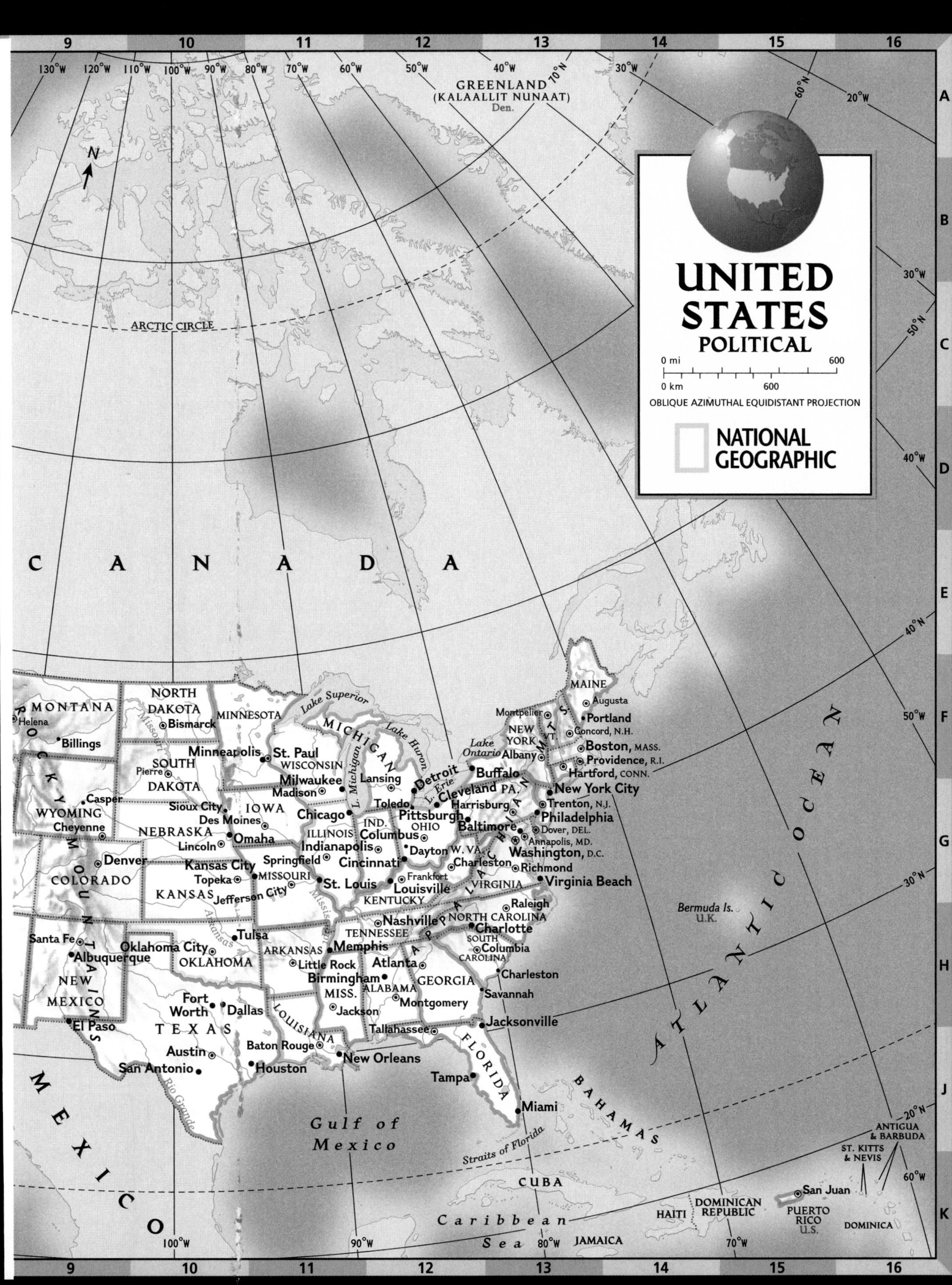
UNITED STATES
POLITICAL
0 mi 600
0 km 600
OBLIQUE AZIMUTHAL EQUIDISTANT PROJECTION
NATIONAL GEOGRAPHIC
GREENLAND (KALAALLIT NUNAAT) Den.
ARCTIC CIRCLE
CANADA
MEXICO
ATLANTIC OCEAN
Gulf of Mexico
Caribbean Sea
Straits of Florida
BAHAMAS
CUBA
JAMAICA
HAITI
DOMINICAN REPUBLIC
PUERTO RICO U.S.
San Juan
DOMINICA
ST. KITTS & NEVIS
ANTIGUA & BARBUDA
Bermuda Is. U.K.
ROCKY MOUNTAINS
APPALACHIAN MTS.
MONTANA
Helena
Billings
WYOMING
Casper
Cheyenne
COLORADO
Denver
NEW MEXICO
Santa Fe
Albuquerque
TEXAS
El Paso
Fort Worth
Dallas
Austin
San Antonio
Houston
NORTH DAKOTA
Bismarck
SOUTH DAKOTA
Pierre
Sioux City
NEBRASKA
Lincoln
Omaha
KANSAS
Topeka
Kansas City
OKLAHOMA
Oklahoma City
Tulsa
MINNESOTA
Minneapolis
St. Paul
IOWA
Des Moines
MISSOURI
Jefferson City
St. Louis
ARKANSAS
Little Rock
LOUISIANA
Baton Rouge
New Orleans
WISCONSIN
Madison
Milwaukee
ILLINOIS
Chicago
Springfield
MICHIGAN
Lansing
Detroit
IND.
Indianapolis
OHIO
Columbus
Toledo
Cleveland
Cincinnati
Dayton
KENTUCKY
Frankfort
Louisville
TENNESSEE
Nashville
Memphis
MISS.
Jackson
ALABAMA
Birmingham
Montgomery
GEORGIA
Atlanta
Savannah
FLORIDA
Tallahassee
Jacksonville
Tampa
Miami
SOUTH CAROLINA
Columbia
Charleston
NORTH CAROLINA
Charlotte
Raleigh
VIRGINIA
Richmond
Virginia Beach
W. VA.
Charleston
PA.
Pittsburgh
Harrisburg
Philadelphia
Baltimore
Dover, DEL.
Annapolis, MD.
Washington, D.C.
NEW YORK
Albany
Buffalo
New York City
Trenton, N.J.
Hartford, CONN.
Providence, R.I.
Boston, MASS.
Concord, N.H.
Montpelier
VT.
N.H.
MAINE
Augusta
Portland
Lake Superior
Lake Michigan
Lake Huron
L. Erie
Lake Ontario
Missouri
Arkansas
Mississippi
Rio Grande

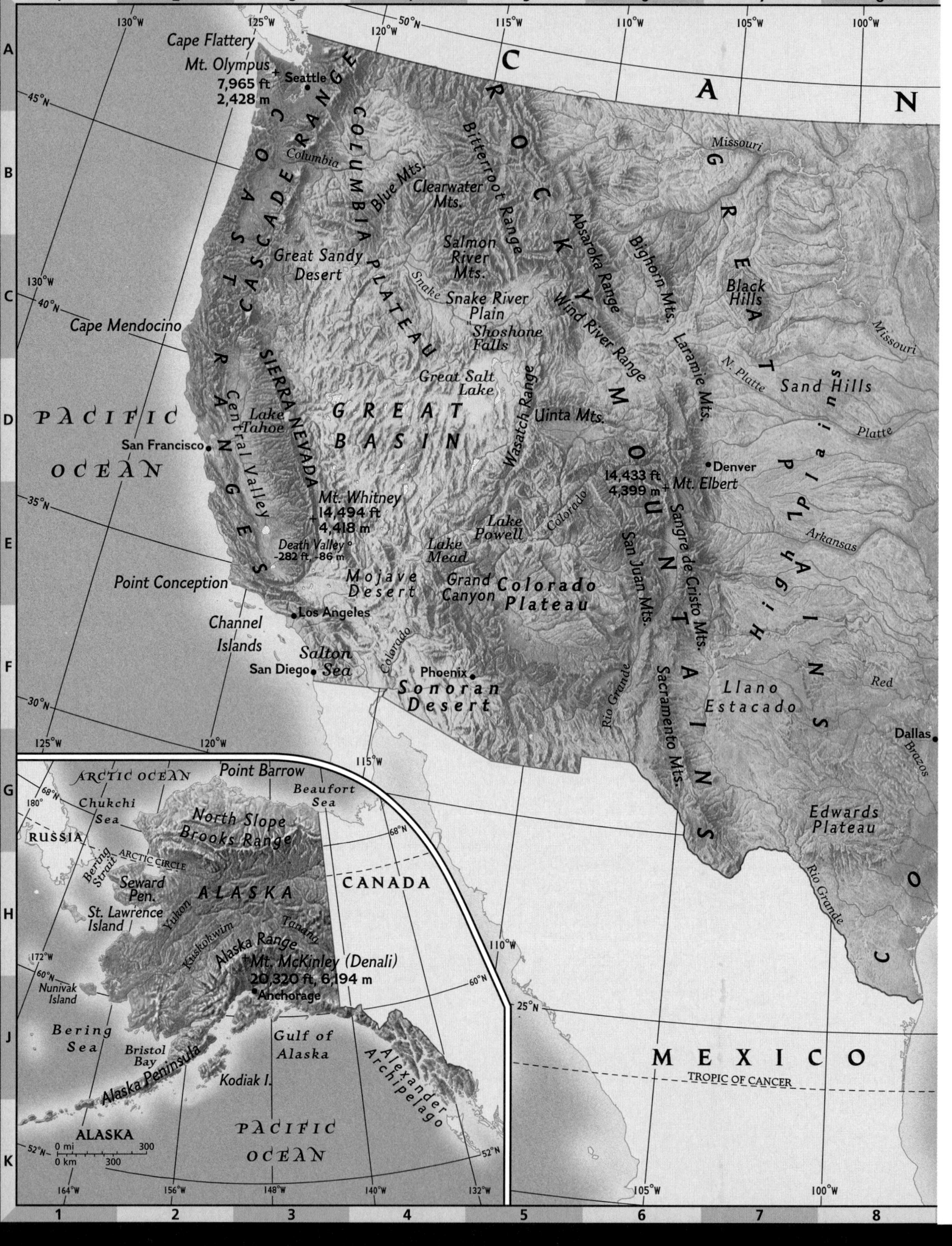

CANADA
PACIFIC OCEAN
Cape Flattery
Mt. Olympus 7,965 ft 2,428 m
Seattle
CASCADE RANGE
COLUMBIA PLATEAU
ROCKY MOUNTAINS
Columbia
Blue Mts.
Clearwater Mts.
Bitterroot Range
Salmon River Mts.
Absaroka Range
Bighorn Mts.
GREAT PLAINS
Missouri
Great Sandy Desert
Snake
Snake River Plain
Shoshone Falls
Wind River Range
Laramie Mts.
Black Hills
Cape Mendocino
COAST RANGES
SIERRA NEVADA
Central Valley
Lake Tahoe
Great Salt Lake
GREAT BASIN
Wasatch Range
Uinta Mts.
N. Platte
Sand Hills
High Plains
Platte
San Francisco
Denver
14,433 ft 4,399 m
Mt. Elbert
Mt. Whitney 14,494 ft 4,418 m
Death Valley -282 ft, -86 m
Lake Powell
Lake Mead
Colorado
Sangre de Cristo Mts.
San Juan Mts.
Arkansas
Point Conception
Mojave Desert
Grand Canyon
Colorado Plateau
Los Angeles
Channel Islands
Salton Sea
San Diego
Phoenix
Sonoran Desert
Rio Grande
Sacramento Mts.
Llano Estacado
Red
Dallas
Brazos
Edwards Plateau
MEXICO
TROPIC OF CANCER
ARCTIC OCEAN
Point Barrow
Beaufort Sea
Chukchi Sea
RUSSIA
North Slope
Brooks Range
ARCTIC CIRCLE
Bering Strait
Seward Pen.
ALASKA
CANADA
St. Lawrence Island
Yukon
Tanana
Kuskokwim
Alaska Range
Mt. McKinley (Denali) 20,320 ft, 6,194 m
Anchorage
Nunivak Island
Bering Sea
Bristol Bay
Gulf of Alaska
Alexander Archipelago
Alaska Peninsula
Kodiak I.
PACIFIC OCEAN
ALASKA
0 mi 300
0 km 300

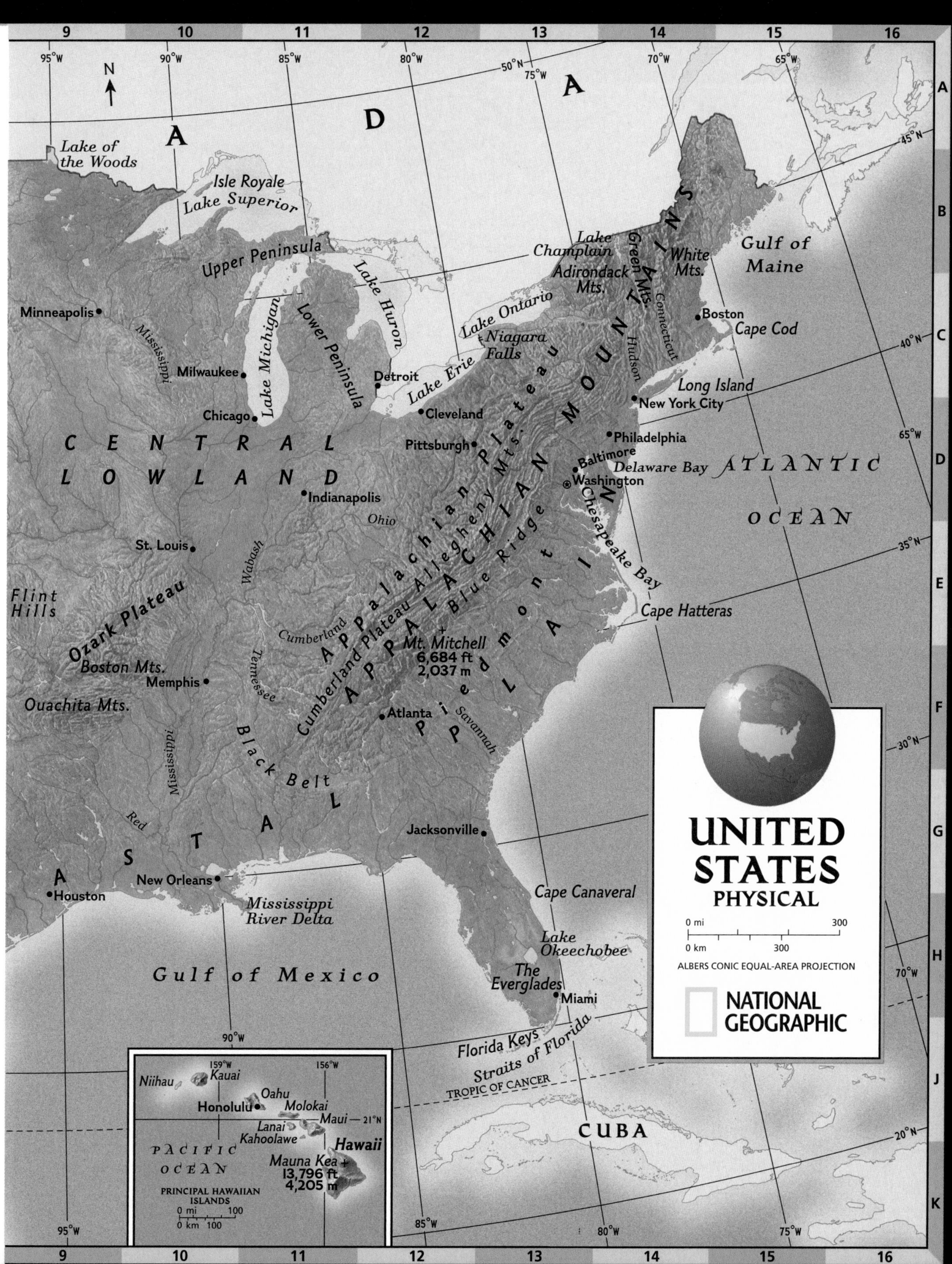
UNITED STATES
PHYSICAL
ALBERS CONIC EQUAL-AREA PROJECTION
NATIONAL GEOGRAPHIC
CENTRAL LOWLAND
APPALACHIAN MOUNTAINS
Appalachian Plateau
Cumberland Plateau
Allegheny Mts.
Blue Ridge
Piedmont
Ozark Plateau
Boston Mts.
Ouachita Mts.
Flint Hills
Black Belt
COASTAL PLAIN
Lake of the Woods
Isle Royale
Lake Superior
Upper Peninsula
Lower Peninsula
Lake Michigan
Lake Huron
Lake Erie
Lake Ontario
Niagara Falls
Lake Champlain
Adirondack Mts.
Green Mts.
White Mts.
Gulf of Maine
Cape Cod
Long Island
Delaware Bay
Chesapeake Bay
Cape Hatteras
ATLANTIC OCEAN
Mt. Mitchell 6,684 ft 2,037 m
Cape Canaveral
Lake Okeechobee
The Everglades
Florida Keys
Straits of Florida
TROPIC OF CANCER
CUBA
Gulf of Mexico
Mississippi River Delta
Minneapolis
Milwaukee
Chicago
Detroit
Cleveland
Pittsburgh
Boston
New York City
Philadelphia
Baltimore
Washington
Indianapolis
St. Louis
Memphis
Atlanta
Jacksonville
New Orleans
Houston
Miami
Mississippi
Ohio
Wabash
Cumberland
Tennessee
Savannah
Red
Hudson
Connecticut
PRINCIPAL HAWAIIAN ISLANDS
Niihau
Kauai
Oahu
Honolulu
Molokai
Maui
Lanai
Kahoolawe
Hawaii
Mauna Kea 13,796 ft 4,205 m
PACIFIC OCEAN

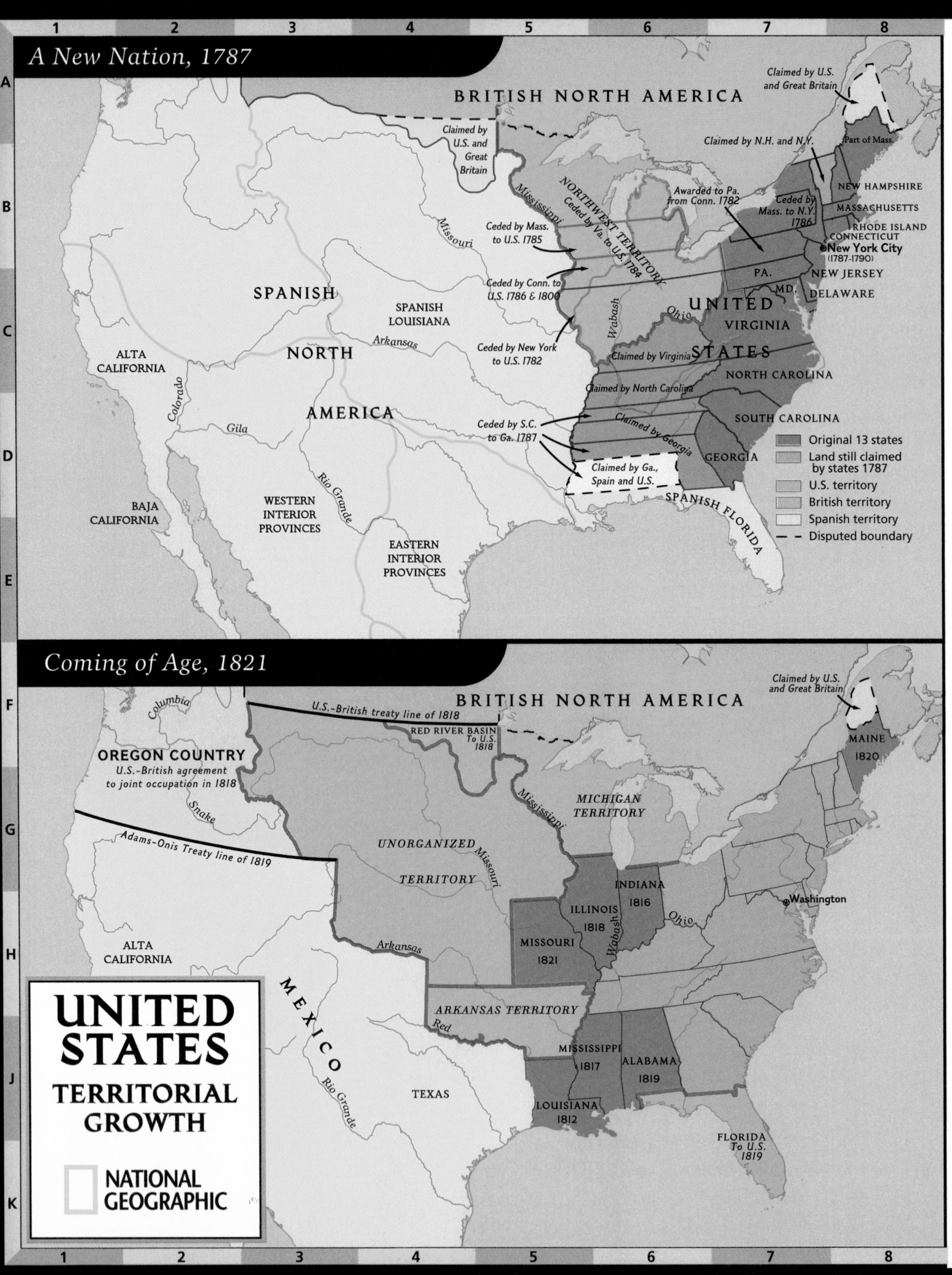

A New Nation, 1787
BRITISH NORTH AMERICA
Claimed by U.S. and Great Britain
Claimed by U.S. and Great Britain
Claimed by N.H. and N.Y.
Part of Mass.
NEW HAMPSHIRE
MASSACHUSETTS
RHODE ISLAND
CONNECTICUT
New York City (1787-1790)
NEW JERSEY
DELAWARE
PA.
MD.
Awarded to Pa. from Conn. 1782
Ceded by Mass. to N.Y. 1786
NORTHWEST TERRITORY Ceded by Va. to U.S. 1784
Ceded by Mass. to U.S. 1785
Ceded by Conn. to U.S. 1786 & 1800
Ceded by New York to U.S. 1782
Ceded by S.C. to Ga. 1787
UNITED STATES
VIRGINIA
NORTH CAROLINA
SOUTH CAROLINA
GEORGIA
Claimed by Virginia
Claimed by North Carolina
Claimed by Georgia
Claimed by Ga., Spain and U.S.
SPANISH FLORIDA
SPANISH NORTH AMERICA
SPANISH LOUISIANA
ALTA CALIFORNIA
BAJA CALIFORNIA
WESTERN INTERIOR PROVINCES
EASTERN INTERIOR PROVINCES
Mississippi
Missouri
Arkansas
Colorado
Gila
Rio Grande
Wabash
Ohio
Original 13 states
Land still claimed by states 1787
U.S. territory
British territory
Spanish territory
Disputed boundary
Coming of Age, 1821
BRITISH NORTH AMERICA
Claimed by U.S. and Great Britain
MAINE 1820
U.S.-British treaty line of 1818
RED RIVER BASIN To U.S. 1818
OREGON COUNTRY
U.S.-British agreement to joint occupation in 1818
Columbia
Snake
Adams-Onís Treaty line of 1819
ALTA CALIFORNIA
MEXICO
TEXAS
Rio Grande
UNORGANIZED TERRITORY
Missouri
Mississippi
Arkansas
Red
MICHIGAN TERRITORY
ILLINOIS 1818
INDIANA 1816
MISSOURI 1821
Wabash
Ohio
Washington
ARKANSAS TERRITORY
MISSISSIPPI 1817
ALABAMA 1819
LOUISIANA 1812
FLORIDA To U.S. 1819
UNITED STATES
TERRITORIAL GROWTH
NATIONAL GEOGRAPHIC

Special Purpose Maps

Some maps are made to present specific kinds of information. These are called **thematic** or **special purpose maps.** They usually show themes or patterns, often emphasizing one subject or theme. Special purpose maps may present climate or natural resources. They may also display historical information, such as battles or territorial changes. The map's title tells what kind of special information it shows. Colors and symbols in the map key are especially important on these types of maps. Special purpose maps are often found in books of maps called atlases.

One type of special purpose map uses colors to show population. Notice the key on the map "Population of the United States, 1820." It indicates that the states with the greatest population are in pink. The map shows these states are along the Atlantic Ocean.

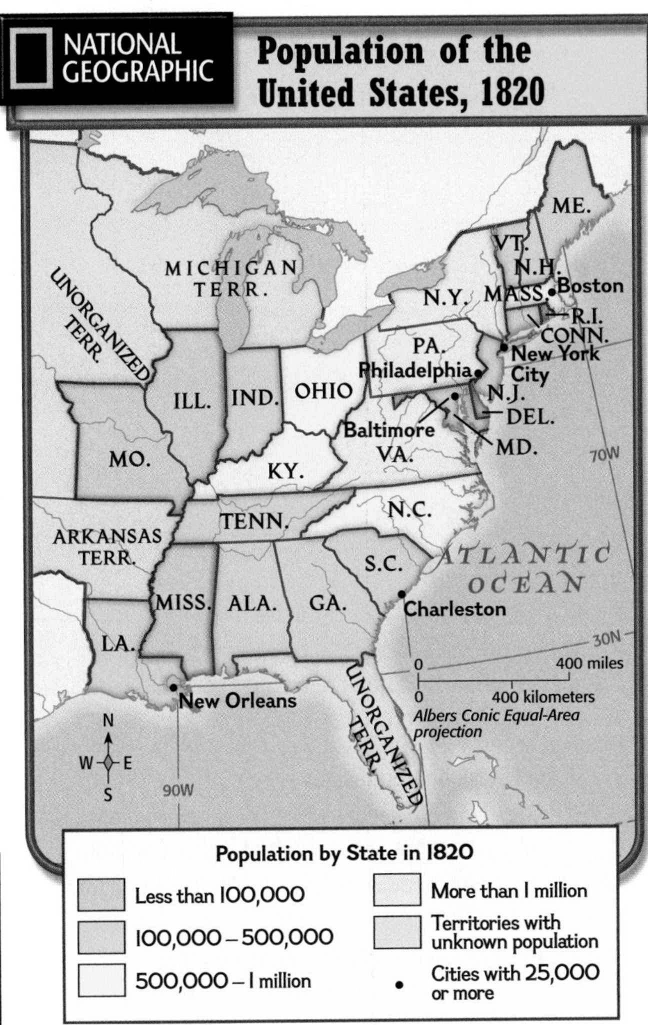

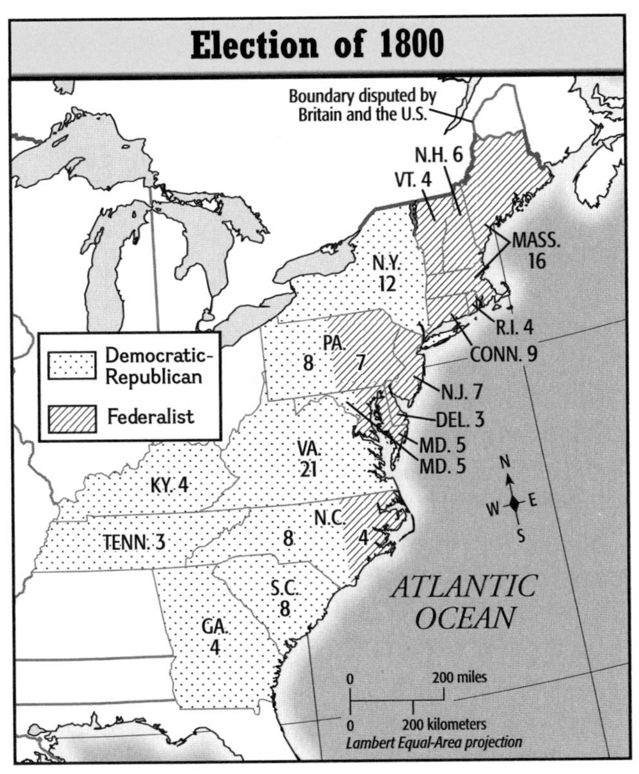

Some special purpose maps, such as "The Election of 1800," are not in color. This map is an example of what you might find on a standardized test or in a newspaper.

absolute location exact location of a place on the earth described by global coordinates

basin area of land drained by a given river and its branches; area of land surrounded by lands of higher elevation

bay part of a large body of water that extends into a shoreline, generally smaller than a gulf

canyon deep and narrow valley with steep walls

cape point of land that extends into a river, lake, or ocean

channel wide strait or waterway between two landmasses that lie close to each other; deep part of a river or other waterway

cliff steep, high wall of rock, earth, or ice

continent one of the seven large landmasses on the earth

cultural feature characteristic that humans have created in a place, such as language, religion, housing, and settlement pattern

delta flat, low-lying land built up from soil carried downstream by a river and deposited at its mouth

divide stretch of high land that separates river systems

downstream direction in which a river or stream flows from its source to its mouth

elevation height of land above sea level

Equator imaginary line that runs around the earth halfway between the North and South Poles; used as the starting point to measure degrees of north and south latitude

glacier large, thick body of slowly moving ice

gulf part of a large body of water that extends into a shoreline, generally larger and more deeply indented than a bay

harbor a sheltered place along a shoreline where ships can anchor safely

highland elevated land area such as a hill, mountain, or plateau

hill elevated land with sloping sides and rounded summit; generally smaller than a mountain

island land area, smaller than a continent, completely surrounded by water

isthmus narrow stretch of land connecting two larger land areas

lake a sizable inland body of water

latitude distance north or south of the Equator, measured in degrees

longitude distance east or west of the Prime Meridian, measured in degrees

lowland land, usually level, at a low elevation

map drawing of the earth shown on a flat surface

meridian one of many lines on the global grid running from the North Pole to the South Pole; used to measure degrees of longitude

mesa broad, flat-topped landform with steep sides; smaller than a plateau

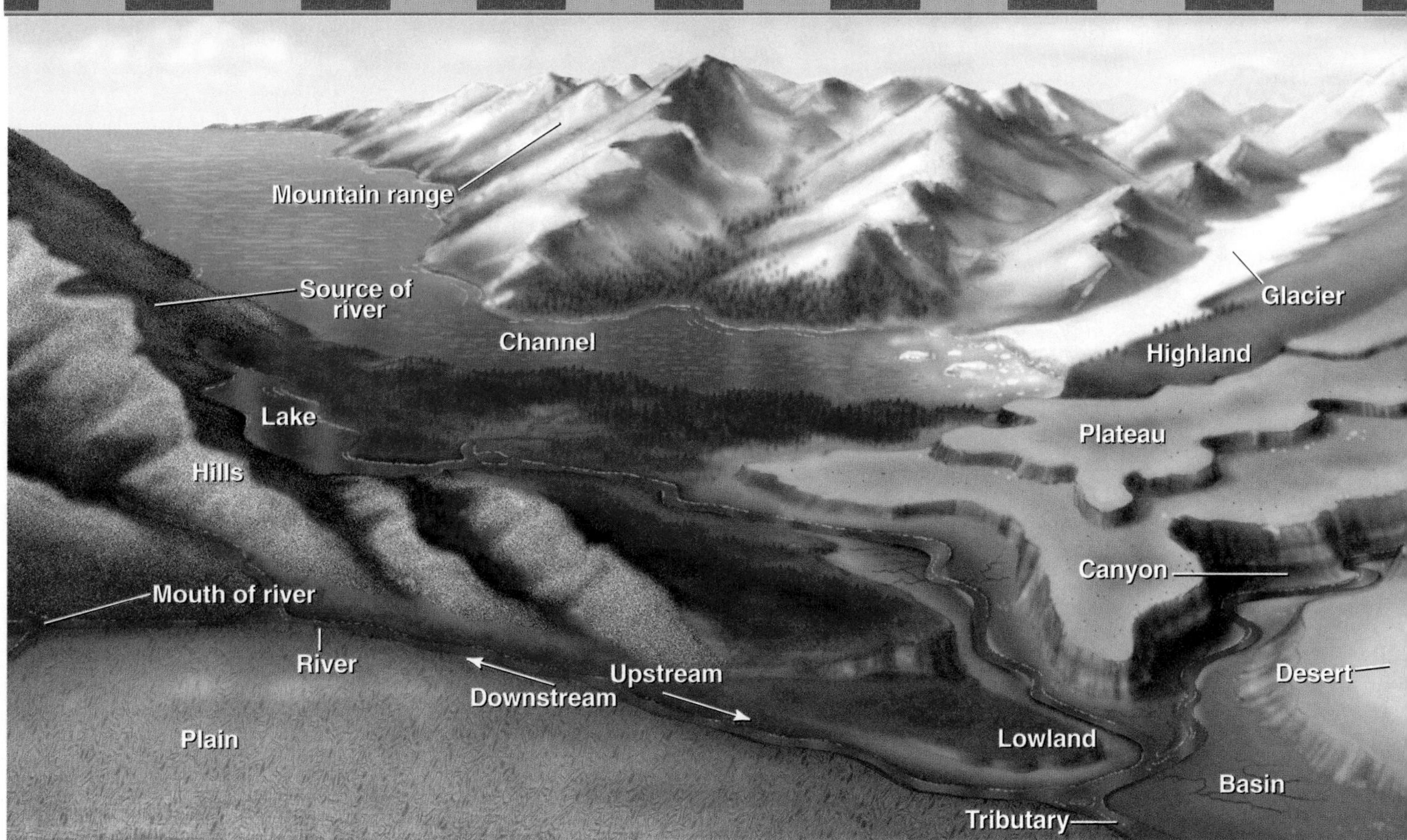

mountain land with steep sides that rises sharply (1,000 feet [305 m] or more) from surrounding land; generally larger and more rugged than a hill

mountain peak pointed top of a mountain

mountain range a series of connected mountains

mouth (of a river) place where a stream or river flows into a larger body of water

ocean one of the four major bodies of salt water that surround the continents

ocean current stream of either cold or warm water that moves in a definite direction through an ocean

parallel one of many lines on the global grid that circle the earth north or south of the Equator; used to measure degrees of latitude

peninsula body of land jutting into a lake or ocean, surrounded on three sides by water

physical feature characteristic of a place occurring naturally, such as a landform, body of water, climate pattern, or resource

plain area of level land, usually at a low elevation and often covered with grasses

plateau area of flat or rolling land at a high elevation, about 300–3,000 feet (91–914 m) high

Prime Meridian line of the global grid running from the North Pole to the South Pole through Greenwich, England; starting point for measuring degrees of east and west longitude

relief changes in elevation over a given area of land

river large natural stream of water that runs through the land

sea large body of water completely or partly surrounded by land

seacoast land lying next to a sea or ocean

sea level position on land level with surface of nearby ocean or sea

sound body of water between a coastline and one or more islands off the coast

source (of a river) place where a river or stream begins, often in highlands

strait narrow stretch of water joining two larger bodies of water

tributary small river or stream that flows into a larger river or stream; a branch of the river

upstream direction opposite the flow of a river; toward the source of a river or stream

valley area of low land between hills or mountains

volcano mountain that is created as liquid rock or ash erupts from inside the earth

Tools of the Historian

A historian is a person who studies and writes about people and events of the past. Historians find out how people lived, what happened to them, and what happened around them. They look for the reasons behind events and study the effects of events.

Have you ever wondered if you could be a historian? To answer that question, you will need to find out how history is researched and written. Historians use a number of skills to research and organize information. You can learn about these skills in the next few pages. As you study this textbook, you will see that the sections listed below will help you understand geography and history.

Scientists looking for evidence of past civilizations

Digging Up The Past

Historians depend on the work of archaeologists. Archaeologists are scientists who unearth the remains of the past.

What Do Archaeologists Study?

- Human and animal bones, seeds, trees
- Pottery, tools, weapons
- Mounds, pits, canals

▲ Prehistoric pottery

▲ Archaeologist at work

How Do They Gather Data?

- Surveys on foot
- Photographs taken from airplanes or satellites
- Ground-penetrating radar
- Plot locations on maps
- Dig for evidence with heavy equipment as well as shovels
- Sonar scanning to find underwater objects

How Do They Interpret Findings?

- Organize artifacts into groups based on similarities
- Compare objects in relation to other objects
- Look for evidence of changes over a period of time
- Date once-living objects by measuring carbon-14 levels
- Use microscopic and biological tests to date objects

◀ Carbon-14 dating

Do Your Own Digging

Research the library and Internet to find information on two archaeological diggings, one past and the other recent. Compare and contrast the methods used in each digging. What changes do you notice in the tools that archaeologists have used over time?

Measuring Time

Historical and Social Sciences Analysis Skills

Chronological and Spatial Thinking

CS1. Students explain how major events are related to one another in time.

Calendars Historians rely on *calendars,* or dating systems, to measure time. Cultures throughout the world have developed different calendars based on important events in their history. Western nations begin their calendar with the year in which Jesus was thought to have been born. The Jewish calendar begins about 3,760 years before the Christian calendar. This is the time when Jewish tradition says the world was created. Muslims date their calendar from the time their first leader, Muhammad, left the city of Makkah for Madinah. This was A.D. 622 in the Christian calendar.

Ancient stone calendar

The dates in this book are based on the Western calendar. In the Western calendar, the years before the birth of Jesus are known as "B.C.," or "before Christ." The years after are called "A.D.," or *anno domini.* This phrase comes from the Latin language and means "in the year of the Lord."

About A.D. 500, a Christian monk, or religious person, developed the Western way of dating events.

Dating Events To date events before the birth of Christ, or B.C., historians count backwards from A.D. 1. There is no year 0. The year before A.D. 1 is 1 B.C. (Notice that A.D. is written before the date, but B.C. is written following the date.) Therefore, a date in the 100 years before the birth of Christ lies between 100 B.C. and A.D. 1.

To date events after the birth of Christ, or A.D., historians count forward, starting at A.D. 1. A date in the first 100 years after the birth of Christ is between A.D. 1 and A.D. 100.

Dating Archaeological Finds One of the most important and difficult jobs for archaeologists is dating the artifacts that they find. Artifacts are objects made by people, such as weapons, tools, or pottery. The earliest artifacts are pieces of hard rock that were chipped into cutting or digging tools or into weapons. By examining artifacts, scientists can learn about the social and military structures of an ancient society.

▲ Pioneers on the Oregon Trail

Miner seeking gold ▶

Relative location tells where a place is, compared with one or more other places. San Francisco is northwest of Los Angeles and southwest of Seattle. Knowing a place's relative location may help a historian understand how it was settled and how its culture developed. For example, people in California have settled in coastal areas and valleys, because inland areas have many mountains or deserts. They also have turned to the sea for food and trade.

Place

"What is it like?" *Place* describes all of the characteristics that give an area its own special quality. These can be physical features, such as mountains, waterways, climate, and plant or animal life. Places can also be described by human characteristics, such as language, religion, and architecture. For example, pioneers on the Oregon and California Trails crossed vast plains, swift rivers, high mountains, and hot deserts to reach their western destinations. When they arrived, they set up farms, homesteads, and towns.

Pioneer chest ▶

Human/Environment Interaction

"What is the relationship between people and their surroundings?" Landforms, waterways, climate, and natural resources all have helped or hindered human activities.

People have responded to their environment, or natural surroundings, in different ways. Sometimes they have adjusted to it. For example, people throughout history have worn light clothing in hot places. At other times, people have changed their environment to meet their needs. For example, some pioneers who went westward set up farms, and others mined for gold and other minerals.

History and Geography

Movement

"How do people in one area affect people in other areas?" Historians answer this question with one word—*movement.* Throughout history, people, ideas, goods, and information have moved from place to place. Movement has brought the world's people closer together.

Transportation—the movement of people and goods—has allowed people to use products that are made thousands of miles away. This has increased the exchange of ideas and cultures. Communication—the movement of ideas and information—has allowed people to find out what is happening in other parts of the world. Unlike in the past, people today receive almost instant communication by radio, television, and the computer.

The movement of people to different places is called migration. Why have people migrated throughout history? Some have chosen to move to seek a better life. Others have been forced to move because of wars, famine, enslavement, or other settlers. For example, many white settlers moved into the southeastern states from the 1820s to the 1840s. They wanted the land held by Native Americans. In 1830 Congress passed the Indian Removal Act to move Native Americans west of the Mississippi River. Under pressure, the Choctaw, Creek, and Chickasaw moved. The Cherokee and the Seminole resisted but in the end many of them were forced to relocate.

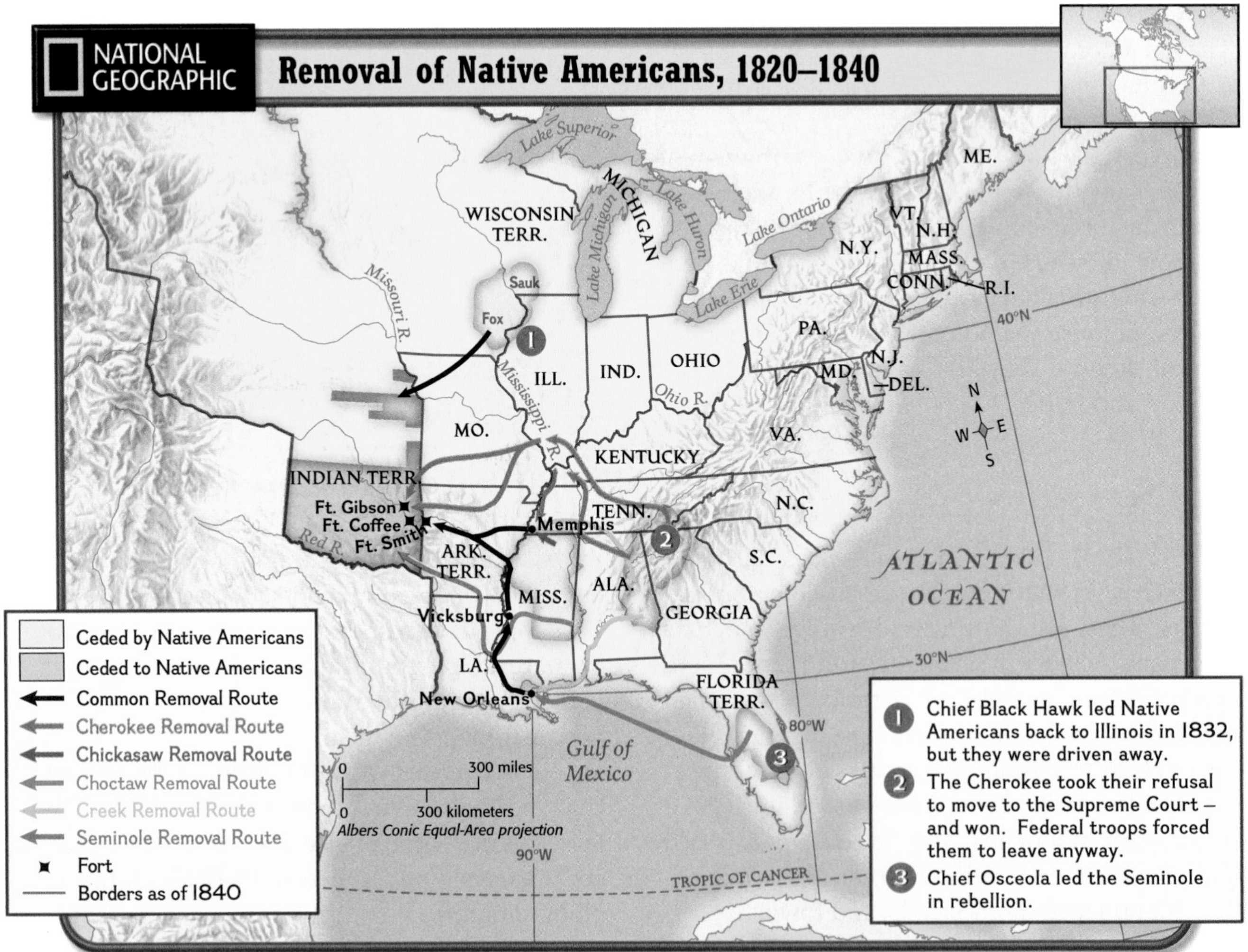

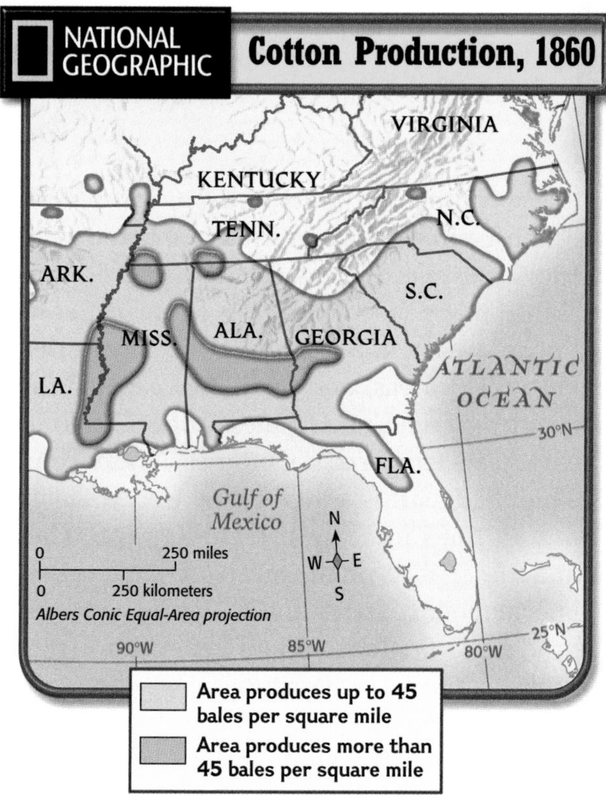

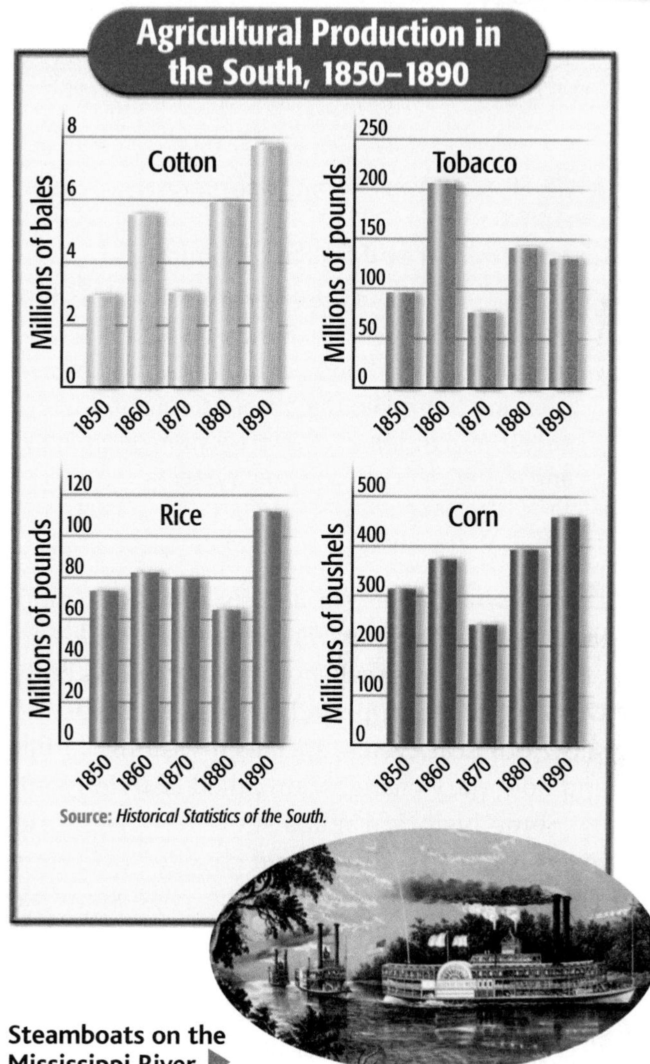

Steamboats on the Mississippi River ▶

Region

"What common characteristics does a certain area share?" Historians often view places or areas as regions. A *region* is an area that is defined by common features. Regions can be defined by physical features, such as mountains and rivers, or by human features, such as religion, language, or livelihood. For example, the South during the 1800s was a largely agricultural region.

Six Essential Elements

Recently geographers have begun to look at geography a different way. They break down the study of geography into *Six Essential Elements.* These elements are:

- The World in Spatial Terms
- Places and Regions
- Physical Systems
- Human Systems
- Environment and Society
- The Uses of Geography

See the information about the Six Essential Elements in the Geography Handbook on pages 39–40. Knowing these elements will help you in your study of history.

Thinking Like a Historian

1. **Identify** How are absolute location and relative location different?
2. **Analyzing Themes** What characteristics do geographers use to describe a place?
3. **Linking History and Geography** Make a list of the Five Themes of Geography. Under each theme, explain how you think geography has affected the history of your community.

What Is a Historical Atlas?

Historical and Social Sciences Analysis Skills

Chronological and Spatial Thinking

CS3. Students should use a variety of maps and documents to identify physical and cultural features of neighborhoods, cities, states, and countries and to explain the historical migration of people, expansion and disintegration of empires, and the growth of economic systems.

Historical Maps An *atlas* is a book of maps that show different parts of the world. A *historical atlas* has maps that show different parts of the world at different periods in history. Maps that show political events, such as invasions, battles, and boundary changes, are called *historical maps.*

Some historical maps show how territories in a certain part of the world changed over time. The maps at the bottom of the page show the territorial size of the United States in 1800 and 1810. By comparing the two maps, you can see how the United States gradually expanded its territory westward from 1800 to 1810.

Both maps use colors to show different political areas: U.S. states, U.S. territories, foreign-ruled areas, and territories claimed but not owned by the United States. Different colored lines indicate territorial boundaries. A heavy blue line highlights areas added to the United States, and gray lines indicate present-day U.S. state boundaries. Labels on the maps present a variety of information. This data includes new states and their dates of admission to the Union, plus recently acquired U.S. territories.

Historical maps show places and events from the past. As you study history, you will use many other kinds of maps. *Thematic maps* deal with specialized information, often on a single topic such as population or land use. A *political map* shows the political boundaries or borders of a state, country, or region.

NATIONAL GEOGRAPHIC **Territorial Growth, 1800–1810**

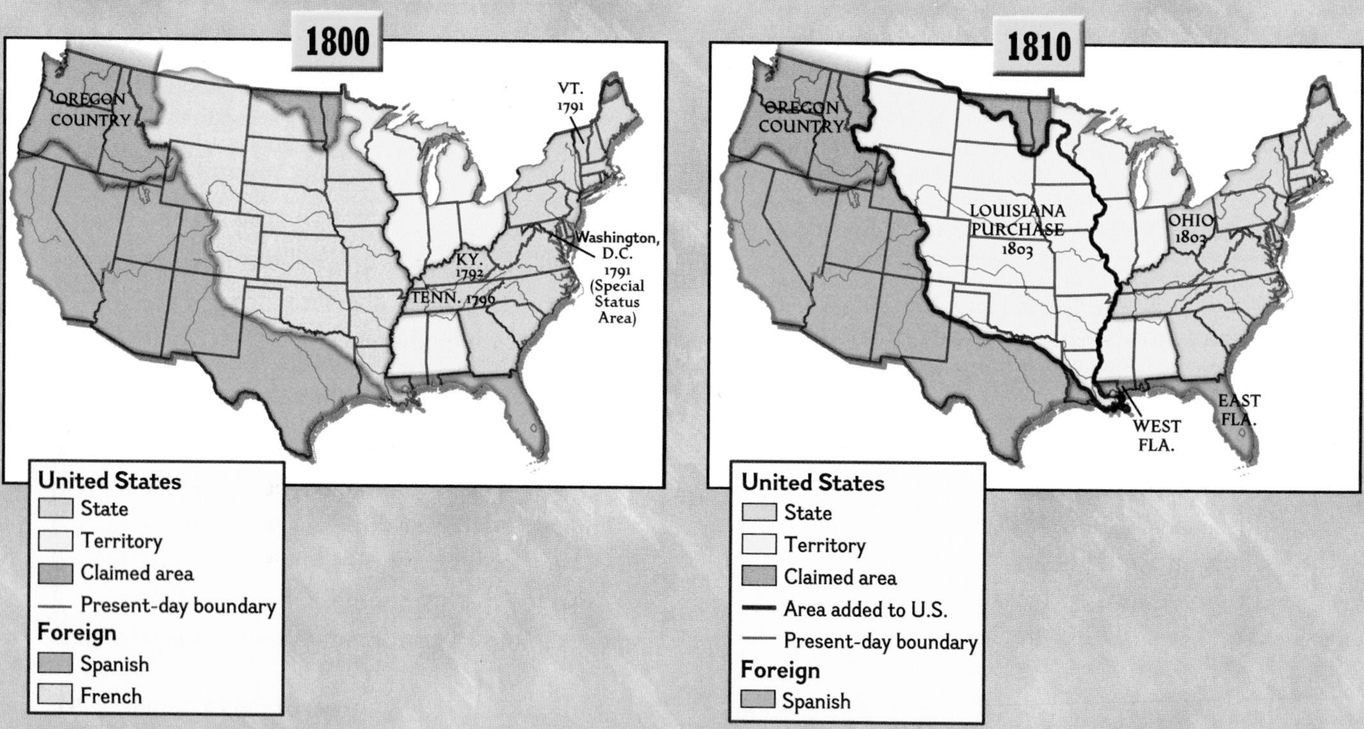

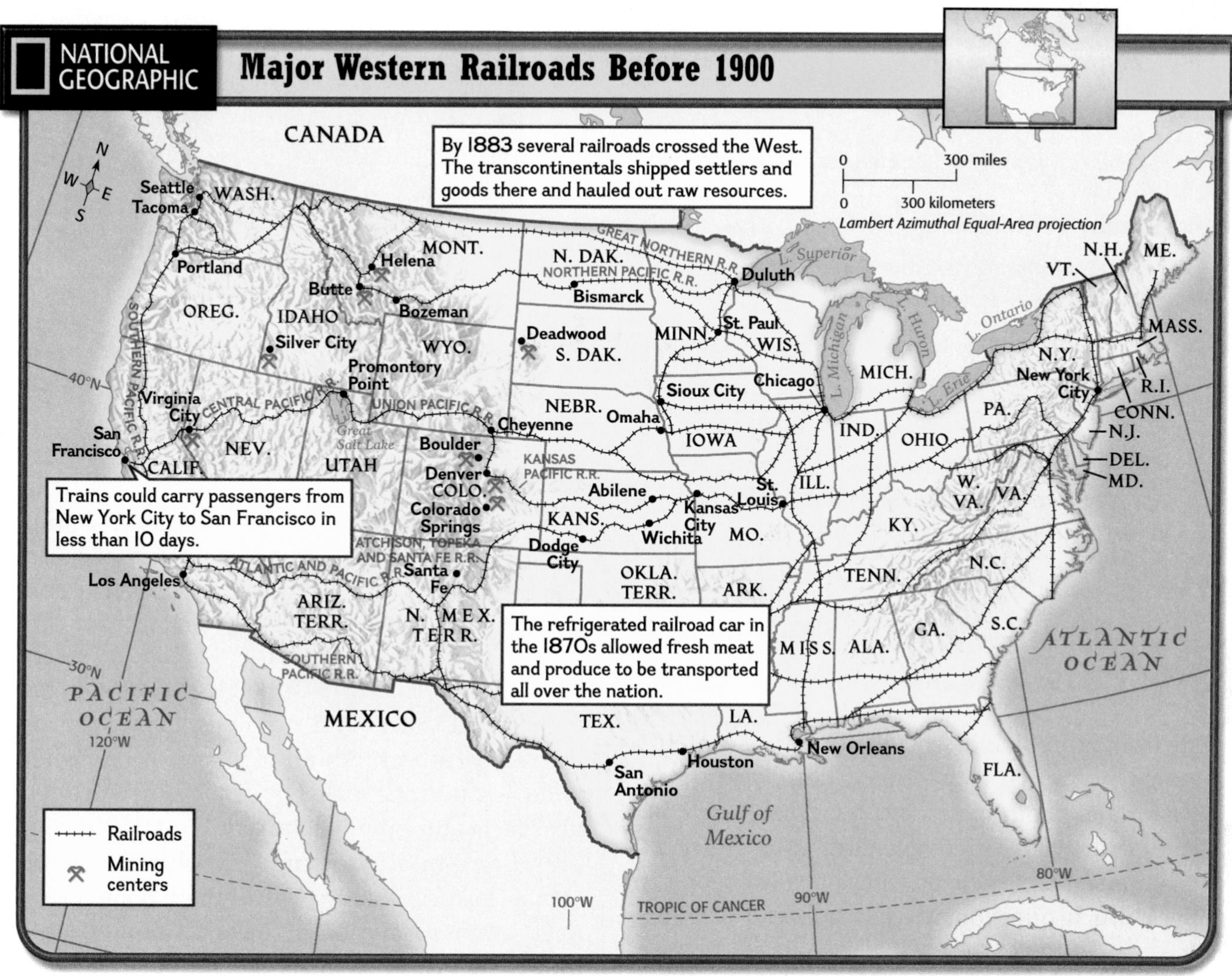

Historical Routes In your study of American history, you will often encounter thematic maps that show movement or routes. On some maps, lines may show *historical routes.* These are roads or courses over which people or goods have traveled all through history. Such routes are often colored or have special markings. On the map above, the black marked lines show major railroad routes in the western United States before 1900.

On maps of historical routes, the key explains what is shown on the maps. This map's key shows railroad routes and mining centers. In addition, boxes on the map provide information about railroad travel during the late 1800s.

Thinking Like a Historian

1. **Analyzing Maps** Look at the map of western railroads. Name one railroad system that extended west to the Pacific Ocean through each of these areas of the country—the North, the central part, and the South.
2. **Reading a Map Key** Look at the map of western railroads. What mining center lay on the Central Pacific Railway?
3. **Analyzing Maps** Select any chapter in your textbook. List the titles of the maps found in that chapter. Beside each map's title, state what kinds of symbols are used in each map key and what they represent.

How Does a Historian Work?

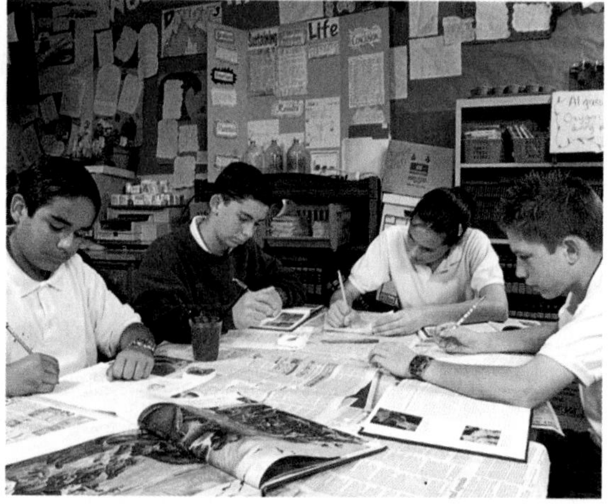

▲ Students studying history

Historical and Social Sciences Analysis Skills

Research, Evidence, and Point of View

HR1. Students frame questions that can be answered by historical study and research.

HR2. Students distinguish fact from opinion in historical narratives and stories.

HR3. Students distinguish relevant from irrelevant information, essential from incidental information, and verifiable from unverifiable information in historical narratives and stories.

Asking Questions About the Past

Historians are like detectives. They look for evidence to solve problems about the past. Historians begin by asking questions, such as: Why did two particular countries go to war? What effect did their fighting have on people's lives? Such questions help historians focus on historical problems. By asking questions, historians can better identify the issues. They also can determine how and why events happened and what the effects of these events were.

Is It Fact or Opinion? Historical sources may contain facts and opinions. A *fact* can be proved, or observed; an *opinion,* on the other hand, is a personal belief or conclusion. We often hear facts and opinions mixed in everyday conversation—in advertising, in political debate, and in historical sources. Although some opinions can be supported by facts, in an argument they do not carry as much weight as facts.

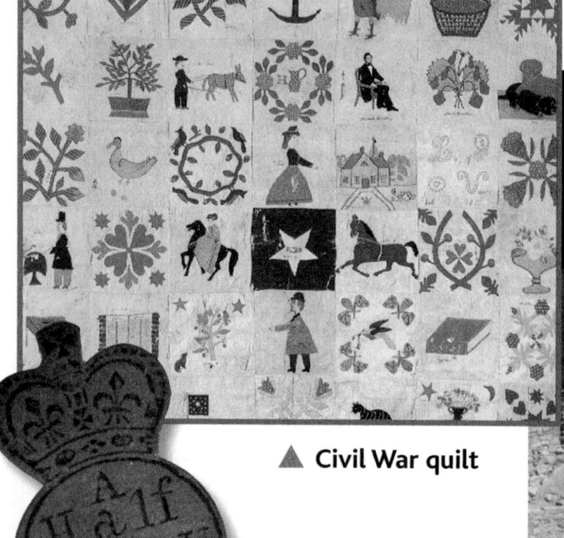

▲ Civil War quilt

◀ Colonial revenue stamp

▼ Native American cliff dwelling

NATIONAL GEOGRAPHIC

3

MAYFLOWER COMPACT

See *Road to Independence* Chapter 2

4

SIGNING THE DECLARATION OF INDEPENDENCE

See *Road to Independence* Chapter 2

George Washington
1732–1799
Leader of the Patriot army
Chapter 2, page 139

Thomas Jefferson
1743–1826
American political leader
Chapter 2, page 150

Benjamin Franklin
1706–1790
American scientist and patriot
Chapter 2, page 151

Abigail Adams
1744–1818
Patriot and supporter of women's rights
Chapter 2, page 155

Expanding Horizons

▼ Mission Santa Barbara in California

Where & When?

1200 — 1450 — 1700

- **1271** Marco Polo travels to China
- **1492** Christopher Columbus sails to the Americas
- **1521** Spanish conquer Aztec Empire
- **1689** English Bill of Rights extends rights

History Online

Chapter Overview Visit ca.hss.glencoe.com for a preview of Chapter 1.

The Big Ideas

Age of Exploration

Exploration and trade spread ideas and goods. In the 1400s, Europeans began to explore other areas of the world. Trade increased and goods, technology, and ideas were exchanged around the world.

Rise of Modern Capitalism

Humans have created various economic systems. Our economic system is usually referred to as free enterprise, or capitalism. Capitalism is based on individual economic freedom. Capitalism developed gradually from economic and political changes in medieval and early modern Europe over hundreds of years.

The Enlightenment

World history has been shaped by significant individuals, groups, ideas, events, eras, and developments. The Scientific Revolution led to new discoveries. Using the scientific method, Europeans of the 1600s and 1700s developed new ideas about society based on reason.

View the Chapter 1 video in the Glencoe Video Program.

FOLDABLES™ Study Organizer

Summarizing Make this foldable to help you learn about European exploration of the Americas.

Step 1 Fold the paper from the top right corner down so the edges line up. Cut off the leftover piece.

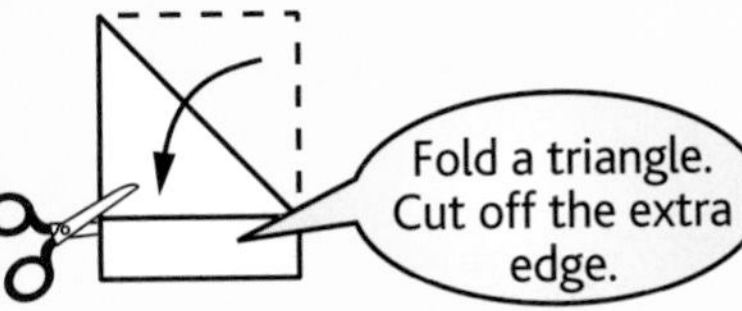

Fold a triangle.
Cut off the extra edge.

Step 2 Fold the triangle in half. Unfold.

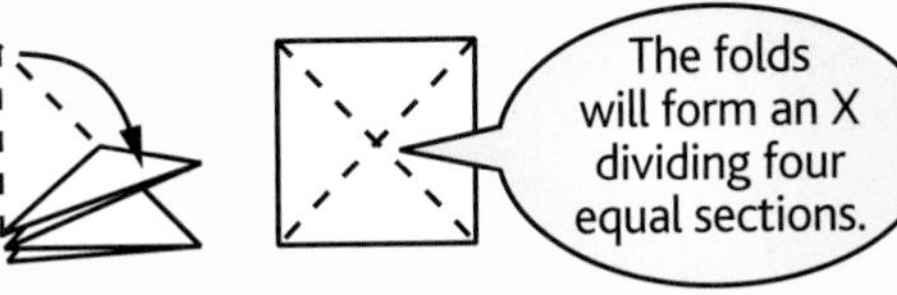

The folds will form an X dividing four equal sections.

Step 3 Cut up one fold line and stop at the middle. Draw an X on one tab and label the other three.

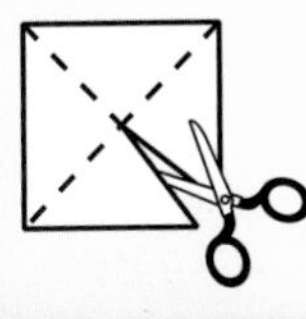

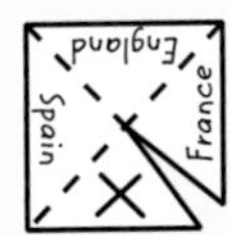

Step 4 Fold the X flap under the other flap and glue together.

Spain
This makes a three-sided pyramid.

Reading and Writing
As you read, ask yourself why England, France, and Spain were exploring the Americas. Write your questions under each appropriate pyramid wall.

Get Ready to Read

Previewing

1 Learn It!

If you know what to expect before reading, it will be easier to understand ideas and relationships presented in the text. Follow these steps to preview your reading assignments.

1. **Look at the title and any illustrations that are included.**
2. **Read the headings, subheadings, and anything in bold letters.**
3. **Skim over the passage to see how it is organized. Is it divided into many parts?**
4. **Look at the graphics—pictures, maps, or diagrams. Read their titles and captions.**
5. **Set a purpose for your reading. Are you reading to learn something new? Are you reading to find specific information?**

Reading Tip

As you preview the chapter, be sure to look over the maps, photographs, and charts.

2 Practice It!

Take some time to preview this chapter. Skim all the main heads and main ideas. With a partner, discuss your answers to these questions.

- Which part of this chapter looks the most interesting to you?
- What do you think will be covered in the next chapter?
- Are there any words in the Main Ideas that are unfamiliar to you?
- Choose one of the Reading Connection questions to discuss with your partner.

Read to Write

Use the information you have gathered through previewing to write a study outline for the chapter.

Europe Gets Ready to Explore

Main Idea **New knowledge and ideas led Europeans to explore overseas.**

Reading Connection Have you ever done something daring or tried something new not knowing how it would turn out? Read to learn how explorers took chances and went to new places.

Christopher Columbus in the Americas

3 Apply It!

Now that you have skimmed the chapter, write a short paragraph describing one thing you want to learn from this chapter.

Age of Exploration

Guide to Reading

History Social Science Standards

WH7.11 Students analyze political and economic change in the sixteenth, seventeenth, and eighteenth centuries (the Age of Exploration, the Enlightenment, and the Age of Reason).

Looking Back, Looking Ahead

Europeans risked dangerous ocean voyages to discover new sea routes. Today, people continue to explore the mysteries of Earth and of space.

Focusing on the Main Ideas

- New knowledge and ideas led Europeans to explore overseas. *(page 81)*
- In search of trade routes, Portuguese explorers began an era of overseas exploration. *(page 84)*
- Rivalries between countries led to increased exploration of North America. *(page 86)*

Meeting People

Marco Polo
Bartholomeu Dias (bahr • THAH • luh • MYOO DEE • AHSH)
Vasco da Gama (VAHS • koh dah GA • muh)
Christopher Columbus
Montezuma (MAHN • tuh • ZOO • muh)

Locating Places

Portugal (POHR • chih • guhl)
Tenochtitlán (tay • NAWCH • teet • LAHN)

Content Vocabulary

technology
astrolabe (AS • truh • LAYB)
circumnavigate (SUHR • kuhm • NA • vuh • GAYT)
conquistador (kahn • KEES • tuh • DAWR)
pueblo (PWEH • bloh)
mission
presidio (prih • SEE • dee • OH)
encomienda (ehn • koh • mee • EHN • da)
Northwest Passage

Academic Vocabulary

culture (KUHL • chuhr)
design (dih • ZYN)

Reading Strategy

Determining Cause and Effect Use a diagram like the one below to identify three reasons Europeans increased overseas exploration.

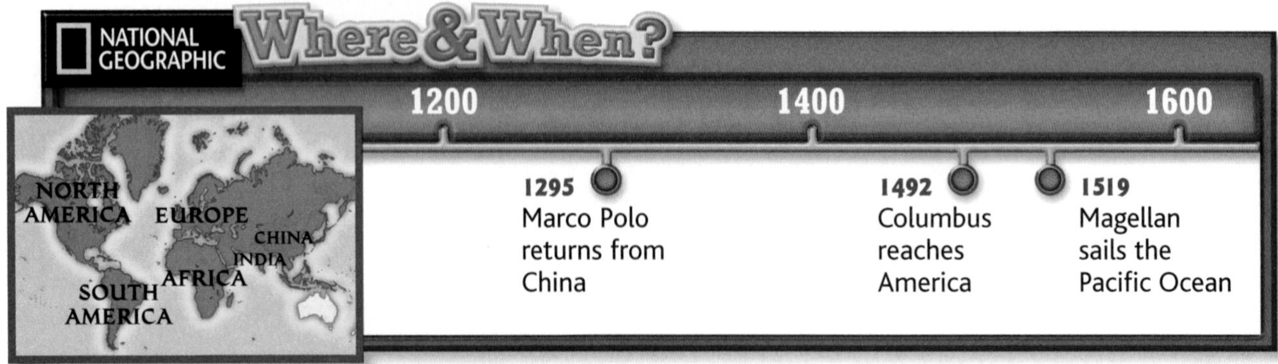

WH7.11.1 Know the great voyages of discovery, the locations of the routes, and the influence of cartography in the development of a new European worldview.

Europe Gets Ready to Explore

Main Idea **New knowledge and ideas led Europeans to explore overseas.**

Reading Connection Have you ever done something daring or tried something new not knowing how it would turn out? Read to learn how explorers took chances and went to new places.

A European Story

In 1271 **Marco Polo** set off from Europe on a great trek across Asia to China. Only 17 years old at the time, Polo journeyed with his father and uncle, both merchants from the Italian city of Venice. Traveling on camels for more than three years, the merchants crossed almost 7,000 miles (11,265 km) of mountains and deserts. Finally they reached the palace of Kublai Khan (KOO•bluh KAHN), the emperor of China. There Marco Polo spent 17 years working for the Khan and learning much about China's advanced **culture.**

When Polo returned from China in 1295, he wrote an account of the marvels of Asia, describing great riches and splendid cities. Polo's *Travels* was eagerly read in Europe and inspired a new age of exploration. Little did Polo realize the effect *Travels* would have. Nearly 200 years later his book about the East would inspire Christopher Columbus and other European explorers to sail in the opposite direction to reach the same destination.

Growth of Trade Marco Polo lived during the Middle Ages, the period in Western Europe that began with the fall of the western Roman Empire and lasted through the 1400s. During this time most Europeans knew little about India, China, or the rest of Asia. They also had no idea that the Western Hemisphere existed. Then, a dramatic series of events occurred that brought Europeans out of their isolation.

From the late 1000s to the early 1300s, Europeans fought a series of crusades, or holy wars, to free the Holy Land where Jesus had lived from the Muslims. The Muslims were followers of Islam, a religion that arose in the Middle East during the A.D. 600s. The Crusades achieved very little for Europeans, but they did increase trade between Europe and the lands to the east. During the time of the Crusades, Marco Polo made his journey. As Polo's story spread and exotic goods from the East appeared in Europe's marketplaces, more people became interested in distant lands. Merchants realized that they could make a fortune selling goods from Asia.

▲ Detail of historic map showing Marco Polo's journey

▲ Kublai Khan presents golden tablets to Marco Polo.

The Compass, c. 1086

European technology improved navigation, but it was the Chinese who invented one of the more important tools for navigation: the compass. Evidence of this technology includes a Chinese document from the year 1086 that tells of sea captains relying on a "south-pointing needle" to help them find their way in foggy weather. The date on the document is more than 100 years earlier than the first recorded use of the compass in Europe.

How does a compass work? It uses a lodestone—a magnetic ore that always points in a north-south direction if allowed to freely rotate. If you know which way is north, you can determine the other directions.

▼ Compasses come in many shapes and sizes.

Centers of Trade Wealthy Europeans clamored for spices, perfumes, silks, and precious stones. Merchants bought goods from Arab traders in the Middle East and sent them overland by caravan to the Mediterranean Sea, then by ship to Italian ports. The cities of Venice, Genoa, and Pisa prospered and became centers of the growing East-West trade. The expansion of trade with Asia made Italian merchants wealthy.

The Rise of Strong Nations During the 1400s, Italian merchants found it harder to get the fabled goods of the East. Political changes in Asia hindered trade between East and West. This made Asian goods more expensive. In areas of western Europe close to the Atlantic Ocean, merchants wanted to expand their businesses through foreign trade. If they could buy spices and silks from the East directly, without going through the Arab and Italian cities, they could earn huge profits. They looked for new routes to East Asia that would bypass the Mediterranean Sea and the Middle East.

Meanwhile, a new type of centralized state was emerging in western Europe. Strong monarchs had come to power in Spain, Portugal, England, and France. They began to establish national laws, courts, taxes, and armies to replace those of local lords. These ambitious kings and queens sought ways to increase trade and make their countries stronger and wealthier. They played an important role in expanding trade and interest in overseas exploration.

New Technology Advances in **technology**—the use of scientific knowledge for practical purposes—paved the way for European voyages of exploration. Maps were a problem for early navigators. By the 1400s, most educated people in Europe knew the world was round, but they only had maps of Europe and the Mediterranean. Most of these maps were inaccurate because they were drawn from the often-mistaken impressions of traders and travelers. Over time, cartographers, or mapmakers, gradually improved their skills.

Using the reports of explorers and information from Arab geographers, mapmakers made more accurate land and sea maps. These maps showed the direction of ocean currents and lines of latitude, which measured the distance north and south of the Equator. Only as sailors began to move beyond the coasts of Europe did they gain information about the actual shape of the earth. By 1500, cartography had reached the point where Europeans had fairly accurate maps of the areas they had explored.

Better Tools and Ships Better instruments were developed for navigating the seas. Sailors could determine their latitude while at sea with an **astrolabe** (AS•truh•LAYB), an instrument that measured the position of the stars. Europeans also improved the magnetic compass, a Chinese invention the Arabs had passed on to Europe in the 1200s. The compass allowed sailors to determine their ship's location when they were far from land.

Advances in ship **design** allowed shipbuilders to build sailing vessels capable of long ocean voyages. The stern rudder and the triangular sail made it possible for ships to sail into the wind. Both of these new features came from the Arabs. In the late 1400s, the Portuguese developed the three-masted caravel. The caravel was a small vessel that sailed faster than earlier ships and carried more cargo and food supplies. It also could float in shallow water, which allowed sailors to explore inlets and to sail their ships up to the beach to make repairs.

✓ Reading Check **Analyze** Why were Marco Polo's travels to China important?

Linking Past & Present

Navigation Tools

Past "Land ho!" The tools that early explorers used to sail the uncharted seas were much different from the instruments used today. One early navigation tool was the astrolabe. A sailor held the astrolabe vertically, located a star through its sights, and measured the star's elevation above the horizon. A ship's approximate location could be identified this way.

▼ Navstar Global Positioning System satellite being launched

▲ Astrolabe

Present Today navigation satellites do the work of an astrolabe—and more! The Navstar Global Positioning System (GPS) is a constellation of orbiting satellites that provides navigation information. Developed by the military, Navstar allows a traveler to find out his or her position anywhere on or above the planet. ***What are some items that help you navigate?***

WH7.11.1 Know the great voyages of discovery, the locations of the routes, and the influence of cartography in the development of a new European worldview.

Exploring the World

Main Idea **In search of trade routes, Portuguese explorers began an era of overseas exploration.**

Reading Connection Do you like traveling to places that you have never been? Read to see why Europeans set off to explore the Americas.

By the mid-1400s, the Italian ports faced increased competition for foreign trade. Powerful countries like **Portugal** (POHR•chih•guhl) and Spain began searching for sea routes to Asia, launching a new era of exploration. These new voyages took sailors down the west coast of Africa, which Europeans had never visited before.

Portugal Leads the Way Prince Henry of Portugal laid the groundwork for a new era of exploration. In about 1420, he set up a center for exploration on the southwestern tip of Portugal. Prince Henry brought astronomers, geographers, and mathematicians to share their knowledge with Portuguese sailors and shipbuilders.

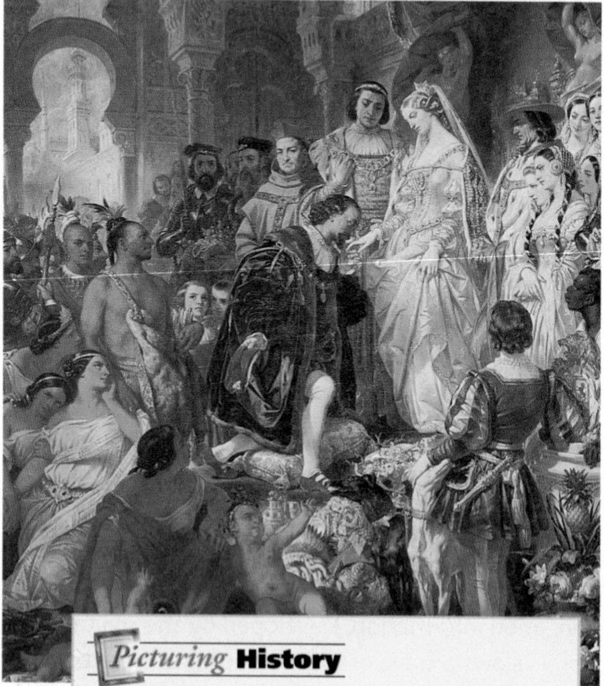

Picturing **History**

Financed by Spain's Queen Isabella, the voyages of Columbus led to an exchange of goods between Europe and the Americas. ***On what island of the Americas did Columbus first land?***

In early 1488, the Portuguese explorer **Bartholomeu Dias** (bahr•THAH•luh•MYOO DEE•AHSH) reached the southern tip of Africa. As Dias approached the area, he ran into a terrible storm that carried him off course and around the southern tip of Africa. Dias wrote that he had been around the "Cape of Storms." On learning of Dias's discovery, King John II renamed this southern tip of land the Cape of Good Hope—he hoped that the passage around Africa might lead to a new route to India.

The first Portuguese voyages to India were made years later. In July 1497, **Vasco da Gama** (VAHS•koh dah GA•muh) set out from Portugal with four ships. Da Gama rounded the Cape of Good Hope and visited cities along the coast of East Africa. In 1498 he reached the port of Calicut, completing the long-awaited eastern sea route to Asia.

Events moved quickly after that. Pedro Alvares Cabral, following Da Gama's route, swung so wide around Africa that he touched Brazil. By claiming land for his king, he gave Portugal a stake in the Americas. Meanwhile, Portuguese ships began to make voyages to India, returning with cargoes of goods.

Columbus Sets Sail While the Portuguese explored Africa, an Italian navigator named **Christopher Columbus** came up with a daring plan to get to Asia. He would sail west across the Atlantic Ocean. At the time, nobody knew that a great landmass blocked the route to Asia.

Desperate for money to make the trip, Columbus obtained support from Queen Isabella of Spain in 1492. The Spanish had been watching the seafaring success of neighboring Portugal with envy. They, too, wanted to share in the riches of Asian trade. Earlier in 1492, the Spanish had driven the Muslims out of Spain. They could now afford to pay for exploration.

Columbus outfitted three ships: the *Niña,* the *Pinta,* and a larger one, the *Santa María.* In 1492 they left Spain and headed west. As the weeks passed, the crew grew desperate. Finally they sighted land—a small island, part of the group now called the Bahamas.

Changes in Banking Meanwhile, many Jews fleeing persecution in Spain settled in port cities in Holland, France, and Germany. There they were granted freedom of worship and offered economic opportunities. Many Jews became financiers and investors as well as importers and shipbuilders.

By the 1600s, governments began to charter, or legally support, banks in return for the banks loaning them money. These government-backed banks accepted deposits of money and charged interest on loans. Before long, the banks began to provide other services. They issued banknotes and checks, making large payments in heavy coins a thing of the past. They acted as money changers, exchanging currencies from other countries.

What Are Joint-Stock Companies? In the 1600s, new ways of doing business developed in Europe. Individual merchants who wanted to invest in exploration often raised money by combining their resources in **joint-stock companies,** organizations that sold stock, or shares, in the venture. This enabled large and small investors to share the profits and risks of a trading voyage. If a loss occurred, investors would lose only the amount they had invested in shares. This sharing of risk provided a stable way of raising **funds** for voyages.

A few joint-stock companies became rich and powerful through government support. For example, the Netherlands entered an era of commercial prosperity upon gaining independence from Spain in 1648. Its government gave the Dutch East India Company a monopoly, or the sole right, to carry out Dutch trade with Africa and the East Indies. The Dutch government also gave the company the power to make war, to seize foreign ships, to coin money, and to set up colonies and forts. In return, the government received customs duties, or taxes on imported goods, from the company's trade.

A New Business Class As gold and silver flowed into Europe from abroad, the supply of coined money increased. At the same time, the nature and goals of business changed. It now came to be seen that the goal of business was to make profits. Individuals known as **entrepreneurs** (AHN • truh • pruh • NUHRZ) combined money, ideas, raw materials, and labor to make goods and profits. Profits were then used to expand the business and develop new ventures.

An entrepreneur in the cloth industry, for example, would buy wool and employ spinners to make the wool into yarn. Weavers and dyers would then be hired to turn the yarn into cloth. Because these tasks were done in the workers' homes, this system became known as the "cottage industry."

The entrepreneur would then sell the cloth on the open market for a price that brought a profit. Of course, entrepreneurs took risks when they put up capital for businesses. They could lose their investment if prices fell or if workers could not produce goods at a specified time or for a specific market.

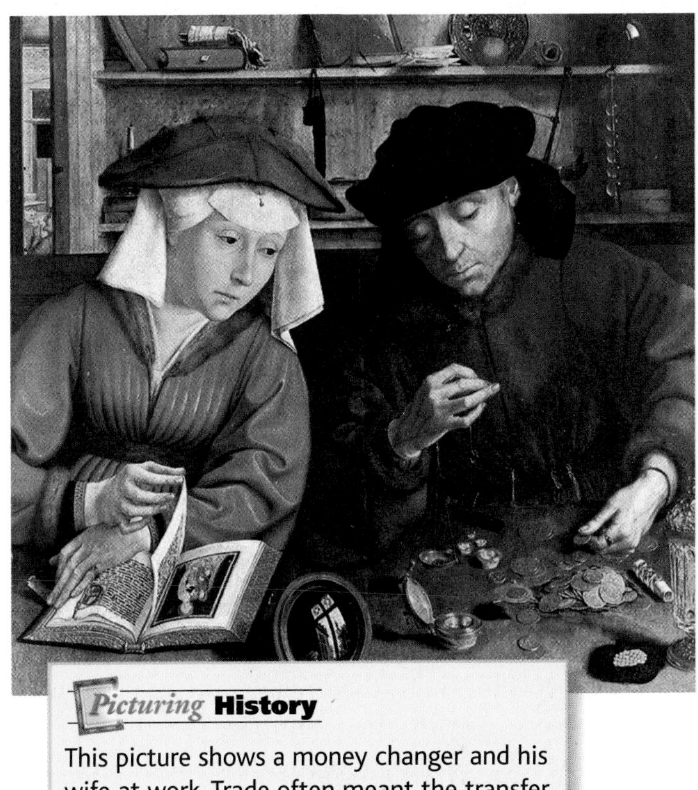

Picturing **History**

This picture shows a money changer and his wife at work. Trade often meant the transfer of money from place to place. ***How did banks help finance trading voyages?***

Reading Check **Explain** What was the advantage of investing in a joint-stock company?

WH7.11.3 Examine the origins of modern capitalism; the influence of mercantilism and cottage industry; the elements and importance of a market economy in seventeenth-century Europe; the changing international trading and marketing patterns, including their locations on a world map; and the influence of explorers and map makers.

Government and Trade

Main Idea **Nations competed to establish colonies in the Americas.**

Reading Connection Suppose your family is thinking about moving to another state. What factors would influence your decision to move? Read on to find out why many Europeans migrated to the Americas.

Governments became closely involved in trade. They believed that a nation's power rested on the wealth obtained from trade. They developed national economic policies to advance trade and become as wealthy as possible.

In the 1600s, the greatest increase in trade took place in the countries bordering the Atlantic Ocean—Portugal, Spain, England, and the Netherlands—in large part because they had the largest overseas empires. Italian cities, such as **Venice** (VEH • nuhs) and **Genoa** (JEH • noh • uh), formerly the leading trade centers in Europe, found themselves cut out of overseas trade as trade routes and fortunes gradually moved westward toward the Atlantic Ocean and the Americas.

What Is Mercantilism? During the 1600s, Europe's trading nations based their policies on an economic theory known as **mercantilism** (MUHR • kuhn • tuh • LIH • zuhm). This theory held that a nation became powerful by building up its supply of **bullion** (BUL • yuhn), or gold and silver. One merchant summed up the general feeling about bullion: "[It is] the sinews of all government, it gives it its pulse, its movement. . . ." Under mercantilism, nations could gain wealth by mining gold or silver at home or overseas.

Primary Sources

The Wealth of Nations

Many nations tried to increase their wealth and power by following the ideas of mercantilism. Putting mercantilism into practice demanded a large amount of government control.

Some economists and writers criticized mercantilism. In his book *The Wealth of Nations* (1776), economist Adam Smith described a system in which government had little to do with a nation's economy. He said individuals left on their own would work for their own self-interest:

> "Every man, as long as he does not violate the laws of justice, is left perfectly free to pursue his own interest his own way, and to bring both his industry and capital into competition with those of any other man, or order of men."

Smith set forth the basic principles of capitalism—that people are free to buy, sell, and produce what they want with little or no government restriction. Smith's ideas influenced the Founders of the United States, who limited the role of government mainly to national defense and keeping the peace.

▲ Gold bullion

Document-Based Question

Does Smith say that there are no limits on a worker "pursuing his own interest"? Explain.

WH7.11.2 Discuss the exchanges of plants, animals, technology, culture, and ideas among Europe, Africa, Asia, and the Americas in the fifteenth and sixteenth centuries and the major economic and social effects on each continent.

How Did Mercantilism Work? Spain sent conquistadors to the Americas to seize the silver and gold mines of the Aztec and Inca Empires. Nations, however, primarily wanted to gain wealth through trade. They wanted to create a favorable balance of trade by **exporting** more goods than they imported. If a nation exported more goods than it imported, more gold and silver flowed in from other nations than went out. This greater wealth meant greater national power and more influence in the world.

Mercantilism provided great opportunities for individual merchants to make money. To increase national wealth, governments often aided businesses that produced export goods. They sold monopolies, which is the total control of an operation free of competition, to producers in certain key industries. They also set tariffs, or taxes on imported goods, to protect local industries from foreign competition.

Quest for Colonies Mercantilism also led to increased rivalry between nations. Mercantilists believed that nations should set up overseas colonies. A **colony** is a settlement of people living in a new territory controlled by their home country. According to mercantilists, colonies are supposed to produce goods that their home country does not have. That way, the home country will not have to import those goods from other countries.

During the 1600s, several countries in Europe, such as England and Spain, competed for overseas territory that could produce wealth. They wanted to acquire colonies in the Americas that could provide valuable resources, such as gold and silver, or raw materials. The colonies would also serve as a place to sell European products.

Reading Check **Analyze** How did mercantilism increase the wealth of countries like Spain?

History Online
Student Web Activity Visit ca.hss.glencoe.com and click on Chapter 1—Student Web Activities for an activity on economic systems.

Global Exchange

Main Idea **Exploration and trade led to a worldwide exchange of products, people, and ideas.**

Reading Connection Think back to the last time you tried a new food or a new way of doing something. Who introduced this new food or idea to you? Read on to find out what happened when new cultures came into contact with one another.

As Europe traded with the world, a global exchange of people, goods, technology, ideas, and even diseases began. We call this transfer the **Columbian Exchange,** after Christopher Columbus.

Trade in Goods This transfer of products from continent to continent brought changes in ways of life throughout the world. Europeans planted many European and Asian grains, such as wheat, oats, barley, rye, and rice, in the Americas. They also brought new animals, such as pigs, sheep, cattle, chickens, and horses. Chickens changed the diet of many people in the Americas, and horses changed the lives of Native Americans. Horses provided a faster way to move from place to place. As a result, Native Americans in North America began hunting buffalo as their main food source.

From Native Americans, Europeans acquired food items such as corn, potatoes, tomatoes, beans, and chocolate, which they brought back to Europe. Corn was used to feed animals. Larger, healthier animals resulted in more meat, leather, and wool. The potato was also important. Europeans discovered that if they planted potatoes instead of grain, about four times as many people could live off the same amount of land.

Other American foods, such as squash, beans, and tomatoes, also made their way to Europe. Tomatoes greatly changed cooking in Italy, where tomato sauces became common. Chocolate was a popular food from Central America. By mixing it with milk and sugar, Europeans created a sweet that is still enjoyed today.

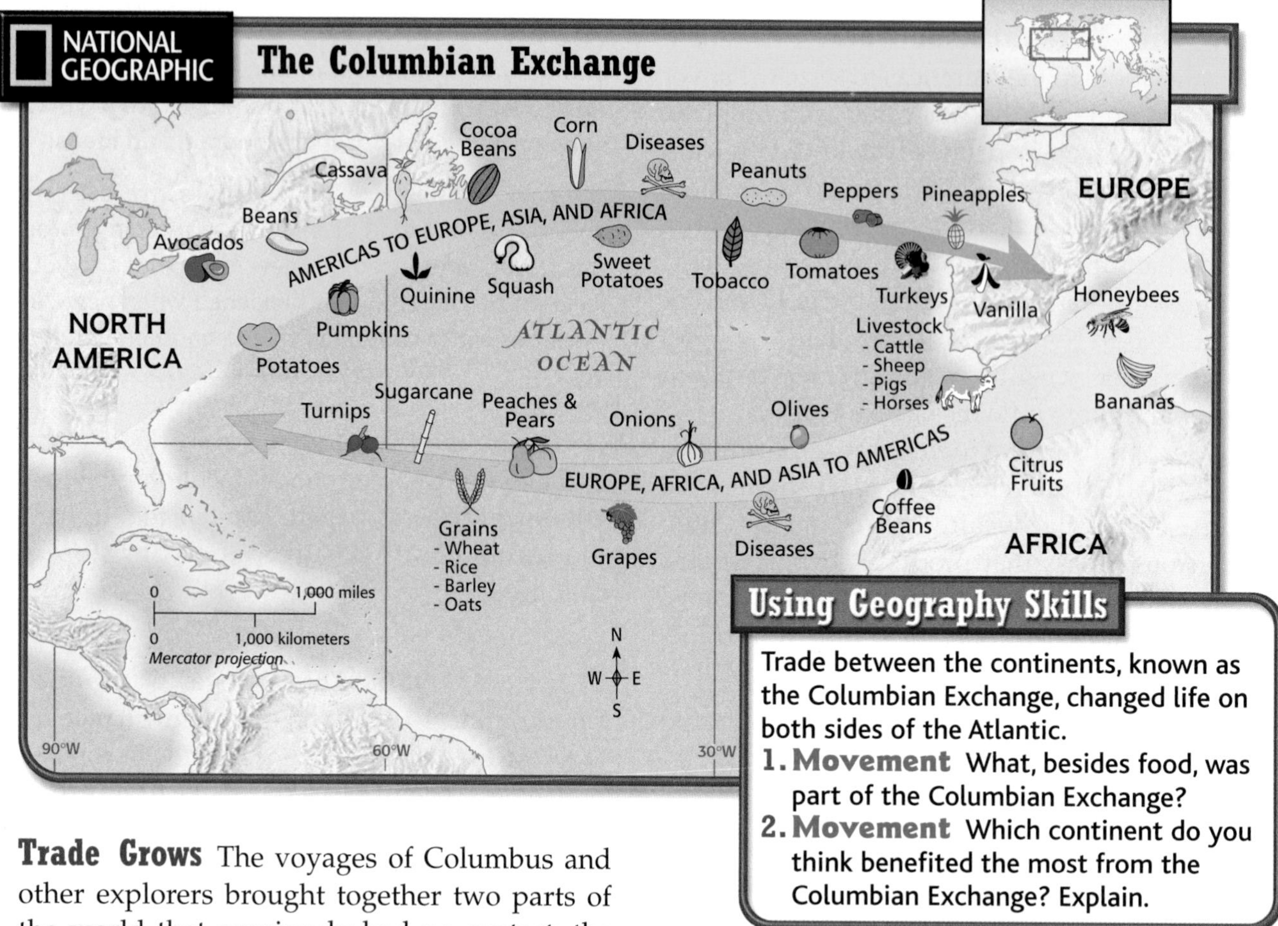

Using Geography Skills

Trade between the continents, known as the Columbian Exchange, changed life on both sides of the Atlantic.

1. **Movement** What, besides food, was part of the Columbian Exchange?
2. **Movement** Which continent do you think benefited the most from the Columbian Exchange? Explain.

Trade Grows The voyages of Columbus and other explorers brought together two parts of the world that previously had no contact: the continents of Europe, Asia, and Africa in one hemisphere and the Americas in the other.

Some American foods, such as chili peppers and peanuts, were taken to Europe, but they also made their way to Asia and Africa where they became popular. Both Europeans and Asians also began smoking tobacco, an American plant.

Foods, such as corn, spread to Asia and Africa, boosting population growth there. From Asia and Africa, Europeans brought to Europe and the Americas tropical products—bananas, coffee, tea, and sugarcane—as well as luxury goods, such as ivory, perfumes, silk, and gems.

Movement of Peoples and Cultures New global trading links increased the movement of people and cultures from continent to continent. Europeans seeking wealth or fleeing economic distress and religious persecution moved to the Americas and other parts of the world. They exchanged food, ideas, and practices with the people living in these areas.

European influences profoundly affected local cultures. European traders spread European languages, and European missionaries taught Christianity and European values. Wealthy Europeans, in turn, developed an interest in the arts, styles, and foods of Asia, especially Chinese porcelain, Indian textiles, and Southeast Asian spices.

With their guns and powerful ships, the Europeans easily defeated Arab fleets and Indian princes. Across Asia, the Europeans forced local rulers to let them set up trading posts. Within a short time, England's East India Company had built an empire in India, and the Dutch East India Company had built an empire in Indonesia.

Not everything exchanged between Europe and America was good. When Europeans arrived in America, they were carrying germs that Native Americans had not previously been exposed to. Many diseases, including smallpox, measles, and malaria, swept across the Americas, killing millions of people.

Beginnings of Slave Trade A huge movement of people also took place after Europeans obtained sugarcane from Asia and began growing it in the Caribbean. To plant and harvest the sugarcane, they enslaved millions of Africans and moved them to the Americas.

Some Spanish settlers made large profits by exporting crops and raw materials back to Spain. In the West Indies, the main exports were tobacco and sugarcane. To raise these crops, the Spanish developed the plantation system. A plantation was a large estate.

The Spanish used Native Americans to work their plantations. The Spanish priest **Bartolomé de Las Casas** (bahr•TOH•loh•may day lahs KAHS•ahs) suggested replacing them with enslaved Africans—a suggestion he bitterly regretted later. He thought the Africans could endure the labor better than the Native Americans.

By the mid-1500s, the Spanish were bringing thousands from West Africa to the Americas. The Portuguese did the same in Brazil. For enslaved Africans, the voyage to America usually began with a march to a European fort on the West African coast. Tied together with ropes around their necks and hands, they were traded to Europeans, branded, and forced to board a ship. An estimated 10 to 12 million Africans were forcibly transported to the Americas between 1450 and 1870.

The Africans who survived the brutal ocean voyage were sold to plantation owners. By the late 1500s, plantation slave labor was an essential part of the economy of the Spanish colonies.

Reading Check **Describe** How did the slave trade come into being?

Study Central Need help understanding the rise of modern capitalism? Visit ca.hss.glencoe.com and click on Study Central.

Reading Summary

Review the Main Ideas

- The introduction of banking and capitalism allowed countries to increase their wealth by financing trading ventures abroad.
- The growth of mercantilism and trade led to the creation of colonies.
- Trade between Europe and Asia and the Americas led to exchanges of people, ideas, and products.

What Did You Learn?

1. What was the Commercial Revolution?
2. What were some of the things Europeans introduced to Native Americans?

Critical Thinking

3. **Explaining** Draw a chart like the one below and explain how each economic concept or action increased the wealth of European nations. CA CS1.

	Effect on European Wealth
Mercantilism	
Joint-stock company	
Slave trade	

4. **The Big Ideas** Explain how exploration brought about great change in Europe and the Americas.
5. **Creative Writing** Imagine you are a member of a trading company on an expedition to the Americas. Describe the people and things you see when you arrive in the Americas. CA 8WA2.1
6. **Analysis** **Analyzing Economics** Write a brief essay about joint-stock companies. Include a definition and an example from the chapter, as well as a modern-day company. Discuss the strengths and weaknesses of this business model. CA HI6.

Section
3

The Enlightenment

Guide to Reading

History Social Science Standards

WH7.11 Students analyze political and economic change in the sixteenth, seventeenth, and eighteenth centuries (the Age of Exploration, the Enlightenment and the Age of Reason).

Looking Back, Looking Ahead

In Section 2, you learned how Europe gained wealth from overseas territories. In this section, you will learn how past civilizations contributed to our scientific, religious, and political thinking today.

Focusing on the Main Ideas

- Ancient cultures laid the foundation of many modern ideas. *(page 99)*
- Religious and philosophical thinkers changed the way people viewed Christianity and the government. *(page 102)*
- Science and the influence of reason led to new innovations in political thought. *(page 105)*

Meeting People

Thomas Aquinas (uh • KWY • nuhs)
Martin Luther
John Calvin
Thomas Hobbes (HAHBZ)
John Locke
Charles de Montesquieu (MAHN • tuhs • KYOO)

Locating Places

Greece
Rome

Content Vocabulary

rule of law
covenant (KUH • vuh • nuhnt)
theology (thee • AH • luh • jee)
Renaissance (REH • nuh • SAHNTS)
scientific method
philosophe (FEE • luh • ZAWF)

Academic Vocabulary

pursue (puhr • SOO)
document (DAH • kyuh • muhnt)
contract
major

Reading Strategy

Organizing Information Re-create the diagram below. List changes in politics, religion, and science mentioned in this section.

	Changes
Politics	
Religion	
Science	

NATIONAL GEOGRAPHIC
Where & When?
1200
1500
1800
EUROPE
CHINA
INDIA
AFRICA
1215
Magna Carta limits power of English king
1689
English Bill of Rights guarantees basic rights
1748
Montesquieu publishes *Spirit of Laws*

WH7.11.4 Explain how the main ideas of the Enlightenment can be traced back to such movements as the Renaissance, the Reformation, and the Scientific Revolution and to the Greeks, Romans, and Christianity.

Europe's Heritage of Ideas

Main Idea **Ancient cultures laid the foundation of many modern ideas.**

Reading Connection Do you chew gum, use an alarm clock to get up for school, or carry an umbrella when it rains? All of these things were originally created by ancient peoples. Read on to see which ideas and inventions originated in ancient cultures.

A European Story

Anton van Leeuwenhoek (LAY • vuhn • hook), a Dutch merchant in the late 1600s, had an unusual hobby that unlocked the door to an unknown world. By carefully grinding very small lenses out of clear glass, van Leeuwenhoek discovered that he could make things look much bigger than they appeared to the naked eye. His most remarkable find was a multitude of tiny microorganisms, which he described as "wretched beasties" with "incredibly thin feet" swimming through a tiny universe.

Leeuwenhoek's microscope captured the imagination of Europeans in the 1600s. His invention was part of the rich heritage of ideas that shaped the course of European history since ancient times. These ideas eventually spread to North America, where they helped shape the English colonies that were arising along the Atlantic seaboard.

The Greeks and Romans The ancient Greeks developed philosophy, or "love of wisdom," because they believed the human mind could understand everything. Greek philosophy led to the study of history, mathematics, and political science. During the 400s B.C., the idea of democracy developed in Athens, one of **Greece's** powerful city-states. The Athenians had a direct democracy, in which people gathered at mass meetings to decide government matters. Every citizen could vote firsthand on laws and policies.

Rome was the next important ancient European civilization. Early Rome began as a republic, a form of government in which the citizens elect their leaders to office. In a republic, the citizens have power. The idea of a republic later shaped the founding of the U.S. government. Another of Rome's chief gifts was the idea of the **"rule of law."** This means that the law should apply to everyone equally and that all people should be treated the same. This understanding of justice is at the basis of the American legal system today.

Judaism and Christianity The Jews were a unique group among the peoples who made up Rome's empire. Most religions of the ancient world worshipped many gods, but the Jews gave their allegiance to one God. The Hebrew Bible describes a **covenant** (KUH • vuh • nuhnt), or agreement between the Jews and their God. In the agreement, God promises to protect the Israelites if they follow his laws. The idea of a covenant, or binding agreement, later influenced the American colonists when they set up their societies in North America.

A major Jewish contribution to the West was the Ten Commandments. Jews believed that God revealed the Ten Commandments to a prophet called Moses. These moral principles found in the Hebrew Bible helped shape the moral laws of many nations.

The Torah, the first five books of the Hebrew Bible

The Ten Commandments told people not to steal, murder, or tell lies about others. They told people to avoid jealousy and to honor their parents. Like the Roman laws, the Ten Commandments reflect the idea of the "rule of law," that laws should apply to everyone equally.

About the A.D. 30s, a Jewish teacher named Jesus of Nazareth preached to Jews living in the Roman provinces of Judaea and Galilee. His message of love and forgiveness helped shape the values many people hold today. Reports of Jesus' resurrection, or rising from the dead, led to a new religion called Christianity.

Christianity soon spread to the European part of the Roman Empire. By A.D. 400, Christianity had become Rome's official religion. After the Roman government fell apart, Christianity survived to shape the civilization of the Middle Ages, the period between Rome's fall and the 1500s.

Advance of Learning While Christianity expanded in Europe, the religion of Islam began in the Arabian Peninsula with the preaching of Muhammad. Islam spread throughout the Middle East, North Africa, and Central Asia. Like Jews and Christians, Muslims—the followers of Islam—believe in one God.

During the Middle Ages, Muslim and Jewish scholars in Islamic lands made significant contributions to the culture of Europe. They saved much of the learning of the ancient world. Europeans in the West had lost this knowledge after the western Roman Empire fell.

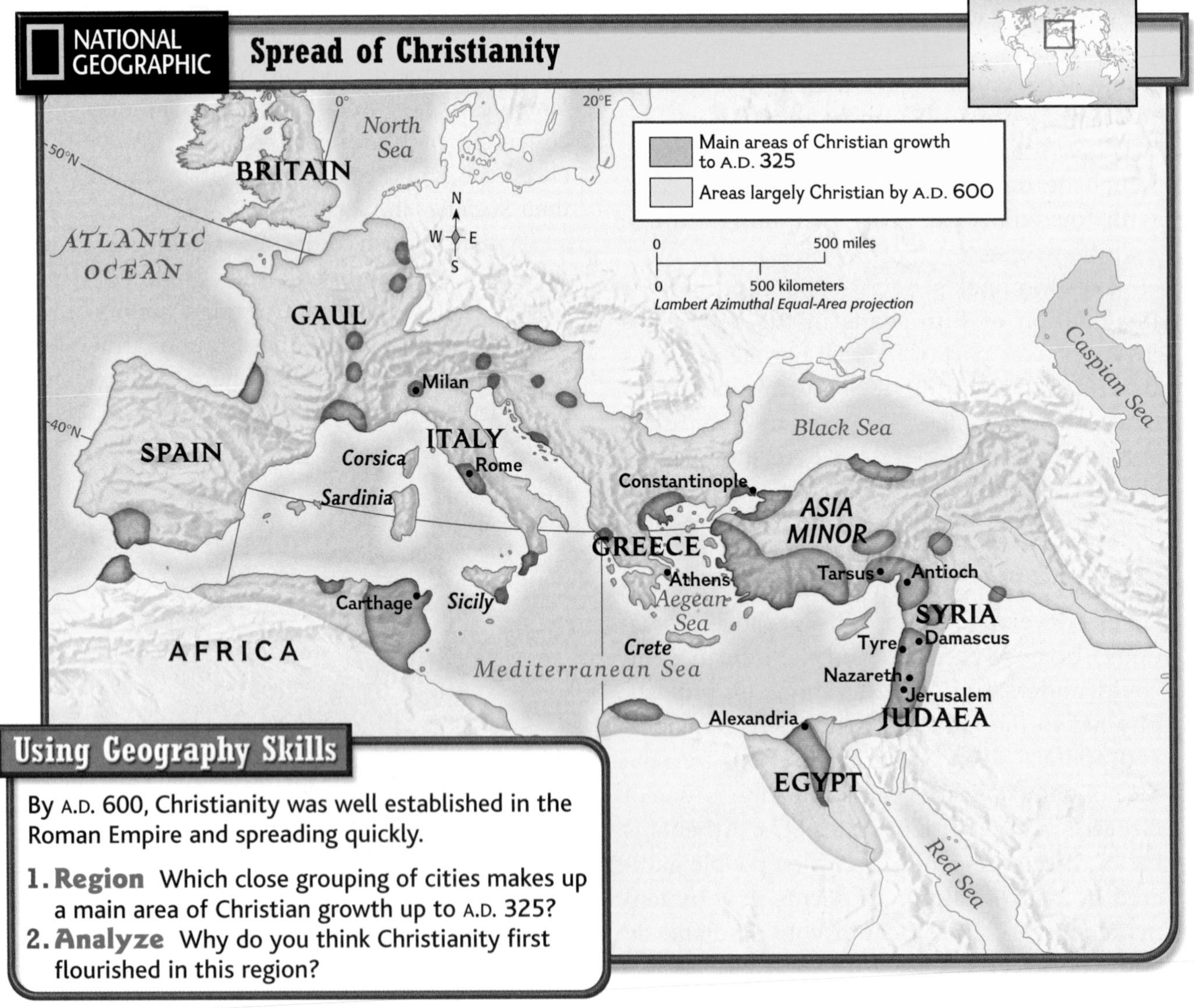

Using Geography Skills

By A.D. 600, Christianity was well established in the Roman Empire and spreading quickly.

1. **Region** Which close grouping of cities makes up a main area of Christian growth up to A.D. 325?
2. **Analyze** Why do you think Christianity first flourished in this region?

Picturing History

Muslim doctors' discoveries helped develop European medicine. ***How did Muslim scholars contribute to the culture of Europe?***

Islamic Influence The Muslims also made many advances in the study of mathematics and medicine, and they introduced the system of Arabic numerals that we use today.

Islamic influences were part of a new wave of learning that shaped Europe during the Middle Ages. Another influence came from universities, which first arose in Europe during the 1100s and 1200s. Universities were self-governing groups of scholars who, in turn, educated and trained new scholars. Because universities enjoyed independence from political and church officials, they could freely investigate knowledge in a wide range of fields, such as theology, law, and medicine.

The first European university appeared in Bologna (boh•LOH•nyah), Italy. A great teacher named Inerius, who taught Roman law, attracted students to Bologna from all over Europe. The first university in northern Europe was the University of Paris. In the late 1100s, a number of students and teachers left Paris and started a university at Oxford, England. Kings, popes, and princes thought it honorable to found new universities. By 1500, there were 80 universities in Europe.

Development of Scholasticism Beginning in the 1100s, a new way of thinking called scholasticism began to change **theology** (thee•AH•luh•jee), or the study of religion and God. Its followers used reason to explore questions of faith.

A Catholic priest named **Thomas Aquinas** (uh•KWY•nuhs) was scholasticism's best-known champion. In the 1200s, Aquinas wrote several works explaining that the Greek philosopher Aristotle would have agreed with many Christian teachings.

What Is Natural Law? Aquinas wrote about government as well as theology, with an emphasis on the idea of natural law. People who believe in natural law think there are some laws that are simply part of human nature. These laws do not have to be made by governments.

Aquinas claimed that natural law gave people certain rights that the government should not take away. These included the right to live, to learn, to worship, and to reproduce. Aquinas's writings on natural law have influenced governments to the present day. Our belief that people have rights can partly be traced to the ideas of Aquinas.

The Latin Language Roman writers influenced later writers in Europe and America, but the language of the Romans, Latin, had a great impact on future generations. Latin became Europe's language for government, trade, and learning until about 1500. Latin became the basis of many modern European languages, including Italian, French, and Spanish.

Reading Check **Describe** What was the importance of the Ten Commandments?

WH7.11.5 Describe how democratic thought and institutions were influenced by Enlightenment thinkers (e.g., John Locke, Charles-Louis Montesquieu, American founders).

New Ideas

Main Idea **Religious and philosophical thinkers changed the way people viewed Christianity and the government.**

Reading Connection Does your family or someone you know attend a church or other place of worship? Read on to find out how religious sects formed in Christianity.

From the 1400s to the 1700s, Europeans gained new knowledge, explored lands overseas, and spread Christianity. Meanwhile, cultural, religious, and political changes took place in their homeland that would have profound effects on the rest of the world.

The Renaissance From about 1350 to 1550, a powerful new spirit emerged in the city-states of Italy and spread throughout Europe. The development of banking and the expansion of trade with Asia made Italian merchants wealthy. These citizens were able to **pursue** an interest in the region's past and learn more about the glorious civilizations of ancient Rome and Greece.

Because they wanted to improve their knowledge of people and the world, Italians studied the classical—ancient Greek and Roman—works with new interest. Scholars translated Greek manuscripts on philosophy, poetry, and science. Influenced by the classical texts, a great many authors began to write about the individual and the universe. Artists studied the sculpture and architecture of the classical world. They especially admired the harmony and balance in Greek art, with its realistic way of portraying people.

This period of intellectual and artistic creativity became known as the **Renaissance** (REH • nuh • SAHNTS). A French word meaning "rebirth," it refers to the renewed interest in classical Greek and Roman learning. Over the next two centuries, the Renaissance spread north, south, and west, reaching Spain and northern Europe in the 1400s.

The Rise of Protestantism Protests against church abuses soon led to a split in western Christianity. In 1517 a German monk named **Martin Luther** criticized the authority of the pope, the leader of the Roman Catholic Church, and many Catholic teachings and practices. Within a few years, Luther had many followers. They broke away from Catholicism to begin their own Christian churches. Martin Luther's protests were the start of a new form of Christianity known as Protestantism.

During the next few years, Luther's religious movement grew. Luther was able to gain the support of many of the German rulers among the numerous states that made up the Holy Roman Empire.

From Germany, Luther's ideas spread rapidly. **John Calvin**, a French religious thinker, also broke away from the Catholic Church. Like Luther, Calvin rejected the idea that good works would ensure a person's salvation. He believed that God had already chosen those who would be saved.

Picturing **History**

Martin Luther and his followers broke away from Catholicism to begin their own Christian churches. ***What new form of Christianity did Luther and his followers start?***

To prove they were saved, Calvin's followers worked hard, behaved well, and obeyed the laws of their towns. In this way, Calvin's ideas, which became known as Calvinism, became a powerful tool in society. His ideas encouraged people to work hard at their business and to behave themselves.

Who Were the Puritans? King Henry VIII replaced the pope as head of the Church in England in 1534. His daughter, Queen Elizabeth I, later made this English, or Anglican, Church Protestant with some Catholic features. Some English Protestants, however, were dissatisfied with Elizabeth's reforms. Known as Puritans, they wanted to "purify" the Anglican Church of its remaining Catholic beliefs and rituals.

Queen Elizabeth I tolerated the Puritans, but when James I became king in 1603, the Puritans faced harder times. James I and the king who came after him, Charles I, persecuted the Puritans. They shut down Puritan churches and jailed Puritan leaders. Many Puritans decided to move to America to practice their religion freely. There they founded colonies that eventually became the American states of Massachusetts, Connecticut, New Hampshire, and Rhode Island.

Royal Power and Citizens' Rights During the 1600s and 1700s, powerful kings and queens ruled most of Europe. Under a system known as absolutism, monarchs held absolute, or total, power. They claimed to rule by divine right, or by the will of God. This meant that rulers did not answer to their people but to God alone.

During the late 1600s, however, political changes began that steadily limited the power of monarchs. In 1688 the English Parliament took action. It forced out King James and placed his daughter Mary and her husband William on the throne. This change, which showed the power of the elected representatives over the monarch, came to be known as the Glorious Revolution.

William and Mary signed an English Bill of Rights in 1689 guaranteeing certain basic rights to all citizens. This **document** became part of the heritage of English law that the American colonists would share. It later inspired the American political leaders who created the American Bill of Rights.

Hobbes and Locke During the 1600s, these political changes sparked a great deal of thought and debate about the purpose of government. Two major English thinkers—**Thomas Hobbes** (HAHBZ) and **John Locke**—developed very different ideas about how England's government should work.

In his book, *Leviathan,* Hobbes argued that absolute monarchy was the best form of government. According to Hobbes, humans were naturally selfish and violent. They could not be trusted to make decisions on their own. Left to themselves, people would make life "nasty, brutish, and short." Therefore, Hobbes said, they needed to obey a government that had the power of a leviathan, or sea monster. To Hobbes, that meant the rule of a king, because only a strong ruler could give people direction.

Another English thinker, John Locke, thought differently. He affirmed citizens' rights and stated that government was answerable to the people. In 1690 he explained many of the ideas of the Glorious Revolution in a book called *Two Treatises of Civil Government.* Locke stated that government should be based on natural law. This law, said Locke, gave all people from their birth certain natural rights. Among them were the right to life, the right to liberty, and the right to own property.

Locke believed that the purpose of government was to protect these rights. All governments, he said, were based on a social **contract,** or an agreement between rulers and the people. If a ruler took away people's natural rights, the people had a right to revolt and set up a new government.

Reading Check **Explain** How did religious changes affect the governments of Europe?

Biography

WH7.11.5 Describe how democratic thought and institutions were influenced by Enlightenment thinkers (e.g., John Locke, Charles-Louis Montesquieu, American founders).

JOHN LOCKE
1632–1704

Born in England, John Locke was a doctor, a philosopher, and a writer. Locke spelled out his political ideas in *Two Treatises of Civil Government,* first published in 1690.

Locke's writings were widely read and discussed in both Europe and America. His ideas deeply influenced the American colonists. Colonial leaders such as Benjamin Franklin, Thomas Jefferson, and James Madison read Locke's writings and discussed his ideas.

Locke and many Enlightenment thinkers believed that God had created an orderly universe governed by established laws. These laws were called natural laws and could be discovered by human reason. By using reason, for example, Sir Isaac Newton, the English physicist, discovered the law of gravity. Natural laws governed not only the physical universe, but also human relations.

The idea that human relations are governed by a set of established laws laid the foundation for the philosophy of natural rights. Locke believed that people in a "state of nature," or a time before the organization of government, had certain basic rights. These included rights to life, liberty, and property.

According to Locke, good government is based on a social contract between the people and the rulers. The people agree to give up some of their freedom and abide by the decisions of their government. In return, the government promises to protect the lives, property, and liberty of the people.

The American colonists accepted Locke's idea that government was legitimate only as long as people continued to consent to it. Both the Declaration of Independence and the Constitution, written nearly a century after Locke lived, reflect Locke's revolutionary ideas.

"All peaceful beginnings of government have been laid in the consent of the people."

—John Locke, *Second Treatise of Civil Government*

Then and Now

Compare the political thought of John Locke to the American form of government. What would Locke support? What would he not support?

WH7.11.5 Describe how democratic thought and institutions were influenced by Enlightenment thinkers (e.g., John Locke, Charles-Louis Montesquieu, American founders). WH7.11.6 Discuss how the principles in the Magna Carta were embodied in such documents as the English Bill of Rights and the American Declaration of Independence.

A New View of the World

Main Idea **Science and the influence of reason led to new innovations in political thought.**

Reading Connection Does your school have a student council? This is usually a group of students who lobby the administration on behalf of the student body. Read on to find out how citizens' rights played a role in governmental reform.

While religious and political changes came to Europe, many European thinkers began to take a more experimental approach to science. They tested new and old theories and evaluated the results. They also began applying reason and scientific ideas to government. They claimed that there was a natural law, or a law that applied to everyone and could be understood by reason. This law was the key to understanding government.

Triumph of Reason During the 1500s, European thinkers began to break with old scientific ideas. They increasingly understood that advances in science could come only through mathematics and experimentation. Scientists, such as Nicolaus Copernicus and Galileo Galilei, disagreed with the ancient view that the earth was the center of the universe. Instead, they held to the idea that the sun was the center of the universe and that the planets moved in orbits around the sun.

Sir Isaac Newton further claimed that the physical universe followed natural laws. He believed that the force of gravity held the entire solar system together by keeping the sun and the planets in their orbits.

The Scientific Method Scientific thought was also influenced by the English thinker Francis Bacon, who lived from 1561 to 1626. Bacon believed that ideas based on tradition should be put aside. He developed the **scientific method,** an orderly way of collecting and analyzing evidence. It is still the process used in scientific research today.

The scientific method is made up of several steps. First, a scientist begins with careful observation of facts and then tries to find a hypothesis, or explanation of the facts. Through experiments, the scientist tests the hypothesis under all possible conditions to see if it is true. Finally, after repeated experiments show that the hypothesis is true, then it is considered a scientific law.

Enlightenment Thinkers As the Scientific Revolution advanced, many educated Europeans came to believe that reason was a much better guide than faith or tradition. To them, reason was a light that revealed error and showed the way to truth. As a result, the 1700s became known as the Age of Enlightenment.

France was the **major** center of the Enlightenment. As the Enlightenment spread, thinkers in France and elsewhere became known by the French word **philosophe** (FEE • luh • ZAWF), which means "philosopher." Most philosophes were writers, teachers, journalists, and observers of society.

The philosophes wanted to use reason to change society. They attacked superstition, or unreasoned beliefs. They also disagreed with Church leaders who opposed new scientific discoveries. The philosophes believed in the individual's right to liberty. They used their skills as writers to spread their ideas across Europe.

Who Were Voltaire and Diderot? One of the greatest thinkers of the Enlightenment was François-Marie Arouet, known as Voltaire (vohl • TAR). Voltaire blamed Catholic Church leaders for keeping knowledge from people in order to maintain the Church's power. Voltaire also opposed the government supporting one religion while forbidding others. He thought people should be free to choose their own beliefs.

Denis Diderot was the French philosophe who did the most to spread Enlightenment ideas. He published a 28-volume encyclopedia. His project, which began in the 1750s, took about 20 years to complete.

Primary Sources

Guarantees of Rights

The Magna Carta and the English Bill of Rights are two important documents that were integral in forming American political thought. Each contributed an essential building block for the American political principles found in the Declaration of Independence, the Bill of Rights, and the Constitution.

The rights of English citizens, referred to in the Magna Carta, is an important principle of American government. This excerpt from the Magna Carta describes the right to a trial by jury:

> "No free man shall be taken, imprisoned, [seized], outlawed, banished, or in any way destroyed, . . . except by the lawful judgment of his peers and by the law of the land."

The English Bill of Rights assured the people of certain basic rights. Among these are:

> "That the freedom of speech and debates or proceedings in Parliament ought not to be impeached or questioned in any court or place out of Parliament."

The founding documents of our nation express these freedoms and the principle of limited government—a government on which strict limits are placed, usually by a constitution.

King John signs the Magna Carta. ▶

DBQ Document-Based Question

The idea of limited government is an important principle of American government. Why must government be limited?

The *Encyclopedia* included a wide range of topics, such as science, religion, government, and the arts. It became an important weapon in the philosophes' fight against traditional ways.

Who Was Montesquieu? In 1748 Baron **Charles de Montesquieu** (MAHN • tuhs • KYOO) published a book called *Spirit of Laws*. In this book, Montesquieu said that England's government was the best because it had a separation of powers. Separation of powers means that power should be divided equally among the branches of government: executive, legislative, and judicial.

The legislative branch would make the laws, and the executive branch would enforce them. The judicial branch would interpret the laws and judge when they were broken. By separating these powers, government could not become too powerful and threaten people's rights.

Who Was Rousseau? By the late 1700s, some European thinkers were starting to criticize Enlightenment ideas. One of these thinkers was Jean-Jacques Rousseau (zhahn zhak ru • SOH). Rousseau claimed that supporters of the Enlightenment relied too much on reason. Instead, people should pay more attention to their feelings.

What Is a Social Contract? According to Rousseau, human beings were naturally good, but civilized life corrupted them. He thought people could improve themselves by living simpler lives closer to nature. In 1762 Rousseau published a book called *The Social Contract*. In this work, Rousseau wrote that a workable government should be based on a social contract. This is an agreement in which everyone in a society agrees to be governed by the general will, or what the people as a whole want.

The Magna Carta In the 1600s and 1700s, ideas of political change spread back and forth across the Atlantic Ocean. The pattern started with the arrival of the first English colonists in North America. They carried with them ideas born of the political struggles in England. By the time the first colonists reached North America, the idea of limited government had become an acceptable part of the English system. The Magna Carta of 1215 had limited royal power and protected nobles from unlawful loss of life, liberty, and property. During the next few centuries, these rights were extended to more and more English people.

The English Bill of Rights In 1689 the English Bill of Rights stated that the monarch could not tax people without Parliament's consent. People had a right to a fair and speedy trial by a jury of their peers. People could also petition the king without fear of being punished. The English colonists in North America shared a belief in these rights with the people of England.

Representative Government From England the American colonists also brought the idea of representative government in which people elect delegates to make laws and conduct government affairs for them. Parliament was a representative assembly that had made laws for England since the mid-1200s. In America colonial legislatures grew directly out of this practice of having representatives pass laws.

For political ideas, the colonists also looked to thinkers of the Enlightenment. John Locke's ideas seemed to fit the colonial experience. Although most had probably never heard of Locke himself, the ideas of natural rights and government responsible to the people became the basis of protest and revolt in the colonies. Colonial leaders, such as Benjamin Franklin, Thomas Jefferson, and James Madison, regarded these ideas as political truths. Locke's ideas became so influential that they have been called the "textbook of the American Revolution."

Reading Check **Summarize** What were the ideas of Charles de Montesquieu?

History Online
Study Central Need help understanding the Enlightenment? Visit ca.hss.glencoe.com and click on Study Central.

Reading Summary

Review the Main Ideas

- Rome and Greece became the basis for much political and scientific thought.
- The Renaissance brought about religious and political changes that sought to increase the rights of human beings.
- Political thinkers argued that citizens had religious, political, and social rights.

What Did You Learn?

1. What was the purpose of the English Parliament?
2. What is the Scientific Method?

Critical Thinking

3. **Contrast** How did the ideas of Hobbes and Locke differ? CA HR3.
4. **Identifying** Who were three of the Enlightenment thinkers?

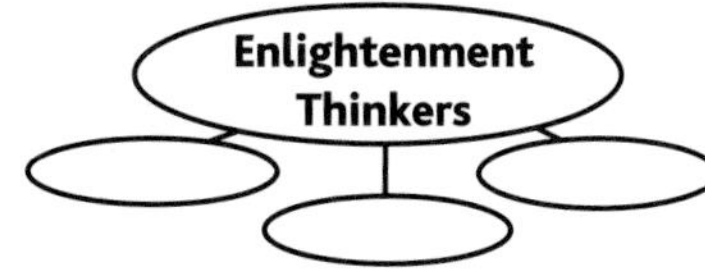

5. **The Big Ideas** How did political, technological, and religious changes affect the formation of the American government? Write a paragraph describing your conclusions. CA HI2.
6. **Persuasive Writing** Imagine you are an English noble in favor of the Magna Carta. Write a letter to the king explaining why he should sign the document. CA 8WA2.4

WH7.11.1 Know the great voyages of discovery, the locations of the routes, and the influence of cartography in the development of a new European worldview.

Analyzing Primary Sources

Cultures in Contact

Before the 1400s, Native Americans had little contact with people from other continents. Improved methods of sea travel and the desire for goods led to the growth of overseas trade in the 1400s and 1500s. During this time, people from Europe came into direct contact with people from the Americas.

Read the passages on pages 108 and 109 and answer the questions that follow.

Columbus lands on San Salvador in October 1492. ▶

Reader's Dictionary

reeds: tall grasses with slim stems that grow in wet areas

bear arms: carry or possess weapons

hawks' bells: small, lightweight bells attached to a trained hawk to help an owner find a lost bird

causeway: a raised road across wet ground or water

Mexico: Tenochtitlán

cues (KYOOS)**:** temples

vein (VAYN)**:** way of thinking

Columbus Crosses the Atlantic

Christopher Columbus left Spain in August 1492 with about 90 sailors on three ships. On October 11 he wrote this in his log:

The crew of the *Pinta* spotted some . . . **reeds** and some other plants; they also saw what looked like a small board or plank. A stick was recovered that looks manmade, perhaps carved with an iron tool . . . but even these few [things] made the crew breathe easier; in fact, the men have even become cheerful.

Other entries in Columbus's log describe the islanders that he met.

They are [a] friendly and well-dispositioned people who **[bear]** no **arms** except for small spears, and they have no iron. I showed one my sword, and through ignorance he grabbed it by the blade and cut himself. . . .

They traded and gave everything they had with good will, but it seems to me that they have very little. . . .

[They] came swimming to our ships and in boats made from one log. They brought us parrots, balls of cotton thread, spears, and many other things, . . . For these items we swapped them little glass beads and **hawks' bells.**

—from *The Log of Christopher Columbus*

Cortés Encounters the Aztec

The soldier and writer Bernal Díaz de Castillo was part of Hernán Cortés's army. These Spaniards fought their way across the Aztec empire to the capital at Tenochtitlán. Castillo wrote the following about what he saw:

And when we saw all those cities and villages built in the water, and other great towns on dry land, and that straight and level **causeway** leading to **Mexico,** we were astounded. These great towns and **cues** and buildings rising from the water, all made of stone, seemed like an enchanted vision. . . . Indeed, some of our soldiers asked whether it was not all a dream. It is not surprising therefore that I should write in this **vein.** It was all so wonderful that I do not know how to describe this first glimpse of things never heard of, seen or dreamed of before. . . .

[In the marketplace], we were astounded at the great number of people and the quantities of merchandise, and at the orderliness and good arrangements that prevailed, for we had never seen such a thing before. . . .

[In the market] they have a building there also in which three judges sit, and there are officials like constables who examine the merchandise. . . .

—from *The Conquest of New Spain*

▲ **Montezuma and Cortés meet after Cortés entered Tenochtitlán.**

DBQ Document-Based Questions

Columbus Crosses the Atlantic

1. What item did the crew take from the sea and examine?
2. How did Columbus's crew react when they saw the objects in the sea?
3. According to Columbus, why did the islander cut himself on the sword?
4. What items did Columbus and his crew exchange with the islanders?

Cortés Encounters the Aztec

5. What surprised Castillo and Cortés's army about the land of the Aztec?
6. Why did some soldiers compare what they saw with a dream?

Read to Write

7. Imagine you are one of the Native Americans who has just met Columbus or Cortés. What do you notice about him? What do you think of him? How do you feel about this meeting? Write a journal entry describing what you observed and how you reacted to this encounter. CA 8WA2.1

Assessment

Standard WH7.11

Review Content Vocabulary

Write the vocabulary word that completes each sentence. Write a sentence for each word not used.

a. technology
b. Renaissance
c. Northwest Passage
d. entrepreneur
e. rule of law
f. mercantilism

1. The ___ states that all people are equal under the law and should be treated as such.
2. England, France, and the Netherlands hoped to find a ___ to Asia.
3. During the ___, many political and religious changes took place.
4. The theory of ___ stated that a country could become prosperous by mining silver and gold found in other countries.

Review the Main Ideas

Section 1 • Age of Exploration

5. What led to the European era of exploration?
6. What were English, French, and Dutch explorers searching for while charting the coast of North America?

Section 2 • Rise of Modern Capitalism

7. What made trading ventures in different countries so difficult?
8. What were the benefits of establishing overseas colonies?

Section 3 • The Enlightenment

9. What is the rule of law?
10. How did John Calvin contribute to religious changes in Europe?
11. What did Copernicus and Galileo believe about the universe?

Critical Thinking

12. **Describe** What was the Columbian Exchange? How did it change Europe and the Americas? CA CS1.
13. **Cause and Effect** Re-create the diagram below. Identify three reasons for the voyages of exploration and three effects that resulted from the exploration. CA HI2.

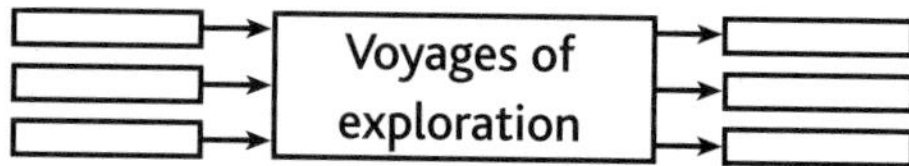

14. **Contrast** How did Judaism differ from most other religions during the Roman era? CA HI2.

Geography Skills

Study the map below and answer the questions that follow. CA CS3.

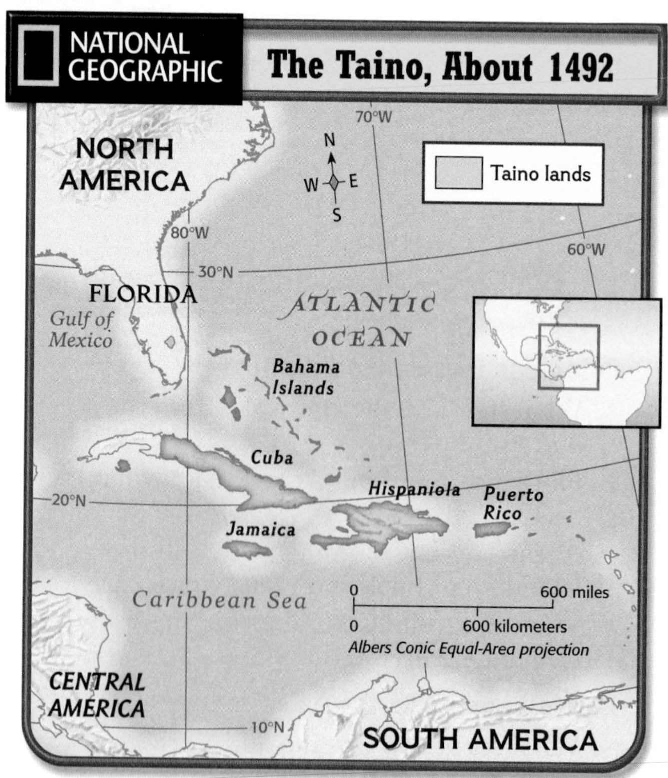

History Online
Self-Check Quiz Visit ca.hss.glencoe.com to prepare for the Chapter 1 test.

15. **Place** What are some of the islands on which the Taino lived?
16. **Location** Between which continents was the Taino homeland located?
17. **Movement** If you traveled from Cuba to Puerto Rico, in what direction would you be going?

Read to Write

18. **The Big Ideas** **Descriptive Writing** Choose an event mentioned in the chapter that had an impact on the Americas. Describe how that event influenced life in the Americas. CA 8WA2.3
19. **Using Your FOLDABLES** Use the information from your completed chapter opener foldable to create a compare-contrast chart of the three countries that were exploring the Americas. Include in the chart their reasons for embarking on explorations, the areas they explored, and the goods and ideas they obtained from the regions. CA CS3.

Using Academic Vocabulary

Read the following sentences and in your own words, write the meaning of the underlined academic vocabulary word.

20. The Magna Carta is an important <u>document</u>.
21. Venice and Genoa became <u>major</u> trading cities.
22. Christopher Columbus hoped that the king and queen of Spain would <u>finance</u> his exploration.
23. Traders wanted to <u>export</u> goods to China and to other areas of the world.

Linking Past and Present

24. **Science Connection** Sir Francis Bacon was the first person to describe the Scientific Method. Describe this method in your own words. Then, describe a modern-day scenario in which scientists are using this method. CA HI3.

Reviewing Skills

25. Review READING SKILL **Previewing** Take a look at the Big Ideas on page 113. Select one and write a paragraph describing the relationship between that idea and something you learned in this chapter. CA CS1. CA 8WA2.2
26. Review ANALYSIS SKILL **Summarize** Describe Montesquieu's theories on government. Contrast these with views held by Thomas Hobbes. CA HI2. CA 8WS1.1

Standards Practice

Read the passage below and answer the following questions.

> The *Legislative cannot transfer the Power of Making Laws* to any other hands. For it being but a delegated Power from the People, they who have it, cannot pass it over to others. The People alone can appoint the Form of the Commonwealth, which is by Constituting the Legislative, and appointing in whose hands that shall be.
>
> —*from* Second Treatise of Civil Government *by John Locke*

27 According to Locke, what branch of government makes the laws?

A judicial
B executive
C legislative
D state governments

28 Who gives government its power?

A the legislature
B the president
C the Supreme Court
D the people

Road to Independence

The Old North Bridge, Concord, Massachusetts

Where & When?

1600 — 1700 — 1800

1620 Mayflower Compact is signed

1682 William Penn plans colony

1775 Boston Tea Party takes place

1781 Americans gain independence with victory at Yorktown

History Online

Chapter Overview Visit ca.hss.glencoe.com for a preview of Chapter 2.

The Big Ideas

Founding the American Colonies

Geography shapes the physical, economic, and political challenges a region faces. Peoples of various cultures and religions settled the early North American colonies.

Life in Colonial America

Geography shapes the physical, economic, and political challenges a region faces. Although the regions of colonial America differed, an American identity was growing.

Trouble in the Colonies

Political ideas and major events shape how people form governments. British policies came into conflict with American ideas about self-government.

War of Independence

Political ideas and major events shape how people form governments. The United States declared independence in 1776, but it took several years of war and turmoil to earn recognition as a new nation.

View the Chapter 2 video in the Glencoe Video Program.

FOLDABLES™ Study Organizer

Cause and Effect Make this foldable to show the causes and effects of the events that led the Americans to declare independence from Great Britain.

Step 1 Fold one sheet of paper in half from side to side.

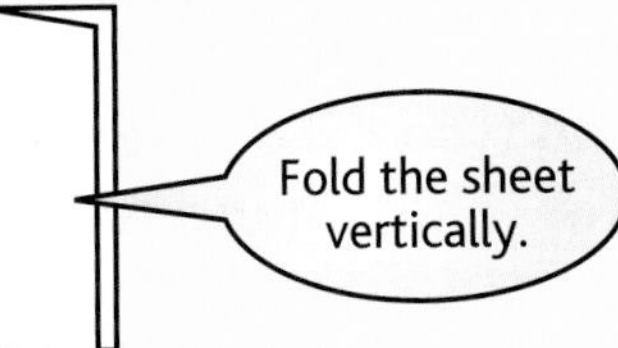
Fold the sheet vertically.

Step 2 Fold again, 1 inch from the top. (Tip: The middle knuckle of your index finger is about 1 inch long.)

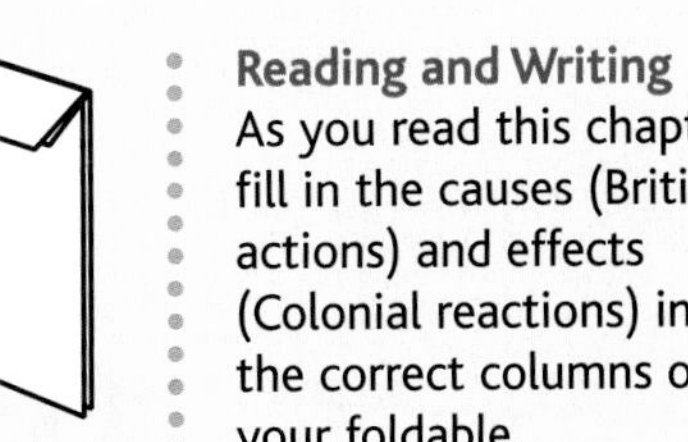

Step 3 Open and label as shown.

British Actions
Colonial Reactions
Draw lines along the fold lines.

Reading and Writing As you read this chapter, fill in the causes (British actions) and effects (Colonial reactions) in the correct columns of your foldable.

Get Ready to Read

Identifying the Main Idea

1 Learn It!

Main ideas are the most important ideas in a paragraph, section, or chapter. Supporting details are facts or examples that explain the main idea. Historical details, such as names, dates, and events, are easier to remember when they are connected to a main idea. Understanding the main idea allows you to grasp the whole picture or story. Read the excerpt below and notice how the author explains the main idea.

Main Idea

Supporting Details

The Spanish, however, did not ignore the lands north of Mexico and the Caribbean. During the 1600s, they built settlements and forts along the northern edge of their American empire. These settlements, such as St. Augustine in Florida and Santa Fe in New Mexico, were intended to keep other Europeans out of Spanish territory. Spanish missionary-priests, such as Junípero Serra (hoo • NEE • puh • ROH SEHR • UH) **and Eusebio Kino** (yoo • SEE • bee • oh), **also headed north. They set up missions, or religious communities, to teach Christianity and European ways to the Native Americans. Missions were set up in New Mexico, Texas, California, and other areas of North America.**

—from page 117

The main idea is often the first sentence in a paragraph but not always.

2 Practice It!

Read the following paragraph. Draw a graphic organizer like the one below to show the main idea and supporting details.

> The Great Awakening is the name for the powerful religious revival that swept through the colonies beginning in the 1730s. Christian ministers such as George Whitefield and Jonathan Edwards preached throughout the colonies, drawing huge crowds. The Great Awakening had a lasting effect on the way in which the colonists viewed themselves, their relationships with one another, and their faith.
>
> *—from page 128*

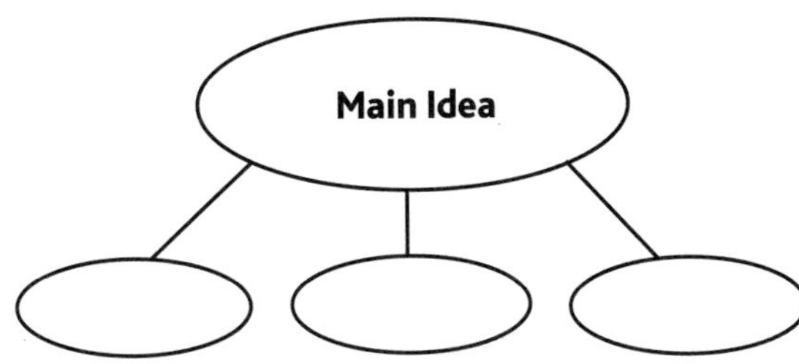

Read to Write

Use the main idea that appears under one of the headings in Section 1 of this chapter as the first sentence in a paragraph. As you read, complete the paragraph with supporting details.

▲ Massachusetts preacher and philosopher Jonathan Edwards

3 Apply It!

Pick a paragraph from another section of this chapter and diagram the main idea as you did above.

Section 1 Founding the American Colonies

Guide to Reading

History Social Science Standards

US8.1 Students understand the major events preceding the founding of the nation and relate their significance to the development of American constitutional democracy.

Looking Back, Looking Ahead

You learned that Europeans explored and began to colonize the Americas in the 1400s and 1500s. In North America, early English colonies faced hardships, but in time they began to flourish.

Focusing on the Main Ideas

- Spain, France, and the Netherlands founded colonies in North America. *(page 117)*
- The first permanent English settlement in North America was at Jamestown. *(page 119)*
- The English established 13 colonies along the east coast of North America. *(page 120)*

Locating Places

New England Colonies
Middle Colonies
Southern Colonies

Meeting People

Samuel de Champlain (sham • PLAYN)
Roger Williams
William Penn

Content Vocabulary

charter
burgess (BUHR • juhs)
Mayflower Compact
constitution (KAHN • stuh • TOO • shuhn)
toleration (TAH • luh • RAY • shuhn)
dissenter (dih • SEHN • tuhr)
persecute (PUHR • sih • KYOOT)
diversity (duh • VUHR • suh • TEE)
debtor (DEH • tuhr)

Academic Vocabulary

survive (suhr • VYV)
grant
military (MIH • luh • TEHR • ee)

Reading Strategy

Classifying Information Create a diagram like the one below with a row for each colony studied in the section. Fill in the names of the colonies and details on why or how the colony was settled.

Colony	Reasons the colony was settled

NATIONAL GEOGRAPHIC Where & When?

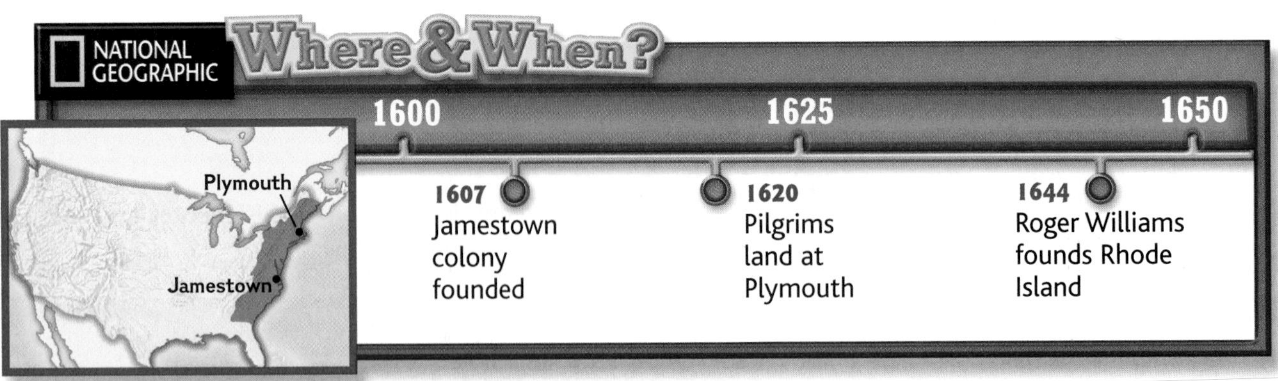
Plymouth
Jamestown
1600
1625
1650
1607 Jamestown colony founded
1620 Pilgrims land at Plymouth
1644 Roger Williams founds Rhode Island

Virginia and the Southern Colonies After early hardships, Virginia prospered from growing tobacco. Wealthy planters held the best land near the coast, so new settlers pushed inland. They increasingly began to settle on land belonging to Native Americans. In 1622 a revolt by a Native American group called the Powhatan Confederation nearly destroyed the colony. Following this revolt, the Virginia Company was accused of mismanaging the colony and lost its charter. In 1624 Virginia became a royal colony, with a governor and council appointed by the king. The House of Burgesses was retained, but its laws now had to receive royal approval. In addition, the Anglican Church was made the official religion of the colony.

Maryland While Virginia struggled and grew, other English colonies were founded in the south. A Catholic noble, George Calvert, who held the title of Lord Baltimore, wanted to set up a safe place for fellow Catholics who faced persecution in England. His dream came true in 1632 when King Charles I gave him a colony north of Virginia. Calvert died before actually receiving the grant. His son Cecilius Calvert, the second Lord Baltimore, took charge of the colony. It was named Maryland after the English queen, Henrietta Maria.

Conflict, however, soon divided Maryland. Protestants as well as Catholics settled in the colony. Soon the Protestants outnumbered the Catholics. To protect Catholics from any attempt to make Maryland a Protestant colony, Lord Baltimore passed a law called the Act of Toleration in 1649. The act granted Protestants and Catholics the right to worship freely. Although the Act initially failed in its goal, it was an early step toward the later acceptance of religious **diversity** (duh • VUHR • suh • TEE), or variety, in the colonies.

The Carolinas In the 1660s, King Charles II issued charters creating a large colony south of Virginia called Carolina. The king gave the colony to a group of eight prominent members of his court. The Carolina proprietors carved out large estates for themselves and provided money to bring colonists over from England.

Picturing **History**

Plantation agriculture became an important part of the economy of the Southern colonies. ***Why did Carolina separate and become two colonies?***

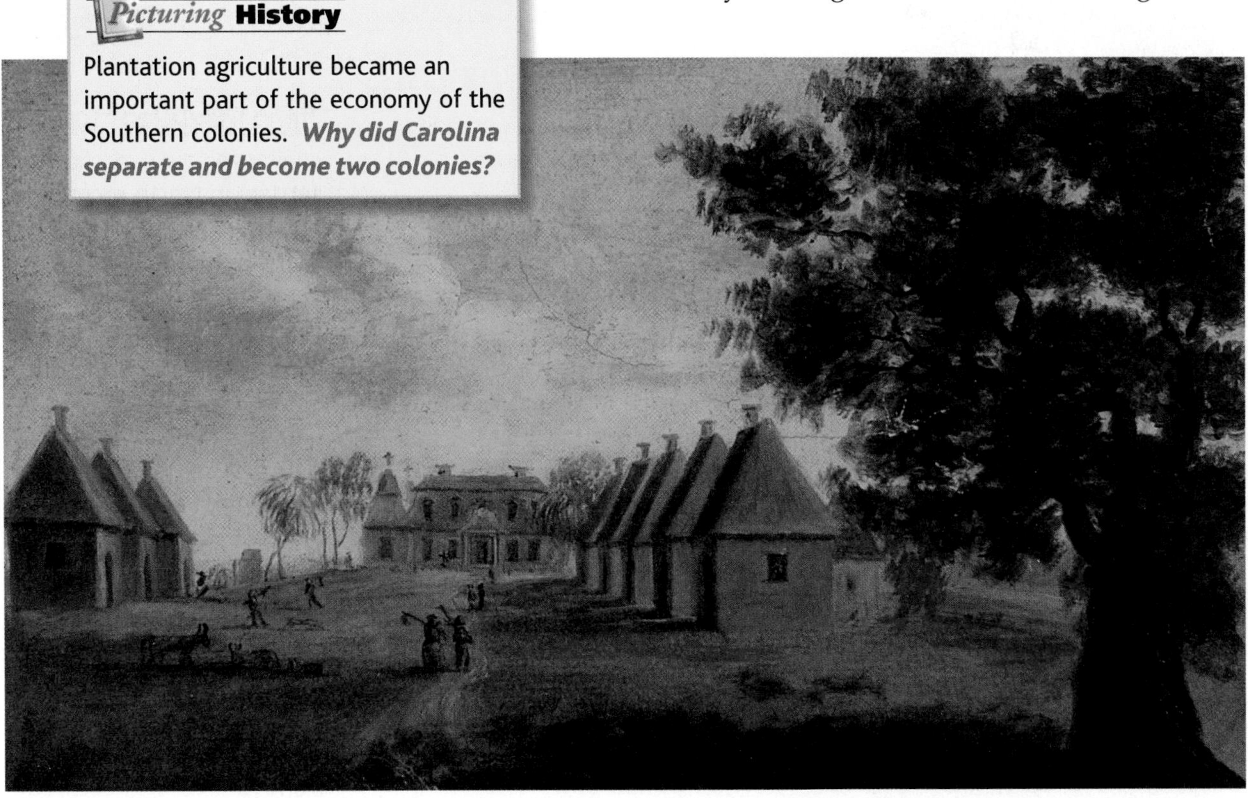

Carolina, however, did not develop according to plan. By the early 1700s, Carolina's settlers wanted a greater role in the colony's government. In 1719 the settlers in southern Carolina seized control from its proprietors. In 1729 Carolina became two royal colonies—North and South Carolina.

Georgia Georgia, the last of the English colonies in America to be established, was founded in 1733. A group led by General James Oglethorpe received a charter to create a colony where English **debtors** (DEH • tuhrs)—people who are unable to repay their debts—could make a fresh start. However, most of Georgia's settlers were poor people from the British Isles or religious refugees from Europe's mainland.

The British government had another reason for creating Georgia. This colony could protect the other British colonies from Spanish attack. Great Britain and Spain had been at war in the early 1700s, and new conflicts over territory in North America were always breaking out. Located between Spanish Florida and South Carolina, Georgia could serve as a **military** barrier against Spain.

Many of the new settlers complained about the limits on the size of landholdings and the law banning slave labor. Oglethorpe reluctantly agreed to lift these bans. Frustrated by the colonists' demands and the colony's slow growth, Oglethorpe turned the colony back over to the king in 1751. By that time, British settlers had been in what is now the eastern United States for almost 150 years. They had lined the Atlantic coast with colonies.

Reading Check **Explain** What was Maryland's Act of Toleration, and why was it important?

History Online
Study Central Need help understanding colonial settlements? Visit ca.hss.glencoe.com and click on Study Central.

Reading Summary

Review the Main Ideas

- A number of European countries, including England, Spain, France, and the Netherlands, founded colonies in North America.
- The English settlers in Jamestown, Virginia, set up a representative government based on what they had known in England.
- The New England, Middle, and Southern Colonies were settled by the English and other Europeans for a variety of reasons, including religious freedom and financial gain.

What Did You Learn?

1. Why did the French originally come to North America?
2. What was the House of Burgesses?

Critical Thinking

3. **Organizing Information** Draw a table like the one below and fill in details about the New England, Middle, and Southern Colonies. CA HR3.

Region	Information
New England	
Middle Colonies	
Southern Colonies	

4. **Analyze** What was the Mayflower Compact and why was it important? CA HI1.
5. **The Big Idea** What challenges did early English settlers in North America face? Write a short essay that summarizes your conclusions. CA 8RC2.0
6. **Expository Writing** Write a short essay describing the importance of the search for religious freedom in the settling of America. Describe the founding of specific colonies in your essay. CA 8WA2.4
7. **Reading Identifying the Main Idea** Using the essay you wrote on the importance of religious freedom, summarize the main idea and supporting points from your essay. CA 8RC2.4

Section 2: Life in Colonial America

Guide to Reading

Looking Back, Looking Ahead

You read how the 13 English colonies were founded. Those colonies continued to grow and develop their own culture and beliefs about government.

Focusing on the Main Ideas

- As the population of the colonies grew, agriculture and trade increased. *(page 126)*
- An American culture, influenced by religion and education, began to develop. *(page 128)*
- Although the American colonies developed some self-government, the British still set many laws, especially those concerning trade. *(page 130)*

Locating Places

New York City
Philadelphia

Meeting People

Benjamin Franklin

Content Vocabulary

subsistence farming
triangular trade
cash crop
indentured servant (ihn • DEHN • shuhrd)
overseer
charter colony
proprietary colony (pruh • PRY • uh • TERH • ee)
royal colony

Academic Vocabulary

adapt
principle (PRIHN • suh • puhl)

Reading Strategy

Organizing Information Use a chart like the one below to describe the differences in the economies of the New England, Middle, and Southern Colonies.

Economic Development		
New England	Middle Colonies	Southern Colonies

History Social Science Standards

US8.1 Students understand the major events preceding the founding of the nation and relate their significance to the development of American constitutional democracy.

NATIONAL GEOGRAPHIC
Who & When?
1700
1750
1800
1700s Thousands of Africans are brought to America
1730s Great Awakening takes root
c. 1760 New York City's population reaches 25,000

African drum

George Whitefield

US8.1 Students understand the major events preceding the founding of the nation and relate their significance to the development of American constitutional democracy.

The Colonies Grow

Main Idea **As the population of the colonies grew, agriculture and trade increased.**

Reading Connection Is your community or region known for any special product, either agricultural or manufactured? Read to find out how the economies of the New England, Middle, and Southern Colonies differed.

An American Story

In 1760 Englishman Andrew Burnaby traveled throughout the North American colonies, observing American life. He could not imagine that these colonies would ever join in union for they were as different from one another as "fire and water," and each colony was jealous of the other.

Commercial New England Although Burnaby believed that the colonies would never unite, the colonies continued to grow. Economic success and religious and political freedoms drew a steady flow of new settlers.

Long winters and thin, rocky soil in New England made large-scale farming difficult. Farmers there practiced **subsistence farming,** which means that they generally produced just enough to meet the needs of their families, with little left over to sell or exchange.

Shipbuilding was an important New England industry. The lumber for building ships came from the forests of New England and was transported down rivers to the shipyards in coastal towns.

Colonial Trade As the center of the shipping trade in America, New England linked the different English American colonies and linked America to other parts of the world. Some ships followed routes that came to be called the **triangular trade** because the routes formed a triangle. On one leg of such a route, ships brought sugar and molasses from the West Indies to the New England Colonies. In New England, the molasses was made into rum. Next, the rum and other manufactured goods were shipped to West Africa where they were traded for enslaved Africans. On the final leg of the route, the enslaved Africans were taken to the West Indies where they were sold to planters. The profit was used to buy more molasses—and the process started over.

Growth of the Middle Colonies The Middle Colonies enjoyed fertile soil and a slightly milder climate than New England's. Farmers in this region cultivated larger areas of land and produced bigger harvests than did New Englanders. In New York and Pennsylvania, farmers grew large quantities of wheat and other **cash crops**—crops that could be sold easily in markets in the colonies and overseas.

Farmers sent cargoes of wheat and livestock to **New York City** and **Philadelphia** for shipment, and these cities became busy ports. By the 1760s, New York, with 25,000 people, and Philadelphia, with 30,000 people, were the largest cities in the American colonies.

Like the New England Colonies, the Middle Colonies also had industries. Some were home-based crafts such as carpentry and flour making. Others included larger businesses such as lumbering, mining, and small-scale manufacturing.

The Middle Colonies attracted many German, Dutch, Swedish, and other non-English settlers. They gave the Middle Colonies a cultural diversity, or variety, that was not found in New England. With the diversity came tolerance for religious and cultural differences.

Plantation Life in the South With their rich soil and warm climate, the Southern Colonies were well suited to the growing of cash crops. These included tobacco, rice, and indigo, a blue flowering plant used to dye textiles. Most cash crops were grown on large farms called plantations. At first planters, or plantation owners, used **indentured servants** (ihn•DEHN•shurd) to work in the fields. Indentured servants were laborers who agreed to work without pay for a certain period of time to pay for their passage to America.

When indentured servants became scarce and expensive, Southern farmers used enslaved Africans instead. Independent small farmers grew corn and tobacco on small farms. They usually worked alone or with their families. Independent small farmers outnumbered the large plantation owners. The plantation owners, however, had greater wealth and more influence. They controlled the economic and political life of the region.

Slavery in the Southern Colonies The slave trade and slavery were major parts of colonial economies. The inhumane part of the triangular trade, shipping enslaved Africans to the Americas, was known as the Middle Passage. Olaudah Equiano, a young African forced onto a ship to the Americas, later described the horror of the voyage across the Atlantic:

> **"We were all put under deck. . . . The stench . . . was so intolerably loathsome, that it was dangerous to remain there for any time. . . . The closeness of the place, and the heat of the climate, added to the number in the ship, which was so crowded that each had scarcely room to turn himself, almost suffocated us. . . ."**
>
> —from *The Interesting Narrative of the Life of Olaudah Equiano*

Most enslaved Africans in the southern colonies lived on plantations. Some of the Africans did housework, but most worked in the fields and often suffered great cruelty. The large plantation owners hired **overseers,** or bosses, to keep the slaves working hard. All the Southern Colonies had slave codes, which were strict rules governing the behavior and punishment of enslaved Africans. All white colonists were encouraged to enforce these laws against enslaved Africans.

African Traditions Although the enslaved Africans had strong family ties, their families were often torn apart. Slaveholders could split up families by selling a spouse, a parent, or a child to another slaveholder. Slaves who worked on plantations found a source of strength in their African roots. They developed a culture that drew on the languages, customs, and religions of their West African homelands.

Some enslaved Africans learned trades such as carpentry, blacksmithing, or weaving. Those lucky enough to be able to buy their freedom joined the small population of free African Americans.

Criticism of Slavery Slavery was one reason for the economic success of the Southern Colonies. That success, however, was built on the idea that one human being could own another. Some colonists did not believe in slavery. Many Puritans refused to hold enslaved people. In Pennsylvania, Quakers and Mennonites condemned slavery. Eventually, the debate over slavery would erupt in a bloody war, pitting North against South.

Reading Check **Explain** Why were the Southern Colonies especially well suited for growing cash crops?

***Picturing* History**

Among the early immigrants to America were some who did not come willingly. Western and Central Africans were taken by force from their homes, shipped across the Atlantic Ocean, and sold as slaves in North and South America. ***What does the term* Middle Passage *refer to?***

US8.1 Students understand the major events preceding the founding of the nation and relate their significance to the development of American constitutional democracy. **US8.1.1** Describe the relationship between the moral and political ideas of the Great Awakening and the development of revolutionary fervor.

An Emerging Culture

Main Idea **An American culture, influenced by religion and education, began to develop.**

Reading Connection What are some things you consider truly American? Perhaps baseball or a summer picnic with hamburgers and hot dogs? Read to find out how the colonists began to form a culture that was different from those European cultures.

Throughout the colonies, people **adapted** their traditions to the new conditions of life in America. Religion, education, and the arts contributed to a new American culture.

The Great Awakening Religion had a strong influence in colonial life. In the 1730s and 1740s, a religious revival called the Great Awakening swept through the colonies. In New England and the Middle Colonies, ministers called for "a new birth," a return to the strong faith of earlier days.

The most important effect of the Great Awakening was greater religious and political freedom in the colonies. More colonists chose their own faith, and the strength of established official churches declined. As a Baptist preacher noted soon after the Great Awakening, "the common people now claim as good a right to judge and act in matters of religion as civil rulers or the learned clergy."

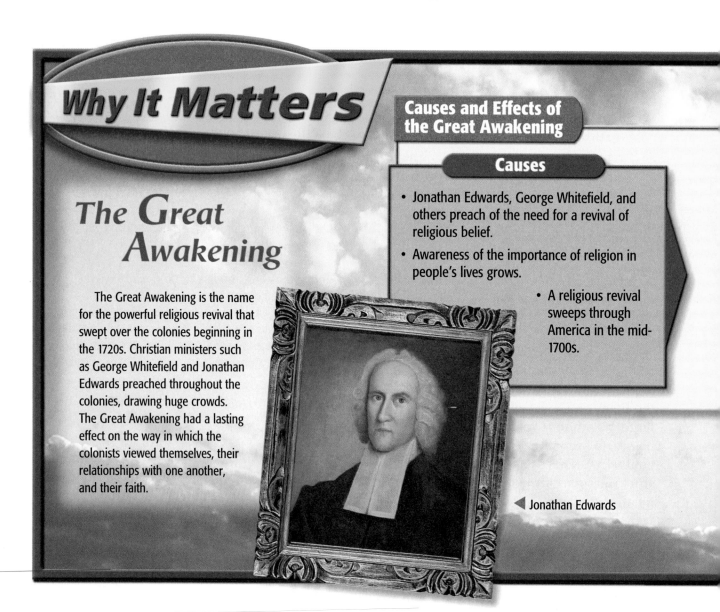

Why It Matters

The Great Awakening

The Great Awakening is the name for the powerful religious revival that swept over the colonies beginning in the 1720s. Christian ministers such as George Whitefield and Jonathan Edwards preached throughout the colonies, drawing huge crowds. The Great Awakening had a lasting effect on the way in which the colonists viewed themselves, their relationships with one another, and their faith.

Causes and Effects of the Great Awakening

Causes

- Jonathan Edwards, George Whitefield, and others preach of the need for a revival of religious belief.
- Awareness of the importance of religion in people's lives grows.
- A religious revival sweeps through America in the mid-1700s.

◀ Jonathan Edwards

The Great Awakening also for the first time united colonists from north to south in a common cause. This paved the way for the rapid spread of political ideas and revolutionary fervor during the struggle for independence.

Education in the Colonies Most colonists valued education. Children were often taught to read and write at home by their parents, even though the daily chores left little time for lessons. In 1647 the Massachusetts Puritans passed a public education law. Each community had to have a teacher whose wages would be paid through taxes. Although some communities did not set up schools, most did. In the Middle Colonies, schooling was not as universal as in New England, but it was widespread. In the Southern Colonies, formal education was generally limited to children of large landowners and professionals such as lawyers and doctors. Even where schools were desired, the widely separated plantations and farms of the South made them impractical. Young children were usually educated by their parents or by tutors.

By modern standards, schools in the American colonies were primitive. Schools had few books, and instruction was given only two or three months a year. Only a small percentage of children received education beyond the primary level. Most girls received little formal education. Despite these shortcomings, few regions of the world had such a high proportion of people who could read or write.

Education was closely related to religion. The first colleges—Harvard, William and Mary, and Yale—were established to train ministers. Six colleges were in operation by 1763; all but two were founded by religious groups primarily for the training of ministers.

By the middle of the 1700s, many educated colonists also were influenced by the Enlightenment. This movement, which began in Europe, spread the idea that knowledge, reason, and science could improve society. The best-known scientist in the colonies was **Benjamin Franklin.** Franklin's greatest services to his fellow Americans would come during the 1770s when he would help guide the colonies to freedom.

Effects

- New religious groups such as the Baptists, Methodists, and Presbyterians take root.
- Emphasis on education grows.
- Belief grows that all people are equal before God.
- Makes Americans more willing to challenge authority prior to the American Revolution.

◀ George Whitefield

The Press in America Schools and colleges spread knowledge. So did books, newspapers, and almanacs. Because paper and type were expensive, most books came from Britain. Newspapers, printed weekly, were mostly four pages in length. Almanacs attracted as many readers as newspapers. In addition to a calendar, dates of holidays, times of sunset and sunrise, almanacs published advice on farming, poems, news of the year, and practical advice.

Reading Check **Analyze** What was the Enlightenment, and what effect did it have in the colonies?

US8.1 Students understand the major events preceding the founding of the nation and relate their significance to the development of American constitutional democracy. US8.1.4 Describe the nation's blend of civic republicanism, classical liberal principles, and English parliamentary traditions.

Colonial Government

Main Idea **Although the American colonies developed some self-government, the British still set many laws, especially those concerning trade.**

Reading Connection How would you feel if your parents or teachers told you that you could only trade lunch snacks or baseball cards with certain people, even if someone else had a better card or dessert they were willing to trade? Read to find out how the British attempted to maintain control over colonial trade.

In Chapter 1, you learned that the English colonists brought with them ideas about government that had been developing in England for centuries. At the heart of the English system were two **principles**—limited government and representative government. As the colonies grew, they relied more and more on their own governments to make local laws.

Picturing History

Colonial legislatures gave some Americans a voice in government. ***What groups were not represented?***

Self-Government in America The 13 colonies began either as charter or proprietary colonies. **Charter colonies,** such as Massachusetts, had a charter, or a grant of rights and privileges, granted by the English monarch to stockholders. **Proprietary colonies** (pruh • PRY • uh • TEHR • ee), such as Pennsylvania, were owned by an individual proprietor or by a small group of proprietors.

Over time, English monarchs began to change colonies into **royal colonies.** Such colonies were under direct English control. In each, Parliament appointed a governor and council, known as the upper house. The colonists selected an assembly, the lower house. The governor and council members usually did what English leaders told them to do. However, this often led to conflicts with the colonists in the assembly, especially when officials tried to enforce tax laws and trade restrictions.

Colonial legislatures gave only some people a voice in government. White men who owned property had the right to vote; however, women, indentured servants, landless poor, and African Americans could not vote. In spite of these limits, a higher proportion of people became involved in government in the colonies than anywhere in the European world. This strong participation gave Americans training that was valuable when the colonies became independent.

British Colonial Policies During the early 1700s, many changes occurred in England and its overseas colonies. In 1707 England united with Scotland and became the United Kingdom. The term *British* came to mean both the English and the Scots. By 1750 Great Britain had become the world's most powerful trading empire.

For many years, Great Britain had allowed the American colonies the freedom to run their local affairs. However, the British government controlled the colonies' trade according to the ideas of mercantilism. The American colonies produced raw materials such as tobacco, rice, indigo, wheat, lumber, fur, deerskin leather, fish, and whale products. These were shipped to Great Britain and traded for manufactured goods such as clothing, furniture, and goods from Asia, including tea and spices.

To control this trade, Britain passed a series of laws called Navigation Acts in the 1650s. Under these laws, the colonists had to sell their raw materials to Britain even if they could get a better price elsewhere. Any goods bought by the colonies from other countries in Europe had to go to England first and be taxed before they could be sent to the Americas. The trade laws also said that all trade goods had to be carried on ships built in Britain or the colonies and that the crews had to be British as well.

Colonial Resistance The colonists at first accepted the trade laws because they were guaranteed a place to sell their raw materials. Later, the colonists came to resent British restrictions. With population in the colonies growing, the colonists wanted to make their own manufactured goods. They also wanted to sell their products elsewhere if they could get higher prices. Many colonial merchants began smuggling, or shipping goods in and out of the country without paying taxes or getting government permission. Controls on trade would later cause conflict between the American colonies and England.

Reading Check **Compare** How did charter colonies and proprietary colonies differ?

Study Central Need help understanding American self-government? Visit ca.hss.glencoe.com and click on Study Central.

Reading Summary

Review the Main Ideas

- As the colonies grew, differing economies developed in the New England, Middle, and Southern Colonies.
- In the colonies, family life, education, and religion were important in the emerging American culture.
- Even with British restrictions, especially on trade, the principle of self-government took a strong hold in the colonies.

What Did You Learn?

1. What was the triangular trade?
2. What were some cash crops grown on southern plantations? What crops were grown on smaller independent farms?

Critical Thinking

3. **Compare and Contrast** Draw a chart like the one below. Fill in details comparing farming in the New England and Southern Colonies. CA HR3.

	Similarities	Differences
New England		
Southern Colonies		

4. **Determining Cause and Effect** What effects did the Great Awakening have on the American colonies? CA HI2.
5. **The Big Ideas** How did geography affect the economies of the three colonial regions? CA CS3.
6. **Descriptive Writing** Imagine you live in New England in the mid-1700s and are visiting cousins on a farm in the Carolinas. Write a letter to a friend at home describing your visit to the farm. CA 8WA2.1

Connecting to the Constitution

US8.1.4 Describe the nation's blend of civic republicanism, classical liberal principles, and English parliamentary traditions. **US8.2.1** Discuss the significance of the Magna Carta, the English Bill of Rights, and the Mayflower Compact.

The Road to Representative Government

Why It Matters **Many of the rights that American citizens enjoy today can be traced back to the political and legal traditions of England. When English people began settling here in the 1600s, they brought with them a tradition of limited and representative government.**

Limited Government By the time the first colonists reached North America, the idea that government was not all-powerful had become an accepted part of the English system. The concept first appeared in the Magna Carta, or Great Charter, that King John was forced to sign in 1215. The Magna Carta established the principle of limited government, in which the power of the **monarch,** or ruler, was limited, not absolute. This document protected the nobles' privileges and upheld their authority. It also granted certain rights to all landholders—rights that eventually came to apply to all English people.

English Parliamentary Traditions The English people had a firm belief in **representative government,** in which people elect delegates to make laws and conduct government. The English Parliament was a representative assembly with the power to make laws. It consisted of two houses, the House of Lords and the House of Commons. American legislatures grew from the English practice of representation.

In the mid-1600s, Parliament and King James II began a struggle for power. In 1688 Parliament removed King James II from the throne and crowned William and Mary to rule.

Thomas Jefferson

"Freedom of religion, freedom of the press, trial by jury, habeas corpus, and a representative legislature . . . I consider as the essentials constituting free government, ..."

—Thomas Jefferson in a letter to Pierre Samuel Dupont de Nemours, 1815

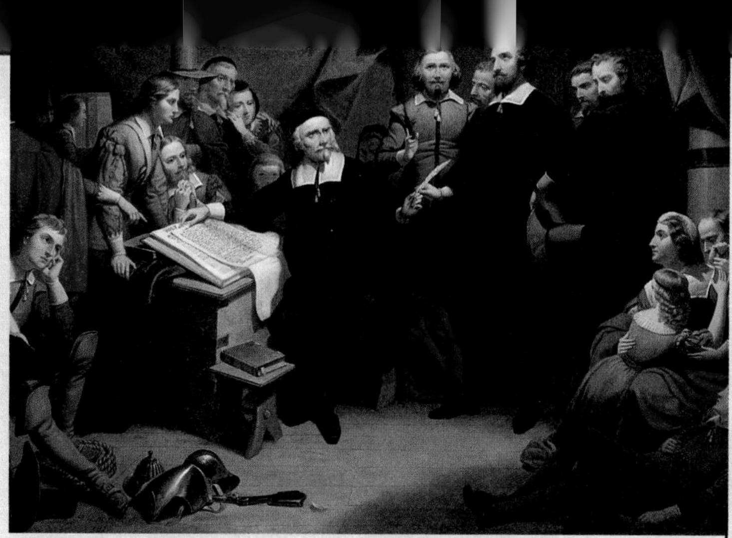

▲ **By signing the Mayflower Compact, the Pilgrims established a set of rules under which they would govern themselves.**

This peaceful transfer of power, known as the Glorious Revolution, changed the idea of government in England. From that time on, no ruler would have more power than the legislature.

The English Bill of Rights To set clear limits to what a ruler could and could not do, Parliament drew up the English Bill of Rights in 1689. The document stated that the monarch could not suspend Parliament's laws; the monarch also could not create special courts, impose taxes, or raise an army without Parliament's consent. The Bill of Rights also declared that members of Parliament would be freely elected and be guaranteed free speech during meetings, that every citizen would have the right to a fair trial by jury in court cases, and that cruel and unusual punishments would be banned.

The English Heritage in America

English settlers in the American colonies established traditions of representative government that they had learned in England. They believed that the ruler was not above the law. They also expected to have a voice in government and other basic rights. Many of the early state constitutions listed the rights of the citizens.

The Virginia House of Burgesses

The first permanent English settlement in North America was Jamestown. At first, the Jamestown colony was managed by a governor and council appointed by the Virginia Company, a group of merchants from London. In 1619, however, the colonists chose two representatives from each community to meet with the governor and his council. These 22 men were called burgesses. They formed the House of Burgesses, which was the first representative assembly, or legislature, in the English colonies. The House of Burgesses had little power, but it marked the beginning of self-government in colonial America.

The Mayflower Compact In 1620, shortly after the House of Burgesses was formed, a new group of colonists, known as the Pilgrims, arrived in America. Even before their ship, the *Mayflower,* reached America, the Pilgrims realized they needed rules to govern themselves if they were to survive in a new land. They drew up a written plan for their government called the Mayflower Compact.

The Mayflower Compact stated that the government would make "just and equal laws . . . for the general good of the colony." The compact set up a direct democracy in which all men would vote and the majority would rule. (As was common at this time, only adult males were permitted to vote.)

The Mayflower Compact established a tradition of direct democracy. Throughout the colonial period—and in parts of New England today—citizens meet at town meetings to discuss and vote on important issues.

Checking for Understanding

1. What is the system of representative government? Where did this system come from?
2. What is important about the Virginia House of Burgesses?

Critical Thinking

3. **Evaluate** The idea of limited government, first established in the Magna Carta, is an important principle of the U.S. Constitution. Do you believe governments should be limited? Why or why not?

Section
3

Trouble in the Colonies

Guide to Reading

History Social Science Standards

US8.1 Students understand the major events preceding the founding of the nation and relate their significance to the development of American constitutional democracy.

Looking Back, Looking Ahead

In the last section, you read about the beginnings of colonial resistance to British colonial policies. British attempts to tax the colonists brought the Americans and British to conflict.

Focusing on the Main Ideas

- Following Britain's victory in the French and Indian War, the British prohibited colonists from moving west of the Appalachian Mountains and taxed the colonists to pay for the war. *(page 135)*
- British actions, including sending more troops to Boston and passing new taxes, brought strong responses from the colonists. *(page 137)*
- After colonial leaders met to discuss their relations with Britain, the first shots of the American Revolution were fired. *(page 139)*

Meeting People

Crispus Attucks
Samuel Adams
John Adams
Patrick Henry
George Washington
King George III
Paul Revere

Content Vocabulary

import
smuggling
boycott
repeal (rih • PEEL)
resolution
militia (muh • LIH • shuh)
minutemen

Academic Vocabulary

convince
violate (VY • uh • LAYT)
correspond

Reading Strategy

Organizing Information Use a diagram like the one below to describe how the Intolerable Acts affected Massachusetts colonists.

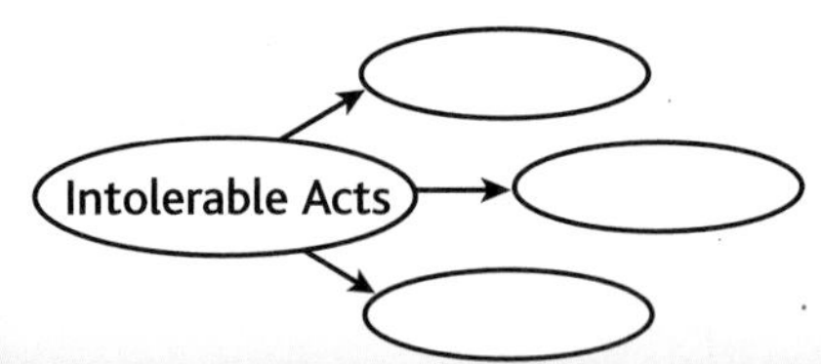
Intolerable Acts

NATIONAL GEOGRAPHIC **Where & When?**

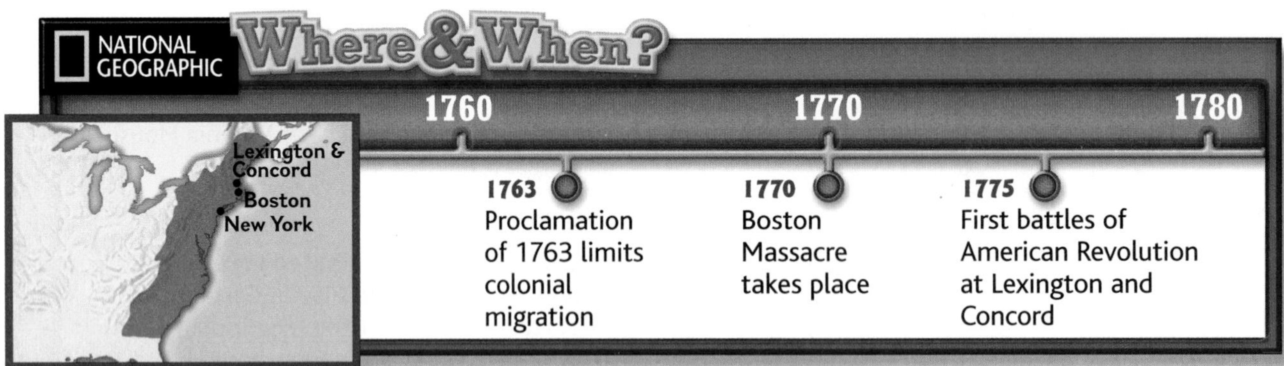
Lexington & Concord
Boston
New York
1760
1770
1780
1763 Proclamation of 1763 limits colonial migration
1770 Boston Massacre takes place
1775 First battles of American Revolution at Lexington and Concord

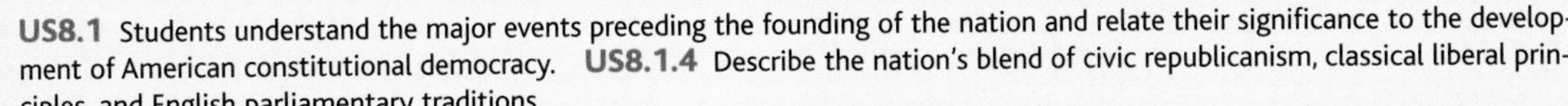

New British Policies

Main Idea **Following Britain's victory in the French and Indian War, the British prohibited colonists from moving west of the Appalachian Mountains and taxed the colonists to pay for the war.**

Reading Connection Have you ever stopped buying a product, perhaps because the manufacturer changed the product or raised its price? Read to find out how the American colonists protested British actions, in part by refusing to buy British products.

An American Story

During the colonial period, Britain and France struggled for control of eastern North America. As their settlements moved inland, both nations claimed the vast territory between the Appalachian Mountains and the Mississippi River. In 1758 writer Nathaniel Ames noted,

> **"The parts of North America which may be claimed by Great Britain or France are of as much worth as either kingdom. That fertile country to the west of the Appalachian Mountains [is the] 'Garden of the World'!"**
>
> —from the *Astronomical Diary and Almanack*, 1758

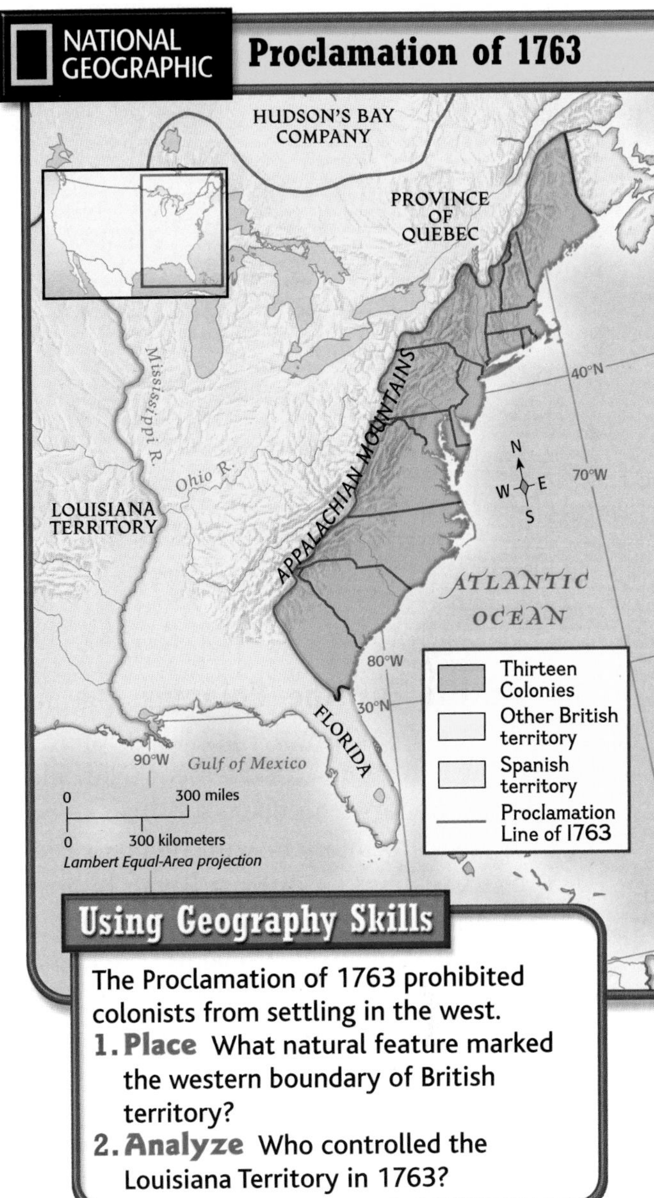

Using Geography Skills

The Proclamation of 1763 prohibited colonists from settling in the west.

1. **Place** What natural feature marked the western boundary of British territory?
2. **Analyze** Who controlled the Louisiana Territory in 1763?

The French and Indian War In 1754 British-French rivalry led to the outbreak of the French and Indian War. Colonial leaders met in Albany, New York, to find a way for the colonies to defend themselves against the French. The leaders adopted the Albany Plan of Union, calling for "one general government" for 11 of the American colonies. However, the plan was not approved. After Britain won the war in 1763, the colonies began to act together. Their united action, however, was directed against Britain itself. What developments brought about this unusual turn of events?

The Proclamation of 1763 Victory in 1763 gained for the British nearly all of France's North American empire. That same year, Britain issued a proclamation that prohibited colonists from moving west of the Appalachian Mountains. Stopping western settlement allowed British officials to control settler movement and avoid a conflict with Native Americans. It also prevented colonists from moving away from the coast—where Britain's important markets and investments were. To protect their interests, the British planned to keep 10,000 troops in America.

The Stamp Act required colonists to buy revenue stamps for newspapers, licenses, and documents. ▶

▼ The snake on the banner symbolized united American resistance to the British.

The British Tax the Colonies Alarmed colonists, however, saw the proclamation as a limit on their freedom of movement. They also feared that the large number of British troops might be used to interfere with their liberties. As a result, feelings of distrust began to grow between Britain and its American colonies.

Britain faced financial problems. The French and Indian War was very costly and left the British government deep in debt. Desperate for money, the British made plans to tax the colonies and tighten trade rules.

In 1764 the British Parliament passed the Sugar Act, which lowered the tax on molasses that had been **imported,** or bought from foreign markets, by the colonists. The British government hoped the lower tax would **convince** the colonists to pay the tax instead of **smuggling.** Smuggling means to trade illegally with other nations. The colonists believed their rights as Englishmen were being **violated.** James Otis, a young lawyer in Boston, argued that:

> **"no parts of [England's colonies] can be taxed without their consent . . . every part has a right to be represented."**
>
> —from *The Rights of the British Colonies*

What Was the Stamp Act? In 1765 Parliament passed another law in an effort to raise money. This law, known as the Stamp Act, placed a tax on newspapers and other printed material. All of these items had to bear a stamp showing that the tax was paid. The colonists were outraged. In October, delegates from nine colonies met in New York at the Stamp Act Congress. They sent a letter to the British government stating that the colonies could not be taxed except by their own assemblies. Colonists refused to use the stamps. They also **boycotted,** or refused to buy, British goods.

In February 1766, Parliament gave in to the colonists' demands and **repealed** (rih•PEELD), or cancelled, the Stamp Act. On the same day, however, it passed the Declaratory Act. This law stated that Parliament had the right to tax and make decisions for the British colonies "in all cases." The colonists might have won one battle, but the war over making decisions for the colonies had just begun.

New Taxes In 1767 Parliament passed another set of tax laws known as the Townshend Acts. In these acts, the British leaders tried to avoid some of the problems the Stamp Act caused. They understood that the colonists would not tolerate internal taxes—those levied or paid inside the colonies. As a result, the new taxes applied only to imported goods, with the tax being paid at the port of entry. The taxed goods, however, included basic items—such as glass, tea, paper, and lead—that the colonists had to import because they did not produce them.

The Colonists React By this time, the colonists were outraged by *any* taxes Parliament passed. They believed that only their own representatives had the right to levy taxes on them. The colonists responded by bringing back the boycott that had worked so well against the Stamp Act. The boycott proved to be even more widespread this time.

Reading Check **Explain** What was the Proclamation of 1763, and why did it anger American colonists?

Meanwhile, impatient to mount and ride,
Booted and spurred, with a heavy stride
On the opposite shore walked Paul Revere.
Now he patted his horse's side,
Now gazed at the landscape far and near,
Then, impetuous, stamped the earth,
And turned and tightened his saddle-girth,[11]
But mostly he watched with eager search
The belfry-tower of the Old North Church,
As it rose above the graves on the hill,
Lonely and spectral[12] and sombre and still.
And lo! as he looks, on the belfry's height
A glimmer, and then a gleam of light!
He springs to the saddle, the bridle he turns,
But lingers and gazes, till full on his sight
A second lamp in the belfry burns!

A hurry of hoofs in a village street,
A shape in the moonlight, a bulk in the dark,
And beneath, from the pebbles, in passing, a spark
Struck out by a steed[13] flying fearless and fleet;
That was all! And yet, through the gloom and the light,
The fate of a nation was riding that night;
And the spark struck out by that steed, in his flight,
Kindled the land into flame with its heat.

He has left the village and mounted the steep,
And beneath him, tranquil and broad and deep,
Is the Mystic,[14] meeting the ocean tides;
And under the alders[15] that skirt its edge,
Now soft on the sand, now loud on the ledge,
Is heard the tramp of his steed as he rides.

[11] **girth:** strap that goes around the body of an animal
[12] **spectral:** ghostly
[13] **steed:** horse
[14] **Mystic:** river that flows into Boston Harbor
[15] **alders:** type of tree

It was twelve by the village clock,
When he crossed the bridge into Medford town.
He heard the crowing of the cock,
And the barking of the farmer's dog,
And felt the damp of the river fog,
That rises after the sun goes down.

It was one by the village clock,
When he galloped into Lexington.
He saw the gilded weathercock[16]
Swim in the moonlight as he passed,
And the meeting-house windows, blank and bare,
Gaze at him with a spectral glare,
As if they already stood aghast[17]
At the bloody work they would look upon.

[16] **weathercock:** a movable device in the shape of a rooster that shows the direction of the wind
[17] **aghast:** shocked

It was two by the village clock,
When he came to the bridge in Concord town.
He heard the bleating of the flock,
And the twitter of birds among the trees,
And felt the breath of the morning breeze
Blowing over the meadows brown.
And one was safe and asleep in his bed
Who at the bridge would be first to fall,
Who that day would be lying dead,
Pierced by a British musket-ball.[18]

[18] **musket-ball:** bullet from a gun

US8.1.2 Analyze the philosophy of government expressed in the Declaration of Independence, with an emphasis on government as a means of securing individual rights (e.g., key phrases such as "all men are created equal, that they are endowed by their Creator with certain unalienable rights"). **US8.1.3** Analyze how the American Revolution affected other nations, especially France.

The American Revolution

Main Idea **America's victory and independence led to revolutions in other parts of the world.**

Reading Connection Has someone else's success ever encouraged you to work harder toward a goal? Read to find out how the American victory over the British led to political revolutions in other colonies.

After the colonial leaders declared independence in July 1776, the war for freedom was unavoidable. The British planned to crush the rebellion by force. Most of the **Patriots**—Americans who supported independence—believed the British would give up after losing one or two major battles.

Not all Americans, however, supported the struggle for independence. Some people were **neutral** (NOO•truhl), taking neither side in the conflict. Still other Americans—known as **Loyalists**—remained loyal to Great Britain. At least one American in five was a Loyalist—perhaps as many as one in three.

Early Campaigns During the summer of 1776, Britain sent 32,000 troops across the Atlantic to New York. The British hoped the sheer size of their army would convince the Patriots to give up. In late August, British armies defeated George Washington's forces on New York's Long Island. By late November, the Patriots had retreated across New Jersey into Pennsylvania. Meanwhile, the British army settled in New York for the winter of 1776, leaving some troops in New Jersey at Trenton and Princeton.

Stationed across the Delaware River from the British camp in New Jersey, Washington saw a chance to catch the British off guard. On Christmas night 1776, Washington took 2,400 troops across the icy river and surprised the enemy at Trenton the next day. The British sent reinforcements, but Washington led his troops away from these soldiers. Washington then marched the army to Princeton, where they drove away the British. One discouraged British soldier wrote in his diary that the American victory made the Americans "all liberty mad again."

History *Through Art*

Washington Crossing the Delaware **by Emanuel Leutze** George Washington led his troops across the Delaware River on Christmas night in a surprise attack on British troops at Trenton. ***What effect did the victory at Trenton have on the American cause?***

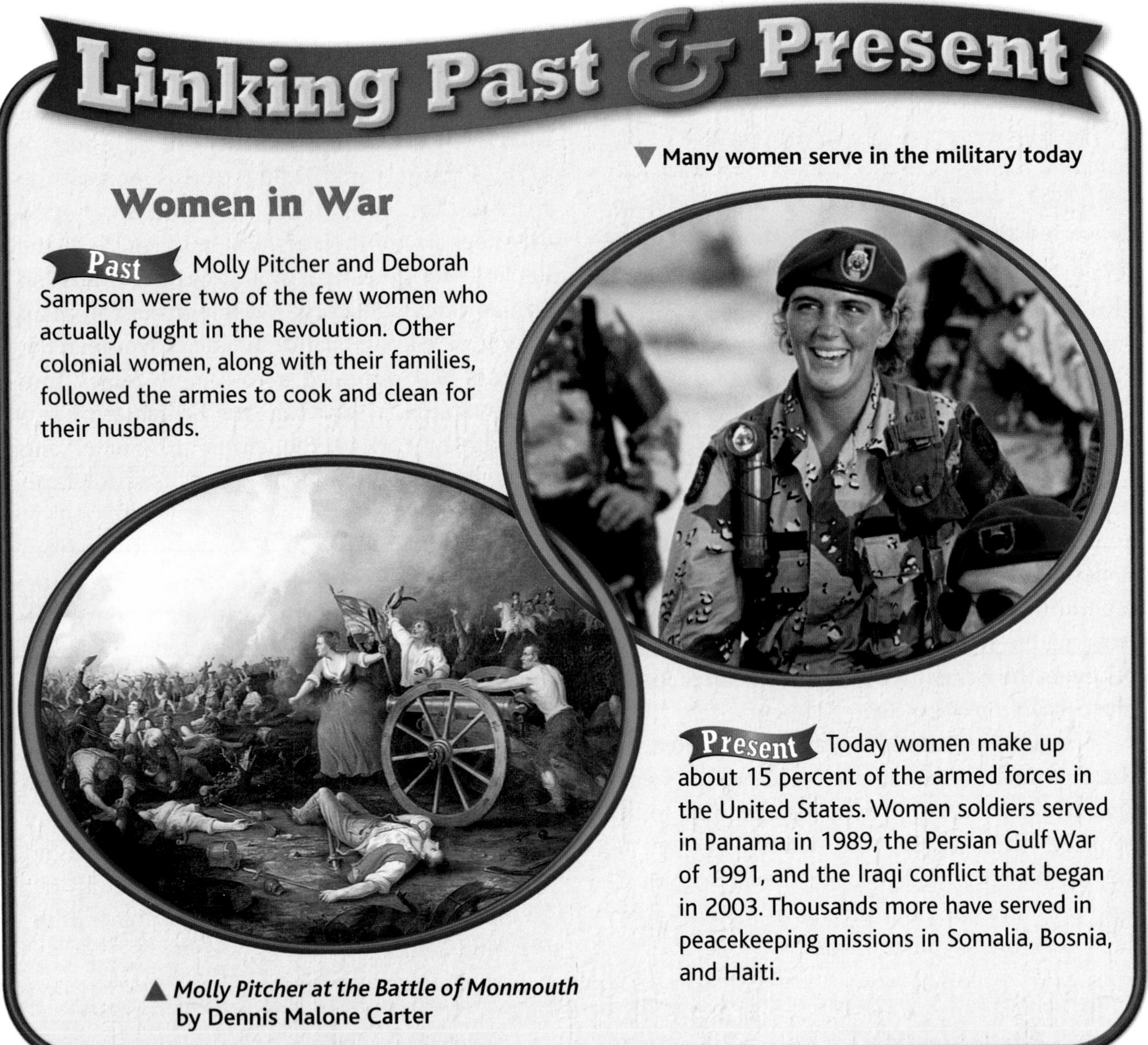

Molly Pitcher and Deborah Sampson were two of the few women who actually fought in the Revolution. Other colonial women, along with their families, followed the armies to cook and clean for their husbands.

▼ Many women serve in the military today

Today women make up about 15 percent of the armed forces in the United States. Women soldiers served in Panama in 1989, the Persian Gulf War of 1991, and the Iraqi conflict that began in 2003. Thousands more have served in peacekeeping missions in Somalia, Bosnia, and Haiti.

▲ *Molly Pitcher at the Battle of Monmouth* by Dennis Malone Carter

The Battle of Saratoga In 1777 the British decided to split New England from the Middle Colonies by taking control of New York's Hudson River valley. The plan called for three British forces to meet at Albany, New York, and destroy the Patriot troops.

A British force under General John Burgoyne advanced southward from Canada. When Burgoyne reached the town of Saratoga in New York, the other two British forces had not arrived. Soon, Burgoyne's forces found themselves surrounded by a larger American army under General Horatio Gates. After a desperate attack, the British realized they were trapped, and Burgoyne surrendered on October 17, 1777. The Battle of Saratoga was the first major American victory in the war.

Winter at Valley Forge As the winter of 1777 approached, other British forces settled in comfort in Philadelphia. Meanwhile, George Washington set up camp at Valley Forge, 20 miles to the west of the British.

Washington and his troops endured a winter of terrible suffering and difficult conditions, lacking decent food, clothing, and shelter. Washington's greatest **challenge** at Valley Forge was keeping the Continental Army together. Yet with strong determination, the Continental Army survived the winter, and conditions gradually improved.

Gaining Allies The victory at Saratoga boosted American spirits. Even more, Saratoga marked a turning point.

The European nations, especially France, realized that the United States might actually win its war against Britain. In 1778 the French declared war on Britain and provided aid to the Americans.

Other European nations also helped the Patriots. Spain declared war on Britain in 1779, and the Spanish governor of Louisiana, **Bernardo de Gálvez,** raised an army. Gálvez's army forced British troops from towns and forts along the Gulf of Mexico. His efforts **secured** the southern frontiers of the United States.

Individual foreigners also helped the Americans. One of the hardy soldiers at Valley Forge was a French nobleman, the **Marquis de Lafayette** (LAH • fee • EHT). Dedicated to the ideas of the Declaration of Independence, Lafayette was a trusted aide to Washington. Two Poles—Thaddeus Kosciusko (kawsh • CHUSH • koh), an engineer, and Casimir Pulaski, a cavalry officer—also helped the Americans. Friedrich von Steuben (STOO • buhn), a former army officer from Germany, turned the ragged Continental Army into a more effective fighting force.

Life on the Home Front The war changed the lives of all Americans, even those who stayed at home. With thousands of men away in military service, women took over the duties that had once been the responsibility of their husbands or fathers. Other women ran their husband's or their own businesses.

The ideals of liberty and freedom that inspired the American Revolution caused some women to question their place in society. Abigail Adams was a dedicated champion of women's interests. She wrote to her husband, John Adams, who was a member of the Second Continental Congress:

> **"I can not say that I think you very generous to the ladies, for whilst you are proclaiming peace and good will to men, emancipating all nations, you insist upon retaining an absolute power over wives."**
>
> —Letter, May 7, 1776

The Revolutionary War ideals of freedom and liberty inspired some white Americans to question slavery. From the beginning of the war, African American soldiers fought for the American cause. To some who were fighting for freedom, both African American and white, the Revolution seemed to bring nearer the day when slavery would be abolished. Vermont, New Hampshire, Massachusetts, and Pennsylvania attempted to end slavery in their states. The issue of slavery would remain unsettled for many years, however.

War in the West and on Sea Along the northwestern frontier, the British and their Native American allies were raiding American settlements. During 1778 and 1779, George Rogers Clark, an officer in the Virginia militia, seized British posts in present-day Illinois and Indiana. Clark's victories strengthened the American position in the West.

Other battles raged at sea. A daring American naval officer, **John Paul Jones,** raided British ports. In September 1779, Jones's ship *Bonhomme Richard* fought the British warship *Serapis.* At one point, Jones's ship was so badly damaged that the British captain asked whether Jones wished to surrender. Jones is said to have answered, "I have not yet begun to fight." In the end the *Serapis* surrendered, making John Paul Jones a naval hero to the American Patriots.

▲ Many soldiers from other countries and about 5,000 African American soldiers fought for American independence.

Struggles in the South By 1778 the British hoped to use sea power and Loyalist support to win victories in the South. By 1780, British forces had seized Savannah and Charles Town. The British, however, could not control their conquered areas. This was due to a new kind of warfare carried out by the Patriots.

As British troops moved through the countryside, small forces of Patriots attacked them. Bands of soldiers suddenly struck and then disappeared. This hit-and-run **technique** of **guerrilla warfare** (guh • RIH • luh) caught the British off guard.

The War Is Won In 1780 the war was at a critical point. Both armies needed a victory to win. This finally came in 1781 at the Battle of Yorktown on the coast of Virginia. The French navy blocked the British from escaping by sea, while American and French forces surrounded and trapped the British inside Yorktown. Realizing they could not win, the British laid down their weapons.

The Treaty of Paris Britain's defeat at Yorktown did not end the Revolutionary War. The fighting dragged on in some areas for two more years. Peace negotiations, however, began in Paris. Benjamin Franklin, John Adams, and John Jay represented the United States. The final settlement, known as the Treaty of Paris, was signed on September 3, 1783.

The Treaty of Paris was a triumph for the Americans. Great Britain recognized the United States as an independent nation. The territory claimed by the new nation extended from the Atlantic Ocean west to the Mississippi River and from Canada in the north to Spanish Florida in the south. The Revolutionary War was over. The creation of a new nation was about to begin.

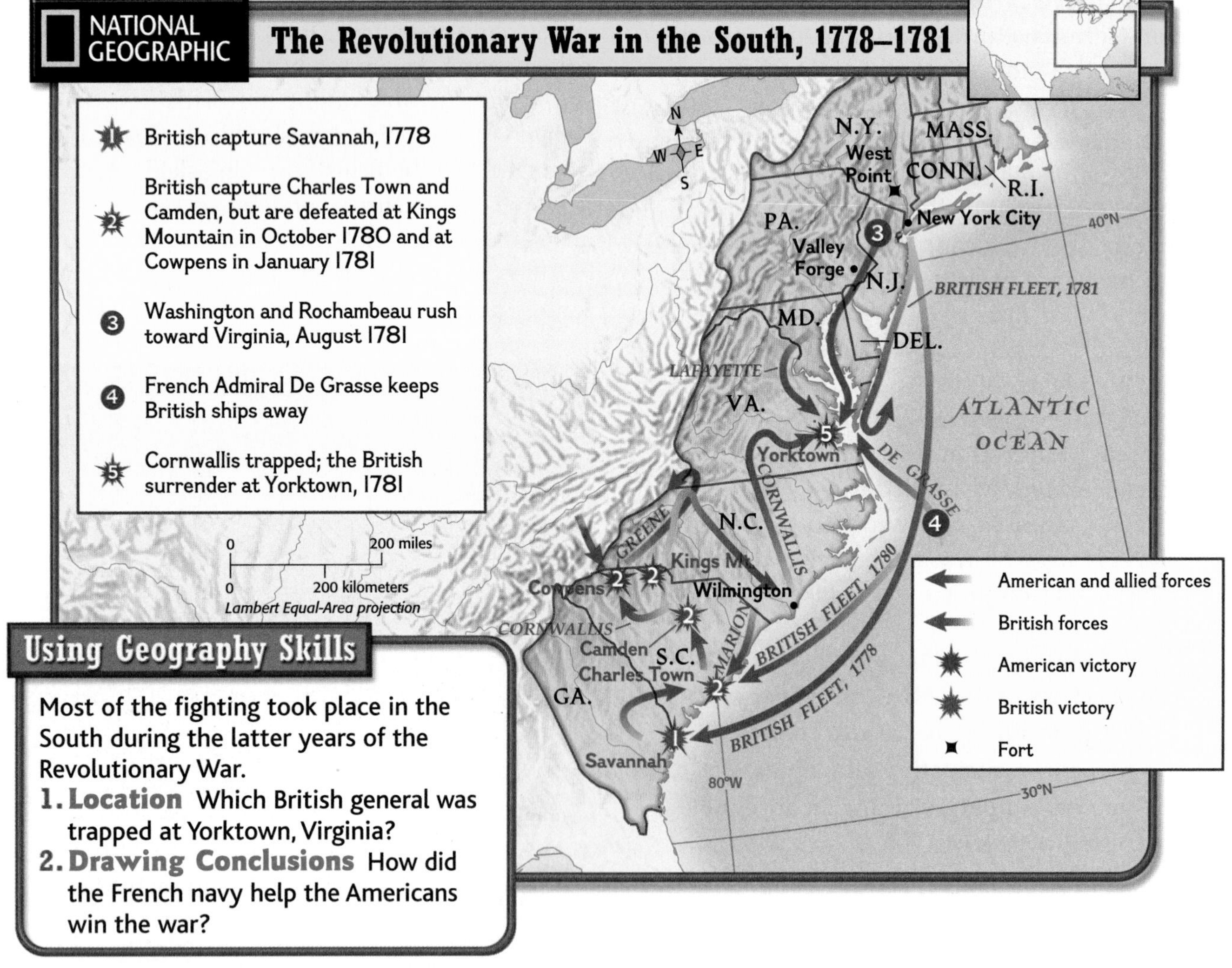

Using Geography Skills

Most of the fighting took place in the South during the latter years of the Revolutionary War.

1. **Location** Which British general was trapped at Yorktown, Virginia?
2. **Drawing Conclusions** How did the French navy help the Americans win the war?

Why the Americans Won How were the Patriots able to win the Revolutionary War? The Americans had several advantages. They fought on their own land, while the British had to bring troops and supplies from far away. The British succeeded in **occupying** cities but had difficulty controlling the countryside. Help from other nations also contributed to the American victory.

Perhaps most important, the American Revolution was a people's movement. Its outcome depended not on any one battle or event but on the determination and spirit of all the Patriots.

A Model for Others In 1776 the American colonists began a revolution, making clear the principles of freedom and rights outlined in the Declaration of Independence. These ideas bounded back across the Atlantic to influence the French Revolution. French rebels in 1789 fought in defense of "Liberty, Equality, and Fraternity." French revolutionaries repeated the principles of the American Declaration of Independence: "Men are born and remain free and equal in rights."

In 1791 the ideals of the American and French revolutions traveled across the Caribbean and the Atlantic to the French-held island colony of Saint Domingue. Inspired by talk of freedom, enslaved Africans took up arms. Led by Toussaint-Louverture, they rejected French rule. In 1804 Saint Domingue—part of present-day Haiti—became the second nation in the Americas to achieve independence from colonial rule.

Reading Check **Summarize** Why was the Battle of Saratoga a turning point in the war?

Study Central Need help understanding the American Revolution? Visit ca.hss.glencoe.com and click on Study Central.

Reading Summary

Review the Main Ideas

- The Second Continental Congress met to discuss governing the colonies and to form the Continental Army to fight the British.
- The Declaration of Independence, written by Thomas Jefferson, declared the American colonies to be a new, independent nation.
- The American victory inspired other peoples to seek independence and rebel against their governments.

What Did You Learn?

1. For what did Thomas Paine argue in *Common Sense?*
2. What was guerrilla warfare, and why was it effective?

Critical Thinking

3. **Organizing Information** Draw a chart like the one below. Fill in the names and dates of major Revolutionary War battles and provide details about each battle. CA CS1. CA CS2.

Battle	What Occurred

4. **Predict** What might have happened if the French had not allied with the colonists during the Revolutionary War? CA CS1.
5. **The Big Ideas** On what laws and political ideas did Jefferson draw when writing the Declaration of Independence? CA HI3.
6. **Math Connection** Examine the list of representatives to the Second Continental Congress on page 167 who signed the Declaration of Independence. Draw a bar graph depicting the number of men representing each state. Use the X-axis for the states and the Y-axis for numbers of men.

You Decide . . .

US8.1 Students understand the major events preceding the founding of the nation and relate their significance to the development of American constitutional democracy.

Independence: Yes or No?

Many American colonists joined the movement for independence. Still, many Americans did not want to break away from Great Britain.

For Independence

Many colonists in the summer of 1775 were not prepared to break away from Great Britain. The colonists resented British taxes. Because they had no representation in Parliament, as people in Great Britain did, the colonists believed that Parliament had no right to tax them. They summarized their feelings with the slogan "No taxation without representation." Most members of the Second Continental Congress wanted the right to govern themselves, but they did not want to break with the British Empire.

By 1776, however, opinion had changed. Frustrated by Britain's refusal to compromise, many Patriot leaders began to call for independence. Influential in swaying the colonists toward the idea of separating from Great Britain was Thomas Paine's pamphlet *Common Sense*, which first appeared in January 1776. Paine made an impassioned appeal:

"I have heard it asserted by some, that as America hath flourished under her former connexion with Great Britain, the same connexion is necessary towards her future happiness. . . . I answer roundly, that America would have flourished as much, and probably much more, had no European power [taken notice of her]. . . . Everything that is right or natural pleads for separation. The blood of the slain, the weeping voice of nature cries, 'TIS TIME TO PART.'"

The Patriots believed that fighting for liberty set an example for others to follow. Ben Franklin wrote to a friend that "our cause is the cause of all mankind, and that we are fighting for their liberty in defending our own."

◀ Thomas Paine

[Resolution of Independence by the United States]

We, therefore, the Representatives of the united States of America, in General Congress, Assembled, appealing to the Supreme Judge of the world for the **rectitude** of our intentions, do, in the Name, and by Authority of the good People of these Colonies, solemnly publish and declare, That these United Colonies are, and of Right ought to be Free and Independent States; that they are Absolved from all Allegiance to the British Crown, and that all political connection between them and the State of Great Britain, is and ought to be totally dissolved; and that as Free and Independent States, they have full Power to levy War, conclude Peace, contract Alliances, establish Commerce, and to do all other Acts and Things which Independent States may of right do.

And for the support of this Declaration, with a firm reliance on the Protection of Divine Providence, we mutually pledge to each other our Lives, our Fortunes and our sacred Honor.

John Hancock
President from Massachusetts

Georgia
Button Gwinnett
Lyman Hall
George Walton

North Carolina
William Hooper
Joseph Hewes
John Penn

South Carolina
Edward Rutledge
Thomas Heyward, Jr.
Thomas Lynch, Jr.
Arthur Middleton

Maryland
Samuel Chase
William Paca
Thomas Stone
Charles Carroll of Carrollton

Virginia
George Wythe
Richard Henry Lee
Thomas Jefferson
Benjamin Harrison
Thomas Nelson, Jr.
Francis Lightfoot Lee
Carter Braxton

Pennsylvania
Robert Morris
Benjamin Rush
Benjamin Franklin
John Morton
George Clymer
James Smith
George Taylor
James Wilson
George Ross

Delaware
Caesar Rodney
George Read
Thomas McKean

New York
William Floyd
Philip Livingston
Francis Lewis
Lewis Morris

New Jersey
Richard Stockton
John Witherspoon
Francis Hopkinson
John Hart
Abraham Clark

New Hampshire
Josiah Bartlett
William Whipple
Matthew Thornton

Massachusetts
Samuel Adams
John Adams
Robert Treat Paine
Elbridge Gerry

Rhode Island
Stephen Hopkins
William Ellery

Connecticut
Samuel Huntington
William Williams
Oliver Wolcott
Roger Sherman

What It Means

Resolution of Independence The Final section declares that the colonies are "Free and Independent States" with the full power to make war, to form alliances, and to trade with other countries.

rectitude *rightness*

What It Means

Signers of the Declaration The signers, as representatives of the American people, declared the colonies independent from Great Britain. Most members signed the document on August 2, 1776.

A Changing World

Native Americans were the first people to live in the Americas. Europeans and enslaved Africans arrived next. In England new ideas about government evolved. English colonists used those ideas to form the United States of America.

	Chapter 1: Expanding Horizons	Chapter 2: Road to Independence
When	• 1200s–1700s	• 1600s–1700s
Where	• Europe • Asia • Africa • Central America • South America • North America	• New England • West Africa • West Indies • Southern Colonies • Middle Colonies • Great Britain

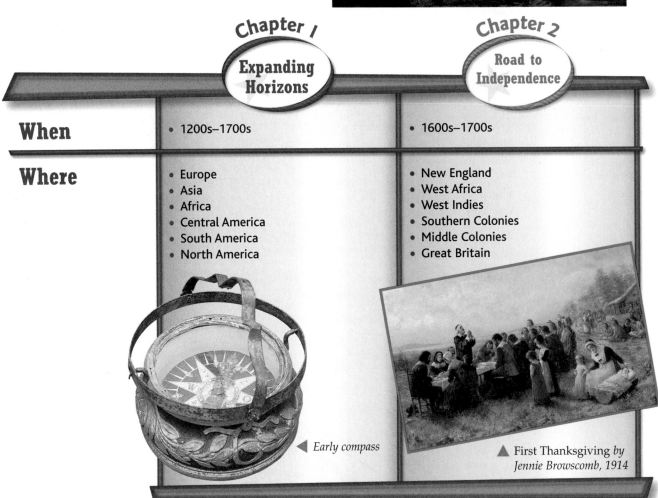

◀ *Early compass*

▲ First Thanksgiving *by Jennie Browscomb, 1914*

	Chapter 1: Expanding Horizons	Chapter 2: Road to Independence
Major Events	• **1215** King John signs Magna Carta • **c. 1400s** Technological advances lead to Age of Exploration and growth of trade • **1492** Columbus reaches the Americas • **1517** Martin Luther's calls for change begin the Reformation • **1521, 1532** Conquistadors conquer Aztec and Inca empires • **1588** English defeat Spanish Armada • **c. 1600s** Governments begin to charter banks • **c. 1600s** Mercantilism becomes basis for national policies • **1689** Bill of Rights guarantees all English people basic rights • **1690** John Locke states that people have rights based on natural law	• **1607** Jamestown is first permanent English colony • **1619** Representatives to House of Burgesses meet • **1620** Pilgrims sign Mayflower Compact • **1730s–1740s** Great Awakening sweeps through English colonies • **1763** Proclamation of 1763 forbids settlement west of Appalachians • **1770** Boston Massacre leads to more boycotts of British goods • **1773** Boston Tea Party protests tax on tea • **1775** First battles of Revolution are fought at Lexington and Concord • **1776** Declaration of Independence is signed • **1781** British surrender at Yorktown
Some Important People	• Christopher Columbus • Queen Elizabeth I • John Locke • Isaac Newton  *Christopher Columbus* ▶	• Roger Williams • Jonathan Edwards • Benjamin Franklin • George Washington
 **How do these events and ideas affect our lives today?**	• School subjects are rooted in Renaissance learning. • Spanish heritage is an important part of North American culture.	• American Patriots supported rights (free speech, religion, press) that we enjoy today.  *Revolutionary War drum and fife* ▲
What was happening in California at this time?	• **1533** Spanish expedition reaches Baja California peninsula • **1542** Juan Cabrillo reaches San Diego Bay • **1579** Francis Drake encounters Coast Miwok people	• **1769** Father Junípero Serra sets up first mission at San Diego • **1776** Juan Bautista de Anza discovers trail from Sonora to San Francisco area  *Juan Bautista de Anza* ▶

Unit
2

Creating a Nation

Why It's Important

After the American Revolution, the new nation struggled to draw up a plan of government. Created to meet the needs of a changing nation, the Constitution has been the fundamental law of the United States for more than 200 years. Many developments of this period shape our lives today.

- The Constitution is central to American life and ideals.
- The Constitution has served as a model for many constitutions all over the world.

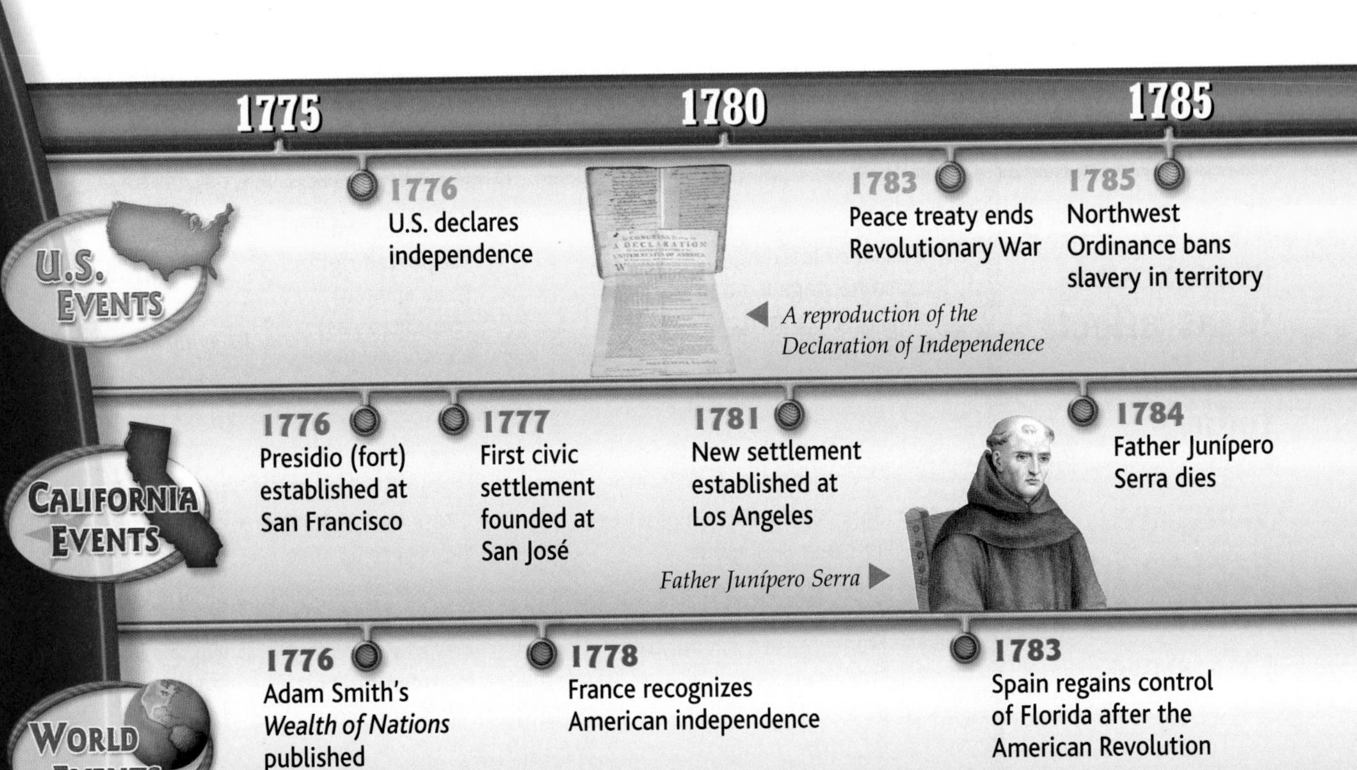
1775
1780
1785
U.S. EVENTS
1776
U.S. declares independence
1783
Peace treaty ends Revolutionary War
1785
Northwest Ordinance bans slavery in territory
CALIFORNIA EVENTS
1776
Presidio (fort) established at San Francisco
1777
First civic settlement founded at San José
1781
New settlement established at Los Angeles
1784
Father Junípero Serra dies
WORLD EVENTS
1776
Adam Smith's *Wealth of Nations* published
1778
France recognizes American independence
1783
Spain regains control of Florida after the American Revolution

A reproduction of the Declaration of Independence

Father Junípero Serra

NATIONAL GEOGRAPHIC

Where in the United States?

1797 Mission San José founded

1800 The Library of Congress, founded in Washington, D.C.

1793 Eli Whitney designs cotton gin in Savannah, Georgia

130°W

PACIFIC OCEAN

ATLANTIC OCEAN

70°W

Gulf of Mexico

N W E S

110°W 90°W 80°W

0 300 miles
0 300 kilometers

Azimuthal Equidistant projection

The U.S. in 1800

- Established States
- British
- U.S. Territory
- French
- Spanish
- Disputed Area

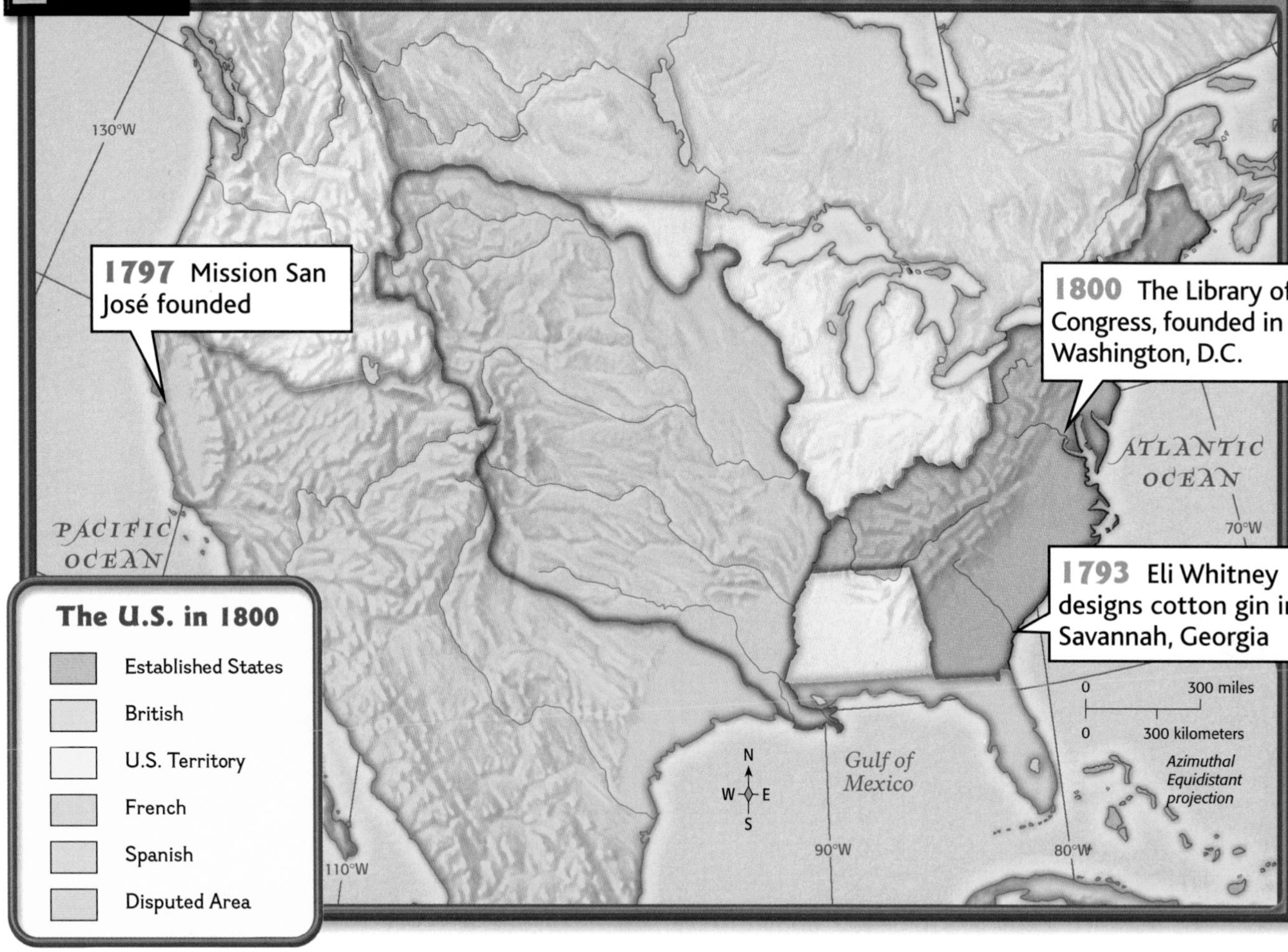

1790 1795 1800

1788
U.S. Constitution ratified

◀ *Eli Whitney*

1793
Eli Whitney designs cotton gin in Savannah, Georgia

▼ *The Library of Congress*

1800
The Library of Congress founded in Washington, D.C.

1791
Mission Santa Cruz established

◀ *San Luis Rey Mission*

1797
Mission San José founded

1798
San Luis Rey founded; it is the 18th of 21 California missions

1789
French Revolution begins

1796
English doctor Edward Jenner invents smallpox vaccine

1799
Rosetta Stone discovered

Unit 2 Places to Locate

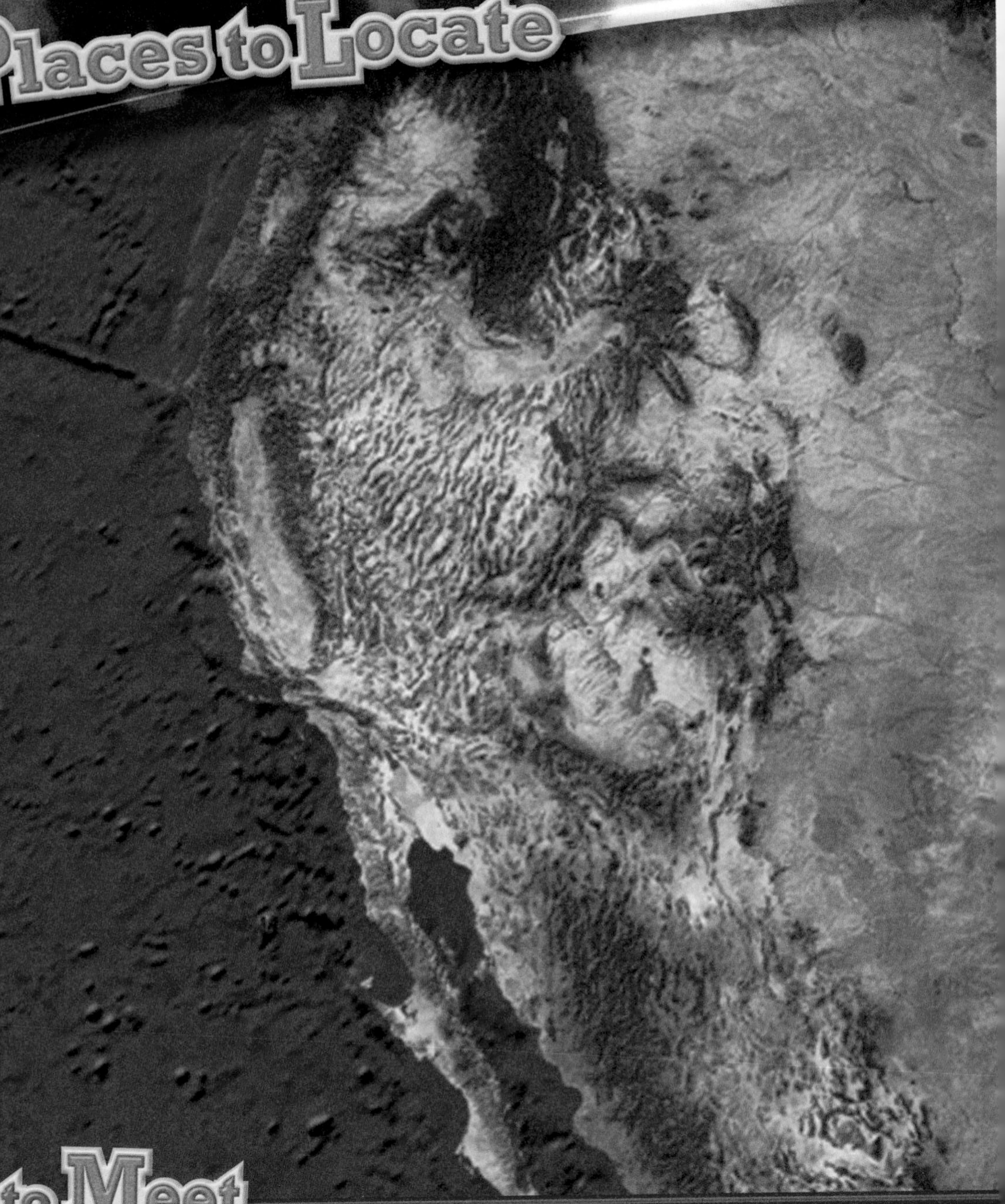

1 The Northwest Territory

See *A More Perfect Union* Chapter 3

2 Shays's Rebellion

See *A More Perfect Union* Chapter 3

People to Meet

Richard Allen
1760–1831
Philadelphia preacher
Chapter 3, page 196

Absalom Jones
1746–1818
Philadelphia preacher
Chapter 3, page 196

James Madison
1751–1836
Architect of the Constitution
Chapter 3, page 198

Roger Sherman
1721–1793
Creator of the Great Compromise
Chapter 3, page 199

NATIONAL GEOGRAPHIC

1
2
3
4

3 INDEPENDENCE HALL

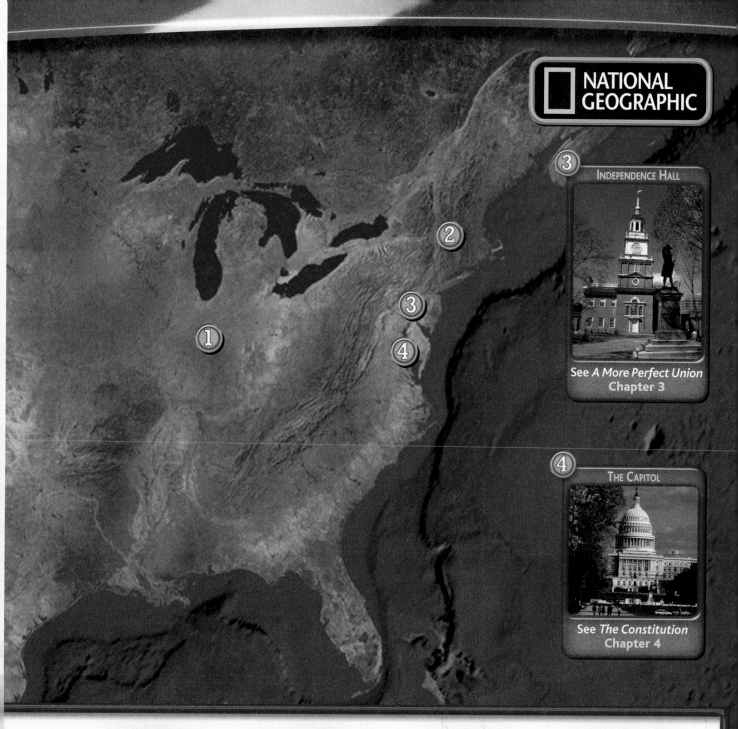

See *A More Perfect Union* Chapter 3

4 THE CAPITOL

See *The Constitution* Chapter 4

George Mason
1725–1792
Political leader
Chapter 3, page 201

Mercy Otis Warren
1728–1814
Political writer
Chapter 3, page 206

Gouverneur Morris
1752–1816
Writer and editor of the Constitution
Chapter 4, page 220

John Marshall
1755–1835
Chief Justice of the Supreme Court
Chapter 4, page 232

A More Perfect Union

Philadelphia's Independence Hall

Where & When?

NORTHWEST TERRITORY

THE UNITED STATES

1770 | 1780 | 1790

1777 Articles of Confederation written

1787 U.S. Constitution signed

1788 U.S. Constitution ratified

History Online
Chapter Overview Visit ca.hss.glencoe.com for a preview of Chapter 3.

The Big Ideas

The Articles of Confederation

Political ideas and major events shape how people form governments. When the American colonies broke their political ties with Great Britain, they faced the task of forming independent governments at both the state and national levels.

Convention and Compromise

A constitution reflects the values and goals of a society that creates it. The new Constitution corrected the weaknesses of government under the Articles of Confederation.

A New Plan of Government

Political ideas and major events shape how people form governments. The United States system of government rests on the Constitution.

View the Chapter 3 video in the Glencoe Video Program.

Compare and Contrast Make this foldable to help you compare the Articles of Confederation to the U.S. Constitution.

Step 1 Fold a sheet of paper from side to side, leaving a 2-inch tab uncovered along the side.

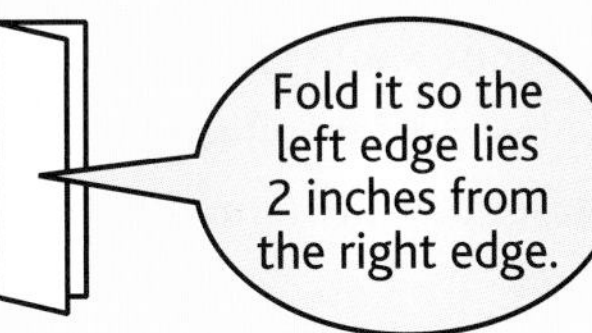

Fold it so the left edge lies 2 inches from the right edge.

Step 2 Turn the paper and fold it into thirds.

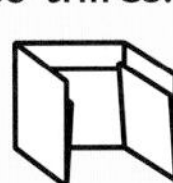

Step 3 Unfold and cut along the two inside fold lines.

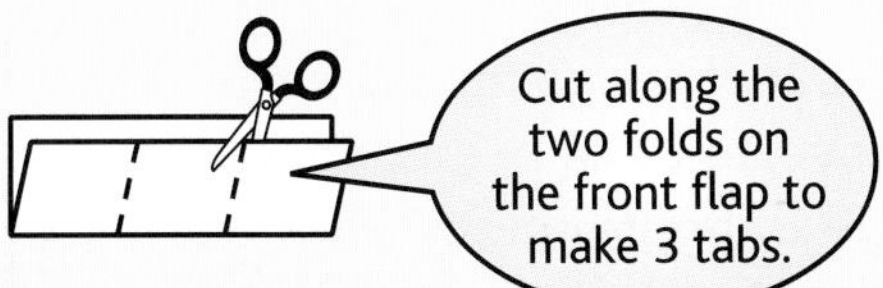

Cut along the two folds on the front flap to make 3 tabs.

Step 4 Label the foldable as shown.

A More Perfect Union

Articles of Confederation | Both | U.S. Constitution

Reading and Writing As you read the chapter, write what you learn about these documents under the appropriate tabs.

Get Ready to Read

Making Connections

1 Learn It!

Good readers make connections between what they are reading and what they know. Some connections are based on personal experiences (text-to-self). Readers also make connections to things they have read in other books (text-to-text). Finally, good readers make connections to things that happen in other places (text-to-world). Making these connections helps you understand words or ideas that are unfamiliar to you and gain knowledge about the world. As you read, ask yourself connecting questions. Are you reminded of something from your life, something you have read, or a person or event in another place or time? Read the paragraph below with these questions in mind.

Text-to-self:
What do you know about how people think and act? What do you think about government?

Framers of the Constitution got many ideas on the nature of people and government from European writers of the Enlightenment. The Enlightenment (ihn•LY•tuhn•muhnt) was a movement of the 1700s that promoted knowledge, reason, and science as the means to improve society.

—from page 203

Text-to-text:
What did you read about the Enlightenment in Chapter 1?

Text-to-world:
What other countries have governments based on ideals of the Enlightenment? How do knowledge, reason, and science impact government today?

Reading Tip

Make connections with important ideas, times, and topics in your life. Connecting helps you remember new information.

2 Practice It!

Read the following paragraphs. Then make a list of connections you made to the ideas in the reading. Compare your lists and discuss your answers with a partner.

Read to Write

Choose one of the connections you made that was different than your partner's or one that you think was more important. Write a paragraph to explain why you made such a connection. Use vivid details.

> The Northwest Ordinance provided a democratic model for national expansion. When the population of a territory reached 60,000, its people could petition, or apply to Congress, for statehood. Each new state would come into the Union with the same rights and privileges as the original 13 states.
>
> The Northwest Ordinance also guaranteed certain rights to people living in the territory. These rights included freedom of religion, property rights, and the right to trial by jury.
>
> —*from page 181–182*

3 Apply It!

As you read this chapter, choose five words or phrases that make a connection to something you already know.

The Articles of Confederation

Guide to Reading

History Social Science Standards

US8.2 Students analyze the political principles underlying the U.S. Constitution and compare the enumerated and implied powers of the federal government.

US8.3 Students understand the foundation of the American political system and the ways in which citizens participate in it.

US8.9 Students analyze the early and steady attempts to abolish slavery and to realize the ideals of the Declaration of Independence.

Looking Back, Looking Ahead

In Chapter 2, you learned about the American Revolution. The United States was now independent, but it remained to be seen whether the new nation could survive.

Focusing on the Main Ideas

- As soon as the Declaration of Independence was signed, the 13 states began writing their own constitutions. *(page 179)*
- Americans realized the necessity of establishing a central, or national, government for the 13 states. *(page 180)*
- The weaknesses of the Articles of Confederation created problems for the new country. *(page 183)*

Locating Places

Appalachian Mountains (A • puh • LAY • chuhn)
Northwest Territory

Meeting People

Robert Morris
John Jay

Content Vocabulary

popular sovereignty (PAH • pyuh • luhr SAH • vuhrn • tee)
bicameral (by • KAM • ruhl)
confederation (kuhn • FEH • duh • RAY • shuhn)
sovereignty (SAH • vuhrn • tee)
ratify (RA • tuh • fy)
ordinance (AWR • duhn • uhnts)
right of deposit (di • PAH • zuht)

Academic Vocabulary

interpret (ihn • TUHR • pruht)
authority (uh • THAHR • uh • tee)

Reading Strategy

Organizing Draw a diagram like the one below. In each oval, list a power you think a national government should have.

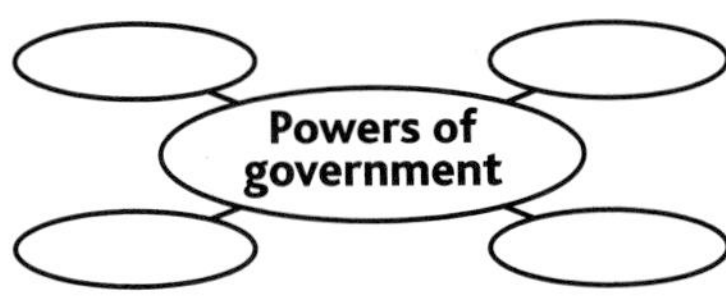

As You Read

Earlier in this story, a very emotional scene took place in the Ashleys' kitchen. Bett angrily told Mistress Ashley that she was leaving and not coming back. The mistress got very upset, cried, and apologized to Bett. Then she told Bett that she could not leave, but Bett did. The following scene is also about Bett's freedom, but it takes place in a courtroom. Think about how the setting affects what people say and do.

Master Noble called Master Ashley to the stand and questioned him: How had he come to own us? Had he seen to it that we were well fed, clothed, and housed? Had he seen to it that we were changed from heathens[1] to Christians? The master answered, "Yes, I have." When Master Reeve said he had no questions, Master Noble said, "I call Mistress Anna Ashley."

There was a stir in the crowd as she made her way to the stand. As always, when she was in public, she was confident and assured. She seemed not to notice anything around her, except once to raise her eyes to the ceiling. She mopped her brow, suffering from the heat. "Will you describe to the court your relationship with your servant, Bett?" her lawyer asked.

"Bett is like one in my family. She was born on my father's land and has been a servant of mine even before I married her master. We have never quarreled, and I have been nothing but kind to her."

I was afraid I was going to start laughing, so I closed my ears and mind to her and held on to keep from being tossed out of the place. How could she sit there pretending that she was a good mistress? I looked at my sister, who sat upright and calm, and I wondered, if asked to disagree with the mistress, would she have the will to do so?

[1] **heathens:** at this time and place, someone who does not believe in the Christian God

Master Reeve said he had no questions for the mistress and called Bett. I could tell that Bett was reluctant. He whispered something to her, and finally she came forward and sat in the seat where the mistress had sat. "Your honor," Master Reeve said, "I would like to prove that the mistress Ashley is not the kind mistress she claims." He then turned to the jury. "The issue here is not whether the Ashleys have been kind. The issue is, do they have the right to hold Bett and Brom as slaves for life?" He turned to Bett. "Has Mistress Ashley ever in any way abused you?"

My sister looked at the judge and then at Lawyer Reeve. She did not speak. The courtroom was hushed, waiting. Answer him! I wanted to say. Why didn't she tell them and show the ugly wound on her arm?

Bett looked at the mistress, who was staring Bett in the face. "Yes, Master Reeve, she is not the kind person she wants people to believe she is. I have been in her household many years and was never paid one pence.[2] We work six days a week and sometimes on the seventh. But whether she is kind or not, the constitution says we have rights to our freedom."

"No further questions," Mr. Reeve said.

Master Noble stood and said, "Bett, you sit here well dressed, in good health, with nothing to even hint at your being anything but blessed[3] to be a servant of the Ashleys." There was applause and sounds of "Hear, hear!"

The judge pounded on his desk. "There must be order in this court. Continue, Mr. Noble."

"You know your master and mistress have been good to you, haven't they, Bett?"

"I object," Lawyer Reeve said. "Whether they were good to her is not the question here."

"Objection sustained."

"Your honor, my worthy opponent asked if she had been abused. May I rephrase the question? What proof can you give to this court of Mistress Ashley's abuse?" Lawyer Noble asked.

My sister looked at the mistress, then at the judge. She did not answer. Was she afraid, thinking What if we lost? What would the master and mistress do to us? I felt cold sweat rolling down my sides. In that room that had been almost unbearably warm, I became chilled.

[2] **pence:** a unit of British money that has very little value

[3] **blessed:** bringing pleasure or good luck

Angry farmers lashed out. Led by **Daniel Shays,** a former Continental Army captain, they forced courts in western Massachusetts to close so judges could not confiscate farmers' lands.

In January 1787, Shays led more than 1,000 farmers toward the federal arsenal in Springfield, Massachusetts, to seize arms and ammunition. The state militia ordered the advancing farmers to halt, then fired over their heads. The farmers did not stop, and the militia fired again, killing four rebels. Shays and his followers scattered, and the uprising was over.

Shays's Rebellion frightened many national leaders. They worried that the government could not control unrest and prevent violence. On hearing of the rebellion, George Washington wondered whether "mankind, when left to themselves, are unfit for their own government." Thomas Jefferson, minister to France at the time, had a different view. "A little rebellion, now and then," he wrote, "is a good thing."

The Issue of Slavery The Revolutionary War brought attention to the contradiction between the American battle for liberty and the practice of slavery. The Southern states accepted the institution of slavery. The plantation system of the South had been built on slavery, and many Southerners feared that their economy could not survive without it.

Although slavery was not a major source of labor in the North, it existed and was legal in all the Northern states. Many individuals and groups began to work to end the institution of slavery. In 1774 Quakers in Pennsylvania organized the first American antislavery society. Six years later, Pennsylvania passed a law that provided for the gradual freeing of enslaved people.

Between 1783 and 1804, Connecticut, Rhode Island, New York, and New Jersey passed laws that gradually ended slavery. Still, free African Americans faced discrimination. They were barred from many public places. Few states gave free African Americans the right to vote.

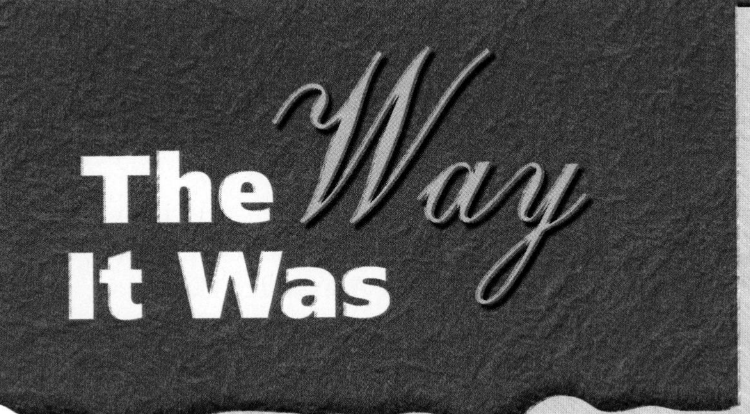

The coneflower is a popular Native American plant. As medicine, it is commonly called Echinacea.

Home Remedies

In an age before germs and proper sanitation were understood, home remedies for illnesses became an everyday part of life in early America. While some folk remedies, such as herbal teas, might have had positive effects, other cures could make the patient worse.

For a venomous snakebite, a part of the snake was placed on top of the wound. This, it was thought, would draw out the poison.

Some remedies used by Native Americans were later adopted by Europeans. The Inca, for example, found that boiling a certain kind of tree bark in water eased the symptoms of malaria. But it was not until the 1900s that the ingredient in the tree bark—quinine—was finally isolated.

Richard Allen and Absalom Jones

Philadelphia preachers Richard Allen and Absalom Jones founded the Free American Society and later set up the first African American churches.

▲ Richard Allen

Born in slavery, Richard Allen was freed and became a Methodist minister. Allen and Absalom Jones founded an independent Methodist church for black members. In the early 1800s, some African American movements encouraged immigration to Africa. Allen and Jones opposed this idea, stating that since

▲ Absalom Jones

"our ancestors (not of choice) were the first successful cultivators of the wilds of America, we their descendants feel ourselves entitled to participate in the blessings of her luxuriant soil. . . . "

—Bethel Church Resolution

DBQ Document-Based Question

Why did Allen and Jones believe African Americans should stay in America even though they had been brought there against their will?

The children of most free blacks had to attend separate schools. Free African Americans established their own institutions—churches, schools, and mutual-aid societies—to seek opportunity.

An increasing number of slaveholders began freeing the enslaved people that they held after the war. Virginia passed a law that encouraged **manumission** (MAN • yuh • MIH • shuhn), the freeing of individual enslaved persons, and the state's population of free African Americans grew.

The abolition of slavery in the North divided the new country on the issue of whether people should be allowed to hold other human beings in bondage. This division came at the time when many American leaders had decided that the Articles of Confederation needed to be strengthened. In the summer of 1787, when state representatives assembled to plan a new government, they compromised on this issue. It would take years of debate, bloodshed, and ultimately a war to settle the slavery question.

A Call for Change The American Revolution had led to a union of 13 states, but it had not yet created a nation. Some leaders believed that a strong national government was the solution to America's problems. They demanded a reform of the Articles of Confederation.

Two Americans who were active in the movement for change were **James Madison,** a Virginia planter, and **Alexander Hamilton,** a New York lawyer. In September 1786, Hamilton proposed calling a convention in Philadelphia to discuss trade issues. He also suggested that this convention consider what possible changes were needed to make the Articles work.

At first, George Washington was not enthusiastic about the movement to revise the Articles of Confederation. When he heard the news of Shays's Rebellion, Washington changed his mind. After Washington agreed to attend the Philadelphia convention, the meeting took on greater significance.

Reading Check **Evaluate** Why did Madison and Hamilton call for a convention in 1787?

US8.2.3 Evaluate the major debates that occurred during the development of the Constitution and their ultimate resolutions in such areas as shared power among institutions, divided state-federal power, slavery, the rights of individuals and states (later addressed by the addition of the Bill of Rights), and the status of American Indians under the commerce clause.

The Constitutional Convention

Main Idea **National leaders worked to produce a new constitution for the United States.**

Reading Connection Why is it important for a nation to establish a set of laws? Read to find out the issues American leaders faced in organizing a new constitution.

The Philadelphia meeting began in May 1787 and continued through one of the hottest summers on record. The 55 delegates included planters, merchants, lawyers, physicians, generals, governors, and a college president. Three of the delegates were under 30 years of age, and one, Benjamin Franklin, was over 80. Many were well educated. At a time when only one white man in 1,000 went to college, 26 of the delegates had college degrees. Native Americans, African Americans, and women were not considered part of the political process, so none attended.

Several men stood out as leaders. The presence of George Washington and Benjamin Franklin ensured that many people would trust the Convention's work. Two Philadelphians also played key roles. James Wilson often read Franklin's speeches and did important work on the details of the Constitution. **Gouverneur Morris,** a powerful speaker and writer, wrote the final draft of the Constitution.

Two revolutionary leaders who had thought deeply about the best form of government were absent. John Adams of Massachusetts and Thomas Jefferson of Virginia were in Europe serving as ambassadors. From Virginia came **Edmund Randolph** and James Madison. Both were keen supporters of a strong national government. Randolph had served in the Continental Congress and was governor of Virginia. Madison's careful notes are the major source of information about the Convention's work. Madison is often called the Father of the Constitution because he was the author of the basic plan of government that the Convention adopted.

▲ Delegates to the Constitutional Convention met in this room at Independence Hall.

Working on the Constitution

The delegates to the Constitutional Convention worked for 116 days (of which they actually met on 89) in a room where the windows were usually shut. None of the delegates wanted anybody to hear what they were doing, because they did not want rumors spread about the form of government upon which they would ultimately decide. Besides, if they opened the windows, hordes of flies would descend upon them. The air became humid and hot by noon of each day.

Biography

US8.2.4 Describe the political philosophy underpinning the Constitution as specified in the Federalist Papers (authored by James Madison, Alexander Hamilton, and John Jay) and the role of such leaders as Madison, George Washington, Roger Sherman, Gouverneur Morris, and James Wilson in the writing and ratification of the Constitution.

JAMES MADISON

c. 1751–1836

Born in 1751, Madison was still a young man at the time of the American Revolution, but his brilliant, incisive mind made him one of the more valuable leaders of the Patriots. After the war, he played a major role at the Constitutional Convention.

As one of the delegates from Virginia, Madison participated in the lengthy, often heated discussions that created a foundation of government. He kept meticulous notes and tried to impress upon the other delegates the need for an effective central government. Power was to be distributed throughout the whole. Every right had to be balanced by a corresponding responsibility.

Madison became the chief architect of the Constitution, and his notes became the best record of what happened at the Convention. There were no official transcripts of the work of the delegates. If Madison had not kept a private diary of the events, historians might know little about what happened in Philadelphia. "Every word *[of the Constitution],*" he later wrote, "decides a question between power and liberty."

After the Constitution went into effect, Madison became a leader of the new national government. In developing the Bill of Rights, he once again was trying to achieve the difficult balance between the rights of the people and the power of government. In 1808 Madison became the fourth president of the United States. Throughout his career, he continued to defend the principle of balance that was built into the Constitution.

"In framing a government . . . you must first enable the government to control the governed; and in the next place, oblige it to control itself."

—James Madison
***The Federalist*, No. 51**

Then and Now

What qualities did Madison possess that made him a leader and an important part of the constitutional process? Do you think these are important qualities for a political leader today? Explain.

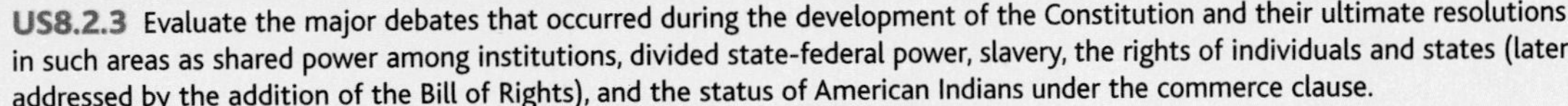

US8.2.3 Evaluate the major debates that occurred during the development of the Constitution and their ultimate resolutions in such areas as shared power among institutions, divided state-federal power, slavery, the rights of individuals and states (later addressed by the addition of the Bill of Rights), and the status of American Indians under the commerce clause.

Organization The Convention began by unanimously choosing George Washington to preside over the meetings. It was also decided that each state would have one vote on all questions. Decisions would be made by a majority vote of those states present. The delegates decided to keep the sessions secret. This decision made it possible for the delegates to talk freely.

The Virginia Plan After the rules were adopted, the Convention opened with a surprise. Edmund Randolph proposed that the delegates create a strong national government instead of revising the Articles of Confederation. He introduced the Virginia Plan, which was largely the work of James Madison.

The plan called for a two-house legislature, a chief executive chosen by the legislature, and a court system. The members of the lower house of the legislature would be elected by the people. The members of the upper house would be chosen by the lower house. In both houses, the number of representatives would be **proportional** (pruh • POHR • shuh • nuhl), or corresponding in size, to the population of each state. This would give Virginia many more delegates than Delaware, the smallest state.

Delegates from small states objected to the plan. They preferred the Confederation system in which all states were represented equally. On June 15 William Paterson of New Jersey presented an alternative plan that revised the Articles of Confederation, which was all the convention was empowered to do.

The New Jersey Plan The New Jersey Plan kept the Confederation's one-house legislature, with one vote for each state. Congress, however, could set taxes and **regulate** trade—powers it did not have under the Articles. Congress would elect a weak executive branch consisting of more than one person. Paterson argued that the Convention should not deprive the smaller states of the equality they had under the Articles.

Reading Check **Explain** Why did some delegates criticize the Virginia Plan?

Compromise Wins Out

Main Idea **The Constitutional Convention broke the deadlock over the form the new government would take.**

Reading Connection Have you and a rival ever set aside your differences to work for a common cause? This happened when American leaders resolved their differences to create a new constitution.

The convention delegates had to decide whether they were simply revising the Articles of Confederation or writing a constitution for a new national government. On June 19 the states voted to work toward a national government based on the Virginia Plan, but they still had to resolve the thorny issue of representation that divided the large and small states.

As the convention delegates struggled to deal with difficult questions, tempers and temperatures grew hotter. How were the members of Congress to be elected? How would state representation be determined in the upper and lower houses? Were enslaved people to be counted as part of the population on which representation was based?

Under Franklin's leadership, the convention appointed a "grand committee" to try to resolve their disagreements. **Roger Sherman** of Connecticut suggested what came to be known as the Great Compromise. A **compromise** is an agreement between two or more sides in which each side gives up some of what it wants.

Sherman proposed a two-house legislature. In the lower house—the House of Representatives—the number of seats for each state would vary according to the state's population. In the upper house—the Senate—each state would have two members.

Another compromise by the delegates dealt with counting enslaved people. Southern states wanted to include the enslaved in their population counts to gain delegates in the House of Representatives.

Linking Past & Present

Symbols of the Nation

Past For Americans, the flag has always had a special meaning. It is a symbol of our nation's freedom and democracy. On June 14, 1777, the Continental Congress designed the first Stars and Stripes. The first flag had 13 stars and 13 stripes. Each star represented a state. Each stripe represented one of the 13 colonies that formed the Union.

▼ The Stars and Stripes today

▲ A legend says that Betsy Ross created the American flag.

Present Many of the symbols through which we express our American identity—heroes, songs, legends, flags, monuments—developed in the early 1800s. Some of our holidays, such as the Fourth of July, and the ways we celebrate them with parades, speeches, and picnics, became established during that time. ***What are other symbols of our nation?***

Objections Are Raised Northern states objected to this idea because enslaved people were legally considered property. Some delegates from Northern states argued that the enslaved, as property, should be counted for the purpose of taxation but not representation. However, neither side considered giving enslaved people the right to vote.

The committee's solution, known as the Three-Fifths Compromise, was to count each enslaved person as three-fifths of a free person for both taxation and representation. In other words, every five enslaved persons would equal three free persons. On July 12, the convention delegates voted to approve the Three-Fifths Compromise. Four days later, they agreed that each state should elect two senators.

Slave Trade The dispute over how to count enslaved people was not the only issue dividing the delegates. The convention needed to resolve another difficult issue that divided the Northern and Southern states. Some Northern delegates wanted to slow the spread of slavery and stop the importation of new slaves. Southern states considered slavery and the slave trade essential to their economies.

To keep the Southern states in the nation, Northerners agreed that the Congress could not interfere with the slave trade until 1808. Beginning that year, Congress could limit the slave trade if it chose to.

Approving the Constitution George Mason of Virginia proposed a bill of rights to be included in the Constitution. Some delegates worried that without the protection of a bill of rights, the new national government might abuse its power. However, most of the delegates believed that the Constitution, with its carefully defined listing of government powers, provided **adequate** protection of individual rights. Mason's proposal was defeated.

The committees finished their work on the Constitution in late summer. On September 17, 1787, the delegates assembled in the Philadelphia State House to sign the document. Franklin made a final plea for approval: "I consent to this Constitution because I expect no better, and because I am not sure, that it is not the best."

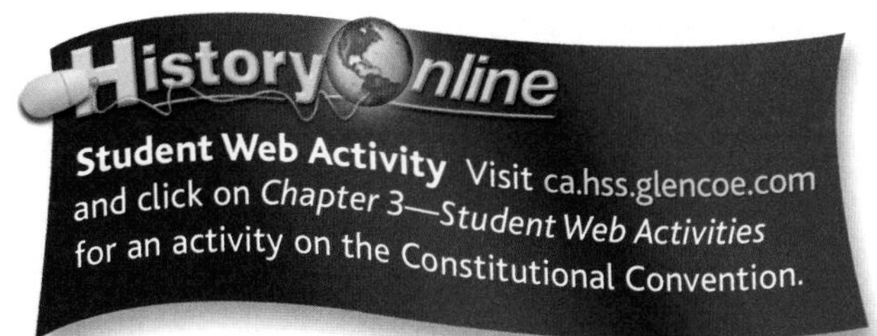

History Online
Student Web Activity Visit ca.hss.glencoe.com and click on Chapter 3—Student Web Activities for an activity on the Constitutional Convention.

Three delegates refused to sign—Elbridge Gerry of Massachusetts, and Edmund Randolph and George Mason of Virginia. Gerry and Mason would not sign without a bill of rights.

The Confederation Congress then sent the approved draft of the Constitution to the states for consideration. To amend the Articles of Confederation had required unanimous approval of the states. The delegates agreed to change the approval process for the Constitution. When 9 of the 13 states had approved, the new government of the United States would come into existence. *(See pages 248–269 for the entire text of the Constitution.)*

Reading Check **Analyze** Who refused to sign the Constitution? Explain why.

History Online
Study Central Need help understanding the Constitutional Convention? Visit ca.hss.glencoe.com and click on Study Central.

Section 2 Review

Reading Summary

Review the Main Ideas

- The government under the Articles of Confederation faced many problems.
- National leaders worked to produce a new constitution for the United States.
- The Constitutional Convention broke the deadlock over the form the new government would take.

What Did You Learn?

1. Explain what caused Shays's Rebellion. What was one effect?
2. According to the Virginia Plan, who elected the members of the lower house?

Critical Thinking

3. **Analyze Information** Re-create the diagram below and identify arguments for and against approving the Constitution. CA HI1.

Ratification	
Arguments for	Arguments against

4. **The Big Ideas** How did the new Constitution reflect the values of the men who wrote it?
5. **ANALYSIS** How did the Great Compromise satisfy both the small and the large states on the question of representation? Why was this compromise important? Write a paragraph summarizing your conclusions. CA CS1.
6. **Persuasive Writing** Write a short speech in favor of either the Virginia Plan or the New Jersey Plan. CA 8LS1.3

A New Plan of Government

Guide to Reading

History Social Science Standards

US8.2 Students analyze the political principles underlying the U.S. Constitution and compare the enumerated and implied powers of the federal government.

US8.3 Students understand the foundation of the American political system and the ways in which citizens participate in it.

Looking Back, Looking Ahead

You read about the compromises that the delegates made to create a new form of government. The Constitution was based on the political ideals of the people who wrote it.

Focusing on the Main Ideas

- Ideas and thinkers of the past influenced the creation of the United States Constitution. *(page 203)*
- The Constitution outlines the responsibilities and the limits of the three branches of government. *(page 204)*
- Americans reacted to the proposed Constitution in different ways. *(page 206)*

Meeting People

John Jay
Mercy Otis Warren

Content Vocabulary

Enlightenment (ihn • LY • tuhn • muhnt)
federalism
article
legislative branch (LEH • juhs • LAY • tihv)
executive branch (ihg • ZEH • kuh • tihv)
judicial branch (ju • DIH • shuhl)
checks and balances
ratify (RA • tuh • FY)
Federalist
Antifederalist

Academic Vocabulary

promote (pruh • MOHT)
conduct (kuhn • DUHKT)

Reading Strategy

Organizing Information Create a diagram to explain how the system of checks and balances works.

	Has check or balance over:	Example
President		
Congress		
Supreme Court		

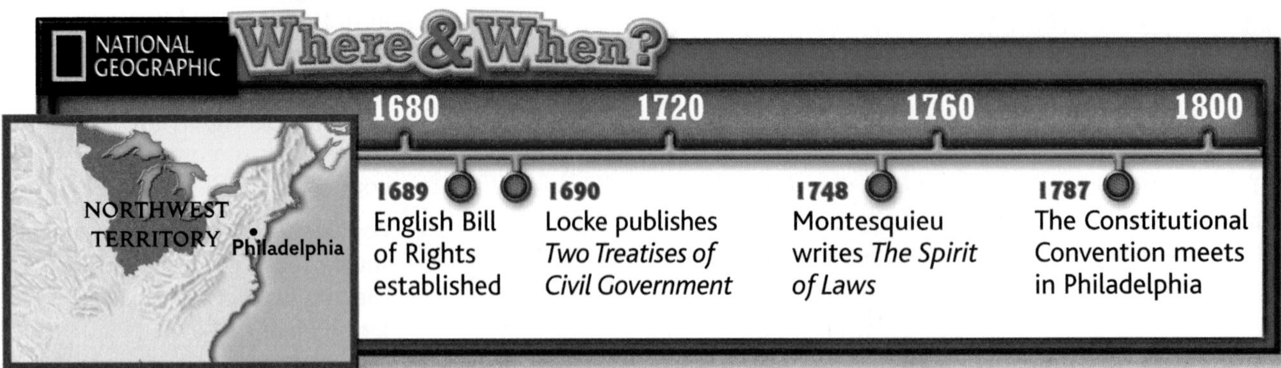

NATIONAL GEOGRAPHIC
Where & When?
NORTHWEST TERRITORY
Philadelphia
1680
1720
1760
1800
1689 English Bill of Rights established
1690 Locke publishes *Two Treatises of Civil Government*
1748 Montesquieu writes *The Spirit of Laws*
1787 The Constitutional Convention meets in Philadelphia

US8.2.1 Discuss the significance of the Magna Carta, the English Bill of Rights, and the Mayflower Compact.

Roots of the Constitution

Main Idea **Ideas and thinkers of the past influenced the creation of the United States Constitution.**

Reading Connection Do you have a role model? Has a person you know influenced you to do better in school or take part in a helping activity? Read to learn about the thinkers who influenced the creation of the Constitution.

An American Story

As Benjamin Franklin was leaving the last session of the Constitutional Congress, a woman asked, "What kind of government have you given us, Dr. Franklin? A republic or a monarchy?" Franklin answered, "A republic, Madam, if you can keep it." Franklin's response indicated that a republic—a system of government in which the people elect representatives to exercise power for them—requires citizens to take an active role.

What Ideas Influenced the Framers?

After four long and difficult months, Franklin and the other delegates had produced a new constitution. The document provided the framework for a strong central government for the United States.

Although a uniquely American document, the Constitution has roots in many other civilizations. The delegates had studied and discussed the history of political development at length—starting with ancient Greece—so that their new government could avoid the mistakes of the past.

The Framers who shaped the document were familiar with the parliamentary system of Britain, and many had participated in the colonial assemblies or their state assemblies. They valued the individual rights guaranteed by the British judicial system. Although the Americans had broken away from Britain, they respected many British traditions.

The Magna Carta (1215) had placed limits on the power of the British monarch. England's lawmaking body, which is called Parliament, emerged as a force that the king had to depend on to pay for wars and to finance the royal government. Like Parliament, the assemblies that developed in the Thirteen Colonies controlled their colony's funds. For that reason, the assemblies had some control over colonial governors.

The English Bill of Rights of 1689 provided another important model for Americans. Many Americans believed that the Constitution also needed a bill of rights.

Enlightenment Thinkers Framers of the Constitution got many ideas on the nature of people and government from European writers of the Enlightenment. The **Enlightenment** (ihn • LY • tuhn • muhnt) was a movement of the 1700s that **promoted** knowledge, reason, and science as the means to improve society. James Madison and other architects of the Constitution were familiar with the work of John Locke and Baron de Montesquieu (mahn • tuhs • KYOO), two important philosophers.

Locke, an English philosopher, believed that all people have natural rights. These natural rights include the rights to life, liberty, and property. Many Americans interpreted natural rights to mean the rights of Englishmen defined in the Magna Carta and the English Bill of Rights.

▲ John Locke

In *The Spirit of Laws* (1748), the French writer Montesquieu declared that the powers of government should be separated and balanced against each other. This separation would keep any one person or group from gaining too much power. Following the ideas of Montesquieu, the Framers of the Constitution carefully specified and divided the powers of government.

Reading Check **Identify** What is a republic?

US8.2.3 Evaluate the major debates that occurred during the development of the Constitution and their ultimate resolutions in such areas as shared power among institutions, divided state-federal power, slavery, the rights of individuals and states (later addressed by the addition of the Bill of Rights), and the status of American Indians under the commerce clause.

The Federal System

Main Idea **The Constitution outlines the responsibilities and limits of the three branches of government.**

Reading Connection Do you think it is important to identify what leaders can and cannot do? Read to find out why the Constitution limits the government and what those limits are.

The Constitution created a federal system of government that divided powers between the national, or federal, government and the states. Under the Articles of Confederation, the states retained their sovereignty. Under the Constitution, the states gave up some of their powers to the federal government while keeping others.

America's *Architecture*

The Old Senate Chamber The U.S. Senate met in the Old Senate Chamber from 1810 until 1859. The two-story chamber is semicircular in shape and measures 75 feet long and 50 feet wide. Two visitors' galleries overlook the chamber. After the Senate moved to its present location, the room was occupied by the Supreme Court from 1860 until 1935. ***Which branches of government conducted business in the chamber?***

Shared Powers **Federalism,** or sharing power between the federal and state governments, is one of the distinctive features of the United States government. Under the Constitution, the federal government gained broad powers to tax, regulate trade, control the currency, raise an army, and declare war. It could also pass laws that were "necessary and proper" for carrying out its responsibilities.

However, the Constitution left important powers in the hands of the states. The states had the power to pass and enforce laws and regulate trade within their borders. They could also establish local governments, schools, and other institutions affecting their citizens.

Supreme Law of the Land The Constitution and the laws that Congress passed were to be "the supreme law of the land." No state could make laws or take actions that went against the Constitution. Any dispute between the federal government and the states was to be settled by the federal courts on the basis of the Constitution. Under the new federal system, the Constitution became the final and supreme authority.

The Organization of Government Influenced by Montesquieu's idea of a division of powers, the Framers divided the federal government into three branches—legislative, executive, and judicial. The first three **articles,** or parts, of the Constitution describe the powers and responsibilities of each branch.

Article I of the Constitution establishes Congress, the **legislative branch** (LEH•juhs•LAY•tihv), or lawmaking branch, of the government. The Congress of the United States is comprised of the House of Representatives and the Senate.

Picturing History

The Supreme Court has the final say in deciding what the Constitution means. ***What types of cases does the Supreme Court hear?***

The powers of Congress include collecting taxes, coining money, and regulating trade. Congress can also declare war and "raise and support armies." Finally, it makes all laws needed to fulfill the functions given to it as stated in the Constitution.

The Executive Branch Memories of King George III's rule made some delegates reluctant to establish a powerful executive, or ruler. Others believed that the Confederation had failed, in part, because it lacked an executive branch or president. They argued that a strong executive would serve as a check, or limit, on Congress.

Article II of the Constitution established the **executive branch** (ihg • ZEH • kuh • tihv), headed by the president, to carry out the nation's laws. The president serves as commander in chief of the armed forces and **conducts** relations with other countries.

The Judicial Branch Article III of the Constitution deals with the **judicial branch** (ju • DIH • shuhl), or court system, of the United States. The nation's judicial power resides in "one supreme Court" and any other lower federal courts that Congress might establish. The Supreme Court and the federal courts hear cases involving the Constitution, laws passed by Congress, and disputes between states.

System of Checks and Balances An important distinctive feature of our government is the separation of powers. The Constitution divides government power among the legislative, executive, and judicial branches. To keep any one branch from gaining too much power, the Framers built in a system of **checks and balances.** The three branches of government have roles that check, or limit, the others so that no single branch can dominate the government.

Both the House and the Senate must pass a bill for it to become law. The president can check Congress by vetoing, or rejecting, the bill. However, Congress can then check the president by overriding, or voting down, the veto. To override a veto, two-thirds of the members of both houses of Congress must vote for the bill.

The system of checks and balances also applies to the Supreme Court. The president appoints Supreme Court justices, and the Senate must approve the appointments.

Over time, the Court became a check on Congress and the president by ruling on the constitutionality of laws and presidential acts. The system has been successful in maintaining a balance of power among the branches of the federal government.

With these revolutionary changes, Americans showed the world that it was possible for a people to change its form of government through discussion and choice—rather than through chaos, force, or war. The rest of the world watched the new nation with interest to see whether its experiment in self-government would really work.

Reading Check **Explain** Why does the Constitution divide government power among the legislative, executive, and judicial branches?

US8.2.2 Analyze the Articles of Confederation and the Constitution and the success of each in implementing the ideals of the Declaration of Independence. **US8.2.4** Describe the political philosophy underpinning the Constitution as specified in the *Federalist Papers* (authored by James Madison, Alexander Hamilton, and John Jay) and the role of such leaders as Madison, George Washington, Roger Sherman, Gouverneur Morris, and James Wilson in the writing and ratification of the Constitution.

The Debate Over Ratification

Main Idea **Americans reacted to the proposed Constitution in different ways.**

Reading Connection Have you taken sides on an important issue? What arguments have you used to support your position? Read to learn about the arguments that Americans used to support or oppose ratification of the Constitution.

The delegates at Philadelphia had produced the Constitution, but its acceptance depended upon the will of the people. Gaining approval of the Constitution, with its radical new plan of government, was not going to be easy.

Before the Constitution could go into effect, nine states needed to **ratify** (RA • tuh • FY), or approve, it. State legislatures set up special ratifying conventions to consider the document. By late 1787 these conventions started to meet. Rhode Island stood apart. Its leaders opposed the Constitution from the beginning and therefore did not call a convention to approve it.

Powers of the Federal Government

	Articles of Confederation	United States Constitution
Declare war; make peace	✔	✔
Coin money	✔	✔
Manage foreign affairs	✔	✔
Establish a postal system	✔	✔
Impose taxes		✔
Regulate trade		✔
Organize a court system		✔
Call state militias for service		✔
Protect copyrights		✔
Take other necessary actions to run the federal government		✔

Understanding Charts

The Articles of Confederation and the U.S. Constitution specified certain powers that would be given to the federal government.

1. Which document allowed the government to organize state militias?
2. **Analyze** In what ways are the two documents similar?

Federalists Supporters of the new Constitution were called **Federalists.** Three of the nation's most gifted political thinkers—James Madison, Alexander Hamilton, and **John Jay**—also backed the Constitution.

Madison, Hamilton, and Jay worked together to write a series of essays explaining and defending the Constitution. These essays appeared in newspapers around the country and were widely read. Called the *Federalist Papers,* they were later published as a book and sent to delegates at the remaining ratifying conventions. Jefferson described the series of essays as "the best commentary on the principles of government which was ever written."

Antifederalists The Federalists called those who opposed ratification **Antifederalists.** Antifederalists criticized the Constitution because it lacked a bill of rights to protect individual freedoms. Antifederalists believed that no government could be trusted to protect the freedom of its citizens. Several state conventions took a stand and announced that they would not ratify the Constitution without the addition of a bill of rights.

Mercy Otis Warren, a Massachusetts opponent of the Constitution, expressed the problem faced by many Antifederalists. She admitted the need for a strong government but feared it.

> **"We have struggled for liberty and made costly sacrifices . . . and there are still many among us who [value liberty] too much to relinquish . . . the rights of man for the dignity of government."**
>
> —Mercy Otis Warren, September 29, 1787

In many ways the debate between Federalists and Antifederalists came down to their different fears. Federalists feared disorder without a strong central government. They believed that more uprisings like Shays's Rebellion would occur without a national government capable of maintaining order. The Antifederalists feared oppression more than disorder. They worried about the concentration of power that would result from a strong national government.

Adopting the Constitution With the promise of a bill of rights, many Americans began to favor the Constitution. Many small states ratified it quickly because they were pleased with equal representation in the new Senate. On June 21, 1788, the ninth state—New Hampshire—ratified it. However, without the support of two critical states—New York and Virginia—the future of the new government was not promising. Neither state had ratified yet, and both had strong Antifederalist groups.

In Virginia, George Washington, James Madison, and Edmund Randolph helped swing a close vote on June 25, 1788. In New York, Alexander Hamilton argued for ratification for six weeks. Finally, on July 26, the Federalists in New York won by only three votes. North Carolina ratified in November 1789, and Rhode Island ratified in May 1790.

After ratification came the celebrations. Boston, New York, and Philadelphia held big parades accompanied by cannon salutes and ringing church bells. Smaller celebrations took place in hundreds of American towns.

The task of creating the Constitution had ended. The Federalists promised to add a bill of rights after the new government took office. Now it was time for the nation to elect leaders and begin the work of government.

Reading Check **Explain** According to the Antifederalists, why was a bill of rights important?

History Online
Study Central Need help understanding the development of the Constitution? Visit ca.hss.glencoe.com and click on Study Central.

Reading Summary

Review the Main Ideas

- Ideas and thinkers of the past influenced the creation of the United States Constitution.
- The Constitution outlines the responsibilities and the limits of the three branches of government.
- Americans reacted to the proposed Constitution in different ways.

What Did You Learn?

1. What influence did John Locke have on American government?
2. Why was the support of New York and Virginia vital to ratifying the Constitution?

Critical Thinking

3. **Compare** Re-create the diagram below. Describe the differences between Federalist and Antifederalist views on the Constitution. CA HR3.

Views on the Constitution	
Federalist	Antifederalist

4. **The Big Ideas** Why did the Framers of the Constitution believe that a division of powers and a system of checks and balances were necessary in a government?
5. **Persuasive Writing** Search your local newspaper for articles that deal with constitutional issues. Select an issue from one of the articles and write a letter to your senator or representatives expressing your opinion about the issue. CA 8WA2.4

You Decide . . .

Ratifying the Constitution

The delegates at Philadelphia had produced the Constitution, but its acceptance depended upon the will of the American people. In each of the 13 states, voters selected delegates to special conventions that would decide whether to accept or reject the new plan of government. Once 9 of the 13 conventions had ratified the Constitution, it could go into effect.

For Ratification

Those who favored the Constitution called themselves Federalists. Federalists wanted a strong government capable of handling the problems facing the United States both at home and abroad. They believed that the new Constitution protected the rights of the states, but gave the central government enough power to function effectively.

James Wilson of Philadelphia was a major force in drafting the Constitution. In a speech to the Pennsylvania Ratifying Convention, Wilson said:

"I am satisfied that anything nearer to perfection could not have been accomplished. If there are errors, it should be remembered, that the seeds of reformation are sown in the work itself, and the concurrence of two thirds of the Congress may at any time introduce alterations and amendments. Regarding it then, in every point of view, with a candid and disinterested mind, I am bold to assert, that it is the best form of government which has ever been offered to the world."

In a series of 85 essays known as *The Federalist Papers*, Alexander Hamilton, James Madison, and John Jay defended the Constitution. In *Federalist*, No. 70, Hamilton argued against the idea of a president with limited or few powers:

"A feeble executive implies a feeble execution of the government. A feeble execution is but another phrase for a bad execution; and a government ill executed, whatever it may be in theory, must be, in practice, a bad government."

Hamilton also believed that a bill of rights would be unnecessary and dangerous. Hamilton wrote that the Constitution gave the national government only limited power. It did not have the power to infringe on the rights of the citizens. Therefore, Hamilton noted, a bill of rights protecting the people's rights is not needed.

Alexander Hamilton ▶

US8.2.4 Describe the political philosophy underpinning the Constitution as specified in the *Federalist Papers* (authored by James Madison, Alexander Hamilton, and John Jay) and the role of such leaders as Madison, George Washington, Roger Sherman, Gouverneur Morris, and James Wilson in the writing and ratification of the Constitution.

Against Ratification

Ratification, however, was not a sure thing. Many people who remembered British tyranny were against a powerful national government. Opponents of the Constitution, called Antifederalists, felt that a strong central government was a threat to liberty.

In the Virginia ratification convention of 1788, Patrick Henry spoke out against the adoption of the Constitution:

"I look upon that paper [the Constitution] as the most fatal plan that could be possibly conceived to enslave a free people."

The Antifederalists' strongest argument, however, was that the Constitution lacked a bill of rights. They feared losing the liberties they had gained during the Revolution and wanted to include a guarantee of those liberties in the Constitution. Mercy Otis Warren wrote that "The rights of the individual should be the primary object of all governments."

George Mason of Virginia refused to sign the Constitution because it did not contain a bill of rights. In a letter explaining his objections to the Constitution, Mason stated that the Constitution has

"no declaration of rights: and the laws of the general government being paramount to the laws and constitutions of the several states, the declarations of rights, in the separate states, are no security. Nor are the people secured even in the enjoyment of the benefit of the common law."

◀ George Mason

You Be The Historian

DBQ Document-Based Questions

1. What group was opposed to ratification of the Constitution? CA HR5.
2. Who argued that the Constitution could be changed if problems arose?
3. What was Hamilton's major argument in *The Federalist*, No. 70? CA HR3.

Analyzing Primary Sources

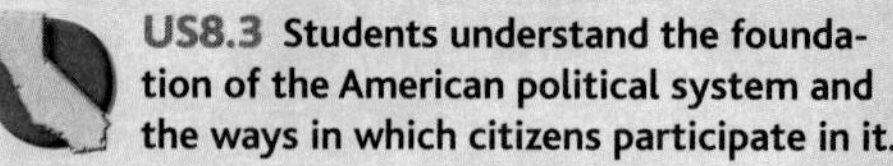

Forming a New Nation

Americans fought for their independence from Great Britain between 1776 and 1783. After the Revolutionary War, a great deal of work needed to be done to establish a new nation. Where would they start? How would they form a new government that served the people better than the last government? To understand the people who called themselves Americans, you can look at letters and writings of the eighteenth century.

Read the passages on pages 210 and 211 and answer the questions that follow.

"Ship of State" float parading through New York during the 1788 ratification

Reader's Dictionary

allies (A • LYS): people or groups joined in alliance or agreement

justice: fairness in the way people are treated or decisions are made

acquainted (uh • KWAYNT • ihd): having some knowledge of something

haughty (HAW • tee): behaving in a superior, arrogant way

appellation (A • puh • LAY • shuhn): the name or title of someone or something

perpetual: occurring over and over

contention (kuhn • TEHN • shuhn): disagreement or competition between rivals

---

The Oneida and the Use of Land

The Oneida Indian Nation fought on the side of the Patriots during the American Revolution. In March 1788, leaders of the Oneida people sent this message to the New York State legislature.

Brothers. We are your **allies,** we are a free people, our chiefs have directed us to speak to you, as such, therefore, open your ears and hear our words.

Brothers. In your late war with the people on the other side of the great water, . . . we fought by your side, our blood flowed together, and the bones of our warriors mingled with yours; . . . [W]e received an invitation to meet some of your chiefs . . . , those chiefs who then met us will doubtless remember how much we were disappointed, when they told us they were only sent to buy our lands. . . .

Brothers. We are determined then never to sell any more; the experience of all the Indian nations to the east and south of us has fully convinced us, that if we follow their example we shall soon share their fate. We wish that our children and grandchildren may derive a comfortable living from the lands which the Great Spirit has given us and our forefathers. . . .

Brothers. We wish you to consider this matter well, and to do us **justice**. . . .

—*Proceedings of the Commissioners of Indian Affairs*

What Is an American?

J. Hector St. John Crèvecoeur of France traveled widely in the American colonies and farmed in New York. His Letters From an American Farmer *was published in 1782.*

I wish I could be **acquainted** with the feelings and thoughts which must . . . present themselves to the mind of an enlightened Englishman, when he first lands on the continent. . . . If he travels through our rural districts he views not the hostile castle, and the **haughty** mansion, contrasted with the clay-built hut and miserable [cabin], where cattle and men help to keep each other warm, and dwell in meanness, smoke, and indigence. A pleasing uniformity of decent competence appears throughout our habitations. The meanest of our log-houses is dry and comfortable. . . . Lawyer or merchant are the fairest titles our towns afford; that of a farmer is the only **appellation** of the rural inhabitants of our country. It must take some time [before] he can reconcile himself to our dictionary, which is but short in words of dignity, and names of honour. . . .

What then is the American, this new man? He is either a European, or the descendant of a European, hence that strange mixture of blood, which you will find in no other country. I could point out to you a family whose grandfather was an Englishman, whose wife was Dutch, and whose son married a French woman, and whose present four sons have now four wives of different nations. . . .

He does not find, as in Europe, a crowded society, where every place is over-stocked; he does not feel that **perpetual** collision of parties, that difficulty of beginning, that **contention** which oversets so many. There is room for everybody in America; has he particular talent, or industry? He exerts it in order to produce a livelihood, and it succeeds. . . .

—*Letters From an American Farmer*

▲ ***The Peale Family*** **by Charles Willson Peale, c. 1770–1773 American artists favored informal scenes over the more formal European styles.**

DBQ Document-Based Questions

The Oneida and the Use of Land

1. Who are the "Brothers" that the Oneida leaders address? Why would the Oneida address legislators in this way?
2. What are the Oneida asking for?
3. What do the Oneida pledge to never do? Why did they make this decision and statement?

What Is an American?

4. How does de Crèvecoeur describe the typical home in the colonies?
5. Why might de Crèvecoeur refer to the American as a "new man"?
6. How are Americans described in comparison to Europeans?
7. What is meant by "there is room for everybody in America"? Is this still true today?

Read to Write

8. What does it mean to have justice in America? What would it look like? How would it work? How would the authors of these documents define justice in their time? How would you define justice in America today? Compare and contrast the ideas from different eras. CA HI3. CA 8WS1.1

Assessment

Standards US8.2 & US8.3

Review Content Vocabulary

Write the vocabulary word that completes each sentence. Write a sentence for each word that is not used.

a. bicameral
b. ratify
c. compromise
d. republic
e. executive branch

1. To resolve their differences, the delegates used ______, with each side giving up something but gaining something else.
2. A legislature divided into two parts, or houses, is called ______.
3. On June 21, 1788, New Hampshire became the ninth state to ______ the Constitution.
4. A(n) ______ is a system of government in which the people elect representatives to exercise power for them.

Review the Main Ideas

Section 1 • The Articles of Confederation

5. What was the purpose of the Articles of Confederation?
6. How did the Northwest Ordinance provide for the country's expansion?

Section 2 • Convention and Compromise

7. According to the Virginia Plan, how was the legislature to be set up?
8. How did the Great Compromise address the issue of representation in Congress?

Section 3 • A New Plan of Government

9. Why did some Americans want a bill of rights added to the Constitution?
10. Why is it important that the powers of government are separated?

Critical Thinking

11. **Identify** What was the purpose of holding secret sessions at the Constitutional Convention? If you had been a delegate, would you have been in favor of secret sessions? Why or why not? CA HI2.
12. **Analyze** Why was a system of checks and balances built into the Constitution? CA HI2.

Geography Skills

Study the map below and answer the following questions. CA CS3.

NATIONAL GEOGRAPHIC **Land Claims in North America, 1783**

History Online
Self-Check Quiz Visit ca.hss.glencoe.com to prepare for the Chapter 3 test.

13. **Place** Who controlled the area in which you live today?
14. **Region** What country held territory directly west of the United States?

Read to Write

15. **The Big Ideas Government and Democracy** Write a short essay discussing the many compromises that are reflected in the final version of the U.S. Constitution. CA 8WS1.1
16. **Using Your FOLDABLES** Use the information you wrote in your foldable to create a fill-in-the blank quiz for a classmate. Write a paragraph about one of the sections, leaving blanks for your classmates to fill in. Also write an answer key. CA 8RC2.0

Using Academic Vocabulary

17. Write two words that are related to the academic vocabulary word *currency*.

Building Citizenship

18. **Interviewing** Interview students from your school and adults from your community to find out what they know about the powers of government specified in the Constitution. Prepare a list of questions to use in your interviews. Compile the answers and present a report to your class. CA HR1.

Reviewing Skills

19. Review READING SKILL **Making Connections** Review the literature excerpt called "Second Daughter." Write a paragraph describing the connections you made while reading. Be sure to include text-to-self, text-to-text, and text-to-world connections. CA 8RC2.0
20. Review ANALYSIS SKILL **Paraphrasing** Select a quotation or primary source from one of the sections in this chapter. Reread it and then paraphrase what you have read. CA HR4.

Standards Practice

Read the passage below and answer the following questions.

> The Senate of the United States shall be composed of two Senators from each State, chosen by the Legislature thereof, for six Years; and each Senator shall have one vote.
>
> —U.S. Constitution, Article I, Section 3.1

21 According to the above excerpt from the U.S. Constitution, by whom were Senators originally chosen?

A other Senators
B members of the U.S. House of Representatives
C the voters of the state
D the state's legislature

22 Each of the states enacted state constitutions in the late 1700s. All state constitutions

A established equal rights for all persons living in the state.
B set up legislative and executive branches of state government.
C granted women the right to vote.
D agreed that states would be supervised by the federal government.

23 The law that established a procedure for surveying and selling the western lands north of the Ohio River was the

A Ordinance of 1785.
B Virginia Plan.
C New Jersey Plan.
D Bill of Rights.

The Constitution

▼ The National Archives, Washington, D.C.

Where & When?

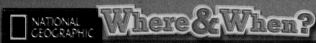

NATIONAL GEOGRAPHIC

1785 — 1790 — 1795

1787 The Constitution is signed

1789 John Jay becomes first Supreme Court Chief Justice

1792 President Washington vetoes a bill from Congress for first time

History Online
Chapter Overview Visit ca.hss.glencoe.com for a preview of Chapter 4.

The Big Ideas

Goals of the Constitution

A constitution reflects the values and goals of the society that creates it. For more than 200 years, the Constitution has provided the framework for the United States government and has helped preserve the basic rights of American citizens.

The Federal Government

Political ideas and major events shape how people form governments. The Constitution provided for a United States government that was set up as three equal branches with different responsibilities.

Citizens' Rights and Responsibilities

Citizen participation is essential to the foundation and preservation of the U.S. political system. Citizens of the United States have certain duties and responsibilities that help maintain our form of government.

View the Chapter 4 video in the Glencoe Video Program.

Know-Want-Learn Make this foldable to determine what you already know, to identify what you want to know, and to record what you learn about the Constitution of the United States.

Step 1 Fold a sheet of paper into thirds from top to bottom.

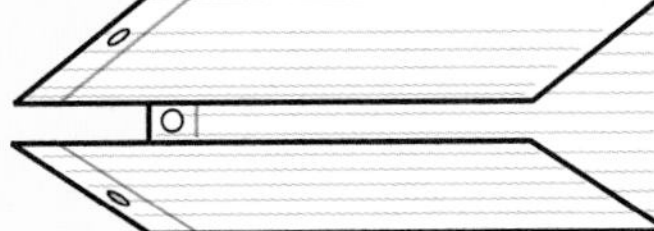

Step 2 Turn the paper horizontally, unfold, and label the three columns as shown.

KNOW: | WANT TO KNOW: | LEARNED:

Reading and Writing
Before you read the chapter, write what you already know about the Constitution in the "Know" column. Write what you want to know about the Constitution in the "Want to Know" column. Then, as you read the chapter, write what you learn in the "Learned" column. Check to see if you have learned what you wanted to know (from the second column).

Get Ready to Read

Summarizing Information

1 Learn It!

Summarizing helps you clarify key points in your own words. You can summarize what you have read by pausing and restating the main ideas of the text. Then answer the key questions *Who? What? Where? When? Why?* and *How?* Read the information under "Major Principles" on page 221. Work with a partner to summarize the main points of what you read.

Did your summary include some of these details?

- **The Constitution rests on seven major principles.**
- **Those principles are: popular sovereignty, republicanism, limited government, federalism, separation of powers, checks and balances, and individual rights.**

As you read, take note of the sections that you may want to go over again.

2 Practice It!

With a partner, read the paragraph below. Then read the sections titled "Rights of American Citizens" on page 235 and "Citizen Participation" on page 236. Work together to make a list summarizing what you read. As you discuss your conclusions, see if you can answer the questions that follow.

Read to Write

Choose two editorials in your local newspaper. Read them carefully and then summarize each writer's main point.

It is the combination of rights, responsibilities, and duties that characterize what it means to be a citizen of a free democratic society. As citizens, we are free to exercise our rights. In return we are expected to fulfill certain duties and responsibilities.

- **What is a citizen?**
- **What are the rights citizens hold?**
- **What is the difference between duty and responsibility?**
- **What is one of the most important responsibilities of citizens?**

Citizens take part in a town hall meeting.

3 Apply It!

As you read this chapter, keep track of the main ideas of each section.

Section 1

Goals of the Constitution

Guide to Reading

History Social Science Standards

US8.2 Students analyze the political principles underlying the U.S. Constitution and compare the enumerated and implied powers of the federal government.

US8.3 Students understand the foundation of the American political system and the ways in which citizens participate in it.

Looking Back, Looking Ahead

You read that the last of the 13 states ratified the Constitution in 1790. The ratifying states had closely examined the goals of and the principles behind the document creating the new government.

Focusing on the Main Ideas

- The Preamble to the Constitution describes six goals for the United States government. *(page 219)*
- The Constitution is based on seven major principles. *(page 221)*
- The Framers wrote the Constitution so that it could be altered or adapted to meet changing needs. *(page 224)*

Content Vocabulary

Preamble
popular sovereignty (SAH • vuhrn • tee)
republicanism
federalism
enumerated powers (ih • NYOO • muh • RAYT • ehd)
reserved powers
concurrent powers (kuhn • KUHR • uhnt)
amendment
implied powers (ihm • PLYD)
judicial review

Academic Vocabulary

function (FUHNG • shuhn)
cooperate (koh • AH • puh • RAYT)
anticipate (an • TIH • suh • PAYT)

Reading Strategy

Organizing Information Use a diagram like the one below to list the seven major principles on which the Constitution is based.

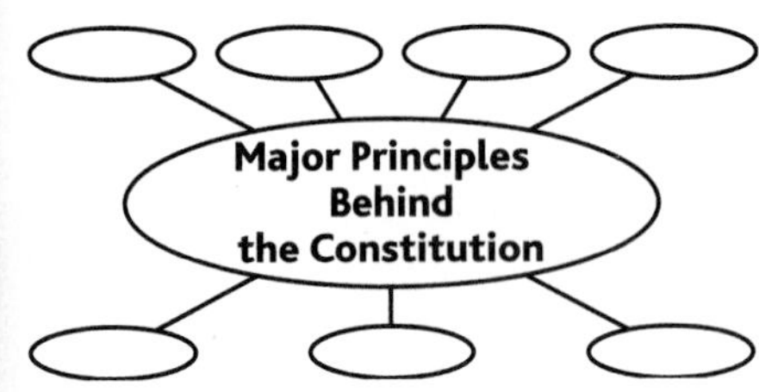
Major Principles Behind the Constitution

NATIONAL GEOGRAPHIC
Who & When?
1785
1795
1805
1786
Shays's Rebellion causes concerns with "domestic tranquility"
1787
Gouverneur Morris writes the Preamble to the Constitution
1803
President Thomas Jefferson increases powers of the presidency

Thomas Jefferson

US8.2.2 Analyze the Articles of Confederation and the Constitution and the success of each in implementing the ideals of the Declaration of Independence. **US8.3.3** Enumerate the advantages of a common market among the states as foreseen in and protected by the Constitution's clauses on interstate commerce, common coinage, and full-faith and credit.

Goals of the Constitution

Main Idea **The Preamble to the Constitution describes six goals for the United States government.**

Reading Connection Just as you often determine goals when working on a project, the creators of the Constitution thought about what they wanted the new government to do for the nation's people. Read to find out the goals set by the Constitution's Framers for the United States government.

An American Story

On September 17, 1787, the delegates to the Constitutional Convention signed the document. When it came Benjamin Franklin's turn to sign, the elderly leader had to be helped forward in order to write his name on the parchment. Tears streamed down his face as he signed. He looked at the carving of the sun on the back of George Washington's chair. "I have often looked at that sun behind the president of the convention without being able to tell whether it was rising or setting," he said, "but now, I have the happiness to know that it is a rising and not a setting sun."

The rising sun that Franklin spoke of was the new government of a very young country, the United States of America.

The Preamble The **Preamble,** or introduction, to the Constitution, written by Gouverneur Morris, begins "We the People." It reflects the basic principle of the new American government—the right of the people to govern themselves. The Preamble also lists six goals for the United States government:

> **"... to form a more perfect Union, establish Justice, insure domestic Tranquility, provide for the common defence [defense], promote the general Welfare, and secure the Blessings of Liberty to ourselves and our Posterity..."**

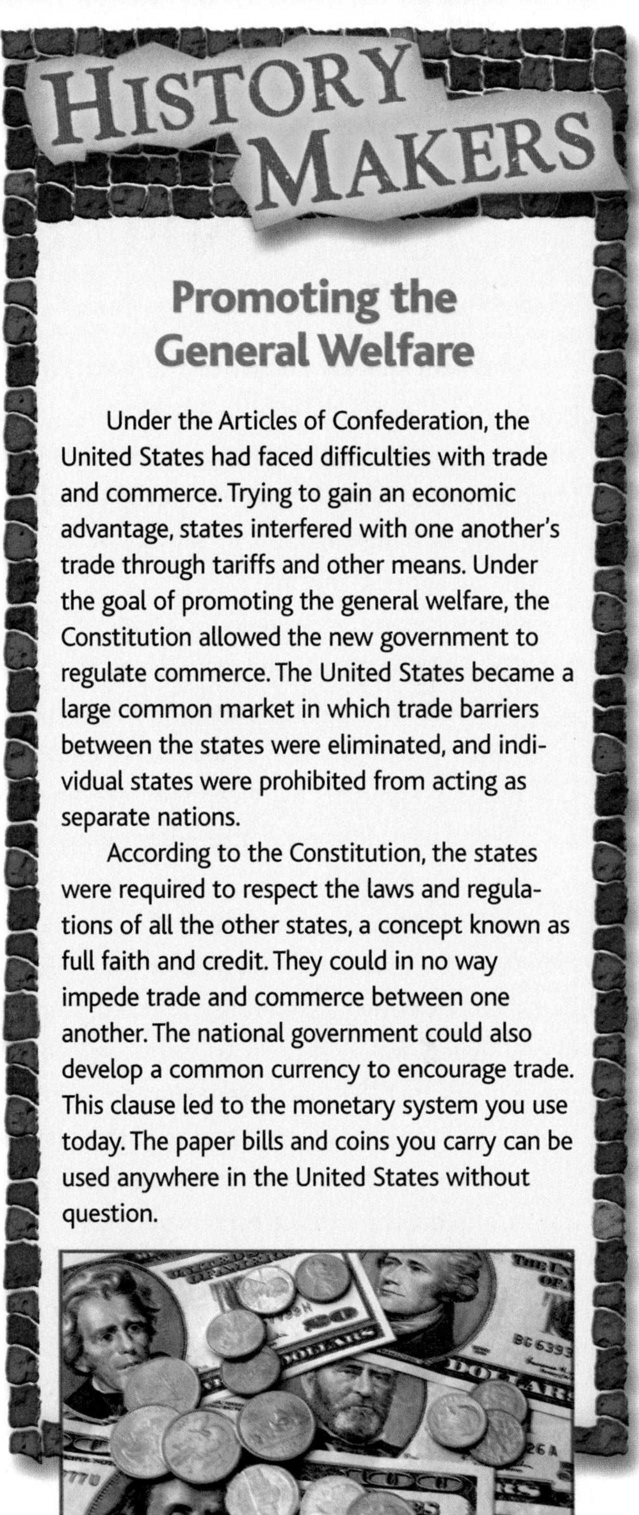

History Makers

Promoting the General Welfare

Under the Articles of Confederation, the United States had faced difficulties with trade and commerce. Trying to gain an economic advantage, states interfered with one another's trade through tariffs and other means. Under the goal of promoting the general welfare, the Constitution allowed the new government to regulate commerce. The United States became a large common market in which trade barriers between the states were eliminated, and individual states were prohibited from acting as separate nations.

According to the Constitution, the states were required to respect the laws and regulations of all the other states, a concept known as full faith and credit. They could in no way impede trade and commerce between one another. The national government could also develop a common currency to encourage trade. This clause led to the monetary system you use today. The paper bills and coins you carry can be used anywhere in the United States without question.

These goals guided the Constitution's Framers as they created the new government. They remain as important today as they were when the Constitution was written.

Biography

US8.2.4 Describe the political philosophy underpinning the Constitution as specified in the *Federalist Papers* (authored by James Madison, Alexander Hamilton, and John Jay) and the role of such leaders as Madison, George Washington, Roger Sherman, Gouverneur Morris, and James Wilson in the writing and ratification of the Constitution.

Gouverneur Morris

1752–1816

A brilliant speaker and writer, Gouverneur Morris was a leader during the American Revolution and the Constitutional Convention. As a young man, Morris devoted himself to education, graduating from King's College in 1768, at the age of 16, and earning a degree in law in 1771.

Morris joined the struggle for American independence although his family supported the Loyalist cause. While his brother served as an officer in the British army, Morris joined the American military despite a physical handicap that left him without the full use of his right arm. Later he lost his left leg in an accident.

In 1778 Morris became one of the youngest delegates to the Continental Congress. At Valley Forge, he had seen "an army of skeletons . . . naked, starved, sick, discouraged," and worked to improve conditions for the soldiers. In 1781 Morris served as an assistant to the Minister of Finance. He developed the system of decimal coinage, or the addition of pennies, nickels, dimes, and quarters to the American dollar.

"We the people of the United States . . ."

—from the *Preamble to the U.S. Constitution*

In 1787 Morris joined the Constitutional Convention as a delegate from Pennsylvania. He was an opponent of slavery and tried to get the Constitutional Convention to ban it. He wrote the inspiring Preamble to the Constitution and helped write and edit much of the rest of the document. Because of his belief in nationalism, Morris changed the first line of the Constitution from "We the people of the states of New Hampshire, Massachusetts, . . ." with all 13 states listed, to "We the people of the United States." James Madison said of Morris: "A better choice [to rework the Constitution] could not have been made."

Then and Now

Although physically impaired, Morris made a significant impact on American history. Can you identify other local or national leaders like him?

[12.] To raise and support Armies, but no Appropriation of Money to that Use shall be for a longer Term than two Years;
[13.] To provide and maintain a Navy;
[14.] To make Rules for the Government and Regulation of the land and naval Forces;
[15.] To provide for calling forth the Militia to execute the Laws of the Union, suppress Insurrections and repel Invasions;
[16.] To provide for organizing, arming, and disciplining, the Militia, and for governing such Part of them as may be employed in the Service of the United States, reserving to the States respectively, the Appointment of the Officers, and the Authority of training the Militia according to the discipline prescribed by Congress;
[17.] To exercise exclusive Legislation in all Cases whatsoever, over such District (not exceeding ten Miles square) as may, by Cession of particular States, and the Acceptance of Congress, become the Seat of Government of the United States, and to exercise like Authority over all Places purchased by the Consent of the Legislature of the State in which the Same shall be, for the Erection of Forts, Magazines, Arsenals, dock-Yards, and other needful Buildings;—And
[18.] To make all Laws which shall be necessary and proper for carrying into Execution the foregoing Powers, and all other Powers vested by this Constitution in the Government of the United States, or in any Department or Officer thereof.

Section 9

[1]. The Migration or Importation of such Persons as any of the States now existing shall think proper to admit, shall not be prohibited by the Congress prior to the Year one thousand eight hundred and eight, but a Tax or duty may be imposed on such Importation, not exceeding ten dollars for each Person.
[2.] The Privilege of the Writ of Habeas Corpus shall not be suspended, unless when in Cases of Rebellion or Invasion the public Safety may require it.
[3.] No Bill of Attainder or ex post facto Law shall be passed.
[4.] No Capitation, or other direct, Tax shall be laid, unless in Proportion to the Census or Enumeration herein before directed to be taken.
[5.] No Tax or Duty shall be laid on Articles exported from any State.
[6.] No Preference shall be given by any Regulation of Commerce or Revenue to the Ports of one State over those of another: nor shall Vessels bound to, or from, one State, be obliged to enter, clear, or pay Duties in another.

Seal of the U.S. Navy

Section 8. Powers Granted to Congress

Elastic Clause The final enumerated power is often called the "elastic clause." This clause gives Congress the right to make all laws "necessary and proper" to carry out the powers expressed in the other clauses of Article I. It is called the elastic clause because it lets Congress "stretch" its powers to meet situations the Founders could never have anticipated.

What does the phrase "necessary and proper" in the elastic clause mean? Almost from the beginning, this phrase was a subject of dispute. The issue was whether a strict or a broad interpretation of the Constitution should be applied. The dispute was first addressed in 1819, in the case of *McCulloch* v. *Maryland*, when the Supreme Court ruled in favor of a broad interpretation.

Section 9. Powers Denied to the Federal Government

Habeas Corpus A writ of habeas corpus issued by a judge requires a law official to bring a prisoner to court and show cause for holding the prisoner. A bill of attainder is a bill that punished a person without a jury trial. An "ex post facto" law is one that makes an act a crime after the act has been committed. *What does the Constitution say about bills of attainder?*

Section 10. Powers Denied to the States

Limitations on Power Section 10 lists limits on the states. These restrictions were designed, in part, to prevent an overlapping in functions and authority with the federal government.

United States coins

Article II. The Executive Branch

Article II creates an executive branch to carry out laws passed by Congress. Article II lists the powers and duties of the presidency, describes qualifications for office and procedures for electing the president, and provides for a vice president.

Vocabulary

appropriations: *funds set aside for a specific use*
emolument: *payment*
impost: *tax*
duty: *tax*

[7.] No Money shall be drawn from the Treasury, but in Consequence of Appropriations made by Law; and a regular Statement and Account of the Receipts and Expenditures of all public Money shall be published from time to time.

[8.] No Title of Nobility shall be granted by the United States: And no Person holding any Office of Profit or Trust under them, shall, without the Consent of the Congress, accept of any present, Emolument, Office, or Title, of any kind whatever, from any King, Prince, or foreign State.

Section 10

[1.] No State shall enter into any Treaty, Alliance, or Confederation; grant Letters of Marque and Reprisal; coin Money; emit Bills of Credit; make any Thing but gold and silver Coin a Tender in Payment of Debts; pass any Bill of Attainder, ex post facto Law, or Law impairing the Obligation of Contracts, or grant any Title of Nobility.

[2.] No State shall, without the Consent of the Congress, lay any Imposts or Duties on Imports or Exports, except what may be absolutely necessary for executing it's inspection Laws: and the net Produce of all Duties and Imposts, laid by any State on Imports and Exports, shall be for the Use of the Treasury of the United States; and all such Laws shall be subject to the Revision and Controul of the Congress.

[3.] No State shall, without the Consent of Congress, lay any Duty of Tonnage, keep Troops, or Ships of War in time of Peace, enter into any Agreement or Compact with another State, or with a foreign Power, or engage in War, unless actually invaded, or in such imminent Danger as will not admit of delay.

Article II

Section 1

[1.] The executive Power shall be vested in a President of the United States of America. He shall hold his Office during the Term of four Years, and, together with the Vice President, chosen for the same Term, be elected, as follows

[2.] Each State shall appoint, in such Manner as the Legislature thereof may direct, a Number of Electors, equal to the whole Number of Senators and Representatives to which the State may be entitled in the Congress: but no Senator or Representative, or Person holding an Office of Trust or Profit under the United States, shall be appointed an Elector.

[3.] The Electors shall meet in their respective States, and vote by Ballot for two Persons, of whom one at least shall not be an Inhabitant of the same State with themselves. And they shall make a List of all the Persons voted for, and of the Number of Votes for each; which List they shall sign and certify, and transmit sealed to the Seat of the Government of the United States, directed to the President of the Senate. The President of the Senate shall, in the Presence of the Senate and House of Representatives, open all the Certificates, and the Votes shall then be counted. The Person having the greatest Number of Votes shall be the President, if such Number be a Majority of the whole Number of Electors appointed; and if there be more than one who have such Majority, and have an equal Number of Votes, then the House of Representatives shall immediately chuse by Ballot one of them for President; and if no person have a Majority, then from the five highest on the List the said House shall in like Manner chuse the President. But in chusing the President, the Votes shall be taken by States, the Representation from each State having one Vote; A quorum for this Purpose shall consist of a Member or Members from two thirds of the States, and a Majority of all the States shall be necessary to a Choice. In every Case, after the Choice of the President, the Person having the greatest Number of Votes of the Electors shall be the Vice President. But if there should remain two or more who have equal Votes, the Senate shall chuse from them by Ballot the Vice President.

[4.] The Congress may determine the Time of chusing the Electors, and the Day on which they shall give their Votes; which Day shall be the same throughout the United States.

[5.] No Person except a natural born Citizen, or a Citizen of the United States, at the time of the Adoption of this Constitution, shall be eligible to the Office of President; neither shall any Person be eligible to that Office who shall not have attained to the Age of thirty five Years, and been fourteen Years a Resident within the United States.

[6.] In Case of the Removal of the President from Office, or of his Death, Resignation, or Inability to discharge the Powers and Duties of the said Office, the Same shall devolve on the Vice President, and the Congress may by Law provide for the Case of Removal, Death, Resignation or Inability, both of the President and Vice President, declaring what Officer shall then act as President, and such Officer shall act accordingly, until the Disability be removed, or a President shall be elected.

[7.] The President shall, at stated Times, receive for his Services, a Compensation, which shall neither be encreased nor diminished during the Period for which he shall have been elected, and he shall not receive within that Period any other Emolument from the United States, or any of them.

[8.] Before he enter on the Execution of his Office, he shall take the following Oath or Affirmation:—"I do solemnly swear (or affirm) that I will faithfully execute the Office of President of the United States, and will to the best of my Ability, preserve, protect and defend the Constitution of the United States."

Section 1. President and Vice President

Former Method of Election The Twelfth Amendment, added in 1804, changed the method of electing the president stated in Article II, Section 1, paragraph 3. The Twelfth Amendment requires that the electors cast separate ballots for president and vice president.

George Washington, the first president

Section 1. President and Vice President

Qualifications The president must be a citizen of the United States by birth, at least 35 years of age, and a resident of the United States for 14 years.

Section 1. President and Vice President

Vacancies If the president dies, resigns, is removed from office by impeachment, or is unable to carry out the duties of the office, the vice president assumes the duties of the president. The Twenty-fifth Amendment sets procedures for presidential succession.

Section 1. President and Vice President

Salary Originally, the president's salary was $25,000 per year. The president's current salary is $400,000 plus a $50,000 nontaxable expense account per year. The president also receives living accommodations in two residences–the White House and Camp David.

Section 2. Powers of the President

Military, Cabinet, Pardons Mention of "the principal officer in each of the executive departments" is the only suggestion of the president's cabinet to be found in the Constitution. The cabinet is an advisory body, and its power depends on the president. Section 2, Clause 1 also makes the president–a civilian–the head of the armed services. This established the principle of civilian control of the military.

Section 2. Powers of the President

Treaties and Appointments An executive order is a command issued by a president to exercise a power which he has been given by the U.S. Constitution or by a federal statute. In times of emergency, presidents sometimes have used the executive order to override the Constitution of the United States and the Congress. During the Civil War, President Lincoln suspended many fundamental rights guaranteed in the Constitution and the Bill of Rights. He closed down newspapers that opposed his policies and imprisoned some who disagreed with him. Lincoln said that these actions were justified to preserve the Union.

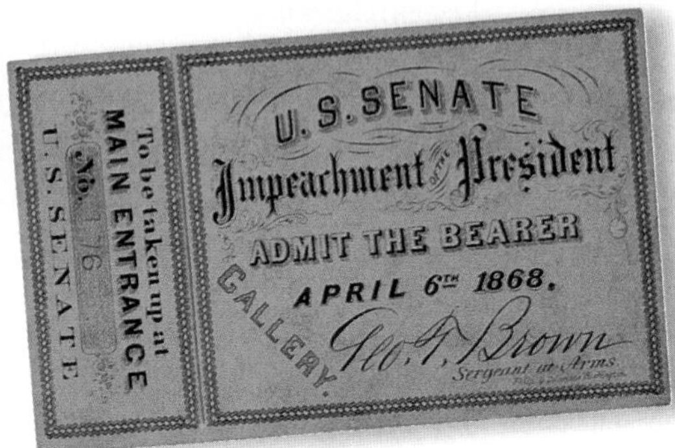

Impeachment ticket

Article III. The Judicial Branch

The term *judicial* refers to courts. The Constitution set up only the Supreme Court but provided for the establishment of other federal courts. The judiciary of the United States has two different systems of courts. One system consists of the federal courts, whose powers derive from the Constitution and federal laws. The other includes the courts of each of the 50 states, whose powers derive from state constitutions and laws.

Section 2

[1.] The President shall be Commander in Chief of the Army and Navy of the United States, and of the Militia of the several States, when called into the actual Service of the United States; he may require the Opinion, in writing, of the principal Officer in each of the executive Departments, upon any Subject relating to the Duties of their respective Offices, and he shall have Power to grant Reprieves and Pardons for Offences against the United States, except in Cases of Impeachment.

[2.] He shall have Power, by and with the Advice and Consent of the Senate, to make Treaties, provided two thirds of the Senators present concur; and he shall nominate, and by and with the Advice and Consent of the Senate, shall appoint Ambassadors, other public Ministers and Consuls, Judges of the supreme Court, and all other Officers of the United States, whose Appointments are not herein otherwise provided for, and which shall be established by Law: but the Congress may by Law vest the Appointment of such inferior Officers, as they think proper, in the President alone, in the Courts of Law, or in the Heads of Departments.

[3.] The President shall have Power to fill up all Vacancies that may happen during the Recess of the Senate, by granting Commissions which shall expire at the End of their next Session.

Section 3

He shall from time to time give to the Congress Information of the State of the Union, and recommend to their Consideration such Measures as he shall judge necessary and expedient; he may, on extraordinary Occasions, convene both Houses, or either of them, and in Case of Disagreement between them, with Respect to the Time of Adjournment, he may adjourn them to such Time as he shall think proper; he shall receive Ambassadors and other public Ministers; he shall take Care that the Laws be faithfully executed, and shall Commission all the Officers of the United States.

Section 4

The President, Vice President and all civil Officers of the United States, shall be removed from Office on Impeachment for, and Conviction of, Treason, Bribery, or other high Crimes and Misdemeanors.

Article III

Section 1

The judicial Power of the United States, shall be vested in one supreme Court, and in such inferior Courts as the Congress may from time to time ordain and establish. The Judges, both of the supreme and inferior Courts, shall hold their Offices during good Behaviour, and shall, at stated Times, receive for their Services, a Compensation, which shall not be diminished during their Continuance in Office.

Section 2

[1.] The judicial Power shall extend to all Cases, in Law and Equity, arising under this Constitution, the Laws of the United States, and Treaties made, or which shall be made, under their Authority;—to all Cases affecting Ambassadors, other public Ministers and Consuls;—to all Cases of admiralty and maritime Jurisdiction;—to Controversies to which the United States shall be a Party;—to Controversies between two or more States;—between a State and Citizens of another State;—between Citizens of different States,—between Citizens of the same State claiming Lands under Grants of different States, and between a State, or the Citizens thereof, and foreign States, Citizens or Subjects.

[2.] In all Cases affecting Ambassadors, other public Ministers and Consuls, and those in which a State shall be Party, the supreme Court shall have original Jurisdiction. In all the other Cases before mentioned, the supreme Court shall have appellate Jurisdiction, both as to Law and Fact, with such Exceptions, and under such Regulations as the Congress shall make.

[3.] The Trial of all Crimes, except in Cases of Impeachment, shall be by Jury; and such Trial shall be held in the State where the said Crimes shall have been committed; but when not committed within any State, the Trial shall be at such Place or Places as the Congress may by Law have directed.

Section 3

[1.] Treason against the United States, shall consist only in levying War against them, or in adhering to their Enemies, giving them Aid and Comfort. No Person shall be convicted of Treason unless on the Testimony of two Witnesses to the same overt Act, or on Confession in open Court.

[2.] The Congress shall have Power to declare the Punishment of Treason, but no Attainder of Treason shall work Corruption of Blood, or Forfeiture except during the Life of the Person attainted.

Article IV

Section 1

Full Faith and Credit shall be given in each State to the public Acts, Records, and judicial Proceedings of every other State. And the Congress may by general Laws prescribe the Manner in which such Acts, Records and Proceedings shall be proved, and the Effect thereof.

Section 2. Jurisdiction

Statute Law Federal courts deal mostly with "statute law," or laws passed by Congress, treaties, and cases involving the Constitution itself.

Section 2. Jurisdiction

The Supreme Court A Court with "original jurisdiction" has the authority to be the first court to hear a case. The Supreme Court primarily has "appellate jurisdiction" and mostly hears cases appealed from lower courts.

Article IV. Relations Among the States

Article IV explains the relationship of the states to one another and to the national government. This article requires each state to give citizens of other states the same rights as its own citizens, addresses admitting new states, and guarantees that the national government will protect the states.

Vocabulary

original jurisdiction: *authority to be the first court to hear a case*

appellate jurisdiction: *authority to hear cases that have been appealed from lower courts*

treason: *violation of the allegiance owed by a person to his or her own country, for example, by aiding an enemy*

Section 3. New States and Territories

New States Congress has the power to admit new states. It also determines the basic guidelines for applying for statehood. Two states, Maine and West Virginia, were created within the boundaries of another state. In the case of West Virginia, President Lincoln recognized the West Virginia government as the legal government of Virginia during the Civil War. This allowed West Virginia to secede from Virginia without obtaining approval from the Virginia legislature.

Section 4. Federal Protection for States

Republic Government can be classified in many different ways. The ancient Greek philosopher Aristotle classified government based on the question: Who governs? According to Aristotle, all governments belong to one of three major groups: (1) autocracy–rule by one person; (2) oligarchy–rule by a few persons; or (3) democracy–rule by many persons. A republic is a form of democracy in which the people elect representatives to make laws and conduct government.

Article V. The Amendment Process

Article V spells out the ways that the Constitution can be amended, or changed. All of the 27 amendments were proposed by a two-thirds vote of both houses of Congress. Only the Twenty-first Amendment was ratified by constitutional conventions of the states. All other amendments have been ratified by state legislatures. *What is an amendment?*

Vocabulary

extradition: *surrender of a criminal to another authority*
amendment: *a change to the Constitution*
ratification: *process by which an amendment is approved*

Section 2

[1.] The Citizens of each State shall be entitled to all Privileges and Immunities of Citizens in the several States.

[2.] A Person charged in any State with Treason, Felony, or other Crime, who shall flee from Justice, and be found in another State, shall on Demand of the executive Authority of the State from which he fled, be delivered up, to be removed to the State having Jurisdiction of the Crime.

[3.] No Person held to Service of Labour in one State, under the Laws thereof, escaping into another, shall, in Consequence of any Law or Regulation therein, be discharged from such Service or Labour, but shall be delivered up on Claim of the Party to whom such Service or Labour may be due.

Section 3

[1.] New States may be admitted by the Congress into this Union; but no new State shall be formed or erected within the Jurisdiction of any other State; nor any State be formed by the Junction of two or more States, or Parts of States, without the Consent of the Legislatures of the States concerned as well as of the Congress.

[2.] The Congress shall have Power to dispose of and make all needful Rules and Regulations respecting the Territory or other Property belonging to the United States; and nothing in this Constitution shall be so construed as to Prejudice any Claims of the United States, or of any particular State.

Section 4

The United States shall guarantee to every State in this Union a Republican Form of Government, and shall protect each of them against Invasion; and on Application of the Legislature, or of the Executive (when the Legislature cannot be convened) against domestic Violence.

Article V

The Congress, whenever two thirds of both Houses shall deem it necessary, shall propose Amendments to this Constitution, or, on the Application of the Legislatures of two thirds of the several States, shall call a Convention for proposing Amendments, which, in either Case, shall be valid to all Intents and Purposes, as Part of this Constitution, when ratified by the Legislatures of three fourths of the several States, or by Conventions in three fourths thereof, as the one or the other Mode of Ratification may be proposed by the Congress; Provided that no Amendment which may be made prior to the Year One thousand eight hundred and eight shall in any Manner affect the first and fourth Clauses in the Ninth Section of the first Article; and that no State, without its Consent, shall be deprived of its equal Suffrage in the Senate.

Article VI

[1.] All Debts contracted and Engagements entered into, before the Adoption of this Constitution, shall be as valid against the United States under this Constitution, as under the Confederation.

[2.] This Constitution, and the Laws of the United States which shall be made in Pursuance thereof; and all Treaties made, or which shall be made, under the Authority of the United States, shall be the supreme Law of the Land; and the Judges in every State shall be bound thereby, any Thing in the Constitution or Laws of any State to the Contrary notwithstanding.

[3.] The Senators and Representatives before mentioned, and the Members of the several State Legislatures, and all executive and judicial Officers, both of the United States and of the several States, shall be bound by Oath or Affirmation, to support this Constitution; but no religious Test shall ever be required as a Qualification to any Office or public Trust under the United States.

Article VI. National Supremacy

Article VI contains the "supremacy clause." This clause establishes that the Constitution, laws passed by Congress, and treaties of the United States "shall be the supreme Law of the Land." The "supremacy clause" recognized the Constitution and federal laws as supreme when in conflict with those of the states.

Article VII

The Ratification of the Conventions of nine States, shall be sufficient for the Establishment of this Constitution between the States so ratifying the Same.

Done in Convention by the Unanimous Consent of the States present the Seventeenth Day of September in the Year of our Lord one thousand seven hundred and Eighty seven and of the Independence of the United States of America the Twelfth. In witness whereof We have hereunto subscribed our Names,

Article VII. Ratification

Article VII addresses ratification and declares that the Constitution would take effect after it was ratified by nine states.

Signers

George Washington, ***President and Deputy from Virginia***

New Hampshire
John Langdon
Nicholas Gilman

Massachusetts
Nathaniel Gorham
Rufus King

Connecticut
William Samuel Johnson
Roger Sherman

New York
Alexander Hamilton

New Jersey
William Livingston
David Brearley
William Paterson
Jonathan Dayton

Pennsylvania
Benjamin Franklin
Thomas Mifflin
Robert Morris
George Clymer
Thomas FitzSimons
Jared Ingersoll
James Wilson
Gouverneur Morris

Delaware
George Read
Gunning Bedford, Jr.
John Dickinson
Richard Bassett
Jacob Broom

Maryland
James McHenry
Daniel of St. Thomas Jenifer
Daniel Carroll

Virginia
John Blair
James Madison, Jr.

North Carolina
William Blount
Richard Dobbs Spaight
Hugh Williamson

South Carolina
John Rutledge
Charles Cotesworth Pinckney
Charles Pinckney
Pierce Butler

Georgia
William Few
Abraham Baldwin

Attest: *William Jackson,*
Secretary

Bill of Rights

The first 10 amendments are known as the Bill of Rights (1791). These amendments limit the powers of government. The First Amendment protects the civil liberties of individuals in the United States. The amendment freedoms are not absolute, however. They are limited by the rights of other individuals. *What freedoms does the First Amendment protect?*

Amendment I

Congress shall make no law respecting an establishment of religion, or prohibiting the free exercise thereof; or abridging the freedom of speech, or of the press; or the right of the people peaceably to assemble, and to petition the Government for a redress of grievances.

Amendment 2

Right to Bear Arms This amendment is often debated. Originally, it was intended to prevent the national government from repeating the actions of the British, who tried to take weapons away from the colonial militia, or armed forces of citizens. This amendment seems to support the right of citizens to own firearms, but the Supreme Court has ruled that it does not prevent Congress from regulating the interstate sale of weapons. *Why is the Second Amendment's meaning debated?*

Amendment II

A well regulated Militia, being necessary to the security of a free State, the right of the people to keep and bear Arms, shall not be infringed.

Amendment III

No Soldier shall, in time of peace be quartered in any house, without the consent of the Owner, nor in time of war, but in a manner to be prescribed by law.

Amendment IV

The right of the people to be secure in their persons, houses, papers, and effects, against unreasonable searches and seizures, shall not be violated, and no Warrants shall issue, but upon probable cause, supported by Oath or affirmation, and particularly describing the place to be searched, and the persons or things to be seized.

Amendment 5

Rights of Accused Persons This amendment contains important protections for people accused of crimes. One of the protections is that government may not deprive any person of life, liberty, or property without due process of law. This means that the government must follow proper constitutional procedures in trials and in other actions it takes against individuals. *According to Amendment V, what is the function of a grand jury?*

Amendment V

No person shall be held to answer for a capital, or otherwise infamous crime, unless on a presentment or indictment of a Grand Jury, except in cases arising in the land or naval forces, or in the Militia, when in actual service in time of War or public danger; nor shall any person be subject for the same offence to be twice put in jeopardy of life or limb; nor shall be compelled in any criminal case to be a witness against himself, nor be deprived of life, liberty, or property, without due process of law; nor shall private property be taken for public use without just compensation.

Vocabulary

quarter: *to provide living accommodations*
probable cause: *police must have a reasonable basis to believe a person is linked to a crime*
warrant: *document that gives police particular rights or powers*
common law: *law established by previous court decisions*
bail: *money that an accused person provides to the court as a guarantee that he or she will be present for a trial*

Amendment VI

In all criminal prosecutions, the accused shall enjoy the right to a speedy and public trial, by an impartial jury of the State and district wherein the crime shall have been committed, which district shall have been previously ascertained by law, and to be informed of the nature and cause of the accusation; to be confronted with the witnesses against him; to have compulsory process for obtaining Witnesses in his favor, and to have the assistance of counsel for his defence.

Amendment 6

Right to a Speedy, Fair Trial A basic protection is the right to a speedy, public trial. The jury must hear witnesses and evidence on both sides before deciding the guilt or innocence of a person charged with a crime. This amendment also provides that legal counsel must be provided to a defendant. In 1963, the Supreme Court ruled, in *Gideon* v. *Wainwright*, that if a defendant cannot afford a lawyer, the government must provide one to defend him or her. *Why is the right to a "speedy" trial important?*

Amendment VII

In Suits at common law, where the value in controversy shall exceed twenty dollars, the right of trial by jury shall be preserved, and no fact tried by a jury, shall be otherwise reexamined in any Court of the United States, than according to the rules of common law.

Amendment VIII

Excessive bail shall not be required, nor excessive fines imposed, nor cruel and unusual punishments inflicted.

Amendment IX

The enumeration in the Constitution, of certain rights, shall not be construed to deny or disparage others retained by the people.

Amendment 9

Powers Reserved to the People This amendment prevents government from claiming that the only rights people have are those listed in the Bill of Rights.

Amendment X

The powers not delegated to the United States by the Constitution, nor prohibited by it to the States, are reserved to the States respectively, or to the people.

Amendment 10

Powers Reserved to the States The final amendment of the Bill of Rights protects the states and the people from an all-powerful federal government. It establishes that powers not given to the national government–or denied to the states–by the Constitution belong to the states or to the people.

Amendment XI

The Judicial power of the United States shall not be construed to extend to any suit in law or equity, commenced or prosecuted against one of the United States by Citizens of another State, or by Citizens or Subjects of any Foreign State.

Amendment 11

Suits Against States The Eleventh Amendment (1795) limits the jurisdiction of the federal courts. The Supreme Court had ruled that a federal court could try a lawsuit brought by citizens of South Carolina against the state of Georgia. This case, *Chisholm* v. *Georgia*, decided in 1793, raised a storm of protest, leading to passage of the Eleventh Amendment.

Amendment 12

Election of President and Vice President The Twelfth Amendment (1804) corrects a problem that had arisen in the method of electing the president and vice president. This amendment provides for the Electoral College to use separate ballots in voting for president and vice president. *If no candidate receives a majority of the electoral votes, who elects the president?*

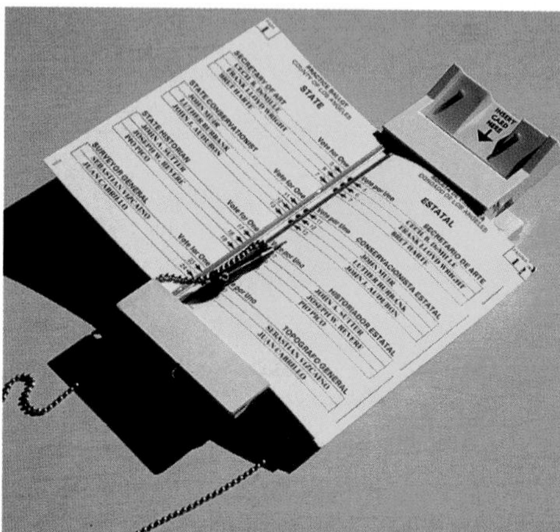

Ballot and ballot marker

Amendment XII

The electors shall meet in their respective states and vote by ballot for President and Vice-President, one of whom, at least, shall not be an inhabitant of the same state with themselves; they shall name in their ballots the person voted for as President, and in distinct ballots the person voted for as Vice-President, and they shall make distinct lists of all persons voted for as President, and of all persons voted for as Vice-President, and of the number of votes for each, which lists they shall sign and certify, and transmit sealed to the seat of the government of the United States, directed to the President of the Senate;—The President of the Senate shall, in the presence of the Senate and House of Representatives, open all the certificates and the votes shall then be counted;—The person having the greatest number of votes for President, shall be the President, if such number be a majority of the whole number of Electors appointed; and if no person have such majority, then from the persons having the highest numbers not exceeding three on the list of those voted for as President, the House of Representatives shall choose immediately, by ballot, the President. But in choosing the President, the votes shall be taken by states, the representation from each state having one vote; a quorum for this purpose shall consist of a member or members from two-thirds of the states, and a majority of all the states shall be necessary to a choice. And if the House of Representatives shall not choose a President whenever the right of choice shall devolve upon them, before the fourth day of March next following, then the Vice-President shall act as President, as in the case of the death or other constitutional disability of the President. The person having the greatest number of votes as Vice-President, shall be the Vice-President, if such number be a majority of the whole number of Electors appointed, and if no person have a majority, then from the two highest numbers on the list, the Senate shall choose the Vice-President; a quorum for the purpose shall consist of two-thirds of the whole number of Senators, and a majority of the whole number shall be necessary to a choice. But no person constitutionally ineligible to the office of President shall be eligible to that of Vice-President of the United States.

Amendment 13

Abolition of Slavery Amendments Thirteen (1865), Fourteen (1868), and Fifteen (1870) often are called the Civil War amendments because they grew out of that great conflict. The Thirteenth Amendment outlaws slavery.

Amendment XIII

Section 1

Neither slavery nor involuntary servitude, except as a punishment for crime whereof the party shall have been duly convicted, shall exist within the United States, or any place subject to their jurisdiction.

Section 2

Congress shall have power to enforce this article by appropriate legislation.

Vocabulary

majority: *more than half*
devolve: *to pass on*
abridge: *to reduce*
insurrection: *rebellion against the government*
emancipation: *freedom from slavery*

Amendment XIV

Section 1

All persons born or naturalized in the United States, and subject to the jurisdiction thereof, are citizens of the United States and of the State wherein they reside. No State shall make or enforce any law which shall abridge the privileges or immunities of citizens of the United States; nor shall any State deprive any person of life, liberty, or property, without due process of law; nor deny to any person within its jurisdiction the equal protection of the laws.

Amendment 14

Rights of Citizens The Fourteenth Amendment (1868) originally was intended to protect the legal rights of the freed slaves. Today it protects the rights of citizenship in general by prohibiting a state from depriving any person of life, liberty, or property without "due process of law." In addition, it states that all citizens have the right to equal protection of the law in all states.

Section 2

Representatives shall be apportioned among the several States according to their respective numbers, counting the whole number of persons in each State, excluding Indians not taxed. But when the right to vote at any election for the choice of electors for President and Vice President of the United States, Representatives in Congress, the Executive and Judicial officers of a State, or the members of the Legislature thereof, is denied to any of the male inhabitants of such State, being twenty-one years of age, and citizens of the United States, or in any way abridged, except for participation in rebellion, or other crime, the basis of representation therein shall be reduced in the proportion which the number of such male citizens shall bear to the whole number of male citizens twenty-one years of age in such State.

Amendment 14. Section 2

Representation in Congress This section reduced the number of members a state had in the House of Representatives if it denied its citizens the right to vote. Later civil rights laws and the Twenty-fourth Amendment guaranteed the vote to African Americans.

Section 3

No person shall be a Senator or Representative in Congress, or elector of President and Vice President, or hold any office, civil or military, under the United States, or under any State, who, having previously taken an oath, as a member of Congress, or as an officer of the United States, or as a member of any State legislature, or as an executive or judicial officer of any State, to support the Constitution of the United States, shall have engaged in insurrection or rebellion against the same, or given aid or comfort to the enemies thereof. But Congress may by a vote of two-thirds of each House, remove such disability.

Amendment 14. Section 3

Penalty for Engaging in Insurrection The leaders of the Confederacy were barred from state or federal offices unless Congress agreed to remove this ban. By the end of Reconstruction all but a few Confederate leaders were allowed to return to public life.

Section 4

The validity of the public debt of the United States, authorized by law, including debts incurred for payment of pensions and bounties for service in suppressing insurrection or rebellion, shall not be questioned. But neither the United States nor any State shall assume or pay any debt or obligation incurred in aid of insurrection or rebellion against the United States, or any claim for the loss or emancipation of any slave; but all such debts, obligations and claims shall be held illegal and void.

Amendment 14. Section 4

Public Debt The public debt acquired by the federal government during the Civil War was valid and could not be questioned by the South. However, the debts of the Confederacy were declared to be illegal. *Could former slaveholders collect payment for the loss of their slaves?*

Amendment 15

Right to Vote The Fifteenth Amendment (1870) prohibits the government from denying a person's right to vote on the basis of race. Despite the law, many states denied African Americans the right to vote by such means as poll taxes, literacy tests, and white primaries. During the 1950s and 1960s, Congress passed successively stronger laws to end racial discrimination in voting rights.

Internal Revenue Service

Amendment 17

Direct Election of Senators The Seventeenth Amendment (1913) states that the people, instead of state legislatures, elect United States senators. *How many years are in a Senate term?*

Section 5

The Congress shall have power to enforce, by appropriate legislation, the provisions of this article.

Amendment XV

Section 1

The right of citizens of the United States to vote shall not be denied or abridged by the United States or by any State on account of race, color, or previous condition of servitude.

Section 2

The Congress shall have power to enforce this article by appropriate legislation.

Amendment XVI

The Congress shall have power to lay and collect taxes on incomes, from whatever source derived, without apportionment among the several States and without regard to any census or enumeration.

Amendment XVII

Section 1

The Senate of the United States shall be composed of two Senators from each State, elected by the people thereof, for six years; and each Senator shall have one vote. The electors in each State shall have the qualifications requisite for electors of the most numerous branch of the State legislatures.

Section 2

When vacancies happen in the representation of any State in the Senate, the executive authority of such State shall issue writs of election to fill such vacancies: *Provided,* That the legislature of any State may empower the executive thereof to make temporary appointments until the people fill the vacancies by election as the legislature may direct.

Section 3

This amendment shall not be so construed as to affect the election or term of any Senator chosen before it becomes valid as part of the Constitution.

Vocabulary

apportionment: *distribution of seats in House based on population*

vacancy: *an office or position that is unfilled or unoccupied*

Amendment XVIII

Section 1

After one year from ratification of this article, the manufacture, sale, or transportation of intoxicating liquors within, the importation thereof into, or the exportation thereof from the United States and all territory subject to the jurisdiction thereof for beverage purposes is hereby prohibited.

Section 2

The Congress and the several States shall have concurrent power to enforce this article by appropriate legislation.

Section 3

This article shall be inoperative unless it shall have been ratified as an amendment to the Constitution by the legislatures of the several States, as provided in the Constitution, within seven years from the date of the submission hereof to the States by the Congress.

Amendment 18

Prohibition of Alcoholic Beverages The Eighteenth Amendment (1919) prohibited the production, sale, or transportation of alcoholic beverages in the United States. Prohibition proved to be difficult to enforce. This amendment was later repealed by the Twenty-first Amendment.

Amendment XIX

Section 1

The right of citizens of the United States to vote shall not be denied or abridged by the United States or by any State on account of sex.

Section 2

Congress shall have power by appropriate legislation to enforce the provisions of this article.

Amendment 19

Woman Suffrage The Nineteenth Amendment (1920) guaranteed women the right to vote. By then women had already won the right to vote in many state elections, but the amendment put their right to vote in all state and national elections on a constitutional basis.

Amendment XX

Section 1

The terms of the President and Vice President shall end at noon on the 20th day of January, and the terms of the Senators and Representatives at noon on the 3d day of January, of the years in which such terms would have ended if this article had not been ratified; and the terms of their successors shall then begin.

Section 2

The Congress shall assemble at least once in every year, and such meeting shall begin at noon on the 3d day of January, unless they shall by law appoint a different day.

Amendment 20

"Lame-Duck" Amendment The Twentieth Amendment (1933) sets new dates for Congress to begin its term and for the inauguration of the president and vice president. Under the original Constitution, elected officials who retired or who had been defeated remained in office for several months. For the outgoing president, this period ran from November until March. Such outgoing officials had little influence and accomplished little, and they were called lame ducks because they were so inactive. *What date was fixed as Inauguration Day?*

Amendment 20. Section 3

Succession of President and Vice President This section provides that if the president-elect dies before taking office, the vice president-elect becomes president.

John Tyler was the first vice president to become president when a chief executive died.

Amendment 21

Repeal of Prohibition Amendment The Twenty-first Amendment (1933) repeals the Eighteenth Amendment. It is the only amendment ever passed to overturn an earlier amendment. It is also the only amendment ratified by special state conventions instead of state legislatures.

Vocabulary

president-elect: *individual who is elected president but has not yet begun serving his or her term*

District of Columbia: *site of nation's capital, occupying an area between Maryland and Virginia*

Section 3

If, at the time fixed for the beginning of the term of the President, the President elect shall have died, the Vice President elect shall become President. If a President shall not have been chosen before the time fixed for the beginning of his term, or if the President elect shall have failed to qualify, then the Vice President elect shall act as President until a President shall have qualified; and the Congress may by law provide for the case wherein neither a President elect nor a Vice President elect shall have qualified, declaring who shall then act as President, or the manner in which one who is to act shall be selected, and such person shall act accordingly until a President or Vice President shall have qualified.

Section 4

The Congress may by law provide for the case of the death of any of the persons from whom the House of Representatives may choose a President whenever the right of choice shall have devolved upon them, and for the case of the death of any of the persons from whom the Senate may choose a Vice President whenever the right of choice shall have devolved upon them.

Section 5

Sections 1 and 2 shall take effect on the 15th day of October following the ratification of this article.

Section 6

This article shall be inoperative unless it shall have been ratified as an amendment to the Constitution by the legislatures of three-fourths of the several States within seven years from the date of its submission.

Amendment XXI

Section 1

The eighteenth article of amendment to the Constitution of the United States is hereby repealed.

Section 2

The transportation or importation into any State, Territory, or possession of the United States for delivery or use therein of intoxicating liquors, in violation of the laws thereof, is hereby prohibited.

Section 3

This article shall be inoperative unless it shall have been ratified as an amendment to the Constitution by conventions in the several States, as provided in the Constitution, within seven years from the date of the submission hereof to the States by the Congress.

Amendment XXII

Section 1

No person shall be elected to the office of the President more than twice, and no person who had held the office of President, or acted as President, for more than two years of a term to which some other person was elected President shall be elected to the office of the President more than once. But this Article shall not apply to any person holding the office of President when this Article was proposed by the Congress, and shall not prevent any person who may be holding the office of President, or acting as President, during the term within which this Article becomes operative from holding the office of President or acting as President during the remainder of such term.

Section 2

This article shall be inoperative unless it shall have been ratified as an amendment to the Constitution by the legislatures of three-fourths of the several States within seven years from the date of its submission to the States by the Congress.

Amendment 22

Limit on Presidential Terms The Twenty-second Amendment (1951) limits presidents to a maximum of two elected terms. It was passed largely as a reaction to Franklin D. Roosevelt's election to four terms between 1933 and 1945.

Presidential campaign buttons

Amendment XXIII

Section 1

The District constituting the seat of Government of the United States shall appoint in such manner as the Congress may direct:

A number of electors of President and Vice President equal to the whole number of Senators and Representatives in Congress to which the District would be entitled if it were a State, but in no event more than the least populous State; they shall be in addition to those appointed by the States, but they shall be considered, for the purposes of the election of President and Vice President, to be electors appointed by a State; and they shall meet in the District and perform such duties as provided by the twelfth article of amendment.

Section 2

The Congress shall have power to enforce this article by appropriate legislation.

Amendment 23

Presidential Electors for the District of Columbia The Twenty-third Amendment (1961) allows citizens living in Washington, D.C., to vote for president and vice president, a right previously denied residents of the nation's capital. The District of Columbia now has three presidential electors, the number to which it would be entitled if it were a state.

Amendment 24

Abolition of Poll Tax The Twenty-fourth Amendment (1964) prohibits poll taxes in federal elections. Prior to the passage of this amendment, some states had used such taxes to keep low-income African Americans from voting. In 1966 the Supreme Court banned poll taxes in state elections as well.

Amendment XXIV

Section 1

The right of citizens of the United States to vote in any primary or other election for President or Vice-President, for electors for President or Vice President, or for Senator or Representative in Congress, shall not be denied or abridged by the United States or any State by reason of failure to pay any poll tax or other tax.

Section 2

The Congress shall have power to enforce this article by appropriate legislation.

Amendment 25

Presidential Disability and Succession The Twenty-fifth Amendment (1967) established a process for the vice president to take over leadership of the nation when a president is disabled. It also set procedures for filling a vacancy in the office of vice president.

This amendment was used in 1973, when Vice President Spiro Agnew resigned from office after being charged with accepting bribes. President Richard Nixon then appointed Gerald R. Ford as vice president in accordance with the provisions of the 25th Amendment. A year later, President Nixon resigned during the Watergate scandal and Ford became president. President Ford then had to fill the vice presidency, which he had left vacant upon assuming the presidency. He named Nelson A. Rockefeller as vice president. Thus individuals who had not been elected held both the presidency and the vice presidency. *Whom does the president inform if he or she cannot carry out the duties of the office?*

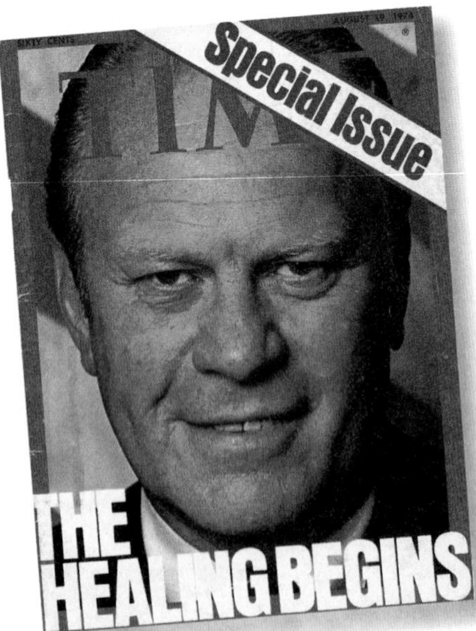

President Gerald Ford

Amendment XXV

Section 1

In case of the removal of the President from office or his death or resignation, the Vice President shall become President.

Section 2

Whenever there is a vacancy in the office of the Vice President, the President shall nominate a Vice President who shall take the office upon confirmation by a majority vote of both Houses of Congress.

Section 3

Whenever the President transmits to the President pro tempore of the Senate and the Speaker of the House of Representatives his written declaration that he is unable to discharge the powers and duties of his office, and until he transmits to them a written declaration to the contrary, such powers and duties shall be discharged by the Vice President as Acting President.

Section 4

Whenever the Vice President and a majority of either the principal officers of the executive departments or of such other body as Congress may by law provide, transmit to the President pro tempore of the Senate and the Speaker of the House of Representatives their written declaration that the President is unable to discharge the powers and duties of his office, the Vice President shall immediately assume the power and duties of the office of Acting President.

Thereafter, when the President transmits to the President pro tempore of the Senate and the Speaker of the House of Representatives his written declaration that no inability exists, he shall resume the powers and duties of his office unless the Vice President and a majority of either the principal officers of the executive department or of such other body as Congress may by law provide, transmit within four days to the President pro tempore of the Senate and the Speaker of the House of Representatives their written declaration that the President is unable to discharge the powers and duties of his office.

Thereupon Congress shall decide the issue, assembling within forty-eight hours for that purpose if not in session. If the Congress, within twenty-one days after receipt of the latter written declaration, or, if Congress is not in session, within twenty-one days after Congress is required to assemble, determines by two-thirds vote of both Houses that the President is unable to discharge the powers and duties of his office, the Vice President shall continue to discharge the same as Acting President; otherwise, the President shall resume the power and duties of his office.

Amendment XXVI

Section 1

The right of citizens of the United States, who are eighteen years of age or older, to vote shall not be denied or abridged by the United States or by any State on account of age.

Section 2

The Congress shall have power to enforce this article by appropriate legislation.

Amendment 26

Eighteen-Year-Old Vote The Twenty-sixth Amendment (1971) guarantees the right to vote to all citizens 18 years of age and older.

Amendment XXVII

No law, varying the compensation for the services of Senators and Representatives, shall take effect, until an election of representatives shall have intervened.

Amendment 27

Restraint on Congressional Salaries The Twenty-seventh Amendment (1992) makes congressional pay raises effective during the term following their passage. James Madison offered the amendment in 1789, but it was never adopted. In 1982 Gregory Watson, then a student at the University of Texas, discovered the forgotten amendment while doing research for a school paper. Watson made the amendment's passage his crusade.

Joint meeting of Congress

Unit
3

Launching the Republic

Why It's Important

With the Constitution in place, the newly chosen government began to set procedures and customs for the country. The nation continued to gain new territory and grow, but faced challenges from other countries, including its old foe, Great Britain. The United States also set foreign policy that would guide its actions for many years.

- The American political process took shape during the country's early years.
- The United States began to establish its place in the world as it gained territory and fought wars with foreign powers.

1780
1790
1800
U.S. EVENTS
1789 Washington becomes first president
1791 Bill of Rights is added to Constitution
1798 Alien and Sedition Acts are passed
1804 Lewis and Clark begin expedition
February 22nd. 1732
December 14th. 1799
CALIFORNIA EVENTS
1796 American ship opens up trade with California
1800 Strong earthquake hits San Diego region
WORLD EVENTS
1789 The French Revolution begins
1804 Napoleon crowns himself emperor of France

Washington banner

Storming of the Bastille

NATIONAL GEOGRAPHIC

Where in the United States?

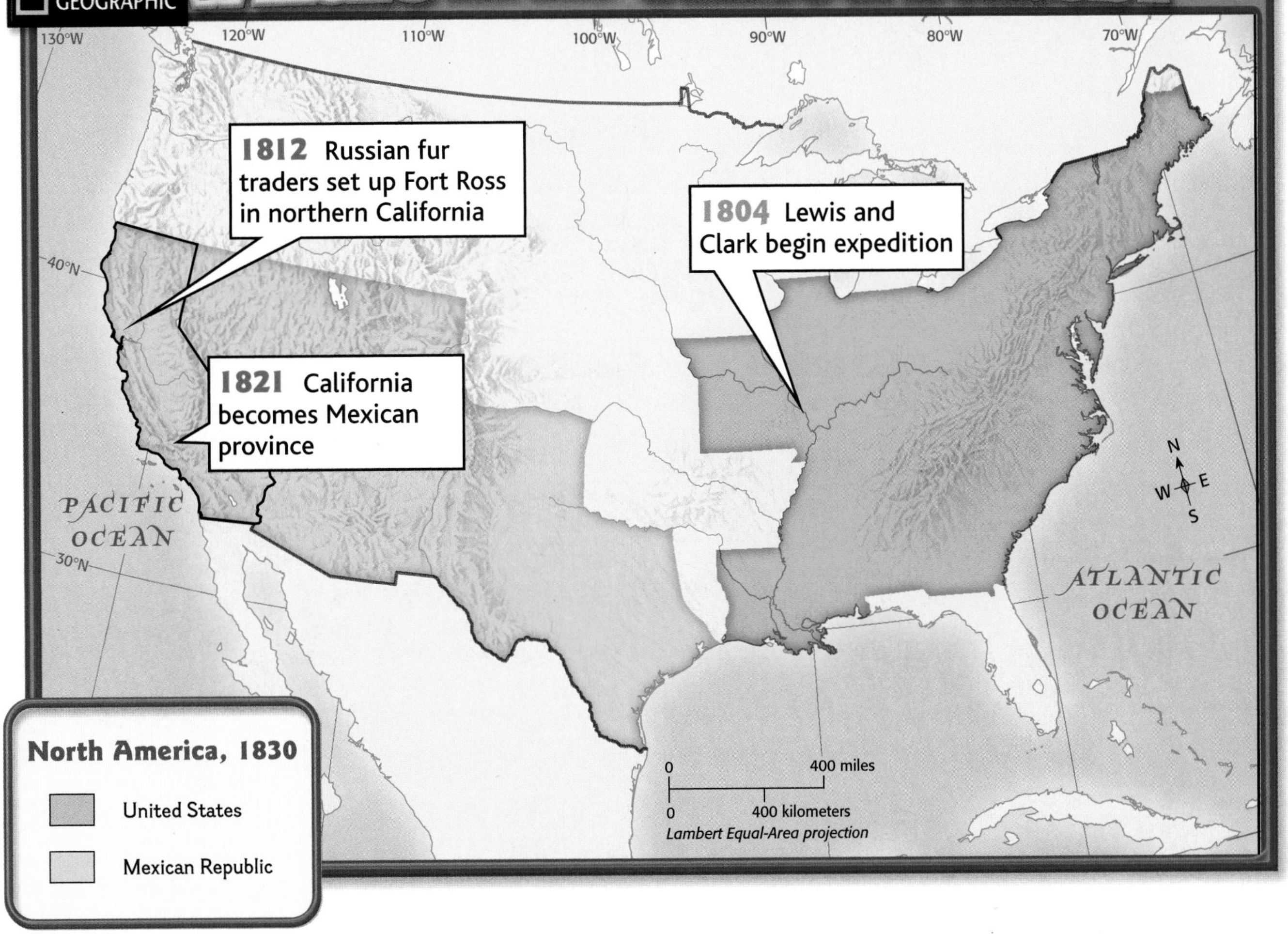

130°W 120°W 110°W 100°W 90°W 80°W 70°W

40°N

30°N

1812 Russian fur traders set up Fort Ross in northern California

1804 Lewis and Clark begin expedition

1821 California becomes Mexican province

PACIFIC OCEAN

ATLANTIC OCEAN

N E S W

0 400 miles
0 400 kilometers
Lambert Equal-Area projection

North America, 1830

- United States
- Mexican Republic

1810 1820 1830

1812
U.S. declares war on Britain

American sailors

1823
Monroe Doctrine is declared

1812
Russian fur traders set up Fort Ross in northern California

1819
Northern California border is set at 42nd parallel

1821
California becomes Mexican province

1824
Rancho economy begins

Fort Ross

Mexican flag

1815
Allies defeat Napoleon at Waterloo

1821
Mexico wins its independence from Spain

1824
Mexico offers land grants to Mexicans and immigrants

Unit 3

Places to Locate

TREATY OF GREENVILLE

See *The Federalist Era*
Chapter 5

MONTICELLO

See *The Age of Jefferson*
Chapter 6

People to Meet

Alexander Hamilton
1755–1804
First Secretary of the Treasury
Chapter 5, page 283

John Adams
1735–1826
First vice president and second president
Chapter 5, page 294

Toussaint Louverture
c. 1743–1804
Haitian revolutionary
Chapter 6, page 313

Sacagawea
c. 1787–1812
Shoshone guide for Lewis and Clark
Chapter 6, page 315

NATIONAL GEOGRAPHIC

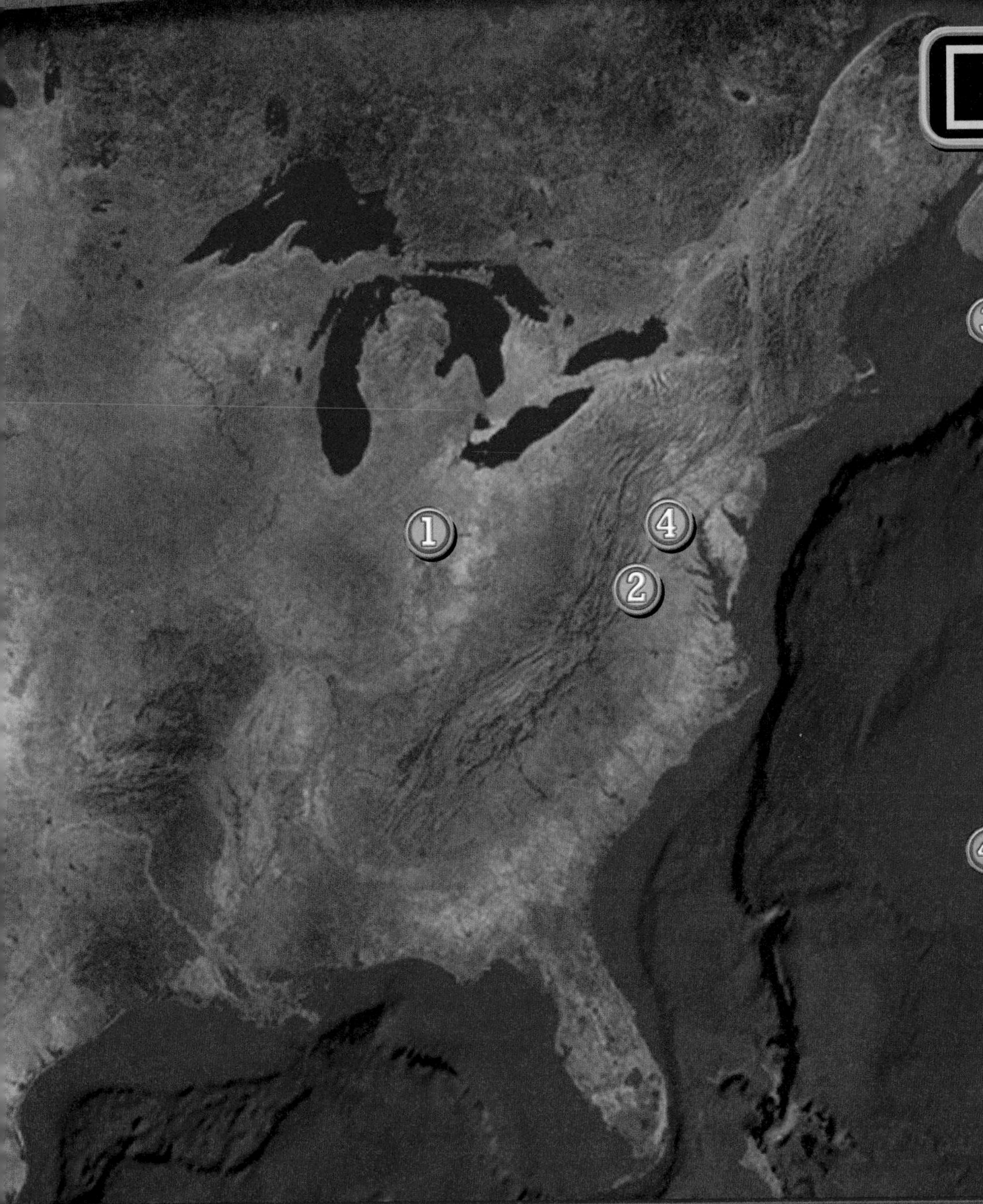

3 LEWIS AND CLARK

See *The Age of Jefferson* Chapter 6

4 BATTLE OF NORTH POINT

See *Foreign Affairs in the Early Republic* Chapter 7

James Fenimore Cooper
1789–1851
American writer
Chapter 6, page 324

Washington Irving
1783–1859
American writer
Chapter 6, page 324

John Calhoun
1782–1850
Political leader
Chapter 7, page 344

Dolley Madison
1768–1849
First lady
Chapter 7, page 357

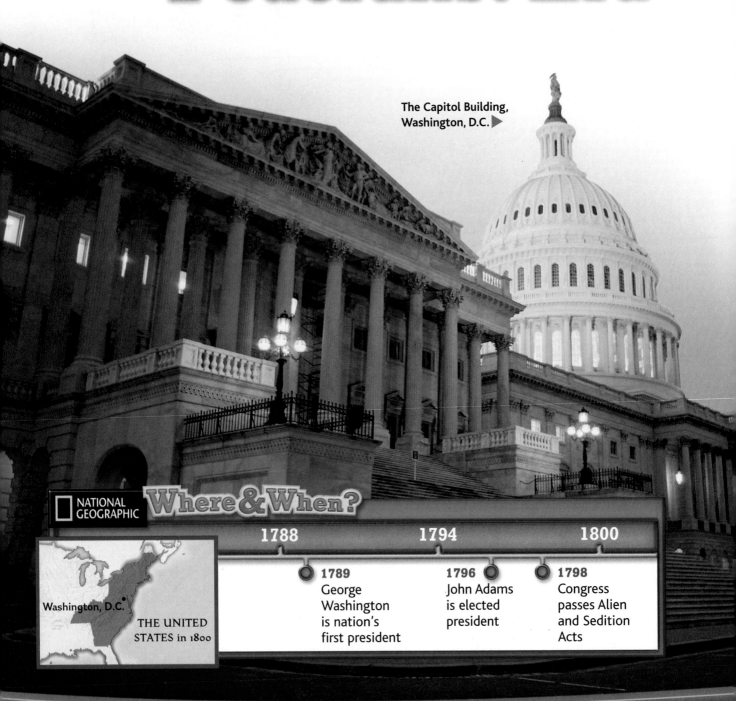

The Federalist Era

The Capitol Building, Washington, D.C. ▶

NATIONAL GEOGRAPHIC

Where & When?

1788 | 1794 | 1800

1789 George Washington is nation's first president

1796 John Adams is elected president

1798 Congress passes Alien and Sedition Acts

History Online
Chapter Overview Visit ca.hss.glencoe.com for a preview of Chapter 5.

The Big Ideas

The First President

Political ideas and major events shape how people form governments. President Washington and the first Congress built a new government.

Early Challenges

Political ideas and major events shape how people form governments. The new American government struggled to keep peace at home and avoid war abroad.

The First Political Parties

Citizen participation is essential to the foundation and preservation of the U.S. political system. By the election of 1796, two distinct political parties with different views had developed.

View the Chapter 5 video in the Glencoe Video Program.

Summarizing Information Make this foldable and use it as a journal to help you record the major events that occurred as the new nation of the United States formed.

Step 1 Fold a sheet of paper from top to bottom.

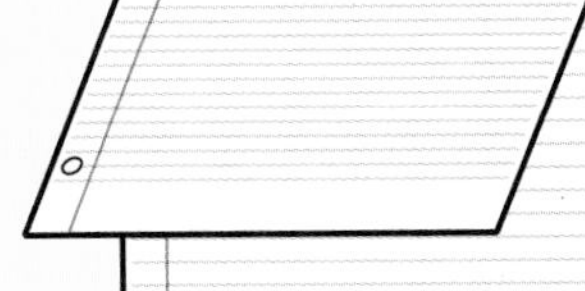

Step 2 Then fold it in half from side to side.

Step 3 Label the foldable as shown.

Reading and Writing As you read the chapter, find the "firsts" experienced by the new nation, and record them in your foldable journal. For example, list the precedents set by President Washington and identify the first political parties.

Get Ready to Read

Recognizing Bias

1 Learn It!

Most people have feelings and ideas that affect their point of view. This viewpoint, or *bias,* influences the way they interpret events. For this reason, an idea that is stated as a fact may really be only an opinion. Recognizing bias will help you judge the accuracy of what you read. You can look for clues to help uncover bias in written form. Read the list below for hints you can use to identify bias.

- **Identify the author of the statement, and examine his or her views and possible reasons for writing the material.**
- **Look for language that reflects an emotion or opinion—words such as *all, never, best, worst, might,* or *should.***
- **Examine the writing for imbalances—focusing on one viewpoint and failing to discuss other perspectives.**

Reading Tip

One way to identify bias is to find out more about the author. Can you find information about the author that will help you understand opinions he or she may express?

2 Practice It!

Look at the two quotes below. Each has a different opinion about "the people." On a separate sheet of paper, restate each opinion in your own words. Discuss your conclusions with a partner.

"The people are turbulent [disorderly] and changing. . . . They seldom judge or determine right."

—*Alexander Hamilton, Federalist, page 292*

Read to Write

Write a paragraph describing a person or event about which you feel very strongly. Now try to write a paragraph about the same person or event without including any personal opinion.

▲ Alexander Hamilton

"I am not among those who fear the people. They, and not the rich, are our dependence [what we depend on] for continued freedom."

—*Thomas Jefferson, Republican, page 293*

▲ Thomas Jefferson

3 Apply It!

Look for examples of bias in comments made by key figures described in the text.

Section 1 The First President

Guide to Reading

History Social Science Standards

US8.3 Students understand the foundation of the American political system and the ways in which citizens participate in it.

US8.4 Students analyze the aspirations and ideals of the people of the new nation.

Looking Back, Looking Ahead

American leaders faced a great challenge. Nobody knew if the political system laid out by the Constitution would work. Many people wondered: Could this new kind of government last?

Focusing on the Main Ideas

- President Washington and the new Congress established the departments in the executive branch, set up the nation's court system, and added the Bill of Rights to the Constitution. ***(page 279)***
- Alexander Hamilton, the secretary of the treasury under Washington, worked to fix financial problems and strengthen the economy. ***(page 281)***

Locating Places

Washington, D.C.

Meeting People

Thomas Jefferson
Alexander Hamilton
Henry Knox
Edmund Randolph
John Jay

Content Vocabulary

precedent (PREH • suh • duhnt)
cabinet
national debt (DEHT)
bond (BAHND)
speculator (SPEH • kyuh • LAY • tuhr)
unconstitutional
tariff (TAR • uhf)

Academic Vocabulary

ultimate (UHL • tuh • muht)
structure
confirm
revenue (REH • vuh • NOO)

Reading Strategy

Classifying Information Use a diagram like the one below to list the actions taken by Congress and Washington's first administration.

Actions	
Washington's First Administration	Congress

NATIONAL GEOGRAPHIC Who & When?

1789
1790
1791
1792
Apr. 30, 1789
Washington takes the oath of office
Sep. 1789
Judiciary Act sets up federal court system
Dec. 1791
Bill of Rights added to the Constitution

George Washington

John Jay

James Madison

US8.4 Students analyze the aspirations and ideals of the people of the new nation.

President Washington

Main Idea **President Washington and the new Congress established the departments in the executive branch, set up the nation's court system, and added the Bill of Rights to the Constitution.**

Reading Connection If you were founding our nation's government, what do you think would be most important? As you read this section, think about the choices that Washington and the new Congress had to make.

An American Story

Celebrations erupted in the streets of Philadelphia, New York, Boston, and Charleston in 1789. News of the Constitution's ratification was greeted with relief and enthusiasm. All that was needed now was a leader to guide the new nation.

On April 6, the new Senate counted the presidential ballots. To no one's surprise, the votes were unanimous. Senator John Langdon wrote to General George Washington: "Sir, I have the honor to transmit to Your Excellency the information of your unanimous election to the office of President of the United States of America." Washington was ready to begin the difficult task of leading the country.

The Nation's First President The 57-year-old president-elect made his way slowly toward New York City, then the nation's capital. After the Constitutional Convention, George Washington had looked forward to a quiet retirement. Instead his fellow citizens elected him to the highest office in the land. On April 30, 1789, Washington took the oath of office as the first president of the United States under the federal Constitution. John Adams became vice president.

Perhaps no office in the new government created more suspicion among the people than the office of president. Many Americans feared that a president would try to become king, but Americans trusted Washington and they believed that it was his leadership that brought them victory in the Revolutionary War. Equally important, he had willingly given up his military power as soon as the war was over to return to his civilian life tending his plantation.

Washington was aware of the difficulties he faced. He knew that the **precedents** (PREH • suh • duhnts), or traditions, he established as the nation's first president would shape the future of the United States. "No slip will pass unnoticed," he remarked. One precedent he established concerned the way people should address him. Vice President Adams supported "His Highness the President of the United States," but **ultimately** it was decided that "Mr. President" would be more appropriate.

Washington and the new Congress also had many decisions to make about the **structure** of government. For example, the Constitution gave Congress the power to establish executive departments, but it did not state whether the department heads would report to the president or to Congress.

The First Congress During the summer of 1789, Congress established three executive departments: a Department of State to take charge of foreign affairs, a Department of the Treasury to handle the nation's finances, and a Department of War to manage the military.

▲ Banner celebrating George Washington

Congress also created the office of attorney general to handle the government's legal affairs and the office of postmaster general to direct the postal service. To head the departments, Washington chose prominent political figures of the day—**Thomas Jefferson** as secretary of state, **Alexander Hamilton** as secretary of the treasury, and **Henry Knox** as secretary of war. He appointed **Edmund Randolph** as attorney general. Washington met regularly with the three department heads and the attorney general, who together became known as the **cabinet.**

According to the Constitution, the Senate must approve presidential appointments to many important positions. However, other issues arose. For example, should the president be able to replace an official that he had appointed and the Senate had **confirmed?** Senators were evenly divided when they voted on the issue.

Vice President Adams broke the tie by voting to allow the president the authority to dismiss cabinet officers without the Senate's approval. This decision strengthened the president's position. It also helped establish the president's authority over the executive branch.

Linking Past & Present

The Electoral College

Past The presidents are not elected directly by the voters, but by a body of representatives called the Electoral College. The Constitution left it up to the states to determine how the electors of the Electoral College are chosen. In the first few presidential elections, the state legislatures chose the electors in many states.

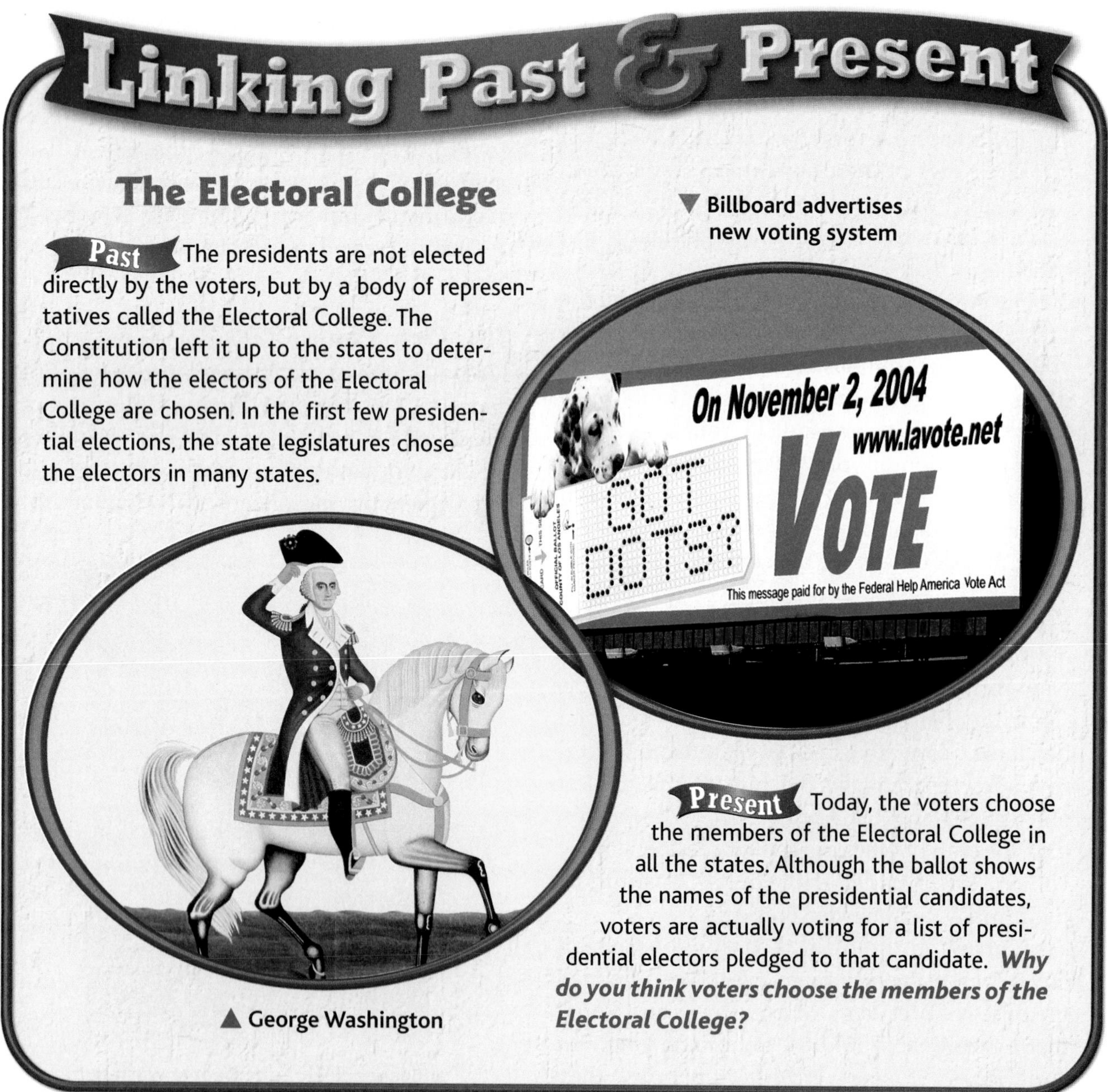
On November 2, 2004
www.lavote.net
GOT DOTS?
VOTE
This message paid for by the Federal Help America Vote Act

▼ Billboard advertises new voting system

▲ George Washington

Present Today, the voters choose the members of the Electoral College in all the states. Although the ballot shows the names of the presidential candidates, voters are actually voting for a list of presidential electors pledged to that candidate. ***Why do you think voters choose the members of the Electoral College?***

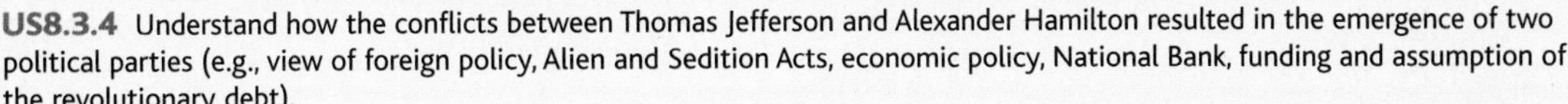
US8.3.4 Understand how the conflicts between Thomas Jefferson and Alexander Hamilton resulted in the emergence of two political parties (e.g., view of foreign policy, Alien and Sedition Acts, economic policy, National Bank, funding and assumption of the revolutionary debt).

What Did the Judiciary Act Do? The first Congress also had to decide how to set up the nation's court system. The Constitution briefly mentioned a supreme court but did not provide details about the court system. This became a job for Congress.

In the Judiciary Act of 1789, Congress established the Supreme Court and the lower federal courts: district courts and courts of appeals. The Supreme Court would be the final authority on many issues. Washington nominated **John Jay** to lead the Supreme Court as chief justice, and the Senate approved Jay's nomination. With the Judiciary Act, Congress had taken the first steps toward creating a strong and independent national judiciary.

The Bill of Rights Americans mistrusted strong central governments. They had fought a revolution to throw off one and did not want to replace it with another. Many people insisted that the Constitution needed to include guarantees of personal liberties. Some states had supported the Constitution on the condition that a bill of rights be added to protect individual rights.

James Madison introduced a set of amendments during the first session of Congress. Congress passed 12 amendments, and the states ratified 10 of them. In December 1791, these 10 amendments were added to the Constitution and became known as the Bill of Rights.

The Bill of Rights protects our individual liberties. Government may not interfere with freedom of speech, press, or religion and must provide a fair and speedy trial for those accused of crimes. The Tenth Amendment protects the rights of states and individuals by saying that powers not specifically given to the federal government "are reserved to the States respectively, or to the people." With the Tenth Amendment, Madison hoped to use the states as an important line of defense against a too-powerful national government. *(See pages 260–261 for the entire text of the Bill of Rights.)*

Reading Check **Describe** Why was the Bill of Rights created?

Strengthening the Economy

Main Idea **Alexander Hamilton, the secretary of the treasury under Washington, worked to fix financial problems and strengthen the economy.**

Reading Connection Have you ever borrowed money from a family member or one of your friends? By doing so, you acquired a debt and had to figure out how and when to pay it back. Hamilton faced a similar challenge with the nation's debt.

Washington himself rarely proposed laws, and he almost always approved the bills that were passed by Congress. The first president concentrated on foreign affairs and military matters and left the government's economic policies to his secretary of the treasury, Alexander Hamilton.

The new nation faced serious financial problems. The **national debt** (DEHT)—the amount the nation's government owed—was growing. The United States owed millions of dollars to France and the Netherlands for loans made during and after the Revolutionary War. The Continental Congress also had borrowed millions of dollars from American citizens.

What Was Hamilton's Plan? In 1790 Hamilton proposed that the new government pay off the millions of dollars in debts owed by the Confederation government to other countries and to individual American citizens. The states had fought for the nation's independence, Hamilton argued, so the national government should pay for the cost of their help. Hamilton also believed that federal payment of state debts would give the states a strong interest in the success of the national government.

Opposition to the Plan Congress readily agreed to pay the money owed to other nations, but Hamilton's plan to pay off the debt to American citizens unleashed a storm of protest. When the government borrowed money during the American Revolution, it issued **bonds** (BAHNDZ)—paper notes promising to repay the money in a certain length of time.

While waiting for the payment, many original bond owners—shopkeepers, farmers, and soldiers—had sold the bonds for less than their value. They were purchased by **speculators** (SPEH • kyuh • LAY • tuhrz), people who take risks with their money in order to make a larger profit. Hamilton proposed that these bonds be paid off at their original value. Opponents believed that Hamilton's plan would make speculators rich.

The original bond owners felt betrayed by Hamilton's proposal. They had lost money on the bonds they had bought in support of the war effort while new bond owners would profit. Opponents in Congress argued that the proposal was contrary to "national justice, gratitude, and humanity."

Even stronger opposition came from the Southern states, which had accumulated much less debt than the Northern states. Southern states complained that they would have to pay more than their share under Hamilton's plan.

History Makers

The Capitol

The Capitol is the seat of the United States Congress in Washington, D.C. Built on a hill popularly called Capitol Hill, the Capitol contains floor space equivalent to more than 16 acres. The dome of the United States Capitol, finished in 1863, is one of the most famous landmarks in the United States. Other important parts of the Capitol include the Rotunda directly under the dome, the Senate Chamber in the north wing, the House chamber in the south wing, and the National Statuary Hall.

▲ The Capitol

Compromise Results in a Capital To win support for his plan, Hamilton worked out a compromise with Southern leaders. They voted for his plan to pay off the state debts, and in return he supported locating the permanent capital in the South. A special district was laid out between Virginia and Maryland along the banks of the Potomac River. This district became **Washington, D.C.** While workers prepared the new city for the federal government, the nation's capital was moved from New York to Philadelphia.

The Fight Over the Bank Hamilton made other proposals for building a strong national economy. He asked Congress to create a national bank, the Bank of the United States. The bank would be a place for the federal government to deposit money raised from taxes. The bank could also provide loans to government and to businesses.

Madison and Jefferson opposed the idea of a national bank. They believed it would give the wealthy too much power over national finances. They also charged that the Bank was **unconstitutional**—that it was inconsistent with the Constitution. Hamilton argued that although the Constitution did not specifically say that Congress could create a bank, Congress still had the power to do so. In the end, the president agreed with Hamilton and signed the bill creating the national bank.

What Is a Tariff? Although most Americans earned their living by farming, Hamilton thought the development of manufacturing would make America's economy stronger. He proposed a **tariff** (TAR • uhf)—a tax on imports—to encourage people to buy American products.

Biography

US8.3.4 Understand how the conflicts between Thomas Jefferson and Alexander Hamilton resulted in the emergence of two political parties (e.g., view of foreign policy, Alien and Sedition Acts, economic policy, National Bank, funding and assumption of the revolutionary debt).

ALEXANDER HAMILTON

1755–1804

Alexander Hamilton was born on the West Indies island of Nevis, where he worked as a clerk as a young man. In 1773 he moved to New York and studied at King's College. Hamilton quickly became involved in the fight for American independence. He impressed General George Washington, who made him one of his aides-de-camp (secretaries). Hamilton and Washington established a strong friendship and Hamilton served his country on the battlefield and in government.

Hamilton was elected to the Continental Congress and was a driving force in the ratification of the Constitution. Hamilton, James Madison, and John Jay wrote a series of essays called *The Federalist Papers* that explained how the new Constitution worked and why it was needed. Hamilton became the nation's first Secretary of the Treasury. He believed that manufacturing and trade were the basis of national wealth and power. He favored policies that would support these areas of the economy.

During Washington's presidency, Hamilton and Secretary of State Thomas Jefferson had some major differences. They disagreed strongly about how the U.S. government should operate. Hamilton was the leader of the Federalist Party, and Jefferson led the Democratic-Republican Party. These two men became, in essence, the founders of today's political parties.

"A feeble executive implies a feeble execution of the government."

—Alexander Hamilton, The Federalist, No. 70

When Jefferson and Aaron Burr tied with 73 electoral votes in the presidential election of 1800, the Federalist-controlled House of Representatives had to choose a president. Hamilton urged his followers to support Jefferson, and Jefferson became the new president. After Burr failed in his bid to become president, he campaigned to become governor of New York in 1804. Hamilton worked actively against Burr. When Burr lost, he blamed his defeat on Hamilton and challenged him to a duel. Hamilton was fatally wounded and died on July 12, 1804, ending the life of one of the nation's most influential leaders.

Then and Now

Which of Hamilton's actions do you think most influenced the nation's government? Explain your reasoning.

Opposition to the Tariff This protective tariff would not only raise revenue for the new national government, but also protect American industry from foreign competition. However, many Americans were against the tariff.

The South, having little industry to protect, opposed protective tariffs. Congress rejected protective tariffs but did pass low tariffs to raise money. By the 1790s, the **revenue** from tariffs provided 90 percent of the national government's income.

Taxes The final part of Hamilton's economic program concerned the creation of national taxes. The government needed additional funds to operate and to make interest payments on the national debt. At Hamilton's request, Congress approved a variety of taxes, including one on whiskey distilled in the United States.

Hamilton and Jefferson Under Alexander Hamilton's economic program, the national government exercised new financial powers. Soon, however, well-organized opposition to Hamilton's political and economic beliefs grew.

The opposition to Hamilton was led by Thomas Jefferson and James Madison. Where Hamilton's policies favored merchants, bankers, and speculators, his opponents spoke for the interests of the farmers and laborers. When Hamilton favored increasing the power of the federal government, Jefferson wanted to limit it. They had a very different vision of what America should become.

Reading Check **Compare** Summarize the arguments for and against protective tariffs.

Study Central Need help understanding Washington's presidency? Visit ca.hss.glencoe.com and click on Study Central.

Section 1 Review

Reading Summary

Review the Main Ideas

- President Washington and the first Congress established the cabinet and a federal court system. The first 10 amendments to the Constitution, the Bill of Rights, were introduced during the first session of Congress.
- Under Secretary of the Treasury Alexander Hamilton, the national government agreed to pay off states' debts, created a national bank, and put in place a number of tariffs and taxes.

What Did You Learn?

1. What challenges did Washington face as the nation's first president?
2. Name one thing Hamilton wanted to do to create a stable economic system and strengthen the economy.

Critical Thinking

3. **Comparing** Re-create the diagram below. Compare the views of Hamilton and Jefferson. In the boxes, write "for" or "against" for each issue. CA HR5.

Issue	Hamilton	Jefferson
National bank		
Protective tariff		
National taxes		

4. **The Big Ideas** What compromise led to acceptance of Hamilton's plan for reducing the national debt? CA HI2.
5. **Expository Writing** Imagine you are choosing the first cabinet members. Write job descriptions for the secretaries of state, treasury, and war. CA 8WA2.5
6. **READING Recognizing Bias** Read Hamilton's quote. Explain in writing why it does or does not contain bias.

"Can a democratic assembly. . . steadily pursue the public good? Nothing but a permanent body can check the imprudence [disregard of others] of democracy." CA HR2.

Section 2 Early Challenges

Guide to Reading

Looking Back, Looking Ahead

The United States needed money to pay its war debts and to finance national growth. Although located an ocean away from Europe, the United States could not hope to exist in isolation. The nation had to respond to overseas pressures.

Focusing on the Main Ideas

- Hamilton's taxes led to rebellion in western Pennsylvania and changed the way the government handled protesters. *(page 286)*
- The new government faced difficult problems in the West. *(page 287)*
- President Washington wanted the nation to remain neutral in foreign conflicts. *(page 288)*

Locating Places

Fallen Timbers
New Orleans

Meeting People

Anthony Wayne
Edmond Genêt (zhuh • NAY)
Thomas Pinckney (PINGK • nee)

Content Vocabulary

neutrality (noo • TRA • luh • tee)
impressment (ihm • PREHS • muhnt)

Academic Vocabulary

transport
maintain

Reading Strategy

Classifying Information As you read the section, re-create the diagram below and list results of government actions during the early Republic.

Government action	Results
Treaty of Greenville	
Proclamation of Neutrality	
Jay's Treaty	
Pinckney's Treaty	

History Social Science Standards

US8.3 Students understand the foundation of the American political system and the ways in which citizens participate in it.

US8.4 Students analyze the aspirations and ideals of the people of the new nation.

US8.3.5 Know the significance of domestic resistance movements and ways in which the central government responded to such movements (e.g., Shays' Rebellion, the Whiskey Rebellion).

The Whiskey Rebellion

Main Idea **Hamilton's taxes led to rebellion in western Pennsylvania and changed the way the government handled protesters.**

Reading Connection Is there a recent government action that you have opposed? What actions did you take? Read to learn what actions the farmers took in regards to the whiskey tax.

An American Story

Far removed from the bustle of trade and shipping along the Atlantic coast, farmers on the western frontier lived quite differently. In fact, western ways seemed almost primitive to travelers from the East. Easterners seemed to notice only the poor roads and the plain diet of corn and salted pork. Living in scattered, isolated homesteads, frontier farmers were proud of their self-reliance. They wanted no "eastern" tax collectors heading their way.

Life in the West In the days before canals and railroads, the Western farmers did not ship their grain east of the Appalachian Mountains because **transporting** the grain was expensive. A wagonload of whiskey was worth much more than a wagonload of grain, so Western farmers distilled their grain into whiskey before they shipped it to market.

The farmers rarely had cash. As a result, most lived on a system of bartering—exchanging whiskey and other items they produced for goods they needed.

The Tax Leads to Protests In 1791 both houses of Congress approved a bill that placed a special tax on whiskey and other alcoholic beverages. Secretary of the Treasury Alexander Hamilton wanted the tax to help prevent the national debt from growing.

The farmers' resistance was mostly peaceful—until July 1794, when federal officers stepped up efforts to collect the tax. Then a large mob of farmers armed with swords, guns, and pitchforks attacked tax collectors and burned down buildings.

The armed protest, called the Whiskey Rebellion, alarmed government leaders as had Shays's Rebellion in 1786. *(See Chapter 3, pages 194–195.)* Now, however, the national government had the taxing and military power that it lacked in 1786. The secretary of the treasury, Alexander Hamilton, urged President Washington to use the full power of the federal government to crush the challenge. The president sent an army of 15,000 across the Appalachian Mountains, only to find that the rebels had already disbanded.

By his action, Washington sent a clear message to those who opposed government actions. If citizens wished to change the law, they had to do so peacefully, through constitutional means such as proposing legislation or using the courts. Otherwise, government would use force when necessary to **maintain** order.

Picturing History

In 1794 President Washington sent nearly 15,000 troops to crush the Whiskey Rebellion. ***What did Washington's action say about the government use of force?***

Reading Check **Explain** How did the Whiskey Rebellion affect the way government handled protesters?

US8.4.1 Describe the country's physical landscapes, political divisions, and territorial expansion during the terms of the first four presidents.

Struggle Over the West

Main Idea **The new government faced difficult problems in the West.**

Reading Connection Imagine you are a member of George Washington's government in 1791. Could you balance the interests of settlers who are moving into the Northwest Territory with the interests of the Native American nations who live there? Read on to see how President Washington handled a similar challenge.

The Native Americans who lived between the Appalachian Mountains and the Mississippi River insisted that the United States had no authority over them.

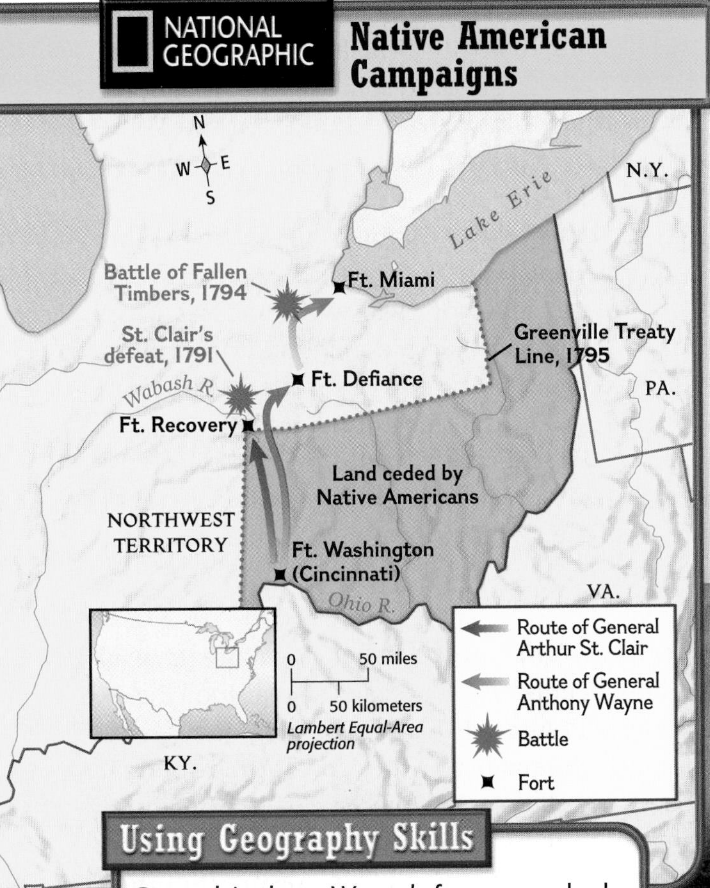

Using Geography Skills

General Anthony Wayne's forces marched north from Fort Washington to fight the Shawnee chief Blue Jacket.

1. **Location** When and where was St. Clair defeated?
2. **Location** On what lake was Fort Miami located?

Armed to defend their lands and encouraged by the British and the Spanish, Native Americans battled settlers over frontier land. Hundreds of people were killed.

Washington sent an army under the command of General Arthur St. Clair to restore order in the Northwest Territory. In November 1791, St. Clair's forces were defeated by Little Turtle, chief of the Miami people. More than 600 American soldiers died in a battle by the Wabash River.

Battle of Fallen Timbers The Native Americans demanded that all settlers north of the Ohio River leave the territory. Washington sent another army headed by **Anthony Wayne,** a former Revolutionary War general, to challenge their demands. In August 1794, his army defeated more than 1,000 Native Americans who fought under Shawnee chief Blue Jacket at the Battle of **Fallen Timbers** (near present-day Toledo, Ohio). The Battle of Fallen Timbers crushed the Native Americans' hopes of keeping their land. In the Treaty of Greenville (1795), the Native Americans agreed to surrender most of their land in present-day Ohio.

Reading Check **Explain** Why did President Washington send troops to the Northwest Territory?

Picturing **History**

Upon signing the Treaty of Greenville, 12 Native American nations received $20,000 worth of goods to share. ***How did the treaty affect white settlement?***

US8.4.2 Explain the policy significance of famous speeches (e.g., Washington's Farewell Address, Jefferson's 1801 Inaugural Address, John Q. Adams's Fourth of July 1821 Address).

Problems With Europe

Main Idea **President Washington wanted the nation to remain neutral in foreign conflicts.**

Reading Connection Have you ever felt like you were in the middle of a disagreement between two other people? Read on to see how President Washington looked for middle ground in a war between Great Britain and France.

Shortly after Washington was inaugurated in 1789, the French Revolution began. At first most Americans cheered upon hearing the news. The French people had helped the Americans in their struggle for independence, and their revolution seemed to reflect many of the ideals of the American Revolution.

By 1793 the French Revolution had turned bloody. The leaders had executed the king and queen of France and thousands of French citizens. Public opinion in the United States started to divide. The violence of the French Revolution offended many Americans. Others hailed the new republic as a copy of the United States.

When Britain and France went to war in 1793, Washington hoped that the nation could maintain its **neutrality** (noo • TRA • luh • tee)—that is, that it would not take sides in the conflict between France and Britain. As time went on, however, remaining neutral became increasingly difficult.

Washington Proclaims Neutrality The French wanted the help of the United States. In April 1793, they sent diplomat **Edmond Genêt** (zhuh • NAY) to the United States. His mission was to recruit American volunteers to attack British ships.

President Washington took action to discourage American involvement. On April 22, he issued a Proclamation of Neutrality. It prohibited American citizens from fighting in the war and barred French and British warships from American ports. Genêt's plans eventually failed, but he did manage to sign up a few hundred Americans to serve on French ships. These ships seized British vessels and stole their cargoes.

Outraged by the French attacks at sea, the British began capturing American ships that traded with the French. The British also stopped American merchant ships and forced their crews into the British navy. This practice, known as **impressment** (ihm • PREHS • muhnt), infuriated the Americans. British attacks on American ships and sailors pushed the nation close to war with Great Britain.

A Controversial Treaty President Washington decided to make one last effort to come to a peaceful solution with Britain. He sent John Jay, chief justice of the Supreme Court, to negotiate.

The British were willing to listen to Jay's proposals. War with the United States would only make it harder to carry on the war with France. In addition, Britain did not want to lose its profitable trade with the United States.

In Jay's Treaty the British agreed to evacuate their forts on American soil, to pay damages for ships they had seized, and to allow some American ships to trade with British colonies in the Caribbean.

Despite these gains, few Americans approved of Jay's Treaty. They protested that the treaty did not deal with the issue of impressment and did not mention British interference with American trade. Although President Washington found fault with Jay's Treaty, he realized it would end an explosive crisis with Great Britain. He sent the treaty to the Senate, which approved it after a fierce debate.

Treaty With Spain When Jay's Treaty was made, Spanish leaders realized that the United States and Great Britain might now join forces to seize Spanish territory in North America. Spain wanted to establish a positive relationship with the United States and was willing to offer concessions. President Washington sent **Thomas Pinckney** (PINGK • nee) to Spain to try to settle the differences between the two nations. In 1795 Pinckney's Treaty gave the Americans free navigation of the Mississippi River and the right to trade at **New Orleans.**

Read to Write

14. **The Big Ideas** **Government and Democracy** Political ideas and major events shape how people form governments. Select an event from this chapter. Write an essay describing how people and ideas affected government through that event. CA 8WS1.1

15. **Using Your FOLDABLES** Review the "American firsts" that you listed in your foldable. Using numbers, rank each first from the most important to the least important. Explain the reasons for your highest and lowest rankings. CA HR3.

Using Academic Vocabulary

16. Read the following sentence and then write the meaning of the underlined word.

    The new federal government was interested in increasing revenue in order to pay off its debts.

Building Citizenship

17. **Research** Work in groups of four to discuss and develop answers to these questions:
    - How does the Bill of Rights reflect the principle of limited government?
    - What are two individual rights protected in the Bill of Rights?
    - Why would it be necessary to change the Constitution? CA 8RC2.0

Reviewing Skills

18. Review READING SKILL **Recognizing Bias** Imagine that you were living in the United States in 1798. Write an editorial to your newspaper that demonstrates bias about your view as to whether the Alien and Sedition Acts violated the U.S. Constitution. Use details from the text and chart about the Alien and Sedition Acts on page 295. CA 8WA2.4

19.  ANALYSIS SKILL **Sequencing** Create a time line that lists key events in President Adams's dispute with France. Write a paragraph analyzing President Adams's handling of this dispute. CA CS2.

Standards Practice

Select the best answer for each of the following questions.

20 Thomas Jefferson and Alexander Hamilton served as members of Washington's

- **A** congress.
- **B** judiciary.
- **C** cabinet.
- **D** military.

21 Which amendment of the Bill of Rights protects the rights of the states?

- **A** First Amendment
- **B** Fifth Amendment
- **C** Sixth Amendment
- **D** Tenth Amendment

22 The XYZ Affair dealt with problems between the United States and

- **A** France.
- **B** Spain.
- **C** Great Britain.
- **D** Canada.

23 Hamilton proposed a national tax on imports, or a(n)

- **A** bond.
- **B** impressment.
- **C** caucus.
- **D** tariff.

The Age of Jefferson

▼ Thomas Jefferson's home, Monticello, in Charlottesville, Virginia

NATIONAL GEOGRAPHIC **Where & When?**

LOUISIANA TERRITORY

1800	1802	1804

- **1801** Jefferson is inaugurated
- **1803** Senate ratifies Louisiana Purchase treaty
- **1804** Lewis and Clark begin expedition

US8.4.2 Explain the policy significance of famous speeches (e.g., Washington's Farewell Address, Jefferson's 1801 Inaugural Address, John Q. Adams's Fourth of July 1821 Address).

Jefferson Becomes President

Main Idea **The election of 1800 showed that power in the United States could be peacefully transferred even when political parties are in disagreement.**

Reading Connection Do you think it is more important for the president to dress formally or casually? Why? Read to learn what changed when Jefferson became president.

An American Story

In 1801 **Washington, D.C.,** was slowly rising from a swampy site on the **Potomac River** (puh • TOH • mihk). The nation's new capital had only two prominent buildings—the president's mansion (later called the White House) and the still-unfinished Capitol. Between them stretched about two miles of muddy streets on which pigs and chickens roamed freely.

Very few people liked being in Washington. It was hot and humid in the summer, and the river and swamps were a breeding ground for mosquitoes. Abigail Adams, the wife of John Adams, called the new capital "the very dirtiest Hole."

The Election of 1800 In 1800 Federalists supported President Adams for a second term and Charles Pinckney of South Carolina for vice president. Republicans nominated **Thomas Jefferson** for president and **Aaron Burr** of New York for vice president.

The election campaign of 1800 differed greatly from campaigns of today. Neither Adams nor Jefferson traveled around the country making speeches. Instead the candidates and their followers wrote letters to leading citizens and newspapers to publicize their views. The letter-writing campaign, however, was not polite.

Federalists charged the Republican Jefferson, who believed in freedom of religion, with being "godless." Republicans warned that the Federalists would bring back monarchy. Federalists, they claimed, only represented the interests of wealthy people with property.

Election Deadlock When members of the Electoral College voted, Jefferson and Burr each received 73 votes. Because of this tie, the House of Representatives had to decide the election. At the time, the electors voted for each presidential and vice-presidential candidate individually rather than voting for a party's candidates as a team.

In the House, Federalists saw a chance to prevent the election of Jefferson by supporting Burr. For 35 ballots, the election remained tied. Finally, at Alexander Hamilton's urging, one Federalist decided not to vote for Burr. Jefferson became president, and Burr became vice president.

To prevent another tie between a presidential and a vice-presidential candidate, Congress passed the Twelfth Amendment to the Constitution in 1803. This amendment, ratified in 1804, **requires** electors to vote for the president and vice president on separate ballots. *(See page 262 for the entire text of the Twelfth Amendment.)*

Jefferson's Inauguration On March 4, 1801, the day of the presidential inauguration, Jefferson dressed in everyday clothes. He left his boardinghouse and walked to the Senate to be sworn in as president. President Adams had slipped out of the presidential mansion and left the city so he would not have to watch Jefferson become president.

In his Inaugural Address, Jefferson tried to reach out to Federalists: "We are all Republicans, we are all Federalists," he said. Then he outlined some of his goals, which included maintaining "a wise and frugal [economical] government" and "the support of state governments in all their rights." He believed that a large federal government threatened liberty and that the states could best protect freedom.

Jefferson believed in reducing the power and size of the federal government. These ideas were similar to the French **philosophy** of **laissez-faire** (LEH • ZAY FEHR), which means "let (people) do (as they choose)."

Reading Check **Describe** What does the Twelfth Amendment to the Constitution require?

US8.4.1 Describe the country's physical landscapes, political divisions, and territorial expansion during the terms of the first four presidents.

Jefferson's Policies

Main Idea **Jefferson worked to limit the scope of the federal government and shift control of the federal courts away from the Federalists.**

Reading Connection How should the federal government balance individual liberty with national interests? Read on to learn of changes Jefferson made to deal with this question.

In 1801, when Jefferson became president, the entire federal government consisted of only a few hundred people. This was exactly how Jefferson thought it should be. (Today nearly 3 million civilians work for the federal government.) In Jefferson's view, the national government should conduct foreign affairs and limit its domestic actions to delivering the mail, collecting customs duties, and taking a census every 10 years.

Jefferson Takes Charge When Jefferson entered office, he surrounded himself with men who shared his Republican principles. His secretary of state was his friend and fellow Virginian, James Madison. For secretary of the treasury, he chose **Albert Gallatin,** a Pennsylvanian with a strong grasp of financial matters.

Jefferson and Gallatin aimed to reduce the national debt that the Federalists had left. They scaled down military expenses by cutting the army by one-third and reducing the navy from 25 to 7 ships. By slashing spending, Jefferson and Gallatin **significantly** lowered the national debt within a few years.

Between the election and Jefferson's inauguration, Federalists in Congress passed the Judiciary Act of 1801. This act increased the number of federal judges. Outgoing President John Adams then filled many positions with Federalists.

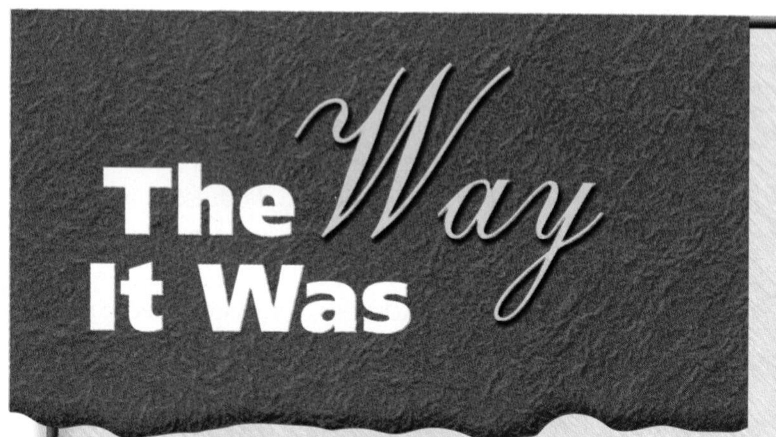

▲ Abigail Adams in the unfinished White House

Washington in 1800

The United States government moved to the new capital city of Washington, D.C., in 1800. Being located along the Potomac River, Washington was expected to emerge as a great trading city, but the plans for a great city had not proceeded very far. The president's house, with laundry sometimes hanging in the unfinished East Room, stood in an open field with two boxlike buildings for executive offices nearby. More than a mile away, across a swamp, stood the partly built Capitol. Members of Congress lived in crowded boardinghouses. The streets were mostly muddy wagon tracks, bordered with the stumps of trees that had been recently cut. Some Americans criticized the choice of Washington as the capital. They believed that the government should move to a larger city.

The judges that President Adams appointed were known as "midnight judges" because Adams supposedly signed appointments for judges until midnight on his last day in office. Through these appointments Adams **ensured** that Federalists would control the courts.

Marbury* v. *Madison The appointments could not take effect, however, until the legal papers (commissions) for these last-minute "midnight judges" were delivered. When Jefferson became president on March 4, a few of the commissions had not yet been delivered. He told Secretary of State Madison not to deliver them. One commission was addressed to William Marbury.

To force the delivery of his commission, Marbury took his case directly to the Supreme Court. Chief Justice **John Marshall** turned down Marbury's claim. Marshall noted that the Constitution did not give the Court jurisdiction to decide Marbury's case.

In his opinion, Marshall set out three principles of **judicial review:** (a) The Constitution is the supreme law of the land. (b) When a conflict arises between the Constitution and any other law, the Constitution must be followed. (c) The judicial branch has a duty to uphold the Constitution. The courts must be able to determine when a federal law conflicts with the Constitution and to nullify, or cancel, unconstitutional laws.

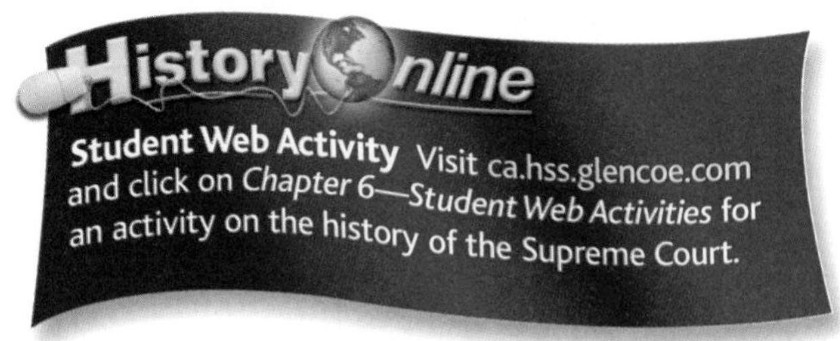

History Online
Student Web Activity Visit ca.hss.glencoe.com and click on Chapter 6—Student Web Activities for an activity on the history of the Supreme Court.

Marshall not only extended the power of the Court, he also broadened federal power at the expense of the states. In *McCulloch* v. *Maryland* (1819), the Court held that the elastic clause allows Congress to do more than the Constitution expressly authorizes it to do. In *Gibbons* v. *Ogden* (1824) the Court held that federal law takes precedence over state law in interstate transportation. *(See the Supreme Court Case Summaries beginning on page 846 for more on these cases.)*

Reading Check **Explain** How did the changes that Jefferson made reflect his views about government?

History Online
Study Central Need help understanding Jefferson's election and his policies? Visit ca.hss.glencoe.com and click on Study Central.

Reading Summary

Review the Main Ideas

- In the presidential election of 1800, Republican Thomas Jefferson defeated Federalist John Adams.
- After taking office as the first Republican president, Jefferson began to implement his party's ideas on how the government should function.

What Did You Learn?

1. Explain how Jefferson cut government spending.
2. Name the court case that established judicial review.

Critical Thinking

3. **Cause and Effect** Re-create the diagram below and list the effects caused by the appointment of the "midnight judges." CA HI2.

Adams appoints judges	→	→

4. **The Big Ideas** How did Jefferson try to calm Federalist fears of Republican rule? CA HI2.
5. **READING Compare and Contrast** Election campaigns have changed since 1800. Write an essay that compares and contrasts current campaigns with those of Jefferson's time. CA CS1.

Connecting to the Constitution

US8.4.3 Analyze the rise of capitalism and the economic problems and conflicts that accompanied it (e.g., Jackson's opposition to the National Bank; early decisions of the U.S. Supreme Court that reinforced the sanctity of contracts and a capitalist economic system of law).

The Supreme Court and the Economy

Why It Matters People in the United States are free to own property; to make a profit; and to make their own choices about what to produce, buy, and sell. The Framers of the U.S. Constitution believed that economic freedom is a basic right of citizens. As a result, the Constitution laid the basis for an economy based on capitalism, or free enterprise.

Although capitalism is the basis of the American economic system, ours is a mixed economy—a system in which the government both supports and regulates private enterprise. Over the years, the American judicial system—headed by the Supreme Court—has made decisions that have encouraged business competition and private property ownership. However, the Court also has expanded the power of the government to regulate, or lay down rules for, the economy as a whole.

The Commerce Power Article I, Section 8 of the Constitution gives Congress the authority to regulate commerce. It is known as the commerce clause. Under the Articles of Confederation, each state jealously guarded its own commerce. Trade barriers among the states restricted commerce and stood in the way of a strong national economy. The Framers of the U.S. Constitution sought to avoid state rivalries by giving Congress the power to regulate all forms of commerce among the states. It also affirmed Congress's right to regulate trade with foreign nations.

"An unlimited power to tax involves, necessarily, a power to destroy; because there is a limit beyond which no institution and no property can bear taxation."

—John Marshall, *McCulloch* v. *Maryland,* 1819

◀ John Marshall

Federalists Support Burr In 1804 the Republican caucus nominated Thomas Jefferson for a second term as president. Jefferson and the Republicans, in doubt about Burr's loyalty to the party, did not nominate Burr for another term as vice president. Instead, they chose George Clinton of New York. Burr then decided to run for governor of New York. Many Federalists supported Burr as they were searching for a powerful ally in New York who would support their plan for the Northern Confederacy. Alexander Hamilton, however, threw his weight against Burr's election.

Burr and Hamilton Alexander Hamilton had never trusted Aaron Burr. Now Hamilton was concerned about rumors that Burr had secretly agreed to lead New York out of the Union. Hamilton called Burr "a dangerous man." When Burr lost the election for governor, he blamed Hamilton and challenged him to a duel. In July 1804, the two men—armed with pistols—met in Weehawken, New Jersey. Hamilton hated dueling and pledged not to shoot at his rival. Burr, however, did fire and aimed to hit Hamilton. Seriously wounded, Hamilton died the next day. Burr fled to avoid arrest on the charge of murder.

The Northern Confederacy Fails With Burr on the run and with almost no support in the New England states, the plans for the Northern Confederacy failed. The results of the election of 1804 showed how thoroughly the Federalists had been discredited. Jefferson and Clinton captured 162 electoral votes to 14 for the Federalist candidates Charles Pinckney and Rufus King.

Reading Check **Summarize** Why did France sell the Louisiana Territory to the United States?

History Online
Study Central Need help understanding the Louisiana Purchase and its exploration? Visit ca.hss.glencoe.com and click on Study Central.

Reading Summary

Review the Main Ideas

- American settlers in the West depended on the use of the lower Mississippi River and the port of New Orleans to trade their farm products. That control was threatened when France gained control of the Louisiana Territory.
- After the purchase of Louisiana from the French, President Jefferson sent Lewis and Clark and others to explore the new territory.

What Did You Learn?

1. Which European countries controlled the Louisiana Territory until 1800?
2. Name the famous Native American woman who Lewis and Clark met along their journey.

Critical Thinking

3. **Organizing Information** Create a diagram like the one below that lists the benefits of acquiring the Louisiana Territory. CA HR3.

4. **The Big Ideas** Why was the French port of New Orleans important to the United States? CA CS2.
5. **Cause and Effect** How could the Lewis and Clark expedition prepare people who wanted to move west? Write a paragraph describing your conclusions. CA HI2.
6. **Analysis** **Assess** What was the relationship between the Louisiana Purchase and political power? How did Jefferson's political opponents react? Write an essay explaining your assessment. CA CS1. CA 8WA2.3.c

US8.4.1 Describe the country's physical landscapes, political divisions, and territorial expansion during the terms of the first four presidents.

GEOGRAPHY & HISTORY

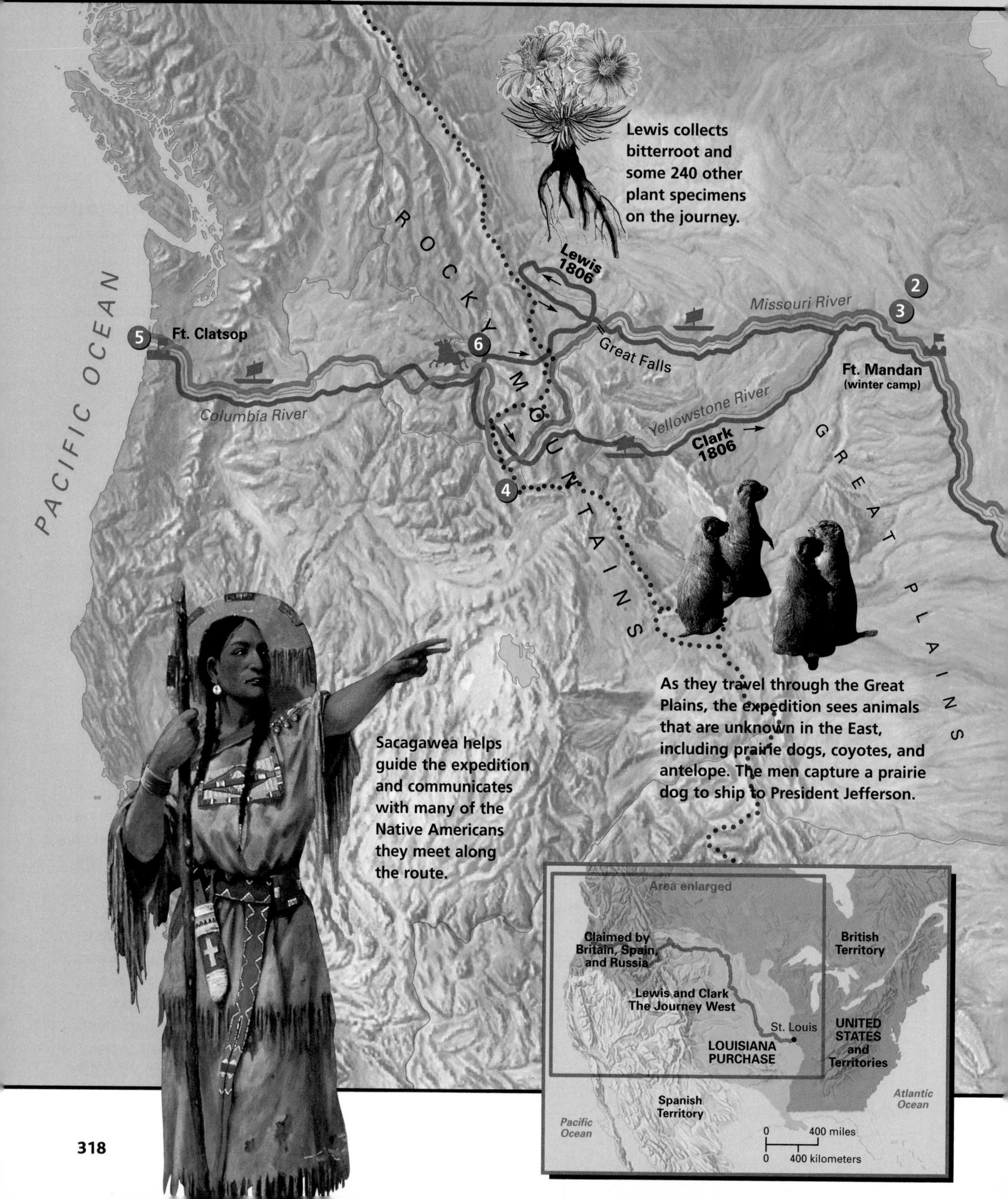

Lewis collects bitterroot and some 240 other plant specimens on the journey.

As they travel through the Great Plains, the expedition sees animals that are unknown in the East, including prairie dogs, coyotes, and antelope. The men capture a prairie dog to ship to President Jefferson.

Sacagawea helps guide the expedition and communicates with many of the Native Americans they meet along the route.

PACIFIC OCEAN
ROCKY MOUNTAINS
GREAT PLAINS
Ft. Clatsop
Columbia River
Lewis 1806
Clark 1806
Missouri River
Great Falls
Yellowstone River
Ft. Mandan (winter camp)
1 2 3 4 5 6

Area enlarged
Claimed by Britain, Spain, and Russia
British Territory
Lewis and Clark The Journey West
St. Louis
LOUISIANA PURCHASE
UNITED STATES and Territories
Spanish Territory
Pacific Ocean
Atlantic Ocean
0 400 miles
0 400 kilometers

Picturing History

Like other artists of the Hudson River School, Frederic Edwin Church showed scenes of nature untouched by settlement. ***How was American art and literature changing during the early 1800s?***

In this passage, Irving describes the terror that Ichabod Crane felt as he came upon the headless horseman late at night:

> **"Mounting a rising ground, which brought the figure of his fellow traveller in relief against the sky, gigantic in height, and muffled in a cloak, Ichabod was horror struck, on perceiving that [the rider] was headless! but his horror was still more increased, on observing, that the head, which should have rested on his shoulders, was carried before him on the pommel of the saddle! His terror rose to desperation; he rained a shower of kicks and blows upon [his horse] Gunpowder, hoping, by a sudden movement, to give his companion the slip—but the spectre started full jump with him. Away, then, they dashed, through thick and thin; stones flying, and sparks flashing, at every bound."**
>
> **—"The Legend of Sleepy Hollow"**

Another New York author, **James Fenimore Cooper,** wrote novels such as *The Last of the Mohicans* and *The Deerslayer.* In these novels, a trapper folk hero of many names—Natty Bumppo, Leatherstocking, Deerslayer, and Pathfinder—is portrayed as strong, brave, resourceful, and honorable. When asked if he had ever shot an enemy that was capable of killing him, Deerslayer responded:

> **"To own the truth, I never did," answered Deerslayer, "seeing that a fitting occasion never offered. The Delawares [a Native American group] have been peaceable since my sojourn with 'em, and I hold it to be [wrong] to take the life of a man, except in open and [generous] warfare."**
>
> —from *The Deerslayer*

Biography

US8.4.4 Discuss daily life, including traditions in art, music, and literature of early national America (e.g., through writings by Washington Irving, James Fenimore Cooper).

WASHINGTON IRVING
1783–1859
JAMES FENIMORE COOPER
1789–1851

In the 1800s, American literature became more "American." Writers, reflecting a sense of national pride, were turning away from European influences and writing about America. Authors such as James Fenimore Cooper and Washington Irving reveal the spirit of the expanding American frontier and of the possibilities for improvement and change.

James Fenimore Cooper ▶

Washington Irving was the first American writer to win international fame. *The Sketch Book* (1820), a collection of stories admired throughout Europe, included Irving's two most famous tales, "Rip Van Winkle" and "The Legend of Sleepy Hollow."

Irving was a born wanderer, even as a child. He later wrote, "I began my travels, and made many tours into foreign parts and unknown regions of my native city, to the frequent alarm of my parents."

Although he wrote many works, Cooper is best known for his novels about Natty Bumppo's frontier life. *The Leatherstocking Tales* is set in the huge expanse of the New York State frontier. Natty Bumppo is a trapper who is forced westward by the movement of settlers into his beloved frontier. Cooper is the first American writer to draw greatly from American history for his setting and characterization. As a result of reading Cooper's novels, generations of children—not only here but in France and Great Britain—gloried in the drama of Native Americans and pioneers on the frontier.

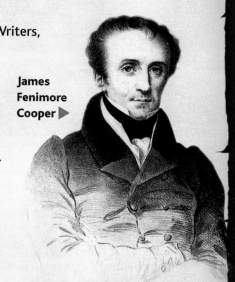

"Should we distrust the man, because his manners are not our manners, and that his skin is dark!"

—from *The Last of the Mohicans*

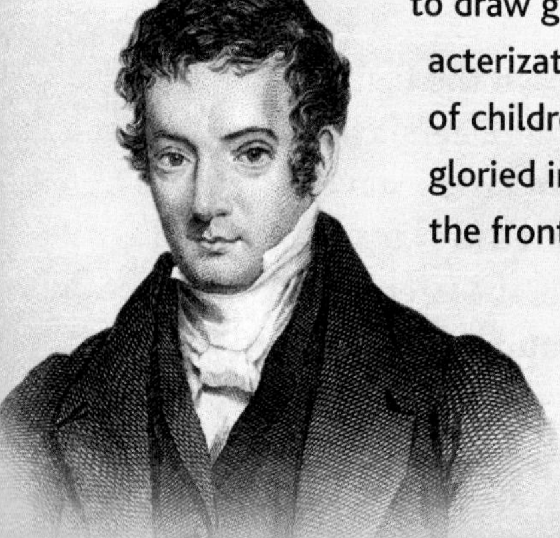

◀ Washington Irving

Then and Now

Why do you think works by Irving and Cooper are still popular today?

Other writers, such as William Cullen Bryant of Massachusetts, wrote poetry. Bryant expressed a love for natural beauty. His poem "Thanatopsis" appeared in 1817. In it, he suggested that by studying nature, people could better understand life and death.

Art During the early 1800s, American artists turned their attention to American people and landscapes. **George Caleb Bingham** painted fur traders, riverboat workers, and political speakers.

Another artist, George Catlin, was one of several artists who lived among the Native Americans and painted scenes of their daily life. Thomas Doughty was one of the first successful landscape painters and a leader of the Hudson River School of painting. This school was made up of artists who liked to paint views of the Catskill Mountains and the Hudson River in New York.

Music In the early 1800s, Americans developed their own forms of music. Instruments such as banjos and pianos were used to play American tunes. Musicals filled with American songs were performed in large cities and in barns, tents, or log cabins throughout the country.

One of the most successful American songwriters was **Stephen C. Foster.** Although born in Pennsylvania, Foster combined African and European music to create **uniquely** American melodies about life in the South, such as "My Old Kentucky Home" and "Swanee River."

Architecture American architects of the early 1800s developed their own forms of building based on the classical styles of ancient Greece and Rome. Classical designs became the model for public buildings all over the country, including the Capitol in Washington, D.C. Thomas Jefferson used classical styles when he planned his home, Monticello, and buildings for the University of Virginia. A style known as Greek Revival also was used for private homes, such as plantation houses in the South.

Reading Check **Describe** What qualities did James Fenimore Cooper give his main character?

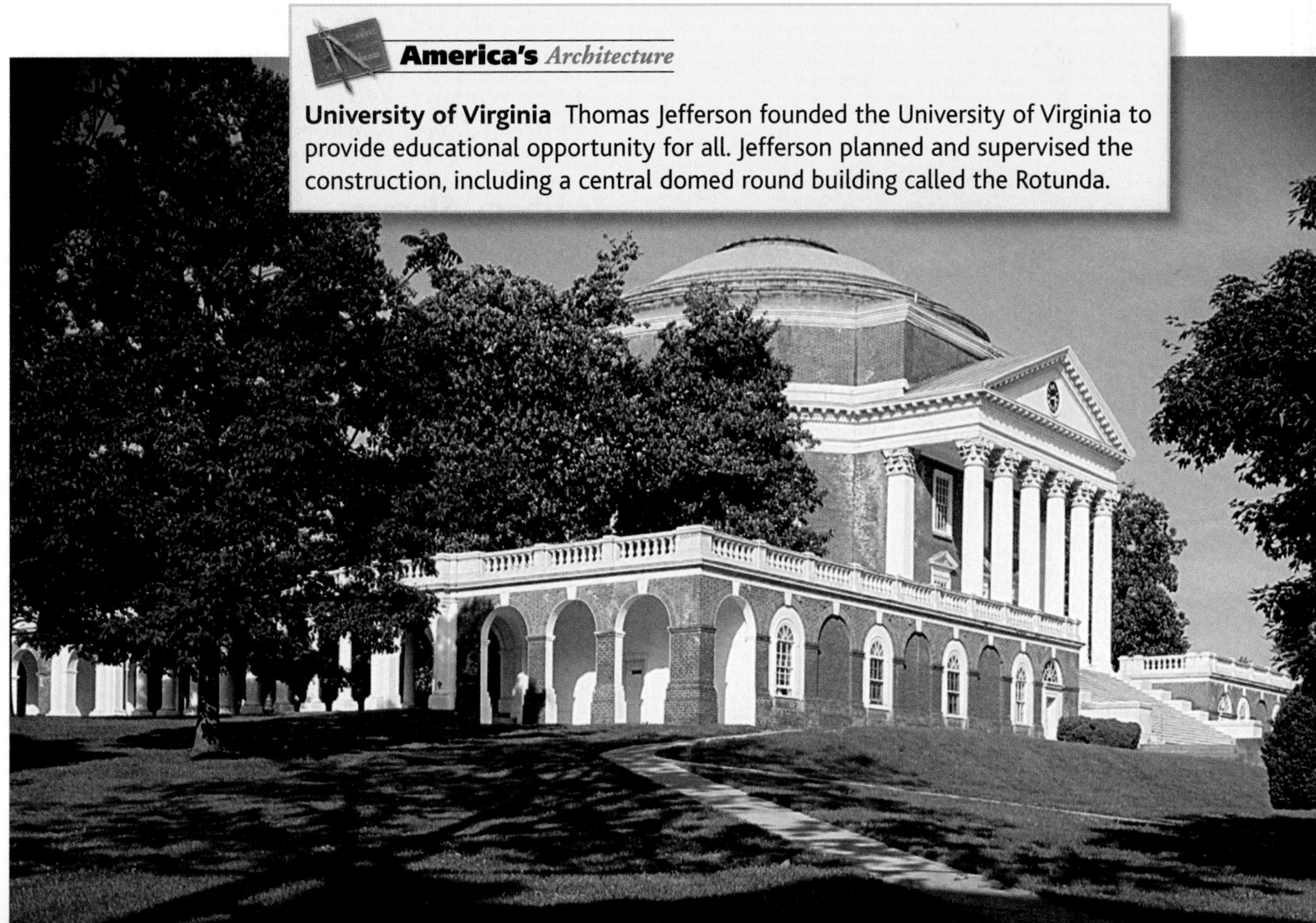

America's *Architecture*

University of Virginia Thomas Jefferson founded the University of Virginia to provide educational opportunity for all. Jefferson planned and supervised the construction, including a central domed round building called the Rotunda.

US8.4.4 Discuss daily life, including traditions in art, music, and literature, of early national America (e.g., through writings by Washington Irving, James Fenimore Cooper).

A Rural Nation

Main Idea **People living in different regions developed different ways to use and farm the land.**

Reading Connection Do you live in a neighborhood that works together? Read on to see how people in the early years of the Republic experienced work and community.

During the early 1800s, most Americans lived in rural areas and made their living on the land. People, however, **occupied** the land in very different ways in different regions of the country.

Farm Life in the North During the early years of the republic, people in the North tended to cluster in villages and towns made up of neat rows of wooden frame houses, churches, and stores. Beyond these settlements were farm communities located within a relatively short traveling distance of each other. Northern farmers cut down forests and created fields marked by hedges or stone walls. They produced enough crops and livestock to sell or exchange in nearby marketplaces for teas, sugar, window glass, and tools.

Farming was the North's major economic activity, but not all rural people in the North worked on the land. Some labored in the small workshops, grain and sawmills, and iron forges that dotted the rural landscape. Others worked as craftspeople or day laborers in nearby towns.

Picturing **History**

Some people in the North lived in villages, but many lived and worked in rural areas. ***What was the major economic activity in the North?***

The South's Plantation Culture While Northerners lived close together, Southerners lived on small farms or large plantations that were widely separated from each other. The South's economy depended on slavery and growing cash crops.

Beginning in the 1790s, the growth at home and in Great Britain of the textile industry turned cotton into a major cash crop throughout the South. Cotton production boomed, leading to an increase in demand for enslaved labor.

Because of their wealth from agriculture, **planters,** or large landowners, became the South's economic and social leaders. However, the planters were few in number. About three out of every four white Southerners was a small farmer who worked a small plot of land and had no enslaved workers.

Southern Slavery In time, slavery became "the peculiar institution" that set the South apart from the rest of the country. Most enslaved people in the South worked on farms and plantations. They labored together from dawn to dusk and were closely supervised. While enslaved men generally worked the fields, enslaved women cooked, cleaned, did laundry, sewed, and cared for the plantation's children.

Still, many enslaved people never saw a farm or plantation. They lived and worked in the South's towns and small cities. Enslaved people also carried out tasks other than farming. Some were coach drivers, household servants, and artisans. Others worked at ironworks or mined gold, coal, or salt.

Picturing History

The South developed an economy based on commercial agriculture. ***What became the major cash crop of the South?***

Wherever they lived, enslaved people formed their own communities. During the evenings, they often shared in song, prayer, and dancing. As one slave recalled, "From sunup to sundown, we belonged to the master; but from sundown to sunup we were our own."

The Rise of Urban Life Most Americans were rural dwellers, but an increasing number of them were living in cities. In the North, cities such as Boston, New York City, and Philadelphia were thriving Atlantic seaports that exported American farm products and imported European manufactured goods. The South had fewer towns and cities than the North. From ports such as New Orleans, Charleston, and Savannah, Southern agricultural goods were shipped to Northern and European markets.

Life in Northern Cities During the early 1800s, America's cities had only a few small industries that made products, such as textiles, shoes, and metal goods. In the North, mills and factories grew and drew in workers from the farms or from overseas. Children also went to work in these industries.

With the rise of industries in the North, the gap between richer and poorer city residents widened. Prosperous merchants and businesspeople controlled urban economic and social life. A middle class of artisans, shopkeepers, and professionals shared modestly in the general prosperity. At the bottom was a growing working class, many of whose members had to struggle to survive. During the early 1800s, rising land values forced the lower classes into increasingly crowded tenements, or rented row houses. Meanwhile, more prosperous urban dwellers stayed in their own detached dwellings in fashionable neighborhoods.

Free African Americans Northern cities attracted many free African Americans during the early 1800s. After the American Revolution, slavery in the North declined. Why did this happen? Farming in the North came to depend on families and paid workers, not enslaved labor. Many northerners came to believe that slavery was **contrary** to the nation's ideals of equality and justice. By 1804 most northern states had passed laws ending slavery.

Still, free African Americans faced many obstacles to full equality. Only a few had voting rights. A small number owned their own homes or businesses. They were excluded from white churches and schools and increasingly from skilled jobs. African Americans responded by building their own churches, schools, newspapers, and charitable and social organizations. They used these institutions to develop their own culture and eventually to demand full freedom and equality.

Reading Check **Identify** What group made up the South's political leaders?

US8.4.1 Describe the country's physical landscapes, political divisions, and territorial expansion during the terms of the first four presidents.

Westward Movement

Main Idea **An increasing number of Americans chose to move west into new territory.**

Reading Connection If you could move somewhere new, where would you go? Would you drive, take a train, or fly to get there? Read to see how Americans in the early Republic realized their dreams on a new frontier.

While the North and South developed different ways of life, Americans in ever larger numbers pushed westward beyond the Appalachian Mountains. They were eager to claim new land and establish farms in the West. They also wanted to escape the growing population and restricting laws and taxes of the East.

How Did the Settlers Travel? Some settlers came to the West by horseback or wagon along difficult overland routes. Others traveled on boats that floated down waterways, such as the Ohio River and the Mississippi River. Upon arrival, settlers had to provide themselves with shelter, food, and clothing. They cut down trees, built log cabins, and cleared the land for farming. As expanding areas of land came under the farmers' plows, forests and wildlife increasingly gave way to human settlement.

What Was Life Like in the West? Living on the frontier was very rigorous. Pioneers wrestled with uncertain climate, limited supplies, and sometimes failing crops. Life could be lonesome. Settlements were far apart and often hard to reach. The few roads that existed were poor, and westerners found it difficult to transport goods and produce to eastern markets.

Despite hardships, pioneers still enjoyed themselves. Weddings, for example, were major events that drew people from the surrounding area. A short ceremony was followed by eating and dancing that lasted for days. The food was usually simple—bread and butter, fried pork, and wild fruits.

Moving West

Rich soil and cheap land drew many farmers to the Northwest. Between 1800 and 1840, thousands of settlers poured into the region.

Once the pioneers arrived, their survival depended upon the long-handled axe and the rifle. With the axe, the farmer cleared trees from the land and fashioned the wood from those trees into cabins and crude furniture.

▲ Life in the West meant work for every member of a pioneer family.

A good rifle was also essential. It was used for defense from enemies—human and otherwise—and for shooting game for food. Until the 1840s, the weapon most settlers chose was the "Kentucky Rifle."

Conflict in the West As the settlers moved farther and farther west; they came into **conflict** with Native American groups that controlled the vast areas of land beyond the Appalachian Mountains. Native Americans were angry that land-hungry settlers began creating farms on tribal hunting grounds. As the pressures of settler expansion increased, Native Americans developed ways of resistance and survival.

Some Native American groups, like the Cherokee, tried to adjust peacefully to American settler ways. To defend their freedom and prevent further loss of land, the Cherokee adopted written laws and a constitution patterned after those of American states. Many Cherokee accepted Christianity and settled down as farmers, mill owners, and shopkeepers. Cherokee culture continued to flourish with the invention of a Cherokee alphabet by Sequoya in 1821. Sequoya developed symbols to represent all syllables in Cherokee speech. Many Cherokee learned how to read and write. Sequoya even published a Cherokee newspaper and translated parts of the Bible into Cherokee. As Cherokee self-confidence grew, so did the hostility of their settler neighbors.

Meanwhile, other Native American groups were opposed to accepting settler ways. Wanting to preserve their traditional culture, the Shawnee and the Creek prepared for armed resistance. In the end, neither peaceful adaptation nor armed resistance was successful. By 1830, Native Americans faced cultural loss, military defeat, or forced **migration** to lands west of the Mississippi River.

Reading Check **Explain** Why were people eager to move west?

History Online
Study Central Need help understanding daily life in early America? Visit ca.hss.glencoe.com and click on Study Central.

Section 3 Review

Reading Summary

Review the Main Ideas

- During Jefferson's presidency, Americans developed a sense of pride, or nationalism.
- Literature, music, art, and architecture began to reflect distinctly American themes.
- Daily life in the young Republic was varied, based on regional differences and ethnicity.
- People were eager to take advantage of new land opportunities in the Louisiana Purchase.

What Did You Learn?

1. What was Jefferson's view of the relationship between education and democracy?
2. What institutions set the South apart from the rest of the country?

Critical Thinking

3. **Comparing** Create a table to describe economic activities and regional distinctions that developed in each area during this period. CA HI1.

	Urban	Rural
North		
South		

4. The Big Ideas Describe how a distinct American identity and culture grew during this period. Be sure to include references to literature, art, music, and architecture. CA 8RC2.0
5. **Creative Writing** Imagine you can travel back in time. You are a newspaper reporter sent to write a story on either farming life in the South or the Native American experience after the Louisiana Purchase. Choose a topic and then identify people of the time to interview. Make a list of questions you would ask them and responses they might give you. CA HR1.

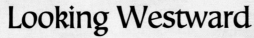

Analyzing Primary Sources

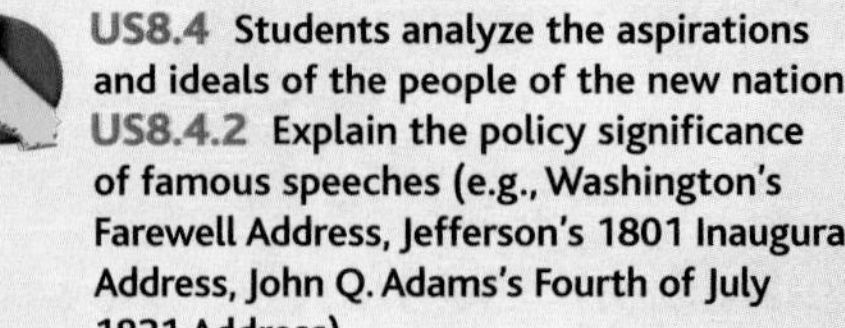

US8.4 Students analyze the aspirations and ideals of the people of the new nation.
US8.4.2 Explain the policy significance of famous speeches (e.g., Washington's Farewell Address, Jefferson's 1801 Inaugural Address, John Q. Adams's Fourth of July 1821 Address).

Looking Westward

The early 1800s was an important time in America. For the first time in modern history, the political power of a country transferred peacefully from one political party to another. It also marked a time of great expansion and change for the United States. The United States looked westward, and also began to look beyond its borders. As you read these primary source selections, think about why this was a time of such rapid growth for the nation.

Meriwether Lewis views the Rocky Mountains. ▶

Reader's Dictionary

maritime (MAR • uh • TYM): bordering on the ocean

garrison (GAR • uh • suhn): fort

pirogue (PEE • ROHG): dugout boat resembling canoes

trodden (TRAH • duhn): stepped

esteem (ihs • TEEM): value

benediction (BEH • nuh • dihk • shuhn): blessing

avarice (A • vuh • ruhs): greed

maxim (MAK • suhm): rule of conduct

California in 1804

Sea captain William Shaler visited the coast of California while engaged in trade with China and recorded his observations.

[The Spanish are] masters of the **maritime** part of the country only. Beyond that range of mountains [the Sierra Madre] the country is remarkably fine, well watered, and covered with forests: these they have not as yet been able to penetrate, on account of their being thickly inhabited by warlike tribes of Indians. I am informed that the government [aims] to establish lines of missions and **garrisons** from San Francisco to New Mexico, and by the country of the Colorado Indians to the same place, and by these means to complete the conquest of the country. But that is a project that does not seem likely to be very soon realized.

—*from Shaler's Journal*

The Explorations of Lewis and Clark

From 1804 to 1806, Meriwether Lewis and William Clark explored and mapped the Louisiana Territory.

Our vessels consisted of six small canoes, and two large [**pirogues**]. This little fleet, altho' not quite so respectable as those of Columbus or Capt. Cook, were still viewed by us with as much pleasure. . . .

We were now about to penetrate a country at least two thousand miles in width, on which the foot of civilized man had never **trodden.** The good or evil it had in store . . . was for experiment yet to determine. . . . [T]he picture which now presented itself to me was a most pleasing one. . . . I could but **esteem** this moment of my departure as among the most happy of my life.

—*from an April 1805 entry in the journal of Meriwether Lewis, as he prepares to leave Fort Mandan on the upper Missouri River*

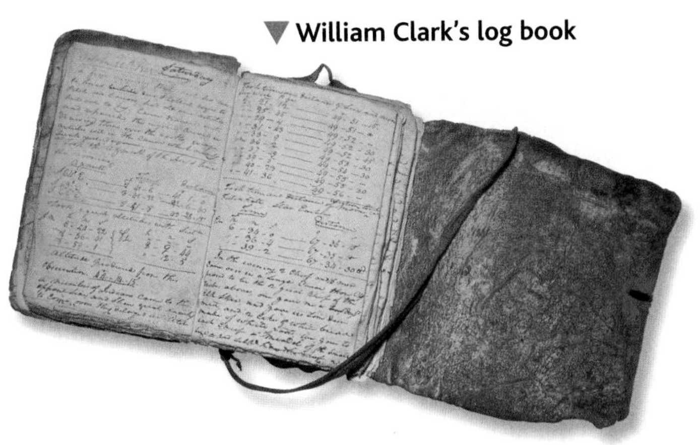
▼ William Clark's log book

Adams's Fourth of July Address

On July 4, 1821, Secretary of State John Quincy Adams took part in a ceremony held at the Capitol. Adams reads an original copy of the Declaration of Independence. He then gives a speech on American freedom and foreign policy.

Wherever the standard of freedom and Independence has been or shall be unfurled, there will her [America's] heart, her **benedictions** and her prayers be. But she goes not abroad, in search of monsters to destroy. She is the well-wisher to the freedom and independence of all. . . . [But if the United States involves itself in the affairs of other nations, even those fighting for freedom, the nation would become involved] in all the wars of interest and intrigue, of individual **avarice,** envy, and ambition, which assume the colors and usurp the standard of freedom. The fundamental **maxims** of her policy would insensibly change from *liberty* to *force*. . . . She might become the dictatress [ruler] of the world. She would be no longer the ruler of her own spirit.

DBQ Document-Based Questions

California in 1804

1. What area of California do the Spanish control?
2. Does Shaler think it will take a long time for the Spanish to settle California? Why or why not?

The Explorations of Lewis and Clark

3. Is Lewis looking forward to the exploration? How can you tell?
4. At the start of their expedition, how many boats did Lewis and Clark have?

Adams's Fourth of July Address

5. Was Adams calling for a stronger U.S. role in other countries' affairs? Explain.

Read to Write

6. Imagine the land that was soon to be settled by American pioneers. What would people need in the 1800s to settle and develop the land? What tools would be required? What skills? How would settlers deal with Native Americans who were already living there? Write a list of things that early settlers would need to bring with them, as well as recommendations for what to do once they arrived. CA 8WA2.6

Assessment

Standard US8.4

Review Content Vocabulary

Define each of the terms below. Use them in a paragraph that discusses government in the early Republic.

1. laissez-faire
2. judicial review

Review the Main Ideas

Section 1 • The Republicans Take Power

3. What was the outcome of the election of 1800?
4. What Federalist measures were ended under Jefferson soon after he took office?

Section 2 • The Louisiana Purchase

5. How far west did U.S. territory extend in 1800?
6. Who sold the Louisiana Territory to the United States? How much did the United States pay for it?
7. How long did Lewis and Clark explore the Louisiana Territory?

Section 3 • Daily Life in Early America

8. What caused the surge of nationalism in the early Republic?
9. What effects did the Second Great Awakening have on American culture?
10. What land-use strategies were practiced by people in the North region?

Critical Thinking

11. **Analyze** Explain the significance of the *Marbury* v. *Madison* decision. Discuss why judicial review is important. CA HI1.
12. **Explore** What was the relationship between the revolt in Santo Domingo and France's interests in North America? How did these events affect U.S. territorial expansion? CA CS1.
13. **Explain** What was the Federalist response to the Louisiana Purchase? What outcomes resulted from this political disagreement? How do you think this might affect future disagreements in the Republic? CA HI3.

Geography Skills

Study the map and answer the questions that follow. CA CS3.

14. **Location** Along what two state borders is Washington, D.C., located?
15. **Location** What city on the map is located approximately 40 miles northeast of Washington, D.C.?

Self-Check Quiz Visit ca.hss.glencoe.com to prepare for the Chapter 6 test.

Read to Write

16. **The Big Ideas Evaluate** Write an essay highlighting the impact of Jefferson's decision to buy the Louisiana Territory. Be sure to include references to politics, geography, trade, and migration. CA 8WS2.4

17. **Narrative Writing** Imagine you were selected to travel with Lewis and Clark. Use the information in this chapter as well as other sources to write letters to your family to describe what you are seeing. CA 8WA2.1

18. **Using Your FOLDABLES** You have been asked to give a speech to a large audience in Washington, D.C. Use the information from your completed chapter opener foldable to write a speech reviewing Jefferson's presidency. CA HR3. CA LS1.0

Using Academic Vocabulary

Synonyms are words that have the same or nearly the same meaning. Choose the synonym that best matches each term's precise meaning.

19. **ensure**
    a. open b. deliver c. guarantee

20. **unique**
    a. ordinary b. huge c. rare

21. **migrate**
    a. travel b. inhabit c. distribute

Reviewing Skills

22. Review READING SKILL **Compare and Contrast** Review the descriptions of rural life in Section 3. Write an essay describing how people lived off the land in the North, South, and West. Note similarities and differences among the regions. CA HR3.

23. Review ANALYSIS SKILL **Predict** How would the Louisiana Purchase affect U.S. relationships with Native American cultures? Make three predictions based on what you've learned about their interactions from colonization through 1803. CA HI2.

Standards Practice

Use the map below to answer the following questions.

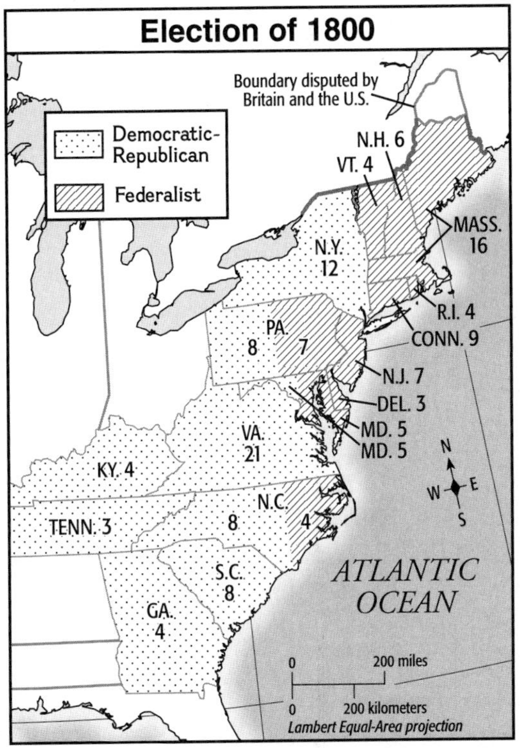

24 **Which of the following statements about the election of 1800 is true?**

A Federalists won Georgia's electoral votes.

B New Hampshire supported the Democratic-Republican ticket.

C Connecticut had seven electoral votes.

D Pennsylvania was one of the states that split its votes.

25 **Which states split their electoral votes between Jefferson and Adams?**

A Pennsylvania and Georgia

B Tennessee and New Hampshire

C North Carolina, New York, and Delaware

D Pennsylvania, Maryland, and North Carolina

Chapter 7

Foreign Affairs in the Early Republic

Fort Niagara in New York

NATIONAL GEOGRAPHIC **Where & When?**

1810	1820	1830

- **1812** War with Great Britain begins
- **1814** The British burn Washington, D.C.
- **1823** Monroe Doctrine is issued

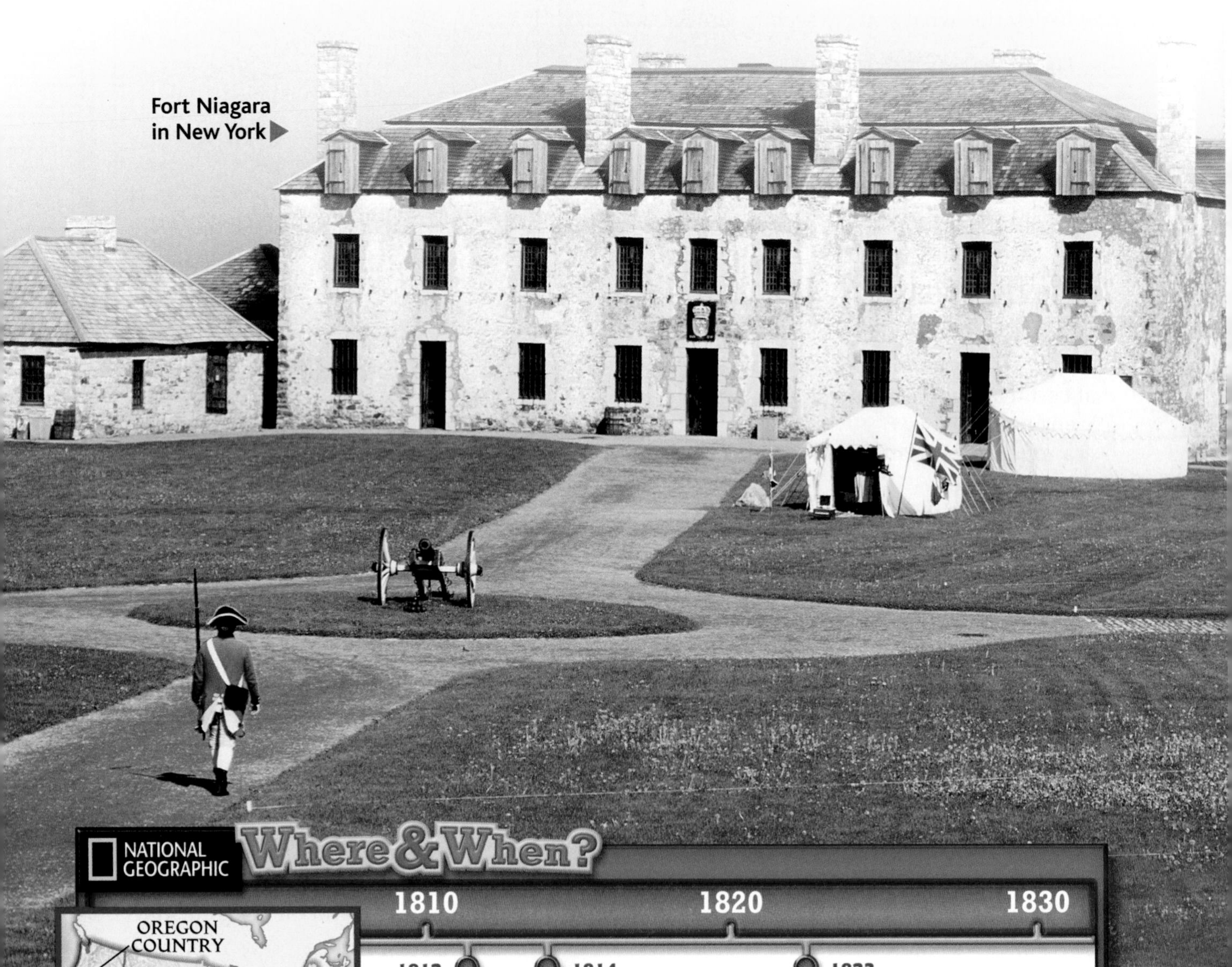

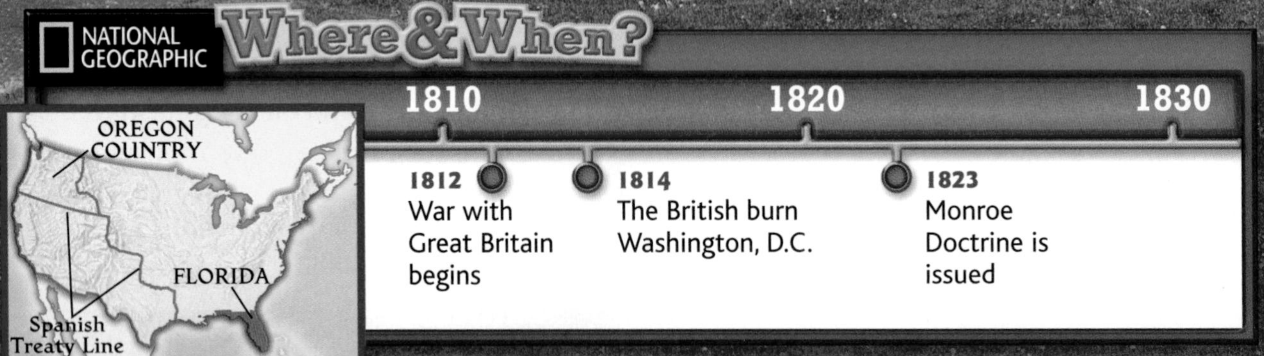

History Online
Chapter Overview Visit ca.hss.glencoe.com for a preview of Chapter 7.

The Big Ideas

A Time of Conflict

Political ideas and major events shape how people form governments. As the United States expanded its trade around the world, it faced a number of foreign challenges.

The War of 1812

Political ideas and major events shape how people form governments. Although the United States gained no territory from its victory in the War of 1812, American self-confidence increased greatly.

Foreign Relations

Political ideas and major events shape how people form governments. The wave of nationalism in Congress and among the American people influenced the nation's foreign affairs.

View the Chapter 7 video in the Glencoe Video Program.

FOLDABLES™ Study Organizer

Identifying Make this foldable to help you identify and learn key terms.

Step 1 Stack four sheets of paper, one on top of the other. On the top sheet of paper, draw a large circle.

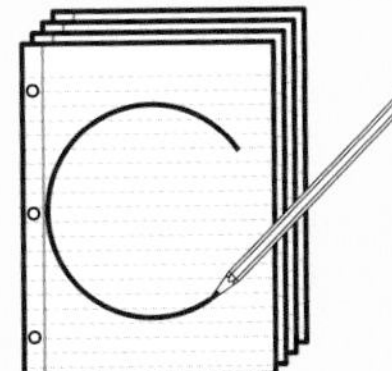

Step 2 With the papers still stacked, cut out all four circles at the same time.

Step 3 Staple the paper circles together at one point around the edge.

Step 4 Label the front circle as shown and take notes on the pages that open to the right.

Reading and Writing
As you read the chapter, write the Content Vocabulary terms for each section in your foldable. Write a definition for each term. Then turn your foldable over (upside down) and write a short sentence using each term on the other side of the pages.

Get Ready to Read

Identifying Cause and Effect

1 Learn It!

Learning to identify causes and effects helps you understand how and why things happen in history. A *cause* is any person, event, or condition that makes something happen. What happens as a result is the *effect*. Use graphic organizers to help you sort and understand causes and effects in your reading. Read the following passage, and see how the information can be sorted.

CAUSE

The warring nations enforced a new strategy.

For two years, American shipping continued to prosper. By 1805, however, the warring nations enforced a new strategy. Britain blockaded the French coast and threatened to search all ships trading with France. France later announced that it would search and seize ships caught trading with Britain.

—*from page 339*

EFFECTS

Britain blockaded the French coast, threatening to search all ships.	France announced it will search and seize all ships trading with Britain.

Reading Tip

To help you make sense of what you read, create different types of graphic organizers that suit your own learning style.

2 Practice It!

History is often a chain of causes and effects. The result, or effect, of one event can also be the cause of another effect. Read the passage called "Frontier Conflicts" from Section 1 on page 341. Then use the graphic organizer below, or create your own to show the chain of causes and effects explained in the passage.

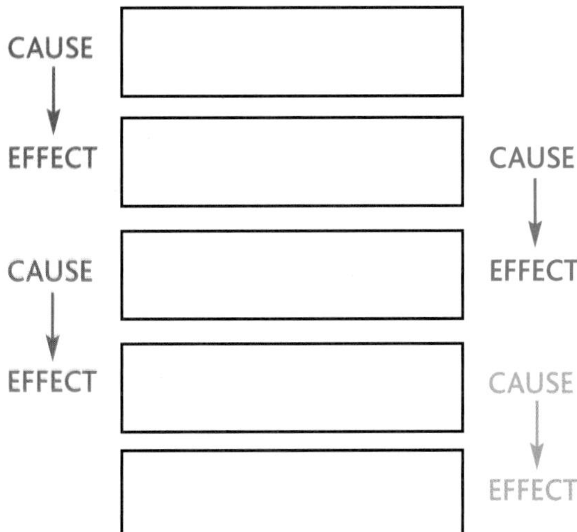

Read to Write

Choose a major event from the chapter. Then write a brief paragraph explaining what caused this event.

▼ American merchant ships

3 Apply It!

Identify causes and effects in the War of 1812 as you read the chapter. Find at least five causes and their effects, and create a graphic organizer to record them.

Section
1

A Time of Conflict

Guide to Reading

History Social Science Standards

US8.5 Students analyze U.S. foreign policy in the early Republic.

Looking Back, Looking Ahead

As the United States began to take a stronger role in world affairs, the new nation faced challenges.

Focusing on the Main Ideas

- In the early 1800s, the livelihoods of many Americans depended on foreign trade, but a war between Great Britain and France threatened U.S. shipping and trade. ***(page 339)***
- President James Madison struggled with trade issues with France and Britain, as well as with tensions between Native Americans and white settlers. ***(page 341)***

Meeting People

Stephen Decatur (dih • KAY • tuhr)
Tecumseh (tuh • KUHM • suh)
The Prophet
William Henry Harrison
Henry Clay
John Calhoun (kahl • HOON)

Locating Places

Barbary Coast states
Virginia
Ohio

Content Vocabulary

tribute (TRIH • byoot)
neutral rights
impressment
embargo (ihm • BAHR • goh)
War Hawks
nationalism

Academic Vocabulary

resolve
guarantee (GAR • uhn • TEE)
strategy
conclude

Reading Strategy

Classifying Information As you read the section, re-create the diagram below and describe in the box the actions the United States took in each of these situations.

U.S. actions
- Demand for tribute
- Attack on *Chesapeake*
- Tecumseh's confederation

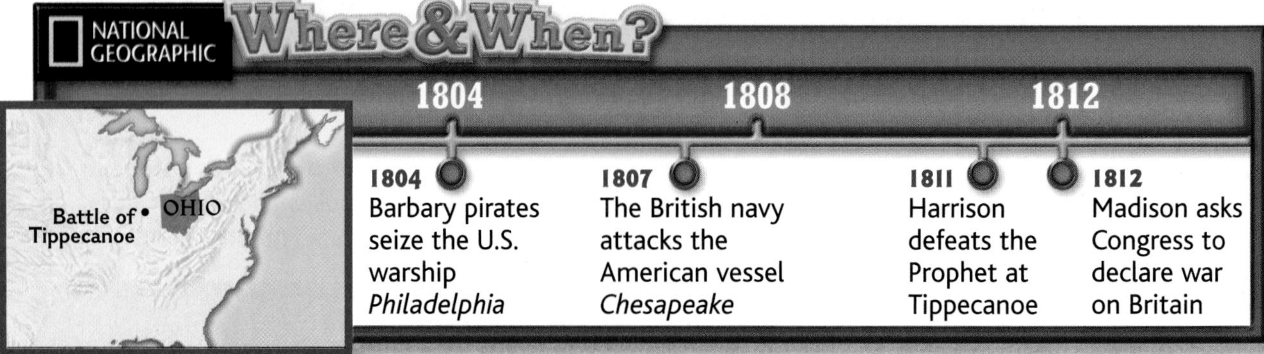
NATIONAL GEOGRAPHIC
Where & When?
Battle of Tippecanoe
OHIO
1804
1808
1812
1804 Barbary pirates seize the U.S. warship *Philadelphia*
1807 The British navy attacks the American vessel *Chesapeake*
1811 Harrison defeats the Prophet at Tippecanoe
1812 Madison asks Congress to declare war on Britain

US8.5 Students analyze U.S. foreign policy in the early Republic.

Freedom of the Seas

Main Idea **In the early 1800s, the livelihoods of many Americans depended on foreign trade, but a war between Great Britain and France threatened U.S. shipping and trade.**

Reading Connection Have you ever traveled by boat? If so, describe the experience. Read to learn what sailors on American merchant ships experienced in foreign seas.

An American Story

By the late 1700s, America faced challenges to its growing trade. In an address to Congress, President Thomas Jefferson described a problem with a country that was raiding American ships, as well as his response to that country.

> **"Tripoli, the least considerable of the Barbary States, had come forward with demands unfounded. . . . The . . . demand admitted but one answer. I sent a small squadron of frigates [warships] into the Mediterranean."**
>
> **—Thomas Jefferson, "First Annual Message to Congress, 1801"**

Barbary Pirates Sailing in foreign seas was dangerous. In the Mediterranean, for example, ships had to be on guard for pirates from Tripoli and the other **Barbary Coast states** of North Africa. For years these Barbary pirates had raided ships in the area. They demanded **tribute** (TRIH • byoot), or protection money, from European governments to let their ships pass safely.

In 1804 the pirates seized the U.S. warship *Philadelphia* and towed it into Tripoli Harbor. They threw the captain and crew into jail. **Stephen Decatur** (dih • KAY • tuhr), a 25-year-old U.S. Navy captain, took action. Slipping into the heavily guarded harbor with a small raiding party, Decatur burned the captured ship to prevent the pirates from using it. A British admiral praised the deed as the "most bold and daring act of the age." Negotiations finally ended the conflict with Tripoli in June 1805. Tripoli agreed to stop demanding tribute, but the United States had to pay a ransom of $60,000 for the release of the American prisoners.

Although the United States had resolved the threat from the Barbary pirates, Americans faced other challenges on the seas. U.S. foreign trade depended on being able to sail the seas freely. By the time Jefferson won reelection in 1804, two powerful European nations were already involved in a war that threatened to interfere with American trade.

Neutral Rights Violated When Britain and France went to war in 1803, America enjoyed a profitable trade with both countries. As long as the United States remained neutral during the war, shippers could continue doing business. A nation not involved in a conflict had **neutral rights**—the right to sail the seas and not take sides.

For two years, American shipping continued to prosper. By 1805 however, the warring nations enforced a new strategy. Britain blockaded the French coast and threatened to search all ships trading with France. France later announced that it would search and seize ships caught trading with Britain.

American Sailors Kidnapped The British needed sailors for their naval war against France. Conditions in the British Royal Navy were terrible. British sailors were poorly paid and fed, and badly treated. Many of them deserted, or ran away. Desperately in need of sailors, the British often used force to get them. British naval patrols claimed the right to stop American ships at sea and search for any sailors on board suspected of being deserters from the British navy.

The British would force sailors on these ships to serve in the British navy. This practice was called **impressment.** Although some of those taken were deserters from the British navy, thousands of native-born and naturalized American citizens were also impressed.

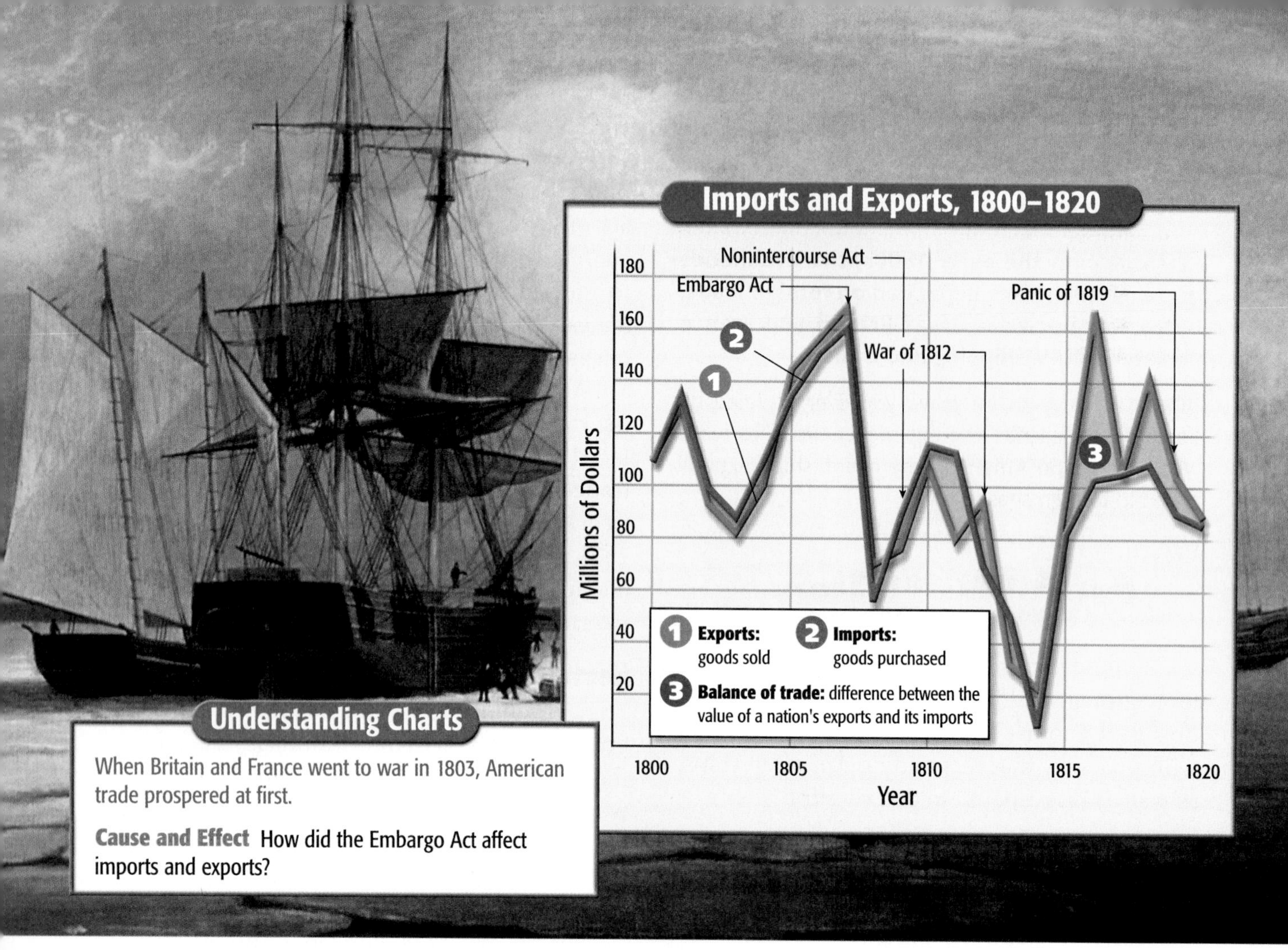

Understanding Charts

When Britain and France went to war in 1803, American trade prospered at first.

Cause and Effect How did the Embargo Act affect imports and exports?

Often the British would wait for American ships outside an American harbor. This happened in June 1807 off the coast of **Virginia.** A British warship, the *Leopard,* intercepted the American vessel *Chesapeake,* and the British demanded to search the ship for British deserters. When the *Chesapeake's* captain refused, the British opened fire, killing 3 and wounding 18.

A Disastrous Trade Ban Britain's practice of impressment and its violation of America's neutral rights led Jefferson to stop some trade with Britain. The attack on the *Chesapeake* triggered even stronger measures. In December 1807, the Republican Congress passed the Embargo Act. An **embargo** (ihm • BAHR • goh) prohibits trade with another country. The embargo banned imports from and exports to all foreign countries.

With the embargo, Jefferson and Madison hoped to hurt Britain but avoid war. They believed the British depended on American agricultural products. As it turned out, the embargo of 1807 was a disaster. The measure wiped out American trade with other nations. Worse, it proved ineffective against Britain. The British simply traded with Latin America for its agricultural goods.

Jefferson Leaves Office Following Washington's precedent, Jefferson made it clear in mid-1808 that he would not be a candidate for a third term. With Jefferson's approval, the Republicans chose James Madison as their candidate for president.

The Federalists again nominated Charles Pinckney and hoped that anger over the embargo would help their party. Pinckney won most of New England, but the Federalist party had little support in other regions. Madison won with 122 electoral votes to Pinckney's 47 votes.

Reading Check **Evaluate** How effective was the Embargo Act? Would such an act work today?

US8.5.1 Understand the political and economic causes and consequences of the War of 1812 and know the major battles, leaders, and events that led to a final peace. **US8.5.3** Outline the major treaties with American Indian nations during the administrations of the first four presidents and the varying outcomes of those treaties.

War Fever

Main Idea **President James Madison struggled with trade issues with France and Britain, as well as with tensions between Native Americans and white settlers.**

Reading Connection Why does tension between different groups occur? Think about this as you read about the conflicts among the various groups in this section.

James Madison became president during a difficult time. At home and abroad, the nation was involved in the embargo crisis. Meanwhile, Britain continued to claim the right to halt American ships, and cries for war with Britain grew stronger.

Closer to War In 1810 Congress passed a law permitting direct trade with either France or Britain, depending on which country first lifted its trade restrictions against America. France's leader Napoleon Bonaparte seized the opportunity and promised to end France's trade restrictions.

Unfortunately for Madison, Napoleon had tricked the American administration. The French continued to seize American ships. Americans were deeply divided. To some it seemed as if the nation was on the verge of war—but it was hard to decide if the enemy should be Britain or France. Madison knew that France had tricked him, but he continued to see Britain as the bigger threat to the United States.

Frontier Conflicts While Madison was trying to decide how to **resolve** the difficulties with European powers, news arrived about problems in the West. **Ohio** had become a state in 1803. Between 1801 and 1810, white settlers continued to press for more land in the Ohio Valley. Now the settlers were moving onto lands that had been **guaranteed** to Native Americans by treaty.

As tensions increased, some Native Americans began renewing their contacts with British agents and fur traders in Canada. Others pursued a new **strategy.** A powerful Shawnee chief named **Tecumseh** (tuh • KUHM • suh) built a confederacy, or union, among Native American nations in the Northwest. Tecumseh believed that a strong confederacy—with the backing of the British in Canada—could put a halt to white movement onto Native American lands. Many Native Americans were ready to follow Tecumseh.

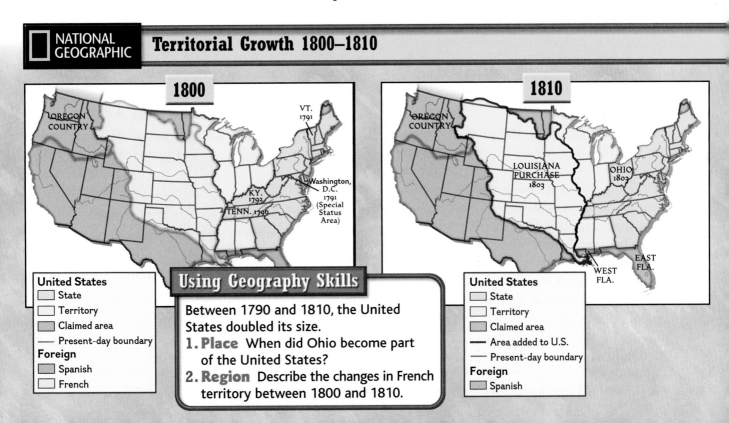

NATIONAL GEOGRAPHIC **Territorial Growth 1800–1810**

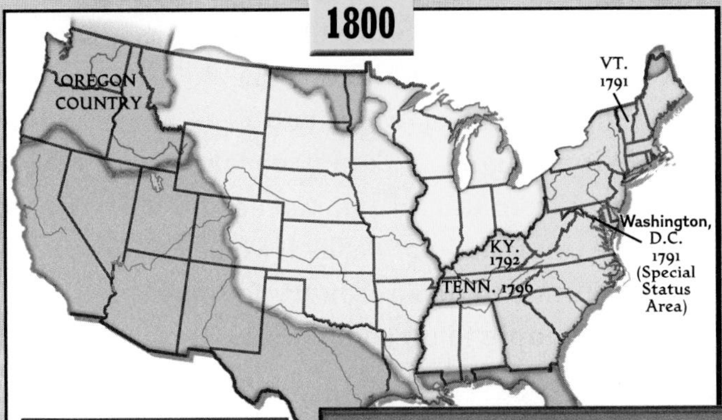

Using Geography Skills

Between 1790 and 1810, the United States doubled its size.

1. **Place** When did Ohio become part of the United States?
2. **Region** Describe the changes in French territory between 1800 and 1810.

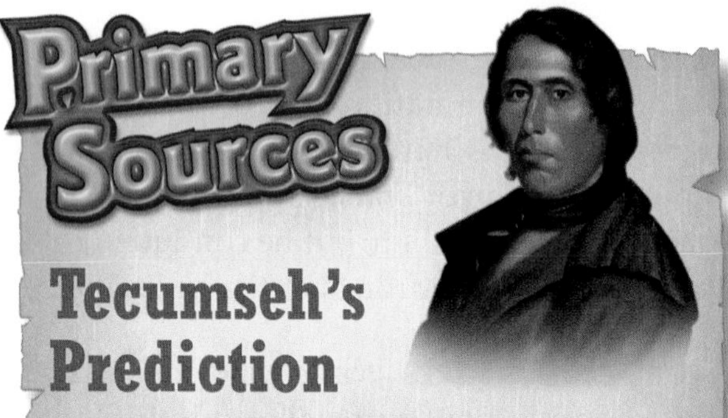

Tecumseh's Prediction

When William Henry Harrison was serving as governor of Indiana, he told Tecumseh that only the president had the authority to return disputed lands to the Native Americans. Tecumseh replied:

> "As the great chief [President Madison] is to determine the matter, . . . I hope the Great Spirit will put sense enough into his head to induce [make] him to direct you to give up this land. It is true he is so far off he will not be injured by the war . . . while you and I will have to fight it out."
>
> —quoted in *The Old Northwest: A Chronicle of the Ohio Valley and Beyond*

Tecumseh's prediction came true.

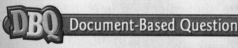

Document-Based Question

Do Tecumseh's words show respect for President Madison? For Harrison? Explain.

Tecumseh and the Prophet A commanding speaker, Tecumseh possessed great political skills. In his view, the U.S. government's treaties with separate Native American nations were worthless. "The Great Spirit gave this great [land] to his red children," he said. Tecumseh felt no one nation had the right to give it away.

Tecumseh had a powerful ally—his brother, Tenskwatawa, known as **the Prophet.** The Prophet urged Native Americans everywhere to return to the customs of their ancestors. They should, he said, give up practices learned from the white invaders—wearing western dress, using plows and firearms, and especially drinking alcohol. The Prophet attracted a huge following among Native Americans. He founded a village at a site in northern Indiana, near present-day Lafayette, where the Tippecanoe and Wabash Rivers meet. It was called Prophetstown.

A Meeting With Harrison The American governor of the Indiana Territory, General **William Henry Harrison,** became alarmed by the growing power of the two Shawnee brothers. He feared they would form an alliance with the British.

In a letter to Tecumseh, Harrison warned that the United States had many more warriors than all the Indian nations could put together.

> **"Do not think that the redcoats can protect you, they are not able to protect themselves."**
>
> —*Messages and Letters of William Henry Harrison*

Tecumseh sent word that he would reply in person.

A few weeks later, Tecumseh came to Harrison and spoke to the white people assembled there:

> **"Brother, . . . Since the peace was made, you have killed some Shawnees, Delawares and Winnebagoes . . . You have taken land from us and I do not see how we can remain at peace if you continue to do so. You try to force red people to do some injury. It is you that are pushing them on to some mischief. You endeavor to make distinctions. You try to prevent the Indians from doing as they wish—to unite."**
>
> —from *Tecumseh, an Indian Moses*

The Battle of Tippecanoe In 1811 while Tecumseh was in the South trying to expand his confederacy, Harrison decided to attack Prophetstown on the Tippecanoe River. After more than two hours of battle, the Prophet's forces fled the area in defeat. The Battle of Tippecanoe was proclaimed a glorious victory for the Americans. Harrison acquired the nickname "Tippecanoe" and his supporters used it as a patriotic rallying cry when he ran for president in 1840.

The Battle of Tippecanoe left about one fourth of Harrison's troops dead or wounded, but the impact on the Native Americans was far greater. Prophetstown was destroyed. The clash also shattered Native American confidence in the Prophet's leadership. Many, including Tecumseh, fled to Canada.

Tecumseh's flight to British-held Canada seemed to prove that the British were supporting and arming the Native Americans. To Harrison and to many white people who settled in the West, there seemed only one way to make the region secure from attack—to drive the British out of Canada and take over the province.

Who Were the War Hawks? Back in the nation's capital, President Madison faced demands for a more aggressive policy toward the British. The most insistent voices came from a group of young Republicans elected to Congress in 1810. Known as the **War Hawks,** they came from the South and the West. The War Hawks pressured the president to declare war against Britain.

Primary Sources

Blue Jacket ▶

Treaties with Native Americans

Many treaties between Native Americans and the U.S. government were signed during the early years of the new nation. These agreements included treaties with the Creeks (1790 and 1814); the Cherokee (1791 and 1794); the Oneida, Tuscarora, and Stockbridge (1794); and the Chickasaw (1805, 1816, and 1818).

Some treaties, like the Treaty of Greenville (1795), were signed to end conflicts. Other treaties ceded Indian land to the United States. White leaders and Indian leaders rarely trusted one another. Shawnee leader Blue Jacket is quoted as saying:

> "From all quarters, we receive speeches from the Americans, and not one is alike. We suppose that they intend to deceive us."
>
> —*American State Papers, Indian Affairs*

The treaties often proved impossible to enforce. Often, white settlers and soldiers crossed into territory and took land that was reserved for Native Americans. Some Native American chiefs were forced to sign a treaty under threat of military force, but they had no intention of abiding by the terms of the treaty. Some chiefs signed only to obtain badly needed items such as food, ammunition, and clothing. In addition, even if a Native American chief signed a treaty, that did not mean that the action was binding on anyone else in the tribe. Other members of the tribe could choose to ignore it.

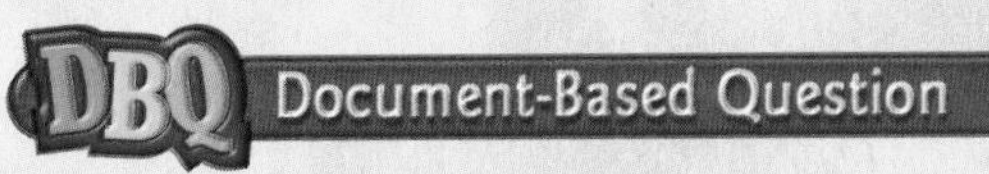

How would you describe Blue Jacket's view of the white leaders?

Biography

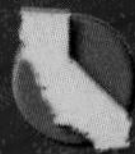

US8.5.1 Understand the political and economic causes and consequences of the War of 1812 and know the major battles, leaders, and events that led to a final peace.

HENRY CLAY

1777–1852

JOHN C. CALHOUN

1782–1850

▲ **Henry Clay**

During their early years in Congress, Henry Clay and John C. Calhoun often joined in support of the young federal government. They were known as War Hawks because of the position they took on the War of 1812. Each argued in stirring speeches the need for a strong army and navy and for the establishment of a national bank.

Both Clay and Calhoun had long, distinguished careers in government. The careers of these two men reflected the conflict between nationalism and sectionalism in the early 1800s.

Born in Virginia, Clay moved to Kentucky, a state that kept him in Congress—and in the center of the political scene—for nearly 50 years. Clay was known as the Great Compromiser for his role in working out various agreements between leaders of the North and South. He served as a Kentucky state legislator, speaker of the U.S. House of Representatives, U.S. senator, and secretary of state.

Clay was a consistent champion of nationalism and devoted his career to strengthening the Union. Although nominated for president three times, the popularity of his opponents and weakness of his political party, the Whigs, kept him from achieving his lifelong goal of winning the presidency.

Calhoun represented South Carolina. He was an influential member of Congress and, at least for a time, a close friend of Henry Clay. Calhoun supported states' rights and the interests of the South. Fearing that the North intended to dominate the South, Calhoun spent the rest of his career trying to prevent the federal government from weakening states' rights and from interfering with the Southern way of life.

◀ **John C. Calhoun**

Then and Now

What political leaders represent the region in which you live? Do you think leaders should represent the views of the citizens who elected them?

Before word of the treaty had reached the United States, one final—and ferocious—battle occurred at New Orleans. In December 1814, British army troops moved toward New Orleans. Awaiting them behind earthen fortifications was an American army led by Andrew Jackson.

On January 8, 1815, the British troops advanced. The redcoats were no match for Jackson's soldiers, who shot from behind bales of cotton. In a short but gruesome battle, hundreds of British soldiers were killed. At the Battle of New Orleans, Americans achieved a decisive victory. Andrew Jackson became a hero, and his fame helped him win the presidency in 1828.

American Nationalism Most New England Federalists had opposed "Mr. Madison's war" from the start. In December 1814, unhappy New England Federalists gathered in Connecticut at the Hartford Convention. A few favored secession. Most wanted to remain within the Union, however. To protect their interests, they drew up a list of proposed amendments to the Constitution.

After the convention broke up, word came of Jackson's spectacular victory at New Orleans, followed by news of the peace treaty. In this moment of triumph, the Federalist grievances seemed unpatriotic. The party lost respect in the eyes of the public. Most Americans felt proud and self-confident at the end of the War of 1812. The young nation had gained new respect from other nations in the world. Americans felt a renewed sense of patriotism and a strong national identity.

Although the Federalist Party weakened, its philosophy of strong national government was carried on by the War Hawks, who were part of the Republican Party. They favored trade, western expansion, the energetic development of the **economy,** and a strong army and navy.

Reading Check **Analyze** Did the Treaty of Ghent resolve any major issues? Explain.

History Online
Study Central Need help understanding the War of 1812? Visit ca.hss.glencoe.com and click on Study Central.

Section 2 Review

Reading Summary

Review the Main Ideas

- While at first unprepared and experiencing setbacks on the battlefield, American forces soon began to gain victories on land and at sea in the War of 1812.
- In 1814 the British succeeded in capturing Washington, D.C., but they lost a number of other important battles, including the one at New Orleans.

What Did You Learn?

1. Who won the Battle of Lake Champlain? Why was it an important victory?
2. What were the effects of the Battle of New Orleans?

Critical Thinking

3. **Determining Cause and Effect** Re-create the diagram below. In the ovals, list four effects that the War of 1812 had on the United States. CA HI2.

Effects of the War of 1812

4. **The Big Ideas** Why did the Federalist Party lose support after the War of 1812? CA CS1.
5. **Creative Writing** Imagine if Francis Scott Key had been at the Battle of New Orleans instead of in Baltimore. Rewrite "The Star-Spangled Banner" based on what occurred in that battle. CA 8WA2.1
6. **Analysis** **Making Connections** Explain the relationship between Britain's war with France and the War of 1812 and the Treaty of Ghent. CA CS1.

TIME NOTEBOOK

What were people's lives like in the past?

What—and who—were people talking about? What did they eat? What did they do for fun? These two pages will give you some clues to everyday life in the U.S. as you step back in time with TIME Notebook.

Profile

SAGOYEWATHA *is the great Iroquois leader some call Red Jacket. Why? Because he fought with the British in the Revolutionary War. Sagoyewatha means "He Causes Them to Be Awake." Below is part of a speech Sagoyewatha delivered in 1805 to a group of religious leaders from Boston:*

"BROTHERS, OUR (*NATIVE AMERICAN*) SEATS were once large and yours (colonists) were small. You have now become a great people, and we have scarcely a place left to spread our blankets. You have got our country but are not satisfied; you want to force your religion upon us....

Brothers, continue to listen. You say there is but one way to worship and serve the Great Spirit. If there is but one religion, why do you white people differ so much about it?...

Brothers, we...also have a religion which was given to our forefathers and has been handed down to us, their children...."

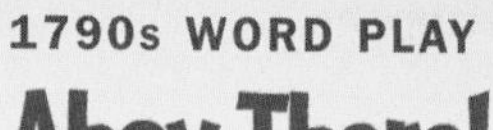
Sagoyewatha

VERBATIM

WHAT PEOPLE ARE SAYING

"We are one."

"Mind your business."

FIRST OFFICIAL U.S. COIN,
sayings are on the front and back of the coin minted in 1787

"I die hard, but I am not afraid to go."

GEORGE WASHINGTON,
on his deathbed in 1799

"My mother and myself begged Mr. Carter not to sell this child out of Fredg [*plantation*], he gave us his word and honor that he would not, but as soon as we left him, he sold the child."

JAMES CARTER,
African American slave of Landon Carter, writing around 1790 about his sister, whom he never saw again

"May the Lord bless King George, convert him, and take him to heaven, as we want no more of him."

REVEREND JOHN GRUBER,
to his Baltimore congregation during the War of 1812

1790s WORD PLAY

Ahoy There!

The U.S.S. *Constitution,* a powerful frigate, or warship, was launched in 1797 with a crew of 450 and 54 cannons. Want to join the crew? First, you must prove you can understand a sailor's vocabulary.
Match each word or phrase in the first column with its original meaning.

1. Keel over
2. Try a new tack
3. Let the cat out of the bag
4. Mind your p's and q's
5. Shipshape

a. Sailors who do wrong are disciplined with a cat-o'-nine-tails whip that's kept in a red sack

b. Putting a ship in for repair

c. Bartenders keep track of what sailors drink and owe by marking numbers under "pints" and "quarts"

d. The course or direction boats take into the wind

e. Good condition

answers: 1. b; 2. d; 3. a; 4. c; 5. e

Where in the United States?

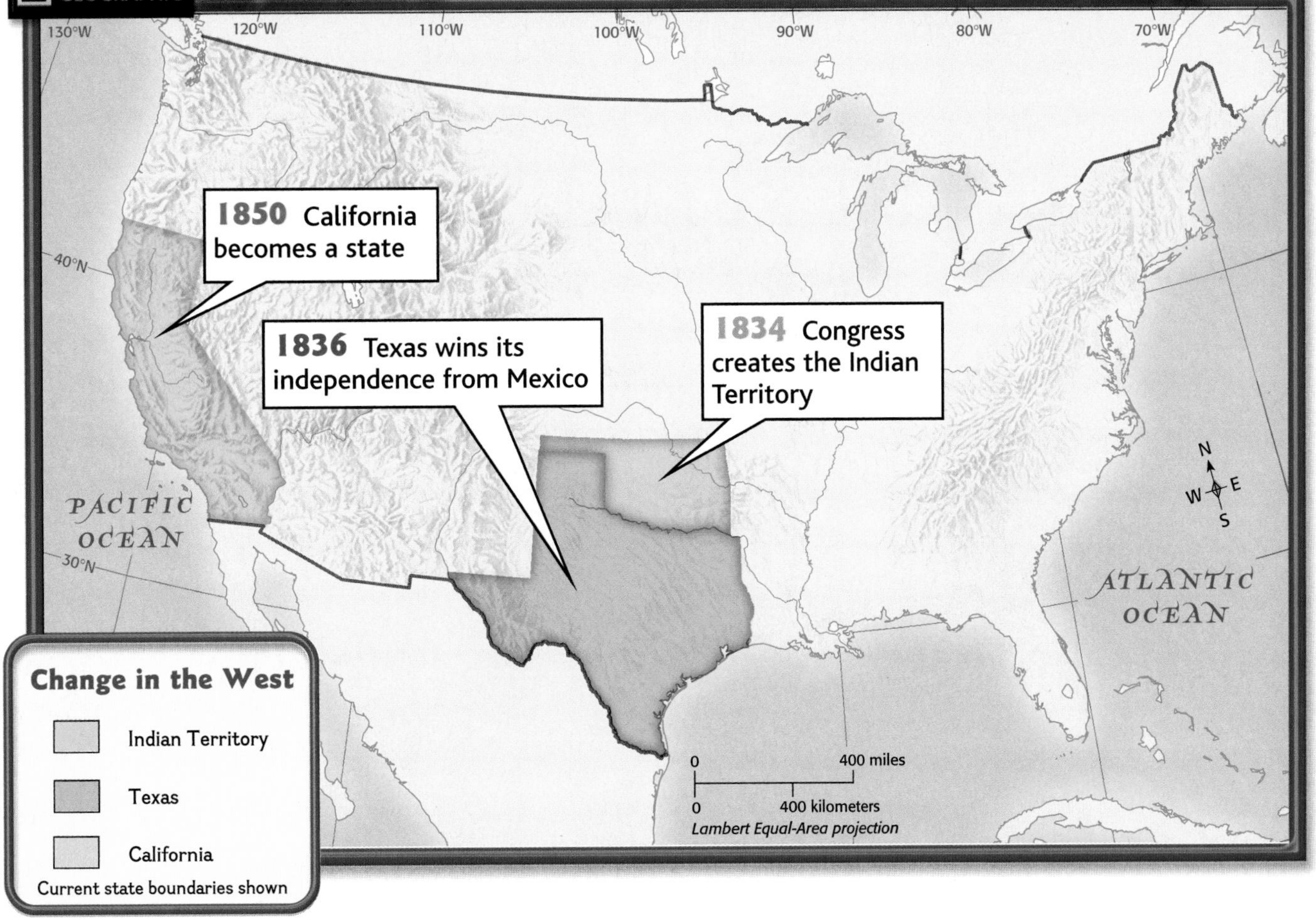

NATIONAL GEOGRAPHIC

130°W 120°W 110°W 100°W 90°W 80°W 70°W

40°N

30°N

1850 California becomes a state

1836 Texas wins its independence from Mexico

1834 Congress creates the Indian Territory

PACIFIC OCEAN

ATLANTIC OCEAN

N S E W

0 400 miles

0 400 kilometers

Lambert Equal-Area projection

Change in the West

- Indian Territory
- Texas
- California

Current state boundaries shown

1835 **1850** **1865**

1832 Jackson challenges the Bank of the United States

1834 Congress creates the Indian Territory

1846 Congress declares war on Mexico

1848 Seneca Falls Convention backs woman suffrage

Lucretia Mott

1834 Mexico begins to break up missions

California Bear flag

CALIFORNIA REPUBLIC

1846 Americans declare California an independent nation

1850 California becomes a state

1833 Great Britain abolishes slavery in its colonies

1836 Texas wins its independence from Mexico

1848 Revolutions sweep through Europe

1850 Tai Ping Rebellion begins in China

Tai Ping Rebellion

Unit 4

Places to Locate

1

ERIE CANAL

See *The Northeast: Building America* Chapter 8

2

TRAIL OF TEARS

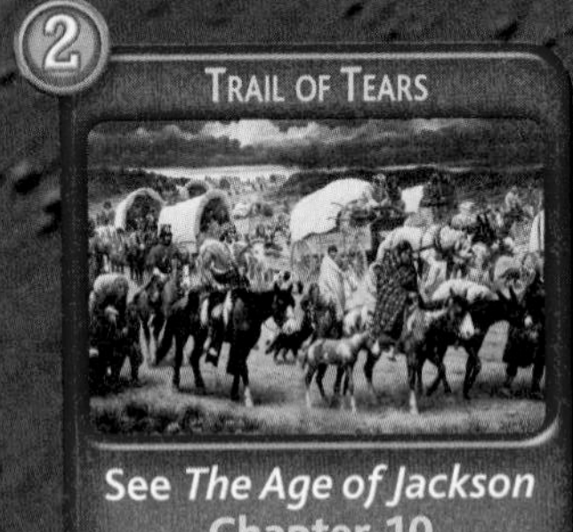

See *The Age of Jackson* Chapter 10

4

3

People to Meet

Eli Whitney
1765–1825
American inventor
Chapter 8, page 384

Dorothea Dix
1802–1887
Prison reformer
Chapter 8, page 405

Elizabeth Cady Stanton
1815–1902
Women's rights activist
Chapter 8, page 409

Harriet Tubman
c. 1820–1913
African American leader
Chapter 9, page 436

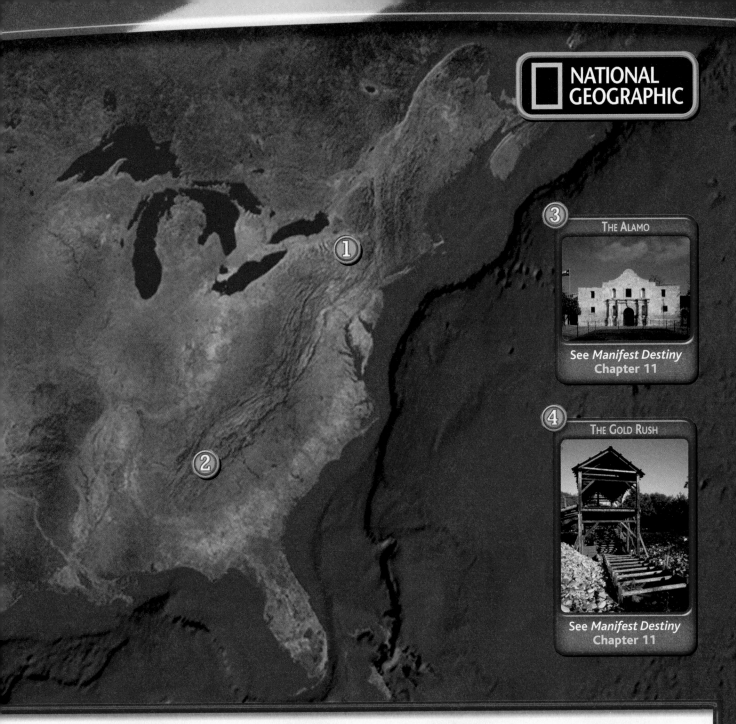

NATIONAL GEOGRAPHIC

3 THE ALAMO

See *Manifest Destiny* Chapter 11

4 THE GOLD RUSH

See *Manifest Destiny* Chapter 11

1

2

Andrew Jackson
1767–1845
Seventh president of the United States
Chapter 10, page 447

Sequoya
c. 1760–1845
Inventor of Cherokee alphabet
Chapter 10, page 453

Osceola
c. 1804–1838
Seminole leader
Chapter 10, page 456

John C. Frémont
1813–1890
American explorer of California
Chapter 11, page 494

Chapter 8

The Northeast: Building Industry

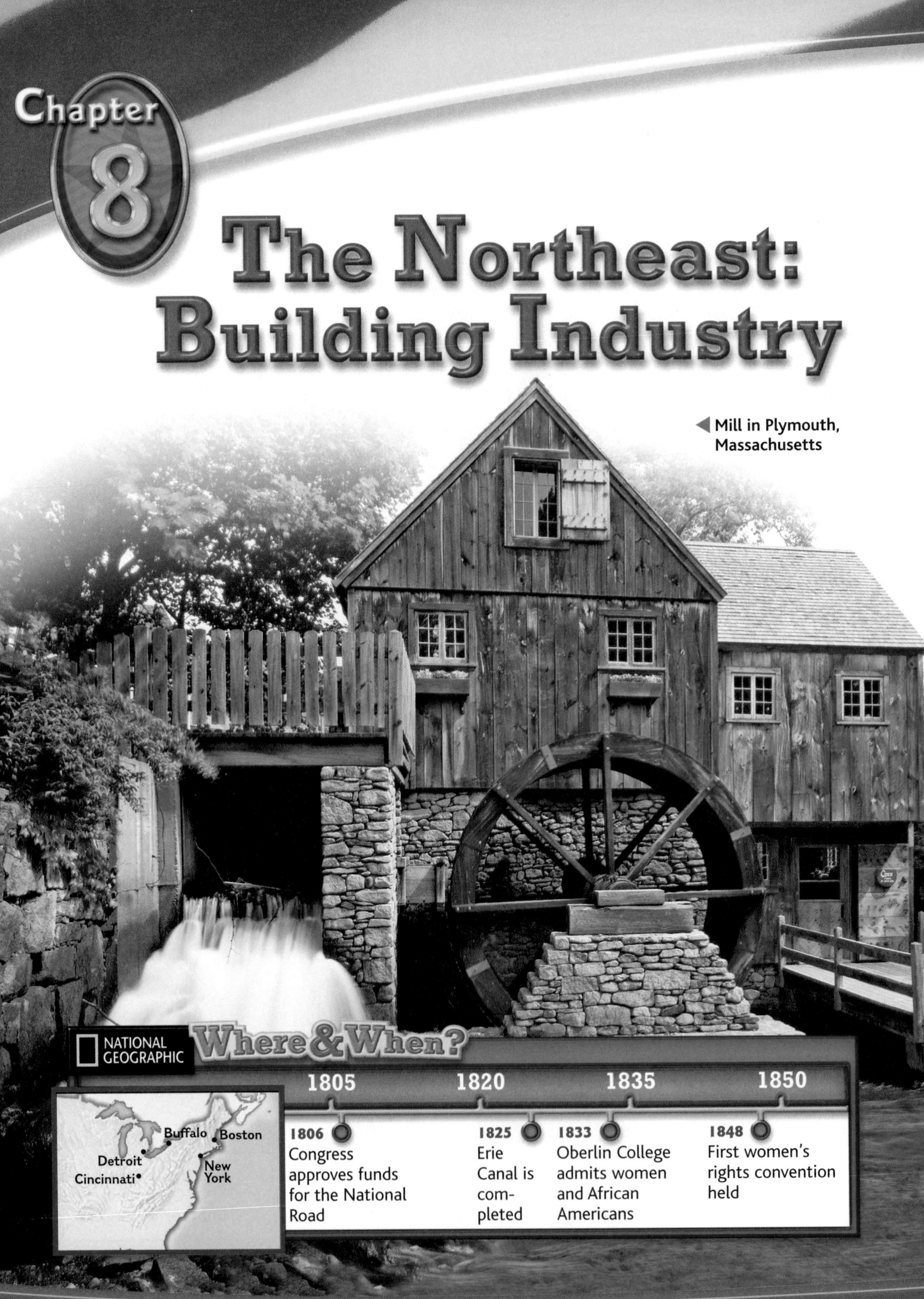
NATIONAL GEOGRAPHIC
Where & When?
1805
1820
1835
1850
1806 Congress approves funds for the National Road
1825 Erie Canal is completed
1833 Oberlin College admits women and African Americans
1848 First women's rights convention held
Buffalo
Boston
Detroit
Cincinnati
New York

Mill in Plymouth, Massachusetts

The Big Ideas

Economic Growth

Geography shapes the physical, economic, and political challenges a region faces. New technology produced the Industrial Revolution.

A System of Transportation

Geography shapes the physical, economic, and political challenges a region faces. Improvements in transportation led to Western settlement.

The North's People

Differences in economic, political, and social beliefs and practices can lead to division within a nation and have lasting consequences. The North saw an increase in industrialism and the growth of cities.

Reforms and Reformers

Reactions to social injustice can lead to reform movements. Many Americans worked for reform in education and other areas.

The Women's Movement

Reactions to social injustice can lead to reform movements. Women lobbied for increased rights and an equal status with men in America.

View the Chapter 8 video in the Glencoe Video Program.

Organizing Make this foldable to organize information from the chapter to help you learn more about the changes in the North.

Step 1 Collect three sheets of paper and place them on top of one another about 1 inch apart.

Step 2 Fold up the bottom edges of the paper to form 6 tabs.

This makes all tabs the same size.

Step 3 When all the tabs are the same size, fold the paper to hold the tabs in place and staple the sheets together. Turn the paper and label each tab as shown.

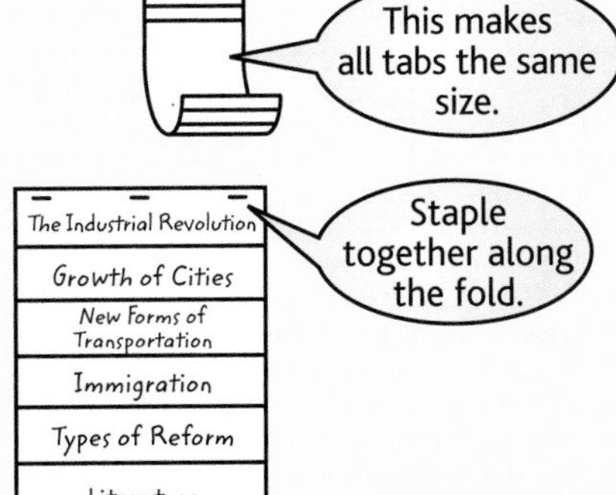

Reading and Writing As you read, use your foldable to write under each appropriate tab what you learned about the people, the economy, and the culture of the North.

Get Ready to Read

Problems and Solutions

1 Learn It!

To explain how and why a person, society, or government made a particular decision in history, authors sometimes use a problem/solution approach in their writing. You can recognize a problem/solution structure by asking three questions. What was the problem? What was the solution? What were the results of that solution? As you read the text below, notice how the author used a problem/solution approach to explain how reformers developed methods to teach people with disabilities.

Some reformers focused on teaching people with disabilities. Thomas Gallaudet (GA • luh • DEHT), who developed a method to educate people who were hearing impaired, opened the Hartford School for the Deaf in Connecticut in 1817.

At about the same time, Dr. Samuel Gridley Howe advanced the cause of those who were visually impaired. He developed books with large raised letters that people with sight impairments could "read" with their fingers. Howe headed the Perkins Institute, a school for the blind, in Boston.

—from page 405

As you read, make a chart listing problems and solutions that are described in the text.

2 Practice It!

As you read this chapter, complete a chart like the one below to show how Americans solved problems by inventing new machines.

Problem		Solution
Need more thread to make cloth	→	Spinning jenny
Cotton bolls difficult to clean	→	
Machine parts are hard to find	→	

Read to Write

Understanding problems and creating solutions is part of everyday life. Can you think of a challenge you have had this week? How have you found solutions? Write a short paragraph describing one of your own problem/solution situations.

▲ Eli Whitney

Cotton gin ▶

3 Apply It!

As you read this chapter, watch for ways that everyday people met the challenges they faced.

Section 1 Economic Growth

Guide to Reading

History Social Science Standards

US8.6 Students analyze the divergent paths of the American people from 1800 to the mid-1800s and the challenges they faced, with emphasis on the Northeast.

Looking Back, Looking Ahead

Beginning in the early 1800s, revolutions in industry brought great changes to the North.

Focusing on the Main Ideas

- New technology led to changes in the way things are made. *(page 383)*
- The growth of factories and trade led to the growth of cities. *(page 386)*

Meeting People

Eli Whitney
Samuel Slater
Francis Cabot Lowell

Content Vocabulary

Industrial Revolution (ihn•DUHS•tree•uhl REH•vuh•LOO•shuhn)
capitalism
capital (KA•puh•tuhl)
free enterprise (EHN•tuhr•PRYZ)
technology (tehk•NAH•luh•jee)
cotton gin
patent (PA•tuhnt)
factory system
interchangeable parts (IHN•tuhr•CHAYN•juh•buhl)

Academic Vocabulary

percent
expand
concentrate (KAHN•suhn•TRAYT)

Reading Strategy

Organizing Information As you read the section, re-create the diagram below and describe in the ovals changes brought about by the Industrial Revolution.

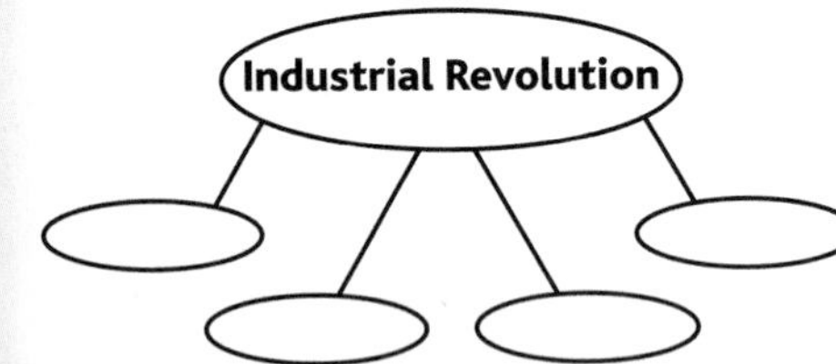
Industrial Revolution

NATIONAL GEOGRAPHIC
Who & When?
1780
1800
1820
1790 Congress passes patent law
1793 Samuel Slater starts cotton mill
1814 Textile plant opens in Waltham, Massachusetts

Velocipede patent

Samuel Slater

US8.6.1 Discuss the influence of industrialization and technological developments on the region, including human modification of the landscape and how physical geography shaped human actions (e.g., growth of cities, deforestation, farming, mineral extraction).

The Growth of Industry

Main Idea **New technology led to changes in the way things are made.**

Reading Connection Do you know someone who works in a factory? What is his or her job like? Read to learn how new technology spurred the Industrial Revolution in New England and what working in mills or factories was like.

From colonial times, most of the people of New England had lived and worked on farms. Work on a new farm was difficult. Eager to plant crops, the farmers first cleared the land. The trees were felled for building materials, fences, and firewood. People believed that trees grew on the most fertile land. As a result, they often cut down all the trees in an area. This created problems. Often the soil eroded without the protection of trees and tree roots.

A New Way of Working During the colonial era, workers were in short supply. Americans learned to develop tools that made work easier and more efficient.

People working in their homes or in workshops made cloth and most other goods. Using hand tools, they produced furniture, farm equipment, household items, and clothing.

In the mid-1700s, however, the way goods were made began to change. These changes appeared first in Great Britain. British inventors created machinery to perform some of the work involved in cloth making, such as spinning. The machines ran on waterpower, so British cloth makers built mills along rivers and installed the machines in these mills. People left their homes and farms to work in the mills and earn wages. The changes this system brought about were so great that this historic development is known as the **Industrial Revolution** (ihn•DUHS•tree•uhl REH•vuh•LOO•shuhn).

The Industrial Revolution The Industrial Revolution began to take root in the United States around 1800, appearing first in New England—Massachusetts, Rhode Island, Connecticut, Vermont, and New Hampshire. New England's soil was poor, and farming was difficult. As a result, some people were willing to leave their farms to find work elsewhere. Also, New England had many rushing rivers and streams. These provided the waterpower necessary to run the machinery in the new factories.

New England's Geography New England's geographic location also proved to be an advantage. It was close to other resources, including coal and iron from nearby Pennsylvania. New England also had many ports. Through these ports passed the cotton shipped from Southern states to New England factories, as well as the finished cloth produced in the North and bound for markets throughout the nation.

A Changing Economy The economic system of the United States is called **capitalism.** Under capitalism, individuals put their **capital** (KA•puh•tuhl), or money, into a business in hopes of making a profit.

Free enterprise (EHN•tuhr•PRYZ) is another term used to describe the American economy. In a system of free enterprise, people are free to buy, sell, and produce whatever they want. They can also work wherever they wish. The major elements of free enterprise are competition, profit, private property, and economic freedom. Business owners have the freedom to produce the products that they think will be the most profitable. Buyers also compete to find the best products at the lowest prices.

▲ American blacksmith, early 1800s woodcut

New Technology Workers, waterpower, location, and capital were key factors in New England's Industrial Revolution. Yet without the invention of new machines and **technology** (tehk•NAH•luh•jee)—scientific discoveries that simplify work—the Industrial Revolution could not have taken place.

Inventions such as the spinning jenny and the water frame, which spun thread, and the power loom, which wove the thread into cloth, made it possible to perform many steps in making cloth by machine, saving time and money. Because these new machines ran on waterpower, most mills were built near rivers.

Another invention greatly increased the production of cotton. In 1793 **Eli Whitney** of Massachusetts invented the **cotton gin,** a simple machine that quickly and efficiently removed seeds from cotton fiber. The cotton gin enabled one worker, usually a slave, to clean cotton as fast as 50 people working by hand.

In 1790 Congress passed a patent law to protect the rights of those who developed "useful and important inventions." A **patent** (PA•tuhnt) gives an inventor the sole legal right to the invention and its profits for a certain period of time. One of the first patents went to Jacob Perkins for a machine to make nails.

TECHNOLOGY & History

Textile Mill

The Lowell factory system was designed to bring work and workers together. A typical Lowell textile mill in 1830 housed 4,500 spindles, 120 power looms, and more than 200 employees under one roof. ***What type of energy powered the mills?***

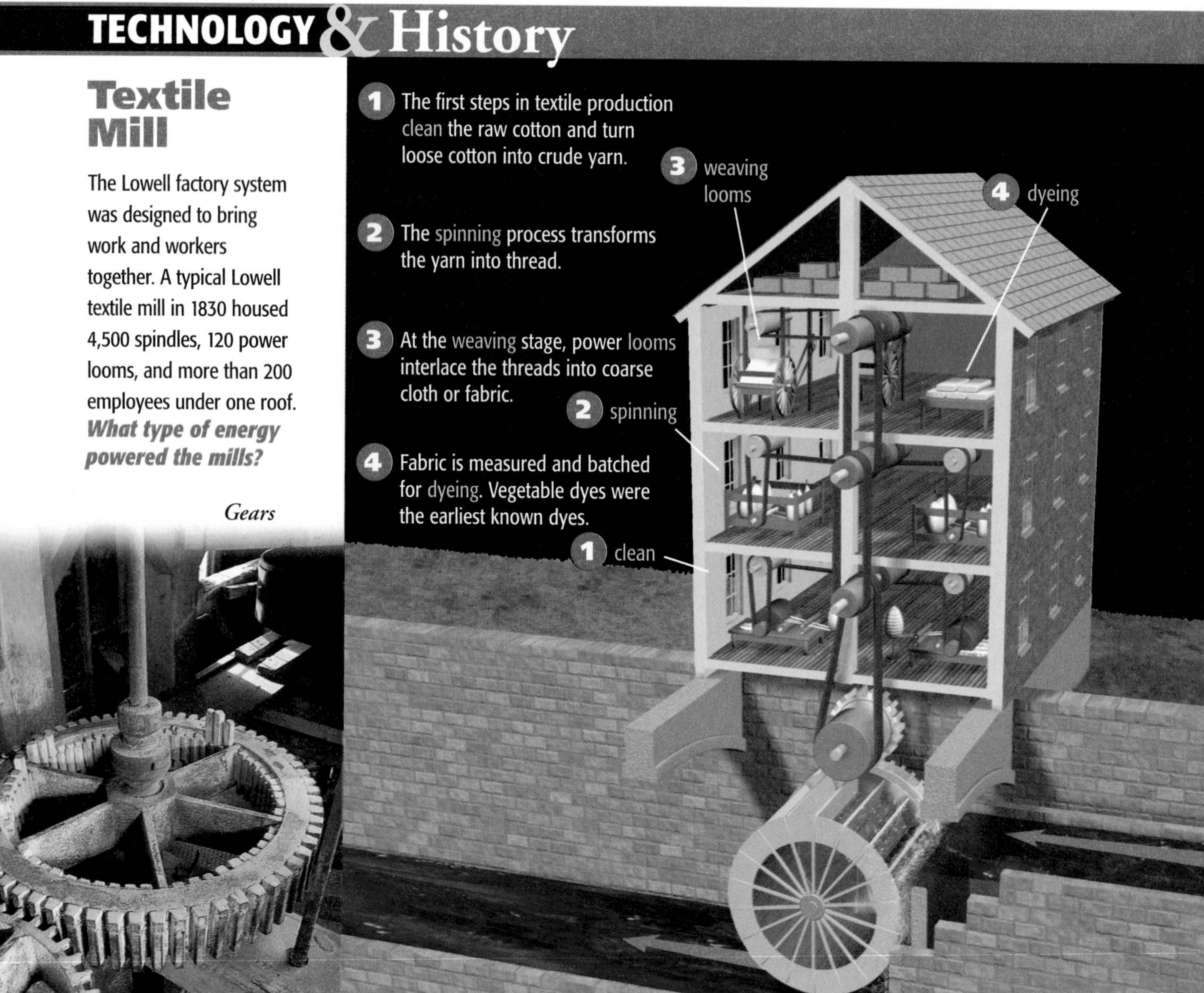

1 The first steps in textile production clean the raw cotton and turn loose cotton into crude yarn.
2 The spinning process transforms the yarn into thread.
3 At the weaving stage, power looms interlace the threads into coarse cloth or fabric.
4 Fabric is measured and batched for dyeing. Vegetable dyes were the earliest known dyes.
3 weaving looms
4 dyeing
2 spinning
1 clean

Gears

New England Factories The British tried to keep their new industrial technology a secret. Great Britain even passed laws prohibiting their machinery as well as their skilled mechanics from leaving the country. However, a few enterprising workers managed to slip away to the United States.

In Britain **Samuel Slater** had worked in a factory that used machines invented by Richard Arkwright for spinning cotton thread. Slater memorized the design of Arkwright's machines and slipped out of Britain. Once in the United States, Slater operated a cotton mill in Pawtucket, Rhode Island, in 1793. There he duplicated all of Arkwright's machines. Using these machines, the mill produced cotton thread. Slater's mill marked an important step in the Industrial Revolution in America.

In 1814 **Francis Cabot Lowell** opened a textile plant in Waltham, Massachusetts. The plan he implemented went several steps beyond Slater's mill. For the first time, all the stages of cloth making were performed under one roof. Lowell's mill launched the **factory system,** a system that brought manufacturing steps together in one place to increase efficiency. The factory system was a significant development in the way goods were made and another important part of the Industrial Revolution. By 1840 many textile mills were operating in the Northeast. Industrialists soon applied factory techniques to the production of lumber, shoes, leather, and other products.

Interchangeable Parts The inventor Eli Whitney started the use of **interchangeable parts** (IHN • tuhr • CHAYN • juh • buhl). These were identical machine parts that could be put together quickly to make a complete product. Because all the parts were alike, they could be manufactured with less-skilled labor and they made machine repair easier. Interchangeable parts opened the way for producing many different kinds of goods on a mass scale and for reducing the price of the goods.

Reading Check **Analyze** Why were the first mills in Great Britain built near rivers?

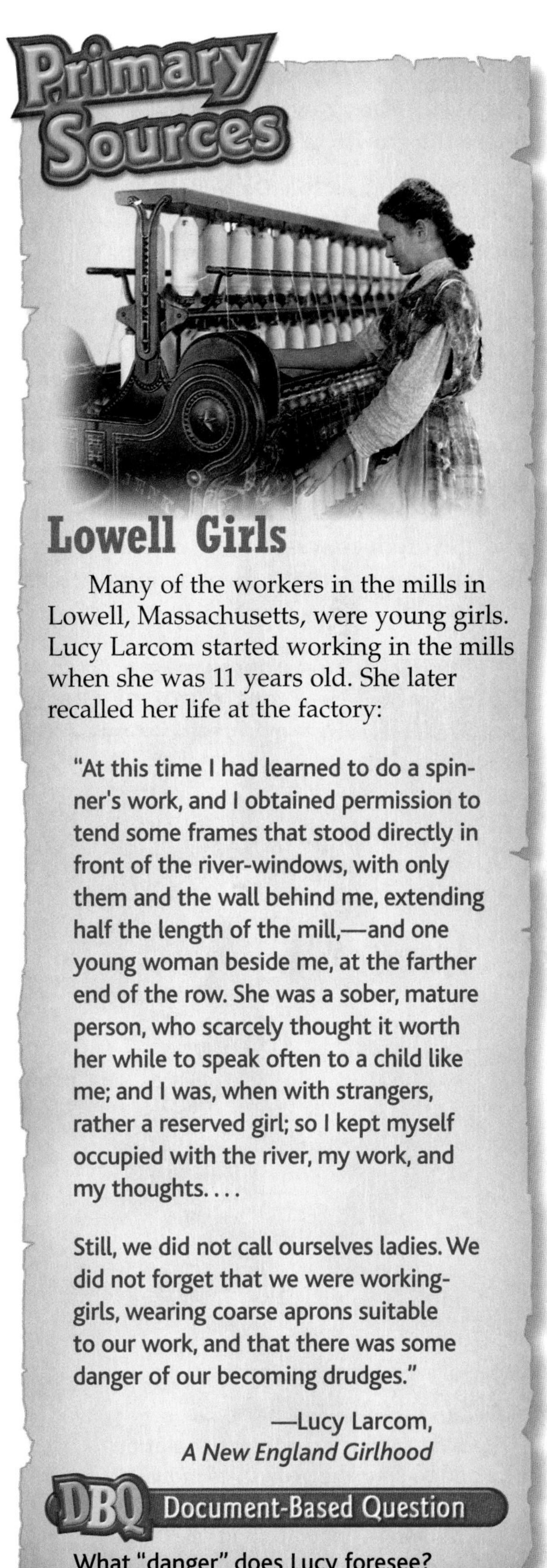

Primary Sources

Lowell Girls

Many of the workers in the mills in Lowell, Massachusetts, were young girls. Lucy Larcom started working in the mills when she was 11 years old. She later recalled her life at the factory:

"At this time I had learned to do a spinner's work, and I obtained permission to tend some frames that stood directly in front of the river-windows, with only them and the wall behind me, extending half the length of the mill,—and one young woman beside me, at the farther end of the row. She was a sober, mature person, who scarcely thought it worth her while to speak often to a child like me; and I was, when with strangers, rather a reserved girl; so I kept myself occupied with the river, my work, and my thoughts. . . .

Still, we did not call ourselves ladies. We did not forget that we were working-girls, wearing coarse aprons suitable to our work, and that there was some danger of our becoming drudges."

—Lucy Larcom,
A New England Girlhood

DBQ Document-Based Question

What "danger" does Lucy foresee?

US8.6.1 Discuss the influence of industrialization and technological developments on the region, including human modification of the landscape and how physical geography shaped human actions (e.g., growth of cities, deforestation, farming, mineral extraction).

A Changing Economy

Main Ideas **The growth of factories and trade led to the growth of cities.**

Reading Connection Do you think you would rather work on a farm or in a factory? Read to learn what caused agriculture to expand at the same time that factories and towns were growing.

Although many New Englanders went to work in factories, most Americans still lived and worked on farms. In the 1820s, more than 65 **percent** of Americans were farmers.

In the Northeast, farms tended to be small, and the produce was usually marketed locally. In the South, cotton production increased dramatically. The demand for cotton had grown steadily with the development of the textile industries of New England and Europe. Southern plantation owners used enslaved workers to plant, tend, and pick the cotton. The cotton gin—which made it possible to clean the cotton faster and less expensively than by hand—encouraged the planters to raise larger crops. Between 1790 and 1820, cotton production soared from 3,000 to more than 300,000 bales a year.

There were also changes in the West. Agriculture in that region **expanded.** Southern farmers seeking new land moved west to plant cotton. Western farmers north of the Ohio River **concentrated** on raising pork and cash crops such as corn and wheat.

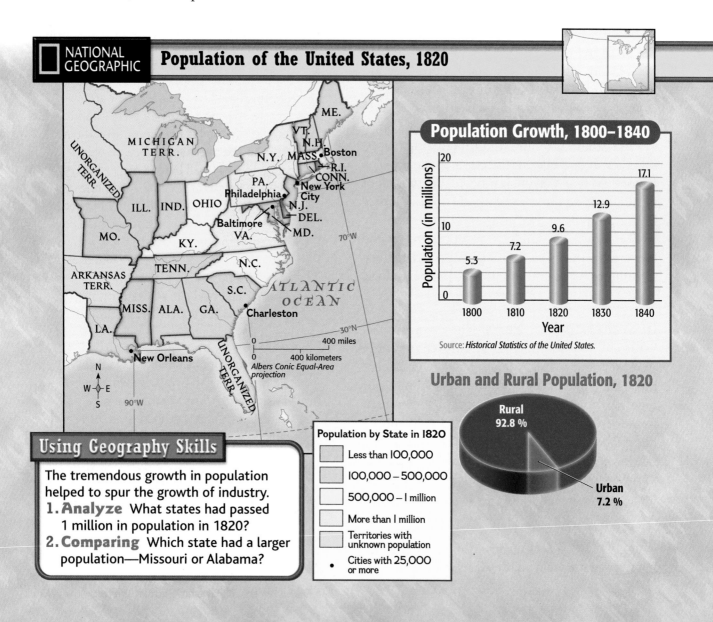

NATIONAL GEOGRAPHIC

Population of the United States, 1820

Population Growth, 1800–1840

Source: *Historical Statistics of the United States.*

Urban and Rural Population, 1820

Using Geography Skills

The tremendous growth in population helped to spur the growth of industry.

1. **Analyze** What states had passed 1 million in population in 1820?
2. **Comparing** Which state had a larger population—Missouri or Alabama?

Biography

US8.6.2 Outline the physical obstacles to and the economic and political factors involved in building a network of roads, canals, and railroads (e.g., Henry Clay's American System).

ROBERT FULTON

1765–1815

Robert Fulton grew up in Lancaster, Pennsylvania. At an early age he created his own lead pencils and rockets. While living in Europe in the late 1790s, Fulton designed and built a submarine called the *Nautilus* to be used in France's war against Britain. Submarine warfare became common later.

Fulton returned to the United States and developed a steamboat engine that was more powerful and provided a smoother ride than previous engines. On August 18, 1807, Fulton's *Clermont* made its first successful run. The *Clermont* made its first voyages on the Hudson River, chugging the 150 miles from New York City to Albany at about five miles per hour.

By demonstrating the usefulness of two-way river travel, Fulton launched the steamboat era. In the years between 1830 and 1850, the steamboat became the most important means of transportation on major rivers.

Steamboats cruised in and out of the Great Lakes, as well as up and down the Mississippi River and its tributaries. By 1850 more than 700 steamboats, also called riverboats, traveled along the nation's waterways.

Fulton designed many other devices such as submarines and steam warships. He also engineered canal systems. Thomas Jefferson and James Madison considered him a mechanical genius with many talents. When the United States went to war with Great Britain in the War of 1812, President Madison said, "I have been asked, on a number of occasions, how the United States could conceivably defeat England, with the resources of its vast empire. I invariably reply, 'The United States has Robert Fulton, and he is all the empire we need.'"

"I have no time to listen to such nonsense."

—Napoleon Bonaparte about Fulton's plans for a steam-powered engine

Then and Now

What modern inventions have changed the way we travel?

US8.6.2 Outline the physical obstacles to and the economic and political factors involved in building a network of roads, canals, and railroads (e.g., Henry Clay's American System).

Canals

Main Idea **Business and government officials came up with a plan to build a canal to link the eastern and western parts of the country.**

Reading Connection Have you ever worked long and hard to build something? Did you feel a sense of accomplishment when you finished? Read to learn the accomplishment of thousands of laborers who worked on the construction of the 363-mile Erie Canal.

Although steamboats represented a great improvement in transportation, their routes depended on the existing river system. Steamboats could not effectively tie the eastern and western parts of the country together.

In New York, business and government officials led by De Witt Clinton came up with a plan to link New York City with the Great Lakes region. They would build a **canal** (kuh•NAL)—an artificial waterway—across New York State, connecting Albany on the Hudson River with Buffalo on **Lake Erie.**

Building the Erie Canal Thousands of laborers, many of them Irish immigrants, worked on the construction of the 363-mile **Erie Canal.** Along the canal, they built a series of **locks**—separate compartments where water levels were raised or lowered. Locks provided a way to raise and lower boats at places where canal levels changed.

After more than two years of digging, the Erie Canal opened on October 26, 1825. Clinton boarded a barge in Buffalo and journeyed on the canal to New York City. As crowds cheered in New York, the officials poured water from Lake Erie into the Atlantic. The East and Midwest were joined.

TECHNOLOGY & History

How a Canal Works

A ship traveling downstream enters a lock and remains there while a gate is closed behind it, creating a watertight chamber. Water is slowly released through the downstream gate to lower the water level in the lock. The downstream gate is then opened, and the ship continues on its way at a lower elevation. To raise a ship, water is added to the lock through the upstream gate. **What happens as a boat travels through each lock of the canal?**

"Get up there mule, here comes a lock
We'll make Rome 'fore 6 'clock
And back we'll go to our home dock
Right back home to Buffalo"

The "lock" in the song verse refers to the Erie Canal. Locks are chambers, with gates at each end, that raise and lower ships to compensate for elevation changes along a waterway.

US8.6.2 Outline the physical obstacles to and the economic and political factors involved in building a network of roads, canals, and railroads (e.g., Henry Clay's American System).

In its early years, the canal did not allow steamboats because their powerful engines could damage the earthen embankments along the canal. Instead, teams of mules or horses hauled the boats and barges. In the 1840s, the canal banks were reinforced to accommodate steam tugboats pulling barges.

The success of the Erie Canal led to an explosion in canal building. By 1850 the United States had more than 3,600 miles of canals. Canals lowered the cost of shipping goods and brought prosperity to the towns along their routes. Canals also created opportunities for new businesses to supply food, shelter, and other necessities to workers—and later to travelers on the canals. Perhaps most important, they helped unite the growing country.

Reading Check **Identify** What two cities did the Erie Canal connect?

Western Settlement

Main Idea **Americans continued to move westward, settling near rivers so they could ship their crops to market.**

Reading Connection What do you do when you get together with your friends? Do you watch a movie or play soccer? Read to learn what kinds of social events western families had in the early 1800s.

Americans moved westward in waves. The first wave began before the 1790s and led to the admission of four new states between 1791 and 1803—Vermont, Kentucky, Tennessee, and Ohio. A second wave of westward growth began between 1816 and 1821. Five new western states were created—Indiana, Illinois, Mississippi, Alabama, and Missouri.

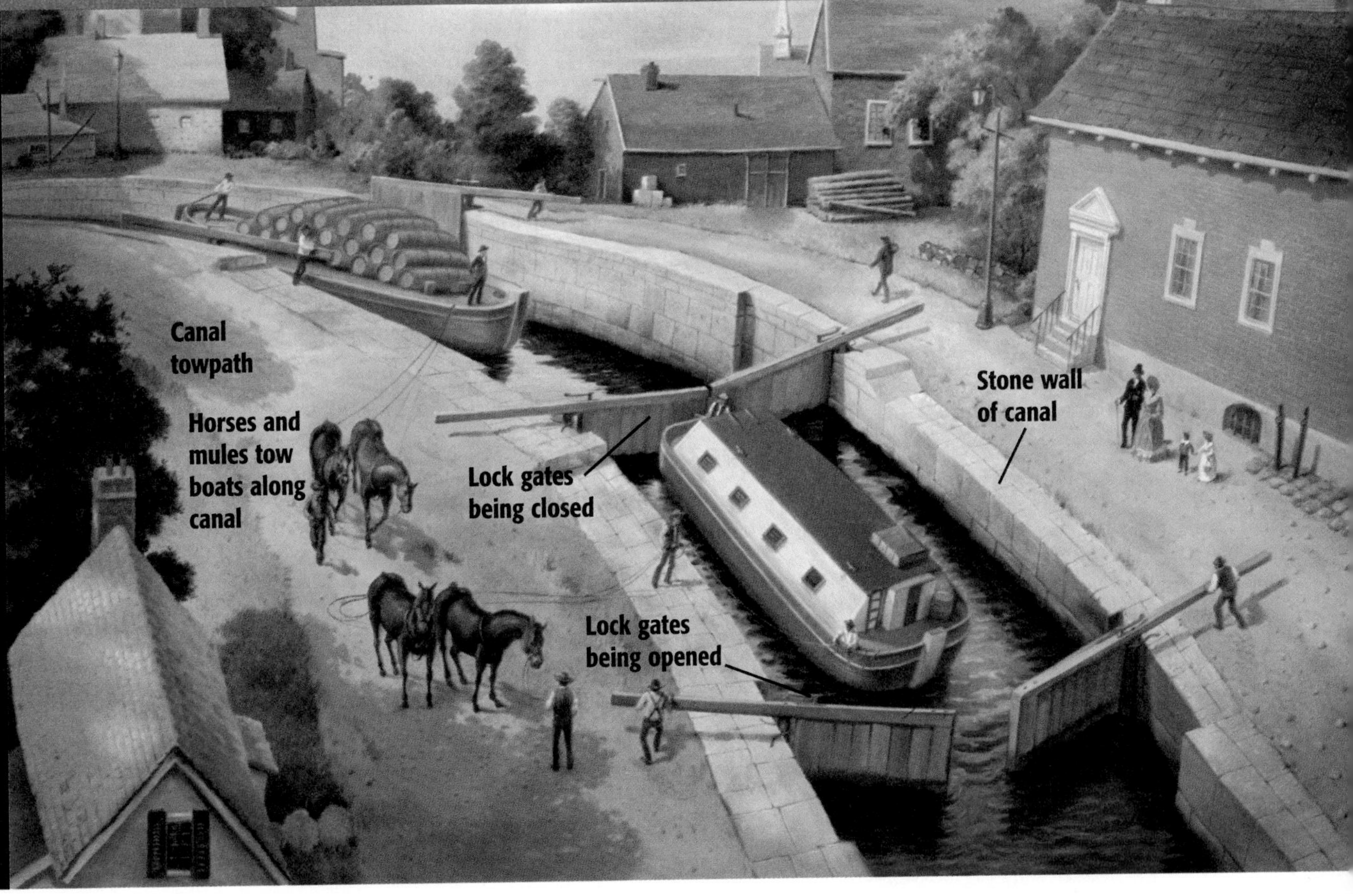

The new states reflected the dramatic growth of the region west of the Appalachians. Ohio, for example, had only 45,000 settlers in 1800. By 1820 it had 581,000.

Pioneer families tended to settle in communities along the great rivers, such as the Ohio and the Mississippi, so that they could ship their crops to market. The expansion of canals, which crisscrossed the land in the 1820s and 1830s, allowed people to live farther away from the rivers.

Pioneer families often gathered together for social events. Men took part in sports such as wrestling. Women met for quilting and sewing parties. Both men and women participated in cornhuskings—gatherings where farm families shared the work of stripping the husks from ears of corn.

Their lives did not include the conveniences of Eastern town life, but the pioneers had not moved to be pampered. They wanted to make a new life for themselves and their families.

Transportation and Daily Life Improved transportation meant that people could now buy goods produced in distant places. Rural Americans could hang curtains sewn from cloth manufactured in the mills of New England. Citizens of Illinois could enjoy the same foods, fashions, and household furnishings as residents of Vermont.

The new transportation changed America in other ways as well. In 1825 Congress established home delivery of letters by mail, and in 1847 the first national postage stamps were created. With the mail came newspapers, which brought national issues to the attention of remote rural communities.

Reading Check **Identify** Which states were formed between 1791 and 1803?

History Online
Study Central Need help understanding the effects of changes in transportation? Visit ca.hss.glencoe.com and click on Study Central.

Reading Summary

Review the Main Ideas

- Settlers used new roads and turnpikes to move west of the Appalachians, and steamboats opened a new era of river travel.
- The success of the Erie Canal led to the building of other canals to link the East and Midwest.
- Although life west of the Appalachian Mountains was often difficult, the population there grew tremendously in the early 1800s.

What Did You Learn?

1. Describe the improvements in transportation during the westward expansion in the early 1800s.
2. What were the benefits of canals in the mid-1800s?

Critical Thinking

3. **Comparing** What forms of communication and transportation linked East to West in the early 1800s? What links exist today? Re-create the diagram below and compare the links. CA CS1.

Links	
Early 1800s	Today

4. **The Big Ideas** How did better transportation affect westward expansion? CA HI2.
5. **Descriptive Writing** Write a newspaper headline along with a brief article describing one of the events discussed in this section, such as a trip on an early steamboat or the opening of the Erie Canal. CA 8WA2.1
6. **Analysis** **Sequencing** Draw a time line identifying major developments in transportation during this period. CA CS2.

Section
3

The North's People

Guide to Reading

Looking Back, Looking Ahead

In Section 2, you learned how advances in transportation changed the geography of America. In Section 3, you will learn about the people and the economy of the North.

Focusing on the Main Ideas

- As industrialism grew in the North, many saw the need for reforms in working conditions. *(page 396)*
- Immigrants entered northern cities from many parts of Europe. They often faced hardships and discrimination upon arriving in America. *(page 398)*

Meeting People

Henry Boyd
Samuel Cornish
John B. Russwurm
Sarah G. Bagley

Content Vocabulary

trade union
strike
prejudice (PREH•juh•duhs)
discrimination (dis•KRIH•muh•NAY•shuhn)
famine (FA•muhn)
nativist (NAY•tih•VIHST)

Academic Vocabulary

shift
manual

Reading Strategy

Determining Cause and Effect As you read the section, re-create the diagram below and list two reasons for the growth of cities.

Growth of Cities

History Social Science Standards

US8.6 Students analyze the divergent paths of the American people from 1800 to the mid-1800s and the challenges they faced, with emphasis on the Northeast.

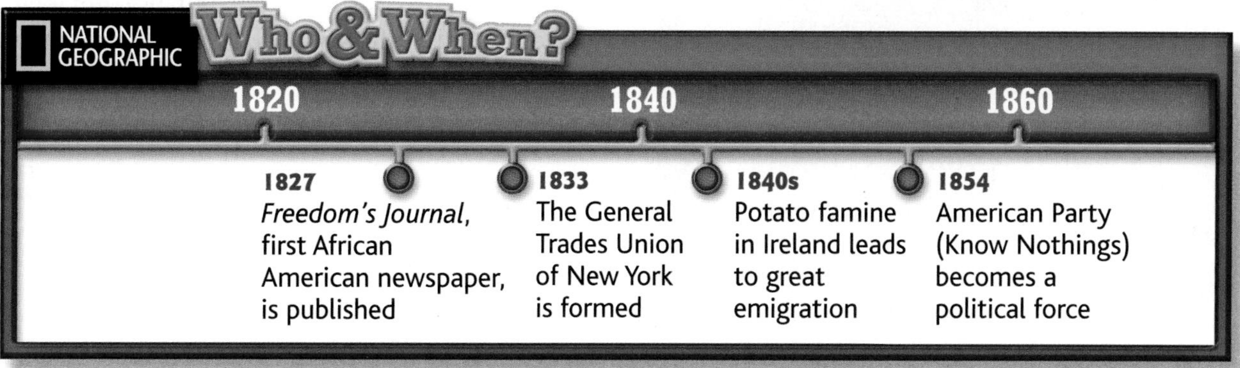
NATIONAL GEOGRAPHIC
Who & When?
1820
1840
1860
1827
Freedom's Journal, first African American newspaper, is published
1833
The General Trades Union of New York is formed
1840s
Potato famine in Ireland leads to great emigration
1854
American Party (Know Nothings) becomes a political force

US8.6.1 Discuss the influence of industrialization and technological developments in the region, including human modification of the landscape and how physical geography shaped human actions. **US8.6.4** Study the lives of black Americans who gained freedom in the North and founded schools and churches to advance their rights and communities.

Northern Factories

Main Idea **As industrialism grew in the North, many saw the need for reforms in working conditions.**

Reading Connection Do you baby-sit or mow lawns to earn money? Do you think the money you earn is fair for the job you perform? Read on to learn about how workers organized to receive better pay and improve working conditions.

An American Story

"At first the hours seemed very long, but I was so interested in learning that I endured it very well; when I went out at night the sound of the mill was in my ears," a Northern mill worker wrote in 1844.

The worker compared the noise of the cotton mill to the deafening roar of Niagara Falls. The roar of machinery was only one of the features of factory life that these workers had to adjust to. Industrialization created new challenges for the men, women, and children who worked in the nation's factories.

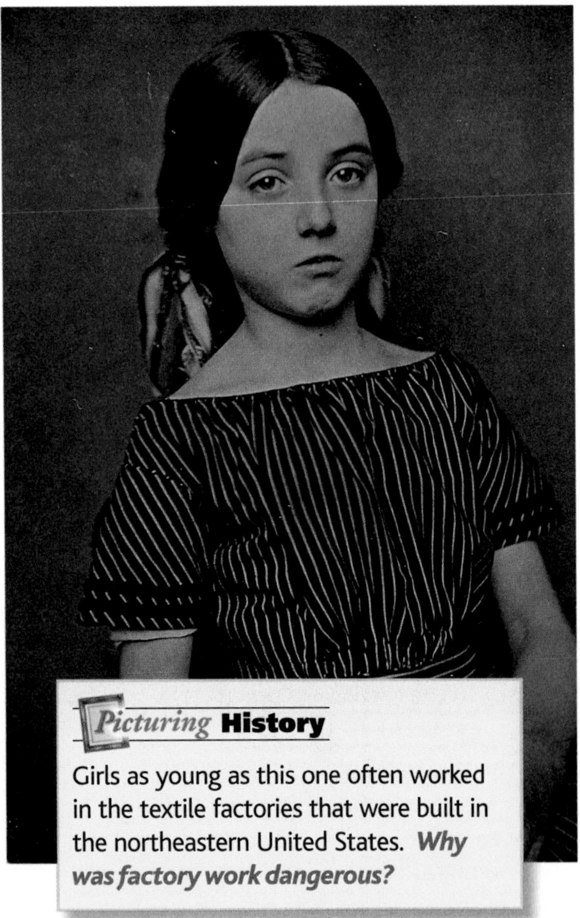

Picturing **History**

Girls as young as this one often worked in the textile factories that were built in the northeastern United States. ***Why was factory work dangerous?***

What Were Working Conditions Like?

Between 1820 and 1860, more and more of America's manufacturing **shifted** to mills and factories. Machines took over many of the production tasks.

In the early 1800s, in the mills established in Lowell, Massachusetts, the entire production process was brought together under one roof, setting up the factory system. In addition to textiles and clothing, factories now produced such items as shoes, watches, guns, sewing machines, and agricultural machinery.

As the factory system developed, working conditions worsened. Factory owners wanted their employees to work longer hours to produce more goods. By 1840 factory employees worked an average of 11.4 hours per day. As the workday grew longer, on-the-job accidents became more common.

Factory work was often dangerous. For example, the long leather belts that connected the machines to the factory's water-powered driveshaft had no protective shields. Workers often suffered injuries such as lost fingers and broken bones from the rapidly spinning belts. Young children working on machines with powerful moving parts were especially at risk.

Workers often labored under unpleasant conditions. In the summer, factories were miserably hot and stifling. The machines gave off heat, and air-conditioning had not yet been invented. In the winter, workers suffered because most factories had no heating.

Factory owners often showed more concern for profits than for the comfort and safety of their employees. Employers knew they could easily replace an unhappy worker with someone else who was eager for a job. No laws existed to regulate working conditions or to protect workers.

Attempts to Organize By the 1830s, workers began organizing to improve working conditions. Skilled workers formed **trade unions**—organizations of workers with the same trade, or skill. Steadily deteriorating working conditions led unskilled workers to organize as well.

In the mid-1830s, skilled workers in New York City staged a series of **strikes,** refusing to work in order to put pressure on employers. Workers wanted higher wages and to limit their workday to 10 hours. Groups of skilled workers formed the General Trades Union of New York.

In the early 1800s, going on strike was illegal. Striking workers could be punished by the law, or they could be fired from their jobs. In 1842 a Massachusetts court ruled that workers did have the right to strike. In other cities and states, workers won some protections. However, it would be many years before workers received federal protection of their right to strike.

African American Workers Slavery had largely disappeared from the North by 1820. However, racial **prejudice** (PREH • juh • duhs)—an unfair opinion that is not based on facts—and **discrimination** (dis • KRIH • muh • NAY • shuhn)—unfair treatment of a group—remained in Northern states. For example, both Rhode Island and Pennsylvania passed laws prohibiting free African Americans from voting.

Most communities would not allow free African Americans to attend public schools and barred them from public facilities, as well. Often African Americans were forced into segregated, or separate, schools and hospitals.

Some African Americans found success in business. **Henry Boyd** owned a furniture manufacturing company in Cincinnati, Ohio. In 1827 **Samuel Cornish** and **John B. Russwurm** founded *Freedom's Journal*, the nation's first African American newspaper. In 1845 Macon B. Allen became the first African American licensed to practice law in the United States.

Women Workers Women took jobs in the developing mills and factories. However, employers discriminated against women, paying them less than male workers. When men began to form unions, they excluded women. Male workers wanted women kept out of the workplace so that more jobs would be available for men.

History *Through Art*

Young Man in White Apron **by John Mackie Falconer** The artist of this painting was known for his watercolors depicting New York City workers such as this African American clerk. ***How did prejudice affect the lives of African Americans in the North?***

Some female workers attempted to organize in the 1830s and 1840s. In Massachusetts the Lowell Female Labor Reform Organization, founded by a weaver named **Sarah G. Bagley,** petitioned the state legislature for a 10-hour day in 1845. Because most of the petition's signers were women, the legislature did not discuss the petition.

Most of the early efforts by women to achieve equality and justice in the workplace failed. They led, however, to later movements to correct the injustices against female workers.

Reading Check **Describe** How did conditions for workers change as the factory system developed?

US8.6.3 List the reasons for the wave of immigration from Northern Europe to the United States and describe the growth in number, size, and spatial arrangement of cities (e.g., Irish immigrants and the Great Irish Famine).

The Rise of Cities

Main Idea **Immigrants entered northern cities from many parts of Europe. They often faced hardships and discrimination upon arriving in America.**

Reading Connection Did you know that the tradition of decorating a tree at Christmas comes from a German tradition? Many of our foods, words, and traditions originated in other countries. Read on to find out how immigrants influenced Northern cities.

The growth of factories helped Northern cities grow. People looking for work moved to the cities, where most of the factories were located. The population of New York City, the nation's largest city, reached 800,000, and Philadelphia's population was more than 500,000 in 1860.

Between 1820 and 1840, communities that had been small villages became major cities, including St. Louis, Pittsburgh, Cincinnati, and Louisville. All of them profited from their location on the Mississippi River or one of the river's branches. These cities became centers of the growing trade that connected the farmers of the Midwest with the cities of the Northeast. After 1830 the Great Lakes became a center for shipping, creating major new urban centers. These centers included Buffalo, Detroit, Milwaukee, and Chicago.

Immigration Immigration, which is the movement of people into a country, increased dramatically between 1840 and 1860. American manufacturers welcomed immigrants, many of whom were willing to work for low pay.

The largest group of immigrants to the United States at this time traveled across the Atlantic from Ireland. Between 1846 and 1860, more than 1.5 million Irish immigrants arrived in the United States, settling mostly in the Northeast. Today, more people of Irish descent live in the United States than in Ireland.

The Irish migration to the United States was brought on by the Great Irish Famine. A **famine** (FA•muhn) is an extreme shortage of food. Potatoes were the main staple of the Irish diet. When a devastating blight, or disease, destroyed Irish potato crops in the 1840s, starvation struck the country. More than 1 million people died from the lack of food and from diseases.

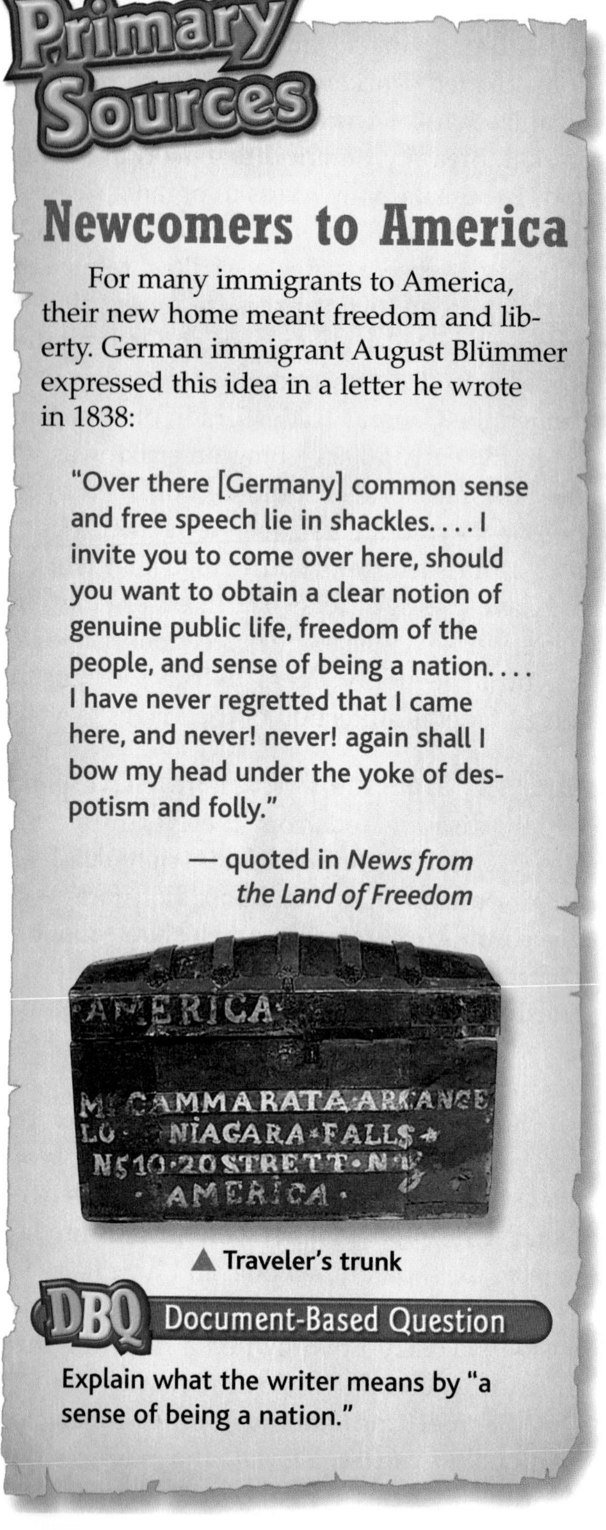

Primary Sources

Newcomers to America

For many immigrants to America, their new home meant freedom and liberty. German immigrant August Blümmer expressed this idea in a letter he wrote in 1838:

> "Over there [Germany] common sense and free speech lie in shackles. . . . I invite you to come over here, should you want to obtain a clear notion of genuine public life, freedom of the people, and sense of being a nation. . . . I have never regretted that I came here, and never! never! again shall I bow my head under the yoke of despotism and folly."
>
> — quoted in *News from the Land of Freedom*

▲ Traveler's trunk

DBQ Document-Based Question

Explain what the writer means by "a sense of being a nation."

Although most of the immigrants had been farmers in Ireland, they were too poor to buy land in the United States. For this reason, many Irish immigrants took low-paying factory jobs in Northern cities. The men who came from Ireland worked in factories or performed **manual** labor, such as working on the railroads. The women became servants and factory workers.

The second-largest group of immigrants in the United States between 1820 and 1860 came from Germany. Some sought work and opportunity. Others had left their homes because of the failure of a democratic revolution in Germany in 1848. During this time, many German Jews came to the United States seeking religious freedom.

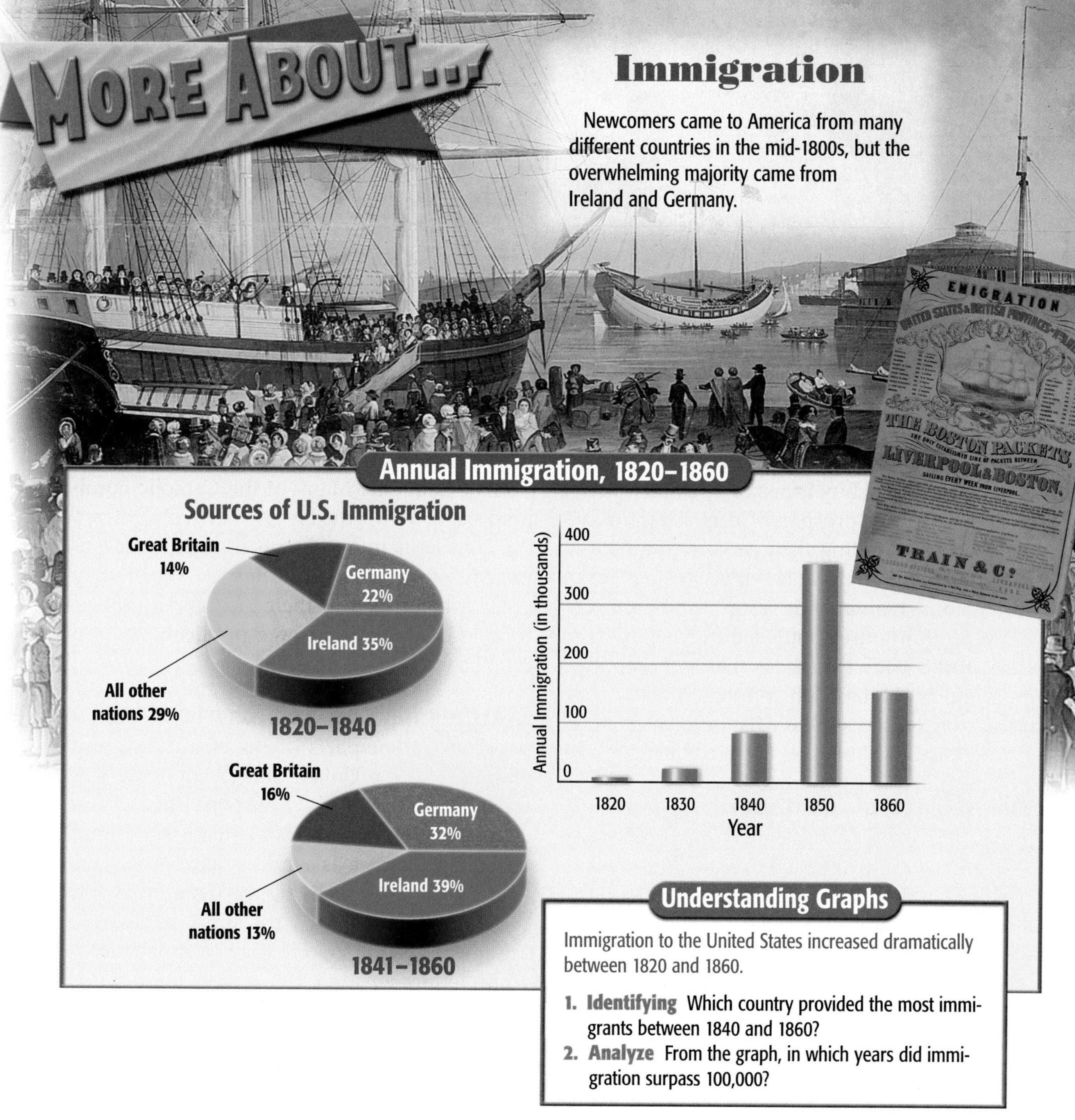

Understanding Graphs

Immigration to the United States increased dramatically between 1820 and 1860.

1. **Identifying** Which country provided the most immigrants between 1840 and 1860?
2. **Analyze** From the graph, in which years did immigration surpass 100,000?

History *Through Art*

Boston Harbor as Seen from Constitution Wharf* by Robert Salmon** In the 1820s and 1830s, artist Robert Salmon recorded the emerging cities and scenic harbors of the young nation. ***What urban centers developed because of their location near the Great Lakes?

Between 1848 and 1860, more than 1 million German immigrants settled in the United States. Many German immigrants arrived with enough money to buy farms or open their own businesses. They prospered in many parts of the country, founding their own communities. Some German immigrants settled in New York and Pennsylvania, but large numbers of German immigrants settled on farms and in cities in the Midwest—areas that were rapidly growing and had job opportunities. The Germans gave a distinctive flavor to such cities as Cincinnati, Milwaukee, and St. Louis.

The Impact of Immigration The immigrants who came to the United States between 1820 and 1860 changed the country. These people brought their languages, customs, religions, and ways of life with them, some of which became part of American culture.

Before the early 1800s, the majority of immigrants to America had been either Protestants from Great Britain or Africans brought forcibly to America as slaves. At the time, the country had relatively few Catholics, and most of them lived around Baltimore, New Orleans, and St. Augustine. Most of the Irish immigrants and about half of the German immigrants were Roman Catholics. Many of the Catholic immigrants of this era settled in cities in the Northeast.

The German immigrants brought their language as well as their religion. When they settled, they lived in their own communities, founded German-language publications, and established musical societies.

Learning About Life in America How did people in other parts of the world find out about life in the United States? One way was through advertising. European agents of railroad companies and steamship lines described America as a land where newcomers could make a better living for themselves and their families. Perhaps the most persuasive arguments for others to come to this country were letters written by recent immigrants to their family and friends. "If you wish to be happy and independent, then come here," wrote a German farmer from his new home in Missouri.

Immigrants Face Prejudice During the colonial period, workers were badly needed in all the colonies and immigrants had been readily accepted in many communities. In the 1830s and 1840s, however, some native-born Americans began to resent the newcomers, especially the Irish immigrants. Some Americans resented them because they dressed and sounded "different" and because they were Catholics.

People who were opposed to immigration were known as **nativists** (NAY • tih • VIHSTS) because they believed that immigration threatened the future of "native"—American-born—citizens. Some nativists accused immigrants of taking jobs from "real" Americans and were angry that immigrants would work for lower wages. Others accused the newcomers of bringing crime and disease to American cities. Immigrants who lived in crowded slums were often targets of this kind of prejudice.

The Know-Nothing Party The nativists formed secret anti-Catholic societies, and in the 1850s they joined to form a new political party: the American Party. By 1854 the party had become a force in American politics. Because members of nativist groups often answered questions about their organization with the statement "I know nothing," their party came to be known as the Know-Nothing Party. They did this to protect the secrecy of their organization.

The Know-Nothings called for stricter citizenship laws—extending the immigrants' waiting period for citizenship from 5 to 14 years—and wanted to ban foreign-born citizens from holding office.

In the mid-1850s, the Know-Nothing movement split into a Northern branch and a Southern branch over the question of slavery. At this time, the slavery issue was also dividing the Northern and Southern states of the nation.

Reading Check **Identify** Which two nations provided the largest number of immigrants to the United States during this era?

Study Central Need help understanding the people and economy of the North? Visit ca.hss.glencoe.com and click on Study Central.

Reading Summary

Review the Main Ideas

- Northern factories grew in the mid-1800s and many workers faced discrimination and unsafe working conditions.
- Immigrants flooded into the North seeking better opportunities than existed in their own countries.

What Did You Learn?

1. What was the nation's largest city in 1860?
2. How did German and Irish immigrants differ in where they settled?

Critical Thinking

3. **Determining Cause and Effect** Re-create the diagram below and list reasons workers formed labor unions. CA HI2.

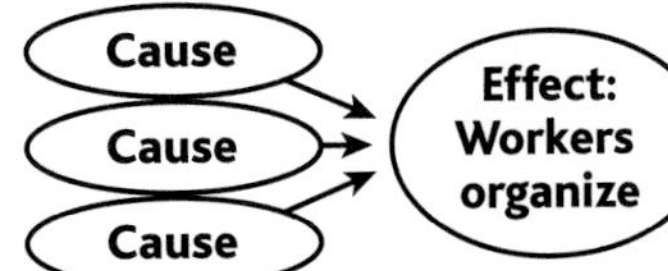

4. **The Big Ideas** Study the graphs on page 399. Did immigration from Ireland increase or decrease after 1840? How did immigration from Germany change? CA CS1.
5. **Expository Writing** Write two paragraphs on being an American: one to defend the nativist point of view and the other to appreciate the value of diversity in immigration. Look through your local newspaper for examples of each point of view. CA 8WA2.1

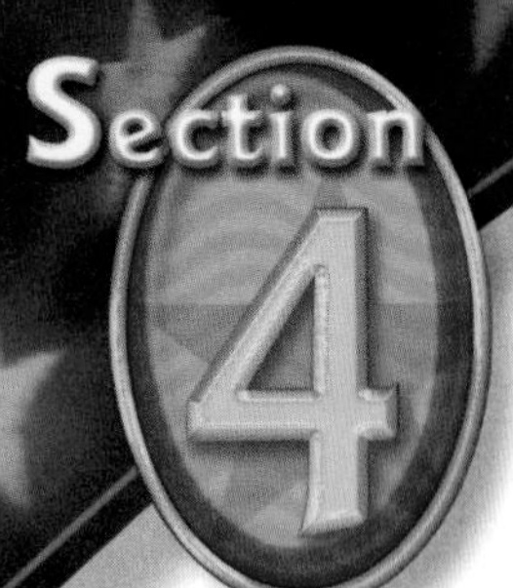

Reforms and Reformers

Guide to Reading

Looking Back, Looking Ahead

In the last section, you learned about what life was like in the Northern cities. In Section 4, you will learn about how reformers worked to make life better for many Americans.

Focusing on the Main Ideas

- Religious and philosophical ideas inspired various reform movements. *(page 403)*
- Reformers wanted to make education accessible to all citizens. *(page 405)*
- A new wave of literature that was distinctly American swept the United States. *(page 406)*

Meeting People

Henry David Thoreau (thuh • ROH)
Ralph Waldo Emerson
Horace Mann
Thomas Gallaudet (GA • luh • DEHT)
Dr. Samuel Gridley Howe
Dorothea Dix
Margaret Fuller
Emily Dickinson

Content Vocabulary

utopia (yu • TOH • pee • uh)
revival
temperance (TEHM • puh • ruhns)
normal school
transcendentalist (TRAN • sehn • DEHN • tuhl • ihst)

Academic Vocabulary

founded
focus
publish

Reading Strategy

Taking Notes Re-create the diagram below and identify these reformers' contributions as you read Section 4.

	Contributions
Horace Mann	
Thomas Gallaudet	
Dorothea Dix	

History Social Science Standards

US8.6 Students analyze the divergent paths of the American people from 1800 to the mid-1800s and the challenges they faced, with emphasis on the Northeast.

NATIONAL GEOGRAPHIC
Who & When?
1820
1835
1850
1825 Robert Owen establishes New Harmony, Indiana
1837 Horace Mann initiates education reform
1843 Dorothea Dix reveals abuses of mentally ill

Horace Mann

Dorothea Dix

American Writers Emerge The transcendentalists were not the only important writers of this time. Many poets created impressive works about American subjects during this period. Henry Wadsworth Longfellow wrote narrative, or story, poems, such as the "Song of Hiawatha." John Greenleaf Whittier in "Snow-Bound" described winter on a New England farm. Edgar Allan Poe, a poet and short-story writer, told tales involving the terrors that lurk in the world of imagination and dreams.

Perhaps the most important poet of the era was Walt Whitman, who **published** a volume of poetry in 1855 called *Leaves of Grass*. Whitman loved nature, the common people, and American democracy, and his famous work reflects these passions. The best-remembered woman poet of the era was **Emily Dickinson,** who wrote simple, personal, deeply emotional poetry.

In a poem called "Hope," Dickinson compares hope with a bird:

> **"'Hope' is the thing with feathers—**
> **That perches in the soul—**
> **And sings the tune without the words—**
> **And never stops–at all—"**
>
> **—Emily Dickinson, "Hope"**

Women writers of the period were generally not taken seriously, yet they were the authors of the most popular fiction. Harriet Beecher Stowe wrote the most successful best-seller of the mid-1800s, *Uncle Tom's Cabin*. Stowe's novel explores the injustice of slavery—an issue that took on new urgency during the age of reform.

Reading Check **Describe** What was one of the subjects that Margaret Fuller wrote about?

History Online

Study Central Need help understanding American literature? Visit ca.hss.glencoe.com and click on Study Central.

Reading Summary

Review the Main Ideas

- Reformers attempted to make the United States a better place for its citizens.
- Reforms in secondary and higher education allowed more Americans to become educated.
- American literature gained a new voice through the writings of Thoreau, Emerson, Dickinson, and others.

What Did You Learn?

1. What did Horace Mann accomplish?
2. How did Thoreau act on his beliefs? What impact might such acts have had on the government?

Critical Thinking

3. **Determining Cause and Effect** Re-create the diagram below and describe two ways the religious movement influenced reform. CA HI2.

Religious movement → [ ] / [ ]

4. **The Big Ideas** Who was Horace Mann, and what was his contribution to public education? How were women and African Americans able to have access to education? Summarize your conclusions in a short essay. CA HI1.
5. **Biography** Using your textbook, the library, and the Internet, learn more about Thomas Gallaudet, Dorothea Dix, or Samuel Gridley Howe. Write a short biography of the person you chose. Include key events in his or her life and the person's impact on the world. CA 8WA2.1

The Women's Movement

Guide to Reading

History Social Science Standards

US8.6 Students analyze the divergent paths of the American people from 1800 to the mid-1800s and the challenges they faced, with emphasis on the Northeast.

Looking Back, Looking Ahead

In Section 4, you learned about the reform movement that swept America in the 1800s. In Section 5, you will learn about how that movement influenced women to lobby for increased rights.

Focusing on the Main Ideas

- Many women believed they should have the same opportunities as men, and they organized to gain these rights. *(page 409)*
- Women made progress in gaining equality in education, marriage laws, and the professional sector. *(page 411)*

Meeting People

Lucretia Mott
Elizabeth Cady Stanton
Susan B. Anthony
Mary Lyon
Elizabeth Blackwell

Content Vocabulary

suffrage (SUH • frihj)
coeducation

Academic Vocabulary

ministry (MIH • nuh • stree)
goal

Reading Strategy

Taking Notes As you read the section, use a chart like the one below to identify the contributions these individuals made to women's rights.

	Contributions
Lucretia Mott	
Elizabeth Cady Stanton	
Susan B. Anthony	

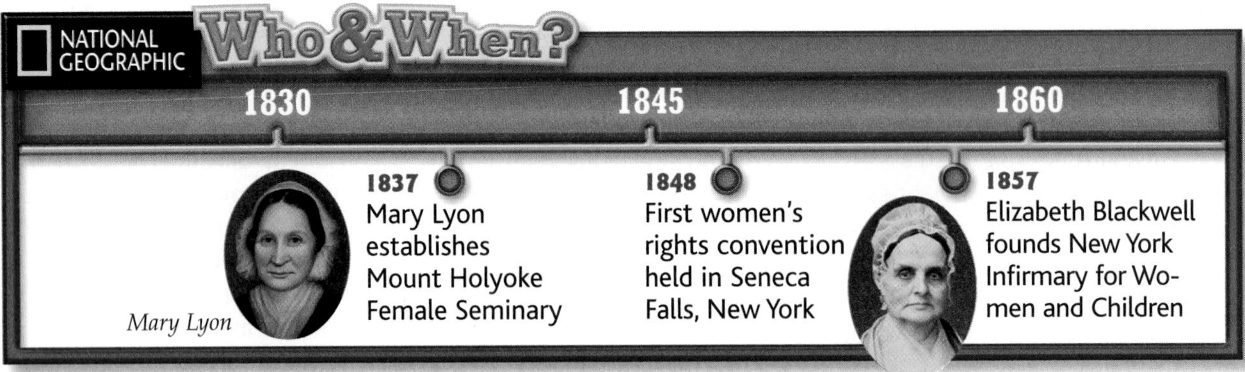
NATIONAL GEOGRAPHIC
Who & When?
1830
1845
1860
1837 Mary Lyon establishes Mount Holyoke Female Seminary
1848 First women's rights convention held in Seneca Falls, New York
1857 Elizabeth Blackwell founds New York Infirmary for Women and Children

Mary Lyon

Lucretia Mott

US8.6.6 Examine the women's suffrage movement (e.g., biographies, writings, and speeches of Elizabeth Cady Stanton, Margaret Fuller, Lucretia Mott, Susan B. Anthony).

Women and Reform

Main Idea **Many women believed they should have the same opportunities as men, and they organized to gain these rights.**

Reading Connection Can you imagine a time when women were not allowed to vote and had limited access to education and jobs? Read on to see how women worked to change their status in America.

An American Story

Women who fought to end slavery began to recognize their own bondage. On April 19, 1850, about 400 women met at a Quaker meetinghouse in the small town of Salem, Ohio. They came together "to assert their rights as independent human beings." One speaker stated: "[W]e should demand our recognition as equal members of the human family."

The Seneca Falls Convention Many women abolitionists also worked for women's rights. Like many of the women reformers, **Lucretia Mott** was a Quaker. Quaker women enjoyed a certain amount of equality in their own communities. Mott gave lectures in Philadelphia calling for temperance, peace, workers' rights, and abolition. Mott also helped fugitive slaves and organized the Philadelphia Female Anti-Slavery Society. At the world antislavery convention in London, Mott met **Elizabeth Cady Stanton.** There the two female abolitionists joined forces to work for women's rights.

In July 1848, Elizabeth Cady Stanton, Lucretia Mott, and a few other women organized the first women's rights convention in Seneca Falls, New York. About 200 women and 40 men attended.

The convention issued a Declaration of Sentiments and Resolutions modeled on the Declaration of Independence. The women's document declared: "We hold these truths to be self-evident: that all men and women are created equal."

The women's declaration called for an end to all laws that discriminated against women. It demanded that women be allowed to enter the all-male world of trades, professions, and businesses. The most controversial issue at the Seneca Falls Convention concerned **suffrage** (SUH•frihj), or the right to vote.

Elizabeth Stanton insisted that the declaration include a demand for woman suffrage, but delegates thought the idea of women voting was too radical. After much debate, the demand for woman suffrage in the United States was included. *(See page 854 of the Appendix for excerpts of the Seneca Falls Declaration.)*

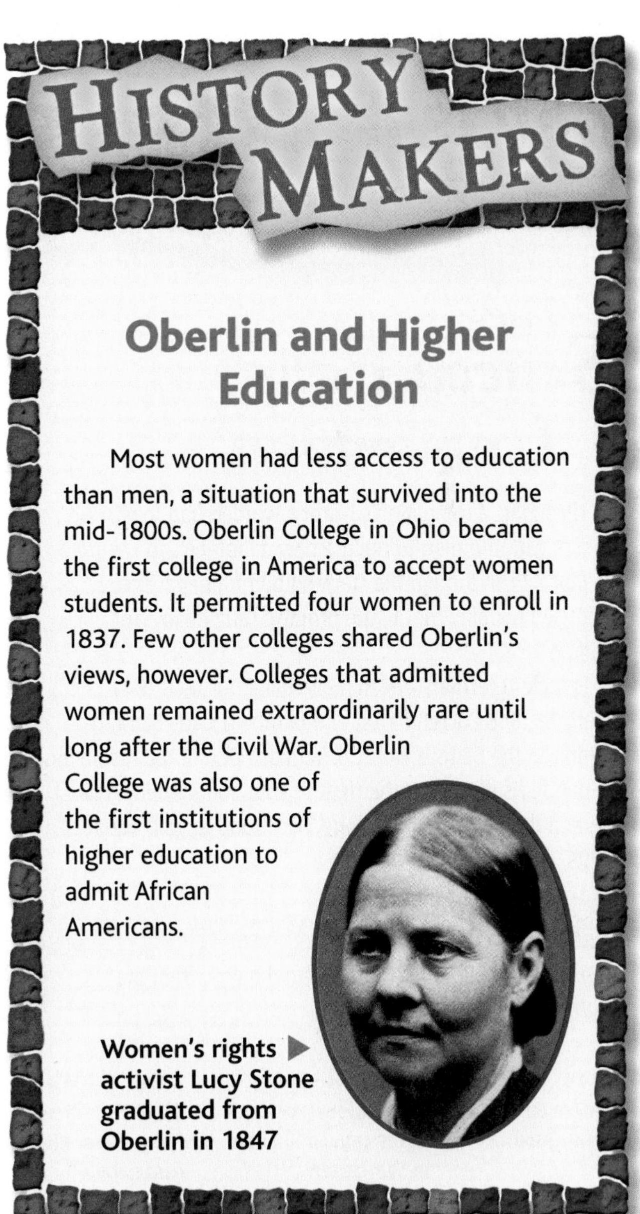

HISTORY MAKERS

Oberlin and Higher Education

Most women had less access to education than men, a situation that survived into the mid-1800s. Oberlin College in Ohio became the first college in America to accept women students. It permitted four women to enroll in 1837. Few other colleges shared Oberlin's views, however. Colleges that admitted women remained extraordinarily rare until long after the Civil War. Oberlin College was also one of the first institutions of higher education to admit African Americans.

Women's rights activist Lucy Stone graduated from Oberlin in 1847

The Women's Rights Movement The Seneca Falls Convention paved the way for the growth of the women's rights movement. During the 1800s, women held several national conventions. Many reformers—male and female—joined the movement.

Susan B. Anthony, the daughter of a Quaker abolitionist in rural New York, worked for women's rights and temperance. She called for equal pay for women, college training for girls, and **coeducation**—the teaching of boys and girls together.

Susan B. Anthony met Elizabeth Cady Stanton at a temperance meeting in 1851. They became lifelong friends and partners in the struggle for women's rights. For the rest of the century, Anthony and Stanton led the women's movement. They worked with other women to win the right to vote, which was granted by several states. It was not until 1920, however, that woman suffrage became a reality everywhere in the United States.

Reading Check **Explain** What is suffrage?

Why It Matters

Raising the Status of Women

The Seneca Falls Convention

Throughout the nation's history, women had fought side by side with the men to build a new nation and to ensure freedom. Even though the Declaration of Independence promised equality for all, the promise rang hollow for women.

Female reformers began a campaign for their own rights. In 1848 Lucretia Mott and Elizabeth Cady Stanton organized the Seneca Falls Convention. One of the resolutions demanded suffrage, or the right to vote, for women. This marked the beginning of a long, hard road to gain equal rights.

Lucretia Mott (below) and Susan B. Anthony were leaders in the effort to allow women a greater role in American society.

"We hold these truths to be self-evident: that all men and women are created equal."
—*Declaration of the Seneca Falls Convention, 1848*

Gaining the Right to Vote, 1848–1920

The Seneca Falls Convention led to the growth of the woman suffrage movement.

- **1848** Seneca Falls Convention
- **1850** First national women's rights convention held in Worcester, Massachusetts
- **1866** Susan B. Anthony forms Equal Rights Association
- **1869** Women granted voting rights in Wyoming Territory
- **1878** Woman suffrage amendment first introduced in U.S. Congress
- **1884** Belva Lockwood runs for president

US8.6.5 Trace the development of the American education system from its earliest roots, including the roles of religious and private schools and Horace Mann's campaign for free public education and its assimilating role in American culture. **US8.6.6** Examine the women's suffrage movement (e.g., biographies, writings, and speeches of Elizabeth Cady Stanton, Margaret Fuller, Lucretia Mott, Susan B. Anthony).

Progress by American Women

Main Idea **Women made progress in gaining equality in education, marriage laws, and the professional sector.**

Reading Connection Laws are often put in place to protect individuals and society—for example, laws against speeding or stealing. How would you feel about laws that barred women from the same privileges as men? Is that fair or discriminatory? Read on to find out how women worked for change.

In the early 1800s, the Industrial Revolution began to change the economic roles of men and women. In the 1700s, most economic activity took place in or near the home because a great many Americans lived and worked in a rural farm setting. Although husbands and wives had separate chores, their main effort was maintaining the farm. By the mid-1800s, these circumstances had started to change, especially in the northeastern states.

Maria Mitchell gained world renown when she discovered a comet in 1847. She became a professor of astronomy and the first woman elected to the American Academy of Arts and Sciences.

Mary Ann Shadd Cary was the first African American woman in the nation to earn a law degree.

Elizabeth Blackwell was the first woman to receive a medical degree in the United States.

Helen Keller overcame the challenges of an illness that left her deaf, blind, and mute to help others with similar disabilities.

Susette La Flesche was a member of the Omaha tribe and campaigned for Native American rights.

1893 → Colorado adopts woman suffrage

1896 → Utah joins the Union, granting women full suffrage

1910–1918 → States including Washington, Kansas, and Michigan adopt woman suffrage

1919 → House and Senate pass the federal woman suffrage amendment

1920 → Tennessee ratifies the Nineteenth Amendment, called the Susan B. Anthony Amendment. It becomes law on August 26, 1920.

Primary Sources

On Equality for Women

Sarah and Angeline Grimké were daughters of a wealthy South Carolina judge and plantation owner. The sisters fought against the institution of slavery. They also spoke out for women's rights. In this passage, Sarah Grimké writes about the differences in pay for men and women.

"There is another way in which the general opinion, that women are inferior to men, is manifested [shown], that bears with tremendous effect on the laboring class, and indeed on almost all who are [obliged] to earn a subsistence [living], whether it be by mental or physical exertion. I allude [refer] to the [unequal] value set on the time and labor of men and of women. A man who is engaged in teaching, can always, I believe, command a higher price . . . than a woman—even when he teaches the same branches [subjects], and is not in any respect superior to the woman. . . . In tailoring, a man [earns] twice or three times as much for making a waistcoat or pantaloons as a woman, although the work done by each may be equally good. In those employments [jobs] which are peculiar to women, their time is estimated at only half the value of that of men. A woman who goes out to wash, works as hard in proportion as a wood sawyer, or a coal heaver, but she is not generally able to make more than half as much by a day's work."

—*Letters on the Equality of the Sexes*

Sarah Grimké ▶

Document-Based Question

What point is Sarah Grimké making about women and men workers in the same occupation?

The development of factories separated the home from the workplace. Men now often left home to go to work, while women tended the house and children.

As the nature of work changed, many Americans began to divide life into two areas of activities—the home and the workplace. Many believed the home to be the proper area for women, partly because of popular ideas about the family. Some also believed that women belonged in the home because the outside world was seen as dangerous and corrupt.

The Great Awakening greatly influenced the American family. For many parents, raising children was a serious responsibility because it prepared young people for a disciplined Christian life. Women often were viewed as kinder and more moral than men, and they were expected to be models of goodness for their children and husbands.

The idea grew that women should be homemakers and should take the main responsibility for raising the sons and daughters. Magazine articles and novels aimed at women supported the value of their role at home.

Opportunities for Education Pioneers in women's education began to call for more opportunity. Early pioneers such as Catherine Beecher and Emma Hart Willard believed that women should be educated for their traditional roles in life. They also thought that women could be capable teachers. Beecher, the daughter of a minister and reformer, wrote a book called *A Treatise on Domestic Economy*. It gave instructions on children, cooking, and health matters. The Milwaukee College for Women set up courses based on Beecher's ideas "to train women to be healthful, intelligent, and successful wives, mothers, and housekeepers."

After her marriage, Emma Willard educated herself in subjects considered suitable only for boys, such as science and mathematics. In 1821 Willard established the Troy Female Seminary in New York. The school taught mathematics, history, geography, and physics, as well as the usual homemaking subjects.

Mary Lyon established Mount Holyoke Female Seminary in Massachusetts in 1837. It was the first institution of higher education for women only. Lyon modeled its curriculum on that of nearby Amherst College.

Marriage and Family Laws During the 1800s, women made some gains in the area of marriage and property laws. New York, Pennsylvania, Indiana, Wisconsin, Mississippi, and the new state of California recognized the right of women to own property after their marriage.

Some states passed laws permitting women to share the guardianship of their children jointly with their husbands. Indiana was the first of several states that allowed women to seek divorce if their husbands were chronic abusers of alcohol.

Breaking Barriers In the 1800s, women had few career choices. They could become elementary school teachers—although school boards often paid lower salaries to women than to men. Breaking into fields such as medicine and the **ministry** was more difficult. Some determined women, however, succeeded in entering these all-male professions.

Hoping to study medicine, **Elizabeth Blackwell** was turned down by more than 20 schools. Finally accepted by Geneva College in New York, Blackwell graduated at the head of her class. She went on to win acceptance and fame as a doctor.

Despite the accomplishments of notable women, gains in education, and changes in state laws, women in the 1800s remained limited by social customs and expectations. The early feminists—like the abolitionists, temperance workers, and other activists of the age of reform—had just begun the long struggle to achieve their **goals.**

Reading Check **Identify** Who established the Troy Female Seminary?

History Online

Study Central Need help understanding the women's movement? Visit ca.hss.glencoe.com and click on Study Central.

Reading Summary

Review the Main Ideas

- The abolitionist movement helped women see the discrimination they encountered in their own lives, and they organized to end this discrimination.
- Women created their own schools and colleges, increased their legal standing in their families, and gained more professional choices.

What Did You Learn?

1. How did the fight to end slavery help spark the women's movement?
2. Discuss three goals of the women's rights movement.

Critical Thinking

3. **Organizing Information** Re-create the diagram below and list the areas where women gained rights.

4. **The Big Ideas** What qualities do you think women such as Susan B. Anthony, Elizabeth Cady Stanton, and Elizabeth Blackwell shared? CA HR3.
5. **Sequencing Information** Study the information on the feature on the Seneca Falls Convention on pages 410–411. When did Wyoming women gain the right to vote? What "first" did Elizabeth Blackwell accomplish? CA CS2.

Analyzing Primary Sources

US8.6 Students analyze the divergent paths of the American people from 1800 to the mid-1800s and the challenges they faced, with emphasis on the Northeast.

Life in the North

In the early 1800s, the northeast United States underwent rapid change. The Industrial Revolution led to new jobs, and new forms of transportation, such as canals and railroads, developed. A Second Great Awakening led to a renewed interest in religion and reform.

Read the passages on pages 414 and 415 and answer the questions that follow.

This scene shows Lockport on the Erie Canal near Buffalo, New York.

Reader's Dictionary

exempted (ihg • ZEHMPT • ihd): excused from something that others must do

pervading (puhr • VAYD • ihng): spreading throughout all parts

melodious (muh • LOH • dee • uhs): having a pleasant sound

tumultuously (tu • MUHL • chuh • wuhs • lee): violently and in confusion

quivered: shook, shivered, trembled

occupation (AH • kyuh • PAY • shuhn): job

station: position in society

packet: passenger boat that usually carries mail and cargo

salons (suh • LAHNZ): sitting rooms

ventilators (VEHN • tuhl • AY • tuhrz): air vents

Religious Camp Meeting

By the 1830s, the Second Great Awakening was in full swing. One revivalist, James Finley, described a revival meeting:

The noise was like the roar of Niagara [Falls]. . . . I counted seven ministers, all preaching at one time, some on stumps, others on wagons . . . no sex nor color, class nor description, were **exempted** from the **pervading** influence of the spirit; even from the age of 8 months to 60 years . . . some of the people were singing, others praying, some crying for mercy . . . some struck with terror . . . others surrounding them with **melodious** song. A peculiar sensation came over me. My heart beat **tumultuously,** my knees trembled, my lips **quivered,** and I felt as though I must fall to the ground.

—James Finley

Camp meetings could attract thousands of people for days of prayer, song, and expressions of faith.

American Notes

British writer Charles Dickens traveled to America in 1842. After returning to England, he published American Notes, *a book about what he had seen in America. In this excerpt, Dickens describes his visit to a factory in Lowell, Massachusetts.*

The rooms in which they worked were as well ordered as themselves. In the windows of some there were green plants, which were trained to shade the glass; in all, there was as much fresh air, cleanliness, and comfort as the nature of the **occupation** would possibly admit of. . . .

They have got up among themselves a periodical called THE LOWELL OFFERING, "a repository of original articles, written exclusively by females actively employed in the mills,"—which is duly printed, published, and sold; and whereof I brought away from Lowell four hundred good solid pages, which I have read from beginning to end. . . .

It is their **station** to work. And they *do* work. They labour in these mills, upon an average, twelve hours a day, which is unquestionably work, and pretty tight work too.

—from *American Notes* by Charles Dickens

Travel on the Erie Canal

This is an 1843 advertisement for traveling on the canal.

—from *Canal Days in America: The History and Romance of Old Towpaths and Waterways*

DBQ Document-Based Questions

Religious Camp Meeting

1. Finley says that the camp meeting is like the roar of Niagara. What is he comparing?
2. Who does the preaching affect?

American Notes

3. According to Dickens, what are conditions in the factory like?
4. How long is the workday?

Travel on the Erie Canal

5. According to the poster, how long does it take to travel from Niagara Falls to Albany if people take a packet boat?
6. What new conveniences do these packet boats have?

Read to Write

7. Review the readings looking for three sentences that are complicated or confusing. Work through each sentence to clarify the meaning for yourself, and then restate that meaning on your paper. CA 8RC2.0

Assessment

Standard US8.6

Review Content Vocabulary

1. Use the following words in a paragraph about the Industrial Revolution.

capital	free enterprise
technology	factory system

Review the Main Ideas

Section 1 • Economic Growth

2. How did the landscape of New England affect how and where people lived in the late 1700s and early 1800s?
3. How did new technology contribute to the growth of the Industrial Revolution?

Section 2 • A System of Transportation

4. How did canals boost the economy of the Great Lakes region?
5. What was the purpose of canal locks?

Section 3 • The North's People

6. Give three reasons why cities grew in the early 1800s.
7. In what ways were women in the workforce discriminated against?
8. Why did immigration from Germany increase after 1848?

Section 4 • Reforms and Reformers

9. What were the founders of utopias hoping to achieve?
10. What problems in society did reformers in the temperance movement blame on alcohol?
11. What were the basic principles of public education?

Section 5 • The Women's Movement

12. What role did Catherine Beecher play in education for women?
13. What was the significance of the Seneca Falls convention?

Critical Thinking

14. **Compare** Discuss an advantage and a disadvantage of city life in the North. CA HR3.
15. **Explain** How did the Industrial Revolution make the United States more economically independent in the early 1800s? CA HI6.

Geography Skills

Study the map below and answer the following questions. CA CS3.

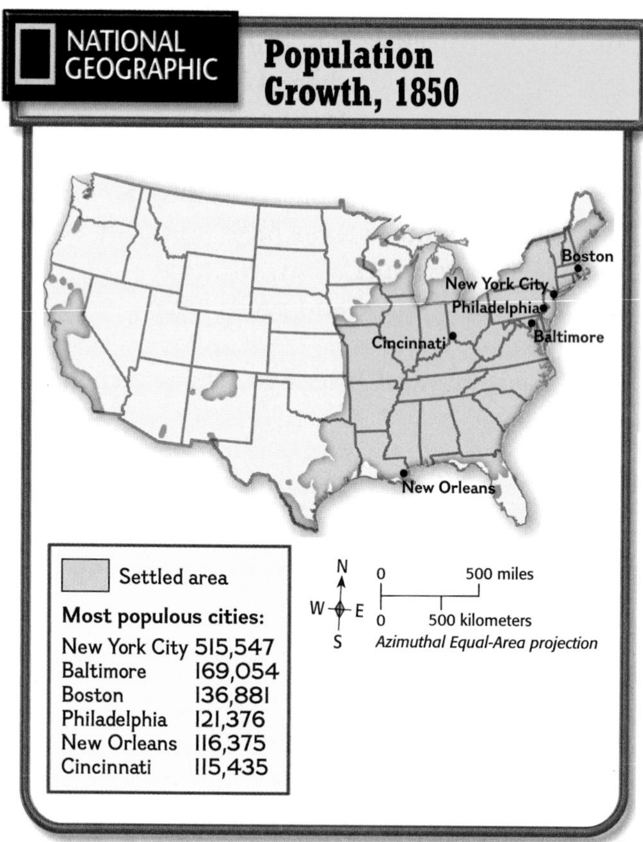

16. **Location** Which city had the largest population in 1850?
17. **Region** Which area of the country was most heavily settled?

Read to Write

18. **The Big Ideas Descriptive Writing** Review Section 2 of the chapter for information about what it was like to live in the Midwest in the early 1800s. Using the information you find, write a postcard to a friend describing your social life. CA 8WA2.1

19. **Using Your FOLDABLES** Use the information you collected in your foldable to create a compare-contrast chart. In your chart, you will assess the roots, goals, and achievements of social reform, educational reform, and the women's rights movement. How are these movements similar? How do they differ? CA HI2.

Using Academic Vocabulary

20. Use two of the following academic vocabulary words to complete the sentence.

focus	expand
manual	goal

As the U.S. economy continued to ___, immigrants provided much of the ___ labor.

Building Citizenship Skills

21. **Explore** Working with two other students, contact a local historical society to learn about your community's history. Prepare a list of questions to ask your historical society. Then interview people in your neighborhood to learn about their roots in the community. Find out when their families first settled there. Write a history of the community and give a copy of it to the historical society. CA CS1.

Reviewing Skills

22. **Review READING SKILL Problems and Solutions** This chapter highlighted various problems, or challenges, that groups of people faced. Choose one group and describe their unique challenges and the ways in which people attempted to face those challenges. CA HI2.

23. **Review ANALYSIS SKILL Describe** Identify and describe the economic impact of canals on the Northeast. CA HI6.

Standards Practice

Use the graph below to answer the following questions.

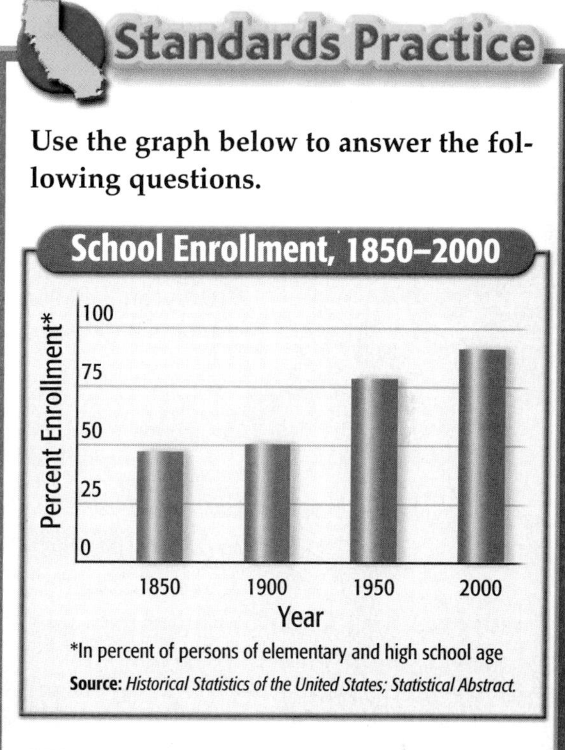

24 According to the graph above, the greatest increase in the percentage of school enrollment occurred between

A 1850 and 1880.
B 1850 and 1900.
C 1900 and 1950.
D 1950 and 2000.

25 Labor unions were formed for all of the following reasons EXCEPT

A to improve workers' wages.
B to protect factory owners from being sued.
C to make factories safer.
D to prevent children from working long hours.

The South

▼ Drayton Hall Plantation, near Charleston, South Carolina

NATIONAL GEOGRAPHIC Where & When?

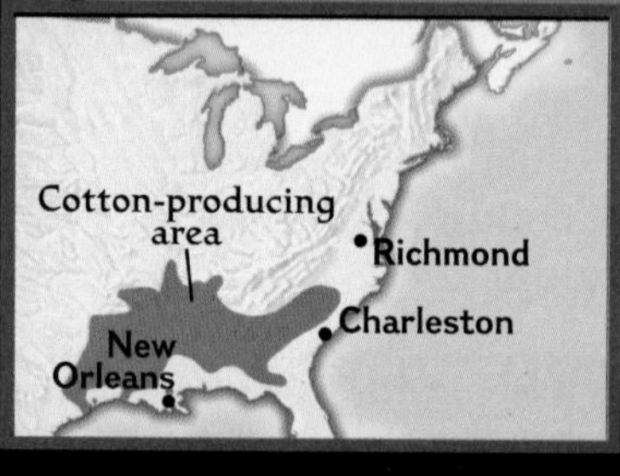

1790 | 1825 | 1860

1793 The cotton gin is invented

1831 Nat Turner's slave revolt strikes fear in Southerners

1860 Baltimore's population is over 200,000

History Online
Chapter Overview Visit ca.hss.glencoe.com for a preview of Chapter 9.

The Big Ideas

Section 1

Southern Cotton Kingdom

Geography shapes the physical, economic, and political challenges a region faces. Cotton was vital to the economy of the South.

Section 2

Life in the South

Geography shapes the physical, economic, and political challenges a region faces. Most of the people in the South worked in agriculture in the first half of the 1800s.

Section 3

The Peculiar Institution

Differences in economic, political, and social beliefs and practices can lead to division within a nation and have lasting consequences. Enslaved African Americans developed a unique culture and fought against slavery.

View the Chapter 9 video in the Glencoe Video Program.

FOLDABLES™ Study Organizer

Summarizing Make this foldable and use it as a journal to help you take notes about the South during the period from 1800 to 1850.

Step 1 Stack four sheets of paper, one on top of the other. On the top sheet of paper, trace a large circle.

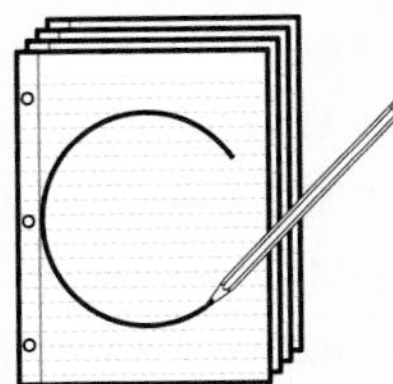

Step 2 With the papers still stacked, cut out all four circles at the same time.

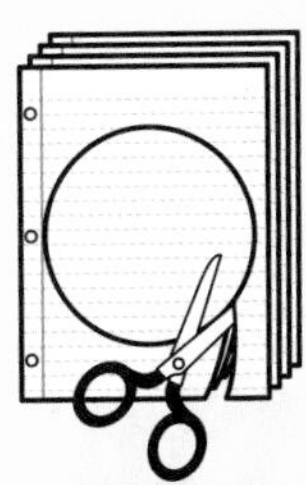

Step 3 Staple the paper circles together at one point around the edge.

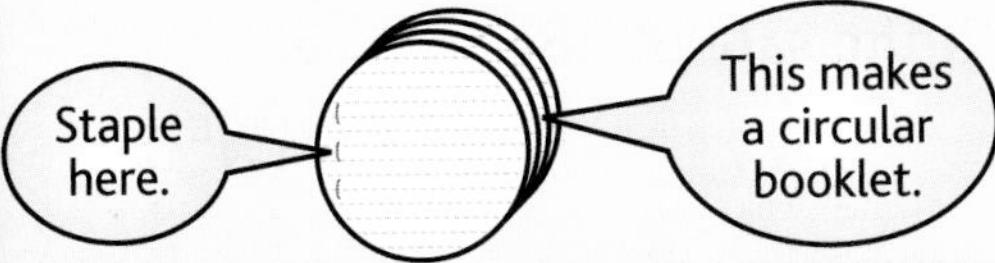
Staple here.
This makes a circular booklet.

Step 4 Label the front cover as shown and take notes on the pages that open to the right.

Living and Working in the South

Reading and Writing As you read the chapter, write what you learn about the South in your foldable.

Get Ready to Read

Questioning

1 Learn It!

One way to understand what you are reading is to interact with the text by asking questions. What questions would you like answered? What are you curious about? As you read, you may be able to locate the answer in the next paragraph or section. Practice asking questions by turning headings into questions. For instance, a heading that reads "Life Under Slavery" can be turned into the question "What was life like under slavery?" Read this selection from Chapter 9. What questions do you have?

> Enslaved people faced constant uncertainty and danger. American law in the early 1800s did not protect enslaved families. At any time, a husband or wife could be sold to a different owner, or a slaveholder's death could lead to the breakup of an enslaved family. Although marriage between enslaved people was not recognized by law, many couples did marry. Their marriage ceremonies included the phrase "until death or separation do us part"—recognizing the possibility that their life together might end with the sale of one spouse.
>
> — *from page 433*

Reading Tip

Good questions start with key words such as *who*, *what*, *when*, *where*, *why*, and *how*.

2 Practice It!

Read the following paragraph, and answer this question with a partner: What were the economic goals of a plantation owner?

The main economic goal for large plantation owners was to earn profits. Such plantations had fixed costs—regular expenses such as housing and feeding workers and maintaining cotton gins and other equipment. Fixed costs remained about the same year after year.

Cotton prices, however, varied from season to season, depending on the market. To receive the best prices, planters sold their cotton to agents in cities such as New Orleans, Charleston, Mobile, and Savannah. The cotton exchanges, or trade centers, in Southern cities were of vital importance to those involved in the cotton economy. The agents of the exchanges extended credit—a form of loan—to the planters and held the cotton for several months until the price rose. Then the agents sold the cotton. This system kept the planters always in debt because they did not receive payment for their cotton until the agents sold it.

—from page 429

Read to Write

Write a *What If* paragraph based on what you read in this chapter. For example, *what if* the South had become industrialized like the North? Your paragraph should answer your *What If* question.

▲ Plantation in the South

3 Apply It!

As you read the chapter, look for answers to section headings that are in the form of questions. For the other sections, turn the headings into questions that you can answer as you read.

Section
1

Southern Cotton Kingdom

Guide to Reading

History Social Science Standards

US8.7 Students analyze the divergent paths of the American people in the South from 1800 to the mid-1800s and the challenges they faced.

Looking Back, Looking Ahead

In the last chapter, you learned about life in and the economy of the Northeastern states. In this section, you will learn about the economy of the South.

Focusing on the Main Ideas

- Unlike the North, the Southern economy remained mainly agrarian. *(page 423)*
- For many reasons, industry developed slowly in the South. *(page 424)*

Locating Places

Upper South
Deep South

Meeting People

Eli Whitney
William Gregg
Joseph Reid Anderson

Content Vocabulary

cotton gin
capital (KA • puh • tuhl)

Academic Vocabulary

predominant (prih • DAH • muh • nuhnt)
sum

Reading Strategy

Comparing As you read the section, re-create the diagram below. In the ovals, give reasons why cotton production grew but industrial growth was slower.

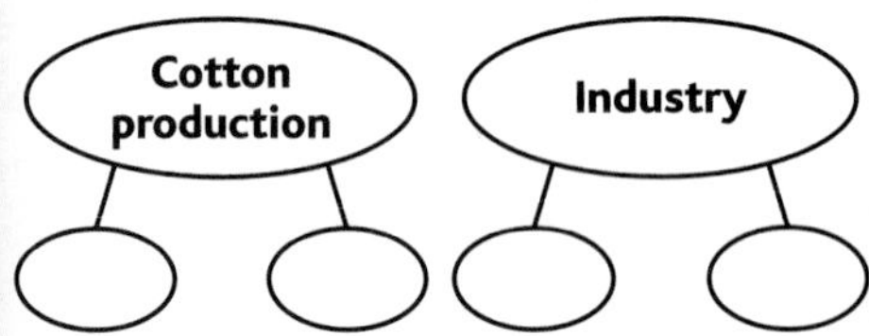
Cotton production
Industry

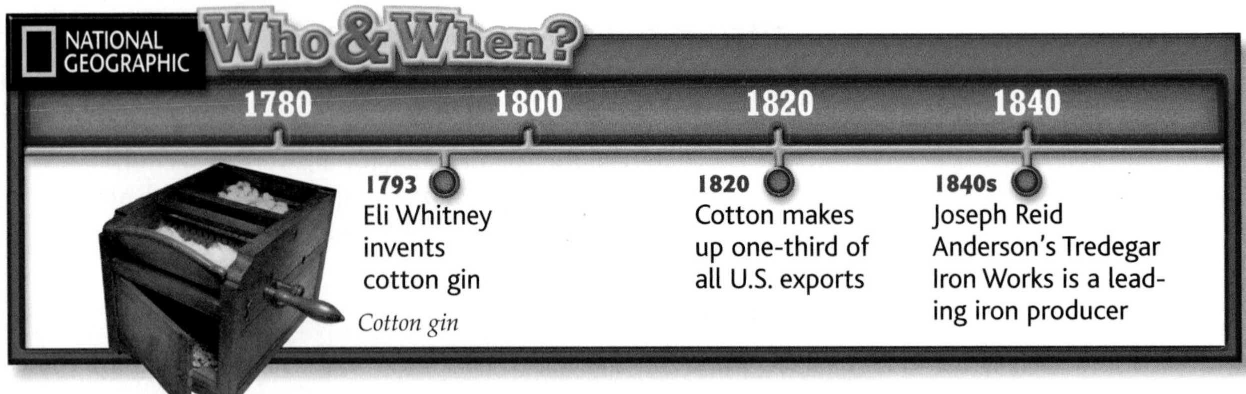
NATIONAL GEOGRAPHIC
Who & When?
1780
1800
1820
1840
1793 Eli Whitney invents cotton gin
1820 Cotton makes up one-third of all U.S. exports
1840s Joseph Reid Anderson's Tredegar Iron Works is a leading iron producer

Cotton gin

US8.7.1 Describe the development of the agrarian economy in the South, identify the locations of the cotton-producing states, and discuss the significance of cotton and the cotton gin.

Rise of the Cotton Kingdom

Main Idea **Unlike the North, the Southern economy remained mainly agrarian.**

Reading Connection Check the label on your pants or shirt. What materials are found in the fabric? Chances are you wear something at least partly made of cotton. Read on to find out how cotton was a major economic asset to the Deep South.

An American Story

Cotton was not the only crop grown in the South, but it was the crop that fueled the Southern economy. Southerners began saying, rightly, "Cotton is king." "Look which way you will, you see it; and see [cotton] moving," wrote a visitor to Mobile, Alabama. "Keel boats, ships, brigs, schooners, wharves, stores, and press-houses, all appeared to be full."

Cotton Rules the Deep South Most Southerners lived along the Atlantic coast in Maryland, Virginia, Tennessee, and North Carolina in what came to be known as the **Upper South.** By 1850 the South had changed. Its population had spread inland to the states of the **Deep South**—Georgia, South Carolina, Alabama, Mississippi, Louisiana, Florida, Arkansas, and Texas.

In colonial times, rice, indigo (a plant used to make blue dye), and tobacco made up the South's main crops. After the American Revolution, demand for these crops decreased. European mills, however, wanted Southern cotton to make into cloth. But cotton was difficult to produce. After cotton was harvested, workers had to painstakingly separate the plant's sticky seeds from the cotton fibers.

In 1793 **Eli Whitney** invented the cotton gin. The **cotton gin** was a compact machine that removed seeds from cotton fibers much more quickly than could be done by hand. Because cotton could be processed more easily, Southern planters wanted to grow more. As a result, they depended on slave labor to plant and pick cotton.

By 1860 the economies of the Deep South and the Upper South had developed in different ways. Both parts of the South were agricultural, but the Upper South still produced tobacco, hemp, wheat, and vegetables. The Deep South was committed to cotton and, in some areas, to rice and sugarcane.

The value of enslaved people increased because of their key role in producing cotton and sugar. In time, the Upper South became a center for the sale of enslaved people.

Reading Check **Describe** What effect did the cotton gin have on the South's economy?

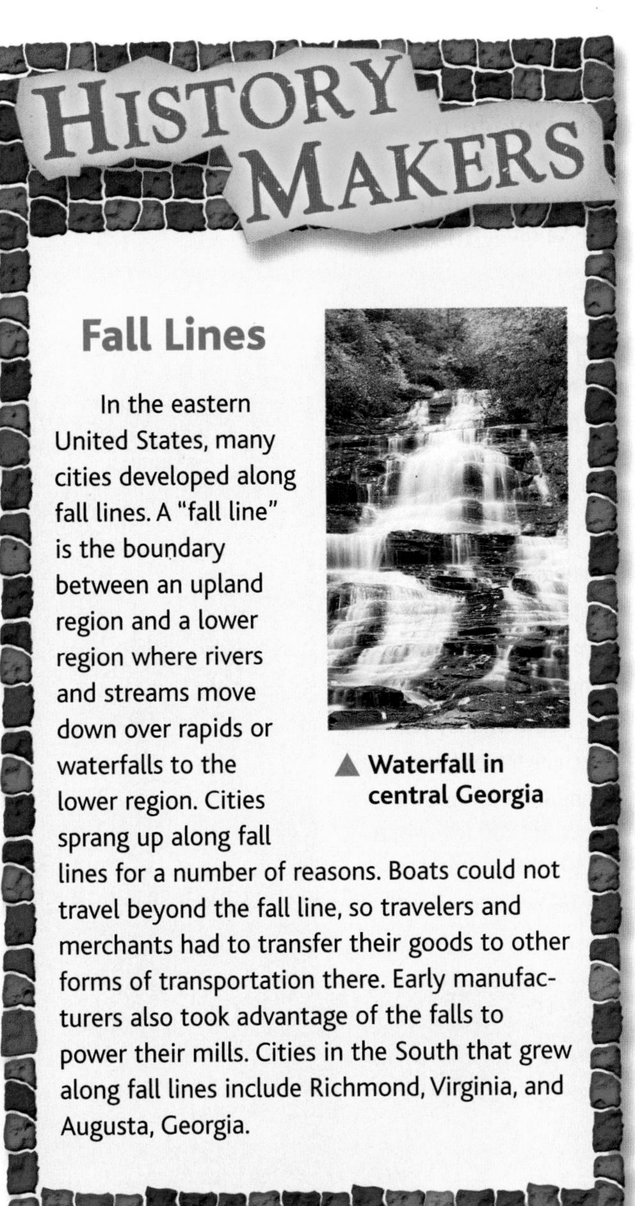

HISTORY MAKERS

Fall Lines

In the eastern United States, many cities developed along fall lines. A "fall line" is the boundary between an upland region and a lower region where rivers and streams move down over rapids or waterfalls to the lower region. Cities sprang up along fall lines for a number of reasons. Boats could not travel beyond the fall line, so travelers and merchants had to transfer their goods to other forms of transportation there. Early manufacturers also took advantage of the falls to power their mills. Cities in the South that grew along fall lines include Richmond, Virginia, and Augusta, Georgia.

▲ Waterfall in central Georgia

US8.7.1 Describe the development of the agrarian economy in the South, identify the locations of the cotton-producing states, and discuss the significance of cotton and the cotton gin.

Industry in the South

Main Idea **For many reasons, industry developed slowly in the South.**

Reading Connection How do you get to school each morning? Do you take the bus or ride in a car, or do you walk to school? Read on to find out what modes of transportation transported people and goods in the South.

The economy of the South prospered between 1820 and 1860. Unlike the industrial North, however, the South remained **predominantly** rural, and its economy became increasingly different from the Northern economy. The South accounted for only a small percentage of the nation's manufacturing in the 1850s. In fact, the entire South produced fewer manufactured goods than the state of Massachusetts.

Barriers to Industry Why was there little industry in the South? One reason was the boom in cotton sales. Because agriculture was so profitable, Southerners remained committed to farming rather than starting new businesses.

Another reason was the lack of **capital** (KA • puh • tuhl)—money to invest in businesses—in the South. To develop industries required money, but many Southerners had their wealth invested in land and slaves. Planters would have had to sell slaves to raise the money to build factories. Most wealthy Southerners were unwilling to do this. They believed that an economy based on cotton and slavery would continue to prosper.

In addition, the market for manufactured goods in the South was smaller than it was in the North. A large portion of the Southern population consisted of enslaved people with no money to buy merchandise. So the limited local market discouraged industries from developing.

TECHNOLOGY & History

The Cotton Gin

In 1793 Eli Whitney visited Catherine Greene, a Georgia plantation owner. She asked him to build a device that removed the seeds from cotton pods. Whitney called the machine the cotton gin—*gin* being short for "engine". **How did the invention of the cotton gin affect slavery?**

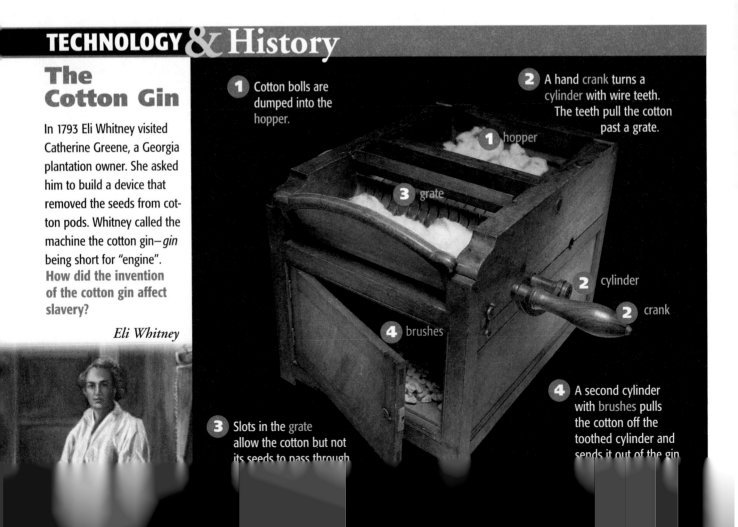

Eli Whitney

1 Cotton bolls are dumped into the hopper.
2 A hand crank turns a cylinder with wire teeth. The teeth pull the cotton past a grate.
1 hopper
3 grate
2 cylinder
2 crank
4 brushes
3 Slots in the grate allow the cotton but not its seeds to pass through.
4 A second cylinder with brushes pulls the cotton off the toothed cylinder and sends it out of the gin.

US8.7.3 Examine the characteristics of white Southern society and how the physical environment influenced events and conditions prior to the Civil War.

Plantations

Main Idea **Plantations varied in size and wealth and contained varying numbers of enslaved people.**

Reading Connection Imagine that you want to open your own business. What things do you need to get your business started? Read on to find out what plantation owners needed to keep their plantations running.

A large plantation might cover several thousand acres. Well-to-do plantation owners usually lived in comfortable but not luxurious farmhouses. They measured their wealth partly by the number of enslaved people they controlled and partly by such possessions as homes, furnishings, and clothing. A small group of plantation owners in the South—about 12 percent of the population—held more than half of the slaves. About half of the planters held fewer than five enslaved workers.

A few free African Americans possessed slaves. The Metoyer family of Louisiana owned thousands of acres of land and more than 400 slaves. Most often, these slaveholders were free African Americans who **purchased** their own family members in order to free them.

Plantation Owners The main economic goal for large plantation owners was to earn profits. Such plantations had **fixed costs**—regular expenses such as housing and feeding workers and maintaining cotton gins and other equipment. Fixed costs remained about the same year after year.

Cotton prices, however, varied from season to season, depending on the market. To receive the best prices, planters sold their cotton to agents in cities such as **New Orleans, Charleston, Mobile,** and **Savannah.** The cotton exchanges, or trade centers, in Southern cities were of vital importance to those involved in the cotton economy. The agents of the exchanges extended **credit**—a form of loan—to the planters and held the cotton for several months until the price rose. Then the agents sold the cotton. This system kept the planters always in debt because they did not receive payment for their cotton until the agents sold it.

Picturing **History**

Although wealthy planters were not numerous, they dominated the economy and political system of the South. ***What were the duties of the wife of a plantation owner?***

History Online

Student Web Activity Visit ca.hss.glencoe.com and click on *Chapter 9—Student Web Activities* for an activity on family life in the South.

Plantation Wives The wife of a plantation owner generally was in charge of watching over the enslaved workers who toiled in her home and tending to them when they became ill. Her responsibilities also included supervising the plantation's buildings and the fruit and vegetable gardens. Some wives served as accountants, keeping the plantation's financial records.

Women often led a difficult and lonely life on the plantation. When plantation agriculture spread westward into Alabama and Mississippi, many planters' wives felt they were moving into a hostile, uncivilized region. Planters traveled frequently to look at new land or to deal with agents in New Orleans or Memphis, so their wives spent long periods alone at the plantation.

US8.7.3 Examine the characteristics of white Southern society and how the physical environment influenced events and conditions prior to the Civil War. **US8.7.4** Compare the lives of and opportunities for free blacks in the North with those of free blacks in the South.

Work on the Plantation Large plantations needed many different kinds of workers. Some enslaved people worked in the house, cleaning, cooking, doing laundry, sewing, and serving meals. They were called domestic slaves. Other enslaved people were trained as blacksmiths, carpenters, shoemakers, or weavers. Still others worked in the pastures, tending the horses, cows, sheep, and pigs. Most of the enslaved African Americans, however, were field hands. They worked from sunrise to sunset planting, cultivating, and picking cotton and other crops. They were supervised by an **overseer** (OH•vuhr•SEE•uhr)—a plantation manager.

Reading Check **Explain** Why were so many slaves needed on a plantation?

Picturing **History**

This photo shows businesses along a street in Atlanta, Georgia, around 1860. ***Why did cities such as Atlanta and Columbia, South Carolina, grow as centers of trade?***

City Life and Education

Main Idea **The South was home to several large cities, and education began to grow in the mid-1800s.**

Reading Connection Imagine living in a town of only a few hundred people. The closest school is miles away—too far to walk—and transportation is not readily accessible. Read on to find out why it was hard for many families to send their children to school in the South.

Although the South was primarily an agricultural region, it was the site of several large cities by the mid-1800s. By 1860 the population of Baltimore had reached 212,000 and the population of New Orleans **exceeded** 165,000. The ten largest cities in the South were either seaports or river ports.

With the coming of the railroad, many other cities began to grow as centers of trade. Among the cities located at the crossroads of the railways were **Columbia,** South Carolina; **Chattanooga,** Tennessee; **Montgomery,** Alabama; Jackson, Mississippi; and **Atlanta,** Georgia. The population of Southern cities included white city dwellers, some enslaved workers, and many of the South's free African Americans.

The cities provided free African Americans with opportunities to form their own communities. African American barbers, carpenters, and small traders offered their services throughout their communities. Free African Americans also founded their own churches and institutions. In New Orleans, many of them were well-educated and prosperous. They used their resources to form an opera company.

Although some free African Americans prospered in the cities, their lives were far from secure. Between 1830 and 1860, Southern states passed laws that limited the rights of free African Americans. Most states would not allow them to migrate from other states. Although spared the horrors of slavery, free African Americans were denied an equal share in economic and political life.

Education Plantation owners and those who could afford to do so often sent their children to private schools. One of the best known was the academy operated by Moses Waddel in Willington, South Carolina. Students attended six days a week. The Bible and classical literature were stressed, but the courses also included mathematics, religion, Greek, Latin, and public speaking.

In many smaller rural areas, classes met in small schoolhouses or in church buildings. School terms lasted only three to four months. Due to poverty, few books were available for study.

During this era, no statewide public school system existed. However, cities such as Charleston, Louisville, and Mobile did establish excellent public schools.

By the mid-1800s, education was growing. Hundreds of public schools were operating in North Carolina by 1860. Even before that, the Kentucky legislature set up a funding system for public schools. Many states in the South also had charity schools. There are schools for students whose parents could not afford to pay.

Although the number of schools and teachers in the South grew, the South lagged behind other areas of the country in literacy, the number of people who can read or write. One reason for this was the geography of the South. Even in the more heavily populated Southern states there were few people per square mile. Virginia and North Carolina had fewer than 15 white inhabitants per square mile. In contrast, Massachusetts had 127 inhabitants per square mile.

It was too great a hardship for many Southern families to send their children great distances to attend school. In addition, many Southerners believed education was a private matter, not a state function; therefore, the state should not spend money on education.

Reading Check **Identify** What Southern city had surpassed 200,000 in population by the year 1860?

History Online
Study Central Need help understanding Southern life in the mid-1800s? Visit ca.hss.glencoe.com and click on Study Central.

Reading Summary

Review the Main Ideas

- Many farmers in the South were yeomen who lived on small farms.
- Many plantations were small and had relatively few slaves.
- By the mid-1800s, the number of cities in the South was increasing, and education was growing.

What Did You Learn?

1. List two differences between yeoman and plantation owners.
2. Explain why some free African Americans might own slaves.

Critical Thinking

3. **Compare** Create a chart like the one below and compare the life of a plantation owner to that of a small farmer. CA HI2.

Plantation Owner	Small Farmer

4. **The Big Ideas** Describe the life of free African Americans in Southern cities. CA CS3.
5. **Descriptive Writing** Study the pictures on pages 429 and 430. Write a paragraph explaining what you think the pictures portray about life in the South. CA 8WA2.4
6. **Analysis** **Explain** Write a short paragraph explaining the relationship between the plantation owner and the cotton exchange. Then, discuss which job you would choose. CA HI6.

Section
3

The Peculiar Institution

Guide to Reading

History Social Science Standards

US8.7 Students analyze the divergent paths of the American people in the South from 1800 to the mid-1800s and the challenges they faced.

US8.9 Students analyze the early and steady attempts to abolish slavery and to realize the ideals of the Declaration of Independence.

Looking Back, Looking Ahead

In Section 2, you learned about the life of Southern whites in the country, as well as about life in Southern cities. In this section, you will learn about slavery and the lives of African Americans in the South.

Focusing on the Main Ideas

- Enslaved African Americans faced many hardships but were able to create family lives, religious beliefs, and a distinct culture. *(page 433)*
- Many enslaved people fought against slavery. *(page 434)*

Meeting People

Nat Turner
Harriet Tubman
Frederick Douglass

Content Vocabulary

spiritual (SPIHR • ih • chuh • wuhl)
slave codes

Academic Vocabulary

constant
communicate

Reading Strategy

Organizing Information Create a chart like the one below to list aspects of African American life in the South.

Way of Life	Aspects
Family Life	
Culture	
Religion	

NATIONAL GEOGRAPHIC
Who & When?
1820
1840
1860
1821 Denmark Vesey plots uprising in South Carolina
1831 Nat Turner leads slave revolt
1850s Harriet Tubman helps enslaved people escape

US8.7.2 Trace the origins and development of slavery; its effects on black Americans and on the region's political, social, religious, economic, and cultural development; and identify the strategies that were tried to both overturn and preserve it (e.g., through the writings and historical documents on Nat Turner, Denmark Vesey).

Life Under Slavery

Main Idea **Enslaved African Americans faced many hardships but were able to create family lives, religious beliefs, and a distinct culture.**

Reading Connection Imagine being taken to a foreign land where you do not speak the language and do not understand the customs. How would you adapt to such a situation? Read on to find out how enslaved Southerners developed family and social ties to cope with their situation.

An American Story

Planters gathered in the bright Savannah sunshine. They were there to bid on a strong slave who could plow their fields. Fear and grief clouded the enslaved man's face because he had been forced to leave his wife and children. Later, he wrote this letter:

> **"My Dear wife I [write] . . . with much regret to inform you that I am Sold to a man by the name of Peterson. . . . Give my love to my father and mother and tell them good Bye for me. And if we Shall not meet in this world, I hope to meet in heaven. My Dear wife for you and my Children my pen cannot Express the [grief] I feel to be parted from you all."**
>
> **—as quoted in *The Black Family in Slavery and Freedom, 1750–1925***

Family Life Enslaved people faced **constant** uncertainty and danger. American law in the early 1800s did not protect enslaved families. At any time, a husband or wife could be sold to a different owner, or a slaveholder's death could lead to the breakup of an enslaved family. Although marriage between enslaved people was not recognized by law, many couples did marry. Their marriage ceremonies included the phrase "until death or separation do us part"—recognizing the possibility that their life together might end with the sale of one spouse.

To provide some measure of stability in their lives, enslaved African Americans established a network of relatives and friends, who made up their extended family. If a father or mother were sold away, an aunt, uncle, or close friend could raise the children left behind. Large, close-knit extended families became a vital feature of African American culture.

African American Culture Enslaved African Americans endured their hardships by extending their own culture, fellowship, and community. They fused African and American elements into a new culture.

The growth of the African American population came mainly from children born in the United States. In 1808 Congress had outlawed the slave trade. Although slavery remained legal in the Southern States, no new slaves could enter the United States. By 1860 almost all the enslaved people in the South had been born there.

These native-born African Americans practiced their African customs. They continued to enjoy African music and dance. They passed traditional African folk stories to their children. Some wrapped colored cloths around their heads in the African style. Although a large number of enslaved African Americans accepted Christianity, they often followed the religious beliefs and practices of their African ancestors as well.

African American Christianity For many enslaved African Americans, Christianity became a religion of hope and resistance. They prayed fervently for the day when they would be free from bondage.

The passionate beliefs of the Southern slaves found expression in the **spiritual** (SPIHR•ih•chuh•wuhl), an African American religious folk song. The song "Didn't My Lord Deliver Daniel," for example, refers to the biblical story of Daniel, who was saved from the lions' den.

US8.7.2 Trace the origins and development of slavery; its effects on black Americans and on the region's political, social, religious, economic, and cultural development; and identify the strategies that were tried to both overturn and preserve it (e.g., through the writings and historical documents on Nat Turner, Denmark Vesey.)

> **"Didn't my Lord deliver Daniel, deliver Daniel, deliver Daniel? Didn't my Lord deliver Daniel, And why [not] every man?"**
>
> — from *Wade in the Water*

Spirituals provided a way for the enslaved African Americans to **communicate** secretly with one another. The spirituals often reflected the connection African American enslaved people felt to enslaved people who were depicted in the Bible. Passed down through the oral tradition, spirituals helped form an African American culture. They also became one of the best-known forms of American music.

Reading Check **Explain** How did the African American spiritual develop?

Resisting Slavery

Main Idea **Many enslaved people fought against slavery.**

Reading Connection How do you react when someone treats you unfairly? Read on to find out how enslaved people resisted.

Enslaved people had few legal rights. Between 1830 and 1860, life under slavery became even more difficult because the **slave codes**—the laws in the Southern states that controlled enslaved people—became more severe. In existence since the 1700s, slave codes were written to prevent the event white Southerners dreaded most—the slave rebellion. For this reason slave codes prohibited slaves from assembling in large groups and from leaving their master's property without a written pass.

Primary Sources

Working the Cotton Fields

Solomon Northup was a free black who was kidnapped and sold into slavery. He picked cotton on a Louisiana plantation for 12 years before winning his freedom. His description of picking cotton follows.

> When a new hand, one unaccustomed to the business, is sent for the first time into the field, he is whipped up smartly, and made for that day to pick as fast as he can possibly. At night it is weighed, so that his capability in cotton picking is known. He must bring in the same weight each night following. If it falls short, it is considered evidence that he has been laggard, and a greater or less number of lashes is the penalty. . . . The hands are required to be in the cotton field as soon as it is light in the morning, and, with the exception of ten or fifteen minutes, which is given them at noon to swallow their allowance of cold bacon, they are not permitted to be a moment idle until it is too dark to see, and when the moon is full, they often times labor till the middle of the night. They do not dare to stop even at dinner time, nor return to the quarters, however late it be, until the order to halt is given by the driver. . . .
>
> —from *Twelve Years a Slave* by Solomon Northup

▲ Solomon Northup

DBQ Document-Based Question

Why do you think it seems like Northup's perspective is that of an outsider?

Living Under Slavery

Enslaved workers reached the fields before the sun came up, and they stayed there until sundown. Planters wanted to keep the slaves busy all the time, which meant long and grueling days in the fields. Enslaved women as well as men were required to do heavy fieldwork. Young children carried buckets of water. By the age of 10, they were considered ready for fieldwork.

Cabins were usually made of small logs, about 10 to 20 feet square. Often, two or three families shared a cabin.

Heavy iron leg shackles were used to punish workers, especially those who tried to run away.

Enslaved people had few personal possessions.

When rented to other masters, enslaved people wore identification tags.

Slave codes also made it a crime to teach enslaved people to read or write. White Southerners believed a slave who did not know how to read and write was less likely to rebel.

Rebellions Some enslaved African Americans did rebel openly against their masters. One was **Nat Turner,** a popular religious leader among his fellow slaves. Turner had taught himself to read and write. In 1831 Turner led a group of followers on a brief, violent rampage in Southhampton County, Virginia, that resulted in the death of at least 55 whites. Nat Turner was hanged, but his rebellion frightened whites and led to more severe slave codes.

Even before the rebellion led by Nat Turner, other enslaved persons had plotted uprisings. In 1800 Gabriel Prosser planned a rebellion to capture Richmond, Virginia, and massacre whites. An informer gave the plot away, and Prosser and 35 others were convicted and executed.

Denmark Vesey, a Charleston, South Carolina, carpenter, who had earlier purchased his freedom, was outraged by the existence of slavery. His reading of the Bible and the Declaration of Independence fueled his hatred of slavery. His 1821 plan for a slave revolt failed when it was betrayed at the last moment by some of his followers.

Biography

US8.9.1 Describe the leaders of the movement (e.g., John Quincy Adams and his proposed constitutional amendment, John Brown and the armed resistance, Harriet Tubman and the Underground Railroad, Benjamin Franklin, Theodore Weld, William Lloyd Garrison, Frederick Douglass).

HARRIET TUBMAN

1820–1913

Born a slave in Maryland, Harriet Tubman worked in plantation fields until she was nearly 30 years old. Then she made her break for freedom, escaping to the North with the help of the Underground Railroad. While jubilant over the success of her escape when she crossed the line from Delaware into Pennsylvania, Tubman's happiness was short-lived. She explained, "I was *free*, but there was no one to welcome me to the land of freedom. . . . [M]y home, after all, was down in Maryland, because my father, my mother, my brothers, my sisters, and friends were there. But I was free and *they should be free!*"

Settling in Philadelphia, Tubman met many abolitionists who shared her desire to bring Southern slaves to the North. Realizing the risks of being captured, Tubman courageously made 19 trips back into the South during the 1850s to help other enslaved people escape. Altogether she assisted about 70 individuals—including her parents—to escape from slavery.

Tubman did not establish the Underground Railroad, but she certainly became its most famous and successful conductor. Tubman was known as the "Moses of her people" for leading slaves to freedom in the North. Despite huge rewards offered in the South for her capture and arrest, Tubman always managed to elude her enemies.

During the Civil War, Tubman assisted the Union army as a nurse and a spy, caring for the sick and wounded and making trips behind enemy lines to scout out Confederate troops. Tubman continued to experience discrimination at the end of the war and was never paid for her services in the army. Despite financial difficulties, Tubman opened her home in New York to African Americans journeying North after the war. Many were sick or near starvation, and she fed them, clothed them, and cared for them. In 1896 Tubman opened a center for the sick and needy on land across from her home. Until her death in 1913, Tubman continued to help those in need and continued to support civil and women's rights.

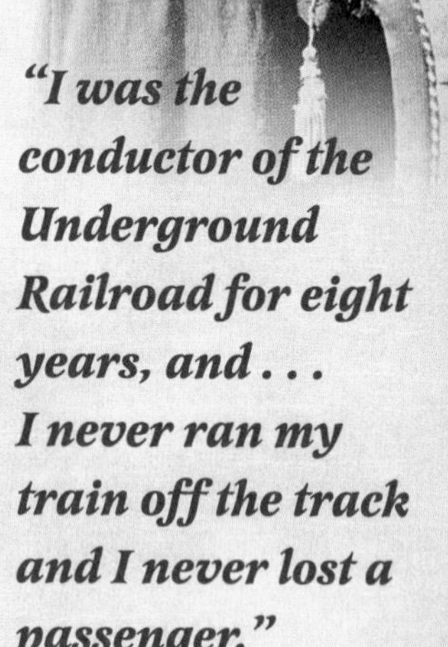

"I was the conductor of the Underground Railroad for eight years, and . . . I never ran my train off the track and I never lost a passenger."

—Harriet Tubman, from *Women's Voices: Quotations by Women*

Then and Now

Many African Americans relied on Tubman and other abolitionists to survive in the North. If a present-day family moved to a new city, what resources could they use to help them find work, shelter, and other necessities?

Other Forms of Resistance Armed rebellions were rare, however. African Americans in the South knew that they would only lose in an armed uprising. For the most part enslaved people resisted slavery by working slowly or by pretending to be ill. Occasionally resistance took more active forms, such as setting fire to a plantation building or breaking tools. Resistance helped enslaved African Americans endure their lives by striking back at white masters—and perhaps establishing boundaries that white people would respect.

Escaping Slavery Some enslaved African Americans tried to run away to the free states in the North. A few succeeded. **Harriet Tubman** and **Frederick Douglass,** two African American leaders who were born into slavery, gained their freedom when they fled to the North.

Yet for most enslaved people, getting to the North was almost impossible, especially from the Deep South. Most slaves who succeeded in running away escaped from the Upper South. The Underground Railroad—a network of "safe houses" owned by free blacks and whites who opposed slavery—offered assistance to runaway slaves. Some slaves ran away to find relatives on nearby plantations or to escape punishment.

Most runaways were captured and returned to their owners. Discipline was usually severe. The most common punishment for captured runaways was whipping.

Even if an enslaved man or woman escaped to the free states in the North, they were not always safe there. In some Northern communities, fugitive slaves were captured and returned to the South. This prevented many slaves from settling in free states and forced them to escape to Canada, where slavery was banned in 1834.

Reading Check **Summarize** Besides rebellions, what other forms did resistance to slavery take?

History Online
Study Central Need help understanding how African Americans in the South lived? Visit ca.hss.glencoe.com and click on Study Central.

Reading Summary

Review the Main Ideas

- Enslaved Southerners developed a culture and religion that had both African and American elements.
- While some enslaved people attempted to rebel openly against slavery, others resisted by running away, refusing to work, or destroying farm tools.

What Did You Learn?

1. Why were extended families vital to African American culture?
2. What was the Underground Railroad?

Critical Thinking

3. **Classify** Re-create the diagram below. In the boxes, briefly explain how the slave codes operated. CA HR3.

Slave Codes	
Education	Assembly

4. **The Big Ideas** Trace the development of the unique elements of African American slave culture in the South. CA HI3.
5. **Summarize** Who were Denmark Vesey and Nat Turner? Write a short paragraph about their efforts against slavery. CA HI1.
6. **Creative Writing** Imagine you are enslaved on a Southern plantation. Write a description of a typical day that you might experience. CA 8WA2.1

Analyzing Primary Sources

US8.7 Analyze the divergent paths of the American people in the South from 1800 to the mid-1800s and the challenges they faced.

Cotton and Slavery in the South

Industry boomed in the North, but agriculture reigned in the South. Cotton was the South's most important crop. The production of cotton depended on a large supply of cheap labor. In the South, enslaved African Americans supplied that labor.

Read the passages on pages 438 and 439 and answer the questions that follow.

Many people copied Eli Whitney's cotton gin and ignored his patent because the gin was so easy to make.

Reader's Dictionary

patent: a document that gives the inventor the sole legal right to an invention for a period of time

miry (MYR • ee)**:** muddy

pigsty: enclosed area where pigs live

speculator (SPEH • kyuh • LAY • tuhr)**:** an individual who buys or sells land in hopes of making a profit

A New Invention

Eli Whitney had invented a workable cotton gin by 1793. One of his next steps was to apply for a patent for the machine. In the following letter, Whitney tells his family, who live in Westboro, Massachusetts, about the progress he is making and his plans.

March 30, 1794

It is with no small satisfaction that I have in my power to inform you I am in good health. I have just returned from Philadelphia. My business there was to lodge a Model of my machine and receive a **Patent** for it. I accomplished everything agreeable to my wishes. I had the satisfaction to hear it declared by a number of the first men in America that my machine is the most perfect & the most valuable invention that has ever appeared in this Country. I have received my Patent. . . .

I wish very much to see you before I go. But should I come to Westboro' now I must neglect my business so much as to lose several Hundred Dollars. If you come [here] I shall be able to show you my machine. I have six of them nearly complete which I expect to carry to the Southward with me. I shall leave this place for Georgia in about twelve or fourteen days at the farthest. . . . Though I have as yet expended much more money than profits of the machine have been heretofore, and am at present a little pressed for money, I am by no means in the least discouraged. And I shall probably gain some honour as well as some profit by the Invention. . . .

—from *The World of Eli Whitney*

The Living Conditions of Enslaved Persons

Josiah Henson was an enslaved person. He escaped and later wrote about his life. In this excerpt, he describes the area where the slaves lived.

We lodged in log huts, and on the bare ground. Wooden floors were an unknown luxury. In a single room were huddled, like cattle, ten or a dozen persons, men, women, and children. . . . Our beds were collections of straw and old rags, thrown down in the corners and boxed in with boards; a single blanket the only covering. . . . The wind whistled and the rain and snow blew in through the cracks, and the damp earth soaked in the moisture till the floor was **miry** as a **pigsty.**

—from *Uncle Tom's Story of His Life. An Autobiography of the Rev. Josiah Henson*

▲ **Slave quarters were usually gathered together in one area of a plantation.**

News From the South

The American Anti-Slavery Society published American Slavery As It Is *by Sarah and Angelina Grimké and Angelina's husband Theodore Weld in 1839. For this book, Weld gathered newspaper ads from Southern papers to show the effects of slavery.*

From the "Richmond (Va.) Compiler," Sept. 8, 1837. Ranaway from the subscriber, Ben. He ran off without any known cause, and *I suppose he is aiming to go to his wife, who was carried from the neighborhood last winter.*

JOHN HUNT.

From the "Jackson (Tenn.) Telegraph," Sept. 14, 1838. Committed to the jail of Madison county, a negro woman, who calls her name Fanny, and says she belongs to William Miller, of Mobile. She formerly belonged to John Givins, of this county, who now owns *several of her children.*

DAVID SHROPSHIRE, Jailor.

From the "Richmond (Va.) Enquirer," Feb. 20, 1838. Stop the Runaway!!!—$25 Reward. Ranaway from the Eagle Tavern, a negro fellow, named Nat. He is no doubt attempting to *follow his wife, who was lately sold to a* ***speculator*** named Redmond. The above reward will be paid by Mrs. Lucy M. Downman, of Sussex county, Va.

Document-Based Questions

A New Invention

1. What has Whitney recently obtained?
2. How successful has Whitney been in making money from the cotton gin?

The Living Conditions of Enslaved Persons

3. How weatherproof are the cabins? Why do you think that?

News From the South

4. According to the ads, why do slaves run away?

Read to Write

5. Imagine that you are living in the early 1800s. You know nothing about slavery. Then you read "The Living Conditions of Enslaved Persons" and "News from the South." Write an editorial to your local newspaper about slavery. What do you think about the fact that there is slavery in the United States? CA 8WS1.1

Assessment

Standard US8.7

Review Content Vocabulary

Write the vocabulary word that best completes each sentence. Write a sentence for each word not used.

a. yeomen
b. capital
c. cotton gin
d. slave codes
e. tenant farmers
f. spiritual

1. The South lacked the ___ needed to develop industries.
2. ___ farmers owned land and lived mostly in the Upper South.
3. A(n) ___ is an African religious folk song.
4. The South's ___ made it difficult for enslaved African Americans to gain an education.

Review the Main Ideas

Section 1 • Southern Cotton Kingdom

5. How did the cotton gin affect cotton production?
6. Why was there little industry in the South?

Section 2 • Life in the South

7. What were the main duties of plantation wives?
8. What obstacles existed to gaining an education in the South?

Section 3 • The Peculiar Institution

9. Why were escaped slaves not always safe in the North?
10. What was the purpose of the slave codes?

Critical Thinking

11. **Analyze** How did enslaved African Americans hold on to their African customs? CA HI1.
12. **Conclude** Why was the production of cotton so lucrative in the South? CA HI6.
13. **Explain** How did African Christianity help slaves cope with their situation? CA HI2.
14. **Summarize** What was life like for most whites in the South? CA HI1.

Geography Skills

The map shows Southern cities with more than 10,000 people in 1850. Study the map and answer the following questions. CA CS3.

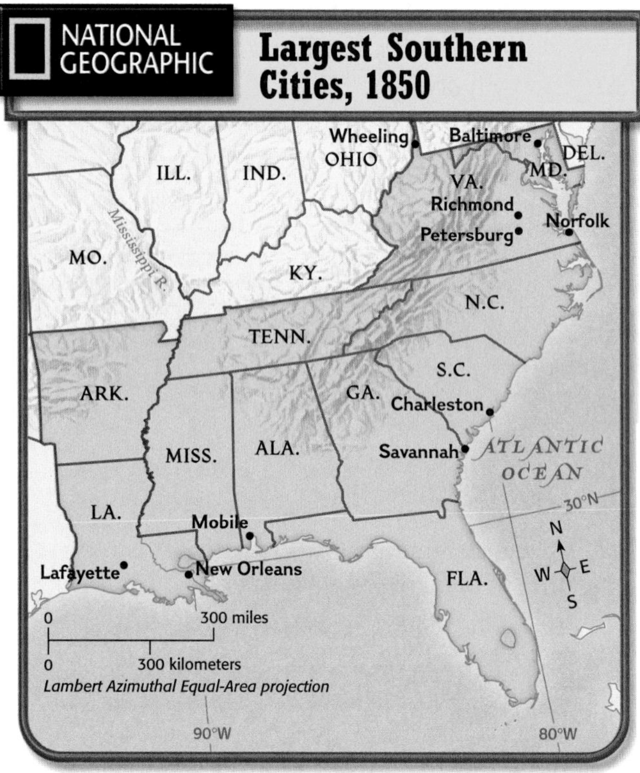

15. **Location** Which state had four of the South's major cities?
16. **Region** Which of the major cities shown were in the Deep South?
17. **Human-Environment Interaction** What do the locations of many of the Southern cities have in common? Why is that significant?

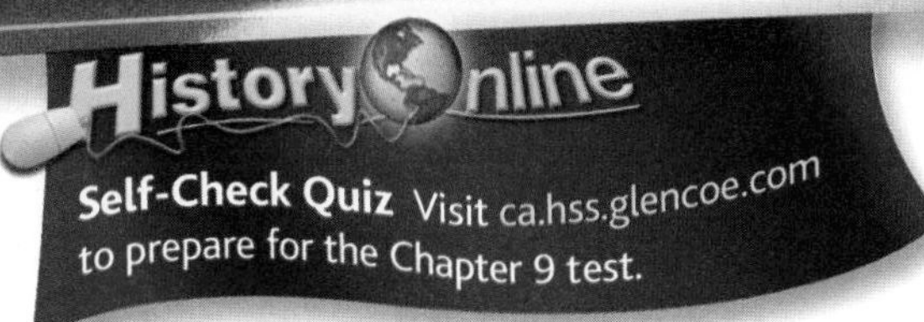

Read to Write

18. The Big Ideas **Expository Writing** Use the Internet or library resources to identify arguments Southerners used to defend slavery. Write a short paper in which you explain why these arguments may have found support in the South. CA 8WA2.3

19. **Narrative Writing** Imagine that you are a slave who has been sold away from your family to another plantation. Write a letter to your family telling them how you feel about your separation. CA 8WA2.1

20. **Using Your** FOLDABLES Use the information you created in your foldable to create a summary of the chapter. In your summary, be sure to cover the main ideas and events that were discussed. CA 8RC1.0

Using Academic Vocabulary

Read the following sentences. Then, in your own words, write the meaning of the underlined academic vocabulary word.

21. The doctor's patients were <u>predominantly</u> elderly.

22. The estimate noted that the cost was not to <u>exceed</u> $75.

Building Citizenship

23. **Explain** Choose an issue you think is important to your community or the nation today. Explain why you think it is important and how you would take steps to resolve that issue. Compare your solutions with steps government officials are taking to address the issue. CA 8WS1.1

Reviewing Skills

24. Review READING SKILL **Asking Questions** Using your local newspaper or an Internet news site, find an article about human rights. Write questions about any elements of the story you do not understand. Then describe how you could get your questions answered. CA 8RC2.0

25.  ANALYSIS SKILL **Inferring** Read the following quote, then identify the region you think the speaker might be from and explain your answer:

"We are an agricultural people. . . . We have no cities—we don't want them. . . . We want no manufactures: we desire no trading, no mechanical or manufacturing classes. As long as we have our rice, our sugar, our tobacco, and our cotton, we can command wealth to purchase all we want." CA HR5

Standards Practice

Select the best answer for each of the following questions.

26 The economy of the Deep South was based on

A growing cotton.
B growing tobacco.
C manufacturing.
D growing vegetables.

27 The white supervisor of enslaved workers on a plantation was known as a(n)

A blacksmith.
B yeoman.
C overseer.
D tenant.

28 The Southern laws that controlled enslaved people were called

A spirituals.
B overseers.
C credits.
D slave codes.

Chapter 10 The Age of Jackson

▼ The White House, Washington, D.C.

NATIONAL GEOGRAPHIC **Who & When?**

1825 — 1835 — 1845

1828 Andrew Jackson elected president

1838 Cherokee begin Trail of Tears

1841 President William Henry Harrison dies in office

History Online

Chapter Overview Visit ca.hss.glencoe.com for a preview of Chapter 10.

The Big Ideas

Jacksonian Democracy

Political ideas and major events shape how people form governments. President Andrew Jackson brought many changes to the American political system.

The Removal of Native Americans

Differences in economic, political, and social beliefs and practices can lead to division within a nation and have lasting consequences. Many Native Americans were forced off their lands in the Southeast.

Jackson and the Bank

Differences in economic, political, and social beliefs and practices can lead to division within a nation and have lasting consequences. Economic issues had a strong effect on politics and government in the mid-1800s.

View the Chapter 10 video in the Glencoe Video Program.

Evaluating Information Make this foldable to help you ask and answer questions about the Jackson era.

Step 1 Fold a sheet of paper in half from side to side, leaving a $\frac{1}{2}$-inch tab along the side.

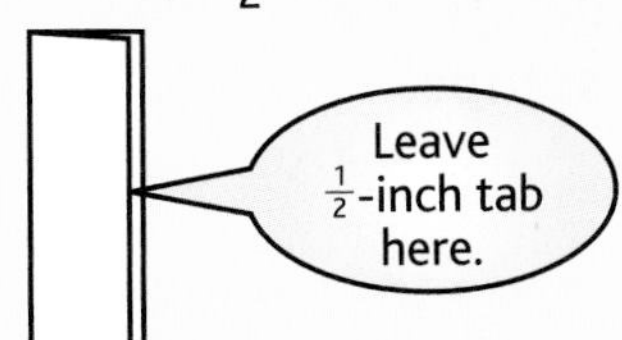

Step 2 Turn the paper and fold it into fourths.

Step 3 Unfold and cut up along the three fold lines.

Step 4 Label your foldable as shown.

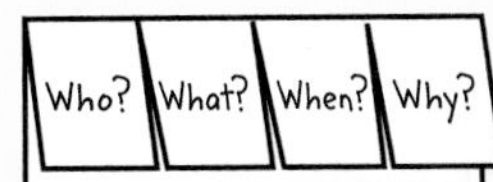

Reading and Writing
As you read, ask yourself "who" Andrew Jackson was, "what" he did, "when" he did it, and "why" it happened. Write your thoughts and facts under each appropriate tab.

Get Ready to Read

Question-and-Answer Relationships

1 Learn It!

Knowing how to find answers to questions will help you on reviews and tests. Some answers can be found in the textbook, while other answers require you to go beyond the text. These answers might be based on knowledge you already have or things you have personally experienced.

How were the Seminole able to resist removal?

They joined forces with a group of African Americans and used guerrilla tactics.

This answer comes directly from the text.

The Seminole people of Florida were the only Native Americans who successfully resisted their removal. . . . The Seminole decided to go to war against the United States instead.

In 1835 the Seminole joined forces with a group of African Americans who had run away to escape slavery. . . . They used guerrilla tactics (guh • RIH • luh), **making surprise attacks and then retreating back into the forests and swamps.**

—from page 455

What are guerrilla tactics? This answer is not directly stated. You need to rely on information you already know or draw conclusions based on how this term is used in the text.

As you read, keep track of questions you answer in the chapter. This will help you remember what you have read.

Justified

John L. O'Sullivan first used the phrase Manifest Destiny in a July 1845 edition of the *United States Magazine and Democratic Review.* In the following article, he promotes the spread of democracy: O'Sullivan supported Manifest Destiny.

"Texas is now ours. Already, before these words are written, her Convention has undoubtedly ratified the acceptance by her Congress, of our proffered invitation into the Union. . . . Her star and her stripe may already be said to have taken their place in the glorious blazon of our common nationality. . . .

. . . The next session of Congress will see the representatives of the new young state in their places in both our halls of national legislation, side by side with those of the old Thirteen.

Why . . . [have] other nations . . . undertaken to intrude themselves into [the question of Texas?] between us and the proper parties to the case, in a spirit of hostile interference against us, for the avowed object of thwarting our policy and hampering our power, limiting our greatness and checking the fulfillment of our manifest destiny to overspread the continent allotted by Providence for the free development of our yearly multiplying millions."

—quoted in *Annexation*

▲ *Spirit of the Frontier* by John Gast

US8.8.2 Describe the purpose, challenges, and economic incentives associated with westward expansion, including the concept of Manifest Destiny (e.g., the Lewis and Clark expedition, accounts of the removal of Indians, the Cherokees' "Trail of Tears," settlement of the Great Plains) and the territorial acquisitions that spanned numerous decades.

You Be The Historian

DBQ Document-Based Questions

1. What does Albert Gallatin think is the real motivation underlying the idea of Manifest Destiny? CA HR3.
2. Imagine you could interview Gallatin and O'Sullivan. Write a list of three questions you could ask each man about his views on Manifest Destiny. CA HR3. CA 8RC2.3

What were people's lives like in the past?

What—and who—were people talking about? What did they eat? What did they do for fun? These two pages will give you some clues to everyday life in the U.S. as you step back in time with TIME Notebook.

Profile

It's 1853, and **AMELIA STEWART** *is heading west to Oregon with her husband and seven children in a covered wagon. How hard can the five-month trip be? Here are two entries from her diary:*

MONDAY, AUGUST 8 We have to make a drive of 22 miles without water today. Have our cans filled to drink. Here we left, unknowingly, our [daughter] Lucy behind, not a soul had missed her until we had gone some miles, when we stopped a while to rest the cattle; just then another train drove up behind us, with Lucy. She was terribly frightened and said she was sitting under the bank of the river when we started, busy watching some wagons cross, and did not know that we were ready. . . .It was a lesson for all of us.

FRIDAY, AUGUST 12 Lost one of our oxen. We were traveling slowly along, when he dropped dead in the yoke. . . .I could hardly help shedding tears, when we drove round this poor ox who had helped us along thus far, and had given us his very last step.

BROWN BROTHERS

MILESTONES

EVENTS OF THE TIME

CLOTHED. Hundreds of miners in 1850 by **LEVI STRAUSS**. Using canvas he originally intended to make into tents, Levi made sturdy, tough pants with lots of pockets—perfect clothing for the rough work of mining. Can you imagine anyone in the city ever wearing them?

BETTMANN/CORBIS

MARCHED. Just under 100 camels in 1857, from San Antonio to Los Angeles, led by hired Turkish, Greek, and Armenian camel drivers. It is hoped the desert beasts will help the U.S. Army open the West.

MAILED. Thousands of letters carried by **PONY EXPRESS** in 1860 from Missouri to California in an extremely short time—only 10 days! Riders switch to fresh horses every 10 or 15 miles and continue through the night, blizzards, and attacks by outlaws.

FRONTIER FOOD

Trail Mix

Hard Tack for a Hard Trip

INGREDIENTS: 3 cups flour • 3 tsp. salt • 1 cup water

Mix all ingredients and stir until it becomes too difficult. Knead the dough; add more flour until mixture is very dry. Roll to 1/2-inch thickness and cut into 3" squares, poke with a skewer [pin] to make several holes in each piece (for easy breaking). Bake 30 minutes in a hot oven until hard. Store for up to 10 years.

Thunder on the Sierra

By Kathy Balmes

Before You Read

The Scene: This part of the story takes place at Señor Sosa's gold claim in the Sierra in 1852.

The Characters: Mateo is a 13-year-old boy who trades with miners in the California gold camps. His pack animals are mules with names, such as Fabio and Cisco. Señor Sosa has a gold claim in the mountains somewhere between the mining camps of Indian Gulch and Poverty Hill.

The Plot: While restocking supplies that he will sell to the gold miners, Mateo agrees to deliver a letter to a Señor Sosa if he can find the man.

Vocabulary Preview

decaying: rotting
ghastly: scary like a ghost or corpse
glossy: shiny on the surface
hue (HYOO): color or shade of color
moan: long, low sound of pain, sorrow, or grief
nauseating (NAW • zhee • AYT • ihng): causing a strong sick feeling in the stomach
stench: strong, bad smell

Has a promise ever led you into an unexpected situation? That's what happened to Mateo.

As You Read

A novel has a main plot that relates to the action in all or almost all of the book. The main plot in Thunder on the Sierra *concerns Mateo's desire to get back his stolen horse. This novel also has subplots, or shorter plots, that occur in part of the story. As you read, think about the subplot that takes place in this excerpt. What is the problem or conflict? How is it resolved? Or is it solved?*

When I first came across Señor Sosa's camp, I thought it was deserted. I had crossed between Indian Gulch and Poverty Hill twice, looking for the man. I was ready to give up when a downpour started, and I saw a broken down shack. As I hobbled[1] and unloaded the mules a short distance away, I heard a low moan. I pushed the door of the shack open. Inside was dark. A nauseating stench, like a decaying corpse, almost knocked me backwards.

"Hello? Who are you?" a weak voice asked in Spanish.

"My name is Mateo."

"You must be an angel. Good. I'm finally dying."

"No. I'm not an angel. I'm an arriero,"[2] I replied.

"My name is Sebástiano Sosa."

I had found my man.

"Are you sick or hurt?" I asked, knowing it must be one or the other.

"Sick."

Even though it was pouring rain, I hesitated to enter the shack.

"Do you have cholera[3] or dysentery[4] or malaria?[5] I have quinine. It can ease malaria."

"I don't have malaria."

---

[1] **hobbled:** tied a rope or strap around two legs
[2] **arriero:** a person who drives mules
[3] **cholera:** very severe diarrhea that can kill the patient
[4] **dysentery:** severe diarrhea
[5] **malaria:** severe chills and fever

I pushed down my fear of the deadly cholera and entered the shack. He had not been able to get up from his bed. His shack smelled of vomit, urine, and diarrhea. I breathed through my mouth to avoid the overwhelming odors.

I had never seen anyone in such awful condition. His bleeding gums made his attempt to smile ghastly. His skin had a purple hue. His arms were swollen to double their normal size. They were black where his blood vessels had broken. He was hideous. But as I moved closer, I could see what was wrong with him.

"What have you been eating?" I asked.

"Nothing lately. Before that only spoiled salt pork and flour fried in grease," he said weakly.

"For how long?" I asked.

"Months," he said.

"Were you always alone?" I said.

"No. I had a partner. We had studied law together before the gold rush. We met again in the diggings.[6] But he gave up this summer. We hadn't found any gold, and our food was running out. He left for San Francisco to start a law firm. I planned to follow him back in a few weeks to become his law partner."

"Why didn't you?" I asked.

"I found gold. Not much. But enough to keep me here panning. After a few months I got sick. My arms and legs swelled. Now it hurts me to move," he said.

"You have scurvy. I've seen it in other camps where the miners don't have good food. You're the worst case I've ever seen."

The watery brown eyes pleaded, "Can you help me?"

"Yes. You need fruits and vegetables. I have some in my packs. I'll stay until you are strong enough to take care of yourself."

The sick man lay back and closed his eyes. "God bless you. You are an angel," he murmured.

I brought him raisins and dried apples from Fabio's pack. I filled his cup with water and fed him. His breath stunk like an animal that had been dead for a month. He could barely chew and swallow. Was I too late?

[6] **diggings:** area where people are looking for gold

"I can't make a fire to cook potatoes and onions for you until the rain stops. I'm going to hike around and see if I can find some wild greens. An old Indian showed me which plants cure scurvy."

I looked around for the plants. But I found nothing.

The rain had stopped by the time I returned. I took dry wood from inside the shack and built a fire outside. I fried a pan full of onions and potatoes. The wonderful aroma floated into the shack.

I brought a plate of vegetables to his bed.

"Smells good," said the grateful man.

"Eat as much as you can. It will make you better."

I fed him. But he wasn't able to chew much.

I noticed a copy of *Robinson Crusoe*[7] and three law books on a crude wooden shelf. The law books reminded me of the letter. *I'll wait until he's stronger,* I thought. *It might be bad news.*

I slept outside the door. I couldn't stand the smell in the shack.

The sick man seemed a little better in the morning and ate more of the onions and potatoes. I heated the dried fruit in water until it became plump and easier for him to swallow.

After breakfast I moved the mules to a new place to graze and informed them that they had the rest of the week off. I returned to the shack.

"Can you walk outside so I can clean your cabin? You can lean on me."

"I'll try," Señor Sosa replied weakly.

After I settled him in the sunshine, I cleaned his shack. Señor Sosa looked spent[8] when I helped him back inside and settled him in his clean bed. He slept all afternoon.

The next morning I helped him peel off his dirty clothes, wash, and put on clean ones. After I fed him lunch I asked, "Would you like me to read you *Robinson Crusoe?*"

"That would ease my suffering, Mateo, my angel."

---

[7] ***Robinson Crusoe:*** story about a man who is marooned on a desert island for many years

[8] **spent:** exhausted

After I had read for about an hour, a movement in a shadowy corner of the cabin caught my eye. I saw a small, sleek[9] animal slink out of a hole under the crude boards and bound gracefully onto Señor Sosa's bed.

"Is that supposed to be in here?" I asked, pointing to the small animal with round, bright eyes. It looked like a tiny raccoon, only cuter, and its coat was softer.

Señor Sosa smiled. "She's my pet," he said as he stroked her velvet fur. "Madalena was my only companion before you came. She's a ringtail. They're so good at catching rats and mice that they're often called miner's cats. This cabin would be overrun with rodents if she didn't eat them."

"She's pretty," I said.

"Madalena has been a great comfort. I figured she'd keep the rodents off my corpse. I'd been warned that one in five miners died in the first year of the gold rush. I didn't believe it. Now I wonder how so many survived."

I reached out a hand to pet the glossy fur. But Madalena darted off the bed and down the hole.

The next morning the lawyer was noticeably healthier. *He's a young man,* I realized with amazement. *It's time,* I decided.

"I have a letter for you," I announced after he fed himself breakfast.

Señor Sosa stared at me in surprise.

"It's from your partner in San Francisco. He said it's important. I kept it until you were strong, in case it's bad news."

"Read it to me, Mateo. I am still weak."

"Yes, señor. The letter is dated September 15, 1852."

"What month is it now, Mateo?"

"December, señor."

"Continue."

I read: " *'My Friend, I hope this letter finds you in good health.'* "

The lawyer snorted. "Go on," he urged.

---

[9] **sleek:** smooth and glossy

Please join me in San Francisco immediately. Because we are Spanish-speaking lawyers, who also speak English, we are needed to help rancheros to prove in court that they own the land they live on.

Disappointed Yankee miners often want land in California. They have pressured the American government to issue the Land Act of 1851. It requires all rancheros to submit proof, within two years, that their land was given to them by the Spanish or Mexican governments. Often the land grants are not well documented so lawyers and courts find it easy to detect some flaw in the titles. Many Californios have already lost part or all of their ranchos. Others don't realize that their ranchos are in danger.

The court's deadline is approaching. I have too much business to handle by myself. It cannot wait. I need your help. Please join me in San Francisco. I anxiously await you.

Sincerely,
Your Partner,
Manuel Torres Vargas

After I finished reading him the letter, we sat in stunned silence. . . .

"I'm leaving here as soon as I'm able. Will you sell me a mule? I have gold. I'll pay you twice what it is worth. That should satisfy its owner. Please?"

"Yes, señor. And I'll sell you the food you will need. Tomorrow I must be on my way. There are miners waiting for supplies."

Responding to the Literature

1. How did Mateo find Señor Sosa?
2. Why did Mateo wait to read the letter to Señor Sosa?
3. **Synthesize** Use the word *scurvy* in a sentence that shows its meaning. You may define scurvy, use it as an example, or compare or contrast it. CA 8RW1.3
4. **Infer** What country were Mateo and Señor Sosa originally citizens of? Give examples from the selection of how the author established this fact. CA 8RC2.0
5. **Read to Write** This excerpt contains one of the subplots in *Thunder on the Sierra*. Describe the subplot. What is the conflict? Is the conflict resolved? Explain. What new conflict does the letter raise? CA 8RL3.2

Reading On Your Own...

Do you want to learn more about Andrew Jackson and the new groups of people who became part of the United States? You might be interested in the following books.

Biography

Andrew Jackson: Frontier President by Nancy Whitelaw describes the life of this colorful frontiersman who became president. She includes his two terms as president and his many firsts in that position. ***The content of this book is related to*** *History–Social Science Standard US8.4.*

Nonfiction

Black Potatoes: The Story of the Great Irish Famine, 1845–1850 by Susan Campbell Bartoletti leads readers through five years of failed potato crops in Ireland. The story of millions of Irish dying and emigrating is told in first-person accounts, news reports, and sketches. ***The content of this book is related to*** *History–Social Science Standard US8.6.*

Nonfiction

In the Days of the Vaqueros: America's First True Cowboys by Russell Freedman tracks the origins of the cowboy back to Spanish Mexico in the 1500s. Freedman describes the equipment and techniques that they developed, their migration to California, and the debt that American settlers owed the vaqueros. ***The content of this book is related to*** *History–Social Science Standard US8.8.*

Historical Fiction

The Journal of Wong Ming-Chung by Laurence Yep recounts the experiences of a Chinese immigrant, nicknamed "Runt," and his uncle during the California Gold Rush. When it becomes clear that there is no Golden Mountain, they develop other ingenious ways to find opportunity in the United States. ***The content of this book is related to*** *History–Social Science Standard US8.8.*

Analyzing Primary Sources

US8.8 Students analyze the divergent paths of the American people in the West from 1800 to the mid-1800s and the challenges they faced.

Going to War With Mexico

The war with Mexico (1846–1848) was supported by President James K. Polk and those who believed in Manifest Destiny. This war was fought to settle the border dispute between the United States and Mexico after Texas declared independence from Mexico. When the Mexican War was over, the United States had gained the vast California and New Mexico territories.

Read the passages on pages 514 and 515 and answer the questions that follow.

Mormons heading west in Conestoga wagon trains ▶

Reader's Dictionary

forbearance (fawr • BAR • uhns): patience, tolerance, or self control

vindicate (VIHN • duh • KAYT): to free from blame or guilt

declivity (dih • KLIHV • uht • ee): a descending slope

lauded (LAWD • ihd): celebrated

extolled (ihk • STOHLD): praised highly

Declaration of War With Mexico

On May 9, 1846, after several Americans were killed by Mexican troops in the borderlands between Texas and Mexico, President James Polk declared to Congress that the United States and Mexico were at war.

The cup of **forbearance** had been exhausted even before the recent information from the frontier of the Del Norte. But now, after reiterated menaces, Mexico has passed the boundary of the United States, has invaded our territory and shed American blood upon the American soil. She has proclaimed that hostilities have commenced, and that the two nations are now at war.

As war exists, and, notwithstanding, all our efforts to avoid it, exists by the act of Mexico herself, we are called upon by every consideration of duty and patriotism to **vindicate** with decision the honor, the rights, and the interests of our country. . . .

The Oregon Trail

In The Oregon Trail, *historian Francis Parkman tells of his encounters during an 1845 journey through the West.*

When we came to the descent of the broad shallow valley . . . an unlooked for sight awaited us. The stream glistened at the bottom, and along its banks were pitched a multitude of tents, while hundreds of cattle were feeding over the meadows. Bodies of troops, both horse and foot, and long trains of wagons, with men, women, and children, were moving over the opposite ridge and descending the broad **declivity** before us. These were the

Mormon battalion in the service of government, together with a considerable number of Missouri Volunteers. The Mormons were to be paid off in California, and they were allowed to bring with them their families and property. . . . to found, it might be, a Mormon empire in California.

Petition for Justice

The Chinese immigrants who came to California during the Gold Rush suffered much prejudice and violence. Chinese merchant Pun Chi describes the discrimination in a petition for justice from Congress.

When your honorable government threw open the territory of California, the people of other lands were welcomed here to search for gold and to engage in trade. The shipmasters of your respected nation came over to our country, **lauded** the equality of your laws, **extolled** the beauty of your manners and customs, and made it known that your officers and people were extremely cordial toward the Chinese. . . . we trusted in your sincerity. Not deterred by the long voyage, we came here presuming that our arrival would be hailed with cordiality and favor. But, alas! what times are these! —when former kind relations are forgotten, when we Chinese are viewed like thieves and enemies, when in the administration of justice our testimony is not received, when in the legal collection of the licenses we are injured and plundered, and villains of other nations are encouraged to rob and do violence to us! Our numberless wrongs it is most painful even to recite.

▲ Engraving of Chinese miners in California

DBQ Document-Based Questions

Declaration of War With Mexico

1. Who does Polk blame for causing the war?
2. Why does Polk believe the United States should go to war with Mexico?

The Oregon Trail

3. What does Parkman see in the valley that is so surprising?
4. Who was working for the government?

Petition for Justice

5. According to Pun Chi, how did Chinese immigrants expect to be treated in America?
6. What injustices were being committed against the Chinese in California?

Read to Write

7. Suppose the United States still had much unsettled western land, with no claims on it and little government or population. Imagine that you are preparing to move to this new territory. Write a letter to your family explaining your reasons and your plans. Use references to the primary sources you just read. CA HI1. CA 8WA2.1

Assessment

Standard US8.8

Review Content Vocabulary

Use the following vocabulary terms to create a newspaper article in which you describe events in the Southwest during this era.

1. emigrant
2. *Tejano*
3. *empresario*
4. ranchero
5. forty-niner

Review the Main Ideas

Section 1 • Westward to the Pacific

6. What agreement did the United States and Great Britain reach about the Oregon Territory?
7. What was Manifest Destiny?

Section 2 • Independence for Texas

8. Who was Stephen Austin? What was his role in early Texas history?
9. What was the outcome of the Battle of San Jacinto?

Section 3 • War With Mexico

10. Some Americans believed that annexing California would benefit national security. Why?
11. Identify the two main causes of the United States's war with Mexico.

Section 4 • New Settlers in California and Utah

12. What started the California Gold Rush?
13. Why did Mormons emigrate to Utah?

Critical Thinking

14. **Determining Cause and Effect** How did economic troubles in the East affect settlement in the Oregon area? CA HI2.
15. **Conclude** How did the war with Mexico change the U.S. border and its land holdings? CA CS3.
16. **Drawing Conclusions** How do you think the government of Mexico reacted to the American idea of Manifest Destiny? CA HR5.
17. **Compare** How did the negotiations between the United States and Britain over the Oregon Territory differ from those between the United States and Mexico over the Southwest? CA HI2.

Geography Skills

Study the routes of the western trails shown on the map. Then answer the questions that follow. CA CS3.

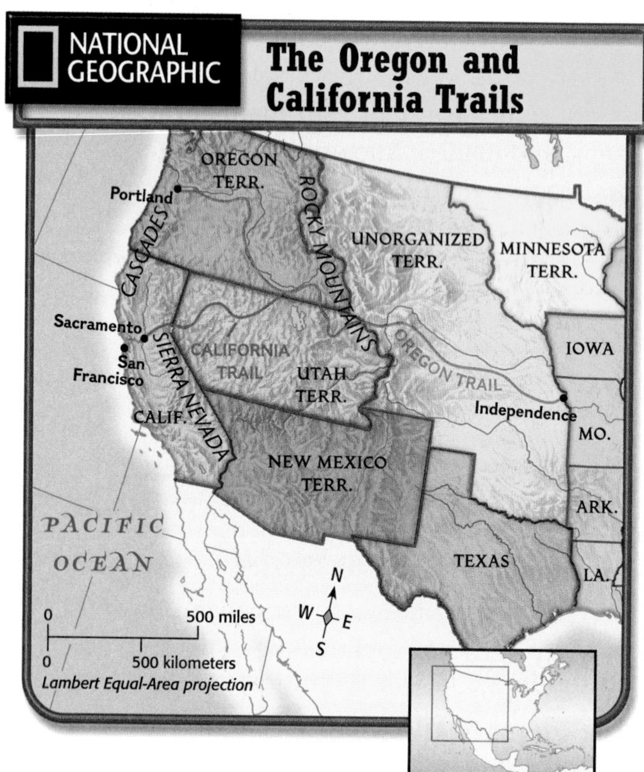

18. **Region** Which mountains did settlers have to cross to reach Oregon's Pacific coast? California's Pacific coast?
19. **Location** In what city did the Oregon Trail begin? In what city did it end?

History Online
Self-Check Quiz Visit ca.hss.glencoe.com to prepare for the Chapter 11 test.

Read to Write

20. The Big Ideas **Evaluate** How did immigration impact the economy and society of Texas, California, and Utah? Write an essay summarizing your conclusions. CA 8WS1.1

21. **Using Your FOLDABLES** Manifest Destiny was a term first used by a reporter in 1845. Was he introducing a new concept for Americans or describing something that settlers had believed since colonial times? Does Manifest Destiny have any modern forms? Explain your conclusions in a short essay. CA 8WA2.4 CA HI3.

Academic Vocabulary

Choose an academic vocabulary word to complete each sentence.

a. range
b. access
c. route
d. vision

22. The United States government was eager to have ___ to the Pacific Ocean.

23. Political leaders had a clear ___ of Manifest Destiny and pursued acquiring new territory for Americans to settle.

Building Citizenship

24. **Analyze** According to the Constitution of the United States, what steps need to be taken in order for new states to enter the Union? Why was Texas admitted by a joint resolution of the Senate rather than by treaty? Explain. CA HI2.

Reviewing Skills

25. Review READING SKILL **New Vocabulary** Write definitions for the words *emigrant* and *immigrant*. Clearly explain what each term means. Then use each of these words in a sentence. CA 8RW1.0

26.  ANALYSIS SKILL **Predicting** Write a paragraph predicting how Manifest Destiny will affect relationships with Native Americans. CA HI2.

Standards Practice

Select the best answer for the following questions.

27 The discovery of gold in California led to which of the following?

A discovery of gold in the Black Hills of the Dakotas
B increased western expansion and foreign immigration
C annexation of California as a slave state
D war with Mexico over the independence of California

28 The Mormons immigrated to the West to

A mine for gold.
B settle Texas.
C escape further religious persecution.
D purchase California from Mexico.

29 Some Northern leaders opposed admitting Texas to the United States because

A Texas was part of Mexico.
B they feared Texas would become a slave state.
C Texans did not want to join the Union.
D they feared Texas would become a free state.

The Young Republic

Between 1800 and 1860, the United States grew stronger as it expanded to the Pacific Ocean. At the same time, the North, the South, and the West developed sectional differences that would affect the country's future.

	Chapter 8 The Northeast: Building Industry	Chapter 9 The South	Chapter 10 The Age of Jackson	Chapter 11 Manifest Destiny
When	• 1790–1850	• 1820–1860	• 1815–1848	• 1819–1858
Where	• New England • the South • the West • New York • the North	• the South • Upper South • Deep South	• the South • the Northeast • Georgia • Alabama • Mississippi • Florida • Indian Territory	• Oregon Country • Texas • Mexico • New Mexico Territory • California • Utah

▲ *The textile mills in Lowell, Massachusetts, employed many young women.*

◀ *Goblet showing Andrew Jackson's log cabin*

	Chapter 8 The Northeast: Building Industry	Chapter 9 The South	Chapter 10 The Age of Jackson	Chapter 11 Manifest Destiny
Major Events	• c.1800 Industrial Revolution • 1807 Steamboat *Clermont* • c. 1820s on Changes in art and literature • 1825 Erie Canal • 1840s–1860s Millions of new immigrants • 1848 Seneca Falls Convention	• 1793 Cotton gin • 1808 End of importing slaves • 1830–1860 More severe slave codes • 1831 Nat Turner's rebellion • 1840s Tredegar Iron Works is a leading iron producer • 1860 South has only one-third of nation's rail lines • 1860 New Orleans has 168,000 people	• 1820s Expansion of voting rights • 1830 Webster-Hayne Debate • 1830 Indian Removal Act • 1832 Nullification Act • 1832 Veto of National Bank • 1835–1842 Seminole wars • 1837 Panic of 1837 • 1838 Trail of Tears	• 1830–1840s American settlers in Oregon • 1835–1836 Texas War for Independence • 1845 Texas statehood • 1846–1847 Mexican War • 1846 Bear Flag Republic • 1846 Mormons migrate to Utah • 1848 California gold rush • 1853 Gadsden Purchase
Some Important People	• Samuel Slater • Francis Cabot Lowell • Robert Fulton • Horace Mann • Henry David Thoreau • Henry Wadsworth Longfellow • Elizabeth Cady Stanton • Susan B. Anthony	• Eli Whitney • William Gregg • Joseph Reid Anderson • Nat Turner • Harriet Tubman • Frederick Douglass	• Andrew Jackson • Henry Clay • John Q. Adams • John C. Calhoun • Daniel Webster • Black Hawk • Osceola • Martin Van Buren	• William Henry Harrison • John Q. Adams • James Polk • Henry Clay • Stephen Austin • Santa Anna • Sam Houston • John Frémont • Zachary Taylor • Joseph Smith • Brigham Young
How do these events and ideas affect our lives today?	• The United States began to emerge as an industrial giant during this period.	• The heritage of discrimination and unequal rights created by slavery still poses problems today.	• Many Native Americans still live on reservations.	• The United States grew from coast to coast during this period.
What was happening in California at this time?	• 1820s Beginning of rancho economy • 1834 Break up of missions starts	• 1846 Bear Flag Revolt	• 1848 Territorial transfer to U.S. • 1848 Discovery of gold	• 1850 California statehood • 1851 Land Law of 1851

◀ *Erie Canal barrel*

◀ *Harriet Tubman*

◀ *Gold nuggets*

Unit 5

Civil War and Reconstruction

Why It's Important

Because of the issue of slavery, relations between the North and the South grew more hostile. Soon the two sides met in the most horrible war the country had ever seen. With the North's victory slavery was ended, but the reunited nation faced key issues that would take many decades to reconcile.

- While the North and South had made several compromises on slavery over the years, the issue eventually split the country.
- The Civil War and Reconstruction freed the slaves, but issues related to civil rights and equal opportunity still exist today.

1820 | 1840

U.S. EVENTS

1820 Congress passes Missouri Compromise

1850 Congress passes Compromise of 1850

Dred Scott ▶

1857 Supreme Court announces *Dred Scott* decision

CALIFORNIA EVENTS

1824 Chumash Indians revolt at California missions

1846 Bear Flag revolt takes place

1850 California is admitted to Union as a free state

WORLD EVENTS

1848 *The Communist Manifesto* is published

1853 Commodore Perry arrives in Japan

Commodore Perry ▶

NATIONAL GEOGRAPHIC

Where in the United States?

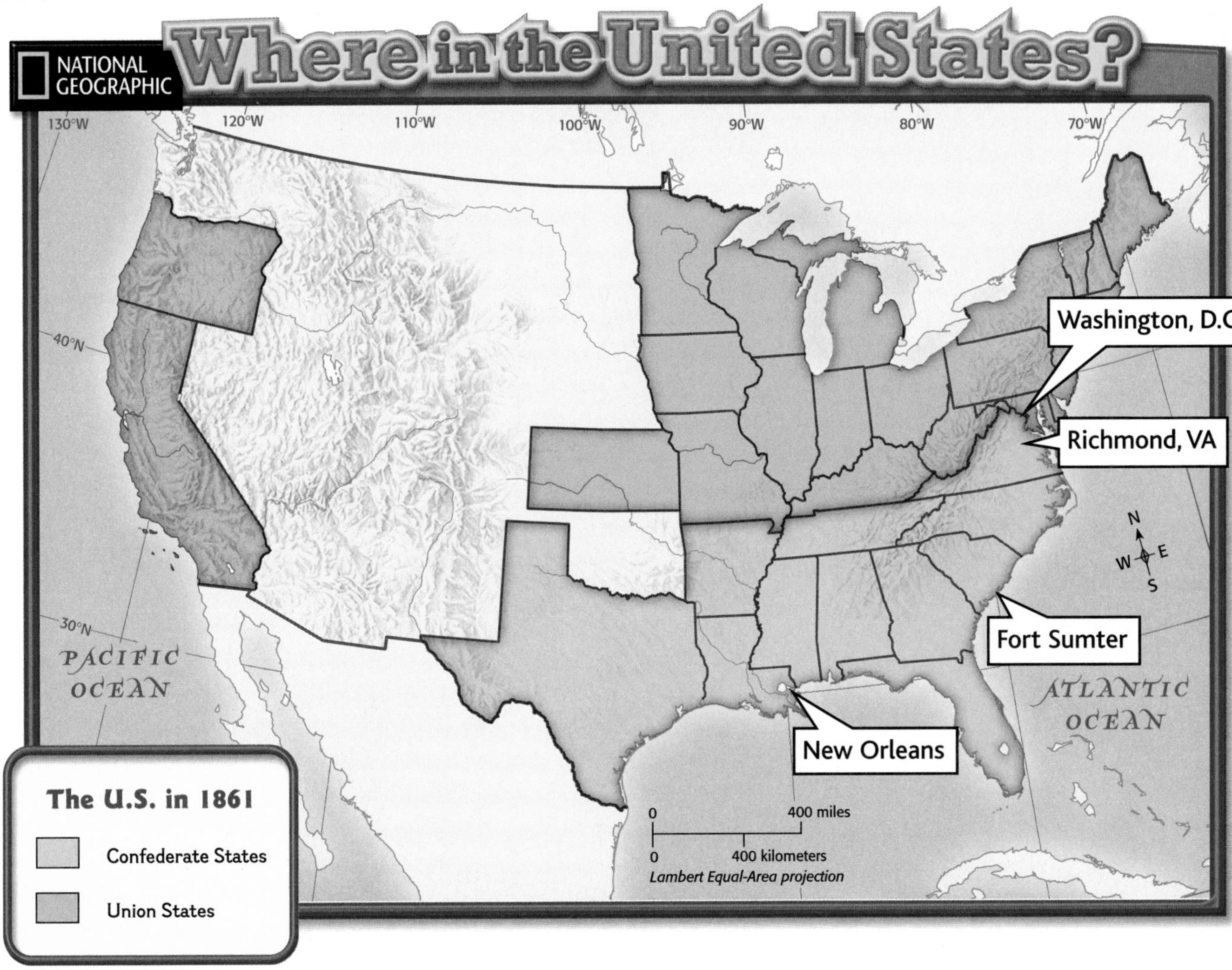

130°W 120°W 110°W 100°W 90°W 80°W 70°W

40°N

30°N

PACIFIC OCEAN

ATLANTIC OCEAN

Washington, D.C.

Richmond, VA

Fort Sumter

New Orleans

N W E S

0 400 miles
0 400 kilometers
Lambert Equal-Area projection

The U.S. in 1861

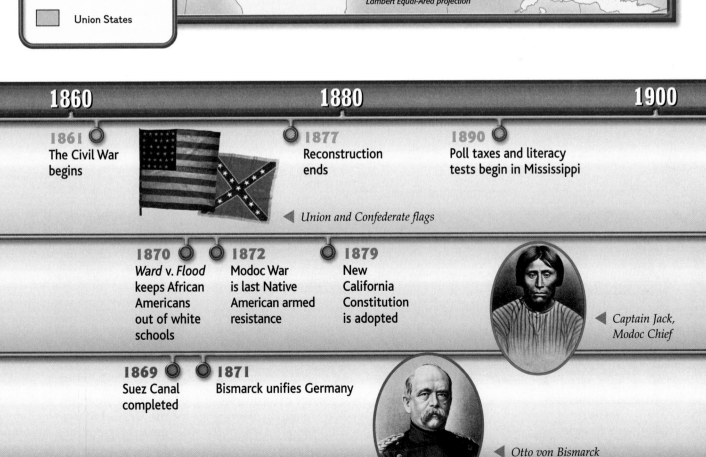

Confederate States

Union States

1860 1880 1900

1861 The Civil War begins

Union and Confederate flags

1877 Reconstruction ends

1890 Poll taxes and literacy tests begin in Mississippi

1870 *Ward* v. *Flood* keeps African Americans out of white schools

1872 Modoc War is last Native American armed resistance

1879 New California Constitution is adopted

Captain Jack, Modoc Chief

1869 Suez Canal completed

1871 Bismarck unifies Germany

Otto von Bismarck

Unit 5

Places to Locate

FORT SUMTER

See *Road to Civil War*
Chapter 12

GETTYSBURG

See *The Civil War*
Chapter 13

People to Meet

Frederick Douglass
c. 1817–1895
African American leader
Chapter 12, page 532

Sojourner Truth
c. 1797–1883
African American leader
Chapter 12, page 532

Dred Scott
c. 1800–1857
Subject of Supreme Court case on slavery
Chapter 12, page 549

Abraham Lincoln
1809–1865
Sixteenth president of the United States
Chapter 12, page 552

NATIONAL GEOGRAPHIC

3 Appomattox Court House

See *The Civil War* Chapter 13

4 Ford's Theater

See *Reconstruction* Chapter 14

Ulysses S. Grant
1822–1885
Union general
Chapter 13, page 611

Robert E. Lee
1807–1870
Confederate general
Chapter 13, page 611

Clara Barton
1821–1912
Civil War nurse
Chapter 13, page 601

Andrew Johnson
1808–1875
Seventeenth president of the United States
Chapter 14, page 628

Road to Civil War

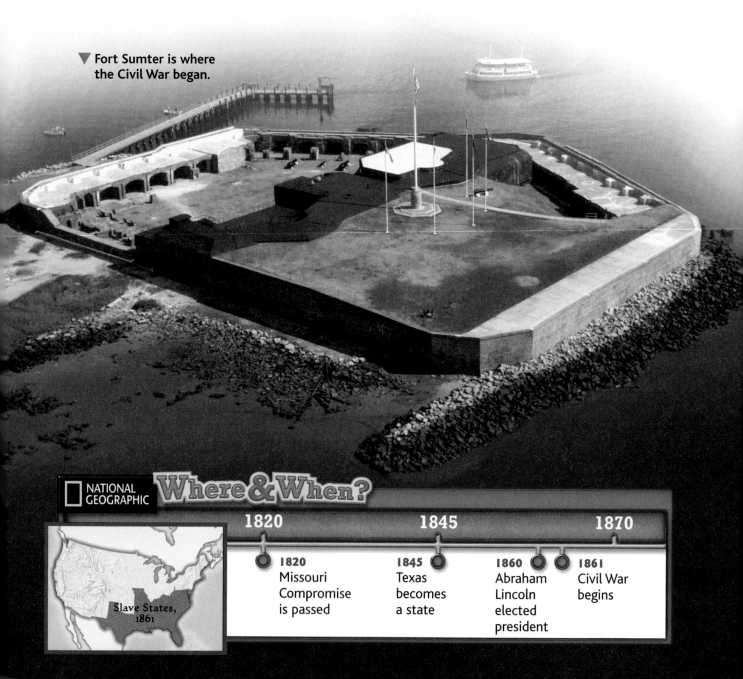

▼ Fort Sumter is where the Civil War began.

NATIONAL GEOGRAPHIC

Where & When?

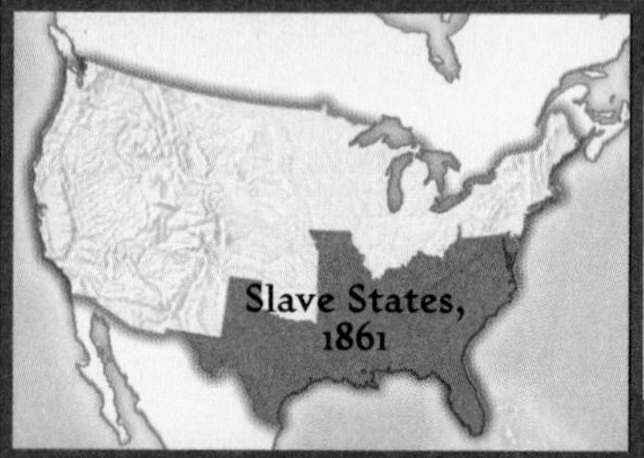

1820 — 1845 — 1870

1820 Missouri Compromise is passed

1845 Texas becomes a state

1860 Abraham Lincoln elected president

1861 Civil War begins

History Online
Chapter Overview Visit ca.hss.glencoe.com for a preview of Chapter 12.

The Big Ideas

Abolitionists

Reactions to social injustice can lead to reform movements. Many reformers turned their attention to eliminating slavery.

Slavery and the West

Differences in economic, political, and social beliefs and practices can lead to division within a nation and have lasting consequences. The question of whether to admit new states as free states or slave states arose.

A Nation Dividing

Differences in economic, political, and social beliefs and practices can lead to division within a nation and have lasting consequences. Growing tensions over slavery eventually led to violence in the new territories.

Challenges to Slavery

Conflict often brings about great change. A new antislavery party and a Supreme Court decision divided the nation further on slavery.

Secession and War

Conflict often brings about great change. In response to Lincoln's election as president, most Southern states left the Union.

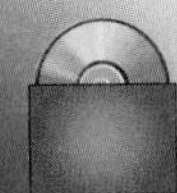

View the Chapter 12 video in the Glencoe Video Program.

Sequencing Events Make and use this foldable to sequence some of the key events that led to the Civil War.

Step 1 Fold a sheet of paper in half from side to side, leaving a $\frac{1}{2}$ inch tab along the side.

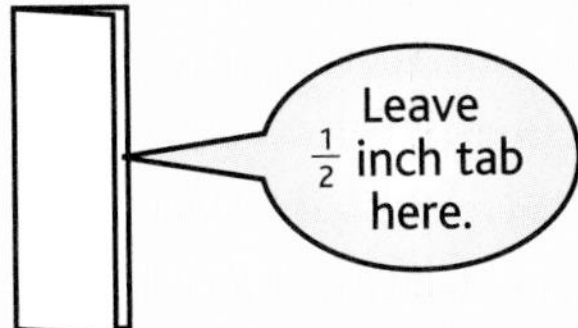

Step 2 Cut the top flap to make 5 tabs.

Step 3 Label your foldable as shown.

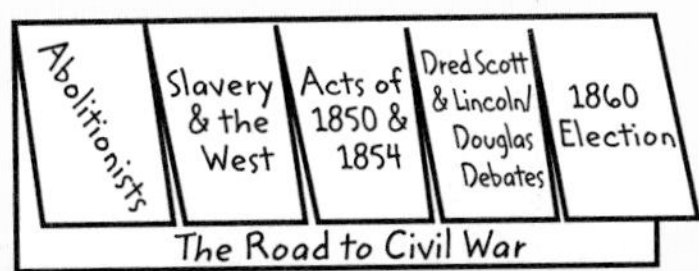

Reading and Writing
As you read, write facts about the events under each appropriate tab of your foldable. How did these events lead to the Civil War?

Get Ready to Read

Making Inferences

READING SKILL

1 Learn It!

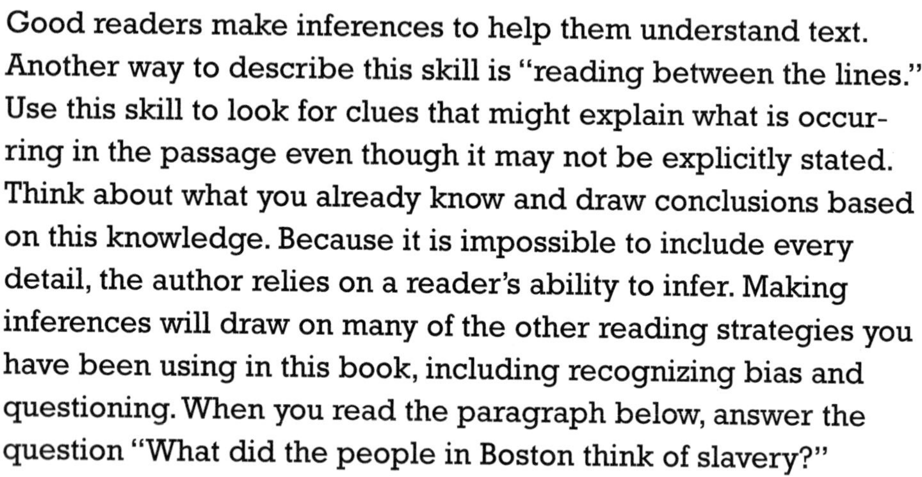

Good readers make inferences to help them understand text. Another way to describe this skill is "reading between the lines." Use this skill to look for clues that might explain what is occurring in the passage even though it may not be explicitly stated. Think about what you already know and draw conclusions based on this knowledge. Because it is impossible to include every detail, the author relies on a reader's ability to infer. Making inferences will draw on many of the other reading strategies you have been using in this book, including recognizing bias and questioning. When you read the paragraph below, answer the question "What did the people in Boston think of slavery?"

> On May 24, 1854, the people of Boston erupted in outrage. Federal officers had seized Anthony Burns, a runaway slave who lived in Boston, to send him back to slavery. Abolitionists tried to rescue Burns from the federal courthouse, and city leaders attempted to buy his freedom. All efforts failed. . . . In a gesture of bitter protest, Bostonians draped buildings in black and hung the American flag upside down.
>
> —*from page 533*

Reading Tip

As you read, ask yourself "What facts or information does the author expect me to already know about this topic?"

2 Practice It!

With a partner, discuss these questions to make more inferences from the passage about Anthony Burns. Be sure to discuss why this account may have been included by the author.

- What was the opinion of the Boston public? The city leaders?
- What message did they want to send to the federal government?
- A flag flown upside down is a naval distress signal. Why did they choose this signal?
- The issue of slavery divided Americans in the 1850s. What are some issues today that divide Americans? What distinguishes a divisive issue from one that can be solved through compromise?

Read to Write

Can you rewrite the passage about Anthony Burns from his perspective? Use the same facts but convey a different impression.

THE
BOSTON SLAVE RIOT,
AND
TRIAL
OF
Anthony Burns,

CONTAINING THE
REPORT OF THE FANEUIL HALL MEETING; THE MURDER OF BACHELDER; THEODORE PARKER'S LESSON FOR THE DAY; SPEECHES OF COUNSEL ON BOTH SIDES, CORRECTED BY THEMSELVES; VERBATIM REPORT OF JUDGE LORING'S DECISION; AND, A DETAILED ACCOUNT OF THE EMBARKATION.

BOSTON:
FETRIDGE AND COMPANY.
1854.

Press of J. S. Potter & Co., 1 Spring Lane and 120 Washington Street.

Pamphlet, 1854

3 Apply It!

As you read this chapter, practice your skill at making inferences by making connections and asking questions. Try to think about the information "between the lines."

Section 1

Abolitionists

Guide to Reading

History Social Science Standards

US8.9 Students analyze the early and steady attempts to abolish slavery and to realize the ideals of the Declaration of Independence.

Looking Back, Looking Ahead

You learned earlier that slave labor was important to the South. You will now read about how groups and individuals worked to end slavery and to free individual enslaved people.

Focusing on the Main Ideas

- By the early 1800s, a growing number of Americans had begun to demand an immediate end to slavery in the South. *(page 529)*
- The issue of slavery became the most pressing social issue for reformers, beginning in the 1830s. *(page 530)*
- Abolitionists established a network of routes and risked their lives to help African Americans escape slavery. *(page 533)*

Meeting People

William Lloyd Garrison
Sarah and Angelina Grimké
David Walker
Frederick Douglass
Sojourner Truth

Content Vocabulary

abolitionist (A • buh • LIH • shuhn • ihst)
Underground Railroad (UHN • duhr • GROWND RAYUHL • ROHD)

Academic Vocabulary

notion (NOH • shuhn)
publication (PUH • bluh • KAY • shuhn)

Reading Strategy

Organizing Information Create a diagram like the one below. As you read the section, identify five abolitionists. Below each name, write a sentence describing his or her role in the movement.

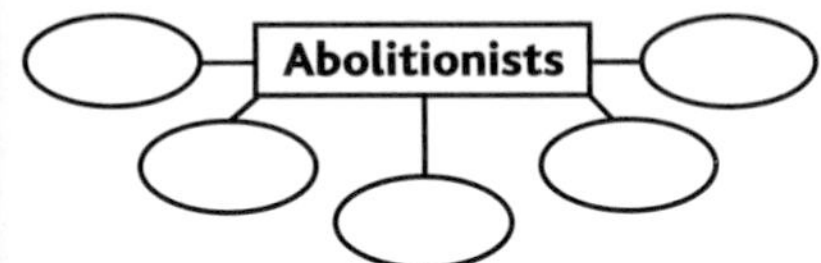
Abolitionists

Where & When?

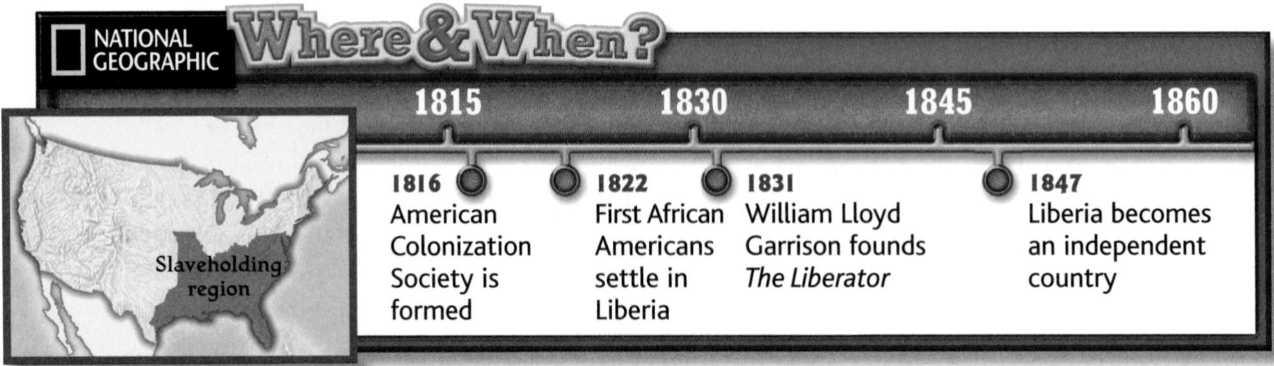
NATIONAL GEOGRAPHIC
Slaveholding region
1815
1830
1845
1860
1816 American Colonization Society is formed
1822 First African Americans settle in Liberia
1831 William Lloyd Garrison founds The Liberator
1847 Liberia becomes an independent country

US8.9 Students analyze the early and steady attempts to abolish slavery and to realize the ideals of the Declaration of Independence.

Early Efforts to End Slavery

Main Idea **By the early 1800s, a growing number of Americans had begun to demand an immediate end to slavery in the South.**

Reading Connection Can you think of an issue that caused disagreement in your family or group of friends? Read to learn how divisive the issue of slavery was to the nation.

An American Story

William Lloyd Garrison, a dramatic and spirited man, fought strongly for the right of African Americans to be free. On one occasion, Garrison was present when Frederick Douglass, an African American who had escaped from slavery, spoke to a white audience about life as a slave. Douglass electrified his listeners with a powerful speech. Suddenly, Garrison leaped to his feet. "Is this a man," he demanded of the audience, "or a thing?" Garrison shared Douglass's outrage at the **notion** that people could be bought and sold like objects.

The spirit of reform that swept the United States in the early 1800s was not limited to improving education and expanding the arts. It also included the efforts of **abolitionists** (A • buh • LIH • shuhn • ihsts) like Garrison and Douglass—members of the growing band of reformers who worked to abolish, or end, slavery.

Even before the American Revolution, some Americans had tried to limit or end slavery. At the Constitutional Convention in 1787, the delegates had reached a compromise on the difficult issue, agreeing to let each state decide whether to allow slavery. By the early 1800s, Northern states had ended slavery, but it continued in the South.

The religious revival and the reform movement of the early and mid-1800s gave new life to the antislavery movement. Many Americans came to believe that slavery was wrong. Yet not all Northerners shared this view. The conflict over slavery continued to build.

Many of the men and women who led the antislavery movement came from the Quaker faith. One Quaker, Benjamin Lundy, wrote:

> **"I heard the wail of the captive; I felt his pang of distress, and the iron entered my soul."**
>
> —from *Historical Collections of Ohio*

Lundy founded a newspaper in 1821 to spread the abolitionist message.

American Colonization Society The first large-scale antislavery effort was aimed at resettling African Americans in Africa or the Caribbean. The American Colonization Society, formed in 1816 by a group of white Virginians, attempted to free enslaved workers gradually by buying them from slaveholders and sending them abroad to start new lives.

The society raised enough money from private donors, Congress, and a few state legislatures to send several groups of African Americans out of the country. Some went to the west coast of Africa, where the society had acquired land for a colony. In 1822 the first African American settlers arrived in this colony, called Liberia, Latin for "place of freedom."

In 1847 Liberia became an independent country. American emigration to Liberia continued until the Civil War. Some 12,000 to 20,000 African Americans settled in the new country between 1822 and 1865.

The American Colonization Society did not halt the growth of slavery. The number of enslaved people continued to increase at a steady pace, and the society could only resettle a small number of African Americans. Furthermore, most African Americans regarded the United States as their home and were not prepared to migrate to another continent. Many were from families that had lived in America for several generations. They simply wanted to be free in American society.

Reading Check **Explain** How did the American Colonization Society fight slavery?

US8.9.1 Describe the leaders of the movement (e.g., John Quincy Adams and his proposed constitutional amendment; John Brown and the armed resistance, Harriet Tubman and the Underground Railroad, Benjamin Franklin, Theodore Weld, William Lloyd Garrison, Frederick Douglass).

The New Abolitionists

Main Idea **The issue of slavery became the most pressing social issue for reformers, beginning in the 1830s.**

Reading Connection Think of a person or a leader whom you admire. Does he or she stand up for others? Read to learn how abolitionists worked to end slavery.

The Movement Changes Reformers realized that the gradual approach to ending slavery had failed. Moreover, the numbers of enslaved persons had sharply increased because the cotton boom in the Deep South made planters increasingly dependent on slave labor. Beginning in about 1830, the American antislavery movement took on new life. Soon it became the most pressing social issue for reformers.

Picturing **History**

In 1831 William Lloyd Garrison began publishing a newspaper called *The Liberator.* ***What was Garrison's position regarding slavery?***

William Lloyd Garrison An abolitionist named **William Lloyd Garrison** stimulated the growth of the antislavery movement. In 1829 Garrison left Massachusetts to work for the country's leading antislavery newspaper in Baltimore. Impatient with the paper's moderate position, Garrison returned to Boston in 1831 to found his own newspaper, *The Liberator.*

Garrison was one of the first white abolitionists to call for the "immediate and complete emancipation [freeing]" of enslaved people. In the first issue of his paper, he wrote: "I will not retreat a single inch—AND I WILL BE HEARD."

Garrison *was* heard. He attracted enough followers to start the New England Anti-Slavery Society in 1832 and the American Anti-Slavery Society the next year. The abolitionist movement grew rapidly. By 1838 the antislavery societies Garrison started had more than 1,000 chapters, or local branches.

The Grimké Sisters Among the first women who spoke out publicly against slavery were **Sarah and Angelina Grimké.** Born in South Carolina to a wealthy slaveholding family, the sisters moved to Philadelphia in 1832.

In the North, the Grimké sisters lectured and wrote against slavery. At one antislavery meeting, Angelina Grimké exclaimed:

> **"As a Southerner, I feel that it is my duty to stand up . . . against slavery. I have seen it—I have seen it."**
>
> **—Angelina Grimké, lecture, 1838**

The Grimkés persuaded their mother to give them their share of the family inheritance. Instead of money or land, the sisters asked for several of the enslaved workers, whom they immediately freed.

The Grimkés and Angelina's husband, abolitionist Theodore Weld, wrote *American Slavery As It Is* in 1839. This collection of firsthand accounts of life under slavery was an influential abolitionist **publication,** selling more than 100,000 copies in its first year.

African American Abolitionists White abolitionists drew public attention to the cause, but African Americans played a major role in the abolitionist movement from the start. The abolition of slavery was an especially important goal to the free African Americans of the North.

Many African Americans in the North lived in poverty in cities. Although they were excluded from most jobs and were often attacked by white mobs, a great many of these African Americans were intensely proud of their freedom and wanted to help those who were still enslaved.

African Americans took an active part in organizing and directing the American Anti-Slavery Society, and they subscribed in large numbers to William Lloyd Garrison's *The Liberator.* In 1827 Samuel Cornish and John Russwurm started the country's first African American newspaper, *Freedom's Journal.* Most of the other newspapers that African Americans founded before the Civil War also promoted abolition.

Born a free man in North Carolina, writer **David Walker** of Boston published an impassioned argument against slavery, challenging African Americans to rebel and overthrow slavery by force. "America is more our country than it is the whites'—we have enriched it with our blood and tears," he wrote.

In 1830 free African American leaders held their first convention in Philadelphia. Delegates met "to devise ways and means for the bettering of our condition." They discussed starting an African American college and encouraging free African Americans to emigrate to Canada.

Primary Sources

Abolishing Slavery

While serving in the House of Representatives, former President John Quincy Adams battled slavery. In 1839 he proposed a constitutional amendment that provided for the abolition of slavery. Its three provisions follow.

John Quincy Adams

1st From and after the 4th of July, 1842, there shall be, throughout the United States, no hereditary slavery;
but on and after that day every child born within the United States, their Territories or jurisdiction, shall be born free.

2d. With the exception of the Territory of Florida, there shall henceforth never be admitted into this Union any State, the constitution of which shall tolerate within the same the existence of slavery.

3d. From and after the 4th of July, 1845, there shall be neither slavery nor slave trade at the seat of Government of the United States.

DBQ Document-Based Questions

1. How would each part of the amendment bring about the end of slavery?
2. Was Adams providing for its immediate or gradual end? Why do you think he chose this method?

Frederick Douglass **Frederick Douglass,** the most widely known African American abolitionist, was born enslaved in Maryland. After teaching himself to read and write, he escaped from slavery in Maryland in 1838 and settled first in Massachusetts and then in New York.

As a runaway, Douglass could have been captured and returned to slavery. Still, he joined the Massachusetts Anti-Slavery Society and traveled widely to address abolitionist meetings. A powerful speaker, Douglass often moved listeners to tears with his message. At an Independence Day gathering, he told the audience:

> **"What, to the American slave, is your [Fourth] of July? I answer; a day that reveals to him, more than all other days in the year, the gross injustice and cruelty to which he is the constant victim. To him, your celebration is a sham . . . your national greatness, swelling vanity; your sounds of rejoicing are empty and heartless . . . your shouts of liberty and equality, hollow mockery."**
>
> —from *Frederick Douglass: Selected Speeches and Writings*

For 16 years, Douglass edited an antislavery newspaper called the *North Star.* Douglass won admiration as a powerful and influential speaker and writer. He traveled abroad, speaking to huge antislavery audiences in London and the West Indies.

Douglass returned to the United States because he believed abolitionists must fight slavery at its source. He insisted that African Americans receive not only their freedom but full equality with whites as well. In 1847 friends helped Douglass purchase his freedom from the slaveholder in Maryland from whom he had fled.

Sojourner Truth "I was born a slave in Ulster County, New York," Isabella Baumfree began when she told her story to audiences. Called

Picturing **History**

Sojourner Truth learned about abolition in 1843 when she was preaching in Massachusetts. ***How did Sojourner Truth get and keep her freedom?***

"Belle," she lived in the cellar of a slaveholder's house. She escaped in 1826 and gained official freedom in 1827 when New York banned slavery. Quaker friends then helped her recover one son who had been sold as a slave. She eventually settled in New York City with her two youngest children. She supported her family by doing domestic work. During this time, she began preaching in the streets.

In 1843 Belle chose a new name. "**Sojourner Truth** is my name," she said, "because from this day I will walk in the light of [God's] truth." She dedicated her life to the movements for abolition and for women's rights.

Reading Check **Explain** Why did Frederick Douglass return to the United States?

US8.9.1 Describe the leaders of the movement (e.g., John Quincy Adams and his proposed constitutional amendment; John Brown and the armed resistance, Harriet Tubman and the Underground Railroad, Benjamin Franklin, Theodore Weld, William Lloyd Garrison, Frederick Douglass).

The Underground Railroad

Main Idea **Abolitionists established a network of routes and risked their lives to help African Americans escape slavery.**

Reading Connection Can you think of an example in recent times when people fled to avoid oppression? Read and find out about the Underground Railroad.

An American Story

On May 24, 1854, the people of Boston erupted in outrage. Federal officers had seized Anthony Burns, a runaway slave who lived in Boston, to send him back to slavery. Abolitionists tried to rescue Burns from the federal courthouse, and city leaders attempted to buy his freedom. All efforts failed. Local militia units joined the marines and cavalry in Boston to keep order. Federal troops escorted Burns to a ship that would carry him back to Virginia and slavery. In a gesture of bitter protest, Bostonians draped buildings in black and hung the American flag upside down.

The Fugitive Slave Act The Fugitive Slave Act of 1850 required all citizens to help catch runaways. Anyone who aided a fugitive could be fined or imprisoned. People in the South believed the law would force Northerners to recognize the rights of Southerners. Instead, enforcement of the law led to mounting anger in the North, convincing more people of the evils of slavery. After passage of the Fugitive Slave Act, slaveholders stepped up efforts to catch runaway slaves.

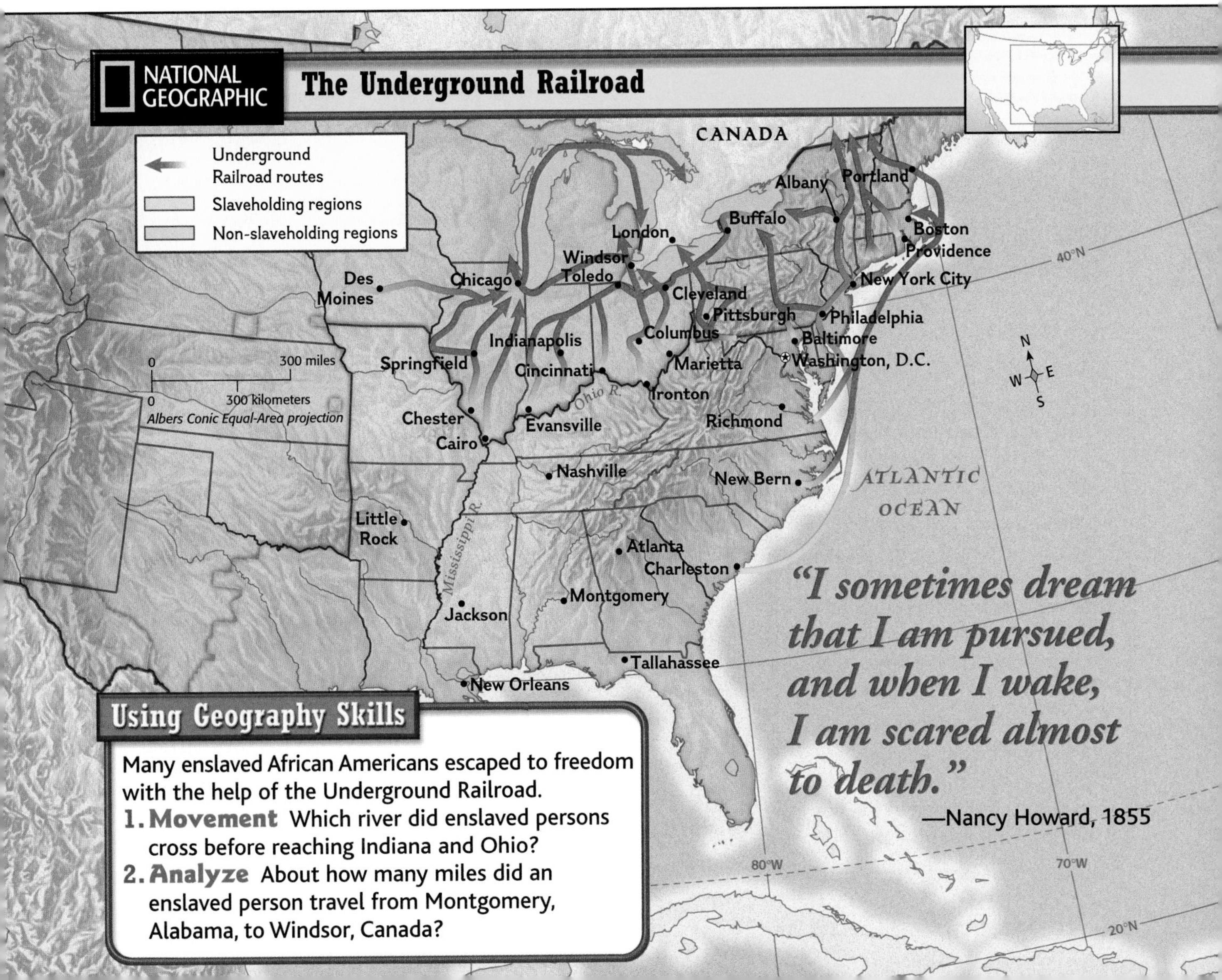

NATIONAL GEOGRAPHIC

The Underground Railroad

Underground Railroad routes
Slaveholding regions
Non-slaveholding regions

0 300 miles
0 300 kilometers
Albers Conic Equal-Area projection

CANADA
ATLANTIC OCEAN
Des Moines
Chicago
Springfield
Chester
Cairo
Indianapolis
Cincinnati
Evansville
Windsor
Toledo
London
Cleveland
Columbus
Marietta
Ironton
Pittsburgh
Buffalo
Albany
Portland
Boston
Providence
New York City
Philadelphia
Baltimore
Washington, D.C.
Richmond
New Bern
Nashville
Little Rock
Atlanta
Charleston
Montgomery
Jackson
Tallahassee
New Orleans
Ohio R.
Mississippi R.
40°N
80°W
70°W
20°N
N
W
E
S

Using Geography Skills

Many enslaved African Americans escaped to freedom with the help of the Underground Railroad.

1. **Movement** Which river did enslaved persons cross before reaching Indiana and Ohio?
2. **Analyze** About how many miles did an enslaved person travel from Montgomery, Alabama, to Windsor, Canada?

"I sometimes dream that I am pursued, and when I wake, I am scared almost to death."

—Nancy Howard, 1855

Slaveholders even tried to capture runaways who had lived in freedom in the North for years. Sometimes they seized African Americans who were not escaped slaves and forced them into slavery.

Resistance to the Law In spite of the penalties, many Northerners refused to cooperate with the law's enforcement. The **Underground Railroad,** a network of free African Americans and whites, helped runaways make their way to freedom. Antislavery groups tried to rescue African Americans who were being pursued or to free those who were captured. In Boston, members of one such group followed federal agents shouting, "Slave hunters—there go the slave hunters." People contributed funds to buy the freedom of African Americans. Northern juries refused to convict those accused of breaking the Fugitive Slave Law.

Harriet Tubman Born as a slave in Maryland, Harriet Tubman worked in plantation fields until she was nearly 30 years old. Then she made her break for freedom, escaping to the North with the help of the Underground Railroad. Settling in Philadelphia, Tubman met many abolitionists who shared her desire to bring Southern slaves to the North. Realizing the risks of being captured, Tubman courageously made 19 trips back into the South during the 1850s to help other enslaved people escape. Altogether she assisted about 70 individuals—including her parents—to escape from slavery. Tubman became the most successful conductor on the Underground Railroad. She was known as the "Moses of her people" for leading slaves to freedom in the North.

Reading Check **Identify** What was the Underground Railroad?

History Online
Study Central Need help understanding abolitionism? Visit ca.hss.glencoe.com and click on Study Central.

Reading Summary

Review the Main Ideas

- In the early 1800s, one major antislavery movement worked to resettle freed slaves in the country of Liberia in Africa.
- The antislavery movement became stronger in the 1830s, spurred on by a number of abolitionists, both white, such as William Lloyd Garrison and the Grimké sisters, and African American, such as Frederick Douglass and Sojourner Truth.
- Abolitionists helped runaway slaves escape, but many others in both the North and the South opposed abolition.

What Did You Learn?

1. Describe the American Colonization Society's solution to slavery.
2. How did William Lloyd Garrison help the abolitionist movement?

Critical Thinking

3. **Organizing Information** Use a diagram like the one below to identify actions that abolitionists took to free enslaved people. CA CS1.

4. **The Big Ideas** What role did Harriet Tubman play in the antislavery movement? CA HI1.
5. **Compare** How did the goals and strategies of the American Colonization Society differ from those of the abolitionist movement? CA HR5.
6. **Reading Making Inferences** Reread the primary source quotes from this section. Write a paragraph that makes inferences to describe each person's views of slavery. CA 8RC2.0

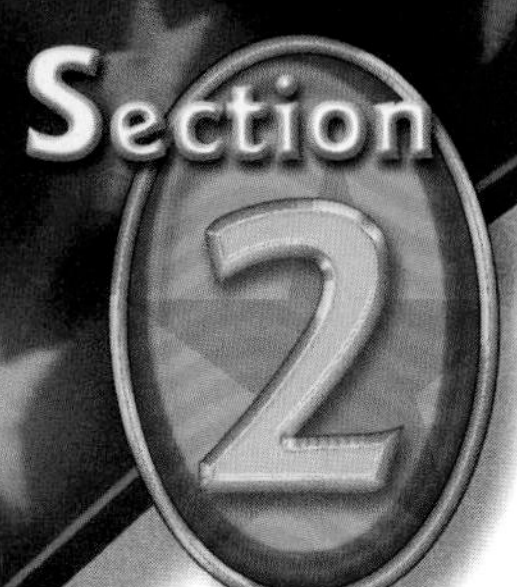
Section
2

Slavery and the West

Guide to Reading

Looking Back, Looking Ahead

As you know, abolitionists tried to end slavery. At the same time, the possible spread of slavery into the West was an issue that repeatedly divided the nation.

Focusing on the Main Ideas

- The Missouri Compromise helped resolve the issue of whether new states would be slave states or free states. *(page 536)*
- The Kentucky Resolution first advanced the doctrine of nullification. *(page 537)*
- In the 1840s, the issue of slavery in new territories was once again at the forefront. *(page 539)*
- Henry Clay presented a plan to settle the slavery debate that resulted in the Compromise of 1850. *(page 541)*

Meeting People

James K. Polk
Millard Fillmore
Stephen A. Douglas

Content Vocabulary

sectionalism (SEHK • shnuh • LIH • zuhm)
nullify (NUH • luh • FY)
protective tariff (pruh • TEHK • tihv TAR • uhf)
fugitive (FYOO • juh • tihv)
secede (sih • SEED)
abstain (uhb • STAYN)

Academic Vocabulary

debate
controversy (KAHN • truh • VUHR • see)
collapse

Reading Strategy

Organizing Information As you read the section, describe how these compromises dealt with the admission of new states.

Admission of New States	
The Missouri Compromise	The Compromise of 1850

History Social Science Standards

US8.9 Students analyze the early and steady attempts to abolish slavery and to realize the ideals of the Declaration of Independence.

US8.10 Students analyze the multiple causes, key events, and complex consequences of the Civil War.

NATIONAL GEOGRAPHIC
Where & When?
Free states and territories, 1850
Washington, D.C.
California admitted 1850
1820
1840
1860
1820 Missouri Compromise is passed
1845 Texas becomes a state
1848 Free-Soil Party nominates Van Buren
1850 Compromise of 1850 diverts war

US8.9.5 Analyze the significance of the States' Rights Doctrine, the Missouri Compromise (1820), the Wilmot Proviso (1846), the Compromise of 1850, Henry Clay's role in the Missouri Compromise and the Compromise of 1850, the Kansas-Nebraska Act (1854), the *Dred Scott* v. *Sandford* decision (1857), and the Lincoln-Douglas debates (1858).

The Missouri Compromise

Main Idea **The Missouri Compromise helped resolve the issue of whether new states would be slave states or free states.**

Reading Connection Do you compete with a nearby school in sports or another activity? If so, you probably feel loyalty to the school you attend. Read to learn how in the early 1800s, differences between the North and South led to sectionalism, which is loyalty to a particular region.

An American Story

"The deed is done. The . . . chains of slavery are forged for [many] yet unborn. Humble yourselves in the dust, ye high-minded citizens of Connecticut. Let your cheeks be red as crimson. On *your* representatives rests the stigma of this foul disgrace." These biting, fiery words were published in a Connecticut newspaper in 1820. They were in response to members of Congress who had helped pave the way for the admission of Missouri as a slaveholding state.

What Is Sectionalism? The request by slaveholding Missouri to join the Union in 1819 caused an angry debate that worried former president Thomas Jefferson and Secretary of State John Quincy Adams. Jefferson called the dispute "a fire-bell in the night" that "awakened and filled me with terror." Adams accurately predicted that the bitter **debate** was "a mere preamble—a title-page to a great tragic volume."

"I know no South, no North, no East, no West, to which I owe any allegiance."

–Henry Clay

Many Missouri settlers had brought enslaved African Americans into the territory with them. By 1819 the Missouri Territory included about 50,000 whites and 10,000 slaves. When Missouri applied to Congress for admission as a state, its constitution allowed slavery.

In 1819 eleven states permitted slavery and eleven did not. The Senate—with two members from each state—was therefore evenly balanced between slave and free states. The admission of a new state would upset that balance.

In addition the North and the South, with their different economic systems, were competing for new lands in the western territories. At the same time, a growing number of Northerners wanted to restrict or ban slavery. Southerners, even those who disliked slavery, opposed these antislavery efforts. They resented the interference by outsiders in Southerners' affairs. These differences between the North and the South grew into **sectionalism** (SEHK • shnuh • LIH • zuhm)—an exaggerated loyalty to a particular region of the country.

Clay's Proposal The Senate suggested a way to resolve the crisis by allowing Missouri's admittance as a slave state while simultaneously admitting Maine as a free state. Maine, formerly part of Massachusetts, had also applied for admission to the Union. The Senate also sought to settle the issue of slavery in the territories for good. It proposed prohibiting slavery in the remainder of the Louisiana Purchase north of 36°30'N latitude.

Speaker of the House Henry Clay of Kentucky skillfully maneuvered the Senate bill to passage in 1820 by dividing it into three proposals. The Missouri Compromise preserved the balance between slave and free states in the Senate and quieted the bitter debate in Congress over slavery. However, this would not last.

Reading Check **Explain** How did sectionalism contribute to the ongoing debate about the admission of states?

US8.10.1 Compare the conflicting interpretations of state and federal authority as emphasized in the speeches and writings of statesmen such as Daniel Webster and John C. Calhoun US8.10.3 Identify the constitutional issues posed by the doctrine of nullification and secession and the earliest origins of that doctrine.

Nullification

Main Idea **The Kentucky Resolution first advanced the doctrine of nullification.**

Reading Connection Have you ever wanted to overturn a decision that you thought was unfair? Read to learn how nullification legally permitted states to overturn unconstitutional laws.

Southerners argued that states could **nullify** (NUH•luh•FY), or legally overturn, federal laws that they considered unconstitutional. The issue of nullification arose again and again in the nation's early history.

Virginia and Kentucky Resolutions Nullification was first expressed in the Virginia and Kentucky Resolutions of 1798–1799. These resolutions, written by Thomas Jefferson and James Madison, declared that the Federalists' Alien and Sedition laws were unconstitutional. *(See page 295-96.)* Jefferson and Madison used the ideas of John Locke and the Tenth Amendment to the Constitution to argue that the federal government had been formed by a contract among the states. The federal government possessed only certain powers. Whenever a state decided that the federal government passed a law that went beyond these powers, the state had the right to nullify the law.

What Was the Hartford Convention? The issue of nullification reappeared during the War of 1812, this time among Federalists in New England. Many New Englanders opposed the war. One reason was that many people there made their living by trade, which was greatly hurt when the war began. Many Federalists also believed that Republicans in the South and West brought about the war. Delegates from the New England states revived the idea of nullification and proposed amendments to the Constitution at a meeting called the Hartford Convention. *(See page 359.)* The Federalists made no progress with their demands, and with the end of the war, the power of the Federalist party declined.

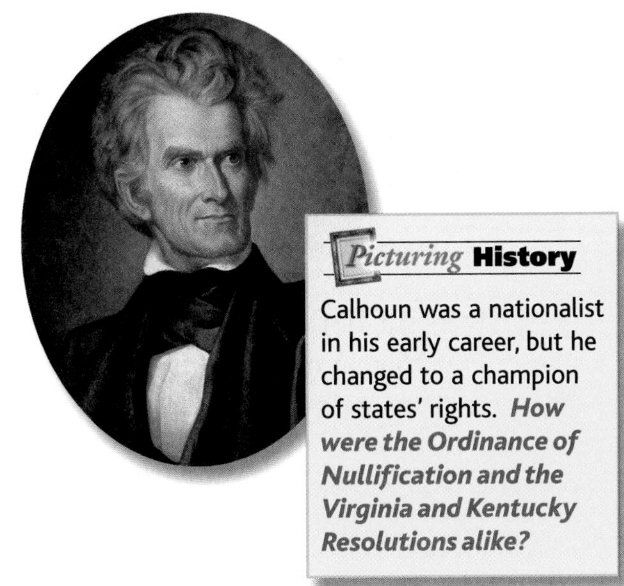

Picturing **History**

Calhoun was a nationalist in his early career, but he changed to a champion of states' rights. ***How were the Ordinance of Nullification and the Virginia and Kentucky Resolutions alike?***

The Tariff Controversy The nullification **controversy** arose again in the 1820s and 1830s, this time over the issue of protective tariffs. **Protective tariffs** (pruh•TEHK•tihv TAR•uhfs) are taxes that are placed on goods that come from another country. Protective tariffs raise the price of goods from other countries. A tax on imported shoes, for example, makes American-made shoes more attractive to consumers.

By the 1820s, most Southerners had become convinced that protective tariffs were harmful to the South. Although such tariffs helped the young industries of the North, they also raised the prices of manufactured goods purchased in the South. People in the South felt that it was unjust for them to bear the expense for the development of another region of the country.

Ordinance of Nullification When Congress passed the tariff of 1828, John C. Calhoun of South Carolina argued that the tariff was "unconstitutional, oppressive, and unjust." Calhoun based his argument on the ideas that Jefferson and Madison had used in defending the Virginia and Kentucky Resolutions. In 1832 Congress passed a new tariff law. Although the tax rates were lower than those of 1828, they were still high. South Carolina called a special convention that voted for an Ordinance of Nullification against the new tariff.

Calhoun had raised an important issue—the supremacy of the national government versus state sovereignty. The states' rights doctrine, first found in the Virginia and Kentucky Resolutions, had taken a giant step toward secession. If states were sovereign, they had a right to secede from the Union.

Can a State Nullify a Law? Early in 1830, Calhoun's doctrine of nullification came before the United States Senate during a debate over land policy. People in the West were angry because of a bill that would limit the sale of western lands. Robert Y. Hayne of South Carolina argued that the western states could nullify the bill if it became law.

Daniel Webster of Massachusetts replied to Hayne. Webster denied that the Constitution was just a compact between the states, to be interpreted as each state chose. On the contrary, he said, only the Supreme Court could decide whether a law was constitutional. Webster argued that the federal government was sovereign, that the Union was perpetual, and that any attempt to dismember it was nothing less than treason. Webster closed with this ringing statement: "Liberty and Union, now and forever, one and inseparable."

In 1833 the nullification crisis was settled by a compromise. The tariff was lowered and, in response, South Carolina withdrew its Ordinance of Nullification. Both sides claimed victory, and the issue was laid to rest—at least temporarily.

Reading Check **Analyze** **Why did the South and the Northeast try to use nullification?**

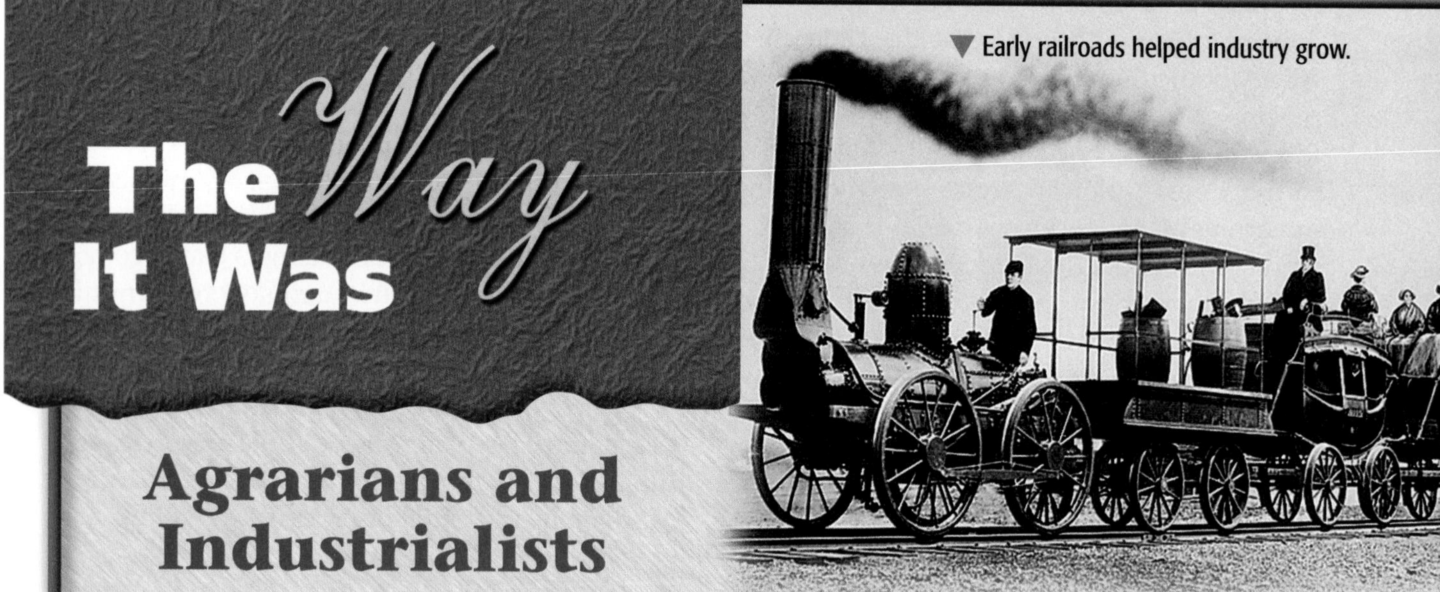

▼ Early railroads helped industry grow.

Agrarians and Industrialists

Sectionalism, the rivalry between one region and another, was based on economic and political interests. One rivalry that developed was between agrarians and industrialists.

Agrarianism

Thomas Jefferson believed that the strength of the United States was its independent farmers. His ideas are sometimes referred to as agrarianism. Jefferson argued that owning land enabled people to be independent. As long as most people owned their own land, they would fight to preserve the Republic.

Jefferson believed that too much of an emphasis on industry and trade would lead to a society that was divided between the rich who owned everything and the poor who worked for wages. He also believed that the wealthy would corrupt the government and threaten the rights and liberties of ordinary people.

US8.9.5 Analyze the significance of the States' Rights Doctrine, the Missouri Compromise (1820), the Wilmot Proviso (1846), the Compromise of 1850, Henry Clay's role in the Missouri Compromise and the Compromise of 1850, the Kansas-Nebraska Act (1854), the *Dred Scott* v. *Sandford* decision (1857), and the Lincoln-Douglas debates (1858).

New Western Lands

Main Idea **In the 1840s, the issue of slavery in new territories was once again at the forefront.**

Reading Connection Can you think of a debate you have been a part of that turned out to be difficult to resolve? Read to learn how Congress continued to struggle with a solution concerning slavery.

For the next 25 years, Congress avoided the issue of slavery's expansion. In the 1840s, however, this heated debate moved back into Congress. Again, the dispute was over slavery in new territories. The territories involved were Texas, which had won its independence from Mexico in 1836, and New Mexico and California, which were still part of Mexico.

Many Southerners hoped to see Texas, where slavery already existed, join the Union. As a result, the annexation of Texas became the main issue in the presidential election of 1844. Democrat **James K. Polk** of Tennessee won the election and pressed forward on acquiring Texas. Texas became a state in 1845. At the same time, support for taking over New Mexico and California also grew in the South. The federal government's actions on these lands led to war with Mexico.

Conflicting Views Just months after the war with Mexico began, Representative David Wilmot of Pennsylvania introduced a proposal in Congress. Called the Wilmot Proviso, it specified that slavery should be prohibited in any lands that might be acquired from Mexico.

During the 1800s, many Americans kept Jefferson's ideal of small, independent farming communities as the model society. Agrarians, particularly in the South, were alarmed at the changes that industrialization was producing in the nation's cities. They viewed independent farming as a way to escape degrading factory work and the unhealthy and overcrowded large cities.

Industrialism

The Industrial Revolution changed the Northeast from a region where families lived and worked together at farming, crafts, and home-based businesses to one in which people earned their livings by working for others in industry. Many Americans believed that manufacturing and trade were the basis of national wealth and power. They favored policies that would support these areas of the economy.

Although industrial growth caused problems, economic progress also made life easier in many ways. Improved transportation and mass production meant that more goods were available to more people. American living standards were surpassing those of European countries.

In the cities, people were beginning to enjoy new comforts and conveniences such as gas streetlights and better sewer systems. Some Americans came to believe that they were living in an age of progress. They expected that new inventions, along with America's abundant resources, would improve life for Americans and set an example for other countries of the world.

▼ Many Americans made their living by farming.

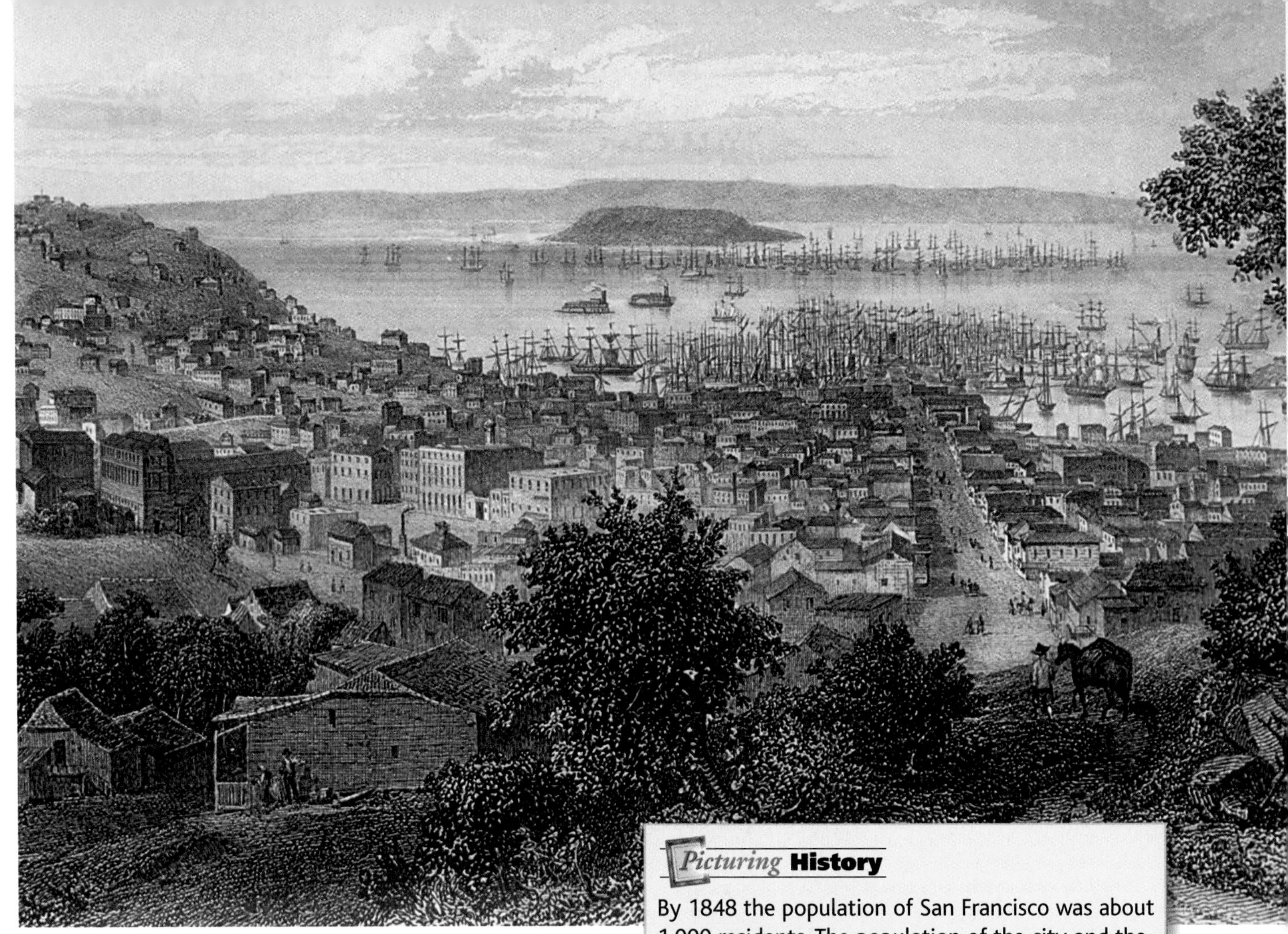

Picturing **History**

By 1848 the population of San Francisco was about 1,000 residents. The population of the city and the California territory would grow greatly during the gold rush. ***What issue during the presidential election campaign of 1848 involved California?***

Southerners protested furiously. They wanted to keep open the possibility of introducing slavery to California and New Mexico. Senator John C. Calhoun of South Carolina countered Wilmot's proposal with another. It stated that neither Congress nor any territorial government had the authority to ban slavery from a territory or regulate it in any way.

Neither Wilmot's nor Calhoun's proposal passed, but both caused bitter debate. By the time of the 1848 presidential election, the United States had acquired the territories of California and New Mexico from Mexico but had taken no action on the issue of slavery in those areas.

The Free-Soil Party The debate over slavery led to the formation of a new political party. In 1848 the Whigs chose Zachary Taylor, a Southerner and a hero of the war with Mexico, as their presidential candidate. The Democrats selected Senator Lewis Cass of Michigan. Neither candidate took a stand on slavery in the territories. They were both afraid of losing votes.

This failure to take a position angered voters. Many antislavery Democrats and Whigs left their parties and joined with members of the old Liberty Party to form the Free-Soil Party. The new party proclaimed "Free Soil, Free Speech, Free Labor, and Free Men," and endorsed the Wilmot Proviso. The party nominated former president Martin Van Buren as its presidential candidate.

Whig candidate Zachary Taylor won the election, receiving 163 electoral votes to 127 for Cass. The Whig's strategy of maintaining neutrality helped them win the election. Van Buren failed to receive a single electoral vote, and captured only 14 percent of the popular vote in the North. However, several candidates of the Free-Soil Party won seats in Congress.

Reading Check **Explain** How was John C. Calhoun's proposal different from the Wilmot Proviso?

The slavery supporters destroyed the town, burned the hotel and the home of the governor, and tore down two newspaper offices. Soon after, forces opposed to slavery retaliated.

"Bleeding Kansas" **John Brown,** a fervent abolitionist, believed God had chosen him to end slavery. When he heard of the attack on Lawrence, Brown went into a rage. He vowed to "strike terror in the hearts of the proslavery people." One night, Brown led four of his sons and two other men along Pottawatomie Creek, where they seized and killed five supporters of slavery.

More violence followed as armed bands roamed the territory. Newspapers began referring to "Bleeding Kansas" and "the Civil War in Kansas." A **civil war** is a conflict between citizens of the same country. Not until October of 1856 did John Geary, the newly appointed territorial governor, stop the bloodshed in Kansas. Geary ordered 1,300 federal troops to suppress the guerrilla forces.

Violence in Congress The violence that erupted in Kansas spilled over to the halls of the U.S. Congress as well. Abolitionist senator **Charles Sumner** of Massachusetts delivered a speech entitled "The Crime Against Kansas." Sumner lashed out against proslavery forces in Kansas. He also criticized proslavery senators, repeatedly attacking Andrew P. Butler of South Carolina.

Two days after the speech, Butler's distant cousin, Representative **Preston Brooks,** walked into the Senate chamber. He hit Sumner again and again over the head and shoulders with a cane. Sumner fell to the floor, unconscious and bleeding. He suffered injuries so severe that he did not return to the Senate for several years. The Brooks-Sumner incident and the fighting in "Bleeding Kansas" revealed the rising level of hostility between North and South.

Reading Check **Predict** Who do you predict will be the combatants if the United States is torn apart by Civil War?

History Online
Study Central Need help understanding the Kansas-Nebraska Act and its effects? Visit ca.hss.glencoe.com and click on Study Central.

Reading Summary

Review the Main Ideas

- The Kansas-Nebraska Act abandoned the provisions of the Missouri Compromise and put in place the doctrine of popular sovereignty to decide the issue of slavery in new territories.
- In Kansas antislavery and proslavery forces came into violent conflict.

What Did You Learn?

1. Who were the border ruffians?
2. How many cast votes in the Kansas elections? How did that compare with the population at the time?

Critical Thinking

3. **Organizing Information** Re-create the diagram below and list the steps that led to bloodshed in Kansas. CA CS1.

Step → Step → Step → Bloodshed in Kansas

4. **The Big Ideas** How did popular sovereignty lead to violence in Kansas? CA HI2.
5. **Predicting Consequences** Could the violence in Kansas have been prevented if Congress had not abandoned the Missouri Compromise? Explain. CA HR3.
6. **Persuasive Writing** Decide whether you would have been for or against the Kansas-Nebraska Act and the concept of popular sovereignty. Then write a newspaper editorial arguing your position. CA 8WA2.4

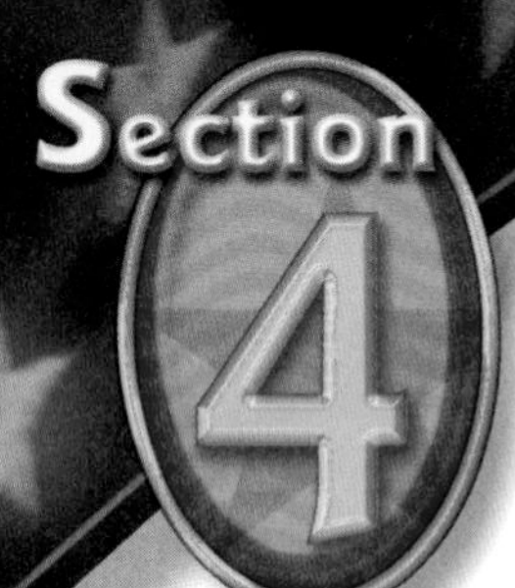
Section
4

Challenges to Slavery

Guide to Reading

Looking Back, Looking Ahead

You learned that the issue of slavery led to civil war in Kansas. You will next read about how slavery led to the founding of a new political party and additional bloodshed.

Focusing on the Main Ideas

- The Supreme Court's decision in the *Dred Scott* case resulted in even more division in the country. ***(page 549)***
- The Lincoln-Douglas debates helped Lincoln emerge as a leader. ***(page 552)***

Meeting People

John C. Frémont
James Buchanan
Dred Scott
Roger B. Taney (TAW•nee)
Abraham Lincoln

Content Vocabulary

arsenal (AHR•suhn•uhl)
martyr (MAHR•tuhr)

Academic Vocabulary

restrict
topic

Reading Strategy

Classifying Information As you read the section, re-create the diagram below and list major events that occurred in each year.

1846	1854	1856	1858

History Social Science Standards

US8.9 Students analyze the early and steady attempts to abolish slavery and to realize the ideals of the Declaration of Independence.

US8.10 Students analyze the multiple causes, key events, and complex consequences of the Civil War.

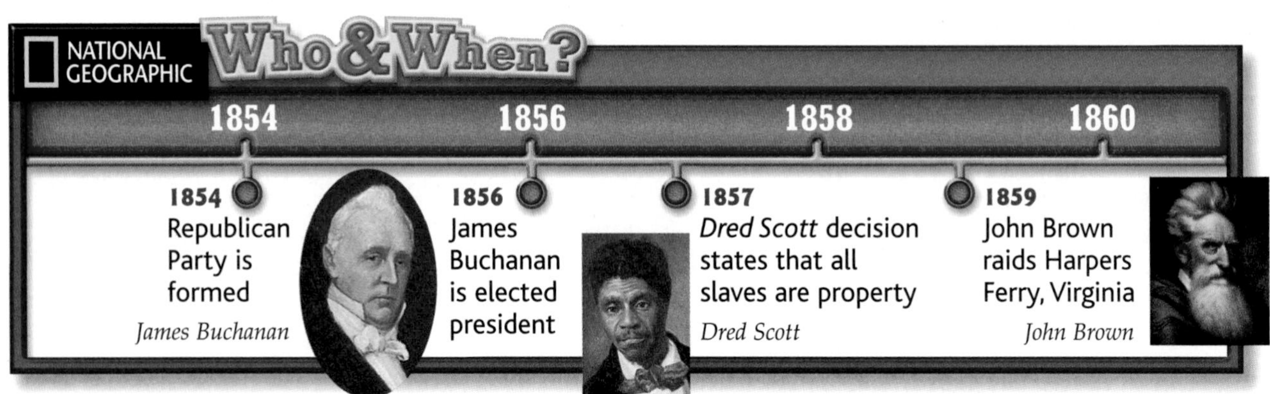
NATIONAL GEOGRAPHIC
Who & When?
1854
1856
1858
1860
1854
Republican Party is formed
James Buchanan
1856
James Buchanan is elected president
1857
Dred Scott decision states that all slaves are property
Dred Scott
1859
John Brown raids Harpers Ferry, Virginia
John Brown

US8.9.5 Analyze the significance of the States' Rights Doctrine, the Missouri Compromise (1820), the Wilmot Proviso (1846), the Compromise of 1850, Henry Clay's role in the Missouri Compromise and the Comprise of 1850, the Kansas-Nebraska Act (1854), the *Dred Scott* v. *Sandford* decision (1857), and the Lincoln-Douglas debates (1858).

The *Dred Scott* Decision

Main Idea **The Supreme Court's decision in the *Dred Scott* case resulted in even more division in the country.**

Reading Connection How would you feel if the Supreme Court decided that you were "property"? Read to find out how the decision in the *Dred Scott* case shocked the nation.

An American Story

Many people considered John Brown to be a radical murderer, but others viewed him as a fighter for the cause of freedom. When he was executed in 1859, a magazine published this imaginative account of Brown's exit from the jail,

> **"a black woman, with her little child in arms, stood near his way. . . . He stopped. . . and with the tenderness of one whose love is as broad as the brotherhood of man, kissed the child. . . ."**
>
> —from *The Anglo-African Magazine*

Why Was the Republican Party Founded?

Even before Brown's raid, other events had driven the North and South further apart. After the Kansas-Nebraska Act, the Democratic Party began to divide along sectional lines, with Northern Democrats leaving the party. Differing views over the slavery issue destroyed the Whig Party.

In 1854 antislavery Whigs and Democrats joined forces with Free-Soilers to form the Republican Party. The Republicans challenged the proslavery Whigs and Democrats, choosing candidates to run in the state and congressional elections of 1854. Their main message was that the government should ban slavery from new territories.

The Republican Party quickly showed its strength in the North. In the election, the Republicans won control of the House of Representatives and of several state governments. In the South, the Republicans had almost no support.

Almost three-fourths of the Democratic candidates from free states lost in 1854. The party was increasingly becoming a Southern party.

The Election of 1856 Democrats and Republicans met again in the presidential election of 1856. The Whig Party, disintegrating over the slavery issue, did not offer a candidate of its own.

The Republicans chose **John C. Frémont** of California as their candidate for president. Frémont had gained fame as an explorer in the West. The party platform called for free territories, and its campaign slogan became "Free soil, free speech, and Frémont."

The Democratic Party nominated **James Buchanan** of Pennsylvania, an experienced diplomat and former member of Congress. The party endorsed the idea of popular sovereignty.

The American Party, or Know-Nothings, had grown quickly between 1853 and 1856 by attacking immigrants. The Know-Nothings nominated former president Millard Fillmore.

The presidential vote divided along sectional lines. Buchanan won the election, winning all of the Southern states except Maryland, and received 174 electoral votes compared to 114 for Frémont and 8 for Fillmore. Frémont did not receive a single electoral vote south of the Mason-Dixon line, but he carried 11 of the 16 free states.

The *Dred Scott* Decision Until 1857 some slaves who had lived in free states or territories were successful when they sued for their freedom. Biddy Mason had done this in California. The case of another slave, Dred Scott, however, went all the way to the Supreme Court. On March 6, 1857, the Court announced a decision about slavery and the territories that shook the nation.

Dred Scott was an enslaved African American who was bought by an army doctor in Missouri, a slave state. In the 1830s, the doctor moved his household to Illinois, a free state, and then to the Wisconsin Territory, where slavery was banned by the Northwest Ordinance of 1787. Later the family returned to Missouri, where the doctor died.

In 1846 with the help of antislavery lawyers, Scott sued for his freedom. He claimed he should be free because he had once lived on free soil. Eleven years later, in the midst of growing anger over the slavery issue, the case reached the Supreme Court.

The Court's Decision The case attracted enormous attention. Although the immediate issue was Dred Scott's status, the Court also had the opportunity to rule on the question of slavery in territories. Many Americans hoped that the Court would resolve the issue for good.

The Court's decision electrified the nation. Chief Justice **Roger B. Taney** (TAW•nee) said that Dred Scott was still a slave. As a slave, Scott was not a citizen and had no right to bring a lawsuit. Taney could have stopped there, but he decided to address the broader issues.

Taney wrote that Scott's residence on free soil did not make him free. An enslaved person was property, and the Fifth Amendment prohibits Congress from taking away property without "due process of law."

Finally, Taney wrote that Congress had no power to prohibit slavery in any territory. The Missouri Compromise—which had banned slavery north of 36°30′N latitude—was unconstitutional. For that matter, so was popular sovereignty. Not even the voters in a territory could prohibit slavery because that would amount to taking away a person's property. In effect, the decision meant that the Constitution protected slavery. *(See page 846 of the Appendix for a summary of the* Dred Scott *decision.)*

Reaction to the Decision Rather than settling the issue, the Supreme Court's decision divided the country even more. Many Southerners were elated. The Court had reaffirmed what many in the South had always maintained: Nothing could legally prevent the spread of slavery. Northern Democrats were pleased that the Republicans' main issue—**restricting** the spread of slavery—had been ruled unconstitutional.

Republicans and other antislavery groups were outraged, calling the *Dred Scott* decision "the greatest crime" ever committed in the nation's courts.

Reading Check **Explain** How did the *Dred Scott* decision regulate the spread of slavery?

FRANK LESLIE'S ILLUSTRATED NEWSPAPER

Picturing **History**

Chief Justice Roger B. Taney (above right) delivered the Supreme Court's ruling in the *Dred Scott* case. The decision made Scott a topic for the nation's press. ***What impression of Scott's family do you get from the engravings shown here?***

Biography

US8.9.6 Describe the lives of free blacks and the laws that limited their freedom and economic opportunities.

Bridget Mason

1818–1891

Born a slave in 1818, Bridget Mason had worked on plantations in Georgia and Mississippi. In 1851 slaveholder Robert Smith moved his family and their 12 slaves to California. Among the slaves were Bridget —or Biddy as she was usually called—and her three children. Smith's plan to start a ranch and mine for gold did not work. In the autumn of 1855, Smith made plans to move to Texas.

Before Smith could leave, charges were filed against him for planning to move enslaved people from California, a free state, to Texas, a slave state. In court, Smith's attorney argued that Biddy and the other slaves had agreed to come to California and were willing to go to Texas.

Before Judge Benjamin Hayes issued his verdict, he wanted to hear how Biddy felt about moving to Texas. Biddy told the judge, "Mr. Smith told me I would be just as free in Texas as here." But she admitted she "always feared this trip to Texas since I first heard of it." In his decision, Hayes said that Biddy and the others were "entitled to their freedom and cannot be held in slavery or involuntary servitude . . . [they] are free forever."

"If you hold your hand closed, nothing good can come in. The open hand is blessed, for it gives in abundance, even as it receives."

—Bridget Mason

In 1856 when Biddy was declared free, she and her family decided to settle in Los Angeles. Biddy first worked as a servant, then was hired by Dr. John Strother Griffin to help care for his patients. Saving her money, she purchased her first home in 1866. Biddy soon bought and sold more property, making money during the mid-1870s when property in Los Angeles was in demand.

Biddy devoted her life to helping others. She helped form the First African Methodist Episcopal Church in 1872, visited jail inmates, and provided food and shelter for the poor. When floods struck the Los Angeles area in the 1880s, Biddy paid to feed the flood victims.

Then and Now

Read the quote above. Can you think of anyone today who lives by that motto? Explain.

US8.10.4 Discuss Abraham Lincoln's presidency and his significant writings and speeches and their relationship to the Declaration of Independence, such as his "House Divided" speech (1858), Gettysburg Address (1863), Emancipation Proclamation (1863), and inaugural addresses (1861 and 1865).

Lincoln and Douglas

Main Idea **The Lincoln-Douglas debates helped Lincoln emerge as a leader.**

Reading Connection If you really wanted something, what risks would you be willing to take? Read to learn how Lincoln, who was nearly unknown, challenged Douglas to a series of debates and emerged as a leader.

In the congressional election of 1858, the Senate race in Illinois was the center of national attention. The current senator, Democrat Stephen A. Douglas, ran against Republican challenger **Abraham Lincoln.** People considered Douglas a likely candidate for president in 1860. Lincoln was nearly an unknown.

Short and powerful, Douglas was called "the Little Giant." He disliked slavery but thought that the controversy over it would interfere with the nation's growth. He believed the issue could be resolved through popular sovereignty.

Born in the poor backcountry of Kentucky, Abraham Lincoln moved to Indiana as a child, and later to Illinois. Like Douglas, Lincoln was intelligent, ambitious, and a successful lawyer. Lincoln started his campaign with a memorable speech, in which he declared:

> **"A house divided against itself cannot stand. I believe this government cannot endure permanently half slave and half free. I do not expect the Union to be dissolved—I do not expect the house to fall—but I do expect it will cease to be divided. It will become all one thing or all the other."**

The Lincoln-Douglas Debates Not as well known as Douglas, Lincoln challenged the senator to a series of debates. Douglas reluctantly agreed. The two met seven times in August, September, and October of 1858 in towns throughout Illinois. Thousands came to these debates. The main **topic,** of course, was slavery.

During the debate at Freeport, Lincoln questioned Douglas about his views on popular sovereignty. Could the people of a territory legally exclude slavery before achieving statehood? Douglas replied that the people could exclude slavery by refusing to pass laws protecting slaveholders' rights. Douglas's response, which satisfied antislavery followers but lost him support in the South, became known as the Freeport Doctrine.

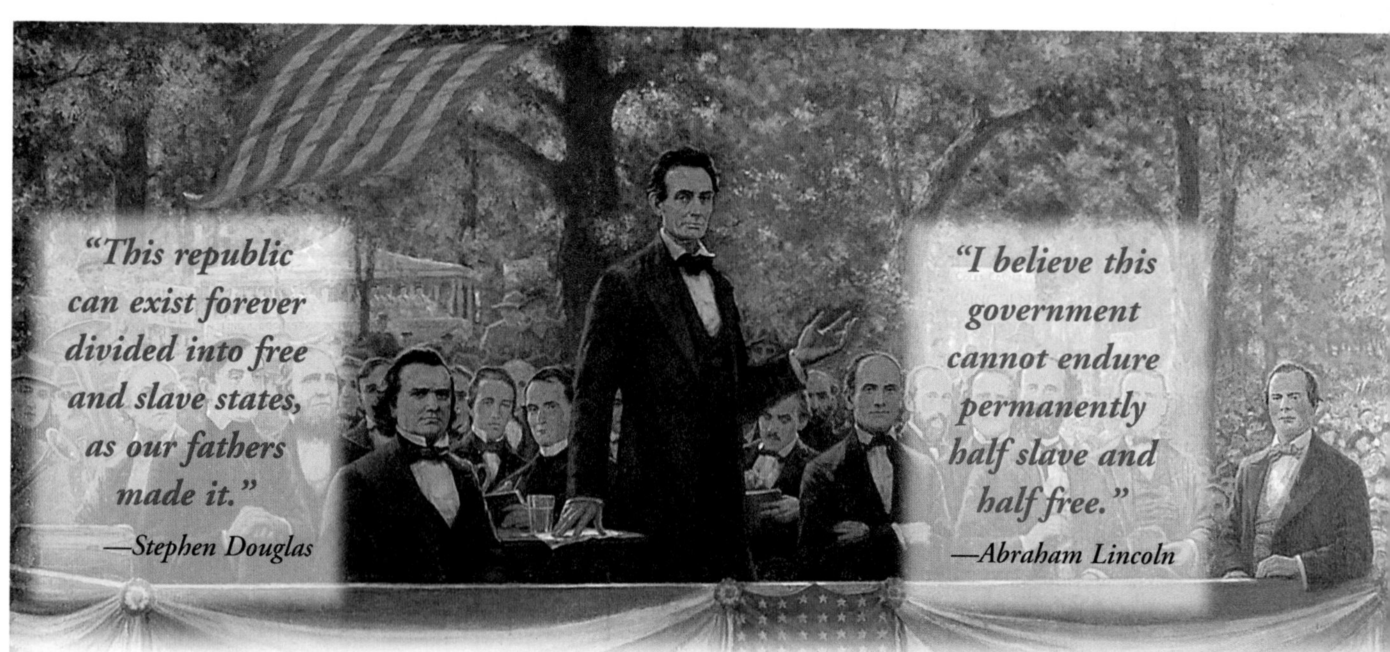

"This republic can exist forever divided into free and slave states, as our fathers made it."
—Stephen Douglas
"I believe this government cannot endure permanently half slave and half free."
—Abraham Lincoln

US8.9.5 Analyze the significance of the States' Rights Doctrine, the Missouri Compromise (1820), the Wilmot Proviso (1846), the Compromise of 1850, Henry Clay's role in the Missouri Compromise and the Compromise of 1850, the Kansas-Nebraska Act (1854), the *Dred Scott* v. *Sandford* decision (1857), and the Lincoln-Douglas debates (1858).

Douglas claimed that Lincoln wanted African Americans to be fully equal to whites. Lincoln denied this. Still, Lincoln said, "in the right to eat the bread . . . which his own hand earns, [an African American] is my equal and the equal of [Senator] Douglas, and the equal of every living man." The real issue, Lincoln said, is "between the men who think slavery a wrong and those who do not think it wrong. The Republican Party thinks it wrong."

Following the debates, Douglas won a narrow victory in the election. Lincoln lost the election, but the debates had earned him a national reputation.

The Raid on Harpers Ferry After the 1858 elections, Southerners began to feel threatened by growing Republican power. In late 1859, an act of violence greatly increased their fears. On October 16, the abolitionist John Brown led 18 men, both whites and African Americans, on a raid on Harpers Ferry, Virginia. His target was an **arsenal** (AHR•suhn•uhl), a storage place for weapons and ammunition. Brown—who had killed five proslavery Kansans in 1856—hoped to start a rebellion against slaveholders by arming enslaved African Americans. His raid was financed by a group of abolitionists.

Brown and his men were quickly defeated by local citizens and federal troops. Brown was convicted of treason and murder and was sentenced to hang. His execution caused an uproar in the North. Some antislavery Northerners, including Republican leaders, denounced Brown's use of violence. Others viewed Brown as a hero. Writer Ralph Waldo Emerson called Brown a **martyr** (MAHR•tuhr)—a person who dies for a cause he believes in.

John Brown's death became a rallying point for abolitionists. When Southerners learned of Brown's connection to abolitionists, their fears of a great Northern conspiracy against them seemed to be confirmed. The nation was nearing disaster.

Reading Check **Identify** What was John Brown's target when he led a raid on Harpers Ferry?

Study Central Need help understanding the nation's division on slavery? Visit ca.hss.glencoe.com and click on Study Central.

Reading Summary

Review the Main Ideas

- The Republican Party became a major political force, while the Supreme Court ruled in the *Dred Scott* case that the spread of slavery could not be restricted.
- Debates between Abraham Lincoln and Stephen Douglas helped put Lincoln in the national spotlight.

What Did You Learn?

1. Discuss the stages in the development of the Republican Party.
2. Who financed John Brown's raid on Harpers Ferry?

Critical Thinking

3. **Organizing Information** Re-create the table shown here, and describe the positions taken by Lincoln and Douglas in their debates. CA HI1.

Lincoln-Douglas Debates	
Lincoln's position	Douglas's position

4. **The Big Ideas** How did the *Dred Scott* decision reverse an earlier ruling made by Congress? CA HI2.
5. **Making Inferences** Why did Lincoln emerge as a leader after the Lincoln-Douglas debates? CA CS1.
6. **Descriptive Writing** Write a short biographical essay on either John Brown, Dred Scott, or Stephen Douglas. Include key events from the person's life that relate to events leading up to the Civil War. CA 8WA2.1.a

Secession and War

Guide to Reading

History Social Science Standards

US8.10 Students analyze the multiple causes, key events, and complex consequences of the Civil War.

Looking Back, Looking Ahead

As you know, the *Dred Scott* decision and John Brown's raid further divided the nation. Read to learn how the election of 1860 affected the possible disaster that faced the country.

Focusing on the Main Ideas

- A split occurred in the Democratic Party, which allowed Lincoln to win the election of 1860. *(page 555)*
- South Carolina led other Southern states in seceding from the Union. *(page 556)*
- The Civil War began when Confederate forces attacked Fort Sumter in South Carolina. *(page 558)*

Locating Places

South Carolina
Fort Sumter

Meeting People

John Crittenden
Jefferson Davis

Content Vocabulary

border states
secession (sih • SEH • shuhn)
states' rights

Academic Vocabulary

eventual (ih • VEHNT • shuh • wuhl)
justify
theory

Reading Strategy

Classifying Information As you read the section, re-create the time line below and list the major events at each time.

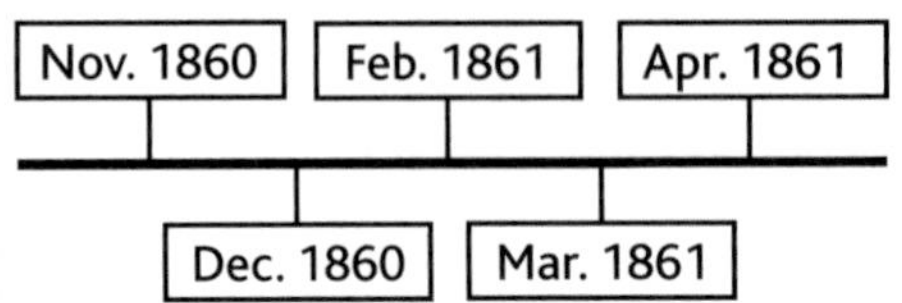

NATIONAL GEOGRAPHIC **Where & When?**

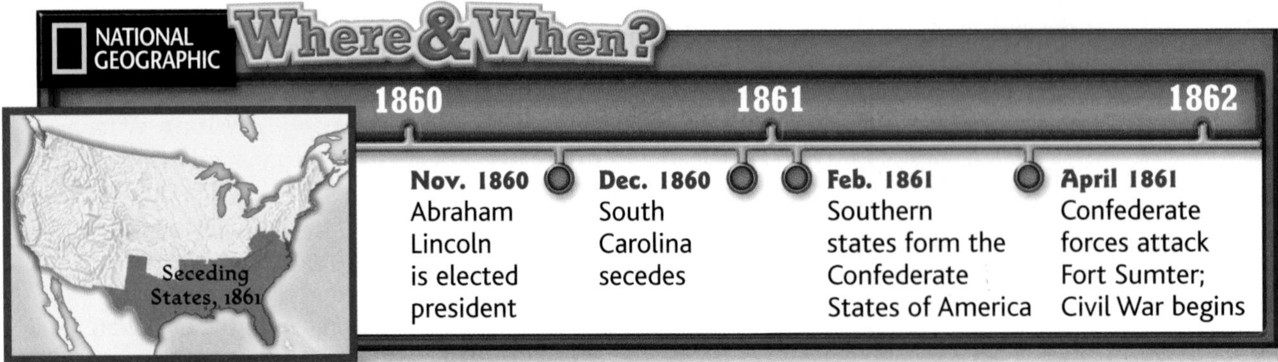

Nov. 1860 Abraham Lincoln is elected president

Dec. 1860 South Carolina secedes

Feb. 1861 Southern states form the Confederate States of America

April 1861 Confederate forces attack Fort Sumter; Civil War begins

US8.10.4 Discuss Abraham Lincoln's presidency and his significant writings and speeches and their relationship to the Declaration of Independence, such as his "House Divided" speech (1858), Gettysburg Address (1863), Emancipation Proclamation (1863), and inaugural addresses (1861 and 1865).

The Election of 1860

Main Idea **A split occurred in the Democratic Party, which allowed Lincoln to win the election of 1860.**

Reading Connection Think of an issue that you feel strongly about. Do you think your views would affect your choice for president? Read to learn how the slavery issue affected the election of 1860.

An American Story

After John Brown's raid on Harpers Ferry, calls for secession grew. South Carolina's *Charleston Mercury* declared "The day of compromise is passed . . . [T]here is no peace for the South in the Union." The *Nashville Union and American* said, "The South will hold the whole party of Republicans responsible for the bloodshed at Harpers Ferry."

Republicans argued that secession was only a scare tactic, aimed at frightening voters from casting their ballot for Abraham Lincoln. To many Southerners, however, Lincoln's election would be a signal that their position in the Union was hopeless.

Many Parties Would the Union break up? That was the burning question in the months before the presidential election of 1860. The issue of slavery **eventually** caused a break in the Democratic Party. Northern Democrats nominated Stephen Douglas for the presidency and supported popular sovereignty. Southern Democrats—vowing to uphold slavery—nominated John C. Breckinridge of Kentucky and supported the *Dred Scott* decision. Southern Democrats denounced John Brown's raid as "among the gravest of crimes." Northern and Southern moderates formed the Constitutional Union Party and nominated John Bell of Tennessee. This party took no position on slavery. However, voters in the North and South would no longer tolerate neutrality on this important issue.

Lincoln Nominated The Republicans nominated Abraham Lincoln. Their platform, designed to attract voters from many quarters, was that slavery should be left undisturbed where it existed, but that it should be excluded from the territories. Many Southerners feared, however, that a Republican victory would encourage slave revolts.

Lincoln Elected Lincoln won a clear majority of the electoral votes—180 out of 303. He received 40 percent of the popular vote. Douglas was second with 30 percent of the vote.

The vote was along purely sectional lines. Lincoln's name did not even appear on the ballot in most Southern states, but he won every Northern state. Breckinridge swept the South, and Bell took most **border states.** These states were located between the North and the South. They were divided over whether to stay in the Union or join the Confederacy. Douglas won only the state of Missouri and three of New Jersey's seven electoral votes.

Reading Check **Examine** What caused the split in the Democratic Party in 1860?

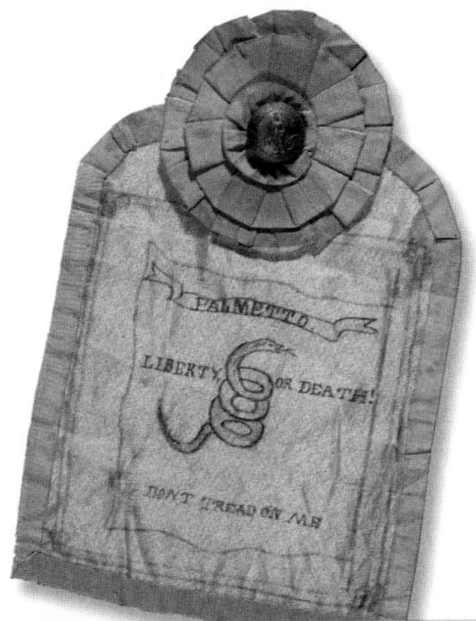

Picturing History

Patriots used these mottos on this secessionist ribbon during the American Revolution. ***What did they mean during the Revolution? Why do you think secessionists used these mottos?***

US8.10.3 Identify the constitutional issues posed by the doctrine of nullification and secession and the earliest origins of that doctrine. **US8.10.4** Discuss Abraham Lincoln's presidency and his significant writings and speeches and their relationship to the Declaration of Independence, such as his "House Divided" speech (1858), Gettysburg Address (1863), Emancipation Proclamation (1863), and inaugural addresses (1861 and 1865).

The South Secedes

Main Idea **South Carolina led other Southern states in seceding from the Union.**

Reading Connection Have you ever been so angry that you needed to leave a room? Read to find out about the South's decision to leave the Union.

In the election of 1860, the more populous North had outvoted the South. The victory for Lincoln was a short-lived one, however, for the nation Lincoln was to lead would soon disintegrate.

Lincoln and the Republicans had promised not to disturb slavery where it already existed. Many people in the South, however, did not trust the party, fearing that the Republican administration would not protect Southern rights. On December 20, 1860, the South's long-standing threat to leave the Union became a reality when **South Carolina** held a special convention and voted to secede.

Attempt at Compromise Even after South Carolina's action, many people still wished to preserve the Union. The question was *how.* As other Southern states debated **secession** (sih • SEH • shuhn)—withdrawal from the Union—leaders in Washington, D.C., worked frantically to fashion a last-minute compromise. On December 18, 1860, Senator **John Crittenden** of Kentucky proposed a series of amendments to the Constitution. Central to Crittenden's plan was a provision to protect slavery south of 36°30′N latitude—the line set by the Missouri Compromise—in all territories "now held or hereafter acquired."

Republicans considered this unacceptable. They had just won an election on the principle that slavery would not be extended in any territories. "Now we are told. . . ," Lincoln wrote,

> **"the government shall be broken up, unless we surrender to those we have beaten."**
>
> —*letter to James T. Hale, January 11, 1861*

Leaders in the South also rejected the plan. "We spit upon every plan to compromise," exclaimed one Southern leader. "No human power can save the Union," wrote another.

The Confederacy By February 1861, Texas, Louisiana, Mississippi, Alabama, Florida, and Georgia had joined South Carolina and also seceded. Delegates from these states and South Carolina met in Montgomery, Alabama, on February 4 to form a new nation and government. Calling themselves the Confederate States of America, or the Confederacy, they chose **Jefferson Davis,** a senator from Mississippi, as their president.

Southerners **justified** secession with the **theory** of **states' rights.** The states, they argued, had voluntarily chosen to enter the Union. They defined the Constitution as a contract among the independent states. Now because the national government had violated that contract—by refusing to enforce the Fugitive Slave Act and by denying the Southern states equal rights in the territories—the states felt justified in leaving the Union.

Reactions to Secession Many Southerners welcomed secession. Senator Albert Brown of Mississippi said in a speech to a Southern audience "disunion is a fearful thing, but emancipation is worse." In Charleston, South Carolina, people rang church bells, fired cannons, and celebrated in the streets. A newspaper in Atlanta, Georgia, said the South "will never submit" and would defend its liberties no matter what the cost.

Other Southerners, however, were alarmed. A South Carolinian wrote, "My heart has been rent [torn] by . . . the destruction of my country—the dismemberment of that great and glorious Union."

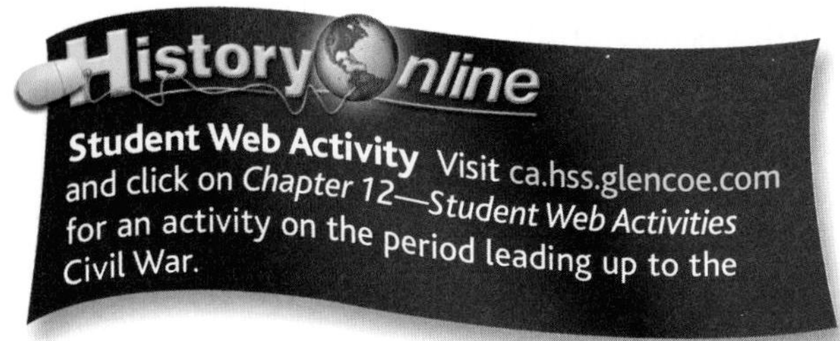
History Online
Student Web Activity Visit ca.hss.glencoe.com and click on *Chapter 12—Student Web Activities* for an activity on the period leading up to the Civil War.

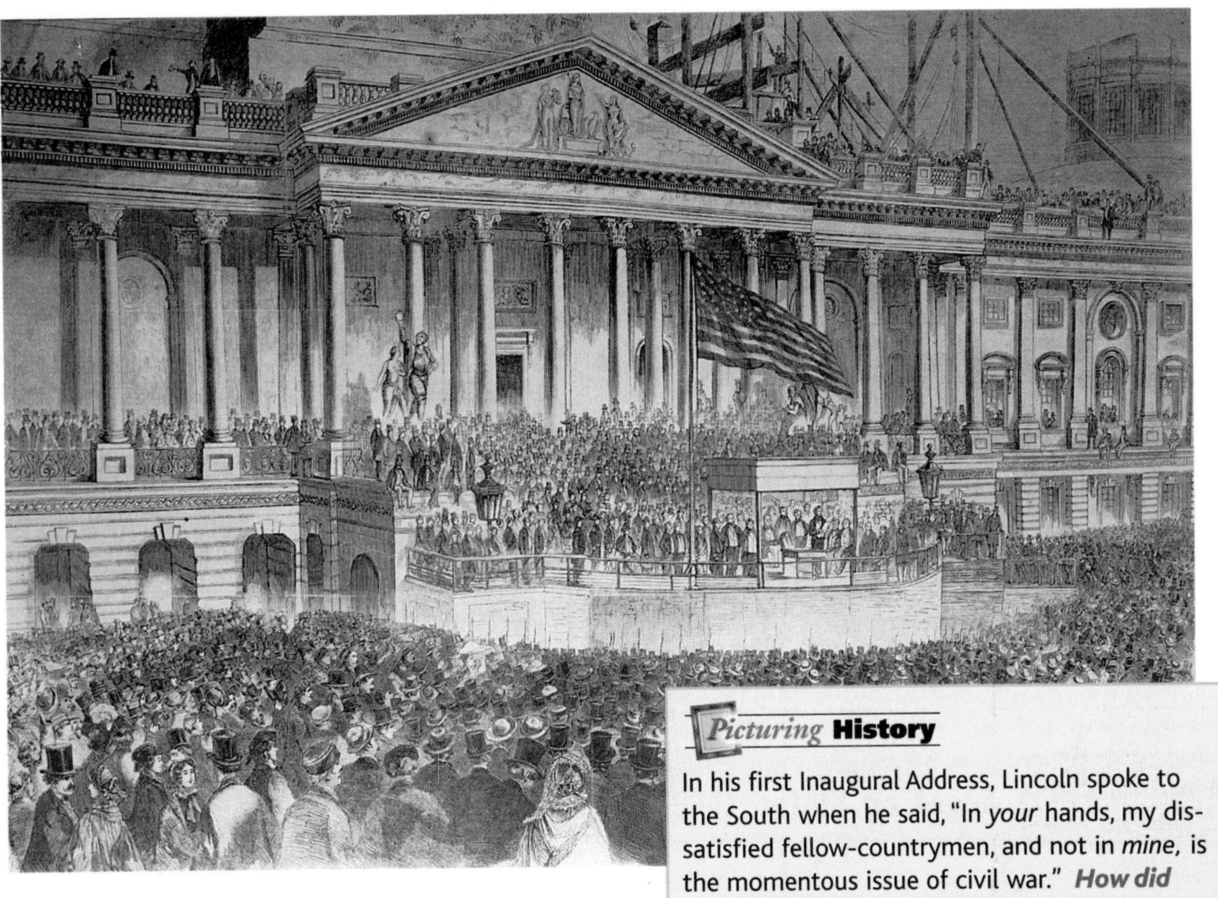

Picturing History

In his first Inaugural Address, Lincoln spoke to the South when he said, "In *your* hands, my dissatisfied fellow-countrymen, and not in *mine*, is the momentous issue of civil war." ***How did Southerners feel about secession?***

Virginian Robert E. Lee expressed concern about the future. "I see only that a fearful calamity is upon us," he wrote.

In the North, some abolitionists preferred to allow the Southern states to leave. If the Union could be kept together only by compromising on slavery, they declared, then let the Union be destroyed. Most Northerners, however, believed that the Union must be preserved. For Lincoln the issue was "whether in a free government the minority have the right to break up the government whenever they choose."

Presidential Responses Lincoln had won the election, but he was not yet president. James Buchanan's term ran until March 4, 1861. In December 1860, Buchanan sent a message to Congress saying that the Southern states had no right to secede. Then he added that he had no power to stop them from doing so.

As Lincoln prepared for his inauguration on March 4, 1861, people in both the North and the South wondered what he would say and do. They wondered, too, what would happen in Virginia, Maryland, North Carolina, Kentucky, Tennessee, Missouri, and Arkansas. These slave states had chosen to remain in the Union, but the decision was not final. If the United States used force against the Confederate States of America, the remaining slave states also might secede. In his Inaugural Address, the new president mixed toughness and words of peace. He said that secession would not be permitted, vowing to hold federal property in the South and to enforce the laws of the United States. At the same time, Lincoln pleaded with the people of the South for reconciliation:

> **"We are not enemies, but friends. We must not be enemies. Though passion may have strained, it must not break our bonds of affection."**
>
> —from *Inaugural Addresses of the Presidents*

Reading Check **Explain** How did the seceding states justify their right to leave the Union?

US8.10.6 Describe critical developments and events in the war, including the major battles, geographical advantages and obstacles, technological advances, and General Lee's surrender at Appomattox.

Fort Sumter

Main Idea **The Civil War began when Confederate forces attacked Fort Sumter in South Carolina.**

Reading Connection Have you ever been startled by a loud noise? Read to learn how Fort Sumter was attacked on April 12, 1861, and what it was like from inside the fort.

The South soon tested President Lincoln's vow to hold federal property. Confederate forces had already seized some United States forts within their states. Although Lincoln did not want to start a war by trying to take the forts back, allowing the Confederates to keep them would amount to admitting their right to secede.

On the day after his inauguration, Lincoln received a dispatch from Major Robert Anderson, the commander of **Fort Sumter,** a United States fort on an island guarding Charleston Harbor. The message warned that the fort was low on supplies and that the Confederates demanded its surrender.

The War Begins Lincoln responded by sending a message to Governor Francis Pickens of South Carolina. He informed Pickens that he was sending an unarmed expedition with supplies to Fort Sumter.

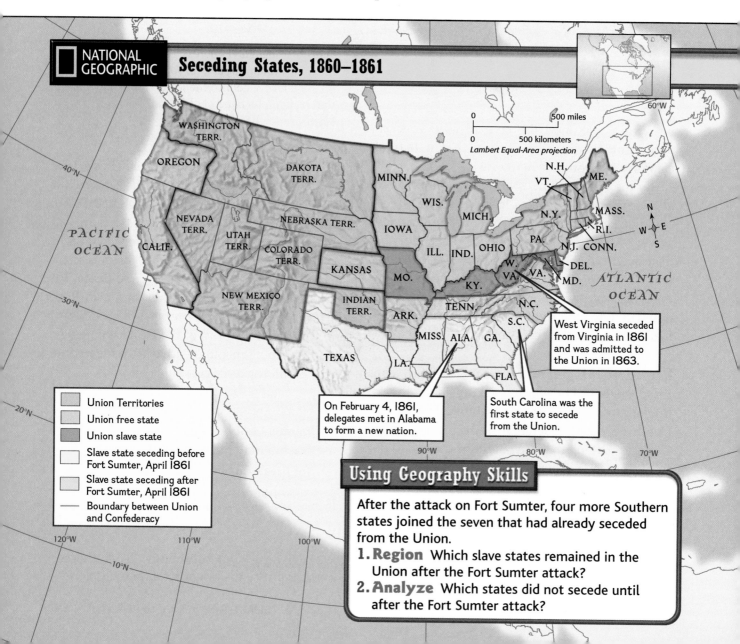

NATIONAL GEOGRAPHIC

Seceding States, 1860–1861

West Virginia seceded from Virginia in 1861 and was admitted to the Union in 1863.

On February 4, 1861, delegates met in Alabama to form a new nation.

South Carolina was the first state to secede from the Union.

- Union Territories
- Union free state
- Union slave state
- Slave state seceding before Fort Sumter, April 1861
- Slave state seceding after Fort Sumter, April 1861
- Boundary between Union and Confederacy

Using Geography Skills

After the attack on Fort Sumter, four more Southern states joined the seven that had already seceded from the Union.

1. **Region** Which slave states remained in the Union after the Fort Sumter attack?
2. **Analyze** Which states did not secede until after the Fort Sumter attack?

Lincoln promised that Union forces would not "throw in men, arms, or ammunition" unless they were fired upon. The president thus left the decision to start shooting up to the Confederates.

Confederate president Jefferson Davis and his advisers made a fateful choice. They ordered their forces to attack Fort Sumter before the Union supplies could arrive. Confederate guns opened fire on the fort early on April 12, 1861. Union captain Abner Doubleday witnessed the attack from inside the fort:

> **"Showers of balls . . . and shells . . . poured into the fort in one incessant stream, causing great flakes of masonry to fall in all directions."**
>
> **—as quoted in *Voices of the Civil War***

High seas had prevented Union relief ships from reaching the fort. The Union garrison held out for 33 hours before surrendering on April 14. Thousands of shots were exchanged during the siege, but no lives were lost on either side. The Confederates hoisted their flag over the fort, and all the guns in the harbor sounded a triumphant salute.

Once Fort Sumter was attacked, both the North and South took action. President Lincoln issued a call for 75,000 troops to fight to save the Union, and volunteers quickly signed up. Meanwhile, volunteers signed up to fight for the South, and Virginia, North Carolina, Tennessee, and Arkansas voted to join the Confederacy. The Civil War had begun.

Reading Check **Explain** What action did Lincoln take after the attack on Fort Sumter?

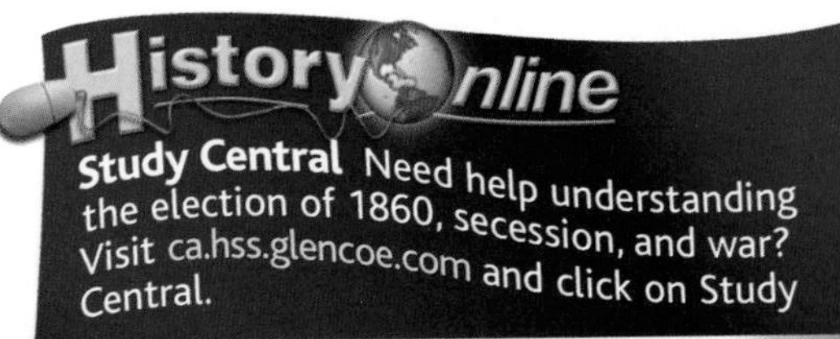

Study Central Need help understanding the election of 1860, secession, and war? Visit ca.hss.glencoe.com and click on Study Central.

Reading Summary

Review the Main Ideas

- In a contest in which votes were split between four candidates, Abraham Lincoln came out the winner of the 1860 presidential election.
- Following Lincoln's election, a number of Southern states seceded from the Union and formed the Confederate States of America.
- The Confederate attack on Fort Sumter in the harbor of Charleston, South Carolina, marked the beginning of the Civil War.

What Did You Learn?

1. What was Senator John Crittenden's last-minute proposal to save the Union?
2. Who served as the president of the Confederate States of America?

Critical Thinking

3. **Sequencing Events** Re-create the diagram below. Fill in the events leading up to the surrender of Fort Sumter and the start of the Civil War. CA CS2.

→	→	→ Fort Sumter Surrenders

4. **The Big Ideas** What role did sectionalism play in Lincoln's victory in the 1860 election? CA CS1.
5. **Drawing Conclusions** Based on what you read, how would you describe President Lincoln's priorities as he took office in March 1861?
6. **Expository Writing** Write a paragraph describing what you consider to be key reasons for the Civil War. CA 8WA2.3

You Decide . . .

US8.10.5 Study the views and lives of leaders (e.g., Ulysses S. Grant, Jefferson Davis, Robert E. Lee) and soldiers on both sides of the war, including those of black soldiers and regiments.

Union or Confederacy?

President Abraham Lincoln and Jefferson Davis, president of the Confederacy, were inaugurated just several weeks apart. These excerpts from their Inaugural Addresses will help you understand differing points of view about secession from the United States in 1861.

Abraham Lincoln—Union

I hold, that . . . the Union of these States is perpetual [forever]. Perpetuity is implied, if not expressed, in the fundamental law of all national governments.

One section of our country believes slavery is right, and ought to be extended, while the other believes it is wrong, and ought not to be extended. This is the only substantial dispute. . . .

Physically speaking, we cannot separate. We cannot remove our respective sections from each other, nor build an impassable wall between them. A husband and wife may be divorced, and go out of the presence, and beyond the reach of each other; but the different parts of our country cannot do this. . . .

In your hands, my dissatisfied fellow countrymen, and not in mine, is the momentous issue of civil war.

—from Abraham Lincoln's First Inaugural Address, March 4, 1861

Abraham Lincoln ▶

Jefferson Davis—Confederacy

Our present condition [as a new confederacy] . . . illustrates the American idea that governments rest upon the consent of the governed, and that it is the right of the people to alter or abolish governments whenever they become destructive of the ends for which they were established. . . . In this they [the people of the Confederacy] merely asserted a right which the Declaration of Independence of 1776 had defined to be inalienable. . . . [I]t is by abuse of language that their act has been denominated [called] a revolution. They formed a new alliance, but within each State its government has remained, the rights of person and property have not been disturbed. . . .

As a necessity, not a choice, we have resorted to the remedy of separation; and henceforth our energies must be directed to the conduct of our own affairs, and the [continuation] of the Confederacy which we have formed. If a just perception of mutual interest shall permit us peaceably to pursue our separate political career, my most earnest desire will have been fulfilled. But if this be denied to us . . . [we will be forced] to appeal to arms. . . .

—from Jefferson Davis's Inaugural Address, February 18, 1861

◀ Jefferson Davis

You Be The Historian

DBQ Document-Based Questions

1. According to Lincoln, what was the major disagreement between the North and South?
2. What did Lincoln compare the United States to? CA HR3.
3. Did Lincoln and Davis say anything in their addresses that was similar? Explain. CA HR3.

Analyzing Primary Sources

US8.9 Students analyze the early and steady attempts to abolish slavery and to realize the ideals of the Declaration of Independence.

Challenging Slavery

In the days leading up to the Civil War, people throughout the United States debated about economics, states' rights, and the institution of slavery. Antislavery society and religious group members were vocal, as were politicians, businesspeople, and plantation owners. In some cases, the voices of both free and enslaved African Americans could be heard.

Read the passages on pages 562 and 563 and answer the questions that follow.

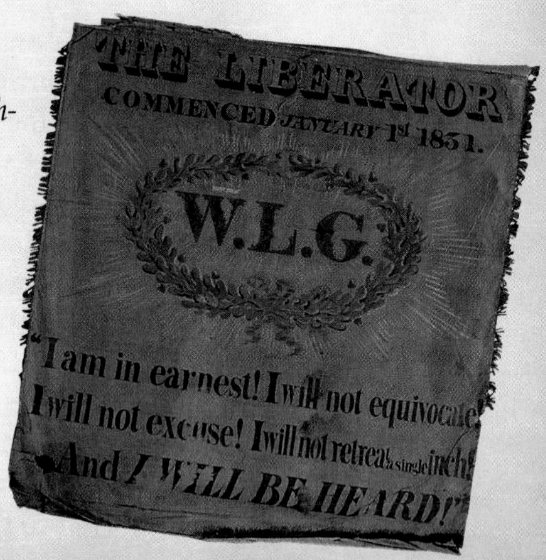

Banner celebrating Garrison's abolitionist newspaper, *The Liberator*

Reader's Dictionary

severity (suh • VEHR • uh • tee): being strict, stern, or harsh

moderation (MAH • duh • RAY • shuhn): limiting or controlling something so as not to be extreme or excessive

ravisher: one who carries somebody or something off by violent force

extricate (EHK • struh • KAYT): to release somebody or something with difficulty from being constrained

equivocate (ih • KWIH • vuh • KAYT): to speak vaguely, especially in order to mislead

dissolution (DIH • suh • LOO • shun): the act or process of dissolving

atone (uh • TOHN): to make amends

The Liberator

Through his newspaper, The Liberator, *abolitionist William Lloyd Garrison demanded the immediate emancipation of all slaves. Founded in 1831 in Boston,* The Liberator *continued publishing antislavery messages under Garrison's leadership for 35 years. In one edition, he wrote:*

[I support] the "self-evident truth" . . . that all men are created equal, and endowed by their Creator with certain inalienable rights. . . .

I am aware that many object to the **severity** of my language; but is there not cause for severity? I *will be* as harsh as truth and as uncompromising as justice. On this subject I do not wish to think or speak, or write with **moderation.** No! No! Tell a man whose house is on fire to give a moderate alarm; tell him to moderately rescue his wife from the hands of a **ravisher;** tell the mother to gradually **extricate** her babe from the fire into which it has fallen—but urge me not to use moderation in a cause like the present. I am in earnest; I will not **equivocate;** I will not excuse; I will not retreat a single inch—AND I WILL BE HEARD. . . .

On the Eve of War

Mrs. Eugene McLean kept a diary of her experiences as an Army officer's wife during the Civil War. This passage describes her thoughts after the fall of Fort Sumter. Her husband joined the Confederate Army.

Strange, strange, strange, how we have accustomed ourselves to the thought, and accept the **dissolution** of the Union as a natural consequence! Whom have we to blame for bringing us to this state . . . ? Wherever the fault lies, I do not envy them their feelings in this hour, and fear both sections will **atone** in mourning and ashes for the crime.

▲ The spiritual is a unique and important part of African American history.

Swing Low, Sweet Chariot

Spirituals—songs of salvation—provided the enslaved African Americans who wrote and sang them with not only a measure of comfort in bleak times but with a means for communicating secretly among themselves. Here is an example of a popular song that was sung by enslaved African Americans at work:

Swing low, sweet chariot,
Coming for to carry me home,
Swing low, sweet chariot,
Coming for to carry me home.
I looked over Jordan, and what did I see,
Coming for to carry me home;
A band of angels coming after me,
Coming for to carry me home.
If you get there before I do,
Coming for to carry me home;
Tell all my friends I'm coming too,
Coming for to carry me home.
Swing low, sweet chariot,
Coming for to carry me home,
Swing low, sweet chariot,
Coming for to carry me home.

—*Selected Famous Negro Spirituals*

Document-Based Questions

The Liberator

1. Who do you think Garrison is referring to when he states that he is aware that many object to the severity of his language?
2. What analogies does Garrison use to make his point about the need for severity over moderation?

On the Eve of War

3. How does the author feel about secession?
4. Does she blame either the Union or the Confederacy for the war? Explain.

Swing Low, Sweet Chariot

5. What does the phrase "swing low, sweet chariot" mean? What is meant by the lines "If you get there before I do . . . Tell all my friends I'm coming too"?
6. Why do you think enslaved African Americans sang this song?

Read to Write

7. Review each of the readings. Do you think these were written to inform, to entertain, to tell a story, or to persuade the reader? Write a one-page paper and give reasons for your answer. CA 8WA2.4

Assessment

Standards US8.9 & US8.10

Review Content Vocabulary

1. Use the following terms to write a brief paragraph describing events in the United States just prior to 1860.
   secede
   fugitive
   civil war
   abolitionist

Review the Main Ideas

Section 1 • Abolitionists

2. How was William Lloyd Garrison effective in the antislavery movement?
3. What was the purpose of the American Colonization Society?

Section 2 • Slavery and the West

4. What was the purpose of the Missouri Compromise?
5. List the five parts of the Compromise of 1850.

Section 3 • A Nation Dividing

6. What was Stephen Douglas's solution to the slavery issue in the Kansas and Nebraska territories?
7. How did abolitionists and African Americans resist the Fugitive Slave Act?

Section 4 • Challenges to Slavery

8. How did Abraham Lincoln become a national figure in politics?
9. What was the *Dred Scott* decision? What did it mean for those opposed to slavery?

Section 5 • Secession and War

10. Why were there four parties and candidates in the presidential election of 1860?
11. How did Lincoln plan to prevent secession?

Critical Thinking

12. **Evaluate** Why was the balance of free and slave states in the Senate such an important issue? CA HR3.
13. **Analyze** What contributions did Frederick Douglass make to the abolitionist movement? Was he successful? Describe your conclusions in a paragraph. CA HI2.

Geography Skills

Study the map below and answer the following questions. CA CS3.

NATIONAL GEOGRAPHIC **Election of 1860**

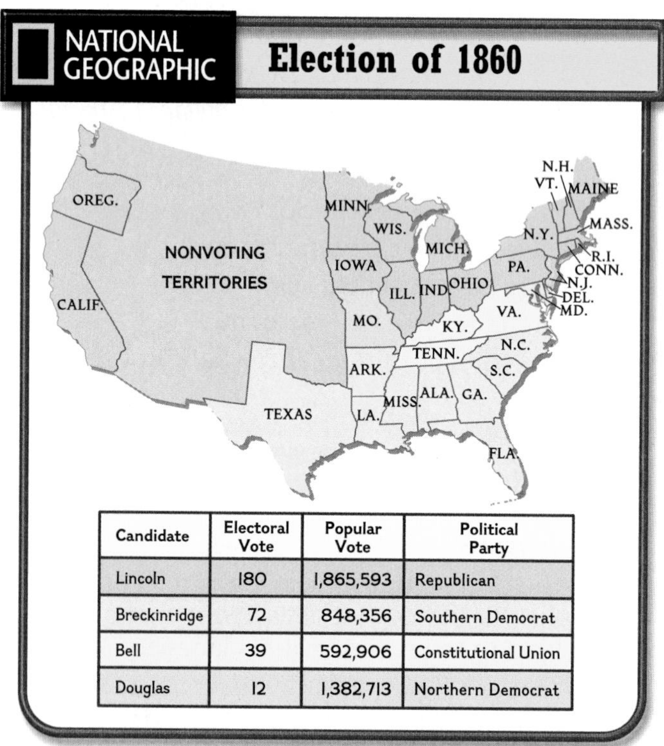

Candidate	Electoral Vote	Popular Vote	Political Party
Lincoln	180	1,865,593	Republican
Breckinridge	72	848,356	Southern Democrat
Bell	39	592,906	Constitutional Union
Douglas	12	1,382,713	Northern Democrat

14. **Location** Which states supported Douglas?
15. **Region** In what region(s) was the Republican Party strongest?
16. **Region** In what region did Breckinridge find support?

History Online

Self-Check Quiz Visit ca.hss.glencoe.com to prepare for the Chapter 12 test.

Read to Write

17. **The Big Ideas** **Conflict and War** Make a list of 10 important events that you read about in this chapter. Select the two events that you think did the most to create conflict between the North and South. Write a one-page essay in which you explain how these events led to war. CA 8WS1.1

18. **Using Your FOLDABLES** Use the information you listed in your foldable to create a brief study guide for the chapter. For each section, your study guide should include at least five questions that focus on the main ideas. CA 8RC2.0

Using Academic Vocabulary

19. Write two words that are related to each of the following academic vocabulary words.
publication **controversy** **inevitable**

Building Citizenship

20. **Making Compromises** With a partner, think of a controversial issue that is a source of disagreement today. Take opposite sides on the issue; then work together to come up with a list of three compromises that would make the solution to this problem acceptable to both sides. CA CS1.

Linking Past and Present

21. **Political Parties** Search the Internet for a list of political parties in existence today. Research to find the date that the party was founded and its current goals. Create a table that briefly summarizes this information. Then compare your table to the political parties discussed in Chapter 12. CA 8WS1.4

Reviewing Skills

22. **Review READING SKILL** **Making Inferences** Reread Jefferson Davis's Inaugural Address on page 561. How do you think Davis feels about his new role? How does he feel about the prospect of war? Write a paragraph explaining your conclusions. CA 8RC2.0

23. **Review ANALYSIS SKILL** **Sequencing Information** Draw two time lines highlighting key figures, dates, and milestones in the abolitionist movement and the political battle over slavery. CA CS2.

Standards Practice

Use the map below to answer the following question.

The Compromise of 1850

OREGON TERR.
MINNESOTA TERR.
UNORGANIZED TERR.
UTAH TERR.
CALIF. (1850)
NEW MEXICO TERR.
N
W
E
S

Free states
Slave states
Territory closed to slaveholding
Territory open to slaveholding
Indian Territory

24 Which of the following statements is true?

A The Compromise of 1850 allowed the Oregon Territory to be open to slaveholding.

B The Compromise of 1850 did not make any land on the Pacific Ocean open to slaveholding.

C The Compromise of 1850 made every state touching the southern border of the United States open to slaveholding.

D The Compromise of 1850 gave the Minnesota Territory the authority to choose whether it would allow slaveholding.

The Civil War

Gettysburg Battlefield ▶

NATIONAL GEOGRAPHIC

Who & When?

1861 — 1863 — 1865

1861 Civil War begins with battle at Fort Sumter

1862 Robert E. Lee commands Confederate army

1863 Emancipation Proclamation issued

1865 War ends; Lincoln assassinated

History Online

Chapter Overview Visit ca.hss.glencoe.com for a preview of Chapter 13.

The Big Ideas

The Two Sides

Differences in economic, political, and social beliefs and practices can lead to division within a nation and have lasting consequences. The Union and the Confederacy prepared for war.

Early Years of the War

Conflict often brings about great change. Neither the Union nor the Confederate forces gained a strong early advantage.

A Call to Freedom

Reactions to social injustice can lead to reform movements. African Americans struggled for their civil rights.

Life During the Civil War

Citizen participation is essential to the foundation and preservation of the U.S. political system. Civilians as well as soldiers had an impact on the war effort.

The Way to Victory

Conflict often brings about great change. Aggressive offensives resulted in a victory for the Union.

View the Chapter 13 video in the Glencoe Video Program.

Organizing Information Make this foldable to help you organize what you learn about the Civil War.

Step 1 Fold a sheet of paper in half from side to side.

Fold it so the left edge lies about ½ inch from the right edge.

Step 2 Turn the paper and fold it into thirds.

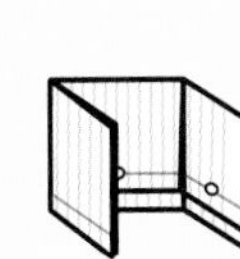

Step 3 Unfold and cut the top layer only along both folds.

This will make three tabs.

Step 4 Label your foldable as shown.

Before the War | During the War | After the War
The Civil War

Reading and Writing As you read the chapter, list events that occurred before, during, and after the Civil War under the appropriate tabs of your foldable.

Get Ready to Read

Evaluation

1 Learn It!

Good readers evaluate information as they read. That means they draw conclusions and determine the significance of events, ideas, and people that they read about. As you read history, ask yourself such questions as:

- What caused this person or group of people to react that way? In the same situation, how did other people in history react?
- What words has the author chosen to describe this event or person? How do these words help me form an opinion?
- Is the information that I'm reading based on fact or opinion?

Keep these questions in mind as you read the excerpt below.

> **Gone were the parades and masses of volunteers, the fancy uniforms, and the optimism of the first years of the war. From 1862 until 1865, the soldiers and civilians faced a grim conflict marked by death, destruction, and wrenching change. What endured on each side was a fierce dedication to its own cause.**
>
> —*from page 605*

Reading Tip

As you read, write down some of your conclusions or opinions in your note-book. When you finish the chapter, go back and review them. Did your conclusions and opinions change?

One Northern advantage was not **obvious** until later. Both sides greatly underestimated Abraham Lincoln. His dedication and intelligence would lead the North to victory.

One of the main advantages for Southerners was fighting in familiar territory—defending their land, their homes, and their way of life.

The military leadership of the South, at least at first, was superior to the North's. Southern families had a strong tradition of military training and service, and military college graduates provided the South with a large pool of officers. Overseeing the Southern effort was Confederate president **Jefferson Davis,** a West Point graduate and an experienced soldier.

The South also faced some disadvantages. It had a smaller population of free men to draw upon in building an army. It also possessed very few factories to manufacture weapons and other supplies, and it produced less than half as much food as the North. With less than half the miles of railroad tracks and vastly fewer trains than the North, the Confederate government had difficulty delivering food, weapons, and other supplies to its troops.

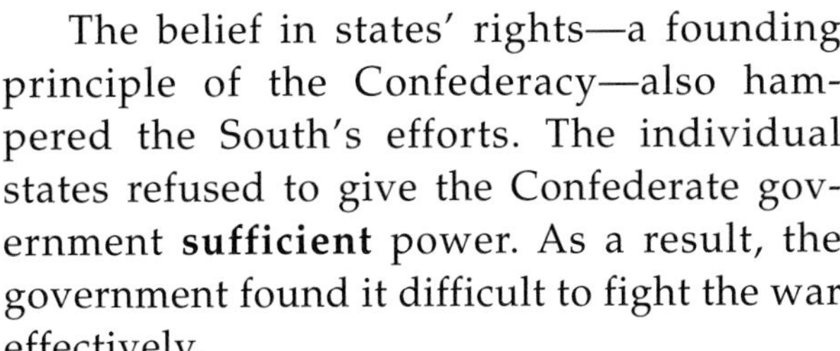

The belief in states' rights—a founding principle of the Confederacy—also hampered the South's efforts. The individual states refused to give the Confederate government **sufficient** power. As a result, the government found it difficult to fight the war effectively.

War Aims and Strategy The North and the South entered the Civil War with different goals. The main goal of the North was to bring the Southern states back into the Union. Ending slavery was not a major Northern goal at first, but this changed as the war continued.

The Union's plan for winning the war included three main strategies. First, the North would **blockade** (blah • KAYD), or close, Southern ports to prevent supplies from reaching the South—and to prevent the South from earning money by exporting cotton. Second, the Union intended to gain control of the Mississippi River to cut Southern supply lines and to divide the Confederacy. Third, the North planned to take control of Richmond, Virginia, the Confederate capital.

For the South, the **primary** aim of the war was to win recognition as an independent nation. Independence would allow Southerners to preserve their traditional way of life—a way of life that included slavery.

To achieve this goal, the South worked out a defensive strategy. It planned to defend its homeland, holding on to as much territory as possible until the North tired of fighting. The South expected that Britain and France, which imported large quantities of Southern cotton, would pressure the North to end the war to restore their cotton supplies.

During the war, Southern leaders sometimes changed strategy and took the **offensive** (uh • FEHN • sihv)—went on the attack. They moved their armies northward to threaten Washington, D.C., and other Northern cities, hoping to persuade the North that it could not win the war.

Reading Check **Compare** What advantages and disadvantages did each side possess?

US8.10.5 Study the views and lives of leaders (e.g., Ulysses S. Grant, Jefferson Davis, Robert E. Lee) and soldiers on both sides of the war, including those of black soldiers and regiments.

American People at War

Main Idea **Soldiers in the Civil War came from every region, and each side expected an early victory.**

Reading Connection What motivates men and women to join the armed forces today? Read to find out about the backgrounds of the soldiers in the Union and Confederate armies.

The Civil War was more than a war between the states. It often pitted brother against brother, parents against their children, and neighbor against neighbor.

American Against American The leaders from both North and South—and their families—felt these divisions. President Lincoln's wife, **Mary Todd Lincoln,** had several relatives who fought in the Confederate army. John Crittenden, a senator from Kentucky, had two sons who became generals in the war—one for the Confederacy and one for the Union. Officers on both sides—including Confederate general **Robert E. Lee,** and Union generals George McClellan and **William Tecumseh Sherman**—had attended the United States Military Academy at West Point, never dreaming that they would one day command forces fighting against each other.

Who Were the Soldiers? Most of the soldiers were young. The average recruit was 25 years old, but about 40 percent were 21 or younger. Ted Upson of Indiana was only 16 when he begged his father to let him join the Union army. His father replied, "This Union your ancestors and mine helped to make must be saved from destruction."

William Stone from Louisiana rushed to join the Confederate army after the attack on Fort Sumter. His sister Kate wrote that he was "wild to be off to Virginia. He so fears that the fighting will be over before he can get there."

Soldiers came from every region and all walks of life. Most, though, came from farms. Almost half of the North's troops and more than 60 percent of the South's had owned or worked on farms. The Union army did not permit African Americans to join at first, but they did serve later. Lincoln's early terms of enlistment asked governors to supply soldiers for 90 days. When the conflict did not end quickly, soldiers' terms became longer.

By the summer of 1861, the Confederate army had about 112,000 soldiers, who were sometimes called **Rebels** (REH • buhlz). The Union had about 187,000 soldiers, or **Yankees** (YANG • keez), as they were also known. By the end of the war, about 850,000 men fought for the Confederacy and about 2.1 million men fought for the Union.

Picturing **History**

The Civil War divided the nation, but it also divided families. ***What did the soldiers from the Union and the Confederacy have in common?***

The Union number included just under 200,000 African Americans. About 10,000 Hispanic soldiers fought in the conflict.

False Hopes When the war began, each side expected an early victory. A Confederate soldier from a town in Alabama expected the war to be over well within a year because "we are going to kill the last Yankee before that time if there is any fight in them still." Northerners were just as confident that they would beat the South quickly.

Some leaders saw the situation more clearly. Northern general William Tecumseh Sherman wrote, "I think it is to be a long war—very long—much longer than any politician thinks." The first spring of the war proved that Sherman's prediction was accurate. From the first battle, both sides learned there would be no quick victory.

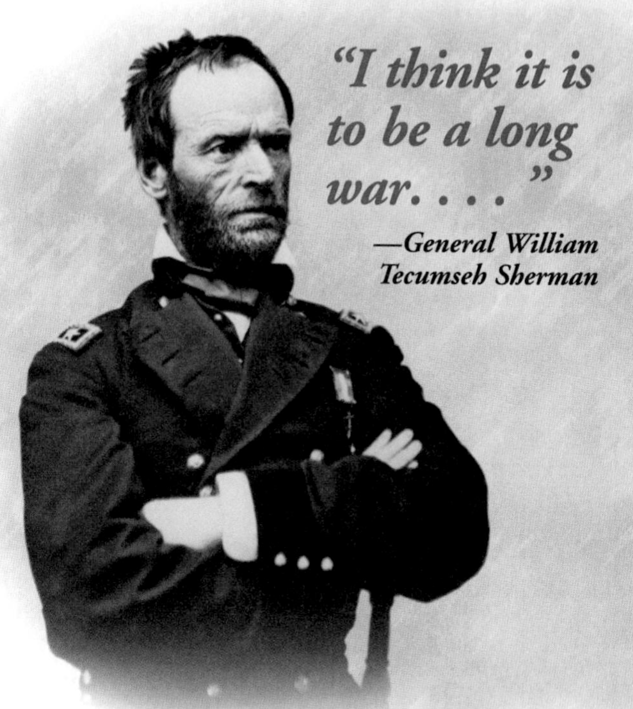

"I think it is to be a long war. . . ."
—General William Tecumseh Sherman

Reading Check **Compare** Which side had the larger fighting force?

History Online
Study Central Need help understanding the start of the Civil War? Visit ca.hss.glencoe.com and click on Study Central.

Section 1 Review

Reading Summary

Review the Main Ideas

- The North hoped to use its large number of soldiers and industry to cut off supplies to the South, and the South planned to fight defensively and win foreign recognition.
- Many of the soldiers from both North and South were young, had come from farms, and mistakenly expected a short war.

What Did You Learn?

1. Why were the border states important to the North and the South?
2. Why was the Civil War especially difficult for families?

Critical Thinking

3. **Comparing** Create a diagram to compare Northern and Southern aims and strategies. CA HR3.

	North	South
Aims		
Strategies		

4. **Analyze** How did a strong belief in states' rights affect the South during the war? CA HI2.
5. **The Big Ideas** How did the South's economy differ from that of the North, and how did it place the South at a disadvantage during the war? CA HI6.
6. **Reading Evaluating Text** Reread the passage at the beginning of Section 1 about Union sergeant Driscoll. Using your evaluation skills, write a short paragraph that explains why the author chose to include this account. How does it relate to what you read in that section? CA 8RC2.0

Section 2 Early Years of the War

Guide to Reading

History Social Science Standards

US8.10 Students analyze the multiple causes, key events, and complex consequences of the Civil War.

Looking Back, Looking Ahead

In 1861, the Union and Confederacy expected a brief war and early victory.

Focusing on the Main Ideas

- The North realized with the first major battle that the war would be a long, difficult struggle. *(page 577)*
- The North set up a blockade along the South's coastline, which caused serious problems for the South. *(page 578)*
- The action shifted to the West after the First Battle of Bull Run as each side reorganized its forces. *(page 579)*
- Battles continued, and after several Southern victories, Lincoln removed General McClellan for his failure to act in these battles. *(page 580)*

Locating Places

Norfolk, Virginia

Meeting People

"Stonewall" Jackson
George B. McClellan
Ulysses S. Grant
David Farragut (FAR•uh•guht)

Content Vocabulary

ironclad
casualty (KAZH•wuhl•tee)

Academic Vocabulary

reinforce (REE•uhn•FOHRS)
abandon (uh•BAN•duhn)
prospect (PRAH•spehkt)
evaluate (ih•VAL•yuh•WAYT)
encounter (ihn•KOWN•tuhr)

Reading Strategy

Classifying Information As you read, describe the outcome of each of these battles on a chart like the one shown.

Battle	Outcome
First Battle of Bull Run (Manassas)	
Monitor v. *Merrimack*	
Antietam	

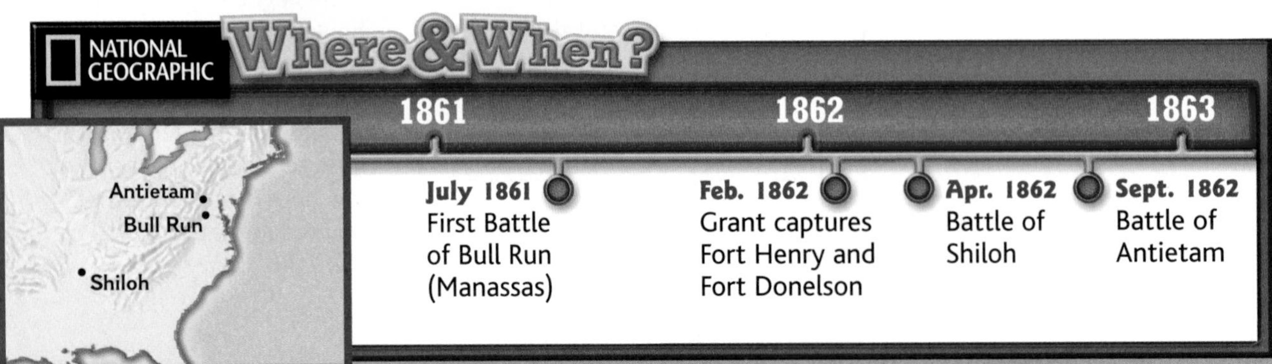

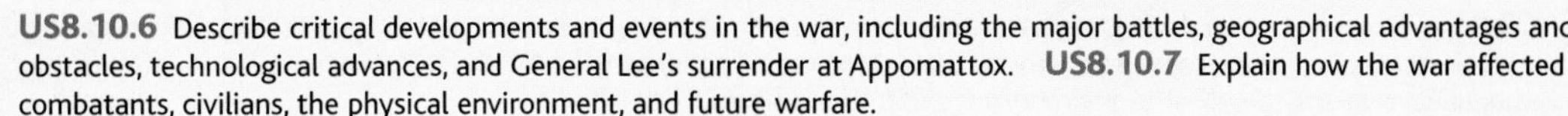

The First Battle

Main Idea **The North realized with the first major battle that the war would be a long, difficult struggle.**

Reading Connection What goes through the mind of a soldier in battle for the first time? Read to learn about the Battle of Bull Run and the soldiers involved.

An American Story

Sunday, July 21, 1861, was a pleasant, sunny day in Washington, D.C. Hundreds of cheerful residents left the city and planned to picnic while watching the first battle between the Union and the Confederate armies. Expecting to see Union troops crush the Rebels, they looked forward to a quick victory. The Confederate soldiers also expected a quick victory.

> **"[The soldiers] carried dress suits with them, and any quantity of fine linen. . . . Every soldier, nearly, had a servant with him, and a whole lot of spoons and forks, so as to live comfortably and elegantly in camp. . . ."**
>
> **—Mary A. Ward,** ***Voices of the Civil War***

First Battle of Bull Run This first major battle of the Civil War was fought in northern Virginia, about five miles from a town called Manassas Junction near Bull Run—a small river in the area. Usually called the First Battle of Bull Run, it began when about 30,000 inexperienced Union troops attacked a smaller, equally inexperienced Confederate force.

The Yankees drove the Confederates back at first. Then the Rebels rallied, inspired by **reinforcements** under General Thomas Jackson. Jackson, who fought the enemy heroically "like a stone wall," became known thereafter as **"Stonewall" Jackson.**

The Confederates surged forward with a strange, unearthly scream that came to be known as the Rebel yell. Terrified, the Northern soldiers began to drop their guns and packs and run. One Union soldier wrote:

> **"As we gained the cover of the woods the stampede became even more frightful, for the baggage wagons and ambulances became entangled with the artillery and rendered the scene even more dreadful than the battle. . . ."**
>
> **—Corporal Samuel J. English, letter to his mother, July 1861**

The Union army began an orderly retreat that quickly became a mad stampede when the retreating Union troops collided with the civilians, fleeing in panic back to Washington, D.C.

A Shock for the North The outcome of the battle shocked the North, but President Abraham Lincoln was ready to act. He issued a call for more volunteers for the army. He signed two bills requesting a total of 1 million soldiers, who would serve for three years. Volunteers soon crowded into recruiting offices. Lincoln also appointed a new general, **George B. McClellan,** to head the Union army of the East—called the Army of the Potomac—and to organize the troops.

Reading Check **Explain** How did the First Battle of Bull Run change expectations about the war?

Civil War cannon

US8.10.6 Describe critical developments and events in the war, including the major battles, geographical advantages and obstacles, technological advances, and General Lee's surrender at Appomattox. **US8.10.7** Explain how the war affected combatants, civilians, the physical environment, and future warfare.

War at Sea

Main Idea **The North set up a blockade along the South's coastline, which caused serious problems for the South.**

Reading Connection Have you ever toured an old warship? Read to learn about the first battle between metal-covered ships.

Even before Bull Run, Lincoln had ordered a naval blockade of Southern ports. An effective blockade would prevent the South from exporting its cotton and from importing the supplies necessary to continue the war.

The blockade caused serious problems for the South. Goods such as coffee, shoes, nails, and salt—as well as guns and ammunition—were in short supply in the South throughout the war.

The *Monitor* Versus the *Merrimack* The South did not intend to let the blockade go unchallenged. Southerners salvaged the *Merrimack*, a Union warship that Northern forces had **abandoned** when Confederate forces seized the naval shipyard in **Norfolk, Virginia.** The Confederates rebuilt the wooden ship, covered it with thick iron plates, and renamed it the *Virginia*.

On March 8, 1862, this **ironclad,** or warship, attacked a group of Union ships off the coast of Virginia. The North's wooden warships could not damage the Confederate ship—shells simply bounced off its sides.

The North sent an iron-clad ship of its own, the *Monitor,* to engage the Confederate ship in battle. On March 9, the two ironclads exchanged fire, but neither ship could sink the other. The Union succeeded in keeping the *Merrimack* in the harbor, so it never again threatened Northern ships. The battle marked a new age in naval warfare—the first battle between two metal-covered ships. Both the North and the South used these ships as models to build more iron-clad ships.

Reading Check **Explain** What was the significance of the battle of the ironclads?

HISTORY MAKERS

Technology of the Civil War

Some historians call the Civil War the first modern war. The Civil War was the first war that featured widespread use of mechanical and electrical equipment. For the first time, troops traveled by railroad. Messages were sent by telegraph. Railroads and telegraphs changed how generals made battlefield decisions. At sea, the battle of ironclad ships changed naval warfare. The *Merrimack* and the *Monitor,* in their famous battle, proved the sturdiness of these metal-covered ships.

In February 1864, the *H.L. Hunley* became the first submarine to sink an enemy warship in combat. *The Hunley,* however, never returned to port. For more than 130 years, the disappearance of the submarine remained a mystery. In August 2000, a team of divers located the long-lost ship, and the *H.L. Hunley* was raised from the waters of Charleston Harbor in South Carolina.

▲ Ironclads marked the beginning of the modern, armored, self-propelled warship.

US8.10.6 Describe critical developments and events in the war, including the major battles, geographical advantages and obstacles, technological advances, and General Lee's surrender at Appomattox.

War in the West

Main Idea **The action shifted to the West after the First Battle of Bull Run as each side reorganized its forces.**

Reading Connection Do you have a nickname, or know someone who does? Read to find out how General Ulysses S. Grant earned his unusual nickname.

After the First Battle of Bull Run in July 1861, the war in the East settled into a stalemate as each side built its strength. Generals focused on training raw recruits, turning civilians into soldiers. For a while, the action shifted to the West.

Early Victories for the North One of the North's primary goals in the West was to gain control of the Mississippi and Tennessee Rivers. This would split the Confederacy and hinder Southern efforts to transport goods.

The Union launched its operations in the West from Cairo, Illinois. The Union commander at Cairo was **Ulysses S. Grant.** Early in 1862, Grant was ordered to move against Confederate forces in Kentucky and Tennessee. On February 6, with the aid of a fleet of newly made ironclads, Grant captured Fort Henry on the Tennessee River. Ten days later, Grant captured Fort Donelson on the Cumberland. When the Confederate commander at Fort Donelson realized he was trapped, he asked Grant for his terms. Grant's reply was:

> **"No terms except an unconditional and immediate surrender can be accepted."**
>
> **—Ulysses S. Grant, note to General Simon Buckner**

"Unconditional Surrender" Grant became the North's new hero. Ulysses S. Grant had earned a new nickname. Grant's victories helped secure the lower Tennessee River. They also opened a path for Union troops to march into Tennessee, Mississippi, and Alabama.

The Battle of Shiloh General Grant and about 40,000 troops then headed south along the Tennessee River toward Corinth, Mississippi, an important railroad junction. In early April 1862, the Union army camped at Pittsburg Landing, 20 miles from Corinth. Nearby was a church named Shiloh. Additional Union forces came from Nashville to join Grant.

Early on the morning of April 6, Confederate forces launched a surprise attack on the Union troops. The Battle of Shiloh lasted two days, with some of the most bitter, bloody fighting of the war. The first day, the Confederates drove Grant and his troops back to the Tennessee River. The second day, the Union forces recovered. Aided by the 25,000 troops from Nashville and shelling by gunboats on the river, they defeated the Confederates, who withdrew to Corinth.

The losses in the Battle of Shiloh were enormous. Together the two armies suffered more than 20,000 **casualties** (KAZH • wuhl • teez)—people who are killed or wounded. Confederate general Johnston also died in the bloodbath.

After their narrow victory at Shiloh, Union forces gained control of Corinth on May 30. Memphis, Tennessee, fell to Union armies on June 6. The North seemed well on its way to controlling the Mississippi River.

New Orleans Falls A few weeks after Shiloh, the North won another important victory. On April 25, 1862, Union naval forces under **David Farragut** (FAR • uh • guht) captured New Orleans, Louisiana, the South's largest city. Farragut, who was of Spanish descent, had grown up in the South but remained loyal to the Union. His capture of New Orleans, near the mouth of the Mississippi River, meant that the Confederacy could no longer use the river to carry its goods to sea. Together with Grant's victories to the north, Farragut's capture of New Orleans gave the Union control of almost the entire Mississippi River.

Reading Check **Analyze** **Why was control of the Mississippi River important to the North and to the South?**

US8.10.5 Study the views and lives of leaders (e.g., Ulysses S. Grant, Jefferson Davis, Robert E. Lee) and soldiers on both sides of the war, including those of black soldiers and regiments. US8.10.6 Describe critical developments and events in the war, including the major battles, geographical advantages and obstacles, technological advances, and General Lee's surrender at Appomattox.

War in the East

Main Idea **Battles continued, and after several Southern victories, Lincoln removed General McClellan for his failure to act in these battles.**

Reading Connection Have you heard the expression "he who hesitates is lost"? Read and find out about a Union general whose hesitancy cost many lives.

While Union and Confederate troops were struggling for control of Tennessee and the Mississippi River, another major military campaign was being waged in the east. General George B. McClellan led the Union army in the east.

McClellan Hesitates In the East, General McClellan was training the Army of the Potomac to be an effective fighting force. An expert at training soldiers, McClellan reorganized and drilled the Army of the Potomac.

However, when faced with the **prospect** of battle, McClellan was cautious and worried that his troops were not ready. He hesitated to fight because of reports that overestimated the size of the Rebel forces. Finally, in March 1862, the Army of the Potomac was ready for action. Its goal was to capture Richmond, the Confederate capital.

Instead of advancing directly overland to Richmond as Lincoln wished, McClellan moved his huge army by ship to a peninsula between the York and the James Rivers southeast of the city. From there he began a major offensive known as the Peninsular Campaign. The operation took many weeks.

Time passed and opportunities to attack slipped away as General McClellan readied his troops and tried to **evaluate** the enemy's strength. Lincoln, constantly prodding McClellan to fight, ended one message with an urgent plea: "You must act." McClellan did not act. His delays allowed the Confederates to prepare their defense of Richmond. At the end of June, the Union forces finally met the Confederates in a series of **encounters** known as the Seven Days' Battles.

In these battles, Confederate general Robert E. Lee took command of the army opposing McClellan. Before the battles began, Lee's cavalry leader, James E.B. (J.E.B.) Stuart, performed a daring tactic. He led his 1,200 troops in a circle around the Union army, gathering vital information about Union positions and boosting Southern morale. Lee's forces eventually drove the Yankees back. The Union troops had failed to capture Richmond.

Gloom in the North Reports from Richmond disheartened the North. Another call was made for volunteers—300,000 this time—but the response was slow. The Southern strategy of making the North weary of war seemed to be working. The defeat had not been complete, however. McClellan's army had been pushed back, but it was larger than Lee's and still only 25 miles from Richmond. President Lincoln ordered him to move his army back to northern Virginia and join the troops led by Major General John Pope.

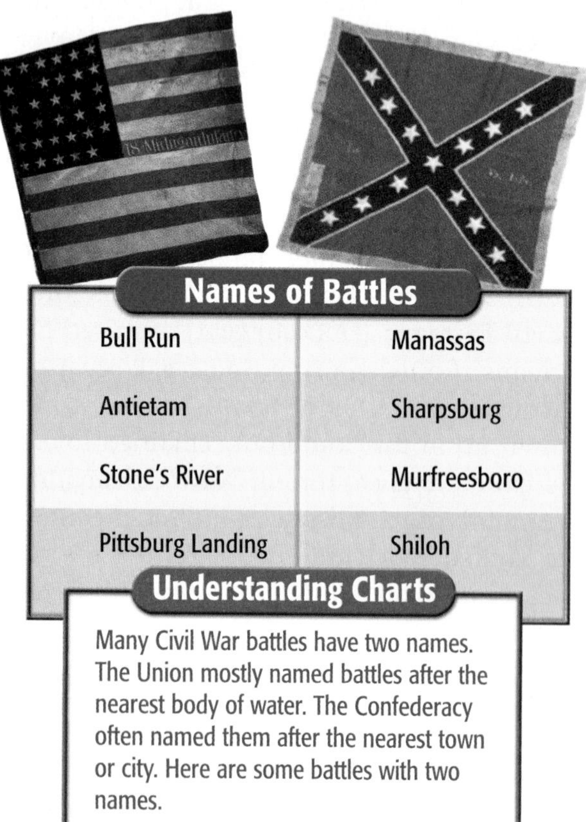

Names of Battles

Bull Run	Manassas
Antietam	Sharpsburg
Stone's River	Murfreesboro
Pittsburg Landing	Shiloh

Understanding Charts

Many Civil War battles have two names. The Union mostly named battles after the nearest body of water. The Confederacy often named them after the nearest town or city. Here are some battles with two names.

Stonewall Jackson's forces moved north to attack Pope's supply base at Manassas. Jackson's troops marched 50 miles in two days and were then joined by the rest of Lee's army. On August 29, 1862, Pope attacked the approaching Confederates and started the Second Battle of Bull Run. The battle ended in a Confederate victory. Richmond was no longer threatened. Instead, the situation of the two sides was completely reversed. Lee and the Confederates now stood only 20 miles from Washington, D.C.

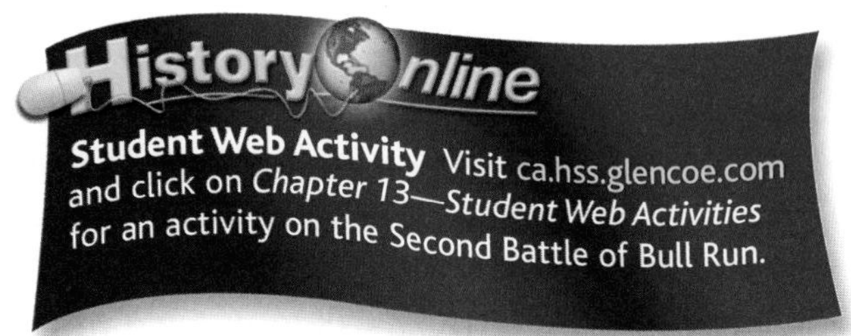
History Online
Student Web Activity Visit ca.hss.glencoe.com and click on Chapter 13—Student Web Activities for an activity on the Second Battle of Bull Run.

NATIONAL GEOGRAPHIC

The Early Battles, 1861–1862

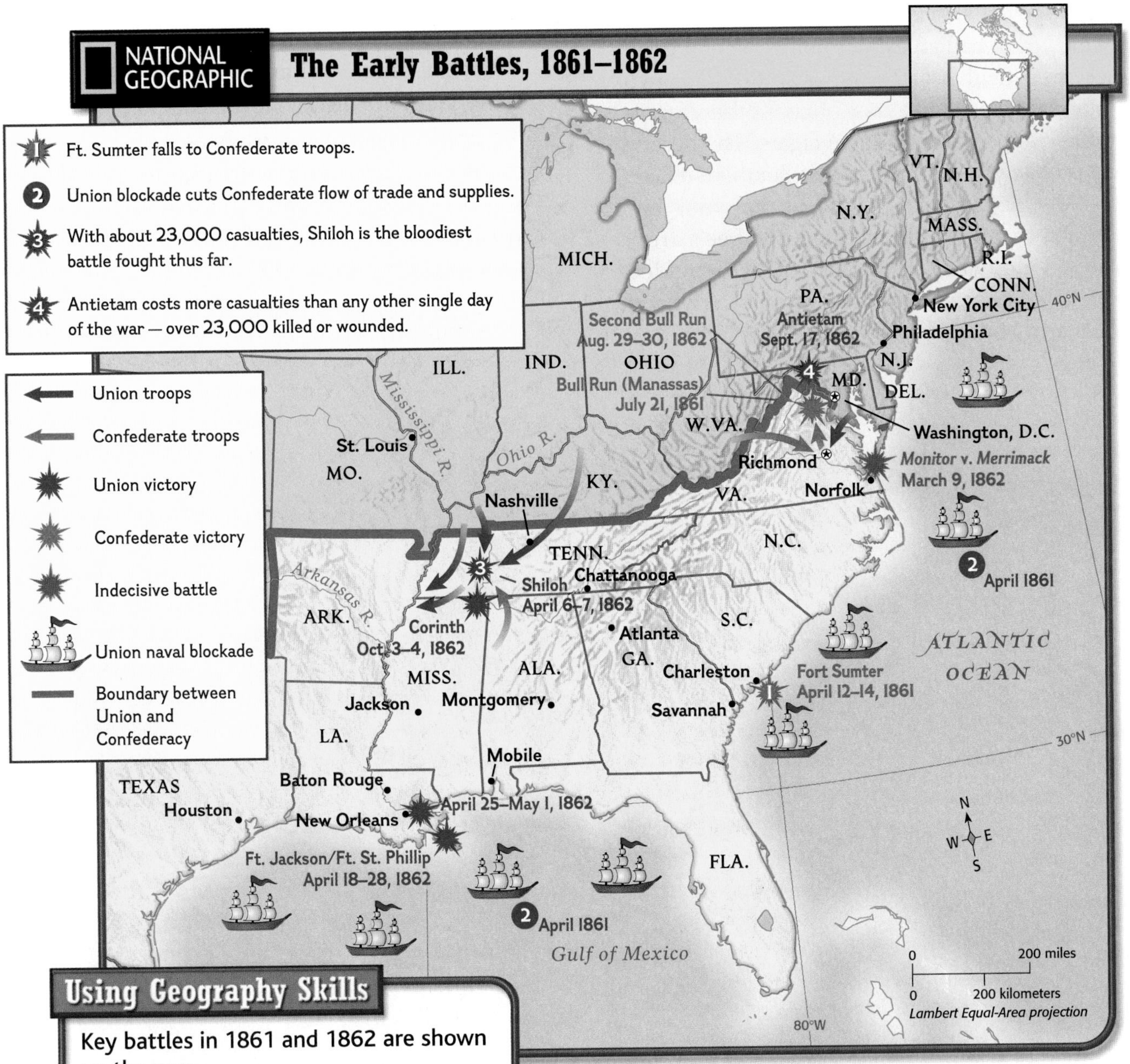

1 Ft. Sumter falls to Confederate troops.

2 Union blockade cuts Confederate flow of trade and supplies.

3 With about 23,000 casualties, Shiloh is the bloodiest battle fought thus far.

4 Antietam costs more casualties than any other single day of the war — over 23,000 killed or wounded.

- Union troops
- Confederate troops
- Union victory
- Confederate victory
- Indecisive battle
- Union naval blockade
- Boundary between Union and Confederacy

Using Geography Skills

Key battles in 1861 and 1862 are shown on the map.

1. **Location** In what state was the Battle of Shiloh fought?
2. **Summarize** In what battles were Confederate forces victorious?

Lee Enters Maryland Following these Southern victories, Confederate president Jefferson Davis ordered Lee to launch an offensive into Maryland, northwest of Washington. He hoped another victory would win aid from Great Britain and France. Lee also issued a proclamation urging the people of Maryland to join the Confederacy.

As Lee's army marched into Maryland in September 1862, McClellan and 80,000 Union troops moved slowly after them. On September 13, the North had an extraordinary piece of good luck. In a field near Frederick, Maryland, two Union soldiers found a copy of Lee's orders for his army wrapped around three cigars. The bundle had probably been dropped by a Southern officer.

Now McClellan knew exactly what Lee planned to do. He also learned that Lee's army was divided into four parts. This provided McClellan with an opportunity to overwhelm Lee's army one piece at a time.

The Battle of Antietam Once again, McClellan was overly cautious. He waited four days before he decided to attack the Confederates. This enabled Lee to gather most of his forces together near Sharpsburg, Maryland, along the Antietam Creek.

The Union and the Confederate armies clashed on September 17 in the Battle of Antietam. It was the single bloodiest day of the entire war. A Union officer wrote that

> **"In the time that I am writing every stalk of corn in [cornfields to the north] was cut as closely as could have been done with a knife, and the slain lay in rows precisely as they had stood in their ranks a few moments before."**
>
> **—Major General Joseph Hooker,** *Eyewitness Accounts*

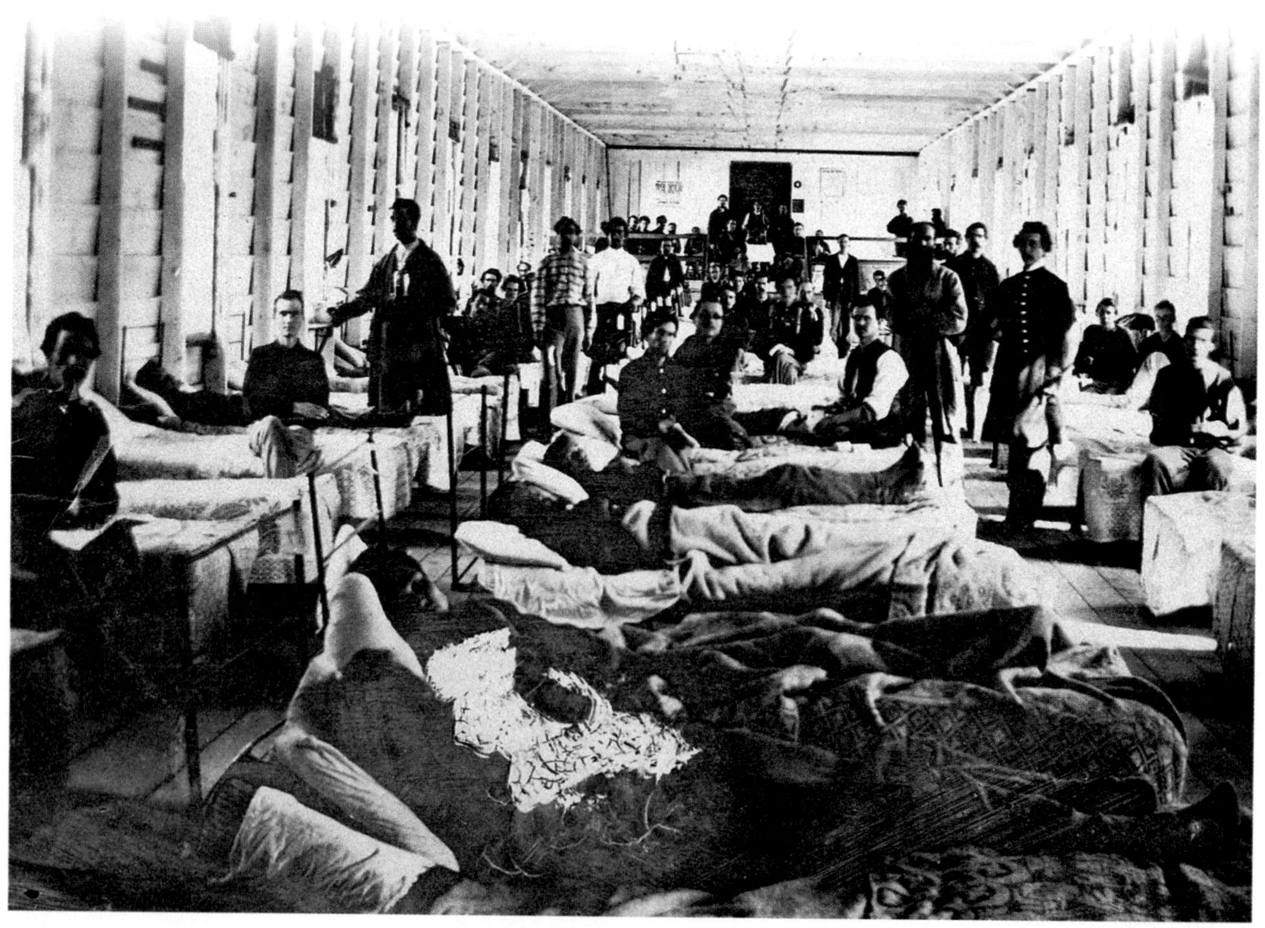

▲ Wounded soldiers at a military hospital at Alexandria, Virginia

By the time the fighting ended, close to 6,000 Union and Confederate soldiers lay dead or dying, and another 17,000 were seriously wounded. Although both armies suffered heavy losses, neither was destroyed.

The day after the battle, Lee withdrew to Virginia. The Confederate retreat allowed the Union troops to claim victory. However, McClellan, who had been ordered by President Lincoln to "destroy the rebel army," did not pursue the Confederate troops. The president, disgusted with McClellan's failure to follow up his victory, removed McClellan from his command in November. Lincoln placed General Ambrose Burnside in command.

The Battle of Antietam was a crucial victory for the Union. The British government had been ready to intervene in the war as a mediator if Lee's invasion had succeeded. It had also begun making plans to recognize the Confederacy in the event the North rejected mediation. With Lee's defeat, the British decided to withhold its support, and the South lost its best chance at gaining international recognition and support.

Antietam had a profound impact on the war. The Army of the Potomac finally gained some confidence, having forced Lee and his soldiers back south. More important, the battle marked a major change in Northern war aims. President Lincoln used the battle to take action against slavery.

Reading Check **Summarize** What was the outcome of the Seven Days' Battles?

History Online
Study Central Need help understanding early battles of the Civil War? Visit ca.hss.glencoe.com and click on Study Central.

Reading Summary

Review the Main Ideas

- Following the first major battle of the war, the Battle of Bull Run, which ended in a Confederate victory, the Union called for more troops and planned for a long war.
- A new era in naval warfare emerged as ironclad ships, belonging to the Union and Confederacy, fought for the first time.
- The Union gained a number of victories in the West as the North and South fought for control of the Mississippi River.
- In the East, the Union faced defeat, although a Confederate invasion of Maryland was turned back at the Battle of Antietam.

What Did You Learn?

1. Explain why the North wanted to blockade the South.
2. Which general won victories for the Union at Fort Henry and Fort Donelson? What nickname did he earn at the second battle?

Critical Thinking

3. **Drawing Conclusions** Why was control of the Mississippi River important? Use a diagram like the one shown here. CA CS3.

4. **Analyze** Why was Union general McClellan not effective as a military commander? CA HI2.
5. **The Big Ideas** What was the importance of the Union victory at the Battle of Antietam?
6. **ANALYSIS** **Analyze** You read about General Lee's battle orders that were dropped and found by a Union soldier. Write a short paragraph explaining the role of chance and error in this discovery and McClellan's use of the information. CA HI4.

Rifles for Watie

By Harold Keith

Before You Read

The Scene: This selection takes place at the Battle of Prairie Grove in northwest Arkansas. The date is December 7, 1862.

The Characters: Jeff Bussey is a private in the First Kansas Regiment of Infantry. His best friends, Noah Babbitt, Bill Earie, and Big Jake Lonegan are all in the same company, and Captain Clardy commands it. Mary and Bess are his sisters, and Ring is his dog. The Union army is under General Blunt.

The Plot: Jeff joined the army to defend his home from Confederate raiders. They were destroying the homes and farms of Union supporters in Kansas. Jeff has wanted to be in a battle since he joined the army.

Vocabulary Preview

acrid: smelling or tasting bitter
din: loud or confused sound
doleful: expressing grief; sad
gaunt: very thin and bony
ominously: in a way that is a sign of future trouble or evil
perplexed: puzzled
ricocheting: hitting a hard surface lightly and bouncing back
sheepishly: acting in an embarrassed way after becoming aware of a mistake

Have you ever wanted to do something because it seemed exciting? Was it as you imagined it would be, or was it different? Jeff is about to have his wish to be in a battle fulfilled. What will it be like?

As You Read

Writers may choose words and events to state an opinion. For example, Jeff lives with Confederates in another part of Rifles for Watie. *During this experience, he discovers that they are no different than any other people. As you read this selection, notice the kinds of words and events the author used. Think about what the writer may be saying concerning war.*

Jeff saw a tiny, circular puff of white smoke blossom above the trees. Then suddenly on the prairie some fifty yards in front of their line, a dash of dust, and something whizzed noisily over their heads, buzzing like a monster bee.

"Blam!"

Jeff dove flat on his stomach. He felt a painful jar as several of his comrades jumped in on top of him to escape the glancing rebel cannon ball.

"Boys, if I ain't flat enough, won't some o' you please jump on me and mash me flatter?" Bill Earie said weakly from the bottom of the pile.

"Git back into line!" Clardy roared sternly. "Eyes front! Stop your cowardly dodging! Any man leaving his station again will be shot!" With the flat[1] of his sword, Clardy spanked a timid recruit in the seat of his pants and pushed another roughly into position.

Sheepishly they re-formed their line. Jeff felt his breathing quicken. He saw another tiny spiral of smoke appear above the tops of the trees. This time a charge of grape[2] came flying overhead, screeching like forty locomotives. Again the men ducked instinctively, but this time only a few left the line.

"It's all right, boys," Jeff heard Bill giggle in his nervous tenor.[3] "Just dodge the biggest of 'em."

---

[1] **flat:** side

[2] **grape:** short for grape shot, which is a group of small iron balls shot from a cannon

[3] **tenor:** a man's singing voice with the highest natural range

Jeff felt a hysterical urge to laugh but discovered that he couldn't. For some strange reason, his throat had gone dry as a bone. The insides of his palms itched, and he could hear his pulse pounding. Again he checked the load in his rifle and was angry at himself. He knew there was nothing wrong with the rifle load.

Furious because he couldn't control his odd behavior, he clenched his jaws and shook his head vigorously. He had looked forward so long to his first battle. And now that the long-awaited moment had finally come, he discovered that some queer species of paralysis[4] had gripped his legs. His chest felt heavy, as if a blacksmith's anvil[5] was weighing it down. It was hard for him to breathe.

Noah looked at him anxiously. "What's the matter, youngster?"

Jeff licked his lips and swallowed once. Perplexed, he shook his brown head. "I don't know. My stomach feels bashful." Embarrassed, he looked around, hoping nobody would get the wrong idea and impute[6] this accursed nervousness to cowardice. He was fiercely determined not to disgrace his family or his county.

Suddenly the Union drums began to roll, loudly and ominously. . . .

"Fall in!"

Obediently Jeff backed into line, dressing up[7] on Noah's tall form next to him. A spiteful[8] crackle of rifle fire, punctuated by the deeper roar of cannon, broke suddenly from the woods. Now the stinking, acrid odor of gunpowder was on the air. A rebel bombshell screeched over their heads, hunting for them. Jeff imagined he could hear it say, "Where-is-yuh, where-is-yuh, where-is-yuh—booooom!"

He began to hear tiny thuds here and there in the ground. They reminded him of the first, isolated dropping of hailstones during a spring storm on the Kansas prairies. Tardily he realized they were rebel rifle bullets.

"Fix bayonets!" Mechanically Jeff groped for the scabbard at his belt. Fingers shaking, he managed to clamp the long knife over the muzzle of his rifle. He shot a quick look at Noah. It was good to have Noah next to him.

"Be ready, youngster! We're goin' in after 'em!" Noah yelled. Jeff pulled a couple of long breaths and felt the goose bumps rising on his arms.

He heard Clardy cursing. Big Jake Lonegan had thrown down his musket and run in terror to the rear. Jeff felt a powerful urge to follow him. He could hear the officers shouting threats, too, but they failed to stop the big sergeant or even to slow him down.

---

[4] **paralysis:** loss of ability to feel or move a body part or parts

[5] **anvil:** heavy metal block that has a flat top on which heated metal objects are hammered into shape

[6] **impute:** to falsely put the responsibility on

[7] **dressing up:** standing in a straight line and at the correct distance

[8] **spiteful:** annoying

Section
3

A Call to Freedom

Guide to Reading

Looking Back, Looking Ahead

As the war continued, African Americans gained opportunities to contribute to the war effort. The Emancipation Proclamation officially permitted African Americans to enlist in the Union army and navy.

Focusing on the Main Ideas

- Lincoln signed the Emancipation Proclamation, which led to the passing of the Thirteenth Amendment freeing enslaved Americans. *(page 592)*
- The Civil War provided opportunities for African Americans to contribute to the war effort. *(page 595)*

Meeting People

Harriet Tubman

Content Vocabulary

emancipate (ih • MAN • suh • PAYT)
ratify (RA • tuh • FY)

Academic Vocabulary

reluctance (rih • LUHK • tuhns)
area

Reading Strategy

Taking Notes As you read the section, complete a table like the one shown describing what the Emancipation Proclamation and the Thirteenth Amendment to the Constitution were meant to accomplish.

	Accomplishments
Emancipation Proclamation	
Thirteenth Amendment	

History Social Science Standards

US8.10 Students analyze the multiple causes, key events, and complex consequences of the Civil War.

NATIONAL GEOGRAPHIC
Who & When?
1862
1863
1864
1865
1862
African Americans begin to serve in Union army
Jan. 1863
Lincoln signs the Emancipation Proclamation
July 1863
Nearly half of the 54th Massachusetts Regiment is wiped out
1865
Thirteenth Amendment is ratified

US8.10.4 Discuss Abraham Lincoln's presidency and his significant writings and speeches and their relationship to the Declaration of Independence, such as his "House Divided" speech (1858), Gettysburg Address (1863), Emancipation Proclamation (1863), and inaugural addresses (1861 and 1865).

Emancipation

Main Idea **Lincoln signed the Emancipation Proclamation, which led to the passing of the Thirteenth Amendment, freeing enslaved Americans.**

Reading Connection Do you recall a time when an announcement had everyone talking? Read and find out about an announcement by Lincoln that changed lives forever.

President Lincoln shook many hands on New Year's Day of 1863, as a reception was held to commemorate the official signing of the Emancipation Proclamation. Diplomats, cabinet members, and army officers filed past the president, and when he finally left the reception, he noted that his arm was very stiff. As the document was presented, Lincoln remarked:

> **"Now, this signature is one that will be closely examined and if they find my hand trembled, they will say 'he had some compunctions [second thoughts].' But, any way, it is going to be done!"**
>
> —from *Lincoln*

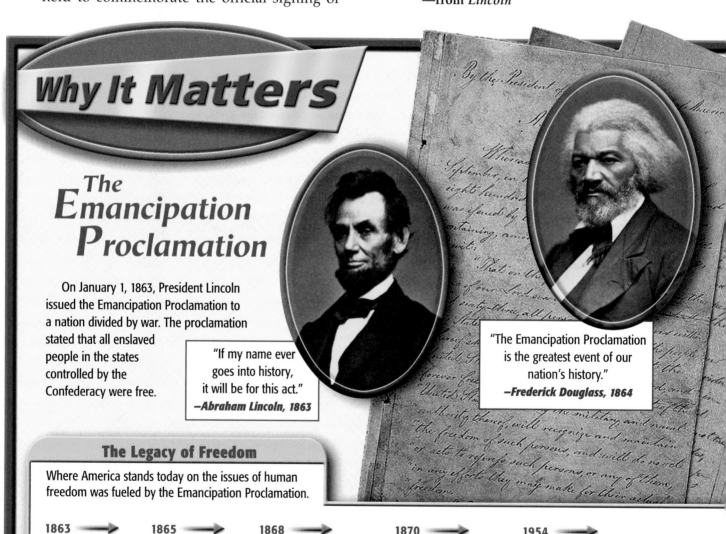

Why It Matters

The Emancipation Proclamation

On January 1, 1863, President Lincoln issued the Emancipation Proclamation to a nation divided by war. The proclamation stated that all enslaved people in the states controlled by the Confederacy were free.

"If my name ever goes into history, it will be for this act."
–Abraham Lincoln, 1863

"The Emancipation Proclamation is the greatest event of our nation's history."
–Frederick Douglass, 1864

The Legacy of Freedom

Where America stands today on the issues of human freedom was fueled by the Emancipation Proclamation.

1863 → Emancipation Proclamation issued

1865 → Thirteenth Amendment abolishes slavery

1868 → Fourteenth Amendment guarantees citizens equal protection

1870 → Fifteenth Amendment strengthens voting rights

1954 → *Brown* v. *Board of Education of Topeka, Kansas* ruling outlaws school segregation

From the start of the war through the brutal Battle of Antietam, the Northerners' main goal was to preserve the Union rather than to destroy slavery. Abolitionists did not control the North, or even the Republican Party. Abraham Lincoln and other Republican leaders insisted on many occasions that they would act only to prevent the expansion of slavery.

Although Lincoln considered slavery immoral, he showed **reluctance** to move against slavery because of the border states. Lincoln knew that making an issue of slavery would divide the people and make the war less popular. In August 1862, Abraham Lincoln responded to pressure to declare an end to slavery.

> **"If I could save the Union without freeing any slave, I would do it; if I could save it by freeing all the slaves, I would do it; and if I could save it by freeing some and leaving others alone, I would also do that. What I do about slavery, . . . I do because I believe it helps to save the Union."**
>
> **—Letter to Horace Greeley, August 22, 1862**

That was his official position. His personal wish was "that all men everywhere could be free."

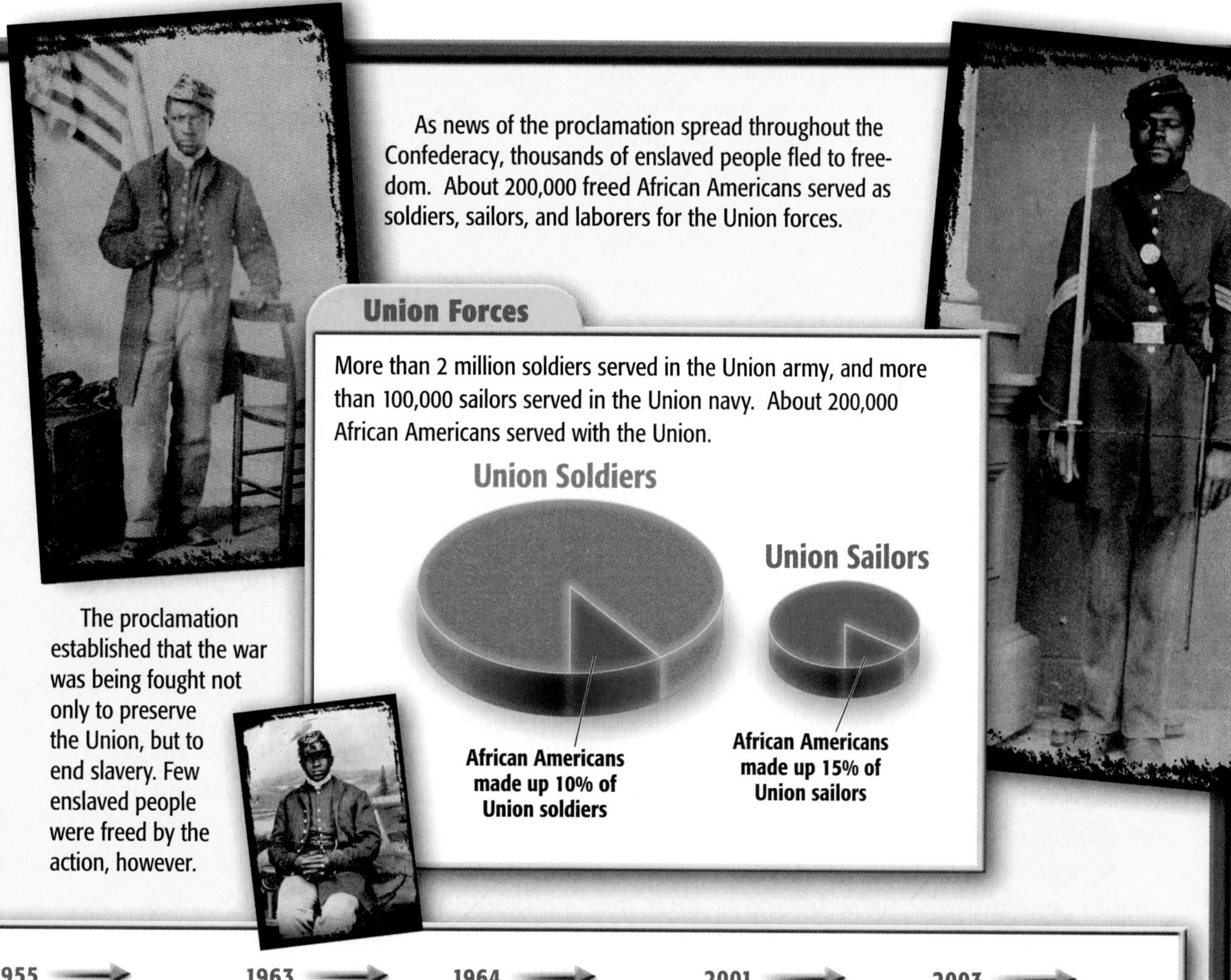

Union Soldiers
Union Sailors
African Americans made up 10% of Union soldiers
African Americans made up 15% of Union sailors

As news of the proclamation spread throughout the Confederacy, thousands of enslaved people fled to freedom. About 200,000 freed African Americans served as soldiers, sailors, and laborers for the Union forces.

Union Forces

More than 2 million soldiers served in the Union army, and more than 100,000 sailors served in the Union navy. About 200,000 African Americans served with the Union.

The proclamation established that the war was being fought not only to preserve the Union, but to end slavery. Few enslaved people were freed by the action, however.

1955 → Rosa Parks refuses to give up her bus seat; Montgomery, Alabama

1963 → March on Washington

1964 → Twenty-fourth Amendment ends use of poll tax; Civil Rights Act passed

2001 → Colin Powell named secretary of state

2003 → Scheduled work on national monument to Martin Luther King, Jr., begins

Changing Attitudes As the war went on, attitudes toward slavery began to change. More Northerners believed that slavery was helping the war effort in the South. Enslaved people in the Confederacy raised crops used to feed the armies and did the heavy work in the trenches at the army camps. In the North's view, anything that weakened slavery struck a blow against the Confederacy.

As early as May 1861, some African Americans in the South escaped slavery by going into territory held by the Union army. In 1861 and 1862, Congress passed laws that freed enslaved people who were held by those active in the rebellion against the Union.

Antietam and the Proclamation Lincoln was keenly aware of the shift in public opinion. He also knew that striking a blow against slavery would make Britain and France less likely to aid the South. Moreover, Lincoln became convinced that slavery helped the South continue fighting. Every enslaved person who worked enabled a white Southerner to fight in the Confederate army.

Lincoln also had political reasons for taking action on slavery. He believed it was important that the president rather than the antislavery Republicans in Congress make the decision on ending slavery. Lincoln told the members of his cabinet:

> **"I must do the best I can, and bear the responsibility."**

By the summer of 1862, Lincoln had decided to **emancipate** (ih • MAN • suh • PAYT)—or free—all enslaved African Americans in the South. He waited for the right moment so that he would not appear to be acting in desperation when the North seemed to be losing the war.

On September 22, 1862, five days after the Union forces turned back the Confederate troops at the Battle of Antietam, Lincoln announced his plan to issue an order freeing all enslaved people in the Confederacy. On January 1, 1863, Lincoln signed the Emancipation Proclamation, which said:

> **". . . all persons held as slaves within any state . . . in rebellion against the United States, shall be then, thenceforward, and forever free."**
>
> **—The Emancipation Proclamation**

Effects of the Proclamation The Emancipation Proclamation applied only to **areas** that the Confederacy controlled. Lincoln knew, however, that many enslaved people would hear about the proclamation. He hoped that knowledge of it would encourage them to run away from their slaveholders. Even before the Emancipation Proclamation, some 100,000 African Americans had left slavery for the safety of the Union. *(See page 855 of the Appendix for the text of the Emancipation Proclamation.)*

Despite the limitations of the Emancipation Proclamation, African Americans in the North greeted it joyfully. On the day it was signed, a crowd of African Americans gathered at the White House to cheer the president. Frederick Douglass wrote, "We shout for joy that we live to record this righteous decree."

The proclamation had the desired effect in Europe as well. The Confederacy had been seeking support from its trading partners, Britain and France. However, the British took a strong position against slavery. Once Lincoln proclaimed emancipation, Britain and France decided to withhold recognition of the Confederacy.

In 1864 Republican leaders in Congress prepared a constitutional amendment to abolish slavery in the United States. In 1865 Congress passed the Thirteenth Amendment, which was **ratified** (RA • tuh • FYD), or approved, the same year by states loyal to the Union. It was this amendment that truly freed enslaved Americans. *(See page 262 for the complete text of the Thirteenth Amendment.)*

Reading Check **Explain** What did the Thirteenth Amendment do that the Emancipation Proclamation did not do?

US8.10.5 Study the views and lives of leaders (e.g., Ulysses S. Grant, Jefferson Davis, Robert E. Lee) and soldiers on both sides of the war, including those of black soldiers and regiments. **US8.10.6** Describe critical developments and events in the war, including the major battles, geographical advantages and obstacles, technological advances, and General Lee's surrender at Appomattox.

African Americans in the War

Main Idea **The Civil War provided opportunities for African Americans to contribute to the war effort.**

Reading Connection How do you think freed African Americans affected the Union war effort? Read to find out how many formerly enslaved people fought against the South during the Civil War.

The Emancipation Proclamation announced Lincoln's decision to permit African Americans to join the Union army. In the South, as well as in the North, the Civil War was changing the lives of all African Americans.

In the South When the war began, more than 3.5 million enslaved people lived in the Confederacy. Making up more than 30 percent of the region's population and the bulk of its workforce, enslaved workers labored on plantations and in vital iron, salt, and lead mines. Some worked as nurses in military hospitals and cooks in the army. By the end of the war, about one-sixth of the enslaved population had fled to areas controlled by Union armies.

The possibility of a slave rebellion terrified white Southerners. For this reason, most Southerners refused to use African Americans as soldiers—for then they would be given weapons.

Near the end of the war, however, the Confederate military became desperate. Robert E. Lee and some others supported using African Americans as soldiers and believed that those who fought should be freed. The Confederate Congress passed a law in 1865 to enlist enslaved people. The war ended before any regiments could be organized.

Helping the North The story was different in the North. At the start of the war, African Americans were not permitted to serve as soldiers in the Union army. This disappointed many free African Americans who had volunteered to fight for the Union.

Yet African Americans who wished to help the war effort found ways to do so. Although the army would not accept them, the Union navy did. African Americans who had escaped slavery often proved to be useful as guides and spies because of their knowledge of the South. Some women, such as **Harriet Tubman,** who had helped dozens escape slavery by way of the Underground Railroad, repeatedly spied behind Confederate lines.

▲ Nearly 200,000 African Americans joined Union forces.

African American Soldiers In 1862 Congress passed a law allowing African Americans to serve in the Union army. By the end of the war, African American volunteers made up nearly 10 percent of the Union army and about 15 percent of the navy. In all, nearly 200,000 African Americans served. About 37,000 lost their lives defending the Union. By becoming soldiers, African Americans were taking an important step toward securing civil rights.

African American soldiers were organized into regiments separate from the rest of the Union army. Most commanding officers of these regiments were white. African Americans received lower pay than white soldiers at first, but protests led to equal pay in 1864.

One of the most famous African American regiments was the 54th Massachusetts, led by white abolitionists. On July 18, 1863, the 54th spearheaded an attack on a Confederate fortification near Charleston, South Carolina. Under heavy fire, the troops battled their way to the top of the fort. The Confederates drove them back with heavy fire. Nearly half of the 54th were wounded, captured, or killed. Their bravery won respect for African American troops.

Many white Southerners, outraged that African American soldiers were fighting for the Union, threatened to execute any they captured. In a few instances, this threat was carried out. However, enslaved workers were overjoyed when they saw that the Union army included African American soldiers. As one African American regiment entered Wilmington, North Carolina, young and old ran through the streets, shouting and praising God. One of the soldiers said, "We could then truly see what we have been fighting for."

Reading Check **Compare** How were African American soldiers treated differently than white soldiers?

History Online

Study Central Need help understanding life for African Americans during the war? Visit ca.hss.glencoe.com and click on Study Central.

Reading Summary

Review the Main Ideas

- The Emancipation Proclamation freed all enslaved African Americans who were living in Confederate states.
- Many free African Americans and African Americans who had escaped from slavery enlisted with the Union army and fought in the war.

What Did You Learn?

1. Summarize President Lincoln's reasons for issuing the Emancipation Proclamation.
2. How did Harriet Tubman help the North?

Critical Thinking

3. **Determining Cause and Effect** Re-create the diagram below and list the factors that caused Lincoln to change his war goals to include freeing enslaved persons. CA HI2.

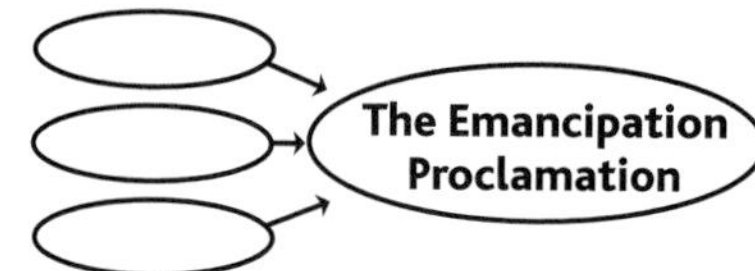

4. **Compare** How did President Lincoln's political stand on slavery differ from his personal stand? CA HR5.
5. **The Big Ideas** Describe the role of African Americans in the Union army. How were they treated, and how did President Lincoln justify their role? CA HI1.
6. **Creative Writing** Write the dialogue for a short play in which enslaved African Americans on a Southern plantation learn of the Emancipation Proclamation and discuss what it means to them. CA 8WA2.1C

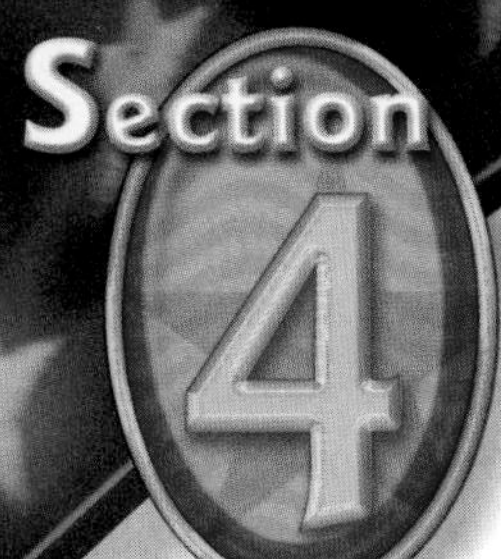

Section 4 Life During the Civil War

Guide to Reading

Looking Back, Looking Ahead

The Civil War affected civilians as well as soldiers. Civilians had an important impact on the war effort.

Focusing on the Main Ideas

- In both the North and the South, civilians and soldiers suffered terrible hardships and faced new challenges. *(page 598)*
- Many Northern and Southern women took on new responsibilities during the war. *(page 599)*
- The war efforts of the Union and the Confederate governments faced opposition. *(page 600)*
- The war created economic problems in the North and in the South. *(page 603)*

Meeting People

Mary Chesnut
Rose O'Neal Greenhow
Belle Boyd
Loretta Janeta Velázquez (vuh • LAS • kwihz)
Dorothea Dix
Clara Barton
Sally Tompkins

Content Vocabulary

habeas corpus (HAY • bee • uhs KAWR • puhs)
draft
bounty
inflation (ihn • FLAY • shuhn)

Academic Vocabulary

distribute (dih • STRIH • byuht)
substitute
occur (uh • KUHR)

Reading Strategy

Classifying Information As you read the section, complete a table like the one shown by describing the roles of these individuals during the war.

Person	Role
Loretta Janeta Velázquez	
Dorothea Dix	
Clara Barton	

History Social Science Standards

US8.10 Students analyze the multiple causes, key events, and complex consequences of the Civil War.

NATIONAL GEOGRAPHIC Who & When?

1861 — 1862 — 1863 — 1864

1861 Union Congress passes income tax

Union soldier

Apr. 1862 Confederate Congress passes draft

Confederate soldier

Mar. 1863 Union passes draft law

July 1863 Angry mobs oppose the draft in New York City

US8.10.5 Study the views and lives of leaders (e.g., Ulysses S. Grant, Jefferson Davis, Robert E. Lee) and soldiers on both sides of the war, including those of black soldiers and regiments.

The Lives of Soldiers

Main Idea **In both the North and the South, civilians and soldiers suffered terrible hardships and faced new challenges.**

Reading Connection How do most movies portray the life of a soldier? Do they make the military life seem exciting and filled with action? Read to find out what life was really like for a Civil War soldier.

A soldier's life was not easy. In touching letters to their families and friends at home, soldiers described what they saw and how they felt—their boredom, discomfort, sickness, fear, and horror.

At the start of the war, men in both the North and the South rushed to volunteer for the armies. Their enthusiasm did not last.

Most of the time, the soldiers lived in camps. Camp life had its pleasant moments of songs, stories, letters from home, and baseball games. Often, however, a soldier's life was dull, a routine of drills, bad food, marches, and rain.

The Reality of War In spite of some moments of calm, the reality of war was never far away. Both sides suffered terrible losses. The new rifles used during the Civil War fired with greater accuracy than the muskets of earlier wars.

Medical facilities were overwhelmed by the thousands of casualties in each battle. After the Battle of Shiloh, many wounded soldiers lay in the rain for more than 24 hours waiting for medical treatment. A Union soldier recalled, "Many had died there, and others were in the last agonies as we passed. Their groans and cries were heart-rending."

Faced with such horrors, many men deserted. About 1 of every 11 Union soldiers and 1 of every 8 Confederates ran away because of fear, hunger, or sickness.

Rebel soldiers suffered from a lack of food and supplies. One reason for Lee's invasion of Maryland in 1862 was to allow his army to feed off Maryland crops. A woman who saw the Confederates march to Antietam recalled the "gaunt starvation that looked from their cavernous eyes."

Reading Check **Explain** Why did many soldiers desert from the armies?

Picturing **History**

Some paintings offered an idealized picture of the Civil War. Photographs provided a chilling account of life—and death—at the front lines. ***In what ways might photographs have affected Americans' view of the war in a way that paintings did not?***

US8.10.7 Explain how the war affected combatants, civilians, the physical environment, and future warfare.

Women and the War

Main Idea **Many Northern and Southern women took on new responsibilities during the war.**

Reading Connection Think of ways the women in your family would be affected by a war in their own backyards. Read to learn the many ways women were affected by the Civil War.

In times of war, people often fill new roles. Women in the North and the South became teachers and office workers, and they managed farms. They also suffered the loss of husbands, fathers, sons, and brothers. As **Mary Chesnut** of South Carolina wrote:

> **"Does anyone wonder [why] so many women die? Grief and constant anxiety kill nearly as many women at home as men are killed on the battle-field."**
>
> —from *Mary Chesnut's Civil War*

Women performed many jobs that helped the soldiers and the armies. They rolled bandages, wove blankets, and made ammunition. Many women collected food, clothing, and medicine to **distribute** to the troops. They also raised money for supplies.

Life at Home For the most part, Northerners saw the war from a distance, since most of the battles took place in the South. News from the battlefront and letters home from the soldiers kept the war in people's minds.

Almost every woman who stayed at home was touched in some way by the war. But while everyday life in the North suffered little disruption, life in the South was dramatically changed.

Those who lived in the paths of marching armies lost crops and homes. As one Southerner noted: the South had depended upon the outside world "for everything from a hairpin to a toothpick, and from a cradle to a coffin." As the war dragged on, shortages became more commonplace.

Picturing **History**

This 1862 photo shows a Union soldier with his family at the front near Washington, D.C. Most soldiers on both sides, however, faced long separations from their families. ***What other hardships did Civil War soldiers face?***

US8.10.7 Explain how the war affected combatants, civilians, the physical environment, and future warfare.

The South ran out of almost everything. Shortages in feed for animals and salt for curing meant that little meat was available. Shortages of meat were matched by shortages of clothing, medicine, and even shelter.

Women as Spies Some women served as spies. Harriet Tubman spied for the North. **Rose O'Neal Greenhow** entertained Union leaders in Washington, D.C., picking up information about Union plans that she passed to the South. Greenhow was caught and exiled to the South.

Belle Boyd, of Virginia, informed Confederate generals of Union army movements in the Shenandoah Valley. Some women disguised themselves as men and became soldiers. A Cuban native, **Loretta Janeta Velázquez** (vuh•LAS•kwihz), of New Orleans, reportedly fought for the South at the First Battle of Bull Run and at Shiloh.

Treating the Sick and Wounded In the Civil War, thousands of women served as nurses. At first many doctors did not want women nurses because they felt that women were too delicate for such work. Men disapproved of women doing what was considered men's work. Also, it was thought improper for women to tend the bodies of unknown men.

Strong-minded women disregarded these objections. In the North, **Dorothea Dix,** the reformer for conditions of prisoners and people with disabilities, organized large numbers of women to serve as military nurses. Another Northerner, **Clara Barton,** became famous for her work with wounded soldiers. In the South, **Sally Tompkins** established a hospital for soldiers in Richmond, Virginia.

Nursing was hard work. Kate Cummings of Alabama, who nursed the wounded in Corinth after the Battle of Shiloh, wrote, "Nothing that I had ever heard or read had given me the faintest idea of the horrors witnessed here."

Reading Check **Describe** What role did Sally Tompkins play in the war effort? Which other women played a similar role in the North?

Opposition to the War

Main Idea **The war efforts of the Union and the Confederate governments faced opposition.**

Reading Connection Can you think of a time when you disagreed or opposed something? Did you take action? Read to learn how various people opposed the Civil War and why.

Both the Union and the Confederate governments faced opposition. Politicians objected to war policies, and ordinary citizens protested the way the war affected their lives.

When the war began, Northern Democrats split into two groups. One group supported most of Lincoln's wartime policies. The other, the "Peace Democrats," favored negotiating with the Confederacy. The Peace Democrats warned that continuing the war would lead to "terrible social change and revolution."

Conflict With the Copperheads Republicans called the Peace Democrats "Copperheads" after a poisonous snake that strikes without warning. When Union armies lost battles, support for the Copperheads rose.

Some Republicans suspected Copperheads of aiding the Confederates. The president ordered the arrest of anyone interfering with the war effort, such as discouraging men from enlisting in the army. Several times Lincoln suspended the right of **habeas corpus** (HAY•bee•uhs KAWR•puhs), which guarantees accused individuals the right to a hearing before being jailed. Lincoln defended his actions, asking:

> **"Must I shoot a simple-minded soldier boy who deserts, while I must not touch a hair of a wily agitator who induces him to desert?"**
>
> **—Letter to Erastus Corning, June 12, 1863**

Enlistments Decline As the war dragged on, fewer men volunteered to serve. Enlisting enough soldiers became a problem, so the Confederacy and the Union tried new measures.

Biography

US8.10.7 Explain how the war affected combatants, civilians, the physical environment, and future warfare.

Clara Barton
1821–1912

When the Civil War began, Clara Barton, a U.S. Patent Office clerk, began collecting provisions for the Union army. In 1862 she began to deliver supplies directly to the front and to tend to the wounded and dying during battle.

The youngest of five children, Barton often felt out of place among her successful older brothers and sisters. When her brother, David, suffered a work-related accident, Barton found her place in the family as David's nurse and caregiver. Her talent for nursing led her into a life in which she was satisfied only when helping and caring for others.

Arriving at the Battle of Antietam to deliver supplies, Barton watched as surgeons dressed the soldiers' wounds with corn husks because they did not have bandages. As the battle raged around her, Barton comforted the wounded and helped the doctors with their work. For her courage, Barton became known as "the angel of the battlefield."

As the Civil War drew to a close, Barton set up an office to assist families and friends looking for missing soldiers and prisoners of war. Thousands of letters came flooding in written by mothers looking for sons and wives looking for husbands. Barton began to publish advertisements in newspapers asking readers to send information on the whereabouts of any soldier listed in the ad. By 1868 she had identified 22,000 missing men.

". . . I shall remain here while anyone remains, and do whatever comes to my hand. I may be compelled to face danger, but never fear it, and while our soldiers can stand and fight, I can stand and feed and nurse them."

—Letter to her father, 1861

Then and Now

Look online or in the phone book to find your local chapter of the Red Cross. Call or e-mail your local office and find out the following information: What kind of work has the chapter recently done? How can volunteers aid the organization?

Draft Laws In April 1862, the Confederate Congress passed a **draft** law that required men between ages 18 and 35 to serve in the army for three years. A person could avoid the draft by hiring a **substitute** to serve in his place.

Union states encouraged enlistment by offering **bounties**—payments to encourage volunteers. In March 1863, when this system failed, the North turned to a draft. All men from age 20 to 45 had to register, and the army drew the soldiers it needed from this pool of names. A person could avoid the draft by hiring a substitute or by paying the government $300.

Protests against the draft erupted in several Northern cities. The worst disturbance took place in New York City in July 1863. Angry mobs, opposed to the draft and to fighting to free African Americans, went on a rampage of burning, looting, and killing. After four days of terror, more than 100 people were dead.

No disturbance as severe took place in the South, but many opposed the draft. The strong opposition led Jefferson Davis, the president of the Confederacy, to proclaim military law and suspend habeas corpus as Lincoln had done early in the war. Davis's action outraged Southerners, who feared that they would lose the liberties for which they had gone to war.

Reading Check **Examine** Why did the governments institute a draft? Why did protests occur in some places?

TECHNOLOGY & History

Civil War Camera

Photographer Mathew Brady and his many assistants recorded the camps, lives, and deaths of soldiers in more than 10,000 photos. **What is the biggest difference between this camera and a more modern one?**

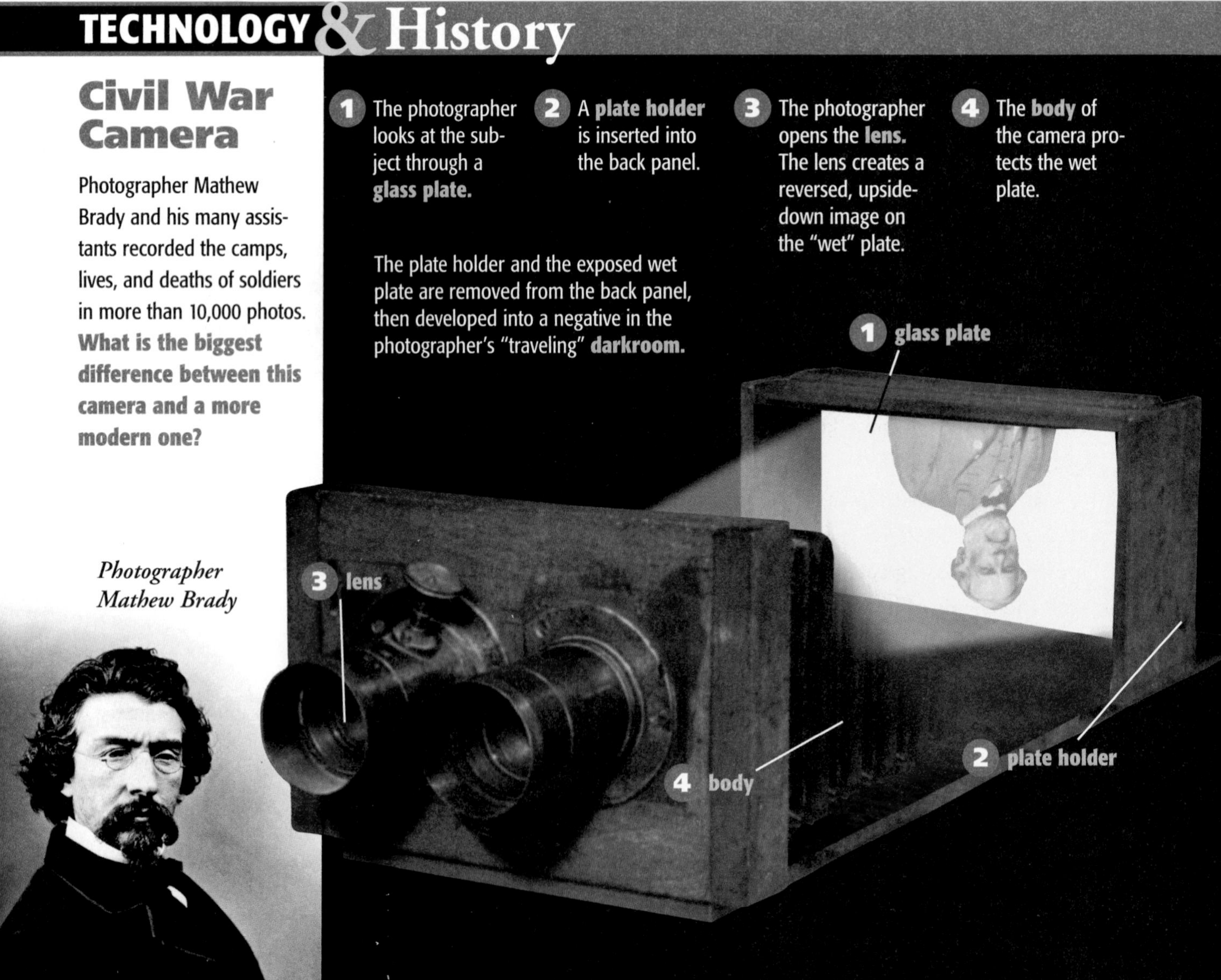

1 The photographer looks at the subject through a glass plate.
2 A plate holder is inserted into the back panel.
3 The photographer opens the lens. The lens creates a reversed, upside-down image on the "wet" plate.
4 The body of the camera protects the wet plate.
The plate holder and the exposed wet plate are removed from the back panel, then developed into a negative in the photographer's "traveling" darkroom.
1 glass plate
3 lens
4 body
2 plate holder

Photographer Mathew Brady

US8.10.7 Explain how the war affected combatants, civilians, the physical environment, and future warfare.

War and the Economy

Main Idea **The war created economic problems in the North and in the South.**

Reading Connection If you had to choose a side to fight for in the Civil War, which side would you choose? Read to learn the effects the war economy had on both the North and South.

The Civil War is often called the first "modern" war because it required the total commitment of resources. Such a war has an impact on every part of life. However, the impact was more devastating on the South than on the North.

The South struggled to carry out its war effort. Its government encouraged factories to supply arms and ammunition, but the South lacked the industry to provide necessities for civilians and for the military.

The economy of the South suffered far more than that of the North. Because most fighting **occurred** in the South, Southern farmland was overrun and rail lines were torn up.

The North's blockade of Southern ports caused severe shortages of essential goods. A scarcity of food led to riots in Atlanta, Richmond, and other cities. **Inflation** (ihn•FLAY•shuhn)—a general increase in the level of prices—was much worse in the South.

These conditions affected soldiers. Worries about their families caused many men to desert. A Mississippi soldier who overstayed his leave to help his family wrote the governor: "We are poor men and are willing to defend our country but our families [come] first."

Reading Check **Explain** What is inflation? **What hardships did inflation cause in the South?**

History Online
Study Central Need help understanding how the war affected daily life? Visit ca.hss.glencoe.com and click on Study Central.

Section 4 Review

Reading Summary

Review the Main Ideas

- Civil War soldiers faced boredom in camp and terrible horrors on the battlefield.
- During the Civil War, women took over men's jobs on farms and in factories. They also served as nurses and spies.
- Opposition to the war was especially strong in the North, and as the war dragged on, both the North and the South faced declining enlistments.
- During the war, the North's economy suffered some, but the South's economy faced ruin as the fighting devastated farmland and rail lines.

What Did You Learn?

1. Why was life on the home front more difficult for Southerners?
2. What do Rose O'Neal Greenhow, Belle Boyd, and Loretta Janeta Velázquez have in common with Harriet Tubman?

Critical Thinking

3. **Analyze** Describe three ways that women in the North and South contributed to the war effort. CA HI1.

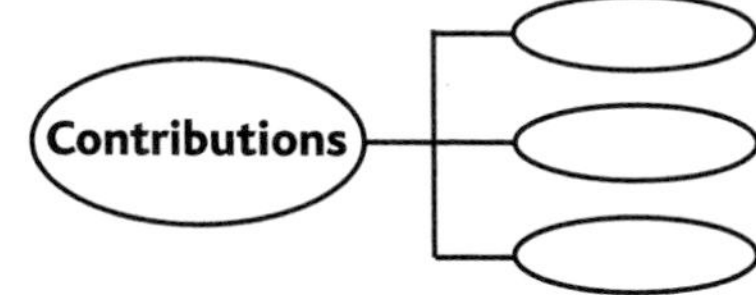

4. **Evaluate** Why do you think President Lincoln believed the Copperheads were a threat to the Union war effort? CA HI2.
5. **The Big Ideas** Describe the methods used by both the North and the South to enlist men into the army in the later years of the war. CA CS1.
6. **Economics** List three sectors of the economy that welcomed women during the Civil War. Describe the jobs women held and contributions they made. CA HI6. CA 8WA2.5

Section
5

The Way to Victory

Guide to Reading

Looking Back, Looking Ahead

The Civil War continued with the Confederacy gaining the upper hand by 1863. However, victories at Gettysburg and Vicksburg turned the tide in favor of the Union.

Focusing on the Main Ideas

- After Confederate victories in Fredericksburg and Chancellorsville, a turning point occurred when Union forces won in Gettysburg and Vicksburg. *(page 605)*
- The end of the war was in sight with Sherman's capture of Atlanta and Grant's pursuit of the Confederates in Virginia. *(page 607)*
- After four years of war that claimed the lives of more than 600,000 Americans, the Northern forces defeated the Southern forces. *(page 610)*

Locating Places

Chancellorsville, Virginia
Vicksburg, Mississippi
Petersburg, Virginia
Mobile Bay
Savannah, Georgia
Appomattox Court House

Meeting People

Ambrose Burnside
Joseph Hooker
George Meade
William Tecumseh Sherman

Content Vocabulary

entrench (ihn • TREHNCH)
total war

Academic Vocabulary

outcome
nevertheless (NEH • vuhr • thuh • LEHS)

Reading Strategy

Organizing Information Use a web like the one shown to describe the strategy Grant adopted to defeat the Confederacy.

Grant's Strategy

History Social Science Standards

US8.10 Students analyze the multiple causes, key events, and complex consequences of the Civil War.

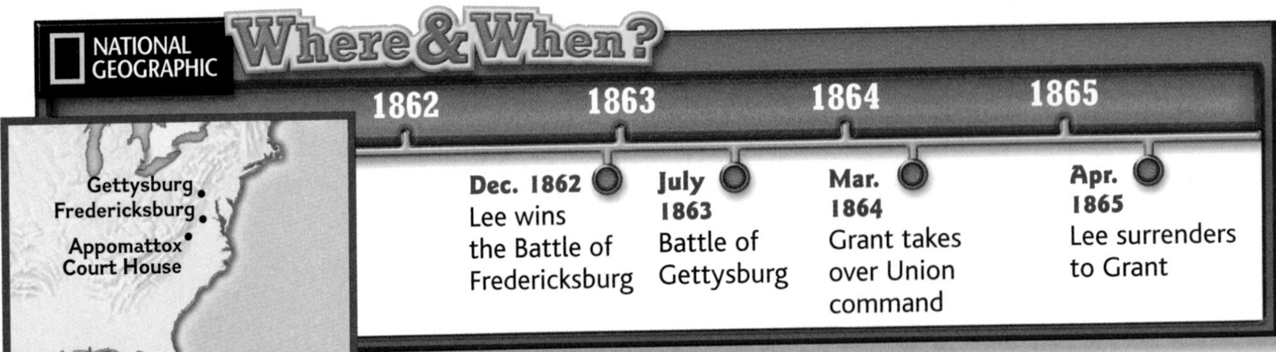
NATIONAL GEOGRAPHIC
Where & When?
1862
1863
1864
1865
Gettysburg
Fredericksburg
Appomattox Court House
Dec. 1862 Lee wins the Battle of Fredericksburg
July 1863 Battle of Gettysburg
Mar. 1864 Grant takes over Union command
Apr. 1865 Lee surrenders to Grant

Lincoln's vice president, Andrew Johnson, became president. Johnson had been a Democrat living in Tennessee before the Civil War. He had served as a mayor and state legislator before being elected to the United States Senate. When Tennessee seceded from the Union, Johnson remained loyal and stayed in the U.S. Senate, making him a hero in the North.

Results of the War The Civil War was the most devastating conflict in American history. More than 600,000 soldiers died, and the war caused billions of dollars of damage, most of it in the South. The devastation had left the South's economy in a state of collapse. Roughly two thirds of the transportation system lay in ruins, with many bridges destroyed and miles of railroad twisted and rendered useless. The war also created bitter feelings among defeated Southerners that lasted for generations.

The war had other consequences as well. The North's victory saved the Union. The federal government was strengthened and was now clearly more powerful than the states. Finally, the war freed millions of African Americans. The end of slavery, however, did not solve the problems that the newly freed African Americans were to face.

Following the war, many questions remained. No one yet knew how to bring the Southern states back into the Union, nor what the status of African Americans would be in Southern society. Americans from the North and the South tried to answer these questions in the years following the Civil War—an era known as Reconstruction.

Reading Check **Identify** Where did General Lee surrender?

History Online
Study Central Need help understanding the conclusion of the war? Visit ca.hss.glencoe.com and click on Study Central.

Section 5 Review

Reading Summary

Review the Main Ideas

- The Confederate army seemed unbeatable after the Battles of Fredericksburg and Chancellorsville, but Northern victories at Gettysburg and Vicksburg turned the tide of the war for the Union.
- In the West, Sherman's army captured Atlanta and marched to the Atlantic coast. In the East, Grant's army maintained a strong offensive against the Confederate army under General Lee.
- In early April 1865, Grant's forces captured Richmond, and Lee's Confederate army surrendered soon after.

What Did You Learn?

1. Identify the reasons that Gettysburg and Vicksburg were important battles.
2. At what Virginia town did Lee defeat Burnside's forces?

Critical Thinking

3. **Analyze** Use a chart like the one shown to explain the significance of each battle listed. CA CS2.

Battle	Importance
Gettysburg	
Vicksburg	
Mobile Bay	
Richmond	

4. **Math Connection** Using the chart on page 608, create two new charts or graphs that communicate the same information in different ways. CA HR3.
5. **The Big Ideas** How did battlefield events affect Lincoln's reelection? CA HI2.
6. **Expository Writing** Refer to Lincoln's Gettysburg Address on page 856. Write an essay discussing Lincoln's ideas on freedom and the importance of saving the Union. CA 8WA2.4

US8.10.6 Describe critical developments and events in the war, including the major battles, geographical advantages and obstacles, technological advances, and General Lee's surrender at Appomattox.

GEOGRAPHY & HISTORY

West Woods

Hagerstown Pike

Dunker Church

This is the area that is shown above.

Potomac River

Hagerstown Pike

Dunker Church

Bloody Lane

Union Headquarters

SHARPSBURG

Confederate Headquarters

Antietam Creek

0 1/2 mile

0 1/2 kilometer

History Online
Self-Check Quiz Visit ca.hss.glencoe.com to prepare for the Chapter 13 test.

Read to Write

16. **The Big Ideas** **Evaluate** Write a short essay that describes the impact that civilians had on the war effort. Include references to both the North and the South. CA 8WS1.1

17. **Paraphrase** To explain his reelection, Lincoln stated, "it was not best to swap horses while crossing the river." Write a paragraph that explains Lincoln's quotation and how it applied to his career. CA 8WA2.2

18. **Using Your FOLDABLES** Use your foldable to write three sentences that summarize the main ideas of this chapter. Share your sentences with the class, and listen to their sentences. Then vote for the one you think best summarizes the chapter. CA 8RC2.0

Using Academic Vocabulary

19. Write a paragraph that uses these academic vocabulary words to describe an event from this chapter:
    a. sufficient
    b. reinforce
    c. encounter

Linking Past and Present

20. **Making Connections** A writ of habeas corpus is a court order that guarantees a person who is arrested the right to appear before a judge in a court of law. During the Civil War, President Lincoln suspended habeas corpus. What recent crisis led to similar actions? Write a short essay describing these actions and why they were taken. CA CS1.

Economics Connection

21. **Compare** Economic differences had always existed between the North and the South. From your reading of Chapter 13, would you say that the North or the South was better equipped economically for war? Explain your reasoning. CA HI6.

Reviewing Skills

22. Review READING SKILL **Evaluation** Review the section called "Total War" on page 609. Write a paragraph that evaluates the effectiveness of this strategy in accomplishing the Union's goals. Take into account the impact of this on the Confederacy and its civilians. CA 8WA2.4

23. Review ANALYSIS SKILL **Sequencing** Draw a time line that includes the major battles you read about in this chapter. Include battle dates, locations, and outcomes. CA CS2.

Select the best answer for each of the following questions.

24 By gaining control of the Mississippi and Tennessee Rivers, the Union was able to

- **A** capture Fort Sumter.
- **B** force the Confederacy to surrender.
- **C** split the Confederacy.
- **D** defeat the Confederate forces at Gettysburg.

25 The Thirteenth Amendment was important because

- **A** it gave women the right to vote.
- **B** it outlawed secession.
- **C** it abolished slavery in the United States.
- **D** limited the President to two terms in office.

Chapter 14 Reconstruction

Ruins of a railroad depot, Charleston, South Carolina

NATIONAL GEOGRAPHIC Who & When?

1860 | 1870 | 1880

1865 President Lincoln is assassinated

1870 Fifteenth Amendment extends voting rights

1877 Reconstruction ends

Members of Congress

History Online

Chapter Overview Visit ca.hss.glencoe.com for a preview of Chapter 14.

The Big Ideas

Reconstruction Plans

Political ideas and major events shape how people form governments. Northern politicians disagreed on how to bring the southern states back into the Union.

Radicals in Control

A constitution reflects the values and goals of the society that creates it. The Radical Republicans in Congress worked to ensure the rights of the newly freed African Americans in the South.

The South During Reconstruction

Political ideas and major events shape how people form governments. African Americans in the South made some gains in government and education, but many white Southerners attempted to limit their rights.

Change in the South

Economic, social, and political changes create new traditions, values, and beliefs. As Reconstruction ended, white Southerners attempted to make economic changes in the South, while restricting the rights of African Americans.

View the Chapter 14 video in the Glencoe Video Program.

FOLDABLES™ Study Organizer

Comparison Make this foldable to help you compare and contrast Reconstruction in the Northen and Southern states.

Step 1 Mark the midpoint of the side edge of a sheet of paper.

Draw a mark at the midpoint.

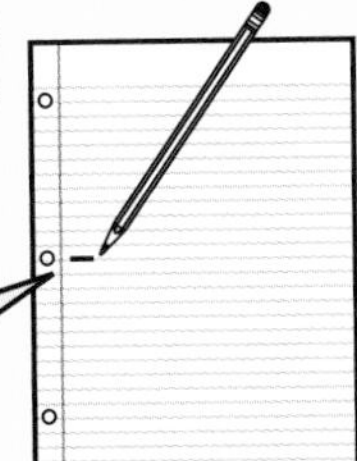

Step 2 Turn the paper and fold the edges in to touch at the midpoint.

Step 3 Turn and label your foldable as shown.

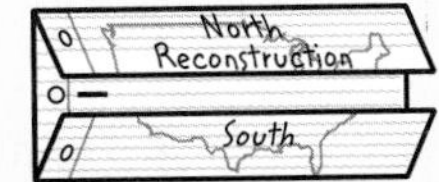

Reading and Writing
As you read the chapter, write facts that show how Reconstruction differed and was the same in the Northern states and Southern states. Write the facts in the appropriate places inside your foldable.

Get Ready to Read

Monitoring and Clarifying

1 Learn It!

Good readers monitor their understanding of text. When a portion of the reading is confusing, good readers use strategies to understand, such as looking up new words, rereading, and reading a bit farther to locate more information. This is called clarifying. As you read, stop and determine which parts were unclear. Identify unfamiliar words, and look on the page for supporting diagrams, maps, or pictures that might help you. Read the following paragraph using these techniques.

What is a reconstruction government? Was it explained earlier in the chapter?

In the 1870s, Reconstruction governments began creating public school systems for both races, which had not existed in the South before the war. Within a few years, more than 50 percent of the white children and about 40 percent of African American children in the South were enrolled in public schools. Northern missionary societies also established academies offering advanced education for African Americans.

—from page 638

What were the children doing who weren't enrolled in public schools?

What is a missionary society? Is it defined in the glossary?

As you read, make a list of words you don't know. Look them up in the dictionary. Practice using them and your vocabulary words in sentences.

2 Practice It!

Read the passage on the Freedmen's Bureau from Section 1. With a partner, see if you can answer the questions below:

> More progress was made in helping freed African Americans. In March 1865, Congress and the president set up a new government agency to help former enslaved persons, or freedmen. It was known as the Freedmen's Bureau.
>
> After the war, the Freedmen's Bureau helped African Americans adjust to freedom. The agency distributed food and clothing, and provided medical services that lowered the death rate among freed African Americans. It also set up schools staffed by Northern teachers such as Charlotte Forten and gave aid to new African American schools of high learning, such as Atlanta University, Howard University, and Fisk University. The bureau helped freed people acquire land or work with fair wages. Although the main goal of the bureau was to aid African Americans, it also helped pro-Union Southerners.
>
> —*from page 626*

Read to Write

Look in your local newspaper or a magazine for an interview with a famous person. Based on what you read, what additional questions would you ask?

▼ Mother and daughter reading

Monitor	Clarify
Were there any unfamiliar words?	Look in a glossary or dictionary
Do you know what the Freedmen's Bureau was?	
Who created the new agency?	Reread selection

3 Apply It!

As you read this chapter, identify one topic or event that you would like explained more fully. Then, do research to find answers to the questions you have. Use your answers to write a paragraph of explanation.

Section
1

Reconstruction Plans

Guide to Reading

History Social Science Standards

US8.11 Students analyze the character and lasting consequences of Reconstruction.

Looking Back, Looking Ahead

You learned that the Civil War ended in a Northern victory but at terrible costs to both sides. Northern politicians needed to figure out how to return the Southern states to the Union and what rights to allow the newly freed African Americans.

Focusing on the Main Ideas

- Differences over how Reconstruction after the Civil War should be carried out divided the government. *(page 625)*
- After Lincoln was assassinated, Johnson became president and announced his plan of "Restoration." *(page 626)*

Meeting People

Thaddeus Stevens
Charlotte Forten
John Wilkes Booth
Andrew Johnson

Content Vocabulary

Reconstruction (REE • kuhn • STRUHK • shuhn)
amnesty (AM • nuh • stee)
radical (RA • dih • kuhl)
freedmen

Academic Vocabulary

period
approach (uh • PROHCH)
deny (dih • NY)
aid

Reading Strategy

Taking Notes As you read the section, re-create the diagram below and describe each of the Reconstruction plans.

Plan	Description
Ten Percent Plan	
Wade-Davis Plan	
Restoration	

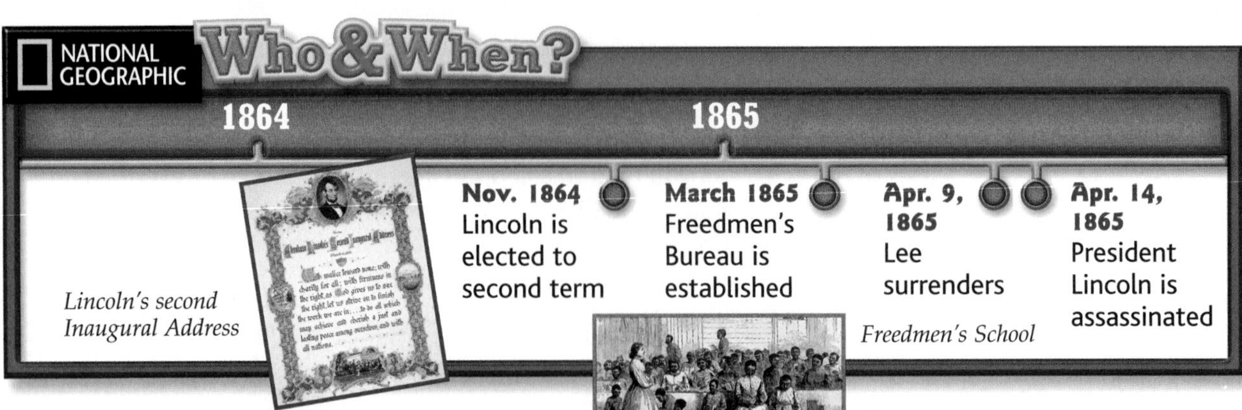
NATIONAL GEOGRAPHIC
Who & When?
1864
1865
Nov. 1864 Lincoln is elected to second term
March 1865 Freedmen's Bureau is established
Apr. 9, 1865 Lee surrenders
Apr. 14, 1865 President Lincoln is assassinated

Lincoln's second Inaugural Address

Freedmen's School

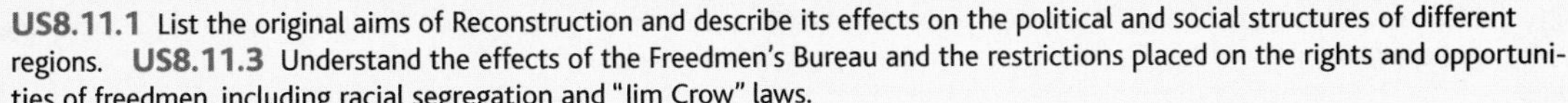

US8.11.1 List the original aims of Reconstruction and describe its effects on the political and social structures of different regions. US8.11.3 Understand the effects of the Freedmen's Bureau and the restrictions placed on the rights and opportunities of freedmen, including racial segregation and "Jim Crow" laws.

Reconstruction Debate

Main Idea **Differences over how Reconstruction after the Civil War should be carried out divided the government.**

Reading Connection How would you have established terms of peace and rebuilding following the Civil War? Read to find out how President Lincoln and the Republicans in Congress disagreed about the treatment of the Southern states as they returned to the Union.

An American Story

When Confederate soldiers—tired, ragged, and hungry—went home at the end of the war, they often returned to a ruined land. Mary Chesnut of South Carolina wrote about what she saw and felt when she traveled:

> **"CAMDEN, S. C., *May 2, 1865.* Since we left Chester nothing but solitude, nothing but tall blackened chimneys, to show that any man has ever trod this road before. This is Sherman's track. It is hard not to curse him. I wept incessantly at first. The roses of the gardens are already hiding the ruins."**
>
> —Mary Chesnut, *A Diary From Dixie*

"We have turned. . . loose four million slaves without a hut to shelter them or a cent in their pockets."

—Thaddeus Stevens in a speech to Congress, December 1865

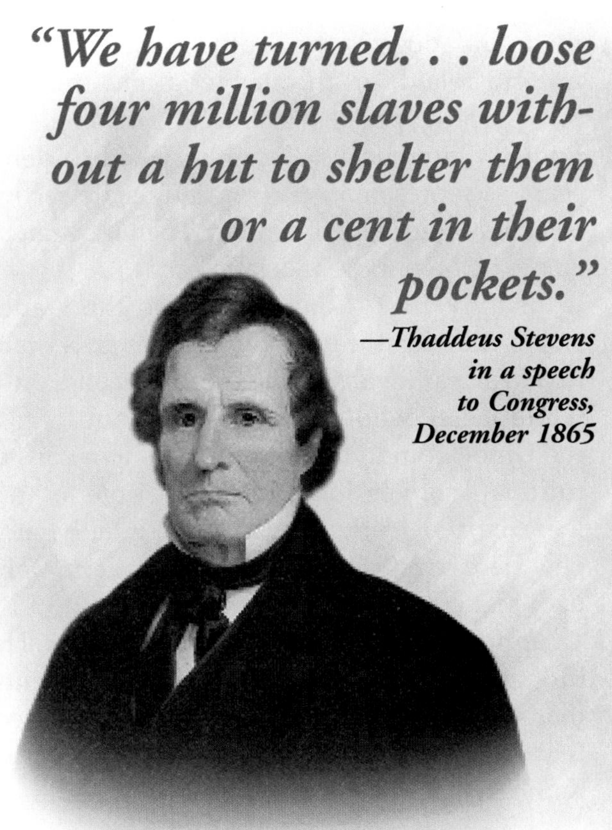

Destruction in the South The war saved the Union but left the South devastated. Cities and plantations were in ruin, and roads, bridges and railroads were destroyed. More than 258,000 Confederate soldiers had died in the war, and illness and injuries weakened thousands more. Americans everywhere agreed that the South needed to be rebuilt, but they disagreed bitterly over how to accomplish it. This **period** of rebuilding is called **Reconstruction** (REE • kuhn • STRUHK • shuhn). This term also refers to the various plans for carrying out the rebuilding.

Lincoln's Plan President Lincoln offered the first plan for accepting the South back into the Union. In December 1863, during the Civil War, the president announced the Ten Percent Plan. When 10 percent of the voters of a state took an oath of loyalty to the Union, the State could form a government and adopt a new constitution that banned slavery.

Lincoln wanted to encourage pro-Union Southerners to run the state governments. He believed that punishing the South would only delay healing the torn nation. The president offered **amnesty** (AM • nuh • stee)—immunity from prosecution—to all white Southerners, except Confederate leaders, who gave loyalty to the Union. In 1864 three states under Union occupation—Louisiana, Arkansas, and Tennessee—set up governments under Lincoln's plan. Some Republicans considered Lincoln's plan too mild. Favoring a more **radical,** or extreme, **approach,** they were called Radical Republicans.

US8.11.5 Understand the Thirteenth, Fourteenth, and Fifteenth Amendments to the Constitution and analyze their connection to Reconstruction.

The Radicals' Plan A leading Radical Republican, **Thaddeus Stevens,** declared that the foundations of the South "must be broken up and relaid, or all our blood and treasure have been spent in vain." Controlled by Radical Republicans, Congress voted to **deny** seats to representatives from any state reconstructed under Lincoln's plan. Then it began to create its own more radical plan.

In July 1864, Congress passed the Wade-Davis Bill. First, most white males in a state had to swear loyalty to the Union. Second, only white males who swore they had not fought the Union could vote for delegates to a constitutional convention. Former Confederates were barred from public office. Finally, any new state constitution had to end slavery. Only then could a state rejoin the Union.

Lincoln refused to sign the bill into law. He did, however, want new state governments that would restore order quickly. He realized that he would have to compromise with the Radical Republicans.

The Freedmen's Bureau More progress was made in helping freed African Americans. In March 1865, Congress and the president set up a new government agency to help former enslaved persons, or **freedmen.** It was known as the Freedmen's Bureau.

After the war, the Freedmen's Bureau helped African Americans adjust to freedom. The agency distributed food and clothing, and provided medical services that lowered the death rate among freed African Americans. It also set up schools staffed by Northern teachers such as **Charlotte Forten** and gave **aid** to new African American schools of higher learning, such as Atlanta University, Howard University, and Fisk University. The bureau helped freed people acquire land or work with fair wages. Although the main goal of the bureau was to aid African Americans, it also helped pro-Union Southerners.

Reading Check **Explain** What was Lincoln's Ten Percent Plan?

Lincoln Is Assassinated

Main Idea **After Lincoln was assassinated, Johnson became president and announced his plan of "Restoration."**

Reading Connection How do you think the loss of a strong leader might impact a nation during a difficult time? Read to find out how the death of Lincoln affected the course of Reconstruction.

A terrible event soon threw the debates over Reconstruction into confusion. On the evening of April 14, 1865, President and Mrs. Lincoln attended a play at Ford's Theater in Washington, D.C. As the Lincolns watched the play from a private box in the balcony, **John Wilkes Booth,** a pro-Confederate actor, entered the box and shot the president in the head. He then leaped to the stage and escaped from the theater. The wounded president died a few hours later.

After fleeing Ford's Theater, Booth rode on horseback to Virginia. There, Union troops tracked him down and cornered him in a barn. When Booth refused to give up, he was shot to death. Booth was part of a small group that had plotted to kill several government officials.

A Nation Mourns News of Lincoln's death shocked the nation. African Americans mourned the death of the man who had helped them win their freedom. Northern whites grieved for the leader who had saved the Union.

A funeral train carried Lincoln's body on a 1,700-mile journey from Washington, D.C., to his home town of Springfield, Illinois. Thousands of people lined the route. At night, bonfires and torches lit the way. By day, bells tolled and cannons fired.

Lincoln's second Inaugural Address, read at the cemetery, reminded Americans of his plan "to do all which may achieve and cherish a just, and a lasting peace, among ourselves, and with all nations." The future, however, was in the hands of those who favored harsher measures against the former Confederacy.

The South During Reconstruction

Guide to Reading

Looking Back, Looking Ahead

You learned that Congress passed the Fourteenth and Fifteenth Amendments to help African Americans gain equal rights. Although African Americans made some gains, most white Southerners refused to recognize their rights.

Focusing on the Main Ideas

- Violence against African Americans and their white supporters took place during Reconstruction. *(page 636)*
- After the Civil War, the South had to rebuild not only its farms and roads, but its social and political structures as well. *(page 638)*

Meeting People

Hiram Revels
Frederick Douglass
Blanche K. Bruce

Content Vocabulary

scalawag (SKA • lih • WAG)
carpetbagger (KAHR • puht • BA • guhr)
corruption (kuh • RUHP • shuhn)
integrate (IN • tuh • GRAYT)
sharecropping (SHEHR • KRAHP • ihng)

Academic Vocabulary

dominate (DAH • muh • NAYT)
brief (BREEF)
region (REE • juhn)
create (kree • AYT)

Reading Strategy

Organizing Information As you read the section, re-create the diagram below and describe improvements in the South in education.

Improvements in education

History Social Science Standards

US8.11 Students analyze the character and lasting consequences of Reconstruction.

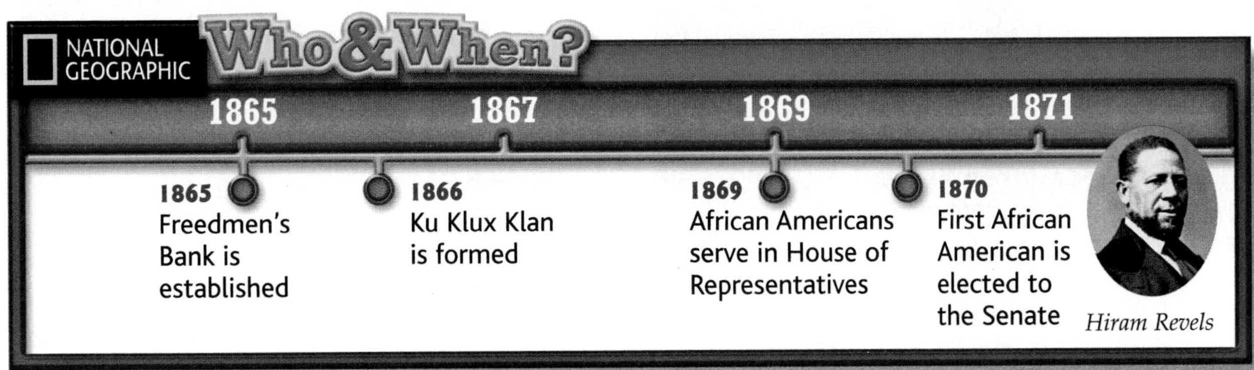
NATIONAL GEOGRAPHIC
Who&When?
1865
1867
1869
1871
1865 Freedmen's Bank is established
1866 Ku Klux Klan is formed
1869 African Americans serve in House of Representatives
1870 First African American is elected to the Senate
Hiram Revels

US8.11.3 Understand the effects of the Freedmen's Bureau and the restrictions placed on the rights and opportunities of freedmen, including racial segregation and "Jim Crow" laws. US8.11.4 Trace the rise of the Ku Klux Klan and describe the Klan's effects.

New Groups Take Charge

Main Idea **Violence against African Americans and their white supporters took place during Reconstruction.**

Reading Connection How might you feel if someone tried to take away your rights through threats and violence? Read to find out how some white Southerners attempted to intimidate African Americans and keep them from voting and exercising their rights.

An American Story

"The dust of our fathers mingles with yours in the same graveyards. . . . This is your country, but it is ours too." So spoke an emancipated African American after the Civil War. Most formerly enslaved people did not seek revenge or power over whites, only respect and equality. The petition of an African American convention in 1865 stated:

> **"We simply desire that we shall be recognized as men; . . . that the same laws which govern *white men* shall direct colored men; . . . that we be dealt with as others, in equity [fairness] and justice."**
>
> **—Address of the Colored State Convention to the People of the State of South Carolina**

Picturing **History**

In 1870 Hiram Revels was elected to the Senate. ***What state did he represent?***

Republicans Take Charge During Reconstruction, the Republicans came to **dominate** Southern politics. Support for the Republican party came from African Americans, white Southerners who backed Republican goals, and white settlers from the North. These groups ran state governments.

African Americans in Government African Americans played an important role both as voters and as officials. In some states, they contributed heavily to Republican victories. African Americans did not control the government of any state, although they **briefly** had a majority in the lower house of the South Carolina legislature. In other Southern states, they held major positions but never in proportion to their numbers.

At the national level, 16 African Americans served in the House of Representatives and 2 in the Senate between 1869 and 1880. **Hiram Revels,** one of the African American senators, was an ordained minister who had recruited African Americans for the Union army. He also started a school for freed African Americans in Missouri and served as a chaplain of an African American regiment in Mississippi. Revels remained in Mississippi after the war and was elected to the Senate in 1870. **Frederick Douglass** was also an important leader who insisted on full equality for African Americans.

Blanche K. Bruce, the other African American senator, also came from Mississippi. A former runaway slave, Bruce taught in an African American school in Missouri when the war began. In 1869 he went to Mississippi and entered politics. He was elected to the Senate in 1874.

By 1876 Republicans held a majority in Congress in only three Southern states—Florida, South Carolina, and Louisiana. During these years, the Republicans had other problems they could not blame on the Democrats. In 1873 a series of political scandals came to light. Investigations uncovered top government officials making unfair business deals, scheming to withhold public tax money, and accepting bribes. One scandal involved the vice president, and another the secretary of war. These scandals further damaged the Grant administration and the Republicans. At the same time, the nation suffered an economic depression. Blame for the hard times fell on the Republicans.

By the time of the congressional elections in 1874, charges of corruption and economic mismanagement had badly weakened the Republican Party. Democrats gained seats in the Senate and won control of the House. For the first time since the Civil War, the Democratic Party controlled a part of the federal government. This situation further weakened Congress's commitment to Reconstruction and protecting the rights of newly freed African Americans.

▼ *Lincoln's funeral carriage*

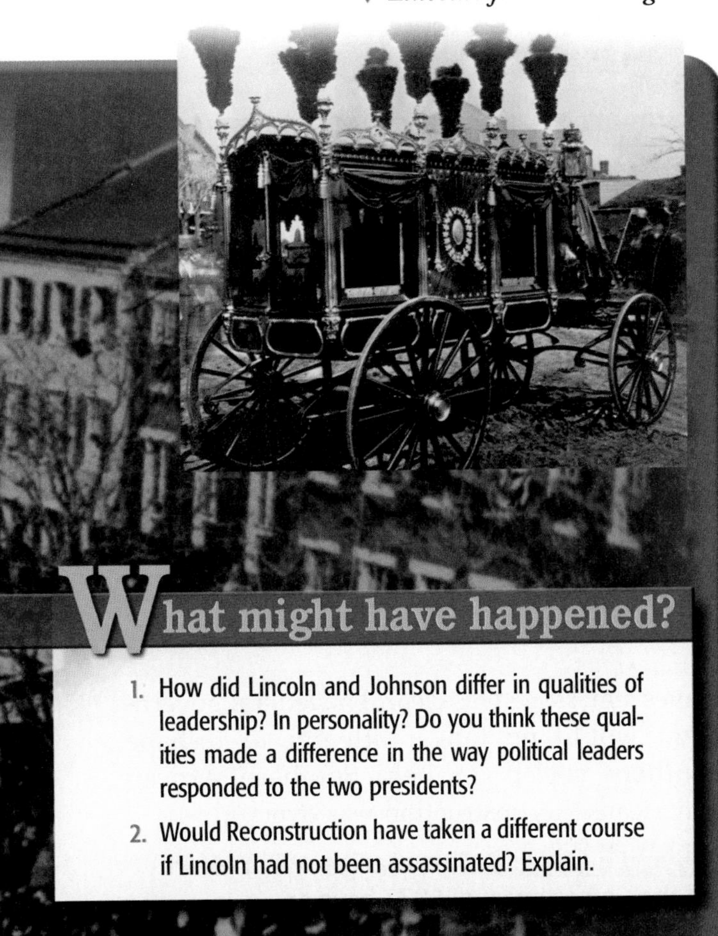

What might have happened?

1. How did Lincoln and Johnson differ in qualities of leadership? In personality? Do you think these qualities made a difference in the way political leaders responded to the two presidents?
2. Would Reconstruction have taken a different course if Lincoln had not been assassinated? Explain.

The Election of 1876 President Grant considered running for a third term in 1876. Most Republican leaders preferred a new candidate—one who could win back the Liberal Republicans and unite the party.

The Republicans nominated **Rutherford B. Hayes,** governor of Ohio, for president. A champion of political reform, Hayes had a reputation for honesty, and he held moderate views on Reconstruction. The Democrats nominated New York governor **Samuel Tilden.** Tilden had gained national fame for fighting political corruption in New York City.

After the election, Tilden appeared to be the winner, receiving almost 250,000 more votes than Hayes. However, disputed returns from Florida, Louisiana, South Carolina, and Oregon—representing 20 electoral votes—kept the outcome in doubt. Tilden had 184 electoral votes, only one short of what he needed to win. Yet if Hayes received all 20 of the disputed votes, he would have the 185 electoral votes required for victory.

In January Congress created a special **commission,** or group, of seven Republicans, seven Democrats, and one independent to review the election results. But the independent resigned, and a Republican took his place. After examining the reports of state review boards, the commission voted 8 to 7 to award all 20 disputed votes, and the election, to Hayes. The vote followed party lines.

Democrats in Congress threatened to fight the decision to award the presidency to Hayes. Inauguration Day approached, yet the country still had no new president. Finally, Republican and Southern Democratic leaders met secretly to work out an agreement.

Disputed Election of 1876

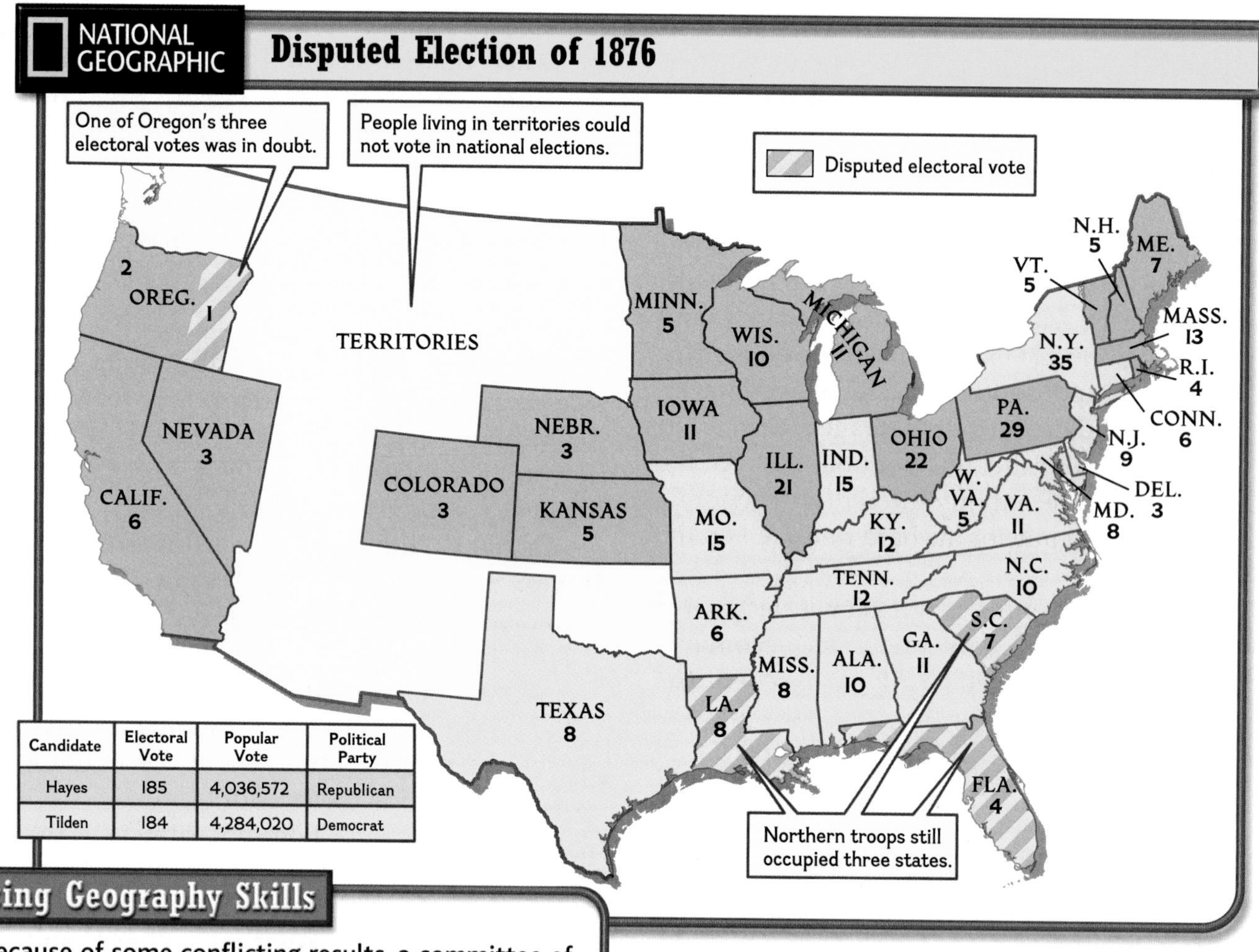

Candidate	Electoral Vote	Popular Vote	Political Party
Hayes	185	4,036,572	Republican
Tilden	184	4,284,020	Democrat

Using Geography Skills

Because of some conflicting results, a committee of 15 members from Congress and the Supreme Court decided the final count in the 1876 election.

1. **Location** Which Southern states sent in election returns that were disputed?
2. **Analyze** By how many electoral votes did Hayes finally win?

Compromise of 1877 Southern Democratic leaders agreed to accept Hayes as president. On March 2, 1877—almost four months after the election—Congress confirmed the verdict of the commission and declared Hayes the winner. He was inaugurated president two days later.

The deal congressional leaders made to settle the election dispute, the Compromise of 1877, included various favors to the South. The new government would give more aid to the region and withdraw all remaining troops from Southern states. The Democrats, in turn, promised to maintain African Americans' rights.

In his Inaugural Address, Hayes declared that what the South needed most was the restoration of "wise, honest, and peaceful local self-government." During a goodwill trip to the South, Hayes announced his intention of letting Southerners handle racial issues. In Atlanta he told an African American audience:

> **"... [your] rights and interests would be safer if this great mass of intelligent white men were let alone by the general Government."**

Hayes's message was clear. The federal government would no longer attempt to reshape Southern society or help Southern African Americans. Reconstruction was over.

Reading Check **Summarize** What effect did the Compromise of 1877 have on Reconstruction?

US8.11.1 List the original aims of Reconstruction and describe its effects on the political and social structures of different regions.

The South After Reconstruction

Main Idea **When Reconstruction ended, many changes took place in the South including a political shift and growth in industry.**

Reading Connection How difficult do you think it would be for an area to change its economy from agricultural to industrial? Read to find out how Southern leaders attempted to create a "New South" with strong industries that could compete with those in the North.

An American Story

John Lynch, a member of Congress who had once been enslaved, spoke these words:

> **"I am treated, not as an American citizen, but as a brute. . . . [A]nd for what? Not that I am unable to or unwilling to pay my way; not that I am obnoxious in my personal appearance or disrespectful in my conduct; but simply because I happen to be of a darker complexion."**
>
> **—quoted in "John Roy Lynch"**

At the end of Reconstruction, many African Americans faced lives of poverty, indignity, and despair.

A New Ruling Party Many Southern whites hated Republicans because of their role in the Civil War and during Reconstruction. When Reconstruction ended, political power in the South shifted from the Republicans to the Democrats.

In some regions, the ruling Democrats were the large landowners and other groups that had held power before the Civil War. In most areas, however, a new ruling class took charge. Among their ranks were merchants, bankers, industrialists, and other business leaders who supported economic development and opposed Northern interference. These Democrats called themselves "Redeemers" because they had "redeemed," or saved, the South from Republican rule.

The Redeemers adopted conservative policies such as lower taxes, less public spending, and reduced government services. They drastically cut, or even **eliminated,** many social services started during Reconstruction, including public education. Their one-party rule and conservative policies dominated Southern politics well into the 1900s.

Rise of the "New South" By the 1880s, forward-looking Southerners were convinced that their region must develop a strong industrial economy. They argued that the South had lost the Civil War because its industry and manufacturing did not match the North's.

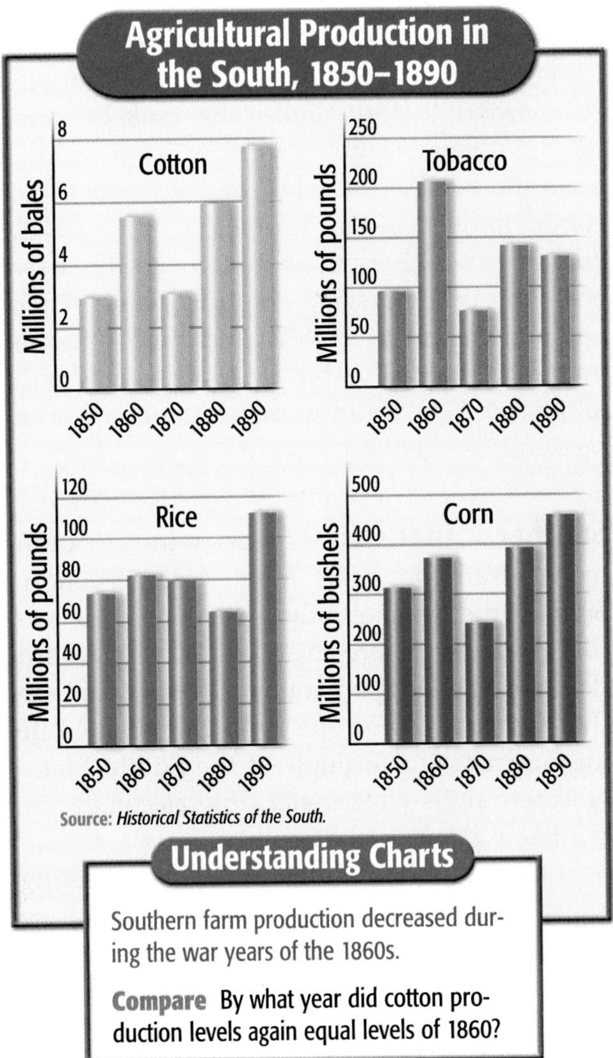

Source: *Historical Statistics of the South.*

Understanding Charts

Southern farm production decreased during the war years of the 1860s.

Compare By what year did cotton production levels again equal levels of 1860?

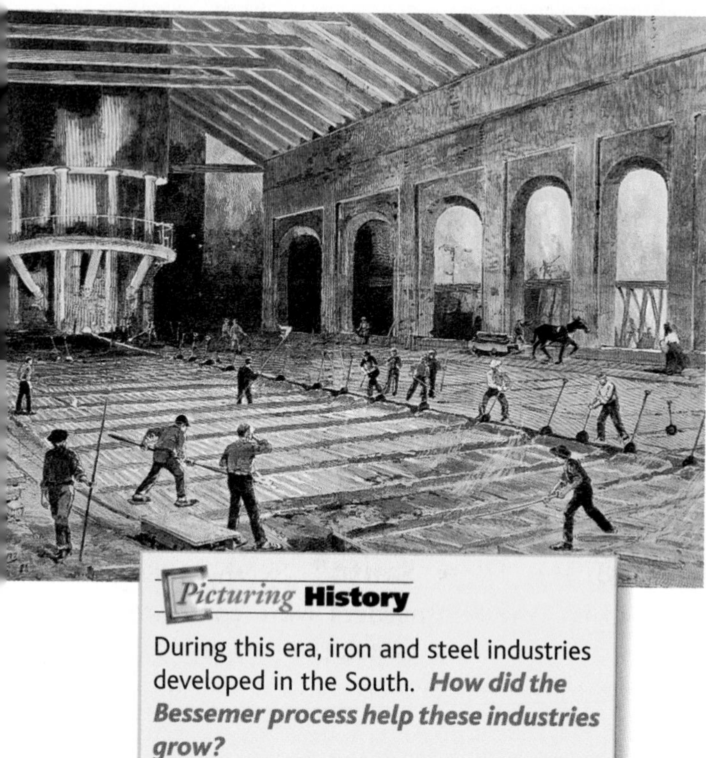

Picturing **History**

During this era, iron and steel industries developed in the South. ***How did the Bessemer process help these industries grow?***

Henry Grady, editor of the *Atlanta Constitution,* headed a group that urged Southerners to "out-Yankee the Yankees" and build a "New South." This New South would have industries based on coal, iron, tobacco, cotton, lumber, and the region's other abundant resources. Southerners would create this new economy by embracing a spirit of hard work and regional pride. In 1886 Grady told a Boston audience that industrial development would allow the New South to match the North in a peaceful competition.

Southern Industries Industry in the South made dramatic gains after Reconstruction. Some of the strongest advances were in the textile industry. Before the Civil War, Southern planters had shipped cotton to textile mills in the North or in Europe. In the 1880s, textile mills sprang up throughout the South. Many Northern mills would later close as companies built new plants in the South.

Other important industries were lumbering and tobacco processing. The tobacco industry was developed largely through the efforts of **James Duke** of North Carolina. Duke's American Tobacco Company eventually controlled almost all tobacco manufacturing.

The iron and steel industry also grew rapidly. In the mid-1800s, William Kelly, an American ironworker, and Henry Bessemer, a British engineer, had developed methods —called the Bessemer process—to inexpensively produce steel from iron. Steel answered industry's need for a sturdy, workable metal. By 1890 Southern mills produced nearly 20 percent of the nation's iron and steel. Much of the industry was in Alabama near deposits of iron ore.

A cheap and reliable workforce helped the South's industry grow. Most factory workers put in long hours for low wages. Sometimes whole families, including children, worked in factories. African Americans worked in the lowest-paying jobs.

More railroads aided the rise of industry. By 1870 the South's war-damaged railroads were largely rebuilt and expanded. Still, the South was not as industrialized as the North. It remained primarily agricultural.

Rural Economy Supporters of the New South also hoped to change Southern agriculture. Their goal was small, profitable farms raising many crops rather than plantations devoted to cotton. A different economy emerged, however. Some plantations were broken up, but large landowners held on to their land. When estates were divided, much of the land went to sharecropping and tenant farming, neither of which was profitable.

Debt also caused problems. Poor farmers used credit to get food and supplies. Merchants who sold on credit charged high prices, and farmers' debts rose. To repay debts, farmers grew **cash crops**—crops that could be sold for money.

Too much cotton, a major cash crop, forced prices down, however. Farmers then had to grow even more cotton to recover their losses. Sharecropping and reliance on one cash crop kept Southern agriculture from advancing. The rural South sank deeper into poverty and debt.

Reading Check **Describe** What happened to prices when too much cotton was produced?

US8.11.3 Understand the effects of the Freedmen's Bureau and the restrictions placed on the rights and opportunities of freedmen, including racial segregation and "Jim Crow" laws. US8.11.5 Understand the Thirteenth, Fourteenth, and Fifteenth Amendments to the Constitution and analyze their connection to Reconstruction.

A Divided Society

Main Idea **As Reconstruction ended, true freedom for African Americans became a distant dream.**

Reading Connection What might it be like to be forced to pass an impossibly difficult test in order to earn a basic right, when others do not have to take the test at all? Read to find out how white Southerners attempted to prevent African Americans from voting.

As Reconstruction ended, African Americans' dreams for justice faded. In the last 20 years of the 1800s, racism became firmly entrenched, and individuals took steps to keep African Americans separated from whites and to deny them basic rights.

Voting Restrictions The Fifteenth Amendment prohibited any state from denying an individual the right to vote because of race. Southern leaders, however, found ways to get around the amendment and prevent African Americans from voting.

Many Southern states required a **poll tax,** a fee that people had to pay before voting. Because many African Americans could not afford the tax, they could not vote. The tax also prevented many poor whites from voting.

What Is a Literacy Test? Another approach was to make prospective voters take a **literacy test** (LIH • tuh • ruh • see) in which they had to read and explain difficult parts of state constitutions or the federal Constitution. Because most African Americans had little education, literacy tests prevented many from voting.

Primary Sources

Jim Crow Laws

Southern communities and states passed laws that enforced segregation between the black and white races.

Railroads The conductor of each passenger train is authorized and required to assign each passenger to the car or the division of the car, when it is divided by a partition, designated for the race to which such passenger belongs. (Alabama)

Restaurants All persons licensed to conduct a restaurant, shall serve either white people exclusively or colored people exclusively and shall not sell to the two races within the same room or serve the two races anywhere under the same license. (Georgia)

Education The schools for white children and the schools for Negro children shall be conducted separately. (Florida)

▲ Business sign of the era

Libraries The state librarian is directed to fit up and maintain a separate place for the use of the colored people who may come to the library for the purpose of reading books or periodicals. (North Carolina)

—*Race, Racism, and the Law*

Document-Based Question

What do these laws have in common?

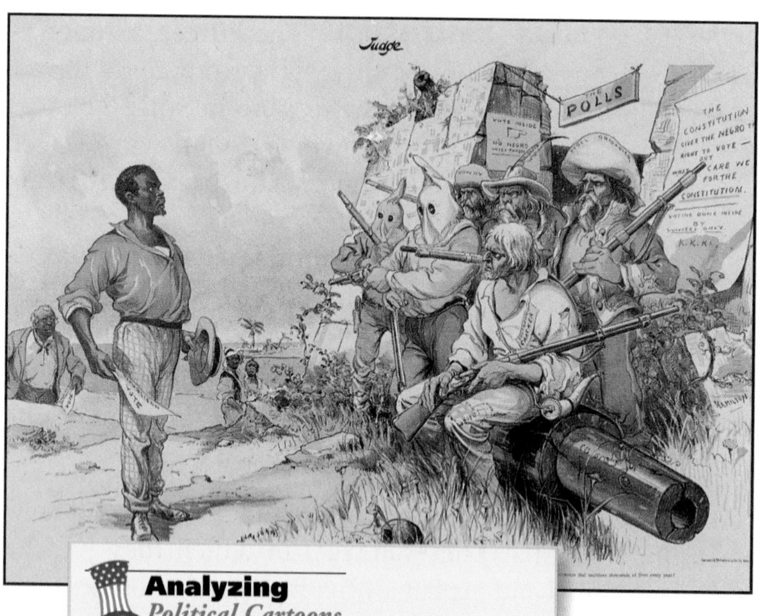

Analyzing *Political Cartoons*

African Americans were often barred from voting. ***What do the people in the cartoon represent?***

Literacy tests could also keep some whites from voting. For this reason, some states passed **grandfather clauses.** These laws allowed individuals who did not pass the literacy test to vote if their fathers or grandfathers had voted before Reconstruction. Because African Americans could not vote until 1867, they were excluded. Georgia enacted a poll tax and other limits as early as 1870. Such laws, however, did not become widespread until after 1889. African Americans continued to vote in some states until the end of the 1800s. Then, voting laws and the constant threat of violence caused African American voting to decline drastically.

Jim Crow Laws Another set of laws hurt African Americans. By the 1890s, **segregation** (SEH • grih • GAY • shuhn), or the separation of the races, was a prominent feature of life in the South.

The Southern states formed a segregated society by passing so-called Jim Crow laws. Taking their name from a character in a song, Jim Crow laws required African Americans and whites to be separated in almost every public place where they might come in contact with each other.

In 1896 the Supreme Court upheld Jim Crow laws and segregation in *Plessy* v. *Ferguson.* The case involved a Louisiana law requiring separate sections on trains for African Americans. The Court ruled that segregation was legal as long as African Americans had access to public facilities or accommodations equal to those of whites. *(See page 849 of the Appendix for a summary of* Plessy v. Ferguson.)

One problem, however, was that the facilities were separate but in no way equal. Southern states spent much more money on schools and other facilities for whites than on those for African Americans. This "separate but equal" doctrine provided a legal foundation for segregation in the South that lasted more than 50 years.

Along with restrictions on voting rights and laws passed to segregate society, white violence against African Americans increased. This violence took many terrible forms, including **lynching** (LIHNCH • ihng), in which an angry mob killed a person by hanging. African Americans were lynched because they were suspected of **committing** crimes—or because they did not behave as whites thought they should behave.

Reconstruction's Impact Reconstruction was both a success and a failure. It helped the South recover from the Civil War and begin rebuilding its battered economy. Yet economic recovery was far from complete. Although Southern agriculture took a new form, the South was still a rural economy, and that economy was still very poor.

Under Reconstruction, African Americans gained greater equality and began creating their own institutions. They joined with whites in new governments, fairer and more democratic than the South had ever seen. This improvement for African Americans did not last long, however.

In the words of African American writer and civil rights leader **W.E.B. Du Bois** (doo BAWIHS),

> **"The slave went free; stood a brief moment in the sun; then moved back again toward slavery."**
>
> —from *Black Reconstruction*

The biggest disappointment of Reconstruction was that it did not make good on the promise of true freedom for freed African Americans. With troop withdrawals and the end of Reconstruction, African Americans lost most of the gains they had made. The South soon created a segregated society.

The Civil War had ended slavery, but the failure of Reconstruction left many African Americans trapped in economic, political, and social circumstances whereby they lost most of their newly gained freedom.

Reading Check **Describe** What is segregation? How was segregation carried out?

▲ W.E.B. Du Bois demanded full political rights for African Americans.

Study Central Need help understanding the end of Reconstruction? Visit ca.hss.glencoe.com and click on Study Central.

Section 4 Review

Reading Summary

Review the Main Ideas

- As support for Reconstruction weakened, Democrats regained power in the South. Reconstruction ended because of a political compromise that allowed Rutherford B. Hayes to become president.
- A number of industries, such as textiles and steel, developed in the South, but agriculture also remained important.
- Following the end of Reconstruction, African Americans in the South lost many of the rights they had briefly gained.

What Did You Learn?

1. Why was the presidential election of 1876 controversial?
2. Who was reelected president in 1872?

Critical Thinking

3. **Organizing Information** Re-create the diagram below and describe how the poll tax and literacy tests restricted voting rights. CA CS1.

Poll tax → ( )

Literacy tests → ( )

4. **Determining Cause and Effect** Explain how the Amnesty Act helped the Democratic Party regain its strength. CA HI2.
5. **The Big Ideas** What ideas led to political changes in the South beginning in the early 1870s? CA CS2.
6. **Analyze** Find two secondary sources that discuss Reconstruction—one from the 1800s and one written in the past 20 years. Identify how the views expressed in the later source are based on new historical information or research. CA HI5.

Connecting to the Constitution

US8.11.5 Understand the Thirteenth, Fourteenth, and Fifteenth Amendments to the Constitution and analyze their connection to Reconstruction.

Citizenship

Why It Matters Today, most people are citizens of the country in which they live. They are community members who owe loyalty to that country. They also expect to be protected by it. Citizens may share a common history, common customs, or common values. They agree to follow the laws and to accept the government's authority.

Who Are U.S. Citizens? Every country has rules about how people gain citizenship. In the United States, a citizen is a person who by birth or by choice owes loyalty to this nation. In the Fourteenth Amendment, the U.S. Constitution states that anyone "born or naturalized in the United States" is a citizen. If you were born in the United States and its territories, you automatically are an American citizen by birth. Foreigners who choose to become U.S. citizens do so through naturalization. **Naturalization** is the legal process by which a person becomes a citizen. Naturalized citizens have all the rights and duties of citizens by birth except the right to be president or vice president.

National and State Citizenship Over the years, the basis of citizenship has changed greatly in the United States. Today, citizenship relates both to the nation as a whole and to the states. This was not always so, however.

The Articles of the Constitution mention citizenship only as a qualification for holding office in the federal government. The Constitution's writers assumed that the states would decide who was or was not a citizen. Their citizens were also citizens of the United States. The exceptions were African Americans and immigrants who became citizens through naturalization.

New American citizens pledging allegiance

"Our Constitution is color-blind, and neither knows nor tolerates classes among citizens. In respect of civil rights, all citizens are equal before the law."

—Justice John Marshall Harlan, 1896

The basis of state citizenship became an issue in the *Dred Scott* v. *Sandford* case in 1857. The Supreme Court, led by Chief Justice Roger Taney, ruled that Dred Scott, an enslaved African American, could not bring a legal suit in a federal court. Taney reasoned that African Americans, whether enslaved or free, were not United States citizens at the time the Constitution was adopted. Therefore, they could not claim citizenship. Only descendants of people who were state citizens at that time, or immigrants who became citizens through naturalization, were U.S. citizens.

The Fourteenth Amendment The *Dred Scott* decision caused great outrage and protest in the North. It added to the tensions that led to the Civil War. After the war ended, many Southern states passed laws that kept African Americans from holding certain jobs, limited their property rights, and restricted them in other ways. To remedy this situation, the Fourteenth Amendment was enacted in 1868.

The new amendment clearly stated what citizenship is at both the national and state levels of government. Overruling the *Dred Scott* decision, the Fourteenth Amendment stated that a United States citizen is anyone "born or naturalized in the United States." This definition included most African Americans. It guaranteed that people of all races born in the United States are citizens, making state citizenship an automatic result of national citizenship.

Denial of Citizens' Rights The Fourteenth Amendment granted citizenship to former enslaved African Americans and their descendants. It also guaranteed their rights as citizens. The amendment did this by requiring every state to grant citizens equal protection under the laws.

Despite this guarantee, African Americans routinely faced **discrimination,** or unfair treatment based on prejudice against a certain group. In the late 1800s, Southern states, for example, passed so-called Jim Crow laws requiring African Americans and whites to be separated in most public places, such as schools. Later, African Americans had to ride in the back of buses and sit in separate sections of restaurants and theaters.

The Supreme Court supported Jim Crow laws in *Plessy* v. *Ferguson* (1896). The Court said the Fourteenth Amendment allowed separate facilities for different races as long as those facilities were equal. For the next 50 years, this decision was used to justify segregation in the United States.

Extension of Citizens' Rights By the 1950s, society's views on racial segregation were beginning to change. In 1954 in the case of *Brown* v. *Board of Education of Topeka,* the Court overturned the ruling of "separate but equal." The justices ruled that racially separate schools are unequal simply because they are separate. The unanimous opinion of the Court found that segregation was a violation of the Fourteenth Amendment's principle of equal protection under the law.

Linda Brown was able to attend the school of her choice after the *Brown* decision. ▶

Checking for Understanding

1. How do people become citizens in the United States?
2. Why did the Supreme Court overturn the "separate but equal" idea in *Brown* v. *Board of Education of Topeka*?

Critical Thinking

3. Why do you think the writers of the Constitution assumed that the states would decide who was or who was not a citizen? CA HI1.
4. How was the promise of the Fourteenth Amendment fulfilled in the mid-twentieth century? CA HI2.

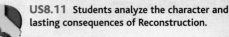

US8.11 Students analyze the character and lasting consequences of Reconstruction.

Reconstruction

Most of the Civil War was waged in the South. After the war, the South faced the huge task of rebuilding. In addition, freed African Americans had to make a new life for themselves. There was also the difficult problem of how to make the former Confederacy and the Union into one nation again.

Read the passages on pages 652 and 653 and answer the questions that follow.

The head of the Freedmen's Bureau (seated at the far right) is pictured with students in a Freedmen's school.

Reader's Dictionary

charge: blame

exterminating (ihk • STUHR • muh • NAYT • ihng): getting rid of completely

emerged: have risen from a low condition

bondage (BAHN • dihj): slavery

plea (PLEE): serious or sincere call for help

quarters: places

The South in Ruins

Newspaper reporter Sidney Andrews toured major Southern cities in the fall of 1865. He wrote the following account about Columbia, South Carolina.

Columbia was doubtless once the gem of the state. . . . What with its broad streets, beautiful shade trees, handsome lawns . . . I can easily see that it must have been a delightful place of residence. No South Carolinian with whom I have spoken hesitates an instant in declaring that [Columbia] was the most beautiful city on the continent; and, as already mentioned, they **charge** its destruction directly to General Sherman.

[Columbia] is now a wilderness of ruins. Its heart is but a mass of blackened chimneys and crumbling walls. Two thirds of the buildings in the place were burned, including, without exception, everything in the business portion. Not a store, office, or shop escaped; and for a distance of three fourths of a mile on each of twelve streets there was not a building left. . . .

The work of clearing away the ruins is going on, not rapidly or extensively, to be sure, but something is doing, and many small houses of the cheaper sort are going up. Yet, at the best, this generation will not ever again see the beautiful city of a year ago.

—from *The South Since the War*

On the Plight of African Americans

In 1867 Frederick Douglass appealed to Congress on behalf of African Americans.

Yet the negroes have marvelously survived all the **exterminating** forces of slavery, and have **emerged** at the end of two hundred and fifty years of **bondage,** not [sad and hateful], but cheerful, hopeful, and forgiving. They now stand before Congress and the country, not complaining of the past, but simply asking for a better future. . . .

It is true that a strong **plea** for equal suffrage might be addressed to the national sense of honor. Something, too, might be said of national gratitude. A nation might well hesitate before the temptation to betray its allies. There is something . . . mean, to say nothing of the cruelty, in placing the loyal negroes of the South under the political power of their Rebel masters. . . . We asked the negroes to [support] our cause, to be our friends, to fight for us, and against their masters; and now, after they have done all that we asked them to do, . . . it is proposed in some **quarters** to turn them over to the political control of the common enemy of the government and of the negro. . . .

▼ Douglass fought for civil rights for newly freed slaves and was active in the women's movement.

What, then, is the work before Congress? . . . In a word, it must [allow African Americans to vote], and by means of the loyal negroes and the loyal white men of the South build up a national party there, and in time bridge the [gap] between North and South, so that our country may have a common liberty and a common civilization.

—*An Appeal to Congress for Impartial Suffrage*

DBQ Document-Based Questions

The South in Ruins

1. To what does Andrews compare Columbia? Why?
2. What does Andrews mean when he writes that "Not a store, office, or shop escaped"?

On the Plight of African Americans

3. According to Douglass, why does the United States owe a debt of gratitude to African Americans?
4. How did Douglass think that Congress could ensure the nation a common liberty and civilization for whites and African Americans?

Read to Write

5. During Reconstruction, some people worked to get African Americans the same rights as whites. List the rights that these primary sources include and others that you know about. Then research the civil rights movement of the 1960s. What right or rights were African Americans seeking at that time? Compare and contrast the rights and the methods used to gain them in the two time periods. CA HR3. CA 8RL3.3

Assessment

Standard US8.11

Review Content Vocabulary

Each of the following statements is false. Replace each word in italics with a content vocabulary word that makes the statement true. Write the correct words on a separate sheet of paper.

___ 1. The reorganization of the Southern states after the war was called *integration.*

___ 2. *Carpetbaggers* were Southern whites who sided with Republicans.

___ 3. To *grant amnesty* is to formally charge with a crime.

___ 4. Fees called *grandfather clauses* were often required before voters could cast their ballots in the south.

Review the Main Ideas

Section 1 • Reconstruction Plans

5. What services did the Freedmen's Bureau provide?
6. Who succeeded Lincoln as president?

Section 2 • Radicals in Control

7. How was the Fourteenth Amendment supposed to help African Americans?
8. What verdict did the Senate reach in the trial of President Johnson?

Section 3 • The South During Reconstruction

9. What role did African Americans play in early Reconstruction politics in the South?
10. What tactic did the Ku Klux Klan use to influence elections in the South?

Section 4 • Change in the South

11. Why was a special commission needed to decide the presidential election of 1876?
12. What Supreme Court decision upheld the legality of segregation so long as "separate but equal" facilities were provided?

Critical Thinking

13. **Analyze** How did the black codes deny rights? CA HI2.
14. **Evaluate** Explain the following quote as it applies to Reconstruction: "The slave went free; stood a brief moment in the sun; then moved back again toward slavery." CA HR5.

Geography Skills

Study the map below and answer the question that follows. CA CS3.

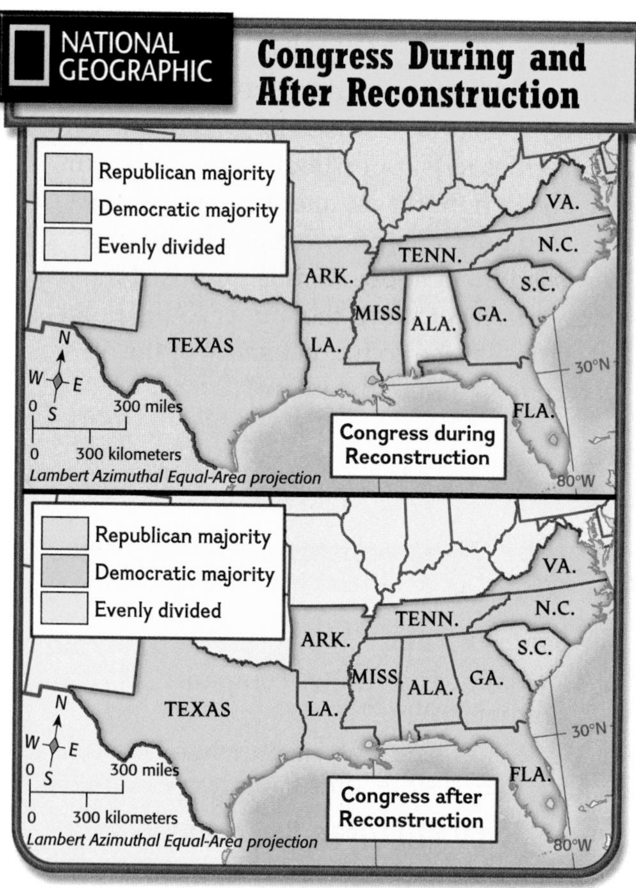

15. **Summarize** Write a paragraph summarizing the changes in congressional representation during and after Reconstruction.

NATIONAL GEOGRAPHIC

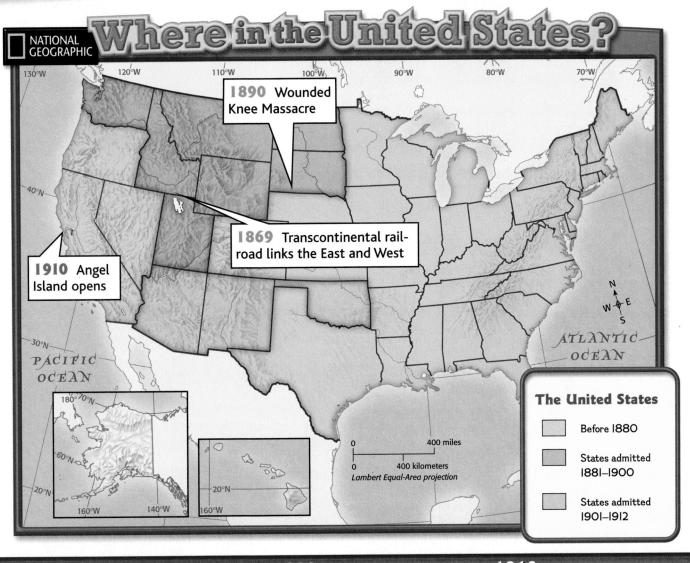

Where in the United States?

130°W 120°W 110°W 100°W 90°W 80°W 70°W

40°N 30°N

1890 Wounded Knee Massacre

1869 Transcontinental railroad links the East and West

1910 Angel Island opens

PACIFIC OCEAN

ATLANTIC OCEAN

N E S W

180° 70°N 60°N 20°N 160°W 140°W

20°N 160°W

0 400 miles
0 400 kilometers
Lambert Equal-Area projection

The United States

- Before 1880
- States admitted 1881–1900
- States admitted 1901–1912

1890 1900 1910

1890 Wounded Knee Massacre

1906 Upton Sinclair publishes *The Jungle*

◀ The Jungle

1913 Seventeenth Amendment is ratified

Devastation following the San Francisco earthquake ▶

1906 San Francisco earthquake and fire occurs

1910 Angel Island opens

1911 Women gain the right to vote in some state elections

1895 Lumière brothers show first projected motion picture films

◀ *Emiliano Zapata*

1911 Zapata leads demand for land reform in Mexico

1914 World War I begins

Unit 6

Places to Locate

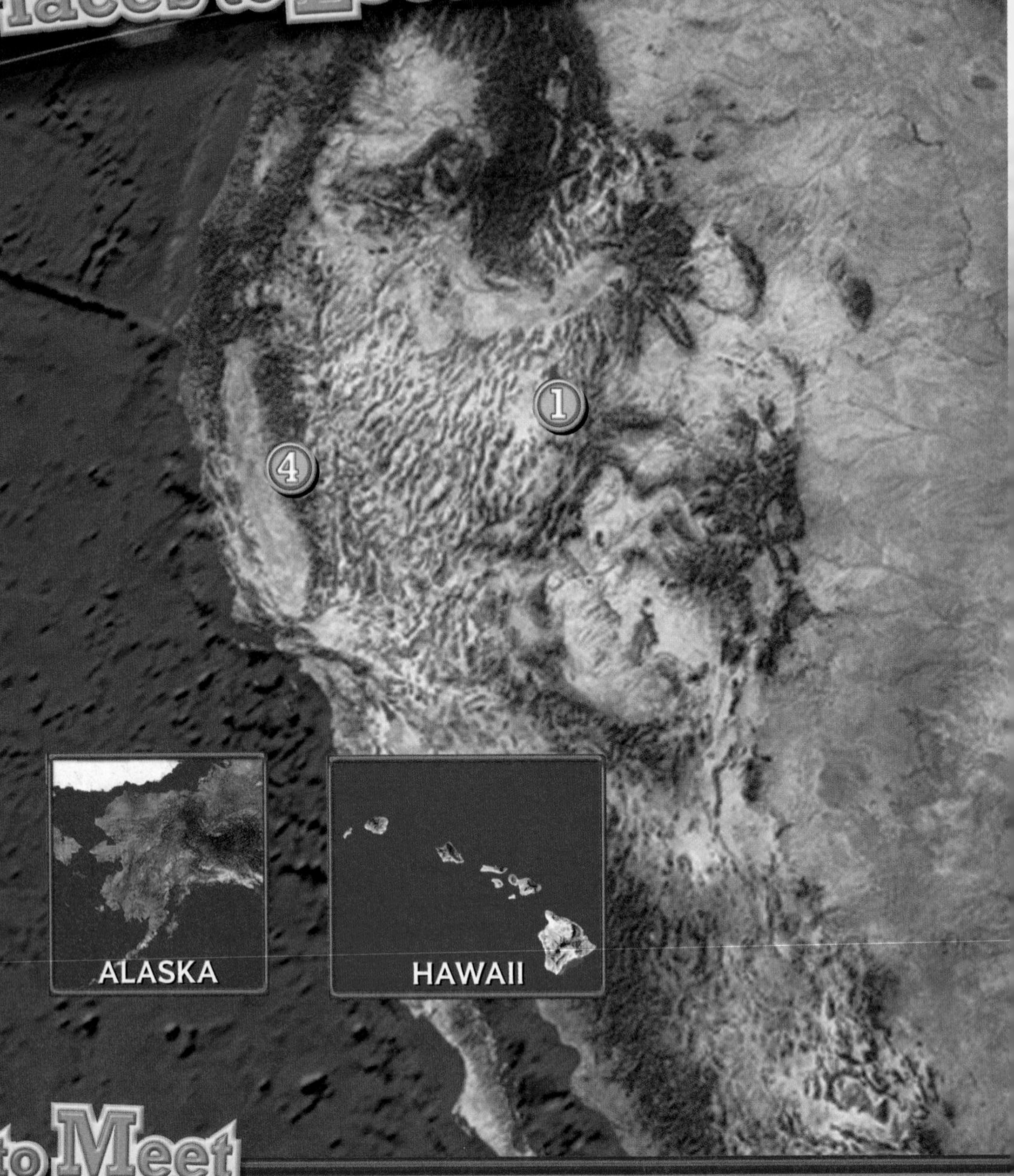

1 PROMONTORY SUMMIT

See *The Western Frontier* Chapter 15

2 THE BROOKLYN BRIDGE

See *America Enters a New Century* Chapter 17

ALASKA

HAWAII

1

4

People to Meet

Chief Joseph
1840–1904
Nez Perce leader
Chapter 15, page 690

Thomas Edison
1847–1931
Inventor
Chapter 16, page 714

Mother Jones
1830–1930
Worker's rights leader
Chapter 16, page 728

Jane Addams
1860–1935
Founder of Chicago's Hull House
Chapter 17, page 753

NATIONAL GEOGRAPHIC

3

2

3

3 CHICAGO SKYSCRAPER

See *America Enters a New Century* Chapter 17

4 YOSEMITE NATIONAL PARK

See *America Enters a New Century* Chapter 17

Booker T. Washington
1856–1915
Equal rights advocate
Chapter 17, page 781

Jacob Riis
1849–1914
Journalist
Chapter 17, page 768

Ida Wells
1862–1931
Journalist
Chapter 17, page 780

W.E.B. Du Bois
1868–1963
Equal rights advocate
Chapter 17, page 781

The Western Frontier

◀ Mother and child in a Wyoming wheat field

NATIONAL GEOGRAPHIC **Who & When?**

1860		1875		1890
1862 Homestead Act gives free land to settlers		**1869** Transcontinental railroad links East and West		**1890** Battle at Wounded Knee; Populist Party forms

Populist Party banner

The Big Ideas

Chapter Overview Visit ca.hss.glencoe.com for a preview of Chapter 15.

The Mining Booms

Geography shapes the physical, economic, and political challenges a region faces. Rail lines and mining speeded the flow of settlers to the West.

Ranchers and Farmers

Geography shapes the physical, economic, and political challenges a region faces. Following the Civil War, settlers began to move west in great numbers.

Native American Struggles

Differences in economic, political, and social beliefs and practices can lead to division within a nation and have lasting consequences. The settlement of white people in the West forced change on the Native Americans of the Plains.

Farmers in Protest

Reactions to social injustice can lead to reform movements. In the late 1800s, farmers began to band together in groups and associations to fight their problems.

View the Chapter 15 video in the Glencoe Video Program.

Evaluating Information Make this foldable to organize information and ask yourself questions as you read about the western frontier of the United States.

Step 1 Fold a sheet of paper in half from side to side, leaving a $\frac{1}{2}$-inch tab along the side.

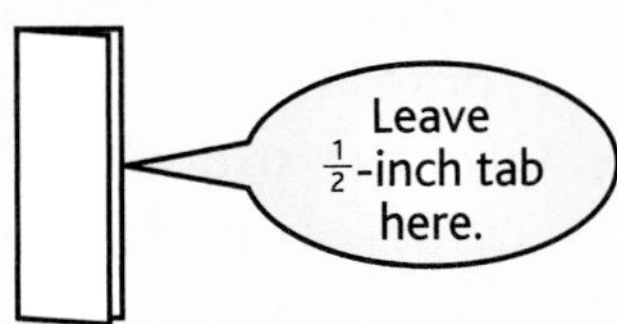

Step 2 Turn the paper and fold it into fourths.

Fold in half, then fold in half again.

Step 3 Unfold and cut along the three fold lines.

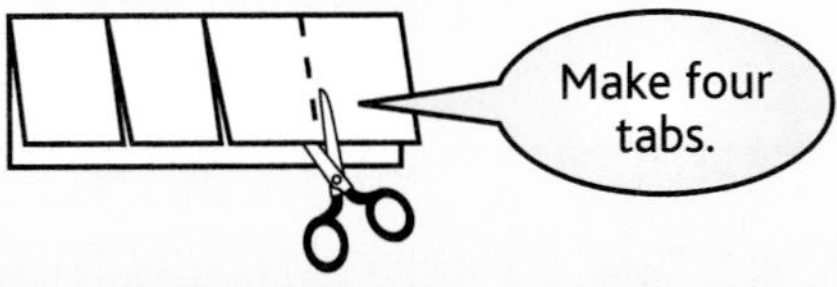

Step 4 Label your foldable as shown.

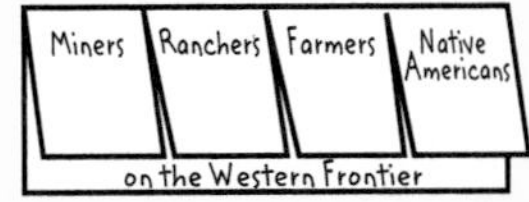

Reading and Writing As you read the chapter, ask yourself and write down questions (under each appropriate tab) about the tragedies and triumphs these four groups of people experienced during the expansion of the western frontier.

Get Ready to Read

Visualizing

1 Learn It!

Creating pictures in your mind as you read—called visualizing—is a powerful aid to understanding. If you can visualize what you read, selections will be more vivid, and you will recall them better later. Authors use descriptive language to create a picture of a person, location, time, or event. These words appeal to the senses and may evoke sights, sounds, or smells. Authors also use words to describe feelings and emotions to make the text come alive to the reader. Good readers take the time to visualize people, places, and events. As you read the following paragraphs, make a picture in your mind of life in a boomtown.

> **Boomtowns were largely men's towns in the early days. Men outnumbered women by two to one in Virginia City, and children made up less than 10 percent of the population.**
>
> **Eager to share in the riches of the boomtowns, some women opened businesses. Others worked as laundresses, cooks, or dance-hall entertainers. Women often added stability to the boomtowns, founding schools and churches and working to make the communities safer.**
>
> *—from page 668*

Look for descriptive words or images in the text to help you form a visual image of what you read.

2 Practice It!

Now read the section below about cowhands. Discuss your impressions with a partner and then reread the selection. Did your visual image change at all?

Read to Write

Think about your favorite place. In writing, describe the picture you have in your mind. Use vivid language and descriptive details.

Many cowhands were veterans of the Confederate army. Some were African Americans who moved west in search of a better life after the Civil War. Others were Hispanics. In fact, the traditions of cattle herding began with Hispanic ranch hands in the Spanish Southwest. These vaqueros (vah • KEHR • ohs) developed many of the skills—riding, roping, and branding—that cowhands used on the drives. Much of the language of the rancher today is derived from Spanish words used by vaqueros for centuries. Even the word *ranch* comes from the Spanish word *rancho*.

The cowhand's equipment was based on the vaquero's equipment too. Cowhands wore wide-brimmed hats to protect themselves from the sun and leather leggings, called chaps, to shield their legs from brush and mishaps with cattle. They used ropes called lariats to lasso cattle that strayed from the herd.

—*from page 674*

Cowhand Nat Love ▶

3 Apply It!

Before you begin reading this chapter, look at all the photographs, maps, and illustrations to help you visualize what you are about to read.

Section
1

The Mining Booms

Guide to Reading

History Social Science Standards

US8.12 Students analyze the transformation of the American economy and the changing social and political conditions in the United States in response to the Industrial Revolution.

Looking Back, Looking Ahead

You read earlier about how the California Gold Rush brought thousands of people to California to try to make their fortunes. In the late 1850s, many more miners headed west as more precious metals were discovered.

Focusing on the Main Ideas

- In the late 1850s, discoveries of gold and silver sent miners flocking to the American West. *(page 667)*
- A number of boomtowns grew quickly in the mining areas of the West. *(page 668)*
- Railroads grew rapidly in the period following the Civil War. *(page 669)*

Locating Places

Pikes Peak
Virginia City, Nevada
Promontory Summit

Meeting People

Leland Stanford

Content Vocabulary

lode (LOHD)
ore
boomtown
vigilante (VIH • juh • LAN • tee)
subsidy (SUHB • suh • dee)
transcontinental (TRANS • kahn • tuhn • EHN • tuhl)

Academic Vocabulary

extract (ihk • STRAKT)
obtain (uhb • TAYN)

Reading Strategy

Analyzing Information As you read the section, re-create the diagram below and explain why these places were significant to the mining boom.

	Significance
Pikes Peak	
Comstock Lode	
Promontory Summit	

NATIONAL GEOGRAPHIC
Where & When?
Central Pacific R.R.
Promontory Summit
Pikes Peak
Union Pacific R.R.
1855
1865
1875
1858
Gold is discovered at Pikes Peak
1869
Transcontinental railroad links East and West
1876
Colorado joins the Union

US8.12.1 Trace patterns of agricultural and industrial development as they relate to climate, use of natural resources, markets, and trade and locate such development on a map.

Mining Is Big Business

Main Idea **In the late 1850s, discoveries of gold and silver sent miners flocking to the American West.**

Reading Connection Have you ever wanted to take part in a great adventure? Read to find out about the gold and silver rushes that lured thousands of Americans into the West.

An American Story

"We'll need no pick or spade, no shovel, pan, or hoe, the largest chunks are 'top of ground. . . . We'll see hard times no more, and want [we'll] never know, when once we've filled our sacks with gold, Way out in Idaho."

—from *Way Out in Idaho*

Miners sang this hopeful song as they headed for new places where gold had been discovered.

Picturing **History**

A miner works the Comstock Lode. ***Where was the Comstock Lode located?***

Searching for Gold and Silver By the mid-1850s, the California Gold Rush had ended. Miners, still hoping to strike it rich, began prospecting in other parts of the West.

In 1858 a mining expedition found gold on the slopes of **Pikes Peak** in the Colorado Rockies. Newspapers claimed that miners were making $20 a day panning for gold—a large sum at a time when servants made less than a dollar a day. By the spring of 1859, about 50,000 prospectors had flocked to Colorado. Their slogan was "Pikes Peak or Bust."

Prospectors skimmed gold dust from streams or scratched particles of gold from the surface of the land. Most of the gold, however, was deep in underground **lodes** (LOHDZ), rich streaks of ore sandwiched between layers of rock. Mining this rock, or **ore,** and then **extracting** the gold required expensive machinery, many workers, and an organized business. Companies made up of several investors had a better chance of getting rich in the goldfields than individual miners did. Mining companies soon replaced the lone miner.

The Comstock Lode In 1859 several prospectors found a rich lode of silver-bearing ore on the banks of the Carson River in Nevada. The discovery was called the Comstock Lode after Henry Comstock, who owned a share of the claim.

Thousands of mines opened near the site, but only a few were profitable. Mining companies reaped the largest share of the profits. When Comstock sold his share of the claim, he received $11,000 and two mules—a huge sum at the time. It was, however, just a tiny fraction of the hundreds of millions of dollars worth of gold and silver pulled from the Comstock Lode strike.

Reading Check **Describe** What was the Comstock Lode?

US8.12.1 Trace patterns of agricultural and industrial development as they relate to climate, use of natural resources, markets, and trade and locate such development on a map.

The Mining Frontier

Main Idea **A number of boomtowns grew quickly in the mining areas of the West.**

Reading Connection Have you ever seen a deserted section of a city where a factory has closed? Read to find out what happened to many mining towns in the West after the gold or silver in nearby mines was gone.

The gold strikes created **boomtowns**—towns that grew up almost overnight around mining sites. The Comstock boomtown was **Virginia City, Nevada.** In 1859 the town was a mining camp. Two years later, it had a stock exchange, hotels, banks, an opera company, and five newspapers.

Boomtowns were lively, and often lawless, places. Money came quickly—and was often spent just as quickly through extravagant living and gambling. A fortunate miner could earn as much as $2,000 a year, about four times the annual salary of a teacher at that time. Still food, lodging, clothing, and other goods were expensive in the boomtowns, draining miners' earnings.

Violence was part of everyday life in boomtowns. Few boomtowns had police or prisons, so citizens sometimes took the law into their own hands. These **vigilantes** (VIH • juh • LAN • tees) dealt out their own brand of justice without benefit of judge or jury, often hanging the accused person from the nearest tree.

Women in the Boomtowns Boomtowns were largely men's towns in the early days. Men outnumbered women by two to one in Virginia City, and children made up less than 10 percent of the population.

Eager to share in the riches of the boomtowns, some women opened businesses. Others worked as laundresses, cooks, or dance-hall entertainers. Women often added stability to the boomtowns, founding schools and churches and working to make the communities safer.

Changing Industry Many mining "booms" were followed by "busts." When the mines no longer yielded ore, people left the towns, and the deserted mine towns became known as ghost towns. At its peak in the 1870s, Virginia City had about 30,000 inhabitants. By 1900 its population had dropped to fewer than 4,000. Toward the end of the rush, gold and silver mining in some places gave way to the mining of other metals. Copper became the key metal found in Montana, New Mexico, and Arizona in the 1870s.

Mining helped the economy, but it hurt the environment. Wildlife was hunted to provide meat for the miners. Mining led to high levels of arsenic and mercury in the ground that contaminated land, lakes, and rivers.

What Were the New States? Frontier areas around the boomtowns eventually became states. Colorado joined the United States in 1876. North Dakota, South Dakota, Washington, and Montana became states in 1889. Wyoming and Idaho were admitted to the Union in 1890.

Reading Check **Explain** Why did the population drop in many boomtowns?

Picturing **History**

The boomtown of Leadville, Colorado, surrounds a settler's cabin that sits in the middle of the main street. ***What happened to many boomtowns when the mines closed?***

US8.12.1 Trace patterns of agricultural and industrial development as they relate to climate, use of natural resources, markets, and trade and locate such development on a map. US8.12.3 Explain how states and the federal government encouraged business expansion through tariffs, banking, land grants, and subsidies.

Railroads Connect East to West

Main Idea **Railroads grew rapidly in the period following the Civil War.**

Reading Connection Would you like to travel across the country by train? Read to find out how the first railroad to connect the east and west coasts was completed in 1869.

The western mines operated far from the industrial centers of the East and Midwest. For this reason, transportation played a vital role in the survival of mining communities. Gold and silver had little value unless they could reach factories, ports, and markets. At the same time, the miners and others in the boomtowns needed shipments of food and other supplies.

Wagon trains and stagecoach lines could not move people and goods fast enough to meet these demands. Railroads could—and did. The nation's railroad network expanded rapidly between 1865 and 1890. During that period, the number of miles of track in the United States grew from about 35,000 to more than 150,000.

Railroad construction was often supported by large government **subsidies** (SUHB • suh • dees)—financial aid and land grants from the government. Railroad executives pushed for free public land on which to lay track because a rail network would benefit the entire nation. The national government and states agreed. In all, the federal government granted more than 130 million acres of land to the railroad companies. Much of the land was purchased or **obtained** by treaties from Native Americans. The government grants included the land for the tracks plus strips of land along the railway, 20 to 80 miles wide. Railroad companies sold those strips of land to raise additional money for construction costs.

TECHNOLOGY & History

Steam Locomotive

Since 1825, when the first steam locomotive was built in the United States, trains have crisscrossed the country. As America's transportation needs increased, so did the miles of railroad track linking its people. **Why do you think steam power was the first power source for locomotives?**

1 The **firebox** burns coal, wood, or sometimes oil.
2 Water in the **boiler,** heated by gases from the firebox, creates steam.
3 The **smokebox** draws hot gases from the firebox and keeps an even fire.
4 In the **steam header tank,** the heated steam expands and creates great pressure.
5 Hot steam is piped to the **pistons.** The pistons power the **drive rods,** which in turn push the **drive wheels.**
22
VIRGINIA & TRUCKEE
1
2
3
4

History *Through Art*

The Race* by Mort Kunstler** The artist is well-known for his realistic paintings about dramatic events in American history. ***What does the painting express about the American West?

States and local communities also helped the railroads. Towns offered cash subsidies to make sure that railroads came to their communities. For example, Los Angeles gave the Southern Pacific Railroad money and paid for a passenger terminal to ensure that the railroad would pass through its town.

Spanning the Continent The search for a route for a **transcontinental** (TRANS•kahn•tuhn•EHN•tuhl) rail line—one that would span the continent and connect the Atlantic and Pacific coasts—began in the 1850s. During the Civil War, the Union government chose a northerly route for the line. The government offered land grants to railroad companies that were willing to build the transcontinental railroad.

The challenge was enormous—laying track for more than 1,700 miles across hot plains and through rugged mountains. Two companies accepted the challenge. The Union Pacific Company began laying track westward from Omaha, Nebraska, while the Central Pacific Company worked eastward from Sacramento, California. The two companies competed fiercely. Each wanted to cover a greater distance in order to receive more of the government subsidies.

The Central Pacific hired about 10,000 Chinese laborers to work on its tracks. The first Chinese were hired in 1865 at about $28 per month. The Union Pacific relied on Irish and African American workers. All workers toiled for low wages in harsh conditions. In the choking heat of summer and the icy winds of winter, they cleared forests, blasted tunnels through mountains, and laid hundreds of miles of track. In the end, the Union Pacific workers laid 1,038 miles of track; Central Pacific workers laid 742 miles over a much harsher terrain.

The Transcontinental Railway On May 10, 1869, construction was completed. A Chinese crew was chosen to lay the final 10 miles of track, which was completed in only 12 hours. The two sets of track met at **Promontory Summit** in Utah Territory.

Leland Stanford, governor of California, drove a final golden spike into a tie to join the two railroads. According to Grenville Dodge, chief engineer for the Union Pacific:

> **"Prayer was offered; a number of spikes were driven in the two adjoining rails. . . . The engineers ran up their locomotives until they touched . . . and thus the two roads were welded into one great trunk line from the Atlantic to the Pacific."**
>
> —from *Mine Eyes Have Seen*

What Effects Did Railroads Have? By 1883 two more transcontinental lines and dozens of shorter lines connected cities in the West with the rest of the nation. The railroads brought thousands of workers to the West. Trains carried metals and produce east and manufactured goods west. As more tracks were laid, more steel was needed, and the demand boosted the nation's steel industry. Coal producers, railroad car manufacturers, and construction companies also thrived as the railroads spread across the West.

Towns sprang up along the rail lines that carried farm goods to market. Some of these towns eventually grew into large cities such as Denver, Colorado. The railroads also brought the next wave of new settlers to the West—cattle ranchers and farmers.

Railroads even changed how people measured time. Before railroads, each community kept its own time. Clocks in Boston, for example, were 11 minutes ahead of clocks in New York. The demand for sensible train schedules, however, changed that. In 1883 the railroad companies divided the country into four time zones. All communities in each zone would share the same time, and each zone was exactly one hour apart from the zones on either side of it. Congress passed a law making this practice official in 1918.

Reading Check **Identify** To what California city did the transcontinental railroad extend?

History Online
Study Central Need help understanding how mining affected railroad growth? Visit ca.hss.glencoe.com and click on Study Central.

Section 1 Review

Reading Summary

Review the Main Ideas

- New discoveries of gold and silver, such as those at the Comstock Lode, brought thousands of miners to the West.
- Many of the boomtowns that developed as miners rushed to the West became ghost towns as the mines became depleted.
- The transcontinental railway connecting the East and West coasts was completed in 1869.

What Did You Learn?

1. Describe life in a boomtown.
2. What are subsidies, and why did the railroads receive them?

Critical Thinking

3. **Determining Cause and Effect** Re-create the diagram below and explain how railroads helped open the West to settlement. CA HI2.

   Coming of the railroad
   Effect | Effect

4. **The Big Ideas** What were the economic effects of building railroads? CA HI6.
5. **Drawing Conclusions** Some boomtowns thrived after the mining boom, but others became ghost towns. Why do you think some towns survived and others did not? CA HR3.
6. **READING Visualizing** Imagine you are a prospector. Write a short paragraph describing what it was like to arrive at Pikes Peak in early summer 1859. Use strong, descriptive language so that your reader can visualize the scene. CA 8WA2.1

Section 2

Ranchers and Farmers

Guide to Reading

History Social Science Standards

US8.11 Students analyze the character and lasting consequences of Reconstruction.

US8.12 Students analyze the transformation of the American economy and the changing social and political conditions in the United States in response to the Industrial Revolution.

Looking Back, Looking Ahead

You learned that the transcontinental railroad linked the East and the West in 1869. The new railroads promoted ranching and farming in the Great Plains and the West.

Focusing on the Main Ideas

- Cattle ranching in Texas became a profitable business once the new railroad reached the Great Plains. *(page 673)*
- The work of the cowhands who drove the cattle north from Texas to the railroads was both difficult and dangerous. *(page 674)*
- Free land and new farming methods brought many settlers to the Great Plains. *(page 676)*

Locating Places

Sedalia, Missouri
Abilene, Kansas
Dodge City, Kansas
Cheyenne, Wyoming

Content Vocabulary

open range
brand
vaquero (vah • KEHR • oh)
homestead (HOHM • STEHD)
sodbuster (SAHD • BUHS • tuhr)
dry farming

Academic Vocabulary

derive (dih • RYV)
acquire (uh • KWYR)

Reading Strategy

Taking Notes As you read the section, re-create the diagram below and list the challenges settlers faced on the Great Plains.

Challenges

Where & When?

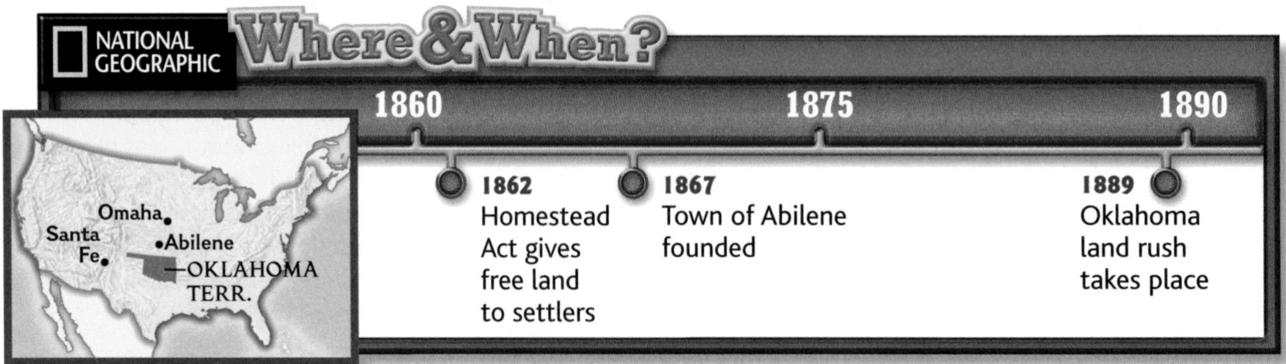
NATIONAL GEOGRAPHIC
Omaha
Santa Fe
Abilene
OKLAHOMA TERR.
1860
1875
1890
1862 Homestead Act gives free land to settlers
1867 Town of Abilene founded
1889 Oklahoma land rush takes place

US8.12.1 Trace patterns of agricultural and industrial development as they relate to climate, use of natural resources, markets, and trade and locate such development on a map.

Cattle on the Plains

Main Idea **Cattle ranching in Texas became a profitable business once the new railroad reached the Great Plains.**

Reading Connection Have you seen large trucks on highways carrying food and supplies to stores? Read to find out about the long, difficult journey that cowhands had to make in order for America's eastern cities to get beef in the mid-1800s.

An American Story

An old Texas cowhand, E.C. Abbott, recalled the early days of riding the trail:

> **"Here [were] all these cheap long-horned steers overrunning Texas; here was the rest of the country crying for beef—and no railroads to get them out. So they trailed them out, across hundreds of miles of wild country that was thick with Indians. . . . In 1867 the town of Abilene was founded at the end of the Kansas Pacific Railroad and that was when the trail really started."**
>
> —from *We Pointed Them North*

The Texas Open Range When the Spanish settled Mexico and Texas, they brought a tough breed of cattle with them. Called longhorns because of their prominent horns, these cattle gradually spread across Texas.

At this time, much of Texas was **open range**—not fenced or divided into lots. Huge ranches covered other areas of the state. Ranchers added to their own herds by rounding up wild cattle. The ranchers burned a **brand,** or symbol, into the animals' hides to show who owned the cattle.

Railroads and Cow Towns Although Texas ranchers had plenty of cattle, the markets for beef were in the North and the East. In 1866 the Missouri Pacific Railroad reached Missouri, and Texas cattle suddenly increased in value. The cattle could be loaded onto trains in Missouri for shipment north and east. Some Texans drove their combined herds—sometimes 260,000 head of cattle—north to **Sedalia, Missouri,** the nearest rail point. Longhorns that had formerly been worth $3 each quickly rose in value to $40.

Cattle drives to cow towns—towns located near railroads to market and ship cattle—turned into a yearly event. Over the next decade, cow towns such as **Abilene, Kansas, Dodge City, Kansas,** and **Cheyenne, Wyoming,** became important rail stations.

What was the Long Drive? The sudden increase in the longhorns' value began what became known as the Long Drive—the herding of cattle 1,000 miles or more to meet the railroads. The drives left Texas in the spring, when there was enough grass along the way to feed the cattle. During the heyday of the "Cattle Kingdom," from the late 1860s to the mid-1880s, the trails carried more than 5 million cattle north.

Reading Check **Explain** Why did the value of cattle increase in the mid-1860s?

Nat Love was one of many African Americans who rode the cattle trails.

US8.12.1 Trace patterns of agricultural and industrial development as they relate to climate, use of natural resources, markets, and trade and locate such development on a map.

Life on the Trail

Main Idea **The work of the cowhands who drove the cattle north from Texas to the railroads was both difficult and dangerous.**

Reading Connection What do you know about cowhands in the old West based on the movies you have seen? Read to find out about the hazards faced by cowhands on the trail and what life in the "Wild West" was really like.

The cattle drives and the cowhands who worked on them captured the imagination of the nation. Cattle driving, however, was hard work. Cowhands rode in the saddle for up to 15 hours every day, in driving rain, dust storms, and blazing sun. Life on the trail was lonely too. Cowhands saw few outsiders.

Spanish Influence Many cowhands were veterans of the Confederate army. Some were African Americans who moved west in search of a better life after the Civil War. Others were Hispanics. In fact, the traditions of cattle herding began with Hispanic ranch hands in the Spanish Southwest. These **vaqueros** (vah•KEHR•ohs) developed many of the skills—riding, roping, and branding—that cowhands used on the drives. Much of the language of the rancher today is **derived** from Spanish words used by vaqueros for centuries. Even the word *ranch* comes from the Spanish word *rancho*.

The cowhand's equipment was based on the vaquero's equipment too. Cowhands wore wide-brimmed hats to protect themselves from the sun and leather leggings, called chaps, to shield their legs from brush and mishaps with cattle. They used ropes called lariats to lasso cattle that strayed from the herd.

Hazards on the Trail During the months on the trail, the cowhands faced violent storms, rustlers who tried to steal cattle, and many other dangers. They had to drive the herds across swift-flowing rivers, where cattle could be lost. One of the greatest dangers on the trail was the stampede, when thousands of cattle ran in panic.

History *Through Art*

Jerked Down* by Charles Russell** Celebrated for his detailed and dramatic scenes of Western life, Charles Russell depicts cowhands on their horses lassoing cattle. ***Where did the traditions of cattle herding begin?

Any sudden sound—a roar of thunder or the crack of a gunshot—could set off the cattle. Then the cowhands had to race on horseback with the stampeding cattle and bring them under control.

African American, Native American, Hispanic, and Anglo cowhands met and worked together. Yet discrimination existed in the West just as it did elsewhere in the nation. Non-Anglo cowhands rarely became trail bosses and often received less pay for their work. Some towns discriminated against Hispanics, segregated African Americans, and excluded Chinese cowhands altogether.

After many tiring weeks on the trail, the cowhands delivered their cattle and enjoyed some time off in cow towns. Cowhands drank and gambled, and got involved in fistfights and gunplay. Some towns, such as Dodge City and Abilene, were rowdy, lawless, and often violent. Eventually, though, they grew into settled, businesslike communities.

Ranching Becomes Big Business Ranchers were building herds in Wyoming, Montana, and other territories. At the same time, sheep ranchers were moving their flocks across the range, and farmers were trying to cultivate crops. Competition over land use and access resulted in range wars. After much loss of life, the range was fenced off with a new invention—barbed wire—which enabled hundreds of square miles to be fenced off cheaply and easily.

At first, ranchers saw barbed wire as more of a threat than an opportunity. They did not want to abandon open grazing and complained when farmers put up barriers that prevented livestock from roaming freely. Soon, however, ranchers used barbed wire to shut out those competing with them for land and to keep their animals closer to sources of food and water. For cowhands, barbed wire ended the excitement of long cattle drives. Ranch hands replaced cowboys.

The Cattle Kingdom Ends As profits from cattle increased, cattle ranching spread north from Texas. On the northern Plains, ranchers crossbred the longhorns with fatter Hereford and Angus cattle to produce hardy, plumper new breeds.

The sturdy crossbred cattle multiplied on open-range ranches. When cattle prices boomed in the early 1880s, ranchers became rich. The boom, however, was soon followed by a bust. Overgrazing depleted the grasslands. In addition, too many cattle glutted the beef market and prices fell. The bitterly cold winters of 1885 and 1886 killed large numbers of cattle.

The price collapse of the mid-1880s marked the end of the "Cattle Kingdom." The cattle industry survived, but was changed forever. Another type of life would rise on the Plains—farming.

Reading Check **Describe** How did the Hispanics influence life in the West?

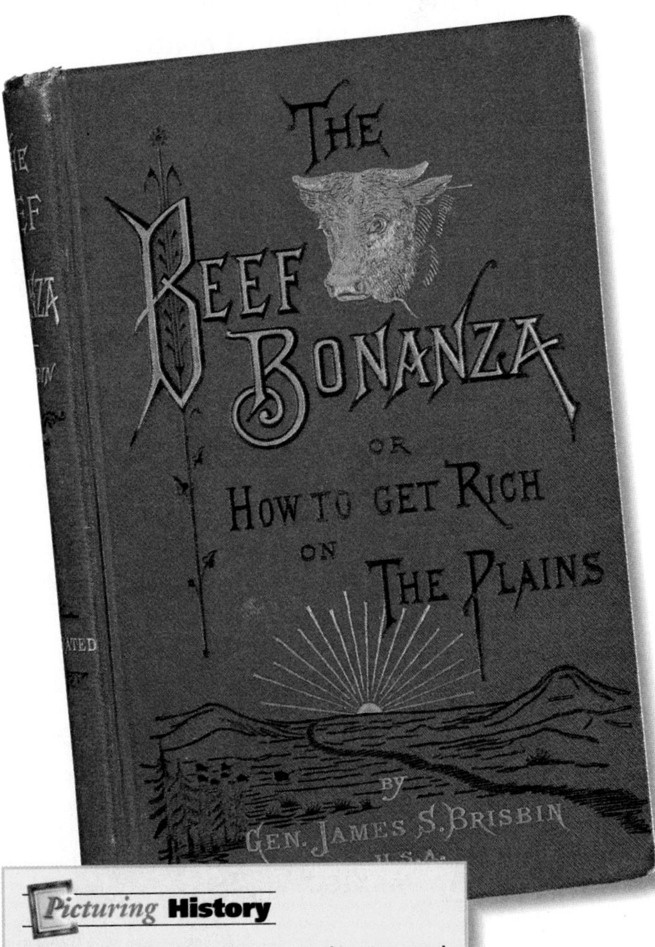

Picturing **History**

Books like *The Beef Bonanza* by General Brisbin helped fuel the cattle boom. ***Why did the cattle boom collapse?***

US8.12.1 Trace patterns of agricultural and industrial development as they relate to climate, use of natural resources, markets, and trade and locate such development on a map.

Farmers Settle the Plains

Main Idea **Free land and new farming methods brought many settlers to the Great Plains.**

Reading Connection Have you ever experienced a drought or flood? Read on to learn about what farmers faced on the Great Plains, including droughts, flooding, plagues of insects, and harsh winters.

The early pioneers who reached the Great Plains did not believe they could farm the dry, treeless area. In the late 1860s, however, farmers began settling there and planting crops. Before long, much of the Plains became farmland. In 1872 a Nebraska settler wrote,

> **"One year ago this was a vast houseless, uninhabited prairie. . . . Today I can see more than thirty dwellings from my door."**
>
> —from *Settling the West*

Several factors brought settlers to the Plains. The railroads made the journey west easier and cheaper. Above-average rainfall in the late 1870s made the Plains better suited to farming. Finally, new laws offered free land.

In 1862 Congress passed the Homestead Act, which gave 160 free acres of land to a settler who paid a filing fee and lived on the land for five years. This federal land policy brought farmers to the Plains to **homestead** (HOHM • STEHD)—earn ownership of land by settling on it.

Homesteading lured thousands of new settlers. Some were immigrants who had begun the process of becoming American citizens and were eligible to file for land. Others were women. Although married women could not claim land, single women and widows had the same rights as men—and they used the Homestead Act to **acquire** property.

Steamship companies went to great lengths to advertise the American Plains in Scandinavia. By 1880 more than 100,000 Swedes and Norwegians had settled in the northern Plains—Minnesota and the Dakotas. The Scandinavian influence remains strong in this region today.

Soon after the Civil War ended, many African American soldiers, called "Buffalo Soldiers," served in the West. Thousands of African Americans also migrated from the Southern states into Kansas in the late 1870s. They called themselves "Exodusters," from the biblical book of Exodus, which describes the Jews' escape from slavery in Egypt.

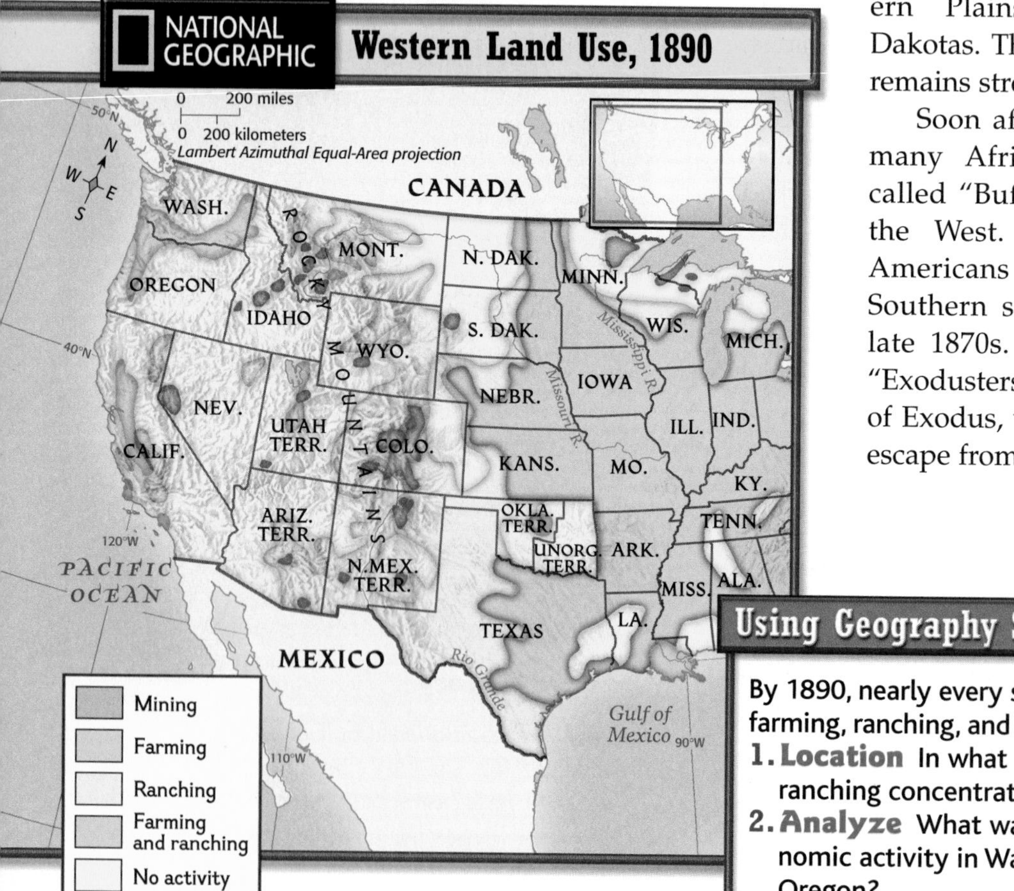

Using Geography Skills

By 1890, nearly every state had developed farming, ranching, and mining regions.

1. **Location** In what region of Texas was ranching concentrated?
2. **Analyze** What was the main economic activity in Washington and Oregon?

Biography

US8.12 Students analyze the transformation of the American economy and the changing social and political conditions in the United States in response to the Industrial Revolution. US8.11.2 Identify the push-pull factors in the movement of former slaves to the cities in the North and to the West and their differing experiences in those regions (e.g., the experiences of the Buffalo Soldiers).

THE BUFFALO SOLDIERS

African Americans had fought in military conflicts since colonial times. Many had served and died during the Civil War.

When Congress set up the peacetime army after the Civil War, it also organized four segregated regiments of African American soldiers and cavalry, the 9th Cavalry, 10th Cavalry, 24th Infantry, and 25th Infantry. Many African Americans joined because of the opportunity for steady pay and a pension. These soldiers first served on the western frontier.

These segregated units answered the nation's call to arms not only in the West, but also in Cuba, the Philippines, Hawaii, and Mexico. They fought in the Indian Wars and served in the western United States from 1867 until 1896. According to legend, the men were called "Buffalo Soldiers" by the Apache and Cheyenne. The name was adopted by the African American soldiers as a sign of honor and respect.

The Buffalo Soldiers did not, however, receive equal treatment from the Anglo American settlers or soldiers. The Buffalo Soldiers were sometimes harassed and abused. Despite being mistreated, these regiments overcame hardships to become among the most decorated military units in the United States Army.

The army, recognizing the courage of the Buffalo Soldiers, presented the Medal of Honor to at least 20 Buffalo Soldiers for service during the wars in the American West. The Buffalo Soldiers also received commendations for their bravery in other wars and conflicts, including the Spanish-American War, World War I, and World War II.

In 1992 Colin Powell, who then served as chairman of the Joint Chiefs of Staff, dedicated a memorial to the Buffalo Soldiers in Fort Leavenworth, Kansas. In recognition, Powell noted that "since 1641 there has never been a time in this country when Blacks were unwilling to serve and sacrifice for America."

▲ Charles M. Young

"Colonel Charles Young . . . stands out as a shining example of the dedication, service, and commitment of the Buffalo Soldiers."

—quoted in Senate Resolution 97, 2001

Then and Now

Research the careers of some of the high-ranking African American officers in today's armed forces.

Picturing History

To survive on the treeless Plains, settlers had to build houses that did not require lumber. A Plains family's first home was usually made of sod, which are rectangular pieces of soil and grass. ***Why did many homesteaders settle in the Plains?***

The Farmers' Frontier The climate of the Plains presented farmers with a great challenge. Generally there was little rainfall, but in some years rain came down in torrents, destroying crops and flooding homesteads. The other extreme—drought—also threatened crops and lives. Fire was another enemy. In times of drought, brushfires swept rapidly through a region, destroying crops, livestock, and homes.

Several times during the 1870s, swarms of grasshoppers swept over the Plains. Thousands of the insects would land on a field of corn. When they left, not a stalk remained.

In winters winds howled across the open Plains, and deep snow could bury animals and trap families in their homes. Families had to plan ahead and store food for the winter.

Farm Families Farming on the Great Plains was a family affair. Men labored hard in the fields. Women often did the same work, but they also cared for the children. A farm wife sewed clothing, made candles, and cooked and preserved food. She often also tended to the children's health and education. When her husband was away—taking the harvest to town or buying supplies—she was responsible for keeping the farm running.

When children grew old enough, they helped in the fields, tended animals, and did chores around the house. Farmwork often kept children from attending school.

Although separated by great distances, people took much pleasure in getting together for weddings, church services, picnics, and other occasions. As communities grew, schools and churches began to dot the rural landscape.

New Farming Methods The Plains could not be farmed by the usual methods of the 1860s. Most parts of the region had little rainfall and too few streams for irrigation. The Plains farmers, known as **sodbusters** (SAHD•BUHS•tuhrs), needed new methods and tools.

One approach, called **dry farming,** was to plant seeds deep in the ground where there was some moisture. Wooden plows could not penetrate the tough layer of sod, but in the late 1870s farmers could use the newly invented, lightweight steel plows to do the job.

The sodbusters had other tools to help them cultivate the Plains—windmills to pump water from deep in the ground and barbed wire fencing. With no wood to build fences, farmers used these wire fences to protect their land.

Dry farming, however, did not produce large crop yields, and the 160-acre grants were too small to make a living. Most farmers needed at least 300 acres, as well as advanced machinery, to make a farm profitable. Many farmers went into debt. Others lost ownership of their farms and then had to rent the land.

What Was the Oklahoma Land Rush? The last part of the Plains to be settled was the Oklahoma Territory, designated by Congress as Indian Territory in the 1830s. After years of pressure from land dealers and settlers' groups, the federal government opened Oklahoma to homesteaders in 1889. Settlers were eager to receive title to 160 acres of land. Their only condition was to remain on, improve, and develop the property for five years.

On the morning of April 22, 1889—the official opening day—more than 10,000 people lined up on the edge of this land. At the sound of a bugle, the homesteaders charged across the border to stake their claims. The eager settlers discovered that some people had already slipped into Oklahoma. These so-called "sooners" had claimed most of the best land. Within a few years, all of Oklahoma was opened to settlement.

Closing the Frontier Not long after the Oklahoma land rush, the government announced in the 1890 census that the frontier no longer existed. Settlement had changed the Plains dramatically. No one felt these changes more keenly than the Native Americans who had lived on the Plains for centuries.

Reading Check **Explain** Why was the Homestead Act important to settlers?

History Online
Study Central Need help understanding ranching and farming on the Great Plains? Visit ca.hss.glencoe.com and click on Study Central.

Section 2 Review

Reading Summary

Review the Main Ideas

- Cattle raised on the open range in Texas were driven north to railroad lines and shipped to eastern markets.
- Cowhands in the American West, who included African Americans, Native Americans, Hispanics, and whites, faced many dangers during cattle drives.
- The Homestead Act helped bring many settlers to the Great Plains.

What Did You Learn?

1. Explain why cow towns developed.
2. What new methods and tools helped settlers successfully farm the Great Plains?

Critical Thinking

3. **Determining Cause and Effect** Re-create the diagram below and explain how the Homestead Act encouraged settlement of the Great Plains. CA HI2.

4. **Analyze** What opportunities did settlement on the Plains provide for women and African Americans? CA HI1.
5. **The Big Ideas** How did geography influence the settlement and economic growth of the Great Plains and American West? CA HI6.
6. **Analysis** In an essay, discuss the growth, life, and decline of the Wild West in American history. Be sure to mention the geographical, economic, and social factors involved in that period in history. CA 8WA2.3

A Lantern in Her Hand

By Bess Streeter Aldrich

Before You Read

The Scene: The homestead in this story is in eastern Nebraska. It is 1874.
The Characters: Will and Abbie Deal set up their homestead in 1868. Mack is their seven-year-old son. The Lutzes are their closest neighbors. The Reinmuellers live a little farther away.
The Plot: Will and his family went to Nebraska because they could own land there. Until this year, they have not had good crops because there has not been enough rain. They have also lived through a prairie fire and blizzards. Will and Abbie still believe, however, that the land is their fortune.

Vocabulary Preview

billowing: bulging or swelling out in the wind
colossal: huge, enormous
diabolical: like a devil; very evil
hazy: unclear because of smoke, dust, or clouds
incredulously: in a way that is unbelieving
perforations: holes
raw: not prepared for use; natural
uncanny: beyond ordinary human means or ability

Have you ever worked hard to make a wish come true? Were you able to reach your goal? Farming is an uncertain business, but it seems that Will and Abbie's hopes may soon be realized.

As You Read

Contrast and vivid description are two tools that writers use to emphasize the importance of an event. As you begin reading this selection, imagine what the homestead looks like. As you continue, pay close attention to the pictures the writer is painting with words. What changes do you see?

The crop of 1874 was the sixth crop and it seemed to give a little more promise than the previous ones. By the twentieth of July, Will had laid by all his corn. Most of his small grain[1] was in the shocks,[2] but one oat field of a few acres was still uncut. Standing there under the July sun, its ripened surface seemed to reflect back the yellow rays. In the afternoon Abbie went out to pick a mess[3] of beans. The garden had come to be Abbie's care. Aside from the potato crop, to which Will attended, she looked after the entire garden. It was quite generally so,—the men bending all their energies to bigger things, the corn and wheat and the stock, with the chickens and the gardens falling to the lot of the wives. Some of the women went into the fields. Christine Reinmueller was out beside Gus many days. Will drew the line at that. "When you have to do that, we'll quit," he said.

Abbie, in her starched[4] sunbonnet, began picking beans for supper. She could see Will and Henry Lutz working together, shocking the last of Henry's oats. To-morrow the two would work together on Will's last stand. It was nice for the men to be so neighborly.

It seemed hazy in the west. By the time she had finished the long rows, a big panful of the yellow pods in her arms, Will had come home from the Lutzes'. In the welcome shade of the house Abbie took off her bonnet, wiped her flushed perspiring face and waited for Will to come up.

"My...it's a scorcher." She looked hot and tired.

In a moment of tenderness, more to be desired because of its rarity, Will picked up Abbie's hands. The slender nails were stubbed and broken,—the grime of the garden was on her tapering fingers. He lifted her hand suddenly and kissed the hollow of it. As his lips touched the calloused palms, his eyes filled with rare tears. He uttered a short swift oath, "I wish you didn't have to, Abbie-girl. It's tough for you. Some day...in a few years...we'll pull out. Weather conditions may change... the land will be high.... You can have better things...and your organ. That singing and painting of yours...maybe we can get to a teacher then...."

---

[1] **small grain:** grains, such as oat, rye, wheat; any grain that is not corn

[2] **in the shocks:** grain stacked in a standing position in a field to dry

[3] **mess:** enough food of one kind to serve as a meal or a dish

[4] **starched:** clothing that has been made stiff

It affected Abbie as it always did. In a moment like that it seemed the end and aim of everything...the family. All her dreams for herself were as nothing. In her own moment of emotion she returned, "We'll make it, Will...don't worry!"

For a moment they stood together looking out over the raw rolling acreage. Even as they looked, the sun darkened and the day took on a grayness. They looked for the storm, and heard it as soon as they saw it,—a great black cloud roar out of the west, with a million little hissing vibrations.[5] Their eyes on the sky, neither moved. Then there was a cessation[6] of the roaring, a soft thud of dropping things, and the cloud of a billion wings lay on the fields.

"Grasshoppers," they said simultaneously, incredulously.

The grasshoppers swarmed over the young waist-high corn and the pasture and the garden. By evening the long rows of sweet corn had been eaten to the plowed ground. The tender vines of the tomatoes were stripped down to the stalk. The buds of the fruit trees were gone. Part of the garden was a memory. The chickens had feasted themselves to the bursting point. Gus Reinmueller, driving up to the door, could hardly control his raring horses, so irritated were they by the bouncing, thumping pests. The farm was a squirming, greenish-gray mass of them.

All evening Will sat by the stove with his head in his hands. It was the first time he had visibly lost his grit. Abbie went over to him and ran her hand through his hair. She tried to think of something to console him. "Don't, Will.... There's one thing we can do. There's the string of pearls. We can always fall back on it. There must be jewelry stores in Omaha that would take it and pay well. You can take the team and make the drive.... You can do it in three days,...and I'll look after things here. When Mother gave the pearls to me, she said 'You'll ne'er starve with them' ...and we won't, Will. We'll sell them for the children's sake."

Will threw her hands away from his hair roughly and stood up. "Hell...no!" He yelled it at her. "I've taken your music away from you and your painting and your teaching and some of your health. But, *by God*,...I won't take your mother's present to you."

He slammed the rough soddie door and went out to the barn.

By the next night the stalks of field corn were skeletons, a few delicate veins of leaves left, like so many white bones bleaching on the desert of the fields. At the end of three days the oat field was stripped almost as bare as the day the plow had finished its work. The young orchard was a graveyard of hopes. Some of the small grain previously harvested had been saved, and luckily, one digging of early potatoes was in the hole in the ground in which Will always kept them. But everything else went through the crunching incisors[7] of the horde. It was as though the little grayish-green fiends[8] became a composite whole,—one colossal insect into whose grinding maw[9] went all the green of the fields and the gardens, all the leaves and tender twigs of the young fruit trees, all the dreams and the hopes of the settlers.

The pests were everywhere. With nightmarish persistence, they appeared in everything. As tightly as Will kept the well covered, he drew them up in the bucket, so that he began

[5] **vibrations:** quick movements back and forth
[6] **cessation:** ending
[7] **incisors:** front teeth that are particularly good for cutting
[8] **fiends:** evil spirits
[9] **maw:** the jaws of an animal that has a huge appetite

going back to the old spring for water. Abbie caught them eating the curtains of the little half-windows and sent them to a fiery death. She was forced to dry the weekly wash around the cook stove, her one attempt to hang it in the sun ending speedily with a dozen perforations in the first billowing garment.

The garden was a total loss. They had tried to save some of the beans by putting gunny-sacks[10] over them and weighting them down with stones from the creek bed. The grasshoppers, after eating the beans, had begun on the gunny-sacks.

"Will they eat the stones, too, Mother?" Mack wanted to know. And they could not laugh at him.

Abbie wrote a letter to her sister Mary, telling of this last hard piece of luck. Even letters were expensive luxuries so that one was made to do for the entire group of relatives back in eastern Iowa. She gave the letter to Will, who said that he would ride over to the little post office in the Lutz store as soon as he had finished caring for the stock. In an hour Will came in holding the letter by a corner. The edges of the envelope had been eaten all the way around with little neat flutings so that the two sides fell apart and the letter fluttered to the floor. The pocket of his old denim coat, where the letter had lain, was flapping down, cut on two sides by the same diabolical jaws.

What could you do? You could not fight them. You could not kill them. They were an army with an uncanny and unnatural power. Abbie looked out upon the devastation[11] of the fields and the garden upon which they both had worked so hard. The hot wind blew over the ruins with Mephistophelean[12] laughter. She looked up at the cloudless blue,—huge cruel, sardonic.[13]

---

[10] **gunny-sacks:** a bag made from coarse heavy material, such as burlap

[11] **devastation:** destruction

[12] **Mephistophelean:** like the proud fallen angel Mephistopheles who is cold-hearted, funny, and sardonic

[13] **sardonic:** making fun in a way that shows someone or something is not important

Responding to the Literature

1. What was Abbie doing when the selection started? What was Will doing?
2. How did Abbie and Will try to save the beans? What happened next?
3. **Analyze** In **foreshadowing** a writer gives clues to prepare readers for what will happen. What did the author foreshadow in this selection? How did she do it? CA 8RL3.6
4. **Explain** What are the literal and figurative meanings of the following sentence? "The young orchard was a graveyard of hopes." CA 8RW1.1
5. **Read to Write** In 500 to 700 words, write a story or describe an incident in your life. Base the narrative on an event related to your local weather, such as a hurricane or blizzard. As an alternative, you may use an environmental issue, such as water pollution or an endangered species. What was life like before and during this incident? Why was the event important? What was your attitude about it? Be sure to include dialogue in the narrative. CA 8WA2.1a,b,c

Reading On Your Own...

Do you want to learn more about life and inventions in the years between the Civil War and 1914? You might be interested in the following books.

Nonfiction

Native Americans and the Reservation in American History by Anita Louise McCormick recounts the history of relations between whites and Native Americans, beginning in the 1600s. McCormick also explains the historical and cultural beliefs that led members of each ethnic group to act as they did. ***The content of this book is related to** History–Social Science Standard US8.12.*

Biography

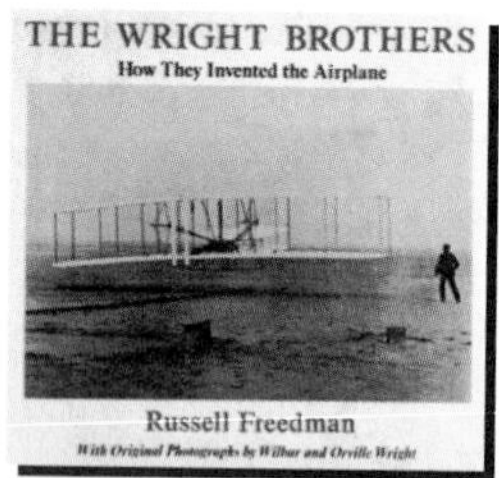

The Wright Brothers: How They Invented the Airplane by Russell Freedman does more than simply describe the brothers' experiments. Freedman has included portions of their journals and letters, plus photos that the brothers took as they documented their experiments. ***The content of this book is related to** History–Social Science Standard US8.12.*

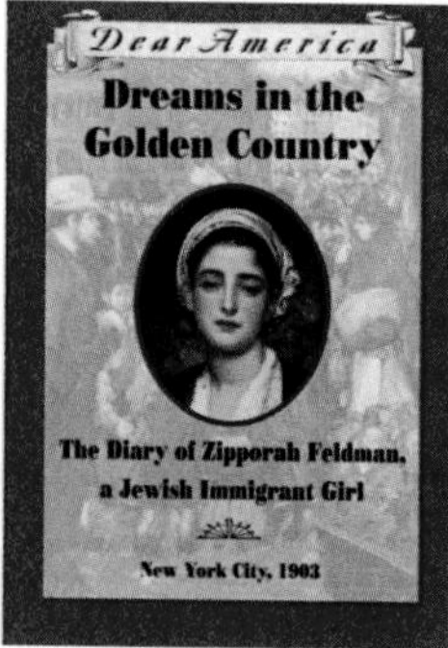

Historical Fiction

Dreams in the Golden Country: The Diary of Zipporah Feldman, a Jewish Immigrant Girl by Kathryn Lasky begins by describing the Feldmans' experience on Ellis Island. As the diary continues, Zipporah tells about their life in New York City in the early 1900s and her hopes for the future. ***The content of this book is related to** History–Social Science Standard US8.12.*

Nonfiction

McGuffey's Fourth Eclectic Reader by William McGuffey starts with directions to the teacher, followed by poetry and prose reading selections for students. This book gives the reader an interesting insight into what students read in the 1800s and why particular pieces were chosen. ***The content of this book is related to** History–Social Science Standard US8.12.*

Native American Struggles

Guide to Reading

Looking Back, Looking Ahead

You learned that following the Civil War, many whites moved to the Great Plains and the American West to mine, ranch, and farm. Many Native American groups, however, already lived in those areas, and the two peoples came into conflict.

Focusing on the Main Ideas

- The Native Americans of the Great Plains lived a nomadic lifestyle while following the great herds of buffalo. *(page 686)*
- During the late 1800s, whites and Native Americans fought while Native Americans tried to preserve their civilizations. *(page 687)*

Locating Places

Oklahoma
Dakota Territory
Black Hills
Little Bighorn River
Wounded Knee

Meeting People

Red Cloud
William Cody
Crazy Horse
Black Kettle
Sitting Bull
George Custer
Geronimo (juh • RAH • nuh • MOH)
Helen Hunt Jackson

Content Vocabulary

nomadic (noh • MA • dihk)
reservation

Academic Vocabulary

despite (di • SPYT)
achieve

Reading Strategy

Determining Cause and Effect As you read the section, re-create the diagram below and describe how Western settlement affected Native Americans.

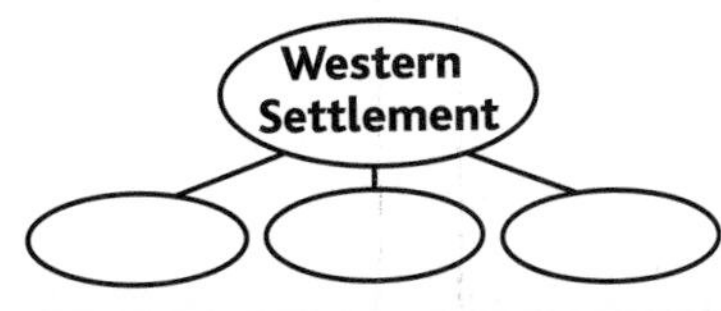

History Social Science Standards

US8.12 Students analyze the transformation of the American economy and the changing social and political conditions in the United States in response to the Industrial Revolution.

US8.12.2 Identify the reasons for the development of federal Indian policy and the wars with American Indians and their relationship to agricultural development and industrialization.

Following the Buffalo

Main Idea **The Native Americans of the Great Plains lived a nomadic lifestyle while following the great herds of buffalo.**

Reading Connection What might it be like to move from place to place throughout the year, following a large herd of animals so that your people could hunt and eat? Read to find out about the lifestyle of the Native Americans of the Great Plains.

In the mid-1850s, miners, railroads, cattle drivers, and farmers came to the Plains. Each new group threatened Native American culture. The Sioux chief **Red Cloud** lamented, "The white children [settlers] have surrounded me and left me nothing but an island."

For centuries the Great Plains was home to many Native American nations. The Omaha and the Osage nations lived in communities as farmers and hunters. The Sioux, the Comanche, and the Blackfeet lived a **nomadic** (noh•MA•dihk) life. They traveled vast distances following their main source of food—the great herds of buffalo that roamed the Great Plains.

Despite their differences, the people of the Plains were similar in many ways. Plains Indian nations, sometimes numbering several thousand people, were divided into bands consisting of up to 500 people each. A governing council headed each band, but most members participated in making decisions.

The women reared the children, cooked, and prepared hides. The men hunted, traded, and supervised the military life of the band. Most Plains Indians practiced a religion based on a belief in the spiritual power of the natural world.

Threats to the Buffalo At one time, the Plains Indians had millions of buffalo to supply their needs. After the Civil War, though, American hunters hired by the railroads began slaughtering the animals to feed the crews building the railroad. The railroad companies also wanted to prevent huge herds of buffalo from blocking the trains. **William Cody,** hired by the Kansas Pacific Railroad, once claimed that he had killed more than 4,000 buffalo in less than 18 months. He became known as Buffalo Bill. Starting in 1872, hunters targeted buffalo to sell the hides to the East, where tanneries made them into leather goods.

Reading Check **Describe** What is a nomadic way of life?

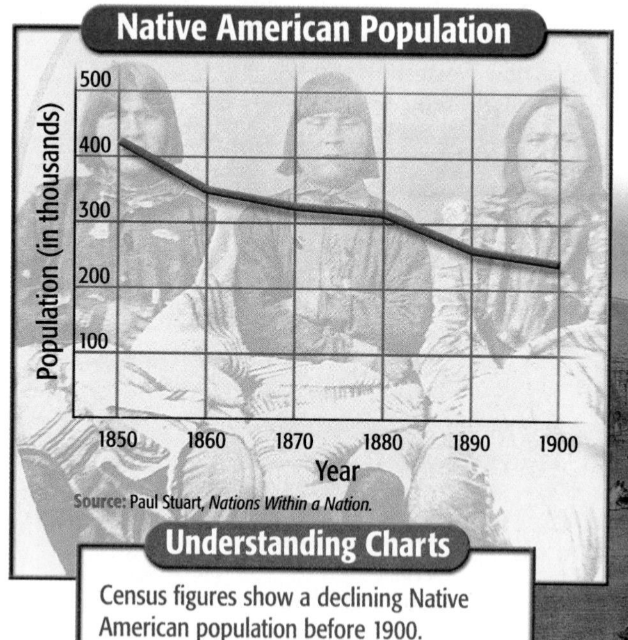

Understanding Charts

Census figures show a declining Native American population before 1900.

Analyze During what 10-year period did the Native American population decline the least?

▲ **Native Americans of the Great Plains settled in one place for only part of the year.**

US8.12.2 Identify the reasons for the development of federal Indian policy and the wars with American Indians and their relationship to agricultural development and industrialization.

Conflict

Main Idea **During the late 1800s, whites and Native Americans fought while Native Americans tried to preserve their civilizations.**

Reading Connection How would you react if the government suddenly forced you to move from your home? Read to find out how Native Americans reacted when settlers moved into their lands and attempted to change the way they lived.

As ranchers, miners, and farmers moved onto the Plains, they deprived Native Americans of their hunting grounds, broke treaties guaranteeing certain lands to the Plains Indians, and often forced them to relocate to new territory. Native Americans resisted by attacking wagon trains, stagecoaches, and ranches. Occasionally, an entire group would go to war against nearby settlers and troops. In the late 1860s, the government pursued a new Indian policy to deal with these challenges.

Reservation Policy In 1867 the federal government appointed the Indian Peace Commission to set policies for Native Americans. The commission recommended moving the Native Americans to a few large **reservations**—tracts of land set aside for them.

One large reservation was in **Oklahoma,** the "Indian Territory" that Congress had created in the 1830s for Native Americans who were relocated from the Southeast. Another one, meant for the Sioux people, was in the **Dakota Territory.** Managing the reservations would be the job of the federal Bureau of Indian Affairs.

Government agents often used trickery to persuade Native American nations to move to the reservations. Many reservations were located on poor land. In addition the government often failed to deliver promised food and supplies, and the goods that were delivered were of poor quality.

A great many Native Americans accepted the reservation policy at first. Many southern Kiowa, Comanche, Cheyenne, and Arapaho agreed to stay on the Oklahoma reservation. Thousands of Sioux agreed to move onto the Dakota reservation in the North.

Pockets of resistance remained, however. Some Native Americans refused to make the move, and some who tried reservation life abandoned it. The stage was set for trouble.

Conflict on the Plains During the 1860s, many armed clashes between Native Americans and whites took place. Minnesota Territory was the site of one especially bloody confrontation. Resentful of the settlers, Sioux warriors, led by Red Cloud, burned and looted white settlers' homes in the summer of 1862. Hundreds died before troops arrived from St. Paul and ended the uprising.

Following the Minnesota uprising, the army sent patrols far out onto the northern Great Plains. This action brought troops into contact with another branch of the Sioux—the nomadic Lakota. The Lakota fought hard to keep control of their hunting grounds, which extended from the Black Hills and the surrounding Badlands—rocky and barren terrain in the western parts of the Dakotas and northwestern Nebraska—westward to the Bighorn Mountains.

▲ Native American buffalo shield

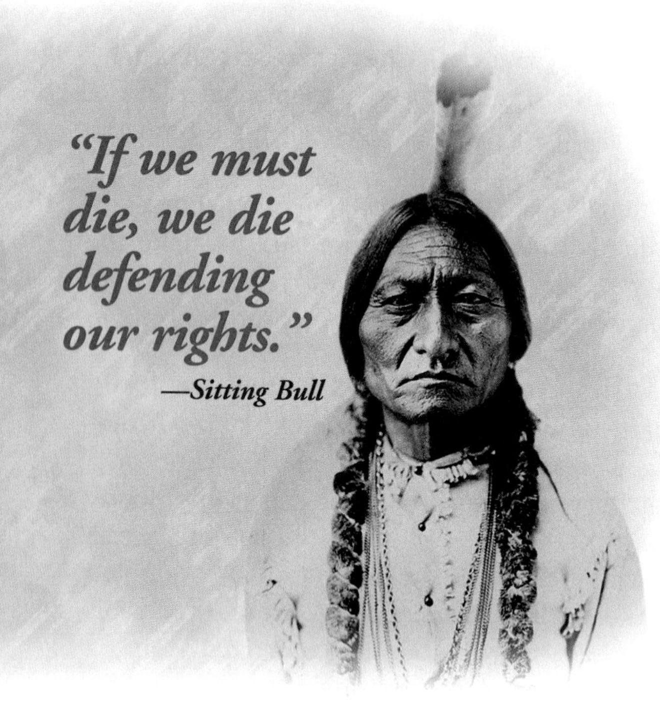

"If we must die, we die defending our rights."
—Sitting Bull

The Sioux, along with Cheyenne and Arapaho warriors, staged a series of attacks from 1865 to 1867. The bloodiest incident occurred on December 21, 1866. Army troops, led by Captain William J. Fetterman, were manning a fort on the Bozeman Trail, used by prospectors to reach gold mines in Montana. A Sioux military leader, **Crazy Horse,** acted as a decoy and lured the troops into a deadly trap. He tricked the fort's commander into sending a detachment of about 80 soldiers in pursuit. Hundreds of warriors were waiting in ambush and wiped out the entire detachment. This incident came to be known as the Fetterman Massacre.

Colorado was another site of conflict. The number of miners who had flocked to Colorado in search of gold and silver grew. Bands of Cheyenne and Arapaho began raiding wagon trains and stealing cattle and horses from ranches. By the summer of 1864, travelers heading to Denver or the mining camps were no longer safe. Dozens of ranches had been burned, and an estimated 200 settlers had been killed. The territorial governor of Colorado ordered the Native Americans to surrender at Fort Lyon, where he said they would be given food and protection.

Although several hundred Native Americans surrendered at the fort, many others did not. In November 1864, Chief **Black Kettle** brought several hundred Cheyenne to negotiate a peace deal. They camped at Sand Creek. Shortly after, Colonel John Chivington led the Colorado Volunteers on an attack on the unsuspecting Cheyenne. Fourteen volunteers and hundreds of Cheyenne died. Retaliation by the Cheyenne was swift, causing widespread uprisings before some of the Cheyenne and Arapaho leaders agreed to stop the fighting in October 1865.

What Occurred at Little Bighorn? Treaties were supposed to bring peace, but tensions remained and erupted in more fighting a few years later. This time the conflict arose over the **Black Hills** of the Dakotas. The government had promised that "No white person or persons shall be permitted to settle upon or occupy" or even "to pass through" these hills. However, the hills were rumored to contain gold. Prospectors swarmed into the area.

The Sioux protested against the trespassers. Instead of protecting the Sioux's rights, the government tried to buy the hills. **Sitting Bull,** an important leader of the Lakota Sioux, refused. "I do not want to sell any land. Not even this much," he said, holding a pinch of dust.

Sitting Bull gathered Sioux and Cheyenne warriors along the **Little Bighorn River** in present-day Montana. They were joined by Crazy Horse, another Sioux chief, and his forces. The United States Army was ordered to round up the warriors and move them to reservations. The Seventh Cavalry, led by Lieutenant Colonel **George Custer,** was ordered to scout the Native American encampment.

Custer wanted the glory of leading a major victory. He divided his regiment and attacked the Native Americans on June 25, 1876. He had seriously underestimated their strength, however. With about 250 soldiers, Custer faced a Sioux and Cheyenne force of thousands. Custer and his entire command lost their lives. News of the army's defeat shocked the nation.

The Native American triumph at Little Bighorn was short-lived. The army soon crushed the uprising, sending most of the Native Americans to reservations. Sitting Bull and his followers fled north to Canada. By 1881, exhausted and starving, the Lakota and Cheyenne agreed to live on a reservation.

Who Were the Nez Perce? Farther west, members of the Nez Perce, led by Chief Joseph, refused to be moved to a smaller reservation in Idaho in 1877. When the army came to relocate them, they fled their homes and traveled more than 1,000 miles. After a remarkable flight to Canada, Chief Joseph realized that resistance was hopeless. Finally, in October 1877, Chief Joseph surrendered, and his followers were moved to reservations.

The Apache Wars Trouble also broke out in the Southwest. The Chiracahua Apache had been moved from their homeland in present-day New Mexico and Arizona to the San Carlos reservation in Arizona in the mid-1870s. Many Apache resented confinement to this reservation. The Apache leader, **Geronimo** (juh • RAH • nuh • MOH), escaped from San Carlos and fled to Mexico with a small band of followers. During the 1880s, he led raids against settlers and the army in Arizona. Army troops pursued Geronimo and his warriors. Several times Geronimo went back to the reservation only to leave again. Geronimo said, "Once I moved about like the wind. Now I surrender to you." In 1886 the Apache leader finally gave up—the last Native American to surrender formally to the United States.

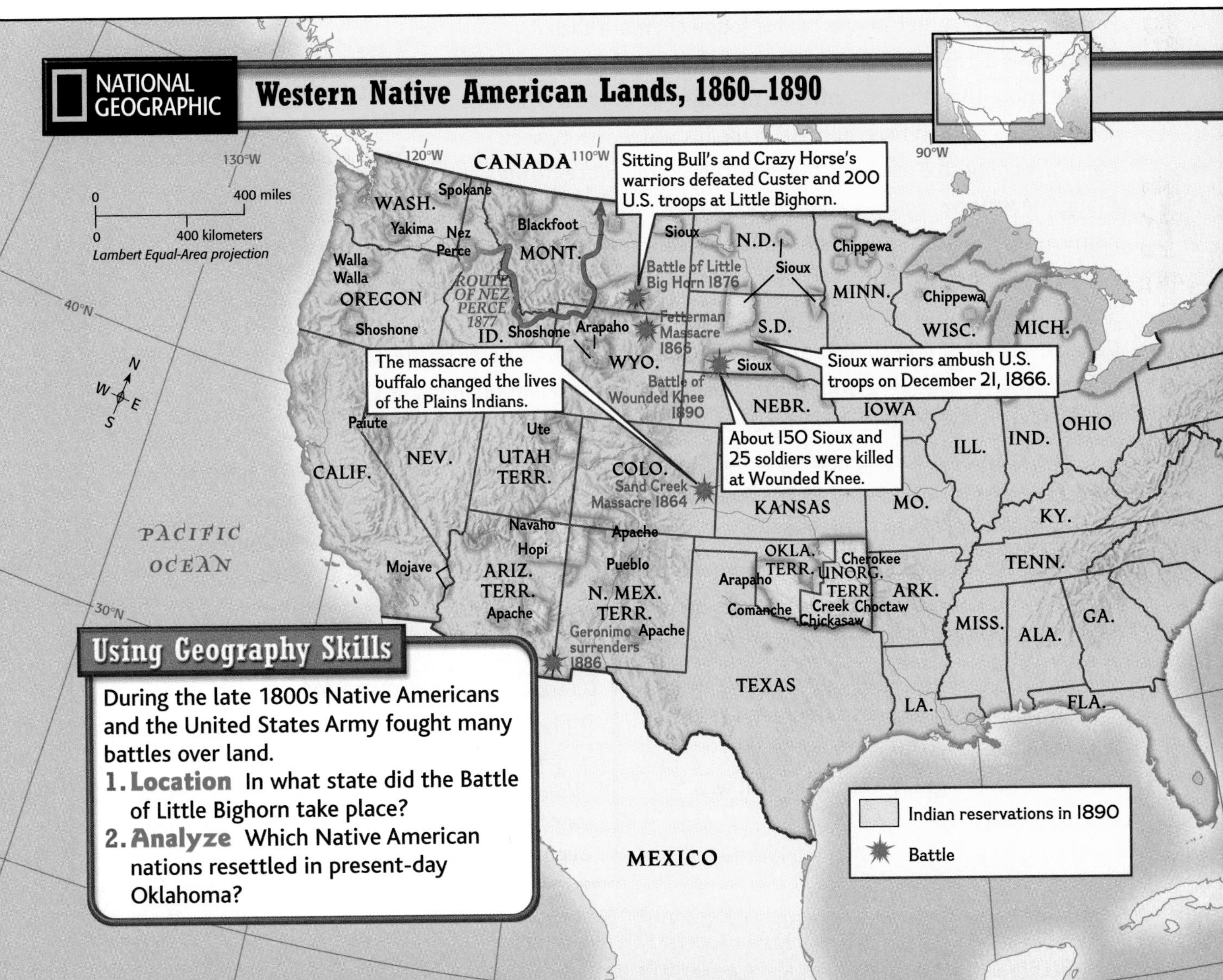

Using Geography Skills

During the late 1800s Native Americans and the United States Army fought many battles over land.

1. **Location** In what state did the Battle of Little Bighorn take place?
2. **Analyze** Which Native American nations resettled in present-day Oklahoma?

Biography

US8.12.2 Identify the reasons for the development of federal Indian policy and the wars with American Indians and their relationship to agricultural development and industrialization.

CHIEF JOSEPH

1840–1904

Chief Joseph was born in 1840 as Hin ma to yah lat k'it, which means Thunder Emerging from the Mountains. He grew up in the Wallowa Valley, located in present-day Oregon. In 1860, when gold was found on Nez Perce land, white settlers flooded into the region. In 1877 the United States government demanded that the Nez Perce give up their lands and move onto a reservation in Idaho. Chief Joseph, hoping to avoid violence, prepared his people for the move. He learned, however, that several young braves had attacked a group of white settlers. Fearing revenge, Chief Joseph led his followers more than 1,000 miles across Oregon, Washington, Idaho, and Montana.

For more than three months he managed to evade a U.S. force 10 times larger than his group. He made his way north toward Canada, hoping to escape the reach of the United States Army. Along the way, he won the admiration of many whites for his humane treatment of prisoners and for his concern for women, children, and the elderly.

In September 1877, the Nez Perce had reached the Bear Paw Mountains in Montana, just 40 miles from the Canadian border. As the Nez Perce rested before their move into Canada, a band of 400 soldiers surrounded the camp. After a fierce battle, Chief Joseph offered to surrender in return for safe passage to the reservation in Idaho. Chief Joseph's words of surrender reflect the tragedy of his people:

"The little children are freezing to death. My people . . . have no blankets, no food. . . . I am tired; my heart is sick and sad. From where the sun now stands I will fight no more forever."

The Nez Perce were taken not to Idaho, but to a swampy tract of land in Kansas. There, unused to the weather and the environment, many fell ill and died. Eventually, the Nez Perce were scattered among reservations in Oklahoma, Idaho, and Washington. Chief Joseph continued to plead with the government to allow his people to return to their land in the Wallowa Valley. His efforts failed, but he is remembered as a great warrior, as well as a man of peace.

"I will fight no more forever."

—Chief Joseph, from *A Patriot's Handbook*

Then and Now

Chief Joseph's reputation as a great leader arose in part from his ability and dignity in battle. Research to find at least three U.S. presidents or other government officials who built their reputations in the military.

A Changing Culture Many things contributed to changing the traditional way of life of Native Americans—the movement of whites onto their lands, the slaughter of the buffalo, United States Army attacks, and the reservation policy. More change came from well-meaning reformers who wanted to abolish reservations and absorb the Native Americans into white American culture.

American reformers such as **Helen Hunt Jackson** were horrified by the massacres of Native Americans and by the cruelty of the reservation system. Describing the whites' treatment of Native Americans in her 1881 book, *A Century of Dishonor,* Jackson wrote:

> **"It makes little difference . . . where one opens the record of the history of the Indians; every page and every year has its dark stain. The story of one tribe is the story of all, varied only by differences of time and place."**
>
> **—Helen Hunt Jackson,**
> ***A Century of Dishonor***

Congress changed government policy with the Dawes Act in 1887. The law aimed to eliminate what white Americans regarded as the two weaknesses of Native American life: the lack of private property and the nomadic tradition.

The Dawes Act proposed to break up the reservations and to end identification with a tribal group. Each Native American would receive a plot of reservation land. The goal was to encourage native peoples to become farmers and, eventually, American citizens. Native American children would be sent to white-run boarding schools. Some of the reservation lands would be sold to support this schooling.

Over the next 50 years, the government divided up the reservations. Speculators acquired most of the valuable land. Native Americans often received dry, gravelly plots that were not suited to farming.

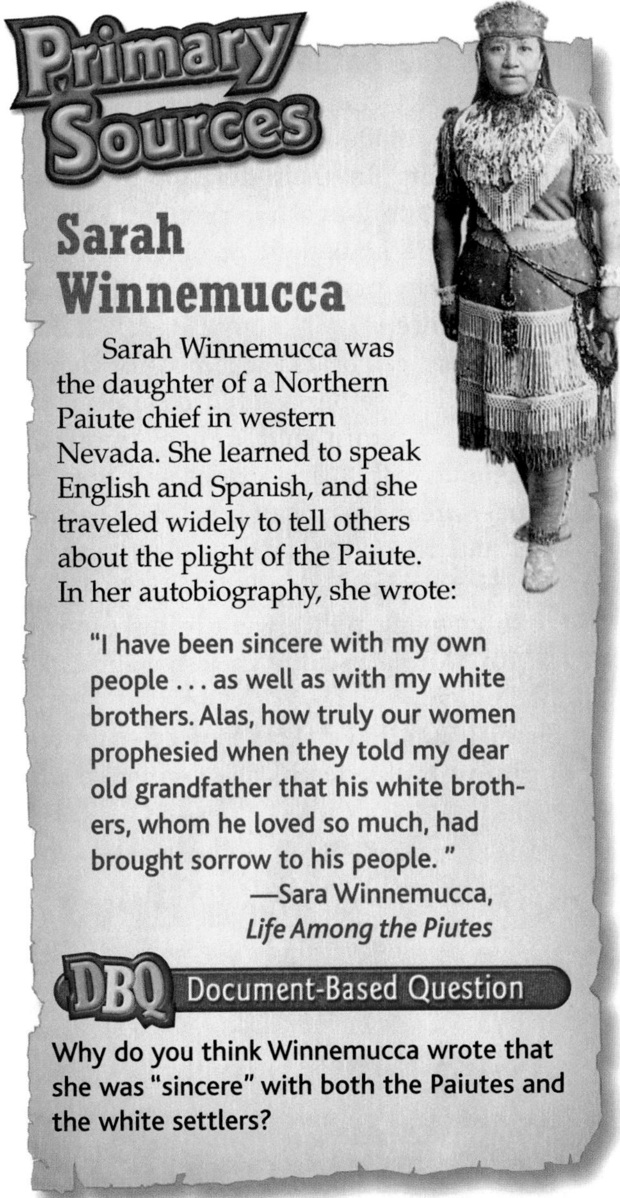

Primary Sources

Sarah Winnemucca

Sarah Winnemucca was the daughter of a Northern Paiute chief in western Nevada. She learned to speak English and Spanish, and she traveled widely to tell others about the plight of the Paiute. In her autobiography, she wrote:

> "I have been sincere with my own people . . . as well as with my white brothers. Alas, how truly our women prophesied when they told my dear old grandfather that his white brothers, whom he loved so much, had brought sorrow to his people."
>
> —Sara Winnemucca,
> *Life Among the Piutes*

DBQ Document-Based Question

Why do you think Winnemucca wrote that she was "sincere" with both the Paiutes and the white settlers?

Cultural Impact This plan failed to **achieve** its goals. Some Native Americans succeeded as farmers or ranchers, but many had little training or enthusiasm for either pursuit. Their land allotments were too small to be profitable. Some Native Americans had adapted to life on reservations and did not want to see it transformed into homesteads. In the end, the Dawes Act did not benefit Native American nations. The culture of the Plains Indians was doomed because it was dependent on buffalo. Once the buffalo were wiped out, Native Americans on the Plains had no means to sustain their way of life and little interest in adopting white American culture in place of their own.

What Was the Battle at Wounded Knee?

The Dawes Act changed forever the Native American way of life and undermined their cultural traditions. In their despair, the Sioux turned in 1890 to Wovoka, a prophet. Wovoka claimed that the Sioux could regain their former greatness if they performed a ritual known as the Ghost Dance.

This ritual celebrated a hoped-for day of reckoning when settlers would disappear, the buffalo would return, and Native Americans would reunite with their deceased ancestors. As the ritual spread, reservation officials became alarmed and decided to ban the dance. Believing that the Sioux chief, Sitting Bull, was the leader of the movement, police went to his camp to arrest him. During a scuffle, they shot and killed Sitting Bull.

Several hundred Lakota Sioux fled in fear after Sitting Bull's death. They gathered at a creek called **Wounded Knee** in southwestern South Dakota. On December 29, 1890, the army went there to collect the Sioux's weapons. No one knows how the fighting started, but when a pistol shot rang out, the army responded with fire. More than 200 Sioux and 25 soldiers were killed.

Wounded Knee marked the end of armed conflict between whites and Native Americans. The Native Americans of the Plains had fought hundreds of battles from 1860 to 1890, but they could fight no more. They depended on the buffalo for food, clothing, fuel, and shelter. When the herds were wiped out, resistance became impossible. The Native Americans had lost their long struggle.

Reading Check **Describe** What was the purpose of the Dawes Act?

History Online
Study Central Need help understanding Native American struggles? Visit ca.hss.glencoe.com and click on Study Central.

Section 3 Review

Reading Summary

Review the Main Ideas

- For centuries, Native Americans lived on the Great Plains. Some were farmers and others were nomadic. The buffalo supplied most of their needs.
- As white settlers continued to migrate and settle the West, Native American civilization was continually threatened. Conflict between the whites and the Native Americans persisted through the late 1800s.

What Did You Learn?

1. Who were Geronimo and Chief Joseph?
2. What was the Ghost Dance?

Critical Thinking

3. **Identifying Central Issues** Re-create the diagram below and identify ways the government reservation policy ignored the needs of Native Americans. CA CS1.

4. **The Big Ideas** How did differences in social beliefs between the white settlers and the Native Americans lead to the conflict that occurred in the West? CA HI1.
5. **Analyze** What two aspects of Native American life was the Dawes Act supposed to eliminate? CA HI2.
6. **Sequence** Draw a time line that lists key developments between the U.S. government and Native American nations from 1860 to 1890. CA CS2.
7. **Creative Writing** From the point of view of a Native American, write a poem describing the Plains Indians' lifestyle or a battle or event that occurred on the Plains. CA 8WA2.1

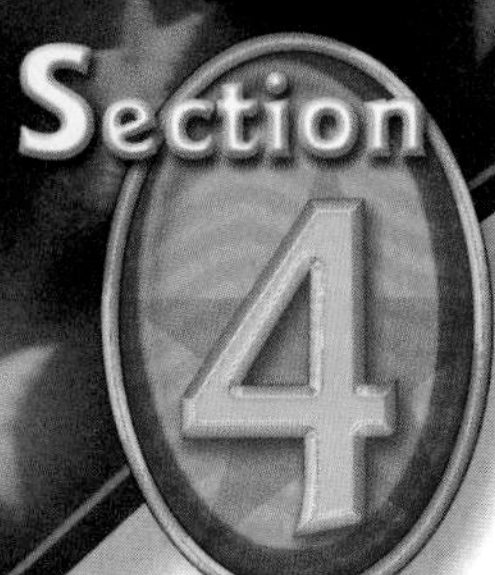

Section 4: Farmers in Protest

Guide to Reading

Looking Back, Looking Ahead
You learned that new farming methods and the defeat of the Native Americans allowed settlers to farm the Great Plains. In time, farmers began to organize to solve problems, such as falling crop prices.

Focusing on the Main Ideas
- When crop prices fell in the late 1800s, farmers began to organize politically. *(page 694)*
- In the 1890s, a political party developed supporting the views of farmers and the common people. *(page 695)*

Locating Places
Omaha, Nebraska

Meeting People
James B. Weaver
Grover Cleveland
William Jennings Bryan
William McKinley

Content Vocabulary
National Grange
cooperative (koh•AH•puh•ruh•tiv)
Populist Party (PAH•pyuh•lihst)
free silver

Academic Vocabulary
decline
dynamic (dy•NA•mihk)

Reading Strategy
Identifying Central Issues As you read the section, re-create the diagram below and identify the problems farmers faced in the late 1800s.

Farmers' problems

History Social Science Standards

US8.12 Students analyze the transformation of the American economy and the changing social and political conditions in the United States in response to the Industrial Revolution.

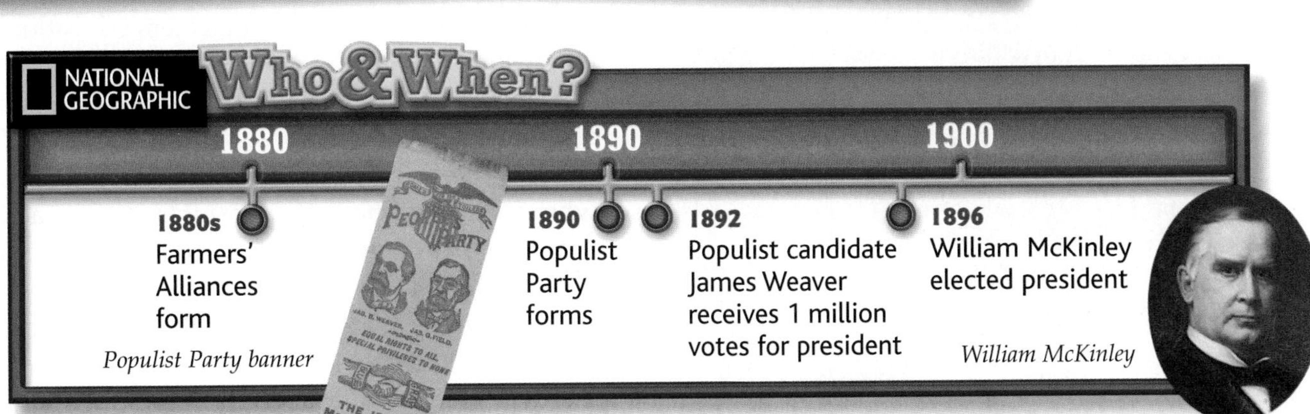
NATIONAL GEOGRAPHIC
Who & When?
1880
1890
1900
1880s Farmers' Alliances form
1890 Populist Party forms
1892 Populist candidate James Weaver receives 1 million votes for president
1896 William McKinley elected president
PEOPLE'S PARTY
EQUAL RIGHTS TO ALL, SPECIAL PRIVILEGES TO NONE
THE ISSUES: MONEY, LAND, AND TRANSPORTATION.

Populist Party banner

William McKinley

US8.12.8 Identify the characteristics and impact of Grangerism and Populism.

The Farmers Organize

Main Idea **When crop prices fell in the late 1800s, farmers began to organize politically.**

Reading Connection Have you heard the expression "strength in numbers"? Read to find out how farmers organized in groups in the late 1800s to help solve the challenges they faced.

An American Story

In the last decades of the 1800s, farmers suffered from falling prices and rising costs. They expressed their frustration in a popular song:

> **"When the banker says he's broke,**
> **And the merchant's up in smoke,**
> **They forget that it's the farmer**
> **feeds them all. . . .**
> **The farmer is the man,**
> **Lives on credit till the fall;**
> **With the interest rates so high,**
> **It's a wonder he don't die,**
> **For the mortgage man's the one**
> **who gets it all."**
>
> **—from "The Farmer Is the Man"**

▲ Honoring the Farmer, 1870s poster

Crop Prices Fall After the Civil War, farming expanded in the West and the South, and more land came under cultivation. The supply of crops grew faster than the demand for them, however, and prices fell steadily. In 1866 a bushel of wheat sold for $1.45. By the mid-1880s, the price had dropped to 80 cents, and by the mid-1890s to 49 cents. At the same time, farmers' expenses—for transporting their goods to market, for seed, and for equipment and other manufactured goods—remained high.

Farmers blamed their troubles on three groups in particular. They resented the railroad companies, which charged farmers high rates to ship their crops. They were angry at the Eastern manufacturers, who charged high prices for their products. They also had problems with bankers.

Farmers needed to borrow money to buy seed, equipment, and other goods. After they sold their crops, they had to pay the high interest rates set by bankers. If crops failed and farmers could not repay the loans, they were in danger of losing their farms.

Farmers with small and middle-sized holdings struggled to survive. Senator William A. Peffer of Kansas summed up the farmers' plight when he noted that the railroad companies "took possession of the land" and the bankers "took possession of the farmer."

What Did the Grange Do? Farmers began to organize in an effort to solve their problems. Within a short time, they created a mass political movement. The first farmers' organization of this period was a network of local organizations that came to be called the **National Grange.** The Grange offered farmers education, fellowship, and support.

Above all, the Grange tried to encourage economic self-sufficiency. It set up "cash-only" **cooperatives** (koh • AH • puh • ruh • tivz), stores where farmers bought products from each other. The cooperatives charged lower prices than regular stores and provided an outlet for farmers' crops. The purpose of the "cash-only" policy was to remove the burden of credit buying that threatened farmers.

Winter in Dakota Territory

Settlers endured challenging living conditions. Laura Ingalls Wilder wrote of her family's experiences during the bitter winter of 1880–81.

Ma said " . . . We must get out the washing while the weather's clear so we can."

All that day Laura and Carrie and Mary looked forward to the [magazine] *Youth's Companions* and often they spoke of them. But the bright day was short. They stirred and punched the clothes boiling on the stove; they lifted them on the broom handle into the tub where Ma soaped them and rubbed them. Laura rinsed them, Carrie stirred the **blueing** bag in the second rinse-water until it was blue enough. Laura made the boiled starch. And when for the last time Ma went out into the cold to hang the freezing wash on the line, Pa had come for dinner.

Then they washed the dishes, they scrubbed the floor and blacked the stove, and washed the inside of the windowpanes. Ma brought in the frozen-dry clothes and they sorted them and sprinkled them and rolled them tightly, ready for ironing. Twilight had come. It was too late to read that day and after supper there was no lamplight because they must save the last of the kerosene.

—from *The Long Winter*

◀ This shirt was part of the Ghost Dance in which the Sioux tried to preserve their way of life.

Indian School

In attempts to "civilize" Native American children, Indian schools were created in several parts of the country. In this passage, Ah-nen-la-de-ni of the Mohawk people describes his first experience in such a school.

After the almost complete freedom of reservation life the cramped quarters and the dull routine of the school were maddening to all us strangers. There were endless rules for us to study and **abide** by, and hardest of all was the rule against speaking to each other in our own language. We must speak English or remain silent, and those who knew no English were forced to be **dumb** or else break the rules in secret. This last we did quite frequently, and were punished, when **detected,** by being made to stand in the "public hall" for a long time or to march about the yard while the other boys were at play.

—from *Witnessing America*

DBQ Document-Based Questions

On the Cattle Trail

1. What seems to be the cowhand's biggest secret?
2. According to the foreman, what is worth the sacrifice of the cowboys' comfort?

Winter in Dakota Territory

3. How many steps were involved in washing the clothes for Laura's family?
4. What activity did Laura and her sisters look forward to doing once their chores were done?

Indian School

5. How does Ah-nen-la-de-ni describe school?
6. What is the hardest rule for the children to follow?

Read to Write

7. Reread the documents to find evidence that shows how each author needed to adapt to a new environment or circumstance. What adjustments did they make? Do they explain why? Write an essay explaining your conclusions. CA 8WA1.1

Assessment

Standard US8.12

Review Content Vocabulary

On a sheet of paper, create a crossword puzzle using the following terms. Use the terms' definitions as your crossword clues.

1. reservations
2. cooperatives
3. vigilantes
4. vaqueros
5. lodes
6. stampedes

Review the Main Ideas

Section 1 • The Mining Booms

7. What was the Comstock Lode?
8. In what ways did the railroads boost the American economy?

Section 2 • Ranchers and Farmers

9. What is a vaquero?
10. What attracted farmers to the Great Plains?

Section 3 • Native American Struggles

11. What actions by whites destroyed the buffalo population?
12. In what present-day state was the Indian Territory located?

Section 4 • Farmers in Protest

13. How did the Grange help farmers?
14. What political reforms did the Populists support?

Critical Thinking

15. **Analyze** How did the rush to find gold and silver spark the creation of new communities in the West? CA CS1.
16. **Economics Link** Why was the Cattle Kingdom dependent on the railroads? CA HI6.
17. **Cause and Effect** Describe the problems that led farmers to organize granges and alliances. CA HI2.

Geography Skills

Study the map below and answer the following questions. CA CS3.

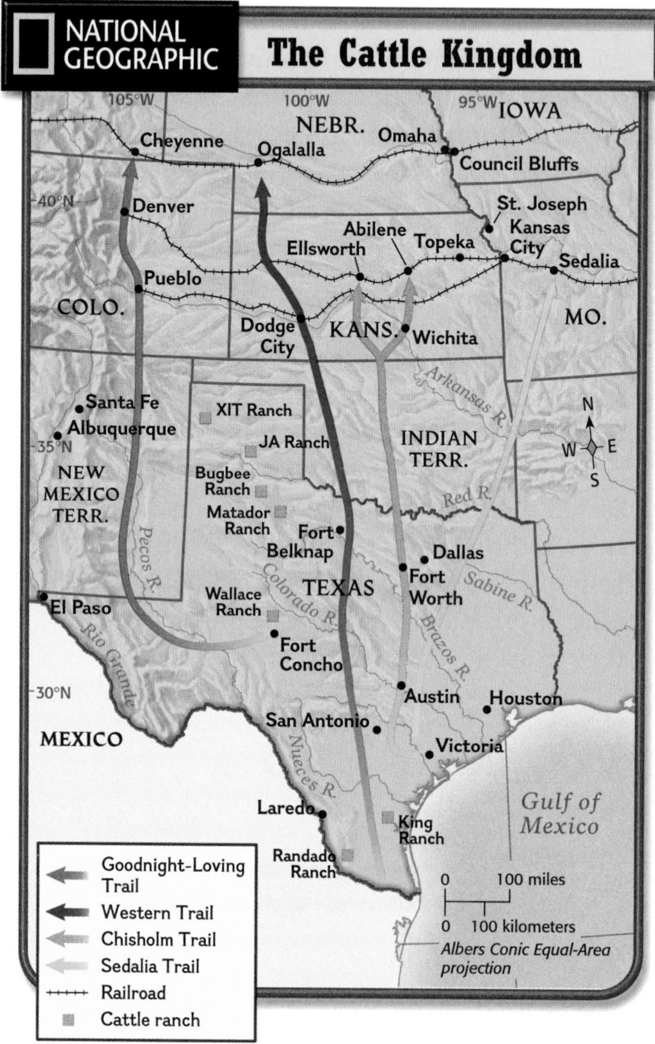

18. **Location** In what part of Texas were most of the large cattle ranches located?
19. **Movement** To which railroad towns did the Goodnight-Loving Trail run?
20. **Movement** Which cattle trails ran though Indian Territory?

Read to Write

21. **The Big Ideas** **Analyze** Briefly discuss the geographic challenges faced by settlers and Native Americans in the American West and Great Plains. How did they overcome the challenges? CA 8WA2.4

22. **Expository Writing** Reread and take notes on the section of the chapter that discusses the chores of a farm woman. Use your notes to create an hour-by-hour schedule to show one day's typical activities for a farm wife living on the Great Plains. CA 8RC2.0

23. **Using Your FOLDABLES** Choose one of the four groups of people you learned about in this chapter. Describe that groups' triumphs and tragedies in a newspaper article you could have written in the late 1800s. CA WS1.1

Using Academic Vocabulary

24. Read the following sentences and write the meaning of the underlined academic vocabulary word.

    Power in a republic is <u>derived</u> from the people.

    New machinery was developed to <u>extract</u> ore from the earth's crust.

Economics Connection

25. **Researching** Research to find information about a Native American reservation in the United States today. Write a report describing one of the major businesses on that reservation. CA HI6. CA 8WA2.3

Reviewing Skills

26. Review READING SKILL **Visualizing** If you lived on the frontier in the late 1800s, would you have been a miner, a rancher, a Native American, or a farmer? Select one and write an essay describing a day in your life. Use clear descriptive language so that your readers have a good visual sense of what your life was like. CA 8WA2.1

27.  ANALYSIS SKILL **Composing** Reread the quote from the farmer's song on page 694. Write a song or poem that a banker or merchant might write. CA HR5.

Standards Practice

Read the passage below and answer the following question.

> Having behind us the producing masses of this nation and the world, supported by the commercial interests, the laboring interests and the toilers everywhere, we will answer their demand for a gold standard by saying to them: You shall not press down upon the brow of labor this crown of thorns, you shall not crucify mankind upon a cross of gold.
>
> —William Jennings Bryan, "Cross of Gold" Speech, 1896

28 By speaking against the gold standard, Bryan was showing his support for the Populist goal of

- A an eight-hour workday.
- B a currency system based on free silver.
- C farmers' cooperatives.
- D an income tax.

29 When Bryan refers to "the producing masses of this nation," he most likely is including

- A farmers.
- B political leaders.
- C manufacturers.
- D Republicans.

Chapter 16: The Growth of Industry

▲ Railroads sped industrialization in the late 1800s.

NATIONAL GEOGRAPHIC **Who & When?**

1870	1890	1910

1870 Rockefeller organizes Standard Oil Company

1876 Bell patents the telephone

1886 Trade unions form AFL

1903 Wright brothers fly first motorized airplane

▲ *Union strikes, such as the Pullman strike of 1894, sometimes turned violent.*

The courts, however, supported employers who challenged state laws that tried to regulate wages and working conditions. In 1905, for example, the Supreme Court ruled in the case *Lochner* v. *New York* that states could not set limits on the working hours of bakery workers. The Court reasoned that the New York law was unconstitutional because it interfered with the right of employers and employees to make contracts, or agreements, about working hours. The Court's reasoning was based on the principle that individuals have "liberty of contract" based on the Fourteenth Amendment.

Protecting Unions and Workers The Great Depression of the 1930s left many American workers without jobs. President Franklin D. Roosevelt's effort to end the Depression included helping labor. One of the most important laws passed by Congress during Roosevelt's administration was the Wagner Act in 1935. This law sought to protect the right of workers to organize and to bargain collectively, or hold contract talks with employers. Under the Wagner Act, companies could not punish a worker because of union activities. Another measure was the Fair Labor Standards Act of 1938. It set the first minimum wage for workers and banned child labor.

Many employers believed that the Wagner Act was unconstitutional, but the Supreme Court upheld the act. In the case *National Labor Relations Board* v. *Jones & Laughlin Steel Corporation* (1937), the Court ruled that local activities of trade unions may affect commerce. Because Congress had the constitutional power to regulate commerce, it could also regulate relations between business and labor. This meant that the National Labor Relations Board created by Congress had the authority to punish businesses involved in interstate commerce that discriminated against union members.

Unions Today During the 1960s and 1970s, several groups, such as government workers and farmworkers, formed new unions. For example, César E. Chávez, a Mexican American labor leader, began to organize farmworkers in California. Chávez founded what is now the United Farm Workers of America (UFW), a union of migrant workers and other farm laborers. Union membership among other Hispanic Americans, African Americans, and women also increased during this period.

Over the years, labor unions—as well as economic prosperity—have raised workers' standards of living. However, as a result of political and economic changes, the number of workers belonging to unions has declined sharply in recent years. Unions face other challenges too. One is defending workers' interests in declining industries that have fewer jobs. Another is protecting the jobs and wages of workers affected by **automation,** or the use of machines to do tasks once performed by people. Despite these difficulties, labor unions remain a powerful force in American life.

Checking for Understanding

1. What reason did the courts of the late 1800s give for finding union leaders guilty of breaking the law?
2. How did the federal government help labor during the Great Depression?

Critical Thinking

3. **Evaluate** Why did the Supreme Court adjust its view on labor in *NLRB* v. *Jones & Laughlin Steel Company*? CA HI2.
4. **Analyze** Restate the Court's reasoning in *Lochner* v. *New York* and predict the ruling's impact on other industries. CA HI6.

Analyzing Primary Sources

US8.12 Students analyze the transformation of the American economy and the changing social and political conditions in the United States in response to the Industrial Revolution.

The Growth of Industry in America

Following the Civil War, the railroads expanded throughout the country. The railroads and inventions created the chance for other industries to grow. Many companies in these industries had long working hours, paid minimal salaries, and provided unsafe working conditions.

Read the passages on pages 732 and 733 and answer the questions that follow.

These women are working on the cloth after it has been woven.

Reader's Dictionary

shaker: person who shook and turned the drill after each blow to keep the drill from getting caught in the rock or the rock dust

haste (HAYST): hurrying too fast

garments (GAHR • muhnts): pieces of clothing

inclined plane: slanted surface

slate: type of rock that is used for chalkboards and roof tiles

John Henry

"John Henry" is a song that railroad men sang as they worked. John Henry hand drilled holes into stone to place dynamite.

When John Henry was a little baby,
Sitting on his pappy's knee,
He grabbed a hammer and a little piece of steel,
Said, "This hammer'll be the death of me,
Lord, Lord,
This hammer'll be the death of me. . . ."

John Henry told his captain,
"A man ain't nothing but a man,
But before I'll let that steam drill beat me down
I'll die with my hammer in my hand,
Lord, Lord,
I'll die with my hammer in my hand."

John Henry said to his **shaker,**
"Now shaker, why don't you sing?
'Cause I'm throwing twelve pounds from my hips on down,
Just listen to that cold steel ring,
Lord, Lord,
Just listen to that cold steel ring."

The man that invented the steam drill,
He thought he was mighty fine,
But John Henry he made fourteen feet
While the steam drill only made nine,
Lord, Lord,
The steam drill only made nine.

John Henry hammered on the mountain
Till his hammer was striking fire,
He drove so hard he broke his poor heart,
Then he laid down his hammer and he died, Lord, Lord,
He laid down his hammer and he died.

They took John Henry to the graveyard,
And they buried him in the sand,
And every locomotive comes rolling by
Says, "There lies a steel-driving man,
Lord, Lord,
There lays a steel-driving man."

—Anonymous in *Annals of America*

The Sweatshop

In factories, people had to work very quickly. In this passage, a young woman described her day in a factory where clothing was made.

At seven o'clock we all sit down to our machines and the boss brings to each one the pile of work that he or she is to finish during the day. . . . This pile is put down beside the machine and as soon as a skirt is done it is laid on the other side of the machine. . . .

The machines go like mad all day, because the faster you work, the more money you get. Sometimes in my **haste** I get my finger caught and the needle goes right through it. . . . We all have accidents like that. . . . Sometimes a finger has to come off. . . .

All the time we are working the boss walks about examining the finished **garments** and making us do them over again if they are not just right. So we have to be careful as well as swift.

—Sadie Frowne, "The Story of a Sweatshop Girl"

Child Labor

Laws forbidding children to work did not exist or were not enforced at this time.

In a little room in this big, black shed—a room not twenty feet square—forty boys are picking their lives away. The floor of this room is an **inclined plane**, and a stream of coal pours constantly in. They work here, in this little black hole, all day and every day, . . . picking their way among the black coals, bending over till their little spines are curved. . . .

Not three boys in this roomful could read or write. Shut out from everything that is pleasant, with no chance to learn, with no knowledge of what is going on about them. . . .

They know nothing but the difference between **slate** and coal.

—from a local Labor Standard Newspaper, St. Clair, Pennsylvania

▲ Young coal miners

DBQ Document-Based Questions

John Henry

1. What does John Henry predict in the first stanza?
2. Who won the contest? How do you know?

The Sweatshop

3. Why do people work quickly at the factory?
4. Why do people have to work carefully?

Child Labor

5. Where do the boys work?
6. What is their job?

Read to Write

7. Make two lists—one labeled Working Conditions and the other Effects of Working Conditions. Use the information in "The Sweatshop," "Child Labor," and what you already know about working conditions at this time to complete the lists. Write a paragraph explaining how you feel about these conditions. Include ideas for how they could be improved. CA 8RC2.3

Assessment

Standard US8.12

Review Content Vocabulary

Write the key term that completes each sentence.

a. standard gauge
b. assembly line
c. horizontal integration
d. trade union
e. rebates

1. Railroads offered ___, or discounts, to their largest customers.
2. Railroad companies adopted 4 feet, 8.5 inches as the width of the railroad track, also known as the ___.
3. The Knights of Labor was a ___ of garment workers.

Review the Main Ideas

Section 1 • Railroads Lead the Way

4. What improvements in railway transportation were brought about by new technology?
5. Why did the American Railway Association divide the country into four time zones?

Section 2 • Inventions

6. What inventions improved communications in the late 1800s?
7. What manufacturing methods did Henry Ford use to make his new automobile affordable?

Section 3 • The Age of Big Business

8. What is vertical integration?
9. What action did Congress take to control trusts and monopolies in response to pressure from the American people?

Section 4 • Industrial Workers

10. What is collective bargaining?
11. How did the Haymarket Riot of 1886 affect public opinion about the labor movement?

Critical Thinking

12. **Conclude** Why did workers think that forming organized labor unions would help them get what they wanted from employers? CA CS1.
13. **Analyze** How did American industry benefit from the growing railroad network in the late 1800s? CA HI2.

Geography Skills

A cartogram is a kind of map used to present statistical information. On a population cartogram the sizes of the states appear in proportion to their populations. Study the population cartogram below and answer the following questions. CA CS3.

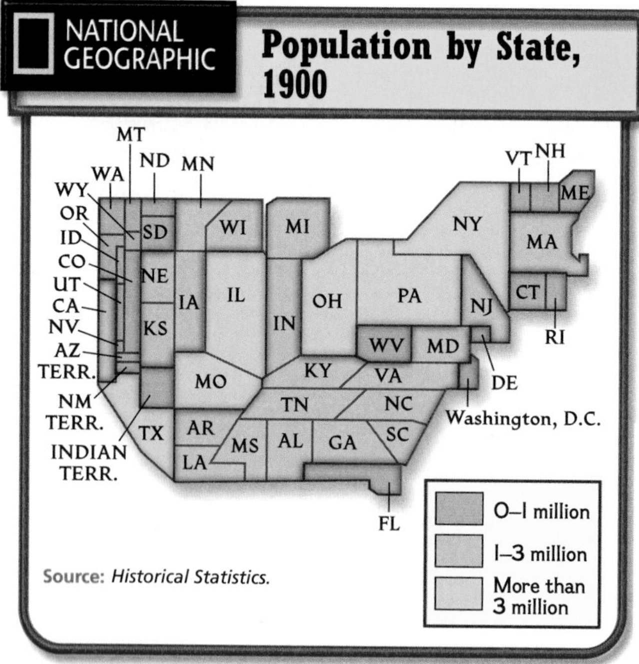

Source: *Historical Statistics.*

14. **Location** Did Florida or Illinois have a larger population 1900?
15. **Location** Did North Dakota have more or fewer people than South Dakota?

History Online
Self-Check Quiz Visit ca.hss.glencoe.com to prepare for the Chapter 16 test.

Read to Write

16. **The Big Ideas Evaluate** In a short essay, describe how the increasing size of corporations was both beneficial and harmful to American business. CA 8WA2.3

17. **Summarize** Review the chapter for information about the four major union strikes between 1877 and 1894. Write a headline for each that might have appeared in newspapers following the strike. CA 8WA2.2

18. **Using Your FOLDABLES** Write a poem, series of journal entries, or short story using the main ideas and supporting details from your completed foldable. CA 8WA2.1

Using Academic Vocabulary

Identify the correct form of the academic vocabulary word to complete each sentence.

technology technological technologically

19. The computer is an example of a ___ advance.

transmit transmits transmitted

20. The reporter used the telegraph to ___ the story to the newspaper.

Building Citizenship

21. **Evaluate** With another student, write a short essay in which you support or criticize labor unions from the point of view of a young person who has just entered the workforce. Note how you think a union could or could not improve your life. Share your essay with the class. CA 8WS1.1

Reviewing Skills

22. **Review Reading Skill Predicting Consequences** How would the growth of industry and new innovations in technology impact preparations for a war? Write a short essay predicting the potential effect. CA 8WA2.3

23. **Review Analysis Skill Organizing Information** Do research to find the dates when the inventions described in this chapter were first created. Also find other inventions created by the inventors mentioned in the chapter, along with their dates of creation. Draw an annotated time line with the information you have found. Be sure to include the importance of each invention. CA CS2.

Standards Practice

Select the best answer for each of the following questions.

24 The development of the transformers that Westinghouse built led to an increase in

A the price of electricity.
B the use of gas to heat homes.
C the use of electricity to power factories.
D imported goods.

25 John D. Rockefeller was the founder of the

A Pennsylvania Railroad.
B United States Steel Corporation.
C Titusville oil well.
D Standard Oil Company of Ohio.

26 The process in which a union represents its workers when negotiating with management is known as

A collective bargaining.
B strikebreaking.
C vertical integration.
D philanthropy.

America Enters a New Century

▼ The growth of American cities continued throughout the twentieth century.

NATIONAL GEOGRAPHIC **Who & When?**

1880 | 1895 | 1910

1882 Chinese Exclusion Act passed

1884 First skyscraper constructed in Chicago

1892 Ellis Island admits immigrants

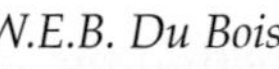

1909 The NAACP is formed

W.E.B. Du Bois

A favorite leisure-time activity for many people was watching and following sports. Baseball became the most popular spectator sport in America. By the turn of the century, both the National and American Leagues had been founded—each made up of teams from major cities. Another popular spectator sport was football, which developed from the English game of rugby. By the 1890s, college games were drawing huge crowds.

Basketball, invented by Dr. James Naismith of Springfield, Massachusetts, also became popular. Naismith developed the game in the 1890s as an indoor winter sport for his YMCA physical education classes. Considered the only major sport that is completely American in origin, basketball soon spread to other countries.

Americans not only watched but also participated in sports. Tennis and golf were enjoyed by the wealthy, usually in exclusive private clubs. Bicycling grew in popularity after the "safety" bicycle was developed. These new bicycles used air-filled rubber tires instead of metal-rimmed wheels.

Large cities had many theaters. Plays performed ranged from serious dramas by Shakespeare to **vaudeville** (VAHD•vihl) shows, which were variety shows with dancing, singing, comedy, and magic acts. Tickets to vaudeville shows were inexpensive, making them very popular. The circus also attracted large crowds. In 1910 the United States had about 80 traveling circuses.

Thomas Edison invented "moving pictures" in the 1880s. The "movies" soon became enormously popular. Some theaters, called nickelodeons, charged five cents to see short films. The nickelodeons were the beginning of today's film industry.

✓ Reading Check **Describe** What elements made up jazz music?

History Online

Study Central Need help understanding changes in American culture? Visit ca.hss.glencoe.com and click on Study Central.

Section 3 Review

Reading Summary

Review the Main Ideas

- In the late 1800s and early 1900s, the number of public schools in the United States increased greatly, and the number of colleges for women and African Americans also grew.
- Newspaper and magazine readership increased greatly, and a number of American writers explored new themes.
- Distinctive styles of American art and music developed, and watching professional sports became a favorite leisure time activity.

What Did You Learn?

1. Describe the new philosophy of education that emerged around 1900.
2. What was yellow journalism?

Critical Thinking

3. **Summarizing Information** Re-create the diagram below and describe the work of each of these writers. CA HR3

Writer	Description of work
Horatio Alger	
Stephen Crane	
Edith Wharton	

4. **The Big Ideas** Explain the correlation between leisure time and the development of the arts. CA HI2.
5. **Analyze** What did supporters of progressive education emphasize? What did they criticize in existing models of education? CA HI1.
6. **Creative Writing** Write a letter to Andrew Carnegie persuading him to establish a public library in your community. Describe the advantages of locating the library in your area and the benefits citizens would receive from his grant. CA 8WA2.1

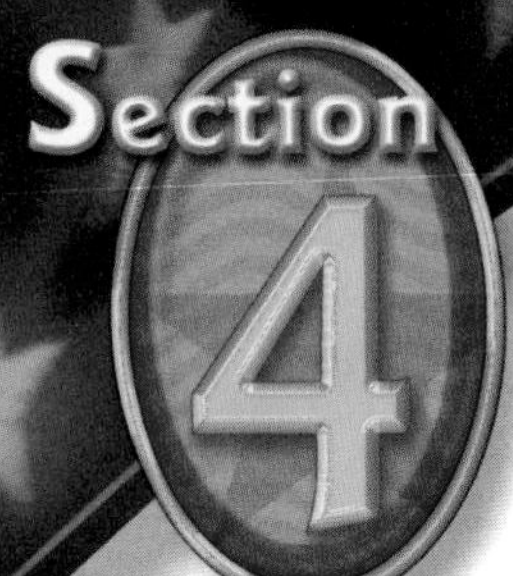

The Progressive Movement

Guide to Reading

Looking Back, Looking Ahead
You learned that America's businesses and cities grew rapidly in the late 1800s. Such rapid growth allowed corruption in business and government to spread.

Focusing on the Main Ideas
- Americans took action against corruption in business and government. *(page 765)*
- New calls for reform were aided by writers who exposed government and business corruption. *(page 767)*
- In the early 1900s, more people received the right to vote, and the government began to regulate industry. *(page 769)*

Meeting People
William M. Tweed
Jacob Riis (REES)
Eugene V. Debs
Lincoln Steffens
Ida Tarbell
Upton Sinclair (sihn • KLEHR)
Robert La Follette (luh FAH • luht)
Theodore Roosevelt

Content Vocabulary
political machine
trust
oligopoly (AH • lih • GAH • puh • lee)
muckraker (MUHK • RAYK • uhr)
primary
initiative (ih • NIH • shuh • tiv)
referendum (REH • fuh • REHN • duhm)
recall
laissez-faire (LEH • ZAY • FEHR)
conservation

Academic Vocabulary
underlie
inspect

Reading Strategy
Organizing Information As you read Section 4, re-create the diagram below and list reforms for each category.

Reforms		
Government	Business	Voting

History Social Science Standards

US8.12 Students analyze the transformation of the American economy and the changing social and political conditions in the United States in response to the Industrial Revolution.

NATIONAL GEOGRAPHIC
Who & When?
1900
1910
1920
1901 Roosevelt becomes president
1904 Ida Tarbell publishes history of Standard Oil
1912 Congress passes the Seventeenth Amendment
1920 Women vote in presidential election for first time

Theodore Roosevelt

Ida Tarbell

US8.12.6 Discuss child labor, working conditions, and laissez-faire policies toward big business and examine the labor movement, including its leaders (e.g., Samuel Gompers), its demand for collective bargaining, and its strikes and protests over labor conditions.

Call for Reform

Main Idea **Americans took action against corruption in business and government.**

Reading Connection What would you think if the members of a school sports team who paid the coach the most money got to be the starting players? Read to find out how reformers worked to prevent unqualified and dishonest people from receiving important government jobs.

Many Americans called for reform in the late 1800s. The reformers, called progressives, had many different goals. These progressive reformers focused on urban problems, government, and business. They claimed that government and big business were taking advantage of the American people rather than serving them.

Fighting Corruption **Political machines**—powerful organizations linked to political parties—controlled local government in many cities. In each ward, or political district within a city, a machine representative controlled jobs and services. This representative was the political boss. A political boss was often a citizen's closest link to local government. Although they did help people, many bosses were dishonest.

Corrupt politicians found numerous ways to make money. They accepted bribes from tenement landlords in return for overlooking violations of city housing codes. They received campaign contributions from contractors hoping to do business with the city. They also accepted kickbacks. A kickback is an arrangement in which contractors padded the amount of their bill for city work and paid, or "kicked back," a percentage of that amount to the bosses.

Some politicians used their knowledge of city business for personal profit. One of the most corrupt city bosses, **William M. Tweed,** known as Boss Tweed, headed New York City's Democratic political machine in the 1860s and 1870s. Boss Tweed led a network of city officials called the Tweed ring.

Analyzing *Political Cartoons*

The Tweed Ring Boss Tweed and New York City officials are shown pointing to one another in response to the question "Who stole the people's money?" On Tweed's right, a man holds a hat labeled "Chairs," a reference to the $179,000 New York City paid for 40 chairs and 3 tables. Other contractors and cheats—their names on their coats—complete the "ring." ***How did political bosses gain votes for their parties?***

TAMMANY RING
"WHO STOLE THE PEOPLE'S MONEY ?" — DO TELL . N.Y.TIMES.
'TWAS HIM.

A Boss Tweed B Peter Sweeny C Richard Connelly D Mayor A. Oakley Hall

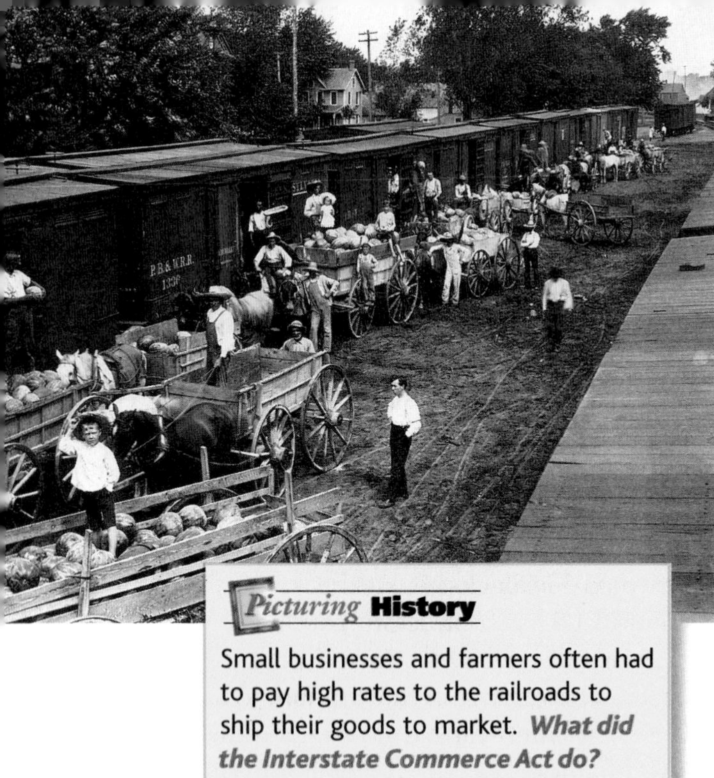

Picturing History

Small businesses and farmers often had to pay high rates to the railroads to ship their goods to market. ***What did the Interstate Commerce Act do?***

The Tweed Ring controlled the police, courts, and some newspapers. Political cartoonist Thomas Nast exposed the Tweed ring's operations in his cartoons for *Harper's Weekly*. Tweed was convicted and sentenced to prison.

To break the power of political bosses, reformers founded organizations such as the National Municipal League in Philadelphia. These groups worked to make city governments more honest and efficient.

What Was the Spoils System? The spoils system—rewarding political supporters with jobs and favors—had been common practice since the time of Andrew Jackson. Also called patronage, the system existed at all levels of government and led to numerous abuses. Many who received government jobs were not qualified. Some were dishonest.

A number of presidents, including Rutherford B. Hayes (1877–1881) and James Garfield (1881), wanted to change the spoils system. Hayes's efforts received little support, and Garfield was assassinated by an unsuccessful office seeker before he could launch his reforms.

When Vice President Chester A. Arthur succeeded Garfield, he tried to end the spoils system. In 1883 Congress passed the Pendleton Act, which established the Civil Service Commission to set up competitive examinations for federal jobs.

Controlling Business During the late 1800s, many Americans came to believe that **trusts,** or combinations of companies, were becoming too large. They believed these trusts had too much control over the economy and the government. This public concern led to new laws.

In 1890 Congress passed the Sherman Antitrust Act, the first federal law to control trusts and monopolies. Supporters of the law hoped it would keep trusts from limiting competition. During the 1890s, however, the government rarely used the Sherman Act to curb business. Instead, it applied the act against labor unions, claiming that union strikes interfered with trade. Not until the early 1900s did the government win cases against trusts by using the Sherman Act.

Reining in the Railroads The railroads functioned as an **oligopoly** (AH•lih•GAH•puh•lee)—a market structure in which a few large companies control the prices of the industry. In 1887 Congress passed the Interstate Commerce Act, which required railroads to charge "reasonable and just" rates and to publish those rates. The act also created the Interstate Commerce Commission (ICC) to supervise the railroad industry.

Lowering Tariffs Reformers also wanted to lower tariffs. Many people believed that high tariffs led to higher prices for goods. In 1890 the Republicans raised tariffs sharply to protect American businesses from international competition. Voters showed their opposition to high tariffs by sending many Democrats to Congress. Grover Cleveland, who became president in 1893, also supported lower tariffs.

Reading Check **Explain** Why did many people want lower tariffs?

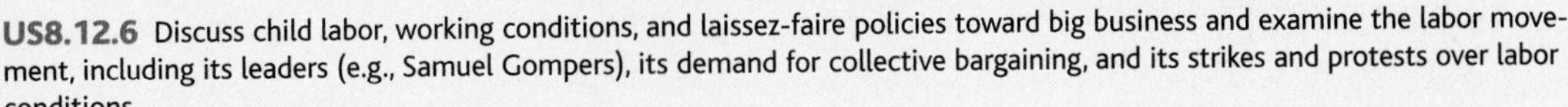

The New Reformers

Main Idea **New calls for reform were aided by writers who exposed government and business corruption.**

Reading Connection Have you ever watched the investigative reporters on your local television news shows? What sorts of problems do they report on? Read to find out about the investigative reporters who wrote about problems in government and business in the early 1900s.

An American Story

Newspaper reporter **Jacob Riis** (REES) shocked Americans with exposés of living conditions in large cities. With words and powerful photographs, Riis vividly portrayed immigrant life in New York City's crowded tenements.

> **"We used to go in the small hours of the morning into the worst tenements to count noses and see if the law against overcrowding was violated, and the sights I saw there gripped my heart until I felt that I must tell of them, or burst."**
>
> —Jacob Riis,
> *The Making of an American*

Socialists and Progressives In the early 1900s, new ideas for correcting injustice and solving social problems emerged among American reformers. Socialism and progressivism were two such ideas.

Socialists believed a nation's resources and major industries should be owned and operated by the government on behalf of all the people—not by individuals and private companies for their own profit. **Eugene V. Debs** helped found the American Socialist Party in 1898. Under Debs's leadership, the party won some support in the early 1900s. Debs ran for president five times but never received more than 6 percent of the popular vote.

During the same period, progressives brought new energy to the reform movement. Like the socialists, many progressives were alarmed by the concentration of wealth and power in the hands of a few. Progressives rejected the socialist idea of government ownership of industries. Instead, they supported government efforts to regulate industry.

They also sought to reform government, to make it more efficient and better able to resist the influence of powerful business interests. Progressives also believed that society had an obligation to protect and help all its members. Many progressive reforms were meant to help those who lacked wealth and influence.

Who Were the Muckrakers? Journalists aided the reformers by exposing injustices and corruption. Investigative reporters wrote stories that brought problems to the attention of the public—and gained readers. These journalists were called **muckrakers** (MUHK•RAYK•uhrz) because they "raked" (exposed) the "muck" (dirt and corruption) **underlying** society.

One of the most effective muckrakers, **Lincoln Steffens,** reported for *McClure's Magazine.* Steffens's articles exposed corrupt machine politics in New York, Chicago, and other cities. **Ida Tarbell,** also writing for *McClure's,* described the unfair practices of the oil trust. Her articles led to public pressure for more government control over big business. In her 1904 book *The History of the Standard Oil Company,* she warned of the giant corporation's power.

In his novel *The Jungle,* published in 1906, **Upton Sinclair** (sihn•KLEHR) described the horrors of the meatpacking industry in Chicago. His vivid descriptions shocked Americans and helped persuade Congress to pass the Meat Inspection Act in 1906. That same year, Congress also passed the Pure Food and Drug Act, requiring accurate labeling of food and medicine and banning the sale of harmful food.

Reading Check **Identify** Who wrote about unfair practices in the oil industry?

Biography

US8.12 Students analyze the transformation of the American economy and the changing social and political conditions in the United States in response to the Industrial Revolution.

Jacob Riis

1849–1914

Jacob Riis came to the United States from Denmark when he was 21. Riis lived in poverty for many years and often made police lodging houses his temporary home. In 1873 Riis began to work as a reporter and photographer for New York City newspapers. In addition to his own experience with poverty, Riis's job allowed him to further witness the poverty in which many lived in New York City.

Riis strongly believed that the poor were not to blame for their situation and felt that something should be done to help them. He realized he could use his newspaper stories to focus attention on the needs of the poor. Riis published many articles about the living conditions in the poorer sections of the city. These articles were accompanied by his photographs or illustrations, which brought to life the circumstances in which the city's inhabitants lived and worked. In 1890 Riis wrote *How the Other Half Lives.* By taking pictures of the tenements, Riis was able to bring the terrible conditions of the slums to the attention of readers. His book helped establish housing codes to prevent the worst abuses.

"The poor we shall always have with us, but the slum we need not have."

—Jacob Riis, *Battle with the Slum*

When Theodore Roosevelt became the city's police commissioner, he asked Riis to present a reform program. Through Riis's efforts, many playgrounds and parks were established in the city. Riis helped make others aware of the problems many urban Americans faced in their daily lives. He was later known as one of the first muckraking journalists, a group of people whose articles and photographs exposed corruption and social problems in American life. Riis served as an example of what individuals could do to lessen these problems.

Then and Now

Are photographs still a powerful means of exposing corruption and injustice? Explain.

US8.12.5 Examine the location and effects of urbanization, renewed immigration, and industrialization (e.g., the effects on social fabrics of cities, wealth and economic opportunity, the conservation movement).

Expanding Democracy

Main Idea **In the early 1900s, more people received the right to vote, and the government began to regulate industry.**

Reading Connection Do you consider protecting public parks and the environment to be an important issue? Read to find out about one of the first American presidents to be concerned with the environment.

In the early 1900s, progressives backed a number of reforms designed to increase the people's direct control of the government. **Robert La Follette** (luh FAH•luht), known as "Fighting Bob," led Wisconsin's reform-minded Republicans. La Follette's greatest achievement was reforming the state electoral system. Candidates for general elections in Wisconsin had been chosen at state conventions run by party bosses. La Follette introduced a direct **primary** election, allowing the state's voters to choose their party's candidates. Reformers in other states copied this "Wisconsin idea."

What Was the Oregon System? The state of Oregon also made important changes in the political process to give voters more power. The reforms in Oregon included a direct primary election and the initiative, the referendum, and the recall.

The **initiative** (ih•NIH•shuh•tiv) allowed citizens to place a measure or issue on the ballot in a state election. The **referendum** (REH•fuh•REHN•duhm) gave voters the opportunity to accept or reject measures that the state legislature enacted. The **recall** enabled voters to remove unsatisfactory elected officials from their jobs. These reforms were called the Oregon System. Other western states soon adopted the reforms.

Picturing **History**

Before the passage of the Nineteenth Amendment, many women campaigned for the right to vote. ***Which was the first state to allow women to vote?***

Theodore Roosevelt board game

McKinley/Roosevelt glass canteen, 1900

The Seventeenth Amendment Progressives also changed the way U.S. senators are elected. The Constitution had given state legislatures the responsibility for choosing senators, but party bosses and business interests often controlled the selection process. Progressives wanted to give the people an opportunity to vote for their senators directly. Support for this idea grew. In 1912 Congress passed the Seventeenth Amendment to the Constitution to provide for the direct election of senators. Ratified in 1913, the amendment gave the people a voice in selecting their representatives. *(See page 264 for the text of the Seventeenth Amendment.)*

The Fight for Suffrage At the Seneca Falls Convention in 1848, women had called for the right to vote. After the Civil War, Congress passed the Fifteenth Amendment, giving voting rights to freed men—but not to women. Some leading abolitionists became suffragists, men and women who fought for woman suffrage, or women's right to vote. The suffragists won their early victories in the West. First as a territory in 1869 and then as a state in 1890, Wyoming led the nation in giving women the vote. Between 1910 and 1913, six other states adopted woman suffrage. By 1919 women could vote in at least some elections in most of the 48 states.

In 1919 Congress voted in favor of the Nineteenth Amendment, which allowed woman suffrage. The amendment was ratified in 1920, in time for women to vote in that year's presidential election. For the first time, American women were able to participate in the election of their national leaders.

"Trustbuster" in the White House

President William McKinley, elected in 1900, was assassinated less than a year later. Suddenly, 42-year-old **Theodore Roosevelt,** the Republican vice president, took over the top office and became the youngest president in the nation's history. When Roosevelt moved into the White House in 1901, he brought progressivism with him.

President McKinley had favored big business, but President Roosevelt was known to support business regulation and other progressive reforms. In 1902 Roosevelt ordered the Justice Department to take legal action against certain trusts that had violated the Sherman Antitrust Act. His first target was the Northern Securities Company, a railroad monopoly formed by financiers J.P. Morgan and James J. Hill to control transportation in the Northwest. The Supreme Court finally decided that Northern Securities had illegally limited trade and ordered the trust to be taken apart.

During the rest of Roosevelt's term as president, he obtained a total of 25 indictments (legal charges) against trusts in the beef, oil, and tobacco industries. Although hailed as a trustbuster, Roosevelt did not want to break up all trusts. As he saw it, trusts should be regulated, not destroyed.

Roosevelt ran for the presidency in 1904, promising the people a Square Deal—fair and equal treatment for all. He was elected with more than 57 percent of the popular vote.

Roosevelt's Policies Roosevelt's "Square Deal" called for a considerable amount of government regulation of business. This contrasted with an attitude toward business that dated back to the presidency of Thomas Jefferson, which was summed up in the phrase **laissez-faire** (LEH • ZAY FEHR). This French term generally means "let people do as they choose."

Roosevelt introduced a new era of government regulation. He supported the Meat Inspection and Pure Food and Drug Acts; these acts gave the Department of Agriculture and the Food and Drug Administration the power to visit businesses and **inspect** their products.

Why Was Conservation Important? Roosevelt held a lifelong enthusiasm for the great outdoors and the wilderness. He believed in the need for **conservation,** the protection and preservation of natural resources. As president, Roosevelt took steps to conserve the country's forests, mineral deposits, and water resources. In 1905 he proposed the creation of the U.S. Forest Service. He pressured Congress to set aside millions of acres of national forests and created the nation's first wildlife sanctuaries. Roosevelt also formed the National Conservation Commission, which produced the first survey of the country's natural resources.

Roosevelt has been called America's first environmental president. While he made conservation an important public issue, Roosevelt also recognized the need for economic growth and development. He tried to strike a balance between business interests and protection of the environment and conservation.

Reading Check **Identify** What reform allowed voters to place a measure on the ballot?

History Online
Study Central Need help understanding the Progressive Movement? Visit ca.hss.glencoe.com and click on Study Central.

Section 4 Review

Reading Summary

Review the Main Ideas

- Americans became angered by corrupt politicians who made money illegally and by large trusts, which began to control the economy and the government.
- Socialists and progressives wanted the government to more tightly control business practices, and reforming journalists exposed injustices and corruption in business.
- Changes led to more political control for common citizens, and the government began to regulate industry and conserve the environment.

What Did You Learn?

1. Explain how the Civil Service Commission helped eliminate the spoils system.
2. What industry did Upton Sinclair describe in his book *The Jungle*?

Critical Thinking

3. **Organizing Information** Re-create the diagram below and show how the Seventeenth Amendment reformed the political process. CA HI3.

Seventeenth Amendment	
Policy before	Policy after

4. **Compare and Contrast** Write a paragraph comparing socialist and progressive views on industry.
5. **Analyze** Examine the political cartoon on page 765. Why are the individuals pointing to someone else? What statement is cartoonist Thomas Nast making about the extent of political corruption in New York City? CA HR4.
6. **The Big Ideas** Write an essay summarizing the role of muckrakers in the reform movement. How would the reform movement have been different if the press were controlled by the government instead of being free? CA 8WA2.3

GEOGRAPHY & HISTORY

WILD WONDERS

GRIZZLY BEARS, WOLVES, MOOSE, CARIBOU, DALL'S SHEEP and many other animals roam Alaska's Denali National Park and Preserve. Larger than Massachusetts, the six-million-acre park includes the highest mountain in North America.

The Alaskan wilderness area set aside as Mount McKinley National Park in 1917 was renamed Denali in 1980 when Congress tripled the size of the park. Denali was the peak's Native American name, meaning "the High One."

The idea of setting aside areas of natural beauty and historic importance for the benefit of the people dates back to the mid-1800s. Before then, Americans had viewed wild places either as obstacles or as a source of natural resources for people to use.

The conservation movement gained popularity in the early 1900s when President Theodore Roosevelt and other conservationists urged Americans to protect natural resources.

Today conservation continues to be an important issue. Although many of us enjoy visiting national parks such as Denali, the parks also serve as refuges for wildlife. Scientists study the plants and animals so that they can protect them. With 430 species of flowering plants, 37 species of mammals, and 156 species of birds, Denali is one of America's great areas of unspoiled wilderness.

Mt. Foraker
17,400 ft. (5,303 m)

Avalanche Spire
10,105 ft. (3,080 m)

Kahiltna Glacier

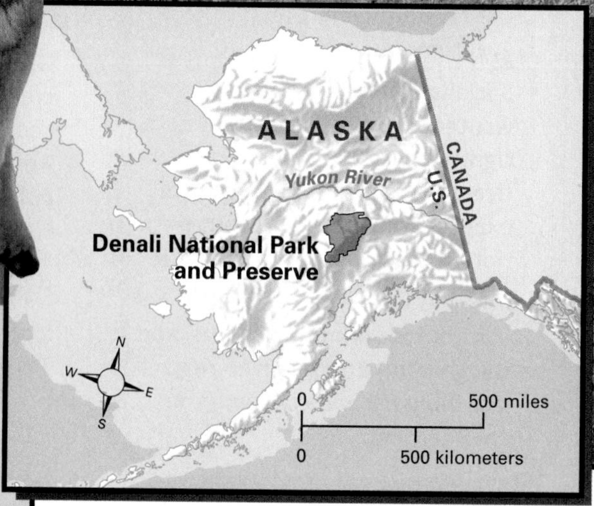

ALASKA

Yukon River

CANADA

U.S.

Denali National Park and Preserve

N
S
E
W

0 500 miles
0 500 kilometers

LEARNING from GEOGRAPHY

1. **Which peaks are higher than 15,000 feet?**
2. **Do you think it is necessary for the government to aid environmental programs? Explain.**

US8.12.5 Examine the location and effects of urbanization, renewed immigration, and industrialization (e.g., the effects on social fabric of cities, wealth and economic opportunity, the conservation movement).

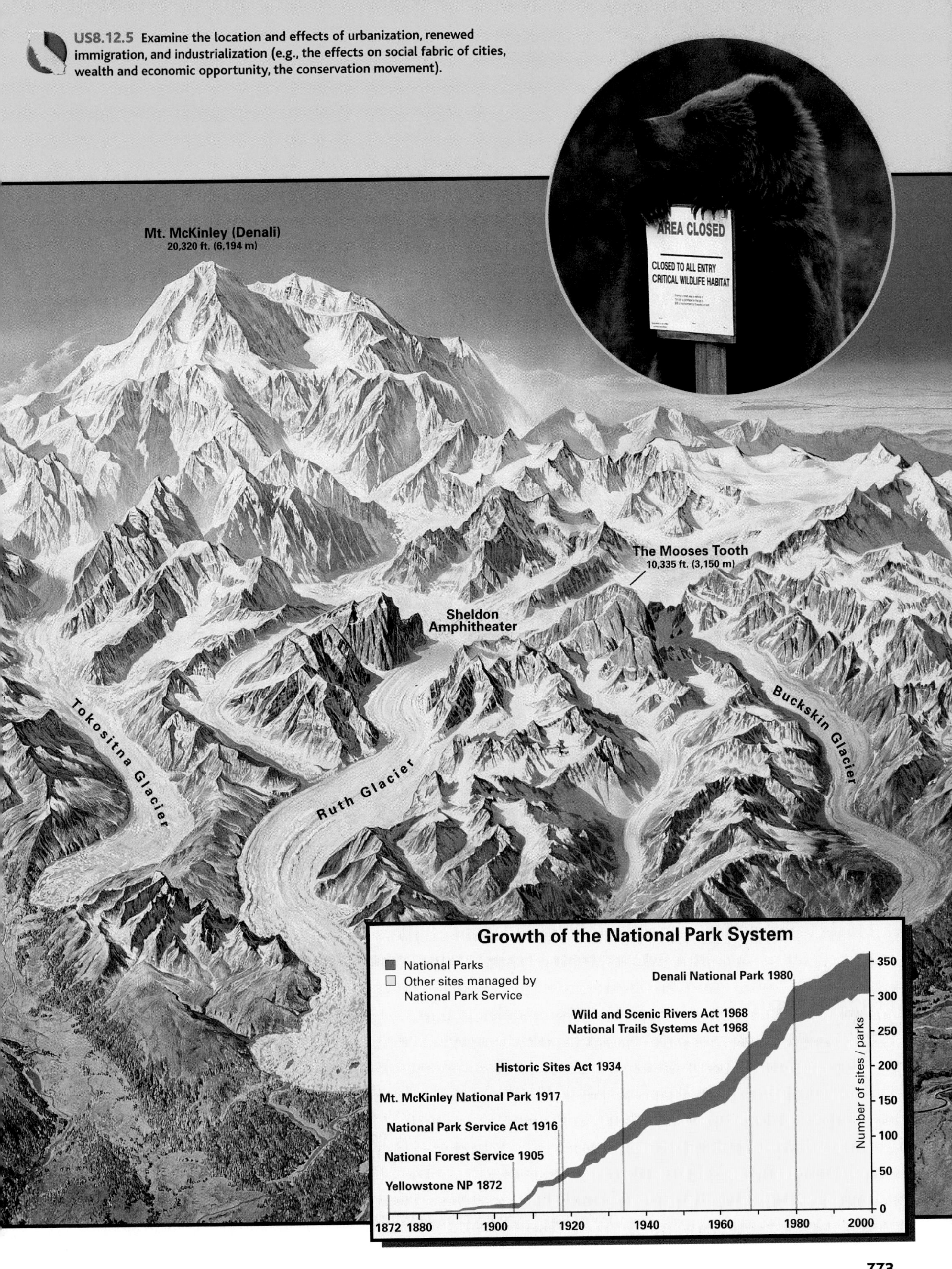

A Changing Nation

Guide to Reading

History Social Science Standards

US8.12 Students analyze the transformation of the American economy and the changing social and political conditions in the United States in response to the Industrial Revolution.

Looking Back, Looking Ahead

You learned that American reformers attempted to reduce corruption in business and government. At the same time, Americans wanted to expand their power and trade around the world.

Focusing on the Main Ideas

- The United States demonstrated its power in areas such as Latin America and the Pacific. *(page 775)*
- Many ethnic and religious minorities in America faced discrimination and even violence. *(page 778)*
- Minority groups in the United States sought to end discrimination and gain equal rights. *(page 780)*

Locating Places

Alaska
Hawaiian Islands
Cuba
Guam
Philippines
Panama

Content Vocabulary

isthmus (IHS • muhs)
discrimination (dihs • KRIH • muh • NAY • shuhn)
ward
barrio (BAHR • ee • OH)

Academic Vocabulary

reject
modify (MAH • duh • FY)
bias (BY • uhs)

Reading Strategy

Analyzing Information As you study Section 5, re-create the diagram below and describe the policies listed.

	Description
Roosevelt Corollary	
Dollar Diplomacy	
Moral Diplomacy	

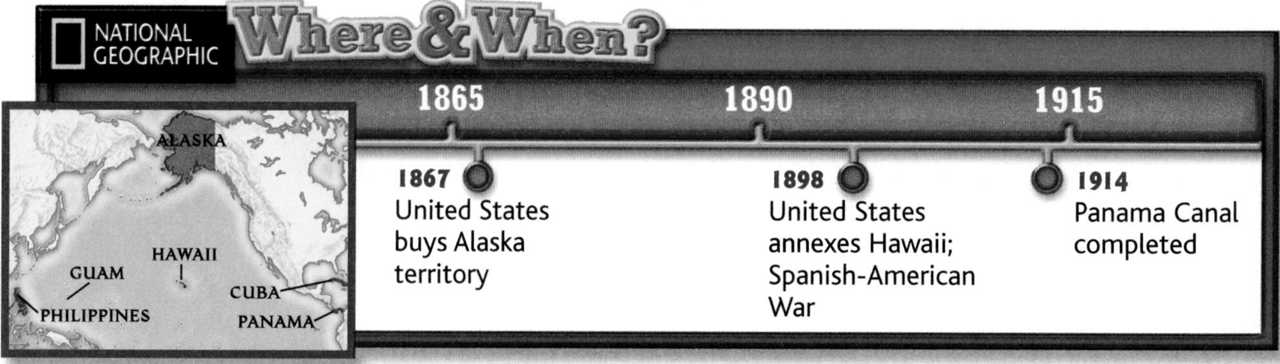

US8.12 Students analyze the transformation of the American economy and the changing social and political conditions in the United States in response to the Industrial Revolution.

American Foreign Policy

Main Idea **The United States demonstrated its power in areas such as Latin America and the Pacific.**

Reading Connection Have you ever wondered how the United States came to include places such as Alaska and Hawaii which are so far from the continental states? Read to find out how the United States expanded its power around the world.

An American Story

In the late 1800s and early 1900s, Americans looked beyond their borders and yearned for an empire. Merchants desired overseas markets, and adventurers wanted another frontier to conquer. Senator Albert Beveridge voiced the feelings of many when he proclaimed in 1900:

> **"The Philippines are ours forever. . . . And just beyond the Philippines are China's illimitable markets. We will not retreat from either. . . . The Pacific is our ocean."**
>
> **—Albert Beveridge, "In Support of an American Empire"**

Goals of Foreign Policy When President George Washington published his Farewell Address in 1796, he advised Americans to increase trade with other countries but to have "as little political connection as possible." Above all else, he warned Americans to "steer clear of permanent alliances with any portion of the foreign world." These principles guided American foreign policy for about 100 years. However, various people interpreted Washington's words in different ways. Some believed he meant that the United States should follow a policy of isolationism, or noninvolvement, in world affairs. Others believed that Washington supported trade with other countries and was not calling for complete isolation from the world.

How Did the United States Expand? Soon after the Civil War, some American leaders began to push for the United States to expand beyond its borders. They believed that acquiring new territories would increase trade and allow the United States to become a world power. In 1867 Secretary of State William Seward negotiated the purchase of **Alaska,** which was Russian territory at the time. At first, many people ridiculed Alaska as "Seward's Ice Box." The discovery of gold there later proved the value of the region's natural resources.

In 1898, during the presidency of William McKinley, the United States annexed—took control of—the **Hawaiian Islands.** The islands provided a base for the American navy. From Hawaii the United States could oversee its trade in Japan and China.

That same year, the United States went to war with Spain. The American press had aroused intense anger by reporting the brutal way that Spain crushed a rebellion in **Cuba.** Almost immediately, fighting extended to Spanish colonies in the Pacific Ocean as well as in Cuba. When the Spanish-American War ended, not only did Cuba gain its independence, but the United States also gained **Guam** and the **Philippines.**

Although about 400 American soldiers died fighting in the war, more than 2,000 died of diseases such as yellow fever, malaria, and other diseases contracted in the tropical climate. The African Americans who served faced the additional burden of discrimination. Serving in segregated units, African Americans battled alongside the Cuban rebel army, in which black and white troops fought as equals.

American Interest in Latin America

Since colonial times, the United States had carried on a flourishing trade with Latin America, including the Caribbean region. Fear of European influence in the region was a factor that led to the Monroe Doctrine in 1823, when President James Monroe warned European nations not to attempt to establish new colonies in North or South America.

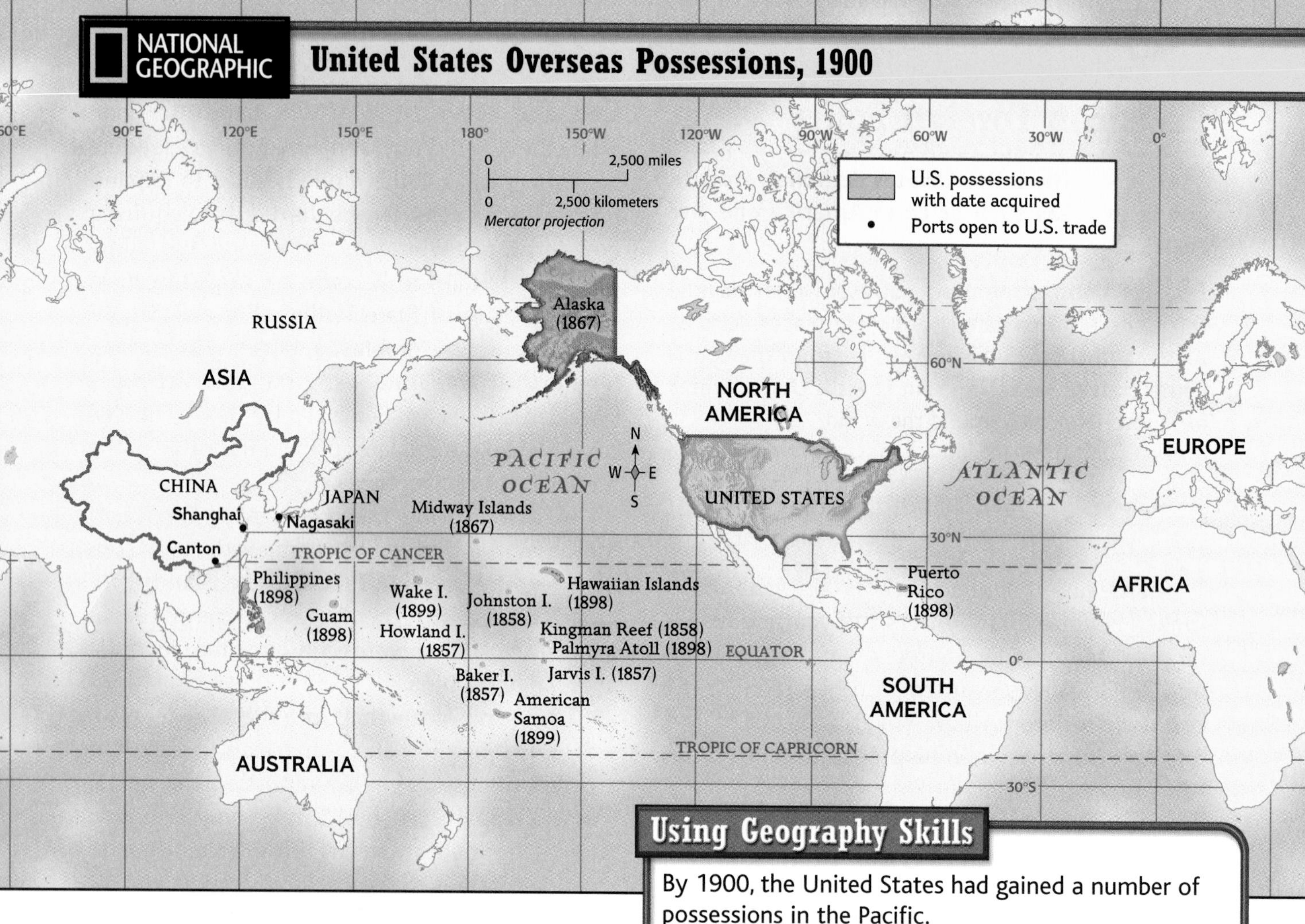

Using Geography Skills

By 1900, the United States had gained a number of possessions in the Pacific.

1. **Location** Locate Puerto Rico, Guam, and the Philippines. Which of these is farthest from the continental United States?
2. **Analyze** When were the Hawaiian Islands acquired?

Theodore Roosevelt, who became President after McKinley's assassination in 1901, worried that instability in the Caribbean region would lead European powers to intervene. In 1902 Venezuela and the Dominican Republic were deeply in debt to European nations. Roosevelt was concerned that European powers would step in to protect their financial interests there.

The president responded to these incidents in 1904 by asserting America's right to act as a "policeman" in Latin America, intervening "however reluctantly . . . in cases of wrong-doing." This policy, known as the Roosevelt Corollary, was an addition to the Monroe Doctrine. Up to that time, the United States had used the Monroe Doctrine only to prevent European intervention in Latin America. Under the Roosevelt Corollary, the United States now claimed the right to intervene in the affairs of Latin American nations whenever those nations seemed unstable. Roosevelt liked to proclaim "Speak softly, but carry a big stick." He meant that he preferred peace, but that he would use force when necessary. Roosevelt put his "big stick" to use to advance U.S. interests in Panama.

The Panama Canal For years the United States and other countries had wanted to build a canal across Central America to connect the Atlantic and Pacific Oceans. An ideal location for such a canal was across the **isthmus** (IHS • muhs) of **Panama.** An isthmus is a narrow strip of land that connects two larger landmasses—in this case, North and South America. Colombia, however, controlled Panama, and the Colombian legislature **rejected** the United States's offer to buy a strip of land across the isthmus.

To obtain the canal site, Roosevelt helped organize a revolt in Panama in 1903. With the help of American marines, the Panamanian rebels overthrew their Colombian rulers and set up their own government. The United States and the new government of Panama quickly signed a canal treaty. For $10 million plus an annual fee, Panama granted Americans control of a strip across the isthmus. Finished in 1914, the Panama Canal ranks as one of the great engineering works of all time.

Taft and Wilson Theodore Roosevelt thought of American power mostly in military terms. His successor in the White House, William Howard Taft, took a different view. Taft hoped to **modify** American foreign policy. He believed that American investments would bring stability to troubled areas of the world, as well as profit and power to the United States, without the need for force. Taft's approach was known as dollar diplomacy.

Elected in 1912, the new president, Woodrow Wilson said he wanted to promote democracy and further the cause of world peace. This new policy was called "moral diplomacy" because its purpose was to help other countries.

The Mexican Revolution From 1884 to 1911, a dictator named Porfirio Díaz, ruled Mexico. A few wealthy landowners dominated Mexican society. Most of the Mexican people were poor and owned no land. In 1911 Francisco Madero, a reformer who called for constitutional government and land reform, forced Díaz from power. Reform came slowly, however, and rebel groups fought against Madero's forces. Madero was captured and murdered and Venustiano Carranza, whose forces had acquired arms from the United States, became Mexico's president.

When the U.S. government came out openly in support of Carranza, rebel leader Pancho Villa retaliated by raiding U.S. border towns, most notably Columbus, New Mexico. American troops under General John J. Pershing crossed the border into Mexico and pursued Villa but were unsuccessful.

The Mexican Revolution had been the first major effort in Latin America to overturn the system of large estates in the hands of the few and raise the living standards for the Mexican people. Out of the revolution emerged historic social and economic reform. The revolution also was responsible for the first big wave of immigration from Mexico to the United States. More than 1 million refugees entered the United States. They influenced the culture and contributed to the economic and political development of the Southwest in particular and the nation as a whole.

Reading Check **Explain** On what principles did Wilson base his foreign policy?

History *Through Art*

Work Trains, Miraflores **by Alson Skinner Clark**
This painting shows the building of the Panama Canal. The stamp commemorates the canal's 25th anniversary. ***What role did the United States play in the independence of Panama?***

US8.12.7 Identify the new sources of large-scale immigration and the contributions of immigrants to the building of cities and the economy; explain the ways in which new social and economic patterns encouraged assimilation of newcomers into the mainstream amidst growing cultural diversity; and discuss the new wave of nativism.

Facing Prejudice at Home

Main Idea **Many ethnic and religious minorities in America faced discrimination and even violence.**

Reading Connection What might it have been like to travel thousands of miles to a new land, hoping to start a new, successful life, only to be told that you could go only to certain schools or hold certain low-paying jobs? Read to learn about the discrimination faced by some new immigrants to the United States around the turn of the century.

During the 1800s the overwhelming majority of Americans were white and Protestant and had been born in the United States. Many Americans believed that the United States should remain a white, Protestant nation. Nonwhite, non-Protestant, and nonnative residents often faced **discrimination** (dihs • KRIH • muh • NAY • shuhn) —unequal treatment because of their race, religion, ethnic background, or place of birth. The government rarely interfered with this discrimination.

Anti-Semitism Many Jewish immigrants came to the United States to escape prejudice in their homelands. Some of them found the same anti-Semitic attitudes in America. Landlords, employers, and schools discriminated against Jewish immigrants. Eastern European Jews faced prejudice both as Jews and as eastern Europeans, whom many Americans regarded as more foreign than western Europeans.

Anti-Catholicism Catholics also faced discrimination because of their religion. America's largely Protestant population feared that Catholic immigrants threatened the "American" way of life. Anti-Catholic Iowans formed the American Protective Association (APA) in 1887.

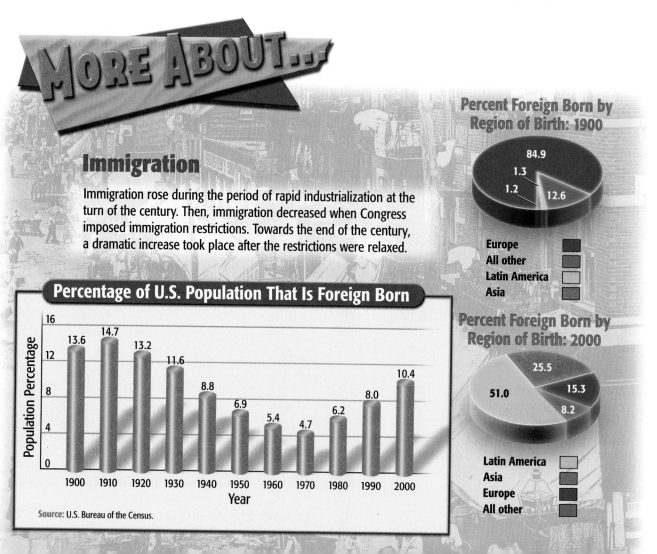

MORE ABOUT...

Immigration

Immigration rose during the period of rapid industrialization at the turn of the century. Then, immigration decreased when Congress imposed immigration restrictions. Towards the end of the century, a dramatic increase took place after the restrictions were relaxed.

Percentage of U.S. Population That Is Foreign Born

Year	Population Percentage
1900	13.6
1910	14.7
1920	13.2
1930	11.6
1940	8.8
1950	6.9
1960	5.4
1970	4.7
1980	6.2
1990	8.0
2000	10.4

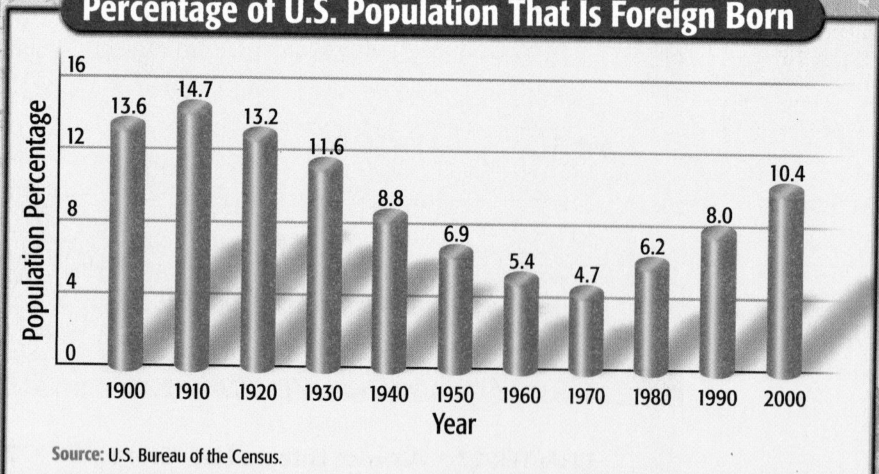

Source: U.S. Bureau of the Census.

Percent Foreign Born by Region of Birth: 1900

Europe	84.9
All other	12.6
Latin America	1.3
Asia	1.2

Percent Foreign Born by Region of Birth: 2000

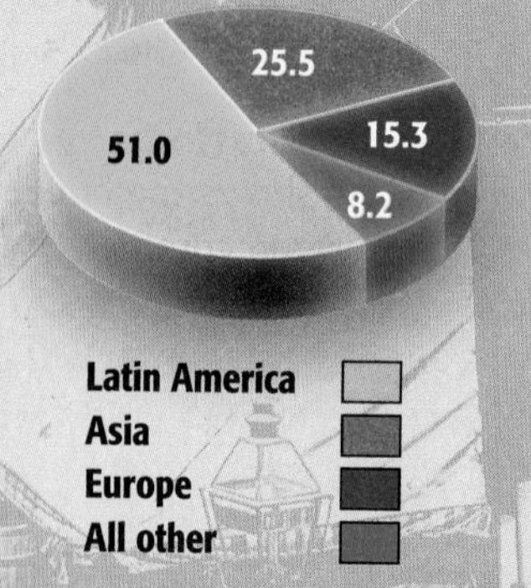

Latin America	51.0
Asia	25.5
Europe	15.3
All other	8.2

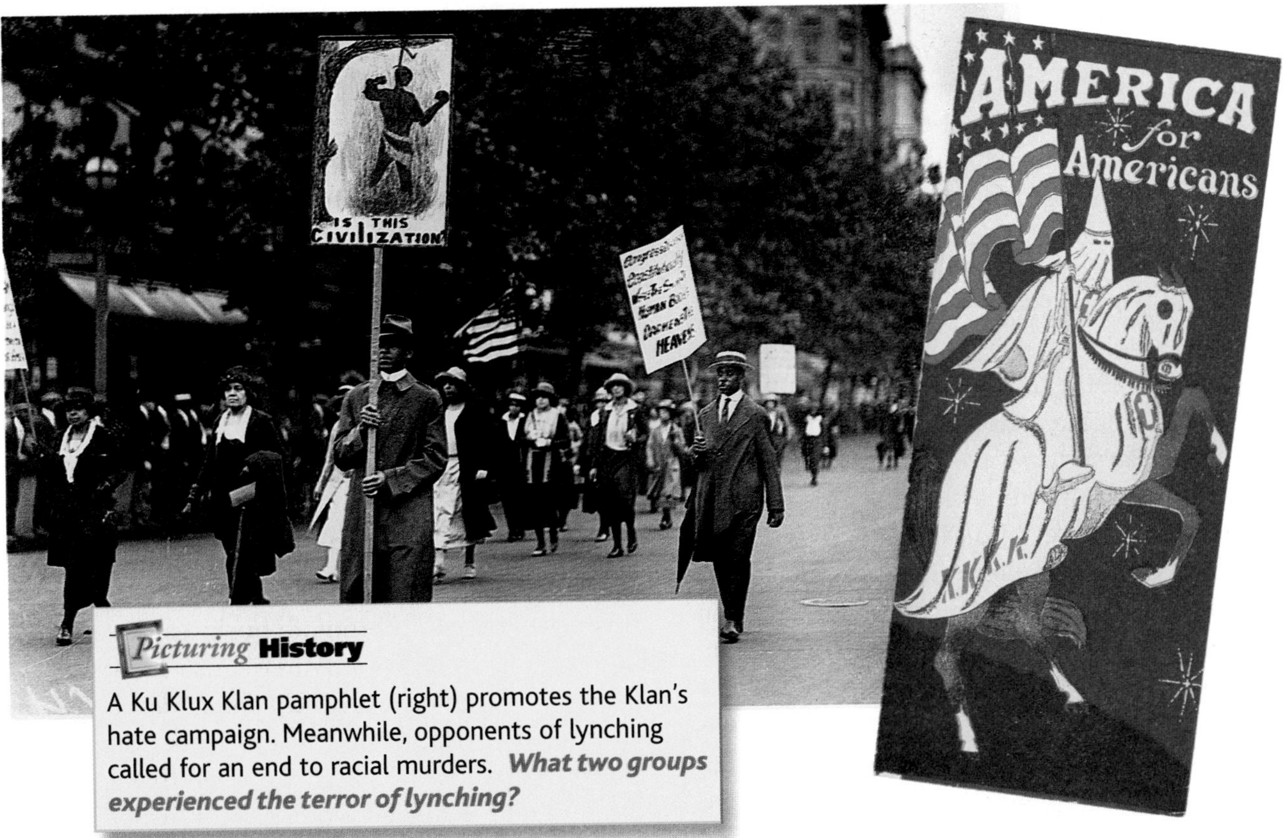

Picturing **History**

A Ku Klux Klan pamphlet (right) promotes the Klan's hate campaign. Meanwhile, opponents of lynching called for an end to racial murders. ***What two groups experienced the terror of lynching?***

By the mid-1890s, the APA claimed a membership of two million, mostly in the West. Among other activities, the APA spread rumors that Catholics were preparing to take over the country.

What Were Anti-Asian Policies? Discrimination was also based on race. In California and other Western states, Asians struggled against prejudice and resentment. White Americans claimed that Chinese immigrants, who worked for lower wages, took away jobs. Congress passed the Chinese Exclusion Act in 1882 to prevent Chinese immigrants from entering the United States.

America's westward expansion created opportunities for thousands of Japanese immigrants who came to the United States to work as railroad or farm laborers. Like the Chinese who had come before them, Japanese immigrants encountered prejudice. California would not allow them to become citizens. In 1906 in San Francisco, the school board tried to make Japanese children attend a separate school for Asians until President Roosevelt stepped in to prevent such segregation.

Roosevelt yielded to a rising tide of anti-Japanese feeling, however, and authorized the Gentlemen's Agreement with Japan in 1907. This agreement restricted Japanese immigration to the United States, but it did not bring an end to anti-Japanese feeling. In 1913 California made it illegal for Japanese immigrants to buy land. Other Western states passed similar laws.

Discrimination Against African Americans

Four-fifths of the nation's African Americans lived in the South. Most worked as rural sharecroppers or in low-paying jobs in the cities. They were separated from white society in their own neighborhoods, schools, parks, restaurants, theaters, and even cemeteries. In 1896 the Supreme Court legalized segregation in the case of *Plessy* v. *Ferguson,* which recognized "separate but equal" facilities.

The Ku Klux Klan, which had terrorized African Americans during Reconstruction, was reborn in Georgia in 1915. The new Klan wanted to restore white, Protestant America. The Klan lashed out against minorities—Catholics, Jews, and immigrants, as well as African Americans.

US8.12.7 Identify the new sources of large-scale immigration and the contributions of immigrants to the building of cities and the economy; explain the ways in which new social and economic patterns encouraged assimilation of newcomers into the mainstream amidst growing cultural diversity; and discuss the new wave of nativism.

Racial Violence People who lost their jobs during the economic depressions of 1893 and 1907 sometimes unleashed their anger against African Americans and other minorities. More than 2,600 African Americans were lynched between 1886 and 1916, mostly in the South. Lynchings were also used to terrorize Chinese immigrants in the West.

Racial violence also occurred in the North, however. A 1908 riot in Springfield, Illinois, Abraham Lincoln's hometown, shocked the nation. A false accusation by a white woman led to the lynching of two African Americans, and dozens more were injured. No one was ever punished for these violent crimes.

Ida B. Wells, the editor of an African American newspaper in Memphis, Tennessee, was forced to leave town after publishing the names of people involved in a lynching. The incident started Wells on a national crusade to stop lynching. Although Congress rejected an anti-lynching bill, the number of lynchings decreased significantly in the 1900s due in great part to activists such as Wells.

Progressivism and Prejudice In the late 1800s and the early 1900s, many Americans held **biased** views. They believed that white, male, native-born Americans had the right to make decisions for all of society.

Most of the progressive reformers came from the middle and upper classes. They saw themselves as moral leaders working to improve the lives of people less fortunate than themselves. Nevertheless, the reforms they supported often discriminated against one group as they tried to help another group.

Trade unions often prohibited African Americans, women, and immigrants from joining. Skilled laborers, these unions argued, could obtain better working conditions for themselves if they did not demand improved conditions for all workers. In spite of these problems, progressive reforms did succeed in improving conditions for many Americans.

Reading Check **Identify** What Supreme Court decision legalized segregation?

Struggle for Equal Opportunity

Main Idea **Minority groups in the United States sought to end discrimination and gain equal rights.**

Reading Connection Have you ever joined a group that worked toward a common cause? Read to find out how some people formed groups to work to end discrimination.

Booker T. Washington, who founded the Tuskegee Institute, believed that if African Americans gained economic power, they would be in a better position to demand equality. Washington founded the National Negro Business League to promote business development among African Americans. In Washington's autobiography, *Up from Slavery,* he counseled African Americans to work patiently toward equality. Washington argued that equality would be achieved when African Americans gained the education and skills to become valuable members of their community.

Other African Americans had different ideas about attaining equality. W.E.B. Du Bois (doo • BAWIHS), an educator and activist, believed that gaining and using the right to vote would best help African Americans succeed. He helped found the National Association for the Advancement of Colored People (NAACP) in 1909. Some African Americans thought that they would be better off in separate societies, either in the United States or in Africa. They founded organizations to establish African American towns and promoted a back-to-Africa movement. These movements were not popular, however.

During the early 1900s, African Americans achieved success in a variety of professions. Chemist George Washington Carver, director of agricultural research at Tuskegee Institute, helped improve the economy of the South through his discoveries of plant products. Maggie Lena founded the St. Luke Penny Savings Bank in Richmond, Virginia. She was the first American woman to serve as a bank president.

Biography

US8.12 Students analyze the transformation of the American economy and the changing social and political conditions in the United States in response to the Industrial Revolution.

Booker T. Washington

1856–1915

W.E.B. Du Bois

1868–1963

▲ **Booker T. Washington**

In the late 1800s and early 1900s, two of the most important African American leaders were Booker T. Washington and W.E.B. Du Bois. Both men had the same goals, but they took different approaches to reaching those goals.

Washington was born into slavery. Later, he attended an industrial school and went on to become a teacher. As a teacher, he developed his own theories about education, which led him to found the Tuskegee Institute.

Washington became an influential leader who advised presidents and governors. He gained support because he was willing—temporarily—to compromise on political rights for African Americans. In return, Washington wanted support for African American schools, economic gains, and an end to violence against African Americans.

W.E.B. Du Bois, the first African American to receive a doctorate degree from Harvard, refused to accept racial inequality. Du Bois helped start the Niagara Movement in 1905 to fight against racial discrimination and demand full political rights and responsibilities for African Americans. Later, Du Bois joined others to form the National Association for the Advancement of Colored People (NAACP). This group today remains a force in the efforts to gain legal and economic equality for African Americans. Du Bois rejected Washington's emphasis on job skills and argued that the right to vote was the way to end racial inequality, stop lynching, and gain better schools. "The power of the ballot we need in sheer self-defense," he said, "else what shall save us from a second slavery?"

◀ **W.E.B. Du Bois**

Then and Now

Why did Washington and Du Bois take the stands they did? Which leaders today have taken stands for equal rights for all?

Native Americans Seek Justice The federal government's efforts to assimilate Native Americans into white society threatened to break down traditional native cultures. In 1910–1911 Native American leaders from around the country formed the Society of American Indians to seek justice for Native Americans, to improve their living conditions, and to educate white Americans about different Native American cultures. Some leaders believed that Native Americans should leave the reservations and make their own way in white society.

Surprisingly, at the time the Fourteenth Amendment was passed, Native Americans, who were considered **wards,** or persons under the legal guardianship of the U.S. government, were not granted citizenship under the amendment. In 1924 Congress reversed this ruling by granting citizenship to all Native Americans who did not possess it.

Mexican Americans Work Together Immigrants from Mexico had long come to the United States as laborers, especially in the West and Southwest. Like the Japanese and other immigrant groups, Mexican Americans encountered discrimination and violence. Relying on themselves to solve their problems, they formed *mutualistas*—self-defense associations—to raise money for insurance and legal help. One of the first *mutualistas* was the Alianza Hispano Americo (Hispanic American Alliance), formed in Tucson, Arizona, in 1894. In labor camps and Mexican neighborhoods called **barrios** (BAHR•ee•OHS), *mutualistas* worked to end overcrowding, poor sanitation, and inadequate public services.

César Chávez Organizes Mexican Workers From the early 1900s on, some efforts were made to organize farmworkers but with little success. In the 1960s, however, César Chávez (CHAH•vehz), born in 1927, finally began making real headway in organizing the workers in the California vineyards and lettuce fields. In 1962 he organized farmworkers into the organization called the United Farm Workers (UFW) and started a five-year strike against California grape growers to force them to recognize the union. The UFW organized a nationwide boycott of table grapes. Sympathetic priests, civic groups, and students aided Chávez in his efforts. In 1965 he launched a strike that led to a nationwide boycott of produce not bearing the label of the United Farm Workers. In 1970, the strikers finally won, and the strike ended in a pact with the growers. By 1975 Chávez and the strikers had convinced the California legislature to pass a bill that gave farmworkers the same rights held by union members elsewhere.

Primary Sources

George Washington Carver

In his studies in botany and agriculture at the Tuskegee Institute, George Washington Carver made a number of amazing discoveries. He found dozens of new uses for plants such as the peanut and sweet potato. A teacher for nearly 50 years, Carver taught his students, often the children of formerly enslaved people, to conserve land and resources.

> The primary idea in all of my work was to help the farmer and fill the poor man's empty dinner pail. . . . My idea is to help the "man farthest down," this is why I have made every process just as simply as I could to put it within his reach.
>
> —George Washington Carver

DBQ Document-Based Question

What was Carver's purpose in much of his work? How did he do this?

Changes and Challenges By 1914 the United States had changed tremendously. Its population had grown and become more urban than rural. The nation had become industrialized, and people traveled by train, automobile, and even airplane.

While the United States had used its power to establish a limited empire in far-off lands, it had steered clear of Europe's arguments and wars. However, the conflict that was growing in Europe by 1914 would develop into a war that would entangle much of the world. Once the United States became involved, its position in the world would change forever.

Looking to the Future Then, as now, Americans approached the future as a free nation committed to the truths expressed in the Declaration of Independence. The Declaration protects the rights of the American people and states that the purpose of government is to protect these rights:

> **"We hold these truths to be self-evident, that all men are created equal, that they are endowed by their Creator with certain unalienable Rights, that among these are Life, Liberty and the pursuit of Happiness. That to secure these rights, Governments are instituted among Men, deriving their just powers from the consent of the governed . . . ."**

Reading Check **Describe** What were *mutualistas?*

Study Central Need help understanding the struggle for equal opportunity? Visit ca.hss.glencoe.com and click on Study Central.

Reading Summary

Review the Main Ideas

- The United States pursued an increasingly international role, especially in Latin America and the Pacific.
- Discrimination and violence were painful, pressing issues for many groups and often went unaddressed by the federal government.
- Minority groups developed strategies for working together to end racial and social discrimination.

What Did You Learn?

1. What was the significance of the Panama Canal?
2. How did the Supreme Court legalize segregation?

Critical Thinking

3. **Summarizing Information** Re-create the diagram below to describe how different minority groups worked toward equality and change. CA HR3.

	Describe
African Americans	
Native Americans	
Mexican Americans	

4. **The Big Ideas** Explain the United States's interest in Latin America. CA CS1.
5. **Describe** What was the impact of African Americans who pioneered new means for achieving equality? Write a paragraph that includes references to Booker T. Washington, George Washington Carver, and Maggie Lena. CA 8WS1.1
6. **Linking Past to Present** Summarize the plight of Mexican farmworkers during this period and the impact of César Chávez later in the century. What was the lasting legacy of his work? CA HI3.

Step Back in Time

What—and who—were people talking about? What did they eat? What did they do for fun? These two pages will give you some clues to everyday life in the U.S. as you step back in time with TIME Notebook.

Profile

BOOKER T. WASHINGTON *Teaching industrial training as a means to success, in 1881 Washington founded the Tuskegee Institute in Alabama. Here is an excerpt from his autobiography,* Up From Slavery.

FROM THE VERY BEGINNING, AT TUSKEGEE, I was determined to have the students do not only the agricultural and domestic work, but to have them erect their own buildings. My plan was to have them, while performing this service, taught the latest and best methods of labour, so that the school would not only get the benefit of their efforts, but the students themselves would be taught to see not only utility in labour, but beauty and dignity. . . . My plan was not to teach them to work in the old way, but to show them how to make the forces of nature—air, water, steam, electricity, horse-power—assist them in their labour.

Booker T. Washington

VERBATIM

WHAT PEOPLE ARE SAYING

"If you pick up a starving dog and make him prosperous, he will not bite you. This is the principal difference between a dog and a man."

MARK TWAIN, *author of* The Adventures of Tom Sawyer

"Speak softly and carry a big stick; you will go far."

PRESIDENT TEDDY ROOSEVELT, *proposing action when asked how the United States will deal with its new far-flung colonies in 1901*

"Give me your tired, your poor, your huddled masses yearning to breathe free."

WORDS BY EMMA LAZARUS, *engraved on the Statue of Liberty in 1903*

"Mountains! Look at them!"

EDWARD CORSI, *10-year-old Italian immigrant on spotting the high-rise buildings in New York City for the first time in 1907*

It's The Law

Two laws were passed in 1902 to deal with the automobile.

1. Tennessee demands all drivers give the public a week's notice before they start any trip.
2. Vermont states an adult waving a red flag has to walk in front of any moving automobile.

MILESTONES

EVENTS AND PEOPLE OF THE TIME

SIGNED UP. Sharpshooter **ANNIE OAKLEY** to Buffalo Bill's Wild West Show in 1885.

FLEW. 19-year-old Cromwell Dixon over the Continental Divide in 1911 in a biplane. At age 14, Dixon was building **DIRIGIBLES** (sausage-shaped balloons), including a model that could be pedaled through the air like a bicycle. Dixon later traveled around the country, flying at state fairs.

Annie Oakley

AMERICAN SCENE

Average Life Spans in 1900

Average life expectancy: **47.3 years**

Male life expectancy: **46.3 years**

Female life expectancy: **48.3 years**

White life expectancy: **47.6 years**

Nonwhite life expectancy: **33.0 years**

0 10 20 30 40 50 years

TRANSPORTATION

Take a Ride in My Car!

Here's what one magazine from the early 1900s recommends you carry in your car at all times:

- **1** Efficient tire pump
- **1** Strong two-gallon can extra gasoline
- **1** Sheet fine sandpaper
- **1** Small, short-handled axe
- **1** Ball asbestos cord
- **4** Half-pound cans of meat or fish
- **2** Pounds sweet chocolate

NUMBERS

U.S. AT THE TIME

12¢ **Price of a dozen eggs in 1910**

$12 **Price of a sewing machine in 1900**

$12 **Lowest price for a steamship ticket from Italy to America in 1905**

$12 **Average weekly salary (seven-day weeks/12-hour days) for arriving immigrants in 1907**

Wright brothers

12 seconds **Air time of Wright brothers' first flight in 1903**

1.2 million **Approximate number of immigrants who entered the U.S. in 1907**

395,000 **Approximate number of immigrants in 1908 who gave up on America and returned home**

50¢ **Price of cheapest seat at baseball's first World Series in 1903**

Analyzing Primary Sources

US8.12 Students analyze the transformation of the American economy and the changing social and political conditions in the United States in response to the Industrial Revolution.

A Time of Change

The United States changed in the late 1800s and early 1900s. Cities grew as people poured into them, looking for work. In addition, reformers investigated the practices of big business.

Read the passages on pages 786 and 787 and answer the questions that follow.

Jane Addams with immigrant children at Hull House in Chicago ▶

Reader's Dictionary

initiative (ih • NIH • shuh • tiv): the first action in a process

ward: an area of a city

sanitary (SA • nuh • TEHR • ee): having to do with cleanliness

foul (FAUL): very dirty

bewildered (bih • WIHL • duhrd): confused

clutches: strong hold of claws

interpretation (ihn • TUHR • pruh • TAY • shuhn): explanation done in an understandable way

asylums (uh • SY • luhms): places for the care of the poor, sick, and insane

gash: long, deep cut

contagion (kuhn • TAY • juhn): spreading of disease

vats: large containers

refuse (REH • FYOOS): garbage

Hull House

In her book, Twenty Years at Hull-House, *Jane Addams describes the area of the city where Hull House is located.*

The policy of the public authorities of never taking an **initiative,** and always waiting to be urged to do their duty, is obviously fatal in a neighborhood where there is little initiative among the citizens. The idea underlying our self-government breaks down in such a **ward.** The streets are inexpressibly dirty, the number of schools inadequate, **sanitary** legislation unenforced, the street lighting bad, the paving miserable and altogether lacking in the alleys and smaller streets, and the stables **foul** beyond description. Hundreds of houses are unconnected with the street sewer.

Addams also explains how settlement houses help disadvantaged people.

We early found ourselves spending many hours in efforts to secure support for deserted women, insurance for **bewildered** widows, damages for injured operators, furniture from the **clutches** of the installment store. The Settlement is valuable as an information and **interpretation** bureau.

It constantly acts between the various institutions of the city and the people for whose benefit these institutions were erected. The hospitals, the county agencies, and State **asylums** are often but vague rumors to the people who need them most. Another function of the Settlement to its neighborhood resembles that of the big brother whose mere presence on the playground protects the little one from bullies.

—from *Twenty Years at Hull-House with Autobiographical Notes*

The Jungle

Upton Sinclair writes about the meatpacking industry in his novel The Jungle.

[Mikolas] is a beef-boner, and that is a dangerous trade, especially when you are on piecework and trying to earn a bride. Your hands are slippery, and your knife is slippery, and you are toiling like mad, when somebody happens to speak to you, or you strike a bone. Then your hand slips up on the blade, and there is a fearful **gash**. And that would not be so bad, only for the deadly **contagion.** The cut may heal, but you never can tell. Twice now; within the last three years, Mikolas has been lying at home with blood poisoning—once for three months and once for nearly seven. The last time, too, he lost his job, and that meant six weeks more of standing at the doors of the packing houses, at six o'clock on bitter winter mornings.

One character, Antanas, has a new job. He must mop up the chemicals used on the meat.

[T]he beef had lain in **vats** full of chemicals, and men with great forks speared it out and dumped it into trucks, to be taken to the cooking room. When they had speared out all they could reach, they emptied the vat on the floor, and then with shovels scraped up the balance and dumped it into the truck. This floor was filthy, yet they set Antanas with his mop slopping the "pickle" into a hole that connected with a sink, where it was caught and used over again forever; and if that were not enough, there was a trap [bend] in the pipe, where all the scraps of meat and odds and ends of **refuse** were caught, and every few days it was the old man's task to clean these out, and shovel their contents into one of the trucks with the rest of the meat!

—from *The Jungle*

A famous muckraking book

DBQ Document-Based Questions

Hull House

1. Why was the area around Hull House in such bad condition?
2. What did Addams mean by comparing the settlement house to a "big brother"?

The Jungle

3. Write three adjectives that describe the working conditions of Mikolas and Antanas.
4. How would you feel about eating meat that comes from a company like the one where Antanas is working? Why?

Read to Write

5. In these writings, Addams reports on social conditions and Sinclair reports on working conditions. Do you think these works were intended to inform or spark reform, or both? How do you think readers responded to these writings? How do you think government officials responded? CA HR3.

Assessment

Standard US8.12

Review Content Vocabulary

For each of the pairs of terms below, write a sentence or short paragraph showing how the two are related.

1. emigrate, ethnic groups
2. slum, settlement house
3. trust, oligopoly

Review the Main Ideas

Section 1 • The New Immigrants

4. What was an immigrant's greatest challenge upon arriving in the United States?
5. What was the goal of the nativist movement?

Section 2 • Moving to the City

6. What were some important advances in transportation?
7. What were tenements and slums?

Section 3 • A Changing Culture

8. What was a land-grant college?
9. Who invented moving pictures?

Section 4 • The Progressive Movement

10. What was the spoils system?
11. What did President Roosevelt do to protect the environment?

Section 5 • A Changing Nation

12. How did the United States expand its territorial interests in the Pacific?
13. What was the Springfield riot of 1908?

Critical Thinking

14. **Explain** Why were minority groups discriminated against during this period? How did these groups respond? CA HI2.
15. **Compare and Contrast** How did Presidents Taft and Wilson differ in their views on international relations? CA HR3.
16. **Cause and Effect** Re-create the diagram below. Describe three ways newcomers to America tried to preserve their culture. CA HI2.

17. **Analyze** Why did leisure time develop for some Americans? How did that affect American culture? CA HI3.

Geography Skills

Study the map below and answer the following questions. CA CS3.

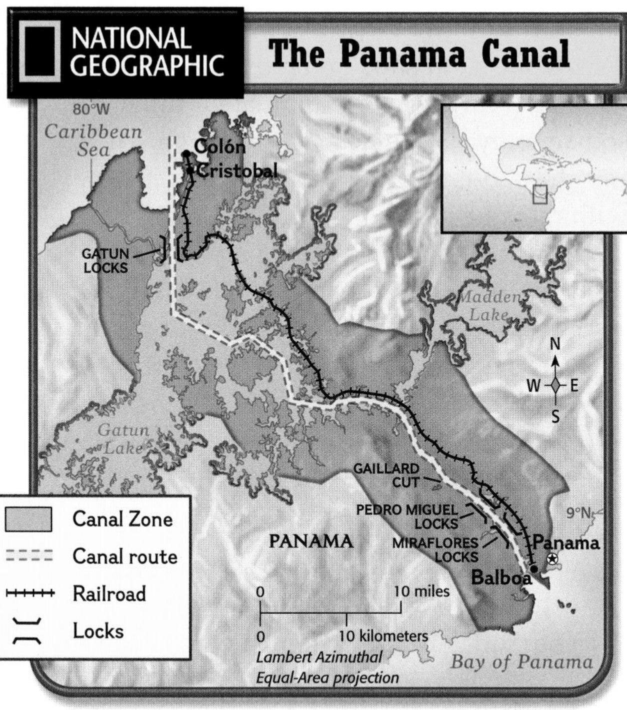

18. **Location** What bodies of water are shown on the map of the Panama Canal?
19. **Movement** Besides the canal, what other form of transportation is shown here?

A Global Struggle

The worldwide depression aided the rise of dictatorships in Europe and Japan. These governments aggressively sought to expand their territories. World War II began when Germany invaded Poland. Britain and France responded by declaring war on Germany. In 1941 the Soviet Union joined the conflict when Germany invaded its territory. The United States entered the war later that year after Japan bombed the U.S. naval base at Pearl Harbor, Hawaii.

World War II, the most destructive war in history, resulted in the deaths of more than 40 million people. More than half of them were civilians, including about 6 million Jews and many others in the Holocaust.

At the end of the war, the United States emerged as one of the strongest nations in the world and the sole possessor of a powerful weapon—the atomic bomb.

▲ **The attack on Pearl Harbor drew the United States into World War II.**

Democracy Versus Communism

The democratic United States and the communist Soviet Union emerged from World War II as the two most powerful nations, struggling for world leadership. This rivalry became known as the Cold War because, although great tensions divided them, the two countries did not actually go to war with each other. Each side tried to gain allies and prove that its system of government—democracy or communism—was better than the other.

The Cold War turned "hot," however, when Communist North Korean soldiers invaded South Korea. United Nations troops led by the United States became involved in the conflict. The Communist Chinese came to the aid of their North Korean ally. The two sides finally agreed to stop fighting. They accepted an armistice line that divided Korea along the existing battlefront.

Review

1. What factors made World Wars I and II different from earlier wars?
2. Why were the 1920s called the Jazz Age? What happened to the U.S. economy at the end of this period?
3. Who was at odds during the Cold War?

1930 — 1940 — 1950

- **1929** Stock market crashes, triggering Great Depression
- **1939** World War II begins in Europe
- **1945** Germany and Japan surrender; World War II ends
- **1950** North Korea invades South Korea

Modern America, 1950 to the Present

From the 1950s to the 1980s, the United States struggled with communism abroad and advanced civil rights at home. Americans prospered, and American culture spread around the globe. In the early 1990s, the Soviet Union collapsed, bringing the Cold War to an end. Meanwhile, new technologies and a changing population transformed America in new ways. Entering the new century, Americans responded to the global spread of terrorism by looking for fresh ways to preserve and protect their ideals in a changing world.

▼ After World War II, more Americans owned cars and homes than ever before.

▲ More than 200,000 people joined the March on Washington in August 1963 to call for civil rights legislation.

America in the 1950s

After years of "going without" during the Great Depression and World War II, Americans hungered for new cars, electronics, appliances, and gadgets. During the 1950s, the American economy began to grow rapidly and steadily. Between 1945 and 1960, the total value of goods and services produced in the United States increased about 250 percent. During the 1950s, 85 percent of new home construction took place in the suburbs—neighborhoods developed just outside of a city.

The Struggle for Civil Rights

In the 1950s, a tide of protest began to rise in America against deeply rooted attitudes of racism and discrimination. This campaign for equality gained momentum in the 1960s. African Americans, women, Hispanic Americans, and Native Americans became more active in seeking equal rights. Leaders such as Martin Luther King, Jr., and César Chávez developed peaceful methods of protest to realize this goal. Although the civil rights movement could not overcome all the obstacles that stood in the way of full equality, it achieved some stunning successes.

Around the World and at Home, 1950–Present

1950 — 1960 — 1970

- **1954** Polio vaccine given to school children
- **1963** March on Washington rallies support for civil rights
- **1973** U.S. ends involvement in Vietnam

Search for Stability

The Vietnam conflict—an effort to defeat communism in Southeast Asia—left scars on America. More than 58,000 U.S. troops died in Vietnam, and thousands more were wounded. The people of Southeast Asia also paid a price for war in Vietnam. Two million Vietnamese and uncounted Cambodians and Laotians were killed. Their villages and towns lay in ruins.

Dramatic change marked the period of the 1960s and 1970s. Faith in government was shaken by presidential scandal. Yet the American system of constitutional government worked and survived. The nation had responsibilities as a world power, faced conflict with the communist world, and carried out ventures in outer space. All of these tasks demanded that the nation learn new ways of carrying out its role in the world. Still, Americans tried to adjust to changes in ways that would assure the future of their democracy.

The attacks of September 11, 2001, shocked Americans, but also united them.

Toward a New Century

The 1980s and 1990s saw the dawn of a new era. With the collapse of communism in Europe, the Cold War came to an end. Relations between East and West changed dramatically. Meanwhile, after centuries of conflict, European nations began to unite economically and politically in the European Union. Worldwide pressure led to the end of apartheid—government-sponsored segregation—and the rise of a multiracial democratic government in South Africa.

At home, new advances in technology, medicine, and industry transformed the American economy. As the United States entered a new century, new challenges emerged. The terrorist attacks on New York City and Washington, D.C. began a new war against global terrorism, as well as renewed commitment to supporting freedom, equality, and democracy in America and abroad.

Review

1. Why did the United States fight a war in Vietnam?
2. What event changed East-West relations beginning in the late 1980s?
3. What new challenge did the United States and the world face at the beginning of the new century?

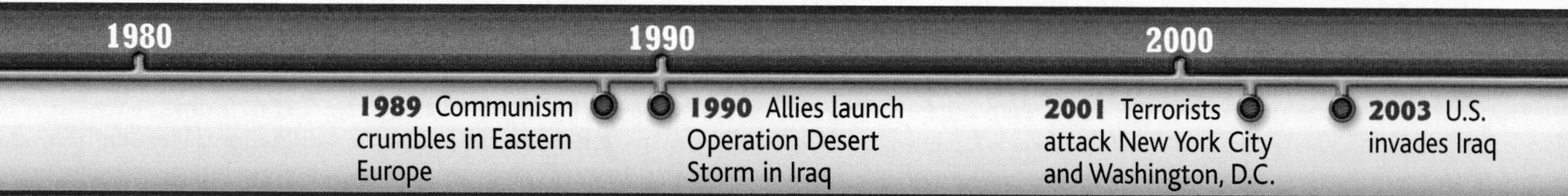
1980
1990
2000
1989 Communism crumbles in Eastern Europe
1990 Allies launch Operation Desert Storm in Iraq
2001 Terrorists attack New York City and Washington, D.C.
2003 U.S. invades Iraq

A Changing Society

▲ Young boys working in a Georgia mill, early 1900s

The Beginnings of Reform

The spirit of reform gained strength in the late 1800s and thrived during the early 1900s. The reformers were confident in their ability to improve government and the quality of life.

Problems in American Society

At the beginning of the 1900s, the United States was a different country than it is today. The vision described in the Declaration of Independence—that all are created equal and possess certain unalienable rights—remained a dream for many Americans. Women could not vote. Laws in many parts of the country enforced racial segregation. People with disabilities were often unable to enjoy the same range of opportunities as other people. Government did little to protect citizens from dangerous medicines, contaminated food, and unfair business practices. There was little concern that our country's air, water, and natural areas were at risk of being polluted or destroyed.

Equal Rights and Reform, 1900–1950

1900 — 1910 — 1920

- **1906** Pure Food and Drug Act passed
- **1916** Keating-Owen Child Labor Act passed
- **1919** Eighteenth Amendment prohibits alcohol
- **1920** Women vote in national election for the first time

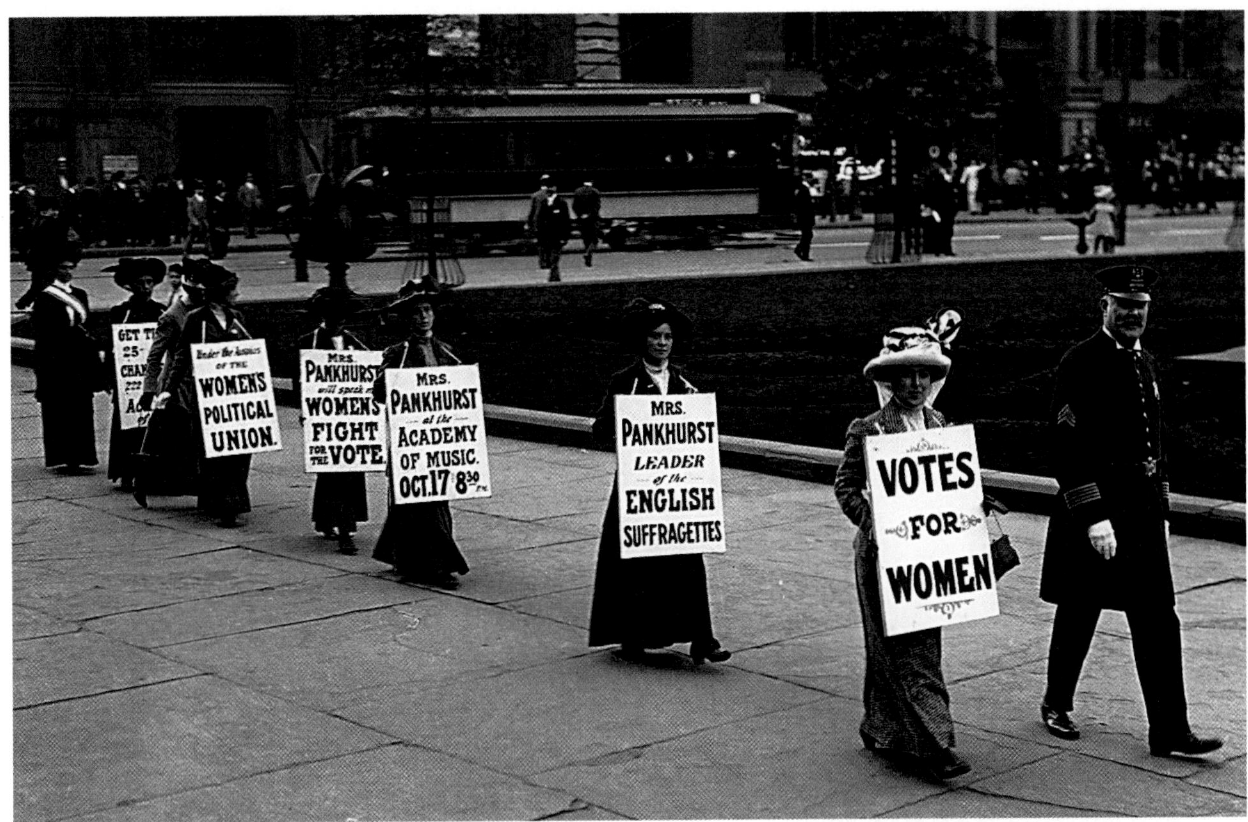

▲ Women march for suffrage in New York City in 1920.

Progressive Reforms

Early in the century, reformers known as Progressives gained influence in local, state, and national government. Progressives believed that government should take a more active role in improving people's lives and solving society's problems.

Some Progressives took aim at political corruption, urban poverty, child labor, or questionable business practices. Others wanted to reform government itself to make it more able to deal with the nation's challenges. Still others wanted to ban the sale and consumption of alcohol. A quarter-century of Progressive reforms left their mark on the nation. As a result, Americans began to look to the government to protect their interests.

Review

1. What impact did Progressive policies have on how Americans perceived their government?
2. Explain the effect of Progressive reforms on the lives of Americans.
3. What reforms would you like to see enacted today? What could you do to make that possible?

1930 — 1940 — 1950

- **1929** Great Depression begins
- **1935** Social Security Act adopted
- **1938** Fair Labor Standards Act passed
- **1944** GI Bill enacted

The Struggle for Equal Rights

Reformers addressed a number of issues in the 1900s, and some of the most difficult struggles were those faced by African Americans and other ethnic groups. Their battles for equal rights led to major changes in American society.

▲ Separate drinking facilities for African Americans and whites

African Americans Face Discrimination

Although amendments to the Constitution guaranteed rights to all Americans, African American and other groups still did not enjoy civil rights, or the rights of full citizenship and equality under the law. In the early 1900s, African Americans routinely faced discrimination. Laws in the South limited their right to vote. Laws in many parts of the nation barred African Americans from attending the same schools as white students. African Americans had to ride in the back of buses, sit in separate sections of restaurants and theaters, and stay in separate hotels. The social separation of races was known as segregation.

African Americans began to campaign actively for civil rights in the 1900s. In 1909 a group of African Americans and whites founded the National Association for the Advancement of Colored People (NAACP). That group sought to end discrimination through legal means. After African Americans fought with American forces in both world wars, the call for equal rights grew even stronger. A major victory in the struggle for civil rights occurred in 1948 when President Harry S. Truman issued an executive order that ended racial segregation in the armed forces.

The Equal Rights Movement, 1900–1970

1900 — 1910 — 1920 — 1930

1909 NAACP formed

1917 African Americans serve as officers during World War I

1930s President Roosevelt appoints 45 African Americans to serve in New Deal agencies

The Civil Rights Era

The landmark 1954 Supreme Court decision *Brown* v. *Board of Education* ruled that segregated schools were unconstitutional. Schools began to desegregate, but the move faced great opposition in some parts of the country. A year later, a young minister led a successful boycott of the segregated Montgomery, Alabama, bus system. His name was Martin Luther King, Jr., and he would become the nation's most important civil rights leader. African Americans and whites protested against segregated facilities in restaurants, at bus and train stations, and in other areas. In many parts of the country, especially the South, the protesters were met with anger and violence.

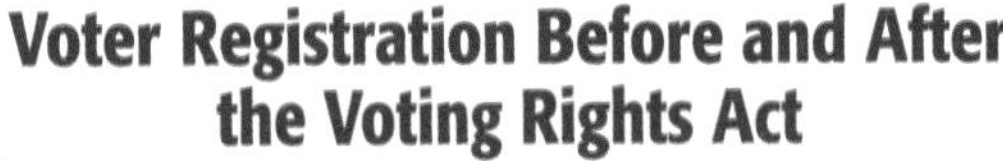

Voter Registration Before and After the Voting Rights Act

- **7% of African American adults registered to vote in Mississippi in 1964 before passage of the Voting Rights Act of 1965**
- **67% of African American adults in Mississippi registered to vote in 1969**
- **70% of white adults registered to vote nationwide in 1964**
- **90% of white adults registered to vote nationwide in 1969**

Source: TIME.

◀ Forcing civil rights protesters to stop their marches, 1963

The Federal Government Takes a Role

Over time, more and more Americans grew sympathetic to the demands for equal rights. The federal government became an ally, passing and enforcing important new laws. These included the Civil Rights Act of 1964 and the Voting Rights Act of 1965. Presidents John F. Kennedy and Lyndon Johnson expressed sympathy for expanding and safeguarding civil rights.

Review

1. How did President Truman demonstrate important leadership for the movement for equality for all people?
2. Who would become the nation's most important civil rights leader?

1940 — 1950 — 1960 — 1970

- **1948** President Truman orders desegregation of U.S. military
- **1954** *Brown* v. *Board of Education*
- **1964** Civil Rights Act passed
- **1965** Voting Rights Act passed

Other Civil Rights Challenges

African Americans were not the only group in American society to face discrimination and inequality. Hispanics, Native Americans, and others also had to struggle to gain equal rights in the 1900s.

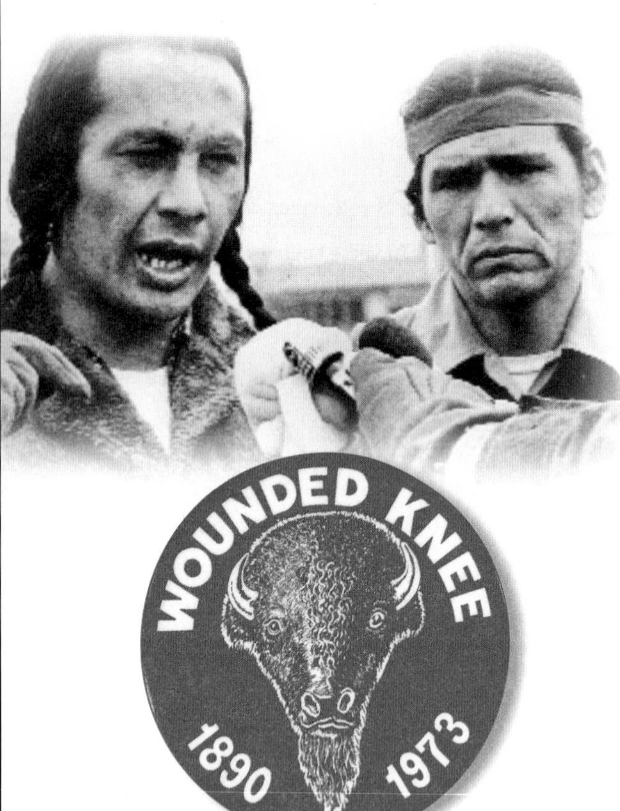

▲ The American Indian Movement protested civil rights violations.

Hispanic Americans Seek Equal Rights

Other groups soon followed African Americans in demanding equal rights. The nation's Hispanic population grew rapidly during the 1960s. Including people of Mexican, Puerto Rican, Cuban, and other backgrounds, Hispanics often faced discrimination and had to cope with limited access to housing, education, and employment.

Many Mexican Americans, the largest Hispanic group, worked on large farms in western states. These farmworkers earned little pay and received few benefits. In the mid-1960s, César Chávez and Dolores Huerta successfully organized the United Farm Workers union in California to fight for better working conditions. Another group, La Raza Unida, organized voters in the Southwest and West.

Native Americans Struggle

Like other groups in the 1950s and 1960s, Native Americans suffered from discrimination in housing, employment, and health care. They, too, began to organize to combat racism and rebuild cultural identity. The American Indian Movement (AIM) led protests, which sometimes turned violent. Working through the federal courts, Native Americans won decisions that helped them establish their economic independence.

Ethnic Groups and Equal Rights

1960 — 1970

- **1963** March on Washington for Equal Rights
- **1966** United Farm Workers formed by César Chávez and Dolores Huerta
- **1970** *La Raza Unida* formed by Jose Angel Gutierrez

A More Aggressive Approach

Most civil rights protesters followed the nonviolent teachings of Martin Luther King, Jr., and other leaders. Others, however, felt that violent opposition should be met with more aggressive methods. Leaders like Malcolm X and Stokely Carmichael endorsed an idea called Black Power, through which African Americans would build economic, political, and cultural strength. Frustration with the slow pace of improvement led to deadly riots in black neighborhoods of some large cities.

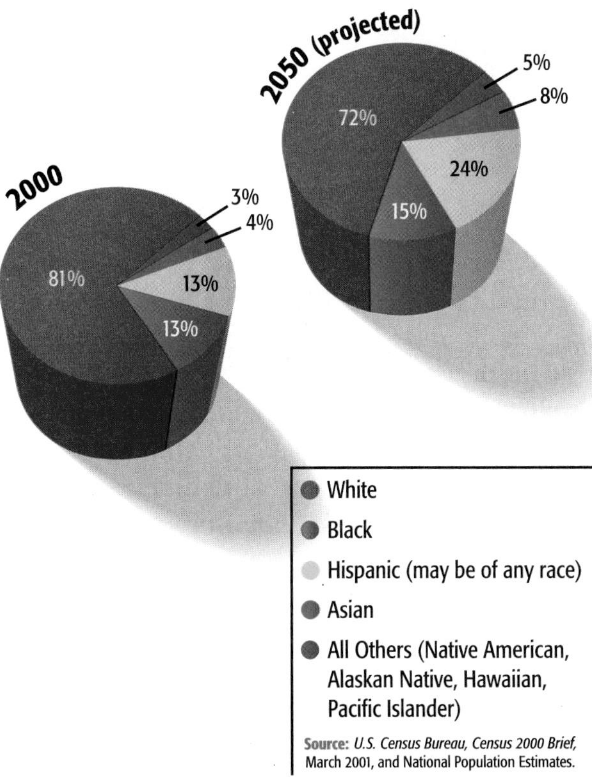

Entering a New Century

By the year 2000, America's ethnic and racial groups had achieved some remarkable successes. African Americans, Hispanics, and Asian Americans held thousands of elected offices throughout the nation. Business and educational leadership grew more diverse as well.

As the 2000s began, the United States had an increasingly diverse population. Hispanic Americans became the fastest growing ethnic group in the country, growing from 22.4 million in 1990 to 35.3 million in 2000. Increased immigration from Latin America, Asia, and Africa also had an impact on the country's population. For the first time since the early 1930s, one out of every ten Americans was foreign-born.

America has become increasingly appreciative of its multicultural heritage and respectful of diversity. Yet economic, social, and political challenges remain, and much still needs to be done.

Review

1. What did Chávez and Huerta do to aid Hispanic farmworkers?
2. How did the methods of Malcolm X and Stokely Carmichael differ from those of Martin Luther King, Jr.?
3. What challenges to civil rights still exist today? What could you do to make a difference?

1980 | 1990 | 2000

1974 Congressional act makes bilingual education available to Hispanic youth

1990 Antonia C. Novello becomes the first female and first Hispanic Surgeon General of the United States

2004 National Museum of the American Indian opens in Washington, D.C.

A Changing Society

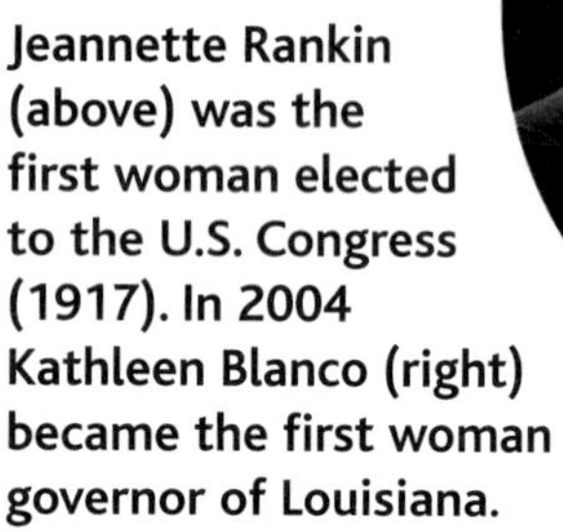

Jeannette Rankin (above) was the first woman elected to the U.S. Congress (1917). In 2004 Kathleen Blanco (right) became the first woman governor of Louisiana.

Into the Mainstream

The 1900s saw important advances in the status of women and people with disabilities. Another significant movement, with roots in the Progressive era, was environmentalism. As multiculturalism became more valued, religious distinctions were increasingly respected as well.

Women: Second-Class Citizens No More

Women pursued equal rights long before the 1900s. Early pioneers like Susan B. Anthony, Elizabeth Cady Stanton, and Lucretia Mott demanded suffrage, or voting rights. Women finally gained the right to vote in 1920, when the Nineteenth Amendment to the U.S. Constitution was approved. During the world wars, many women went to work outside the home. They began to demand the same rights and treatment as men. In the 1960s, women pressed for better educational opportunities, workplace equality and flexibility, and easier access to health care under the leadership of groups like the National Organization for Women (NOW). An Equal Rights Amendment (ERA) passed in both houses of Congress in 1972 but was never ratified by enough states to become law.

▲ **Demonstrators urging equal access for people with disabilities**

Gaining Access for All Americans

Like women, people with disabilities often could not fully participate in American life. In 1990 the Americans with Disabilities Act (ADA) outlawed discrimination against people with physical or mental disabilities. Access ramps were added to buildings, and closed-caption TV programs became common.

Protecting All Americans, 1890–Present

1890 | 1905 | 1920 | 1935

- **1890** Women have right to vote in Wyoming
- **1905** U.S. Forest Service created
- **1916** Mosque established in Detroit, Michigan
- **1920** Women gain right to vote nationally

Rise of Environmentalism

Activists in the 1960s and 1970s turned their attention to another challenge: protecting the earth's resources. Environmentalism was not new. Leaders such as Theodore Roosevelt and John Muir had warned Americans of the need to protect natural places. Groups like the Sierra Club (founded in 1892) and the U.S. Forest Service (created in 1905) worked to protect natural areas. A landmark 1962 book by Rachel Carson, *Silent Spring*, sounded an alarm about pesticides that grew into the environmental movement. Soon, the federal government, through its new Environmental Protection Agency (EPA) and laws like the Wilderness, Clean Air, and Endangered Species Acts, took on the responsibility of safeguarding the environment.

Religious Diversity

One of the founding ideals of the United States was religious tolerance. As more people immigrated to the United States, the variety of religious beliefs also grew. Today, almost every religion has followers in the United States. In the period following the terrorist attacks on New York and Washington, D.C. in 2001, Americans wanted to show their respect for all religious faiths. This marked a time of great national unity and mutual tolerance. Annually, the president recognizes January 16 as Religious Freedom Day to commemorate the passage of the 1786 Virginia Statute for Religious Freedom, written by Thomas Jefferson.

Religious Membership in the United States*

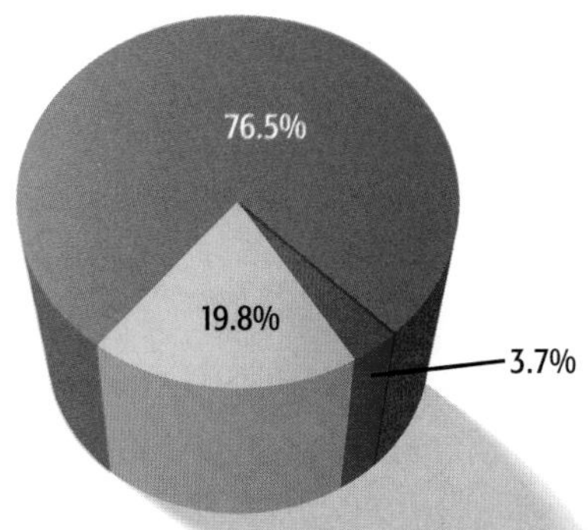

- Christian Religious Groups– more than 159 million, including:

Catholic	50.9 million
Baptist	33.8 million
Methodist/Wesleyan	14.2 million
Lutheran	9.6 million
Presbyterian	5.6 million
Pentecostal/Charismatic	4.4 million
Episcopalian/Anglican	3.5 million

- Other Religious Groups– more than 7.7 million, including:

Jewish	2.8 million
Muslim/Islamic	1.1 million
Buddhist	1.0 million

- Other/No religion specified

* Based on adult population

Source: *American Religious Identification Survey,* 2001; The Graduate Center of the City University of New York.

Review

1. What did the Americans With Disabilities Act accomplish?
2. What government agency was created to protect the environment?
3. What can you do to safeguard religious liberty?

1950 | 1965 | 1980 | 1995

1962 *Silent Spring* published by Rachel Carson

1970 Environmental Protection Agency formed

1981 Sandra Day O'Connor is first woman appointed to U.S. Supreme Court

New Roles, New Faces

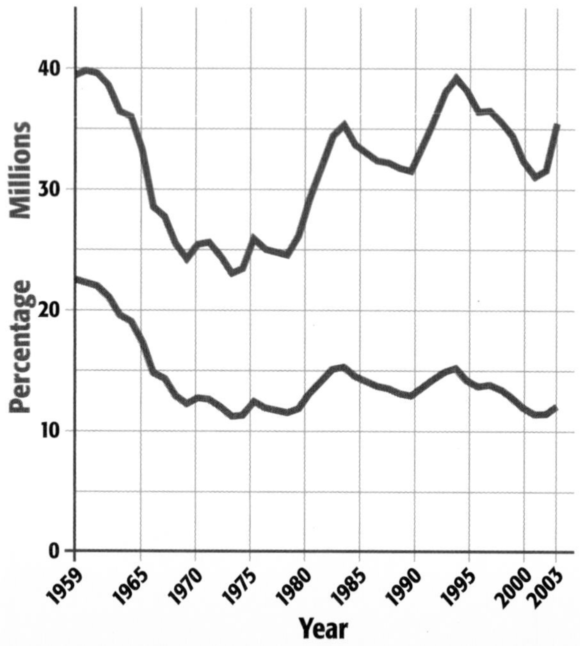

Source: U.S. Bureau of the Census.

Economic Growth

Manufacturing in the United States increased greatly in the late 1800s. During this period, the American economy changed from one that was primarily agricultural to one based on industry. The country's economy continued to grow tremendously in the 1900s.

An Industrial Powerhouse

Around the beginning of the 1900s, the United States surpassed Great Britain and Germany to become the world's leading industrial nation. By the end of the century, the U.S. economy had expanded so much that it was almost twice as large as the world's second largest, China's.

Mass production was the key to the growth of America's industrial might. This form of large-scale manufacturing increased supply and lowered costs to consumers. Thanks to Henry Ford's assembly line, automobiles became affordable for millions of consumers. His ideas were quickly put into place in other industries.

Depression and War

The production of consumer goods; heavy manufacturing; and processing of natural resources such as coal, iron, and oil grew at a rapid pace in the early 1900s. However, the Great Depression of the 1930s handcuffed the U.S. economy for a decade. Industrial production and agriculture fell steeply. Then in the early 1940s, manufacturing rebounded to supply the military during World War II.

An Expanding and Changing Economy, 1900–Present

1900 — 1915 — 1930 — 1945

- **1908** Ford's Model T is sold to the public
- **1912** Department of Labor created
- **1929** Stock market crash triggers Great Depression
- **1938** Fair Labor Standards Act passed
- **1941** U.S. enters World War II; economic growth surges

High-Tech Revolution

The 1950s and 1960s saw continued growth in the U.S. economy. In the 1970s, the nation faced economic roadblocks, such as high inflation, unemployment, and increased energy costs. By the 1980s, a new element had emerged to recharge America's economy—technology. Centered in California, the technology revolution transformed the infrastructure of business. Advances in computers, communications, and other high-tech fields led the U.S. economy—and society—into the next century.

The Income Gap Remains

Not all Americans have benefited from the expanding economy. Although the middle class has grown over the century, millions of people remain in poverty. The federal poverty level in 2003 was set at an income of $18,810 for a family of four. One in eight Americans, or 12.5 percent, lived at or below the poverty level. (See graph on page 806.) African Americans and children were more likely than others to be living in poverty.

One way the federal government has chosen to deal with poverty is the minimum wage. Since 1938, the government has required employers to pay a minimum hourly wage. (See graph above.) Today, younger workers may be paid less than minimum wage for their first 90 days on the job.

Federal Minimum Wage

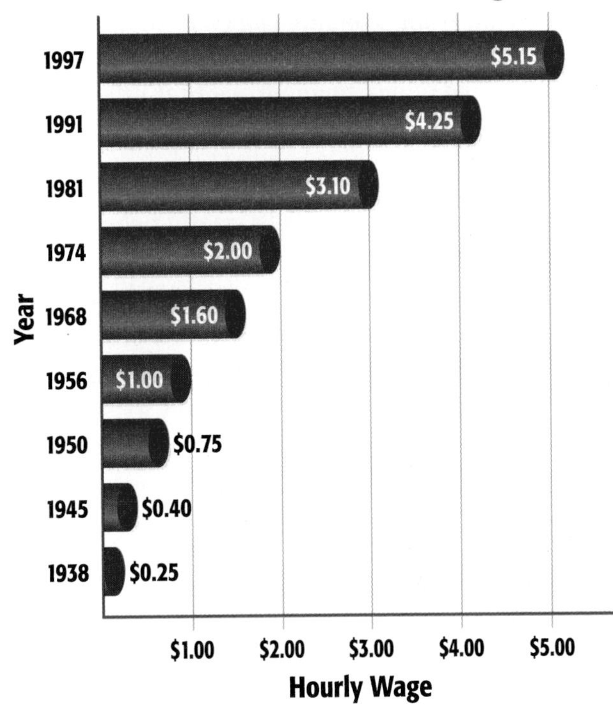

Source: http://usgovinfo.about.com/library/blminwage.htm

During the Great Depression, many Americans could not find work.

Review

1. What was the technology revolution?
2. About how many Americans live at or below the federal poverty level?
3. Why has American industry changed so much over the past century?

1960 1975 1990 2005

1970s Oil embargo and inflation hurt U.S. economy

1975 First personal computers are sold

1994 NAFTA creates huge free trade zone

Changing Nature of Work

As the American economy changed, so did the way the people of the United States worked. In the 1900s, the types of jobs held by most workers shifted from jobs that created goods to positions that offered services.

Moving to the Cities

At the beginning of the 1900s, many people were still moving from farms to the rapidly growing cities. Improved farm machinery made it possible to grow more crops using fewer workers. The higher wages paid in the cities also attracted workers. Many of those moving to the cities found work in newly opened factories. These workers became known as blue collar workers. Others found jobs in offices, schools, stores, and other nonfactory settings and were called white collar workers. By 1920 more than half of all Americans lived in towns or cities.

The Service Economy

Another significant change that took place during the twentieth century was the shift from manufacturing jobs to service industry jobs. Service jobs are those that provide services to people and businesses. They include banking and insurance, communications, retail sales, health care, education, and government. Today, most of the total economic activity of California and much of the United States is made up of this type of business.

▼ America's workforce is diverse with jobs in many different fields.

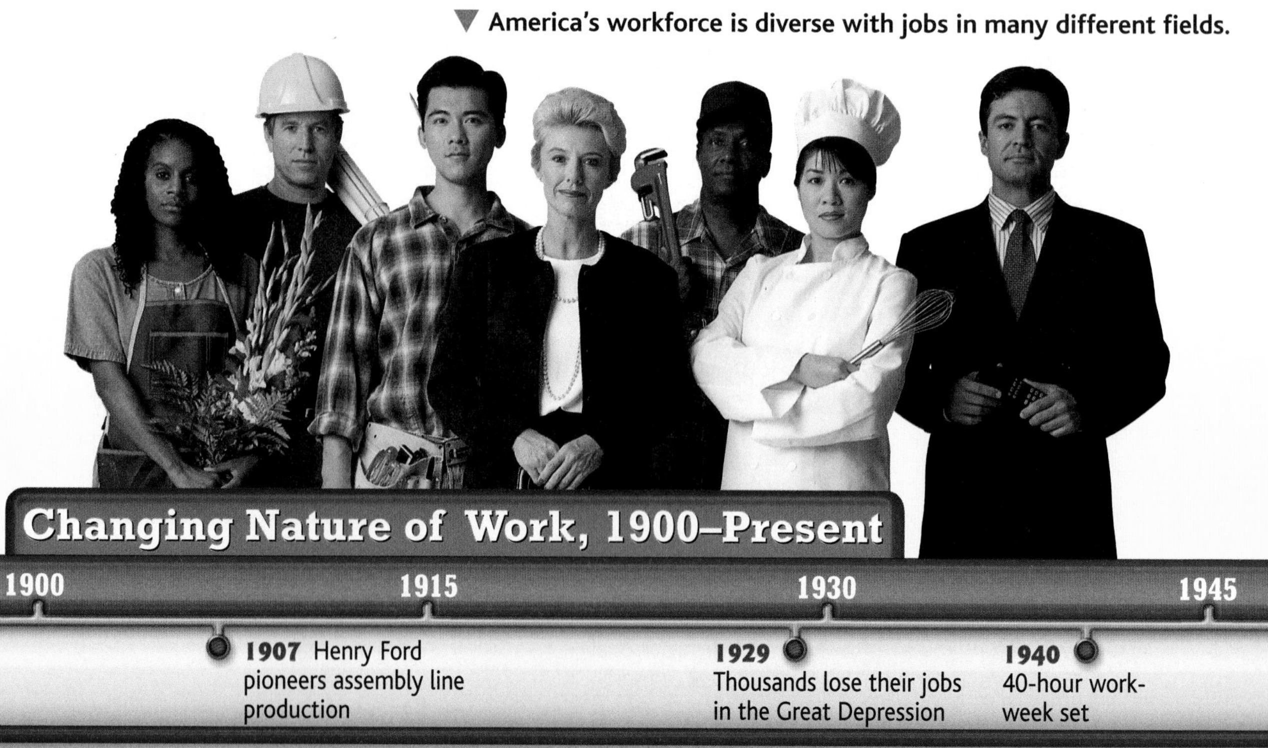
Changing Nature of Work, 1900–Present
1900
1915
1930
1945
1907 Henry Ford pioneers assembly line production
1929 Thousands lose their jobs in the Great Depression
1940 40-hour work-week set

Number of Employees in Selected Professions, 1910 and 2002

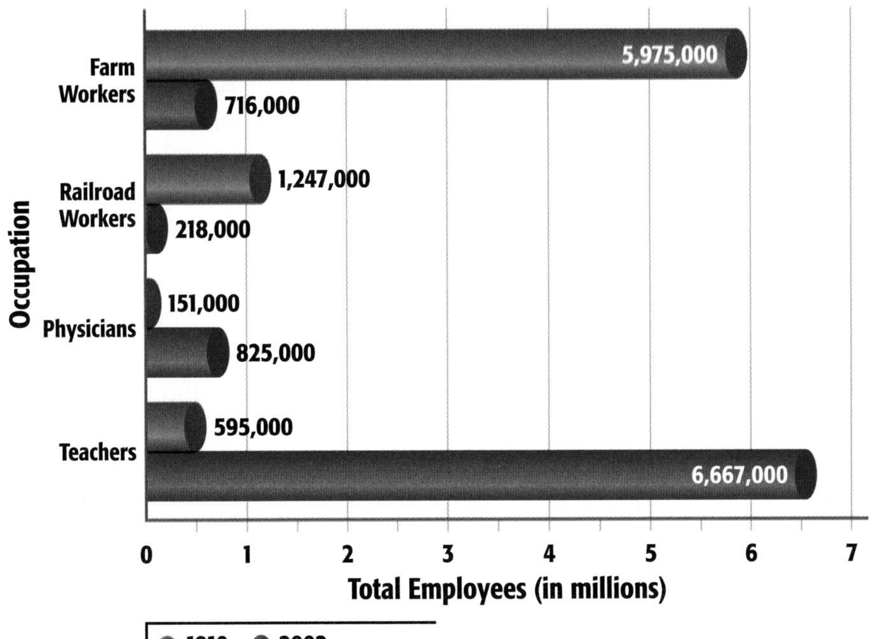

1910 2002

Sources: *Historical Statistics of the United States; Statistical Abstract of the United States,* 2003.

▼ World War II created opportunities for women.

Women Enter the Work Force

During the last century, many women entered the full-time workforce during economic boom times and especially during the two world wars. Often, these women would have to give up their jobs in order to make room for men needing work. Beginning in the 1960s, the women's liberation movement created a broader understanding of women's roles in the workplace. Many more women entered the working world, and they began to rise into positions that had not been possible before. Still, women generally earn less than men in the same profession. Today women are free to pursue their dreams in education, career, and family in ways that would have been hard to imagine in the past.

Review

1. What is the difference between jobs in manufacturing and in the service industry?
2. Why did so many people leave farming as a way of life?

1960 | 1975 | 1990 | 2005

1956 White-collar workers outnumber blue-collar workers for the first time

1970 About 86 million people are in the U.S. workforce

1999 About 140 million people are in the U.S. workforce

2003 Women make up about 47% of the workforce

Changes in Education

The changes in American society and the economy also led to changes in education in the United States. Americans realized that success in an increasingly industrial and technological society required a higher level of education for all citizens.

Increases in School Enrollment

By 1900, the United States achieved the goal of providing public elementary education to all children. At that time, however, only a small number of teenagers went on to high school or college. One major development in education was the dramatic rise in high school and college enrollment. Today, about 53 million students are enrolled in the nation's public and private schools. Another 15.3 million attend colleges and universities.

High School Enrollment

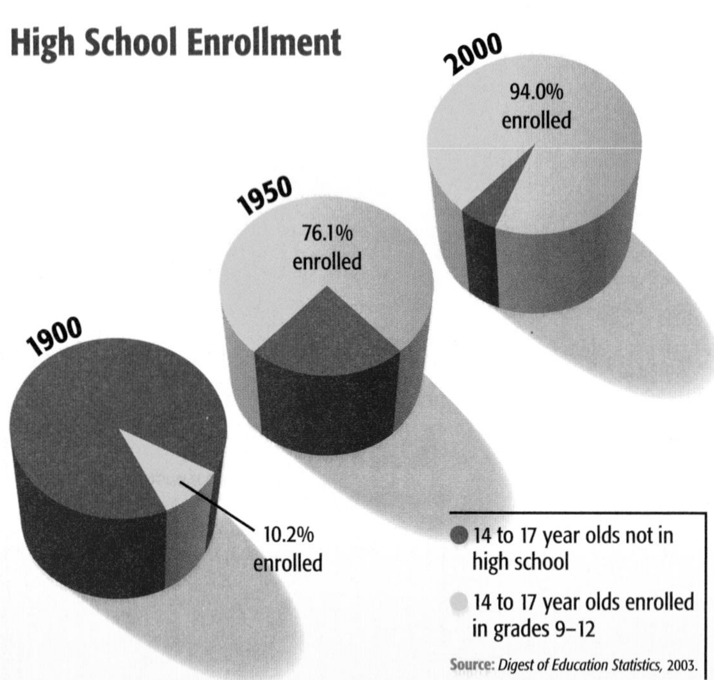

Source: *Digest of Education Statistics*, 2003.

Changes in the Classroom

The early 1900s brought far-reaching changes to public school education in the United States. Most students studied only reading, writing, and arithmetic. In the 1900s, schools became less formal and emphasized a well-rounded education that was able to meet the needs of individual children. Subjects were broadened to include geography, history, and science.

By 2000, technological advances promised more breakthroughs in education. Computers were increasingly common in schools. Technology made it possible for students to have access to more information than ever before. Students became empowered to learn on their own as well as in the classroom.

Changing Nature of Education, 1900–Present

1900 | 1915 | 1930 | 1945

1900 16.9 million children in U.S. public and private schools

1917 Smith-Hughes Act passed, providing federal funds for high school vocational education

Education and Government

Public education in the United States has historically been the responsibility of state and local governments. The federal government has expanded its role in education since the mid-1900s. It worked to ensure that every state provides equal educational opportunities for all citizens. In the mid-1950s, the U.S. Supreme Court ruled that public schools segregated by race were "inherently unequal" and ordered desegregation of schools. This ruling led to other measures to ensure equal educational opportunities for women, people with disabilities, and people who do not speak English.

Government has provided large amounts of money for education. This trend started after World War II, when Congress began granting funds to armed forces veterans to attend colleges and other schools. In the 1960s, Congress began passing laws to aid local schools and to improve the education of children from low-income families.

Since the 1980s, government leaders have worked to raise educational standards. In 2001 the No Child Left Behind Act introduced new federal requirements for student testing and measures for holding schools accountable for student progress.

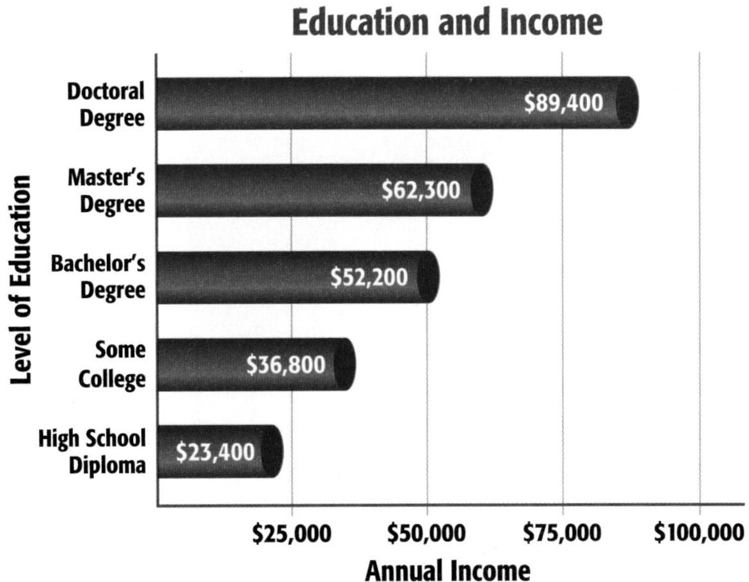

Source: National Center for Education Statistics.

Education and Income

As more Americans enrolled in schools during the twentieth century, education became a powerful social and economic force. Most Americans now expect schools to provide children with skills, values, and behaviors that will help them become responsible and productive citizens. Statistics show that people with a higher level of education make more money than those with less education.

Review

1. How did the classes taught in schools change in the 1900s?
2. How has the federal government increased its role in education?
3. Do you think the educational system prepares a person well for a role in society today? Explain.

1960 | 1975 | 1990 | 2005

1954 U.S. Supreme Court declares segregated schools unconstitutional

1979 Congress establishes the U.S. Department of Education

2001 No Child Left Behind Act passes

Rights and Responsibilities

Our System of Taxation

It is the combination of rights and responsibilities that characterizes what it means to be a citizen of a free and democratic society. As citizens, we are free to exercise our rights. In return, we are expected to fulfill certain responsibilities. One of a citizen's responsibilities is paying his or her fair share of taxes.

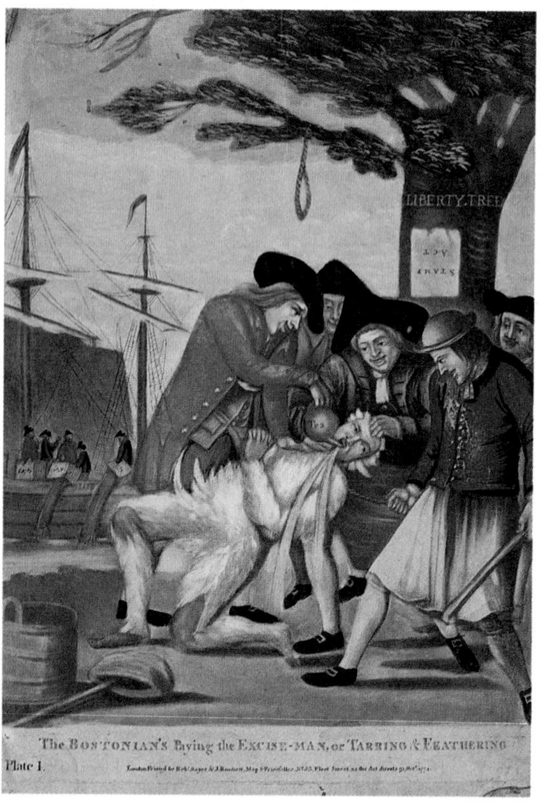

LIBERTY TREE
The BOSTONIAN'S Paying the EXCISE-MAN, or TARRING & FEATHERING
Plate I.

▲ American colonists protested against British taxes.

Paying Taxes

Taxes have been with us since the founding of our nation. British taxes that the colonists considered unfair were major causes of the American Revolution. Until the beginning of the 1900s, taxes were relatively low, as was government spending. Then, in 1913 the Sixteenth Amendment to the Constitution was passed. It allowed the federal government to tax the incomes of individuals and businesses. Since that time, income tax rates have gone up and down. This kind of tax, however, has been the government's primary way to get money to pay for its programs.

How Do Governments Pay for Their Programs?

Governments collect other kinds of taxes and fees as well. Social Security and Medicare taxes pay for retirement and medical benefits for older people. Most states, including California, use a sales tax to earn money. Real estate property taxes usually help pay for local schools. Excise taxes are special taxes that are attached to specific items. Tariffs are a kind of tax paid by foreign companies on goods they export to the United States. Poll taxes are taxes people pay to vote. These were made illegal in 1964 by the passage of the Twenty-fourth Amendment.

Taxation, 1900–Present

1900 — 1915 — 1930 — 1945

1913 Sixteenth Amendment gives U.S. government the power to tax incomes

1935 Tax levied on employers and workers to fund Social Security

What Is Service Learning?

Performing important tasks that meet real community needs forms the basis of service learning. Service learning projects can be organized as a partnership between your school and your community. Examples of these projects are refurbishing parks, teaching younger children to read, and sharing your time with nursing home residents. Service learning requires an investment of your time as well as your talents. You and your team play an active role in planning the project and deciding how to use your skills and talents to complete your tasks.

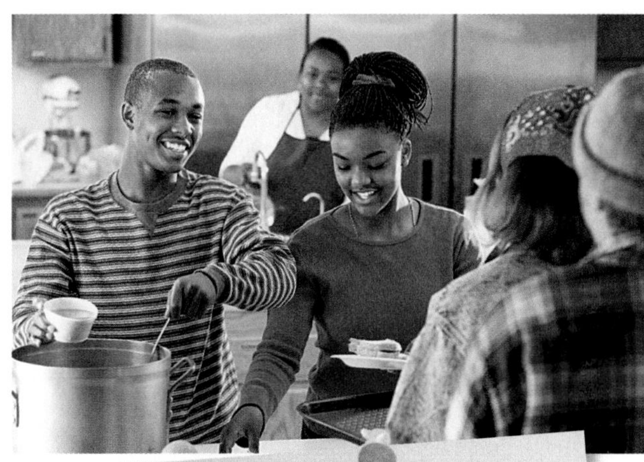

Why Should I Participate?

You can make a difference. Share your knowledge and skills to help others in your school and community. You will cultivate new knowledge and develop new skills. A well-planned project gives you opportunities to practice your rights and responsibilities as a citizen. You take part in setting the goals of the project. You decide what you will do and how you will do it. An effective service learning project also provides time to share your thoughts about the service experience with others.

When you take part in your community and civic life, you not only help others, you also protect your rights. Supreme Court Justice Learned Hand expressed this view during an "I Am An American Day" celebration in 1944. His words are just as true today:

"Liberty lies in the hearts of men and women; when it dies there, no Constitution, no court, can even do much to help it."

Volunteer Opportunities

- ✓ Read to an elderly person
- ✓ Collect litter in your school yard
- ✓ Recycle at home
- ✓ Circulate a petition
- ✓ Put up a poster announcing Earth Day
- ✓ Bring groceries to a shut in

How Do I Get Involved?

Many students are already taking part in service learning. National organizations such as AmeriCorps and Learn and Serve America are always looking for volunteers. Forty-eight states are administering service learning programs through their state education agencies, and at least 64 percent of all public schools had students participating in community service activities recognized by the schools. By exploring the needs of your community, you can plan and organize your own service learning project.

Review

1. What is service learning?
2. Why should you get involved in your community?
3. How could your community be positively impacted by increased participation by its citizens?

Appendix

Contents

What Is an Appendix?

An appendix is the additional material you often find at the end of books. The following information will help you learn how to use the Appendix in **Discovering Our Past: The American Journey to World War I.**

SkillBuilder Handbook

The **SkillBuilder Handbook** offers you information and practice using critical thinking and social studies skills. Mastering these skills will help you in all your courses.

Presidents of the United States

In this resource you will find information of interest on each of the nation's **presidents.**

Supreme Court Case Summaries

The **Supreme Court Case Summaries** discuss important Supreme Court cases. The summaries are listed in alphabetical order and include a summary of the facts of the case and its impact.

Documents of American History

This collection contains some of the most important writings in American history. Each **document** begins with an introduction that describes the author and places the selection within its historical context.

California Standards Handbook

Take time to review what you have learned in this book by using the **California Standards Handbook.** The handbook lists all the content standards listed in each chapter and challenges you with a question about each.

Glossary

A **glossary** is a list of important or difficult terms found in a textbook. Since words sometimes have other meanings, you may wish to consult a dictionary to find other uses for the term. The glossary gives a definition of each term as it is used in the book. The glossary also includes page numbers telling you where in the textbook the term is used.

Spanish Glossary

A **Spanish glossary** contains everything that an English glossary does, but it is in Spanish.

Gazetteer

A **gazetteer** (GA • **zuh** • **TIHR**) is a geographical dictionary. It lists some of the largest countries, cities, and several important geographic features. Each entry also includes a page number telling where this place is mentioned in this book.

Index

An **index** is an alphabetical listing that includes the subjects of the book and the page numbers where those subjects can be found. The index in this book also lets you know that certain pages contain maps, graphs, photos, or paintings about the subject.

Acknowledgements and Photo Credits

This section lists literary credits and/or photo credits for the book. You can look at this section to find out where the publisher of this textbook obtained the permission to use excerpts from other books or a photograph.

Test Yourself

Use the Appendix to answer these questions.

1. Who was the sixth president of the United States?
2. What was the Supreme Court's decision in *Marbury* v. *Madison*?
3. What was the purpose of issuing the Seneca Falls Declaration?
4. California standard US8.9.2 deals with the ending of slavery in early state constitutions. Where does this textbook discuss that topic?
5. What does the expression "favorite son" mean?

SkillBuilder Handbook

Contents

Taking Notes and Outlining

Why Learn This Skill?

One of the best ways to remember something is to write it down. Taking notes—writing down information in a brief and orderly form—not only helps you remember, but it also makes your studying easier.

1 Learning the Skill

There are several styles of note taking, but all explain and put information in a logical order. As you read, identify and summarize the main ideas and details that support them and write them in your notes. Paraphrase, or state in your own words, the information rather than copying it directly from the text. Using note cards or developing a personal "shorthand"—using symbols to represent words—can help.

You may also find it helpful to create an outline when taking notes. When outlining written material, first read the material to identify the main ideas. In textbooks, section headings provide clues to main topics. Then identify the subheadings. Place supporting details under the appropriate heading. The basic pattern for outlines is as follows:

Main Topic
- I. First idea or item
  - A. First detail
    - 1. Subdetail
    - 2. Subdetail
  - B. Second detail
- II. Second idea or item
  - A. First detail
  - B. Second detail
    - 1. Subdetail
    - 2. Subdetail
- III. Third idea or item, and so forth

2 Practicing the Skill

Look back at Chapter 6, Section 2. Take notes about the section and use these notes to create an outline of the main ideas, as shown at the bottom of the left column.

3 Applying the Skill

Scan a local newspaper for a short editorial or article about your local government. Take notes by using shorthand or by creating an outline. Summarize the article, using only your notes.

Reading a Time Line

Why Learn this Skill?

Knowing the relationship of time to events is important in studying history. A time line is a visual way to show the flow of dates and events. On most time lines, years are evenly spaced. For example, a time line showing 1,000 years might be divided into ten 100-year sections. Each event on a time line appears beside the date when the event took place.

1 Learning the Skill

To read a time line, follow these steps:

- Find the dates on the opposite ends of the time line to know the time span. Also note the intervals between dates on the time line.
- Study the order of events.
- Analyze relationships among events or look for trends.

Magellan

2 Practicing the Skill

Analyze the time line about Magellan, which is at the bottom of the page. Use the time line to answer the questions below.

1. What time span is represented?
2. How many years does each of the sections represent?
3. Did Magellan's voyage to the Spice Islands occur before or after his voyage to the Philippines?
4. How long did it take for Magellan's men to go around the world?

3 Applying the Skill

List 10 key events that have occurred in your life and the dates on which these events occurred. Write the events in chronological order on a time line.

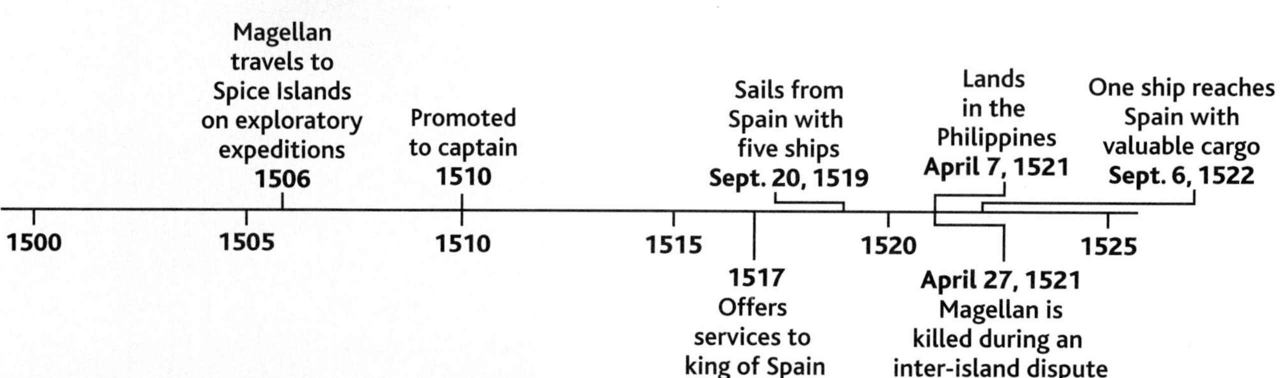
Magellan travels to Spice Islands on exploratory expeditions 1506
Promoted to captain 1510
Sails from Spain with five ships Sept. 20, 1519
Lands in the Philippines April 7, 1521
One ship reaches Spain with valuable cargo Sept. 6, 1522
1500
1505
1510
1515
1520
1525
1517 Offers services to king of Spain
April 27, 1521 Magellan is killed during an inter-island dispute

Understanding the Parts of a Map

Why Learn This Skill?

Maps can direct you down the street or around the world. There are as many different kinds of maps as there are uses for them. Being able to read a map begins with learning about its parts.

1 Learning the Skill

Maps usually include a key, a compass rose, and a scale bar. The map key explains the meaning of special colors, symbols, and lines used on the map.

After reading the map key, look for the compass rose. It is the direction marker that shows the cardinal directions of north, south, east, and west.

A measuring line, often called a scale bar, helps you estimate distance on a map. The map's scale tells you what distance on the earth is represented by the measurement on the scale bar. For example, 1 inch (2.54 cm) on the map may represent 100 miles (160.9 km) on the earth.

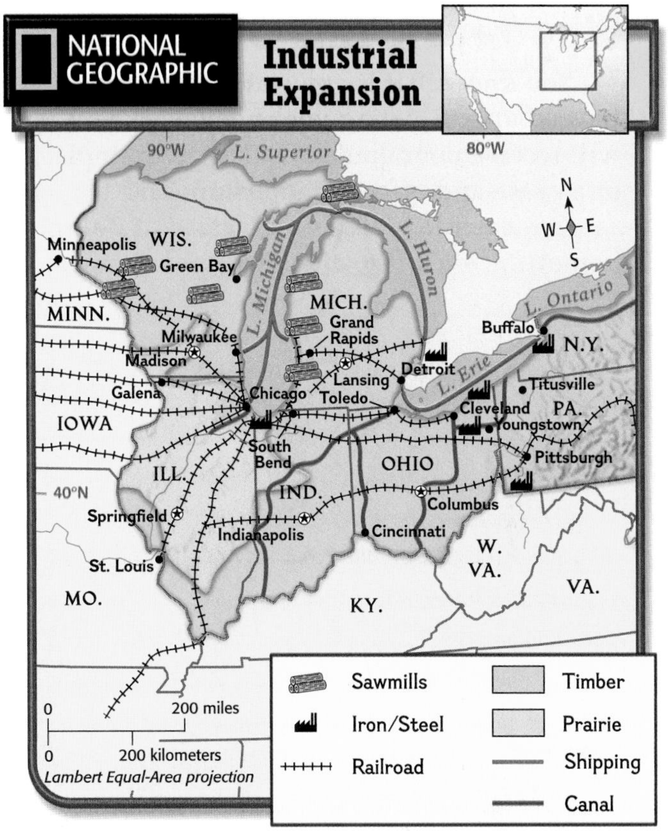

NATIONAL GEOGRAPHIC **Industrial Expansion**

2 Practicing the Skill

The map on this page shows industrial expansion in the late 1800s. Look at the parts of this map, and then answer the questions that follow.

1. What information is given in the key?
2. Which states have the most sawmills?
3. What direction would you travel from Springfield, Illinois, to Columbus, Ohio?
4. About how many miles is the route from Pittsburgh to Chicago?

3 Applying the Skill

Picture a mental image of your house or room. Draw a map showing the location of various areas. Include a map key explaining any symbols or colors you use. Also include a scale bar explaining the size of your map compared to the real area. Finally, add a compass rose and title to your map.

Understanding Cause and Effect

Why Learn This Skill?

You know that if you watch television instead of completing your homework you will receive poor grades. This is an example of a cause-and-effect relationship. The cause—watching television instead of doing homework—leads to an effect—poor grades.

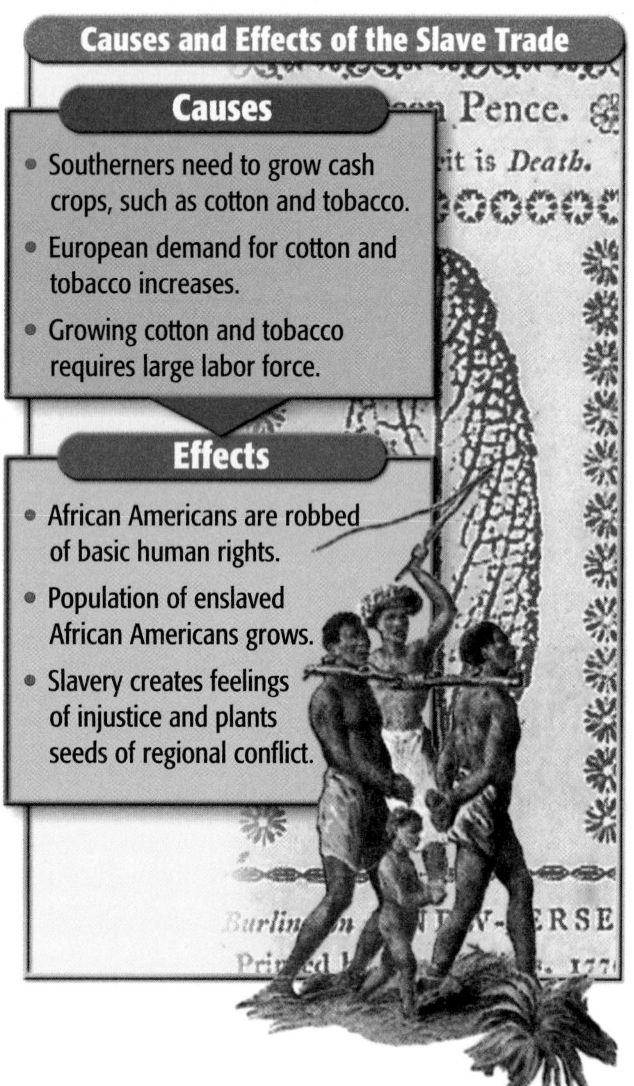

Causes and Effects of the Slave Trade
Causes
• Southerners need to grow cash crops, such as cotton and tobacco.
• European demand for cotton and tobacco increases.
• Growing cotton and tobacco requires large labor force.
Effects
• African Americans are robbed of basic human rights.
• Population of enslaved African Americans grows.
• Slavery creates feelings of injustice and plants seeds of regional conflict.
Pence.
it is Death.

1 Learning the Skill

A *cause* is any person, event, or condition that makes something happen. What happens as a result is known as an *effect*.

These guidelines will help you identify cause and effect.

- Identify two or more events.
- Ask questions about why events occur.
- Look for "clue words" that alert you to cause and effect, such as *because, led to, brought about, produced,* and *therefore.*
- Identify the outcome of events.

2 Practicing the Skill

Study the cause-and-effect chart about the slave trade on this page. Think about the guidelines listed. Then answer the questions below.

1. What were some causes of the development of slavery in the South?
2. What were some of the short-term, or immediate, effects of enslaving Africans?
3. Read the second cause and second effect on the chart. How might these events be related?

3 Applying the Skill

Read an account of a recent event or chain of events in your community newspaper. Determine at least one cause and one effect of that event. Show the cause-and-effect relationship in a chart.

Making Comparisons

Why Learn This Skill?

Suppose you want to buy a portable compact disc (CD) player, and you must choose among three models. You would probably compare characteristics of the three models, such as price, sound quality, and size to figure out which model is best for you. When you study American history, you often compare people or events from one time period with those from a different time period.

1 Learning the Skill

When making comparisons, you examine two or more groups, situations, events, or documents. Then you identify similarities and differences. For example, the chart on this page compares two documents, specifically the powers each gave the federal government.

When making comparisons, you first decide what items will be compared and determine which characteristics you will use to compare them. Then you identify similarities and differences in these characteristics.

2 Practicing the Skill

Analyze the information on the chart on this page. Then answer the following questions.

1. What items are being compared?
2. Which document allowed the government to use state militias?
3. Which document allowed the government to regulate trade?
4. In what ways are the two documents different?
5. In what ways are the two documents similar?

Powers of the Federal Government

	Articles of Confederation	United States Constitution
Declare war; make peace	✔	✔
Coin money	✔	✔
Manage foreign affairs	✔	✔
Establish a postal system	✔	✔
Impose taxes		✔
Regulate trade		✔
Organize a court system		✔
Call state militias for service		✔
Protect copyrights		✔
Take other necessary actions to run the federal government		✔

3 Applying the Skill

On the editorial page of your local newspaper, find two letters to the editor that express different viewpoints on the same issue. Read the letters and identify the similarities and differences between the two points of view.

Drawing Inferences and Conclusions

Why Learn This Skill?

Have you ever heard someone say, "You can't judge him on face value"? It means that people, things you see, or things you read might not be as they appear to be. There might be a double or hidden meaning to what you see or hear.

1 Learning the Skill

To infer means to evaluate information and arrive at a conclusion. Inferences are ideas that are not directly stated. Making inferences involves reading between the lines to interpret what you are reading. You must then use your own knowledge and common sense to draw a conclusion.

Use the following steps to help you draw inferences and make conclusions:

- Read carefully for stated facts and ideas.
- Apply related information that you may already know to make inferences.
- Use your knowledge and insight to develop conclusions about these facts.

James Madison

2 Practicing the Skill

Read the passage below and answer the questions that follow.

Quite often the British would lie in wait for American ships outside an American harbor. This happened in June 1807 off the coast of Virginia. A British warship, the *Leopard,* intercepted the American vessel *Chesapeake* and demanded to search it for British deserters. When the captain of the *Chesapeake* refused, the British opened fire, killing 3, wounding 18, and crippling the American ship.

As news of the attack spread, Americans reacted with an anti-British fury not seen since the Revolutionary War. Secretary of State James Madison called the attack an outrage.

1. What facts are given in the passage?
2. What can you infer about James Madison's political policy regarding Britain?
3. Knowing what you know about this period in America's past, what conclusions can you draw about how this incident relates to British and U.S. relations?

3 Applying the Skill

Choose a poem, or a quote found in a newspaper, that you think has more than one meaning. Share your selection with a classmate. Ask your classmate to infer the hidden meaning.

Predicting Consequences

Why Learn This Skill?

Did you ever wish you could see into the future? Predicting future events is very difficult. You can, however, develop skills that will help you identify the logical consequences of decisions or actions.

1 Learning the Skill

As you read in your book, think about what might come next. What you think will happen is your prediction. What happens as a result of an event is called a consequence.

Follow these steps to help you accurately predict consequences.

- Review what you already know by listing facts, events, and people's responses. The list will help you recall events and how they affected people.
- Ask yourself what prior knowledge you have about the events that are described.
- Use your knowledge and observations of similar situations. In other words, ask yourself, "What were the consequences of a similar decision or action that occurred in the past?"
- Map out all possible consequences or outcomes. Analyze each of the potential consequences by asking, "How likely is it that this will occur?"

2 Practicing the Skill

Read the paragraphs at the top of the next column. They are about the first presidency under the new Constitution. Then answer the questions that follow.

The new United States government faced many challenges during Washington's presidency. To limit the growing debt, Alexander Hamilton proposed the repayment of bonds issued during the American Revolution, the creation of a national bank, and the imposition of taxes on whiskey and other merchandise.

Each of these proposals encountered opposition. Southern states had amassed less debt during the war than Northern states. The Southern states felt that they would be paying more than their share to help end the debt. Many Americans feared that the creation of a national bank would take power away from state governments and make the rich wealthier. The tax on whiskey caused problems for farmers who lived by bartering and could not pay a monetary tax. While Washington and Hamilton were able to compromise with the opposition on most of these proposals, discontent still existed among many in the new United States.

1. Predict what you think is most likely to occur between discontented Americans and the government.
2. Explain why you made the prediction that you did.

3 Applying the Skill

Read newspapers for articles about an event that affects your community. Make an educated prediction about what will happen. Explain your reasoning.

Sequencing and Categorizing Information

Why Learn This Skill?

Sequencing is placing facts in the order in which they happened. Categorizing means grouping information by related facts and ideas. Both help you organize large quantities of information.

1 Learning the Skill

Follow these steps to learn sequencing and categorizing skills.

- When sequencing look for dates or clue words that describe chronological order: *in 2004, the late 1900s, first, then, finally, after,* and so on.
- Sequencing can be seen in time lines or graphs where information covers several years.
- To put information in categories, look for topics and facts that can be grouped together with similar characteristics. If the information is about farming, one category might be *tools of farming*.
- List these categories, or characteristics, as the headings on a chart.
- As you read, look for details and fill them in under the proper categories on the chart.

◀ Immigrants from China and Japan arrived in the late 1800s.

2 Practicing the Skill

Read the passages below and then answer the questions that follow.

- Before 1865 most immigrants to the United States—except for the enslaved—came from northern and western Europe.
- In the mid-1880s the pattern of immigration started to change. Large groups of "new" immigrants arrived from eastern and southern Europe.
- By 1907 only about 20 percent of immigrants came from northern and western Europe, while 80 percent came from southern and eastern Europe.
- After 1900 immigration from Mexico also increased. In addition many people came to the United States from China and Japan.

1. What information can be organized by sequencing?
2. What categories could you use to organize the information in the above list? What facts could be placed under each category?

3 Applying the Skill

Look at the Geographic Dictionary on pages 46–47. Record terms that would fit into the category "bodies of water." Also, find two newspaper articles about a local issue. Sequence or categorize the information in a chart.

Writing a Paragraph

Why Learn This Skill?

Paragraphs are the building blocks of an essay or other composition. Each paragraph is a unit—a group of sentences about a single topic or idea.

1 Learning the Skill

Most well-written paragraphs share four characteristics.

1. First, a paragraph expresses one main idea or is about one subject. A topic sentence states that main idea. The topic sentence may be located at the beginning, the middle, or the end of a paragraph.
2. Second, the rest of the sentences in a paragraph support the main idea. The main idea may be developed by facts, examples, and reasons.
3. Third, the sentences are arranged in a logical order.
4. Fourth, transitional words link sentences within the paragraph. These words can also link one paragraph with the next. Examples include *next, then, finally, also, because, however,* and *as a result.*

2 Practicing the Skill

Use the following sentences to build a paragraph containing a topic sentence and other sentences that give supporting details. Put the sentences in a logical order and add transitional words if you need to. Underline your topic sentence.

- Many such women became role models.
- Women also gained more free time as technology made housework easier.
- Their responsibilities at home lessened as families became smaller, more children spent the day at school, and men worked away from home.
- The situation of middle-class women changed during the late 1800s.
- Many more middle-class women were gaining higher education.
- These changes created the "new women"—a popular term for educated, up-to-date women who pursued interests outside of their homes.
- Many leaders of the urban reform movement were middle-class women.

3 Applying the Skill

Choose a topic concerning the Progressive Movement and write a paragraph about it. Then rewrite the paragraph with its sentences out of order. Exchange papers with a classmate. Have him or her find the topic sentence.

A suffragist asking for the right to vote

Analyzing Information

Why Learn This Skill?

Have you ever heard someone say, "Don't believe everything you read"? To be an informed citizen, you have to analyze information carefully as you read to make sure you understand the meaning and the intent of the writer.

1 Learning the Skill

Follow these steps to learn how to analyze.

- Identify the subject or topic of the information.
- How is the information organized? What are the main points?
- Think about how reliable the source of the information is.
- Summarize the information in your own words. Does the information agree with or contradict something you already know?

Kit Carson

2 Practicing the Skill

Read the paragraph below that is from a Public Broadcasting System biography of Kit Carson. Then answer the questions that follow.

As was the case with many white trappers, Carson became somewhat integrated into the Indian world; he traveled and lived extensively among Indians, and his first two wives were Arapahoe and Cheyenne women. Carson was evidently unusual among trappers, however, for his self-restraint and temperate lifestyle. "Clean as a hound's tooth," according to one acquaintance, and a man whose "word was as sure as the sun comin' up." He was noted for an unassuming manner and implacable [firm] courage.

1. Was the information easy to understand? Explain.
2. Consider the source of the information. Does that make it seem more valid or less valid? Why?
3. Summarize the paragraph in a sentence of your own.
4. What is the main point of the paragraph?

3 Applying the Skill

Choose an article from a news magazine. Read it and analyze the information. Answer questions 1–4 as they apply to the article.

Distinguishing Fact From Opinion

Why Learn This Skill?

Suppose a friend says, "Our school's basketball team is awesome. That's a fact." Actually, it is not a fact; it is an opinion. Knowing how to tell the difference between a fact and an opinion can help you analyze the accuracy of political claims, advertisements, and many other kinds of statements.

1 Learning the Skill

A fact answers a specific question such as: What happened? Who did it? When and where did it happen? Why did it happen? Statements of fact can be checked for accuracy and proven.

An opinion, on the other hand, expresses beliefs, feelings, and judgments. Although it may reflect someone's thoughts, it is not possible to prove or disprove it.

An opinion often begins with phrases such as *I believe, I think, probably, it seems to me,* or *in my opinion.* It often contains words such as *might, could, should,* and *ought* and superlatives such as *best, worst,* and *greatest.* Judgment words that express approval or disapproval—such as *good, bad, poor,* and *satisfactory*—also usually indicate an opinion.

To distinguish between a fact and an opinion, ask yourself these questions:

- Does this statement give specific information about an event?
- Can I check the accuracy of this statement?
- Does this statement express someone's feelings, beliefs, or judgment?
- Does the statement include phrases such as *I believe,* superlatives, or judgment words?

2 Practicing the Skill

Read each numbered statement below. Tell whether each is a fact or an opinion, and explain how you arrived at your answer.

1. Paul Revere rode to Lexington with the news that the British soldiers were coming.
2. The British were the most feared soldiers in the world at that time.
3. The Daughters of Liberty opposed the Tea Act of 1773.
4. The Boston Tea Party raiders should have sunk the tea ships.
5. George III was a foolish king.

▲ Paul Revere's Ride

3 Applying the Skill

Analyze 10 advertisements. List the topics of each and at least three facts and three opinions presented in the ads.

Recognizing Bias

Why Learn This Skill?

Cats make better pets than dogs. If you say this, then you are stating a bias. A bias is a prejudice. It can prevent you from looking at a situation in a reasonable or truthful way. Recognizing bias will help you judge the accuracy of what you read.

1 Learning the Skill

Each of us has feelings and ideas that affect our point of view. Our opinions, or biases, influence how we interpret events. Therefore, an idea that is stated as a fact may really be only an opinion. There are several clues to look for in order to recognize an author's bias.

- Identify the author and examine his or her views and possible reasons for writing the material.
- Look for language that reflects an emotion or opinion—words such as *all, never, best, worst, might,* or *should.*
- Examine the writing for imbalances—discussing only one viewpoint and failing to provide equal coverage for other possible viewpoints.

◀ William McKinley

2 Practicing the Skill

In the excerpt below, President William McKinley explains his decision to annex—add to U.S. territories—the Philippines. Read the excerpt. Answer the questions that follow.

> I walked the floor of the White House night after night until midnight; and I am not ashamed to tell you gentlemen, that I went down on my knees and prayed [to] Almighty God for light and guidance more than one night. And one night late it came to me this way—I don't know how it was, but it came. . . . [T]hat there was nothing left for us to do but to take them all, and to educate the Filipinos, and uplift and civilize and Christianize them, and by God's grace do the very best we could by them, as our fellow-men for whom Christ also died. . . , and the next morning I sent for the chief engineer of the War Department (our map-maker), and I told him to put the Philippines on the map of the United States. . . , and there they will stay while I am President!

1. Imperialism consists of the actions one nation takes to control a weaker nation. Is McKinley stating a pro- or anti-imperialist bias? Which statements indicate bias?
2. What is the main reason McKinley wants to annex the Philippines?
3. What might people today think of this speech?

3 Applying the Skill

Look through the letters to the editor in your local newspaper. Write a short report analyzing one of the letters for evidence of bias.

Analyzing Library and Research Resources

Why Learn This Skill?

Imagine that your teacher has sent you to the library to write a report on the history of the Civil War. Knowing how to choose good sources for your research will help you save time in the library and write a better report.

1 Learning the Skill

Not all sources will be useful for your report on the Civil War. Even some sources that involve topics about the Civil War will not always provide the information you want. In analyzing sources for your research project, choose items that are nonfiction and that contain the most information about your topic.

When choosing research resources ask yourself these questions:

- Is the information up-to-date?
- Does the index have several pages listed for the topic?
- Is the resource written in a way that is easy to understand?
- Are there helpful illustrations and photos?

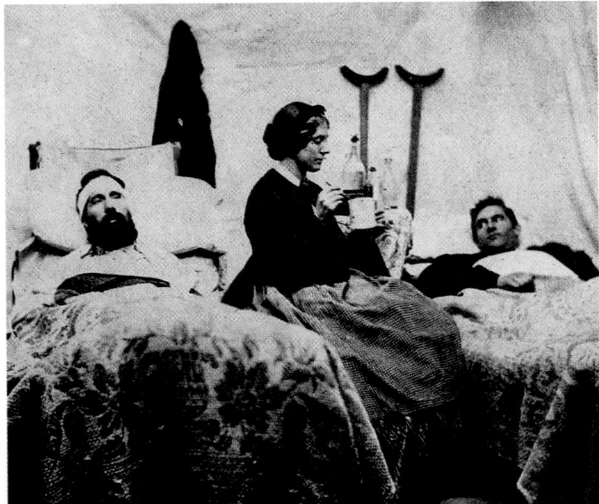

Women made dramatic contributions to the Civil War by acting as nurses to the wounded.

2 Practicing the Skill

Look at the following list of sources. Which would be most helpful in writing a report on the Civil War? Explain your choices.

1. A biographical dictionary of U.S. presidents
2. A history of America's Civil Rights Struggle
3. A photographic essay of the Civil War
4. A history of the United States from 1492–1900
5. The "C" volume of an encyclopedia
6. A history of the Republican Party in America
7. A historical atlas of the United States
8. A children's storybook about America in the 1800s
9. A book on the rise and fall of the South
10. A history of United States economic policy

3 Applying the Skill

Go to your local library or use the Internet to create a bibliography of sources you might use to write a report on the Civil War. List at least five sources.

SkillBuilder Handbook

Analyzing Primary Source Documents

Why Learn This Skill?

Historians determine what happened in the past by combing through bits of evidence to reconstruct events. These pieces of evidence are called primary sources. They are often first-person accounts from someone who saw or lived through what is being described. Examining primary sources can help you understand history.

1 Learning the Skill

Primary sources are records of events made by the people who witnessed them. They include letters, diaries, photographs and pictures, news articles, and legal documents.

To analyze primary sources, follow these steps:

- Identify when and where the document was written.
- Read the document for its content and try to answer the five "W" questions:

  Who is it about?
  What is it about?
  When did it happen?
  Where did it happen?
  Why did it happen?
- Identify the author's opinions.

▲ Choctaw forced from their land

2 Practicing the Skill

The primary source that follows comes from Speckled Snake, an elder of the Creek Nation, in 1829. He was more than 100 years old at the time he said these words. Read the quote, then answer the questions that follow.

> Brothers! I have listened to many talks from our Great Father. When he first came over the wide waters, he was but a little man. . . . But when the white man had warmed himself before the Indians' fire and filled himself with their hominy, he became very large. With a step he bestrode the mountains and his feet covered the plains and the valleys. His hand grasped the eastern and the western sea, and his head rested on the moon. Then he became our Great Father. Brothers, I have listened to a great many talks from our Great Father. But they always began and ended in this—"Get a little further; you are too near me."

1. What events is Speckled Snake describing?
2. Who was affected by these events?
3. What is Speckled Snake's general feeling toward the white man?

3 Applying the Skill

Find a primary source from your past—a photograph, a report card, an old newspaper clipping, or your first baseball card. Bring this source to class and explain what it shows about that time in your life.

Interpreting a Political Cartoon

Why Learn This Skill?

You have probably heard the saying, "A picture is worth a thousand words." For more than 200 years, political cartoonists have drawn pictures to present their opinions about a person or event. Learning to interpret political cartoons can help you understand issues of both the past and present.

1 Learning the Skill

Political cartoons state opinions about particular subjects. To illustrate those opinions, cartoonists provide clues, using several different techniques. They often exaggerate a person's physical features or appearance in a special effect called caricature. A caricature can be positive or negative, depending on the artist's point of view.

Cartoonists often use symbols to represent something else. The bald eagle is often shown in political cartoons as a symbol of the United States. Sometimes cartoonists help readers interpret their message by adding labels or captions.

To interpret a political cartoon, follow these steps:

- Read the caption and any other words printed in the cartoon.
- Analyze each element in the cartoon.
- Identify the clues: What is happening in the cartoon? Who or what is represented by each part of the drawing? Are there any symbols? To whom or what do they refer?
- Study all these elements to decide the point the cartoonist is making.

2 Practicing the Skill

Study the cartoon below and read the information about Jim Crow laws on pages 647–648. Then answer the following questions.

1. Are the white people in the cartoon friendly or unfriendly toward the African American? Explain.
2. What does the sign "POLLS" tell you about where the people are?
3. Who are the people represented in the cartoon?
4. What message do you think the cartoonist is trying to send?

3 Applying the Skill

Bring to class a copy of a political cartoon from a recent newspaper or magazine. Explain the cartoonist's point and the tools used to express it.

Analyzing News Media

Why Learn This Skill?

Every citizen needs to be aware of current issues and events to make good decisions when exercising citizenship rights.

1 Learning the Skill

To get an accurate profile of current events, you must learn to think critically about the news. The steps below will help you think critically.

- First, think about the source of the news story. Reports that reveal sources are more reliable than those that do not. If you know the sources, you can evaluate them. Can all facts be verified?
- Many news stories also interpret events. Such analyses may reflect a reporter's biases. Look for biases as you read or listen to news stories.
- Ask yourself whether the news is evenhanded and thorough. Is it reported on the scene or secondhand? Does it represent both sides of an issue? The more sources cited for a fact, the more reliable it usually is.

Alexander Graham Bell makes the first phone call.

2 Practicing the Skill

Below is an excerpt from an 1891 *New York Times* newspaper article. The article states that the Bell Company did not renew a patent on their telephone.

Read the excerpt below and answer the questions that follow.

THE TELEPHONE MONOPOLY

It is incredible that the Fifty-second Congress will pass an act to authorize the Bell Company to bleed for another seventeen years the public that has enriched the proprietors of that monopoly for nearly that period. ... But behind the company and the Congress there is the long-suffering public, ... [it] will unquestionably take a lively interest in killing off members who dare to support the pretensions of this arrogant and rapacious [greedy] monopoly."

1. What point is the article trying to make?
2. Does the article reflect bias or strong opinion? Explain.

3 Applying the Skill

Think of an issue in your community on which public opinion is divided. Read newspaper features and editorials about the issue and listen to television reports. What biases can you identify? Which reports are the most reliable?

Honoring America

For Americans, the flag has always had a special meaning. It is a symbol of our nation's freedom and democracy.

Flag Etiquette

Over the years, Americans have developed rules and customs concerning the use and display of the flag. One of the most important things every American should remember is to treat the flag with respect.

- The flag should be raised and lowered by hand and displayed only from sunrise to sunset. On special occasions, the flag may be displayed at night, but it should be illuminated.
- The flag may be displayed on all days, weather permitting, particularly on national and state holidays and on historic and special occasions.
- No flag may be flown above the American flag or to the right of it at the same height.
- The flag should never touch the ground or floor beneath it.
- The flag may be flown at half-staff by order of the president, usually to mourn the death of a public official.
- The flag may be flown upside down only to signal distress.
- The flag should never be carried flat or horizontally, but always carried aloft and free.
- When the flag becomes old and tattered, it should be destroyed by burning. According to an approved custom, the Union (stars on blue field) is first cut from the flag; then the two pieces, which no longer form a flag, are burned.

The American's Creed

I believe in the United States of America as a Government of the people, by the people, for the people, whose just powers are derived from the consent of the governed; a democracy in a republic; a sovereign Nation of many sovereign States; a perfect union, one and inseparable; established upon those principles of freedom, equality, justice, and humanity for which American patriots sacrificed their lives and fortunes.

I therefore believe it is my duty to my Country to love it; to support its Constitution; to obey its laws; to respect its flag, and to defend it against all enemies.

The Pledge of Allegiance

I pledge allegiance to the Flag of the United States of America and to the Republic for which it stands, one Nation under God, indivisible, with liberty and justice for all.

Supreme Court Case Summaries

The following summaries give details about important Supreme Court cases.

Brown v. *Board of Education* (1954)

In *Brown* v. *Board of Education of Topeka, Kansas*, the Supreme Court overruled *Plessy* v. *Ferguson* (1896) making the separate-but-equal doctrine in public schools unconstitutional. The Supreme Court rejected the idea that truly equal but separate schools for African American and white students would be constitutional. The Court explained that the Fourteenth Amendment's requirement that all persons be guaranteed equal protection of the law is not met simply by ensuring that African American and white schools "have been equalized...with respect to buildings, curricula, qualifications and salaries, and other tangible factors."

The Court then ruled that racial segregation in public schools violates the Equal Protection Clause of the Constitution because it is inherently unequal. In other words, nothing can make racially segregated public schools equal under the Constitution because the very fact of separation marks the separated race as inferior. In practical terms, the Court's decision in this case has been extended beyond public education to virtually all public accommodations and activities.

Dred Scott v. *Sandford* (1857)

Dred Scott was taken by slaveholder John Sandford to the free state of Illinois and to the Wisconsin Territory, which had also banned slavery. Later they returned to a slave state, Missouri. Several years later, Scott sued for his freedom under the Missouri legal principle of "once free, always free." In other words, under state law enslaved people were entitled to freedom if they had lived in a free state at any time. Missouri courts ruled against Scott, but he appealed the case all the way to the United States Supreme Court.

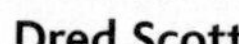
Dred Scott

The Supreme Court decided this case before the Fourteenth Amendment was added to the Constitution. (The Fourteenth Amendment provides that anyone born or naturalized in the United States is a citizen of the nation and of his or her state of residence.) The court held that enslaved African Americans were property, not citizens, and thus had no rights under the Constitution. The decision also declared that it was unconstitutional to prohibit slavery in the territories. Many people in the North were outraged by the decision, which moved the nation closer to civil war.

Gibbons v. *Ogden* (1824)

Thomas Gibbons had a federal license to operate a steamboat along the coast, but he did not have a license from the state of New York to travel on New York waters. He wanted to run a steamboat line between Manhattan and New Jersey that would compete with Aaron Ogden's company. Ogden had a New York license. Gibbons sued for the freedom to use his federal license to compete against Ogden on New York waters.

Gibbons won the case. The Supreme Court made it clear that the authority of Congress to regulate interstate commerce (among states) includes the authority to regulate intrastate commerce (within a single state) that bears on, or relates to, interstate commerce.

Before this decision, it was thought that the Constitution would permit a state to close its borders to interstate commercial activity—which, in effect, would stop such activity in its tracks. This case says that a state can regulate purely internal commercial activity, but only Congress can regulate commercial activity that has both intrastate and interstate dimensions.

Gideon v. *Wainwright* (1963)

After being accused of robbery, Clarence Gideon defended himself in a Florida court because the judge in the case refused to appoint a free lawyer. The jury found Gideon guilty. Eventually, Gideon appealed his conviction to the United States Supreme Court, claiming that by failing to appoint a lawyer the lower court had violated his rights under the Sixth and Fourteenth Amendments.

The Supreme Court agreed with Gideon. In *Gideon* v. *Wainwright* the Supreme Court held for the first time that poor defendants in criminal cases have the right to a state-paid attorney under the Sixth Amendment. The rule announced in this case has been refined to apply whenever the defendant, if convicted, can be sentenced to more than six months in jail or prison.

Korematsu v. *United States* (1944)

After the Japanese bombing of Pearl Harbor in 1941, thousands of Japanese Americans on the West Coast were forced to abandon their homes and businesses, and they were moved to internment camps in California, Idaho, Utah, Arizona, Wyoming, Colorado, and Arkansas. The prison-like camps offered poor food and cramped quarters.

In 1983 Fred Korematsu (center) won a reversal of his conviction.

The Supreme Court's decision in *Korematsu* v. *United States* supported the authority of the federal government to move Japanese Americans, many of whom were citizens, from designated military areas that included almost the entire West Coast. The government defended the so-called exclusion orders as a necessary response to Japan's attack on Pearl Harbor. Only after his reelection in 1944 did President Franklin Roosevelt rescind the evacuation orders, and by the end of 1945 the camps were closed.

Marbury v. *Madison* (1803)

During his last days in office, President John Adams, a Federalist, appointed William Marbury and several other men as judges. This action angered the incoming Democratic-Republican president Thomas Jefferson. Jefferson then ordered James Madison, his secretary of state, not to deliver the commissions, thus blocking the appointments. William Marbury sued. He asked the Supreme Court to order Madison to deliver the commission that would make him a judge.

The Court ruled against Marbury, but more importantly, the decision in this case established one of the most significant principles of American constitutional law. The Supreme Court held that it is the Court itself that has the final say on what the Constitution means. This right is known as judicial review. It is also the Supreme Court that has the final say in whether or not an act of government—legislative or executive at the federal, state, or local level—violates the Constitution.

McCulloch v. *Maryland* (1819)

Following the War of 1812, the United States experienced years of high inflation and general economic turmoil. In an attempt to stabilize the economy, the United States Congress chartered a Second Bank of the United States in 1816. Maryland and several other states, however, opposed the competition that the new national bank created and passed state laws taxing its branches.

In 1818, James McCulloch, head of the Baltimore branch of the Second Bank of the United States, refused to pay the tax to the state of Maryland. The case worked its way through the Maryland state courts all the way to the United States Supreme Court.

The Supreme Court declared the Maryland tax unconstitutional and void. More importantly, the decision established the foundation for expanded Congressional authority. The Court held that the necessary and proper clause of the Constitution allows Congress to do more than the Constitution expressly states it may do. The decision allows Congress to enact nearly any law that will help it achieve any of its constitutional duties. For example, Congress has the express authority to regulate interstate commerce. The necessary and proper clause permits Congress to do so in ways not actually specified in the Constitution.

Miranda v. *Arizona* (1966)

In 1963, police in Arizona arrested Ernesto Miranda for kidnapping. The court found Miranda guilty on the basis of a signed confession. The police admitted that neither before nor during the questioning had Miranda been advised of his right to consult with an attorney before answering any questions or of his right to have an attorney present during the interrogation.

In 1963, the arrest of Ernesto Miranda (right) led to a landmark decision.

Miranda appealed his conviction, claiming that police had violated his right against self-incrimination under the Fifth Amendment by not informing him of his legal rights during the questioning.

Miranda won the case. The Supreme Court held that a person in police custody cannot be questioned unless told that he or she has: 1) the right to remain silent, 2) the right to an attorney (at government expense if the accused is unable to pay), and 3) that anything the person says after stating that he or she understands these rights can be used as evidence of guilt at trial. These rights have come to be called the Miranda warning. They are intended to ensure that an accused person in custody will not unknowingly give up the Fifth Amendment's protection against self-incrimination.

New York Times Company v. *United States* (1971)

In June 1971, the *New York Times* published its first installment of the "Pentagon Papers," a classified document about government actions in the Vietnam War era. The secret document had been leaked to the *Times* by antiwar activist Daniel Ellsberg, who had previously worked in national security for the government. President Richard Nixon went to court to block further publication of the Pentagon Papers. The *New York Times* appealed to the Supreme Court to allow it to continue publishing without government interference.

The Supreme Court's ruling in this case upheld earlier decisions that established the doctrine of prior restraint. This doctrine protects the press (broadly defined as radio and television, newspapers, filmmakers and distributors, etc.) from government attempts to block publication. Except in extraordinary circumstances, the press must be allowed to publish.

Plessy v. *Ferguson* (1896)

In the late 1800s, railroad companies in Louisiana were required by state law to provide "separate-but-equal" cars for white and African American passengers. In 1890 a group of citizens in New Orleans selected Homer Plessy to challenge that law. In 1892, Plessy boarded a whites-only car and refused to move. He was arrested. Plessy appealed to the Supreme Court, arguing that the Louisiana separate-but-equal law violated his right to equal protection under the Fourteenth Amendment.

Homer Plessy lost the case. The Plessy decision upheld the separate-but-equal doctrine used by Southern states to perpetuate segregation following the Civil War. The court ruled that the Fourteenth Amendment's equal protection clause required only equal public facilities for the two races, not equal access to the same facilities. This decision was overruled in 1954 by *Brown* v. *Board of Education of Topeka, Kansas* (discussed previously).

Roe v. *Wade* (1973)

Roe v. *Wade* challenged restrictive abortion laws in both Texas and Georgia. The suit was brought in the name of Jane Roe, an alias used to protect the privacy of the plaintiff.

In this decision, the Supreme Court ruled that females have a constitutional right under various provisions of the Constitution—most notably, the due process clause—to decide whether or not to terminate a pregnancy. The Supreme Court's decision in this case was the most significant in a long line of decisions over a period of 50 years that recognized a constitutional right of privacy, even though the word *privacy* is not found in the Constitution.

United States v. *Nixon* (1974)

In the early 1970s, President Nixon was named an unindicted coconspirator in the criminal investigation that arose in the aftermath of a break-in at the offices of the Democratic Party in Washington, D.C. A federal judge had ordered President Nixon to turn over tapes of conversations he had with his advisers about the break-in. Nixon resisted the order, claiming that the conversations were entitled to absolute confidentiality by Article II of the Constitution.

The decision in this case made it clear that the president is not above the law. The Supreme Court held that only those presidential conversations and communications that relate to performing the duties of the office of president are confidential and protected from a judicial order of disclosure. The Court ordered Nixon to give up the tapes, which revealed evidence linking the president to the conspiracy to obstruct justice. He resigned from office shortly thereafter.

Worcester v. *Georgia* (1832)

State officials in Georgia wanted to remove the Cherokees from land that had been guaranteed to them in treaties. Samuel Worcester was a Congregational missionary who worked with the Cherokee people. He was arrested for failure to have a license that the state required to live in Cherokee country and for refusing to obey an order from the Georgia militia to leave Cherokee lands. Worcester then sued the state of Georgia. He claimed that Georgia had no legal authority on Cherokee land because the United States government recognized the Cherokee in Georgia as a separate nation.

The Supreme Court agreed with Worcester by a vote of 5 to 1. Chief Justice John Marshall wrote the majority opinion which said that Native American nations were a distinct people with the right to have independent political communities and that only the federal government had authority over matters that involved the Cherokee.

President Andrew Jackson supported Georgia's efforts to remove the Cherokee to Indian Territory and refused to enforce the court's ruling. After the ruling Jackson remarked, "John Marshall has made his decision. Now let him enforce it."

The Magna Carta

The Magna Carta, signed by King John in 1215, marked a decisive step forward in the development of constitutional government in England. Later, it became a model for colonists who carried the Magna Carta's guarantees of legal and political rights to America.

1\. . . . [T]hat the English Church shall be free, and shall have its rights undiminished, and its liberties unimpaired. . . . we have also granted, for us and our heirs for ever, all the liberties written out below, to have and to keep for them and their heirs, of us and our heirs:

39\. No free man shall be seized or imprisoned, or stripped of his rights or possessions, or outlawed or exiled, or deprived of his standing in any other way, nor will we proceed with force against him, or send others to do so, except by the lawful judgement of his equals or by the law of the land.

40\. To no one will we sell, to no one deny or delay right or justice.

41\. All merchants may enter or leave England unharmed and without fear, and may stay or travel within it, by land or water, for purposes of trade, free from all illegal exactions, in accordance with ancient and lawful customs. This, however, does not apply in time of war to merchants from a country that is at war with us.

42\. In future it shall be lawful for any man to leave and return to our kingdom unharmed and without fear, by land or water, preserving his allegiance to us, except in time of war, for some short period, for the common benefit of the realm.

60\. All these customs and liberties that we have granted shall be observed in our kingdom in so far as concerns our own relations with our subjects. Let all men of our kingdom, whether clergy or laymen, observe them similarly in their relations with their own men.

63\. . . . Both we and the barons have sworn that all this shall be observed in good faith and without deceit. Witness the abovementioned people and many others. Given by our hand in the meadow that is called Runnymede, between Windsor and Staines, on the fifteenth day of June in the seventeenth year of our reign.

◀ **Illuminated manuscript, Middle Ages**

The Mayflower Compact

On November 21, 1620, 41 colonists aboard the Mayflower drafted this agreement. The Mayflower Compact was the first plan of self-government enacted in the English colonies.

IN The Name of God, Amen. We, whose names are underwritten, the Loyal Subjects of our dread Sovereign Lord King James, by the Grace of God, of Great Britain, France, and Ireland, King, Defender of the Faith, & c. Having undertaken for the Glory of God, and Advancement of the Christian Faith, and the Honour of our King and Country, a Voyage to plant the first colony in the northern Parts of Virginia; Do by these Presents, solemnly and mutually in the Presence of God and one another, covenant and combine ourselves together into a civil Body Politick, for our better Ordering and Preservation, and Furtherance of the Ends aforesaid: And by Virtue hereof do enact, constitute, and frame, such just and equal Laws, Ordinances, Acts, Constitutions, and Offices, from time to time, as shall be thought most meet and convenient for the general Good of the Colony; unto which we promise all due Submission and Obedience. In Witness whereof we have hereunto subscribed our names at Cape Cod the eleventh of November, in the Reign of our Sovereign Lord King James of England, France, and Ireland, the eighteenth and of Scotland, the fifty-fourth. Anno Domini, 1620

The Federalist, No. 10

James Madison wrote several articles supporting ratification of the Constitution. Below, Madison argues for the idea of a federal republic.

By a faction, I understand a number of citizens . . . who are united and actuated by some common impulse . . . adversed to the rights of other citizens. . . .

The inference to which we are brought is, that the CAUSES of faction cannot be removed, and that relief is only to be sought in the means of controlling its EFFECTS. . . .

A republic, by which I mean a government in which the scheme of representation takes place, . . . promises the cure for which we are seeking. . . .

The two great points of difference between a democracy and a republic are: first, the delegation of the government, in the latter, to a small number of citizens elected by the rest; secondly, the greater number of citizens, and greater sphere of country, over which the latter may be extended.

▲ James Madison

The effect of the first difference is . . . to refine and enlarge the public views, by passing them through the medium of a chosen body of citizens, whose wisdom may best discern the true interest of their country, and whose patriotism and love of justice will be least likely to sacrifice it to temporary or partial considerations.

Washington's Farewell Address

At the end of his second term as president, George Washington spoke of the dangers facing the young nation. He warned against the dangers of political parties and sectionalism, and he advised the nation against permanent alliances with other nations.

Citizens by birth or choice of a common country, that country has a right to concentrate your affections. The name of American, which belongs to you, in your national capacity, must always exalt the just pride of patriotism more than any appellation derived from local discriminations. With slight shades of difference, you have the same religion, manners, habits, and political principles. You have in a common cause fought and triumphed together. . . .

In contemplating the causes which may disturb our Union, it occurs as matter of serious concern that any ground should have been furnished for characterizing parties by *geographical* discriminations. . . .

No alliances, however strict between the parts, can be an adequate substitute. They must inevitably experience the infractions and interruptions which all alliances in all times have experienced. . . .

▲ George Washington

The great rule of conduct for us, in regard to foreign nations, is in extending our commercial relations to have with them as little *political* connection as possible. . . .

. . . I anticipate with pleasing expectations that retreat in which I promise myself to realize . . . the sweet enjoyment of partaking, in the midst of my fellow citizens, the benign influence of good laws under a free government, the ever favorite object of my heart, and the happy reward, as I trust, of our mutual cares, labors, and dangers.

The Star-Spangled Banner

During the British bombardment of Fort McHenry during the War of 1812, a young Baltimore lawyer named Francis Scott Key was inspired by the sight to write the words to "The Star-Spangled Banner." Although it became popular immediately, it was not until 1931 that Congress officially declared this song our national anthem.

O! say can you see by the dawn's early light,
What so proudly we hail'd at the twilight's last gleaming;
Whose broad stripes and bright stars, through the perilous fight,
O'er the ramparts we watch'd were so gallantly streaming;
And the rockets' red glare, the bombs bursting in air,
Gave proof through the night that our flag was still there;
O! say does that star-spangled banner yet wave,
O'er the land of the free, and the home of the brave.

Documents

US8.5

What Is the Standard? → Where Can I Find It?

What Is the Standard?	Where Can I Find It?
US8.5 **Students analyze U.S. foreign policy in the early Republic.**	**Chapter 7** covers Standard US8.5 and explores how the United States met challenges in trade, foreign relations, and war in the early 1800s.
US8.5.1 **Understand the political and economic causes and consequences of the War of 1812 and know the major battles, leaders, and events that led to a final peace.**	**Chapter 7, Sections 1, 2, and 3** The United States was drawn into the conflict between Britain and France, eventually leading to war with Britain. Hard-fought battles on land and sea resulted in a victory for the United States and a new wave of American nationalism. **(Review pages 341–345, 354–359, 363–365, 368–369.)**
US8.5.2 **Know the changing boundaries of the United States and describe the relationships the country had with its neighbors (current Mexico and Canada) and Europe, including the influence of the Monroe Doctrine, and how those relationships influenced westward expansion and the Mexican-American War.**	**Chapter 7, Section 3** In the first half of the 1800s, the United States gained territory through war and treaties with other nations. The Monroe Doctrine was an attempt to limit European interventions in the Americas. **(Review pages 363–367.)**
US8.5.3 **Outline the major treaties with American Indian nations during the administrations of the first four presidents and the varying outcomes of those treaties.**	**Chapter 7, Section 1** As white Americans settled in Native American territories, conflict continued to develop between the two peoples. Treaties were made, but were often set aside or ignored. **(Review page 343.)**

Standards Practice

1 What did the Adams-Onís Treaty accomplish?

A It established the border between the United States and Canada.

B It ended the War of 1812.

C It established new trade relations with Spain.

D It resolved territorial disputes between Spain and the United States.

US8.6

What Is the Standard?	Where Can I Find It?
US8.6 Students analyze the divergent paths of the American people from 1800 to the mid-1800s and the challenges they faced, with emphasis on the Northeast.	**Chapter 8** covers Standard US8.6, and describes major developments in immigration, transportation, and industrialization in the United States.
US8.6.1 Discuss the influence of industrialization and technological developments on the region, including human modification of the landscape and how physical geography shaped human actions (e.g., growth of cities, deforestation, farming, mineral extraction).	**Chapter 8, Section 1** As new technology emerged in manufacturing, the economy of the Northeast became increasingly industrial. At the same time, cities developed along transportation routes like rivers and newly built roads. **(Review pages 383–387.)** **Chapter 8, Section 1** Americans used the natural resources at their disposal to provide for their families or create new industry. **(Review page 383.)**
US8.6.2 Outline the physical obstacles to and the economic and political factors involved in building a network of roads, canals, and railroads (e.g., Henry Clay's American System).	**Chapter 8, Section 2** In the early 1800s, leaders in the northeast promoted internal improvements, such as the building of the National Road and a canal system, to help the development of trade and industry. The invention of the steam engine and the railroad led to a revolution in transportation. **(Review pages 389–394.)**
US8.6.3 List the reasons for the wave of immigration from Northern Europe to the United States and describe the growth in the number, size, and spatial arrangements of cities (e.g., Irish immigrants and the Great Irish Famine).	**Chapter 8, Section 3** Many people from northern Europe migrated to the Northeast United States because of economic or political unrest in their home countries. Both the development of cities and the culture of the Northeast were affected by these newcomers. **(Review pages 398–401.)**
US8.6.4 Study the lives of black Americans who gained freedom in the North and founded schools and churches to advance their rights and communities.	**Chapter 8, Section 3** As slavery died out in the Northeast, African Americans tried to realize the ideals of freedom and developed institutions that reflected their needs and interests. **(Review page 397.)**

US8.6 *cont.*

What Is the Standard?	Where Can I Find It?
US8.6.5 Trace the development of the American education system from its earliest roots, including the roles of religious and private schools and Horace Mann's campaign for free public education and its assimilating role in American culture.	**Chapter 8, Section 4** Education played an increasingly important role in the young Republic and took on many different forms, including new colleges and schools for students with disabilities. **(Review page 405.)**
US8.6.6 Examine the women's suffrage movement (e.g., biographies, writings, and speeches of Elizabeth Cady Stanton, Margaret Fuller, Lucretia Mott, Susan B. Anthony).	**Chapter 8, Section 5** Women were eager to share in the ideals of the Declaration of Independence, and a movement to give women the right to vote developed. Women also made gains in education and in their legal rights related to marriage and family. **(Review pages 409–413.)**
US8.6.7 Identify common themes in American art as well as transcendentalism and individualism (e.g., writings about and by Ralph Waldo Emerson, Henry David Thoreau, Herman Melville, Louisa May Alcott, Nathaniel Hawthorne, Henry Wadsworth Longfellow).	**Chapter 8, Section 4** As American identity evolved, themes in art, writing, and music became distinctive. American authors created and explored new themes like transcendentalism and individualism. **(Review pages 406–407.)**

Standards Practice

1 What was the relationship between the Irish potato famine and the United States in the mid-1800s?

A The famine created a devastating shortage of food, causing more than 1.5 million Irish immigrants to come to the United States.

B The famine limited trade between the United States and Ireland.

C The famine caused a revolt among Irish in New York City.

D The famine inspired new farming technology in the United States.

2 Henry David Thoreau and Ralph Waldo Emerson belonged to a group of writers known as the

A Fundamentalists.

B Constitutionalists.

C Federalists.

D Transcendentalists.

US8.7

What Is the Standard?	Where Can I Find It?
US8.7 Students analyze the divergent paths of the American people in the South from 1800 to the mid-1800s and the challenges they faced.	**Chapter 9** covers Standard US8.7 as it explores the distinctive elements of the South's economy and culture, as well as the institution of slavery.
US8.7.1 Describe the development of the agrarian economy in the South, identify the locations of the cotton-producing states, and discuss the significance of cotton and the cotton gin.	**Chapter 9, Section 1** The production of cotton defined large-scale Southern agriculture, especially in the Deep South, while small independent farmers grew varied crops. **(Review pages 423–425.)**
US8.7.2 Trace the origins and development of slavery; its effects on black Americans and on the region's political, social, religious, economic, and cultural development; and identify the strategies that were tried to both overturn and preserve it (e.g., through the writings and historical documents on Nat Turner, Denmark Vesey).	**Chapter 9, Section 3** Slavery had an immense impact on the lives and culture of African Americans, and others, in the South. Enslaved people resisted slavery in a number of ways, including rebellions. **(Review pages 433–437.)**
US8.7.3 Examine the characteristics of white southern society and how the physical environment influenced events and conditions prior to the Civil War.	**Chapter 9, Section 1** The culture of white Southerners was primarily defined by small tenant farming or plantation farming. Cities were generally smaller than in the North, and industry played a much smaller role in the Southern economy. **(Review pages 423–431.)**
US8.7.4 Compare the lives of and opportunities for free blacks in the North with those of free blacks in the South.	**Chapter 9, Section 3** Free African Americans faced prejudice and discrimination in both the North and the South. **(Review page 430.)**

Standards Practice

1 The cotton gin was invented by Eli Whitney in 1793. How did the new technology change cotton production?

A It led to agricultural growth in the North.

B It contributed to the industrialization of the South.

C It dramatically increased the amount of cotton that could be processed.

D It reduced dependence on slave labor.

US8.8

What Is the Standard?	Where Can I Find It?
US8.8 Students analyze the divergent paths of the American people in the West from 1800 to the mid-1800s and the challenges they faced.	**Chapters 10 and 11** cover Standard US8.8 as they trace the development of the American West as a region with political, geographic, and cultural impact on the United States as a whole. Additional information can be found in **Chapter 15.**
US8.8.1 Discuss the election of Andrew Jackson as president in 1828, the importance of Jacksonian democracy, and his actions as president (e.g., the spoils system, veto of the National Bank, policy of Indian removal, opposition to the Supreme Court).	**Chapter 10, Sections 1 and 3** Andrew Jackson promised "equal protection and equal rights" to all, and a spirit of equality spread through American politics and government. His opposition to the National Bank was seen as supportive of the common people, rather than the wealthy. **(Review pages 447–448, 459–460.)** **Chapter 10, Section 2** Despite a Supreme Court ruling to the contrary, Jackson pursued a policy of Indian Removal to open lands for white settlement and to ensure security on the frontier. **(Review pages 453–457, 463.)**
US8.8.2 Describe the purpose, challenges, and economic incentives associated with westward expansion, including the concept of Manifest Destiny (e.g., the Lewis and Clark expedition, accounts of the removal of Indians, the Cherokees' "Trail of Tears," settlement of the Great Plains) and the territorial acquisitions that spanned numerous decades.	**Chapter 11, Section 1** Once the United States reached an agreement to gain control of the Oregon Country, American settlers streamed to the Far West despite many difficulties. Soon Americans came to believe that they should occupy the entire continent. **(Review pages 471–475.)**
US8.8.3 Describe the role of pioneer women and the new status that western women achieved (e.g., Laura Ingalls Wilder, Annie Bidwell; slave women gaining freedom in the West; Wyoming granting suffrage to women in 1869).	**Chapter 11, Section 4** Annie Bidwell, a California pioneer, dedicated her life to social and agricultural reform. **(Review page 502.)** **Chapter 15, Section 2** On the frontier, women enjoyed new freedoms and became farmers, business owners, and community leaders. **(Review pages 676–679.)**
US8.8.4 Examine the importance of the great rivers and the struggle over water rights.	**Chapter 11, Section 2** As settlers moved into the American West, rivers were an important resource for transportation, irrigation, and eventually energy production. **(Review pages 488–489.)**

US8.8 *cont.*

What Is the Standard?	Where Can I Find It?
US8.8.5 **Discuss Mexican settlements and their locations, cultural traditions, attitudes toward slavery, land-grant system, and economies.**	**Chapter 11, Section 3** Following Mexico's independence from Spain, Spanish missions in the Southwest were abolished and an economy based on large ranches developed. **(Review pages 492–494.)**
US8.8.6 **Describe the Texas War for Independence and the Mexican-American War, including territorial settlements, the aftermath of the wars, and the effects the wars had on the lives of Americans, including Mexican Americans today.**	**Chapter 11, Section 2** Settlers in Texas fought for independence from Mexico and created a new nation before becoming a state in the Union. **(Review pages 481–487.)** **Chapter 11, Section 3** The Mexican-American War resolved territorial disputes between the United States and Mexico and resulted in America's acquisition of additional territories, including California. **(Review pages 491–497.)**

Standards Practice

1 The Treaty of Guadalupe Hidalgo of 1848 is significant because

A Mexico gave up all claims to Texas, California, and New Mexico.
B it ended the Texas War for Independence.
C it created a new trade relationship between the United States and Mexico.
D Spain gave up all claims to Florida.

2 The slogan "Fifty-four Forty or Fight" referred to which of the following territories?

A Texas
B Oregon
C Florida
D California

3 Relations between Mexico and the United States were strained because the United States insisted that the Texas-Mexico border was the

A Nueces River.
B Pacific Ocean.
C Mississippi River.
D Rio Grande.

US8.9

What Is the Standard? → Where Can I Find It?

What Is the Standard?	Where Can I Find It?
US8.9 Students analyze the early and steady attempts to abolish slavery and to realize the ideals of the Declaration of Independence.	**Chapter 12** covers the efforts to ban or limit slavery as the United States expanded in the early 1800s. Additional information can be found in **Chapters 3, 6, 8, and 9.**
US8.9.1 Describe the leaders of the movement (e.g., John Quincy Adams and his proposed constitutional amendment, John Brown and the armed resistance, Harriet Tubman and the Underground Railroad, Benjamin Franklin, Theodore Weld, William Lloyd Garrison, Frederick Douglass).	**Chapter 12, Section 1** The courageous leadership of many people gave the abolition movement increasing power and effectiveness. For example, William Lloyd Garrison stimulated the growth of the antislavery movement. The most widely known African American abolitionists were Frederick Douglass and Harriet Tubman. **(Review pages 529–534.)**
US8.9.2 Discuss the abolition of slavery in early state constitutions.	**Chapter 3, Section 2** Between 1783 and 1804, states, such as Connecticut, Rhode Island, New York, and New Jersey, passed laws that gradually ended slavery. **(Review pages 195–196.)**
US8.9.3 Describe the significance of the Northwest Ordinance in education and in the banning of slavery in new states north of the Ohio River.	**Chapter 3, Section 1** The Northwest Ordinance outlawed slavery in territory north of the Ohio River, marking the United States' first attempt to make slavery illegal. **(Review page 182.)** **Chapter 6, Section 3** Education was a vital part of a healthy democracy, and it was provided for in the Northwest Ordinance. **(Review page 321.)**
US8.9.4 Discuss the importance of the slavery issue as raised by the annexation of Texas and California's admission to the union as a free state under the Compromise of 1850.	**Chapter 12, Section 2** Pro-slavery leaders wanted to preserve their balance of power in Congress and resisted the admission of new states where slavery would not be legal. Political disagreement was often heated and divisive. **(Review pages 539–542.)**

US8.9 *cont.*

What Is the Standard?	Where Can I Find It?
US8.9.5 Analyze the significance of the States' Rights Doctrine, the Missouri Compromise (1820), the Wilmot Proviso (1846), the Compromise of 1850, Henry Clay's role in the Missouri Compromise and the Compromise of 1850, the Kansas-Nebraska Act (1854), the *Dred Scott* v. *Sandford* decision (1857), and the Lincoln-Douglas debates (1858).	**Chapter 12, Section 2** The possible spread of slavery into the West was an issue that repeatedly divided the nation. The South affirmed states' rights, while political decisions, such as the Missouri Compromise, the Wilmot Proviso, and the Compromise of 1850, were proposed or implemented to deal with the spread of slavery. **(Review pages 536, 539–542.)** **Chapter 12, Section 3** The Kansas-Nebraska Act resulted from another dispute over slavery in Congress. **(Review page 544.)** **Chapter 12, Section 4** The Supreme Court's decision in the *Dred Scott* case and the Lincoln-Douglas debates called attention to the issue of slavery as the nation moved to the brink of conflict. **(Review pages 549–553.)**
US8.9.6 Describe the lives of free blacks and the laws that limited their freedom and economic opportunities.	**Chapter 8, Section 3 and Chapter 12, Section 4** In the North, free African Americans were barred from schools and public facilities; some African Americans, however, were successful in the business world. **(Review pages 397, 551.)** **Chapter 9, Section 2** Cities allowed free African Americans in the South to form their own communities, but laws limited their rights. **(Review page 430.)**

Standards Practice

1 Which abolition leader escaped slavery in Maryland and settled in the North?

- **A** David Walker
- **B** Frederick Douglass
- **C** William Lloyd Garrison
- **D** Angelina Grimké

2 What principle did the Supreme Court establish in the *Dred Scott* decision?

- **A** It made the sale of slaves illegal.
- **B** It ruled slavery illegal west of the Mississippi River.
- **C** It declared that slaves were not people and therefore could be legally traded as property.
- **D** It set a profit limit on the sale of slaves.

US8.10

What Is the Standard?	Where Can I Find It?
US8.10 Students analyze the multiple causes, key events, and complex consequences of the Civil War.	**Chapters 12 and 13** cover the Civil War, including the road to war, the political and constitutional crisis of secession, the slavery debate, and the impact of the war on daily life in both the North and South.
US8.10.1 Compare the conflicting interpretations of state and federal authority as emphasized in the speeches and writings of statesmen such as Daniel Webster and John C. Calhoun.	**Chapter 12, Section 2** Daniel Webster declared that the federal government was sovereign and supported a strong Union, while John C. Calhoun was a champion of states' rights. **(Review pages 537–538.)**
US8.10.2 Trace the boundaries constituting the North and the South, the geographical differences between the two regions, and the differences between agrarians and industrialists.	**Chapter 13, Section 1** The North and South were distinct regions with marked differences in economy, transportation, and geography. The North had a larger population and more industry and resources. The South remained largely agricultural. **(Review pages 571–573.)**
US8.10.3 Identify the constitutional issues posed by the doctrine of nullification and secession and the earliest origins of that doctrine.	**Chapter 12, Section 2** After the Constitution's ratification, different leaders threatened to reject federal laws or leave the Union, for example, in the Virginia and Kentucky Resolutions, the Hartford Convention, and the tariff controversy. **(Review pages 537–538.)** **Chapter 12, Section 5** Some Southerners justified secession based on the contract theory of the Constitution. **(Review page 556.)**
US8.10.4 Discuss Abraham Lincoln's presidency and his significant writings and speeches and their relationship to the Declaration of Independence, such as his "House Divided" speech (1858), Gettysburg Address (1863), Emancipation Proclamation (1863), and inaugural addresses (1861 and 1865).	**Chapter 12, Section 4** Lincoln expressed concern about the morality of slavery and emphasized the need to preserve the Union in his "House Divided" speech. **(Review pages 552–553.)** **Chapter 12, Section 5 and Chapter 13, Section 5** Lincoln articulated his ideals of freedom and unity in his two inaugural addresses. **(Review pages 557, 560, 610.)** **Chapter 13, Sections 3 and 5** In 1863, Lincoln made significant statements about freedom in the Emancipation Proclamation and the Gettysburg Address. **(Review pages 592–594, 607.)**

US8.10 *cont.*

What Is the Standard?	Where Can I Find It?
US8.10.5 Study the views and lives of leaders (e.g., Ulysses S. Grant, Jefferson Davis, Robert E. Lee) and soldiers on both sides of the war, including those of black soldiers and regiments.	**Chapter 12, Section 5 and Chapter 13, Section 1** Confederate President Jefferson Davis believed in states' rights. **(Review pages 561, 573.)** **Chapter 13, Sections 2 and 5** Battlefield decisions by Ulysses S. Grant changed the course of the war for the North. **(Review pages 579, 606–611.)** **Chapter 13, Sections 1, 2, and 5** Robert E. Lee was an effective Confederate general, but he could not lead his armies to ultimate victory. **(Review pages 574, 580–583, 605–606, 610–611.)** **Chapter 13, Section 3** In both the North and South, soldiers suffered terrible hardships. Black soldiers were kept from battle early in the war, but eventually were an important part of the Union army. **(Review pages 592–593, 595–596.)**
US8.10.6 Describe critical developments and events in the war, including the major battles, geographical advantages and obstacles, technological advances, and General Lee's surrender at Appomattox.	**Chapter 13, Sections 1 and 5** Although both the North and South had advantages and disadvantages, the North was in a better overall position to fight the Civil War. Aggressive offensives by the Union finally resulted in the Confederacy surrendering at Appomattox. **(Review pages 572–573, 605–613.)**
US8.10.7 Explain how the war affected combatants, civilians, the physical environment, and future warfare.	**Chapter 13, Sections 1 to 5** The Civil War became a "total war" that affected soldiers and civilians alike. **(Review pages 574, 582, 595–596, 598–601, 609–610.)** **Chapter 13, Sections 2 and 5** The use of new technology made the Civil War one of the first of the modern wars. The Civil War had a devastating effect on the countryside—for example, Sherman's march across Georgia. **(Review pages 578–579, 609–610.)**

Standards Practice

1 Who was the leader of the Confederate Army during the Civil War?

A Thomas "Stonewall" Jackson
B Jefferson Davis
C Robert E. Lee
D Ulysses S. Grant

2 Why was the Battle of Vicksburg an important turning point in the Civil War?

A The Confederacy surrendered.
B Confederacy captured Pennsylvania.
C The North gained control of Virginia.
D It split the South in two.

US8.11

Where Can I Find It?

What Is the Standard?	Where Can I Find It?
US8.11 Students analyze the character and lasting consequences of Reconstruction.	**Chapter 14** covers the aftermath of the Civil War in different regions of the country. Additional information can be found in **Chapters 15 and 17.**
US8.11.1 List the original aims of Reconstruction and describe its effects on the political and social structures of different regions.	**Chapter 14, Sections 1 and 2** The plan for Reconstruction developed by the Radical Republicans was much harsher than that proposed by Lincoln. Johnson's opposition to Radical Reconstruction led to his impeachment. **(Review pages 625–628, 631–634.)** **Chapter 14, Section 3** Reconstruction policies enabled African Americans and anti-Confederate groups to serve in Southern governments. New schools were built in the South for African Americans. **(Review pages 636–639.)**
US8.11.2 Identify the push-pull factors in the movement of former slaves to the cities in the North and to the West and their differing experiences in those regions (e.g., the experiences of Buffalo Soldiers).	**Chapter 14, Section 4; Chapter 15, Section 2; and Chapter 17, Section 2** Some African Americans left the restrictions of the South to settle or serve as soldiers on the western frontier. Others migrated from the South to seek economic opportunities in Northern cities. **(Review pages 641, 676–677, 751.)**
US8.11.3 Understand the effects of the Freedmen's Bureau and the restrictions placed on the rights and opportunities of freedmen, including racial segregation and "Jim Crow" laws.	**Chapter 14, Section 1** During the Reconstruction period, the Freedmen's Bureau brought food, clothing, medical services, and education to former enslaved persons. **(Review page 626.)** **Chapter 14, Sections 2 and 4** As Reconstruction lost its effectiveness, new legal and cultural barriers were erected against freedoms for black Americans. **(Review pages 630, 647–649.)**
US8.11.4 Trace the rise of the Ku Klux Klan and describe the Klan's effects.	**Chapter 14, Sections 3 and 4** Some Southerners used violence to undermine freedom for African Americans. The KKK carried out acts of terror to keep African Americans from exercising their rights. **(Review pages 638, 648.)**

US8.11 *cont.*

What Is the Standard? → Where Can I Find It?

US8.11.5 Understand the Thirteenth, Fourteenth, and Fifteenth Amendments to the Constitution and analyze their connection to Reconstruction.

Chapter 14, Sections 1 and 2 Through the Thirteenth, Fourteenth, and Fifteenth Amendments, Republican leaders in Congress sought to extend and protect the rights of African Americans. **(Review pages 628, 631, 634.)**

Standards Practice

1 How could former Confederate States reenter the Union under the Reconstruction Act of 1867?

A through a majority vote of the population
B by ratifying the Fourteenth Amendment and submitting a new state constitution for approval by Congress
C by giving freed slaves the right to vote
D by signing an oath of loyalty

2 What did the Fifteenth Amendment do?

A It forbade states from denying the vote on the basis of race.
B It gave citizenship to formerly enslaved African Americans.
C It ended slavery in the United States.
D It gave the right to vote to former Confederates.

3 Northern whites who settled in the South and supported Republican policies were known as

A sharecroppers.
B segregationists.
C carpetbaggers.
D Redeemers.

US8.12

What Is the Standard?	Where Can I Find It?
US8.12 Students analyze the transformation of the American economy and the changing social and political conditions in the United States in response to the Industrial Revolution.	**Chapters 15, 16, and 17** discuss the impact of the Industrial Revolution on ranching, farming, manufacturing, urbanization, and settling the West.
US8.12.1 Trace patterns of agricultural and industrial development as they relate to climate, use of natural resources, markets, and trade and locate such development on a map.	**Chapter 15, Sections 1 and 2** New discoveries of gold and silver brought miners to the West. Cattle raised on the open range in Texas were driven north to railroad lines and shipped to eastern markets. The Homestead Act brought farmers to the West. **(Review pages 667–671, 673–679.)** **Chapter 16, Sections 1, 2, 3** After the Civil War, railroads brought about the faster transport of goods and people. The American economy shifted from agriculture to industry as the nation realized it had the necessary materials for growth. A map on page 710 shows major railroads and mining centers. **(Review pages 707–711, 717, 719–723.)** **Chapter 17, Section 4** During the early 1900s, the federal government began to regulate America's growing industry. **(Review pages 766, 770–771.)**
US8.12.2 Identify the reasons for the development of federal Indian policy and the wars with American Indians and their relationship to agricultural development and industrialization.	**Chapter 15, Section 3** White settlement of the West led to conflict with and forced changes on Native Americans. The federal government set up policies to protect the agricultural and mining interests of settlers and to relocate Native Americans. **(Review pages 685–692.)**
US8.12.3 Explain how states and the federal government encouraged business expansion through tariffs, banking, land grants, and subsidies.	**Chapter 15, Section 1** Government grants to the railroad companies included land for tracks and strips of land along railways. Cash subsidies from local governments also helped the growth of railroads. **(Review pages 669–670.)** **Chapter 17, Section 4** The federal government passed high tariffs that protected industries from foreign competition but led to higher prices for goods. **(Review page 766.)**

US8.12 *cont.*

What Is the Standard?	Where Can I Find It?
US8.12.4 **Discuss entrepreneurs, industrialists, and bankers in politics, commerce, and industry (e.g., Andrew Carnegie, John D. Rockefeller, Leland Stanford).**	**Chapter 16, Sections 1 and 3** Business leaders, such as Carnegie, Rockefeller, and Stanford, gained control of various industries and turned them into successful businesses. **(Review pages 708, 720–723.)**
US8.12.5 **Examine the location and effects of urbanization, renewed immigration, and industrialization (e.g., the effects on social fabric of cities, wealth and economic opportunity, the conservation movement).**	**Chapter 17, Sections 1, 2, and 4** During the late 1800s and early 1900s, large numbers of immigrants came to America in search of jobs and settled in neighborhoods in large urban areas. As city populations rose, cities faced health and crime problems and a growing gap between the rich and poor. Urban growth saw the introduction of new buildings, more public transportation, and city parks. Conservation also became an important issue. **(Review pages 741–747, 751–756, 771–773.)**
US8.12.6 **Discuss child labor, working conditions, and laissez-faire policies toward big business and examine the labor movement, including its leaders (e.g., Samuel Gompers), its demand for collective bargaining, and its strikes and protests over labor conditions.**	**Chapter 16, Section 4** Industrial workers labored long hours for low pay, often in unsafe conditions. Because government favored big business, workers formed labor unions to advance their interests. Union strikes sometimes turned violent. **(Review pages 725–729, 730–731.)** **Chapter 17, Section 4** Reformers sought to improve working conditions and control big business. **(Review pages 765–768.)**
US8.12.7 **Identify the sources of large-scale immigration and the contributions of immigrants to the building of cities and the economy; explain the ways in which new social and economic patterns encouraged assimilation of newcomers into the mainstream amidst growing cultural diversity; and discuss the new wave of nativism.**	**Chapter 17, Sections 1 and 3** Immigrants who arrived in America came from many different countries. They often settled in urban ethnic neighborhoods and contributed their labor and cultures. Schools helped to bring immigrant children into the mainstream. Americans in the nativist movement called for laws to limit immigration. **(Review pages 741–749, 758–763.)**
US8.12.8 **Identify the characteristics and impact of Grangerism and Populism.**	**Chapter 15, Section 4** When crop prices fell in the late 1800s, farmers formed the Grange to protect their interests. In the 1890s the Populist Party developed to represent the views of farmers and common people. Although the party did not last long, Populists got many new laws passed. **(Review pages 694–697.)**

US8.12 *cont.*

What Is the Standard? → Where Can I Find It?

US8.12.9 Name the significant inventors and their inventions and identify how they improved the quality of life (e.g., Thomas Edison, Alexander Graham Bell, Orville and Wilbur Wright).

Chapter 16, Section 2 The electric lightbulb (Edison), the telephone (Bell), and the airplane (the Wright brothers) were among the new inventions that changed the lives of Americans during the late 1800s and early 1900s. **(Review pages 713–717.)**

Standards Practice

1 Why did Great Plains farmers have to use new methods and tools?

A Factories were far away, and farmers had to fend for themselves.
B The Great Plains were dry and had a tough layer of sod.
C The Mississippi River often flooded vast areas of the Great Plains.
D Labor strikes in the East blocked the shipment of goods westward.

2 What factor was most likely to inspire migration to urban centers in the late 1800s?

A affordable housing
B libraries and museums
C employment opportunities
D education

3 Poor, run-down neighborhoods in urban areas are known as

A suburbs.
B settlements.
C subways.
D slums.

California Standards Handbook Answer Key

The answers to the California Standards Handbook presented on the previous pages are listed below. Use this answer key to check your understanding of the material covered in your grade 8 social studies course.

US8.1
page 863

1 D

US8.2
page 865

1 C

2 B

US8.3
page 867

1 B

2 C

3 D

US8.4
page 868

1 C

US8.5
page 869

1 D

US8.6
page 871

1 A

2 D

US8.7
page 872

1 C

US8.8
page 874

1 A

2 B

3 D

US8.9
page 876

1 B

2 C

US8.10
page 878

1 C

2 D

US8.11
page 880

1 B

2 A

3 C

US8.12
page 883

1 B

2 C

3 D

Glossary

This glossary includes all the yellow highlighted and boldfaced vocabulary words from your text. Content vocabulary (those words highlighted in yellow in your text) are words that relate to history content. Academic vocabulary (those words **boldfaced** in your text) are words that will help you understand all of your school subjects. Academic vocabulary is shown here with an asterisk (*).

*__abandon__ to give up completely or desert (p. 578)

abolitionist a person who strongly favors doing away with slavery (p. 529)

abstain to not take part in some activity, such as voting (p. 542)

*__access__ a way or means of approach (p. 471)

*__accommodate__ make suitable for or to provide help (p. 752)

*__accompany__ to attend as a companion (p. 296)

*__achieve__ to reach an aim or goal (p. 691)

*__acquire__ obtain or take possession of something (p. 676)

*__adapt__ to fit a new situation (p. 128)

*__adequate__ enough to satisfy a particular requirement (p. 201)

*__aid__ to provide with help (p. 626)

alien an immigrant living in a country in which he or she is not a citizen (p. 295)

amendment an addition to a formal document such as the Constitution (p. 223)

amnesty the granting of pardon to a large number of persons; protection from prosecution for an illegal act (p. 625)

annex to add a territory to one's own territory (p. 486)

*__annual__ occurs once a year (p. 472)

*__anticipate__ to look forward to (p. 224)

Antifederalists individuals who opposed ratification of the Constitution (p. 206)

*__approach__ a way to deal with an issue (p. 625)

appropriate to set something aside for a particular purpose, especially funds (p. 227)

*__area__ part of a country (p. 594)

arsenal a storage place for weapons and ammunition (p. 553)

article a part of a document, such as the Constitution, that deals with a single subject (p. 204)

*__aspect__ a certain way something appears or may be regarded (p. 744)

*__assemble__ to collect in one place or group together (p. 354)

assembly line a production system with machines and workers arranged so that each person performs an assigned task again and again as the item passes before him or her (p. 717)

*__assign__ to be given a specific role or responsibility (p. 296)

assimilate to absorb a group into the culture of a larger population (p. 744)

*__assist__ giving help when needed (p. 91)

*__assume__ to take on a special quality or responsibility (p. 231)

astrolabe an instrument used by sailors to observe positions of stars (p. 83)

*__authority__ power of influence over others (p. 180)

*__available__ easy or possible to obtain (p. 322)

barrio a Spanish-speaking neighborhood in a city, especially in the southwest U.S. (p. 782)

*__benefit__ something that does good to a person or thing (p. 759)

*__bias__ an attitude that always favors one way of feeling or acting over another (p. 780)

bicameral consisting of two houses, or chambers, especially in a legislature (p. 179)

black codes laws passed in the South just after the Civil War aimed at controlling freedmen and enabling plantation owners to exploit African American workers (p. 630)

blockade cut off an area by means of troops or warships to stop supplies or people from coming in or going out; to close off a country's ports (p. 573)

bond a note issued by the government, which promises to pay off a loan with interest (p. 281)

boomtown a community experiencing a sudden growth in business or population (pp. 503, 668)

border ruffians Missourians who traveled in armed groups to vote in Kansas's election during the mid-1850s (p. 546)

border states the states between the North and the South that were divided over whether to stay in the Union or join the Confederacy (pp. 555, 571)

bounty money given as a reward, such as to encourage enlistment in the army (p. 602)

boycott to refuse to buy items from a particular country (p. 136)

brand a symbol burned into an animal's hide to show ownership (p. 673)

* **brief** not very long (p. 636)

bullion gold or silver in the form of bars (p. 94)

bureaucracy system in which nonelected officials carry out laws and policies (p. 449)

burgesses elected representatives to an assembly (p. 119)

cabinet a group of advisers to the president (p. 280)

Californios Mexicans who lived in California (p. 496)

canal an artificial waterway (p. 392)

capital money for investment (pp. 383, 424)

capitalism an economic system based on private property and free enterprise (pp. 91, 383)

carpetbaggers name given to Northern whites who moved South after the Civil War and supported the Republicans (p. 638)

cash crop farm crop raised to be sold for money (pp. 126, 646)

casualty a military person killed, wounded, or captured (p. 579)

caucus a meeting held by a political party to choose their party's candidate for president or decide policy (pp. 293, 449)

cede to give up by treaty (p. 497)

census official count of a population (p. 389)

* **challenge** a demanding task (p. 154)

charter a document that gives the holder the right to organize settlements in an area (p. 119)

charter colony colony established by a group of settlers who had been given a formal document allowing them to settle (p. 130)

checks and balances the system in which each branch of government has a check on the other two branches so that no one branch becomes too powerful (p. 205)

circumnavigate to sail around the world (p. 85)

citizen a person who owes loyalty to and is entitled to the protection of a state or nation (p. 236)

civil war conflict between opposing groups of citizens of the same country (p. 547)

coeducation the teaching of male and female students together (p. 410)

* **collapse** to fall down suddenly (p. 542)

collective bargaining discussion between an employer and union representatives of workers over wages, hours, and working conditions (p. 727)

colony a settlement of people living in a new territory but controlled by their home country (p. 95)

Columbian Exchange exchange of goods, ideas, and people between Europe and the Americas (p. 95)

commission a group of persons directed to perform some duty (p. 643)

* **commit** to perform an action (p. 648)

* **communicate** to transmit information, thought, or feeling so it is received and understood (p. 434)

* **community** a group of people with common interests, especially when living together (p. 501)

compromise agreement between two or more sides in which each side gives up some of what it wants (p. 199)

* **concentrate** giving most attention to one central idea (p. 386)

* **concept** principle or idea (p. 491)

* **conclude** to come to a final decision (p. 345)

concurrent powers powers shared by the states and the federal government (p. 222)

* **conduct** manage or control the direction of relations between two or more parties (p. 205)

Conestoga wagon sturdy vehicle topped with white canvas and used by pioneers to move west (p. 313)

confederation a voluntary association of independent states (p. 180)

***confirm** to support or agree to (p. 280)

***conflict** a disagreement or struggle (p. 329)

conquistador Spanish explorer in the Americas in the 1500s (p. 86)

conservation the protection and preservation of natural resources (p. 771)

***consist** made up of (p. 354)

consolidation the practice of combining separate companies into one (p. 707)

***constant** happening a lot or all the time (p. 433)

constituents people that members of Congress represent (p. 227)

constitution a formal plan of government (p. 121)

***contract** an agreement between people (p. 103)

***contrary** the exact opposite (p. 327)

***contrast** showing the difference between two things when they are compared (p. 292)

***contribute** help to cause an event or situation (p. 460)

***controversy** a lot of disagreement or argument about something, usually because it affects something or someone (p. 537)

***convert** change from one to another (p. 710)

***convince** make a person believe by arguing or showing facts (p. 136)

***cooperate** to work with others to get a task done (p. 221)

cooperative store where farmers bought products from each other; an enterprise owned and operated by those who use its services (p. 694)

corporation a business in which investors own shares (p. 719)

***correspond** to communicate by letters (p. 137)

corruption dishonest or illegal actions (p. 638)

cotton gin a machine that removed seeds from cotton fiber (pp. 384, 423)

court-martial to try by a military court (p. 365)

covenant a formal agreement, or promise, between two or more people (p. 99)

***create** to make or produce (p. 638)

credit a form of loan; ability to buy goods based on future payment (p. 429)

***culture** a way of life of a group of people who share similar beliefs and customs (p. 81)

***currency** money (p. 194)

D

***debate** a verbal argument (p. 536)

debtor person or country that owes money (p. 124)

***decline** to become less in value (p. 695)

decree an order given by one in authority (p. 482)

demilitarize to remove armed forces from an area (p. 363)

***demonstrate** show by examples (p. 365)

***deny** refuse to accept (p. 626)

depression a period of low economic activity and widespread unemployment (pp. 194, 460)

***derive** the origin of something, such as a word, from which another has developed (p. 674)

***design** the creation of something according to a plan (p. 83)

***despite** without taking any notice of or being influenced by (p. 686)

***device** an object or machine which has been invented to fulfill a particular purpose (p. 713)

***devote** to use space, area, or time for a particular purpose (p. 492)

***diminish** to be reduced in size or importance (p. 238)

disarmament removal of weapons (p. 363)

discrimination unfair treatment of a group; unequal treatment because of a person's race, religion, ethnic background, or place of birth (pp. 397, 778)

dissenter person who disagrees with or opposes established views (p. 121)

***distinct** clearly different from one another (p. 291)

***distribute** to divide among several or many (p. 599)

diversity variety or difference (p. 123)

dividend a stockholder's share of a company's profits, usually as a cash payment (p. 719)

***document** an important paper (p. 103)

***dominate** having great influence over all others (p. 636)

draft the selection of persons for military service (p. 602)

Glossary

dry farming a way of farming dry land in which seeds are planted deep in the ground where there is some moisture (p. 678)

due process of law idea that the government must follow procedures established by law and guaranteed by the Constitution (p. 235)

***dynamic** to be energetic and forceful in presentation (p. 697)

***economy** the money system of a country, region, or community (p. 359)

***eliminate** to remove or get rid of (p. 645)

emancipate to free from slavery (p. 594)

embargo an order prohibiting trade with another country (p. 340)

emigrant a person who leaves a country or region to live elsewhere (p. 474)

emigrate to leave one's homeland to live elsewhere (p. 742)

empresario a person who arranged for the settlement of land in Texas during the 1800s (p. 481)

***enable** to make possible (p. 634)

encomienda system of rewarding conquistadors with tracts of land and the right to tax and demand labor from Native Americans who lived on the land (p. 88)

***encounter** an unexpected meeting (p. 580)

***enforce** to make people obey a law or to accept a new situation (p. 641)

Enlightenment movement during the 1700s that spread the idea that knowledge, reason, and science could improve society (p. 203)

***enormous** very big (p. 313)

***ensure** to make sure or certain (p. 309)

entrenched occupying a strong defensive position (p. 605)

entrepreneur someone who starts their own business (p. 93)

enumerated powers powers belonging only to the federal government (p. 222)

***environment** the combination of the soil, climate and living things that influence the survival of a plant, animal, or human being (p. 239)

***equip** to supply with necessary tools to work properly (p. 390)

***establish** to set up (p. 363)

***ethnic** relating to a large group of people classed according to common racial, national, or cultural origin or background (p. 761)

ethnic group a minority that speaks a different language or follows different customs than the majority of people in a country (p. 742)

***evaluate** judge the quality or amount (p. 580)

***eventual** happening or existing at a later time or at the end, especially after a lot of effort or problems (p. 555)

***exceed** to go beyond the limits (p. 430)

executive branch the branch of government, headed by the president, that carries out the nation's laws and policies (p. 205)

***expand** open up or spread out in terms of size, number or amount (p. 386)

***exploit** to use unfairly for one's own advantage (p. 641)

***export** to sell goods abroad (p. 95)

***extract** to remove (p. 667)

factory system system bringing manufacturing steps together in one place to increase efficiency (p. 385)

famine an extreme shortage of food (p. 398)

favorite son candidate that receives the backing of his home state rather than of the national party (p. 447)

***federal** national government (p. 453)

federalism the sharing of power between federal and state governments (pp. 204, 222)

Federalists supporters of the Constitution (p. 206)

***finance** providing funds or capital (p. 91)

fixed costs regular expenses such as housing or maintaining equipment that remain about the same year after year (p. 429)

***focus** to concentrate on a central point (p. 405)

forty-niners people who went to California during the gold rush of 1849 (p. 501)

***found** establish (p. 403)

free enterprise the freedom of private businesses to operate competitively for profit with minimal government regulation (p. 383)

free silver the unlimited production of silver coins (p. 696)

freedman a person freed from slavery (p. 626)

frigate warship (p. 355)

fugitive runaway or trying to run away (p. 541)

***function** to work or serve towards a particular goal (p. 221)

***fund** a sum of money saved, collected, or provided for a particular purpose (p. 93)

***generation** individuals born and living at the same time (p. 314)

Gilded Age the name associated with America in the late 1800s, referring to the extravagant wealth of a few and the terrible poverty that lay underneath (p. 752)

***goal** an aim or purpose (p. 413)

grandfather clause a clause that allowed individuals who did not pass the literacy test to vote if their fathers or grandfathers had voted before Reconstruction began; an exception to a law based on preexisting circumstances (p. 648)

***grant** giving consent or permission (p. 122)

***guarantee** a promise that some condition will be fulfilled (p. 341)

guerrilla tactics referring to surprise attacks or raids rather than organized warfare (p. 455)

guerrilla warfare a hit-and-run technique used in fighting a war; fighting by small bands of warriors using tactics such as sudden ambushes (p. 156)

habeas corpus a legal order for an inquiry to determine whether a person has been lawfully imprisoned (p. 600)

homestead to acquire a piece of U.S. public land by living on and cultivating it (p. 676)

horizontal integration the combining of competing firms into one corporation (p. 720)

impeach to formally charge a public official with misconduct in office (pp. 227, 633)

implied powers powers not specifically mentioned in the Constitution (pp. 224, 292)

import to buy goods from foreign markets (p. 136)

impressment forcing people into service, as in the navy (pp. 288, 339)

indentured servant laborer who agreed to work without pay for a certain period of time in exchange for passage to America (p. 126)

Industrial Revolution the change from an agrarian society to one based on industry which began in Great Britain and spread to the United States around 1800 (p. 383)

***inevitable** impossible to avoid (p. 546)

inflation a continuous rise in the price of goods and services (p. 603)

initiative the right of citizens to place a measure or issue before the voters or the legislature for approval (p. 769)

injunction a court order to stop an action, such as a strike (p. 729)

***inspect** to examine closely (p. 771)

integrate to end separation of different races and bring into equal membership in society (p. 638)

interchangeable parts uniform pieces that can be made in large quantities to replace other identical pieces (p. 385)

***interpret** explain the meaning (p. 179)

***intervene** to come between (p. 229)

***invest** to commit money in order to receive a profit (p. 719)

***involve** to contain or include (p. 236)

ironclad armored naval vessel (p. 578)

***isolate** to set or keep apart from others (p. 760)

***issue** a matter that is in dispute between two or more parties (p. 450)

isthmus a narrow strip of land connecting two larger land areas (p. 776)

***item** a good or a product (p. 504)

***job** duty or work done for pay (p. 725)

joint occupation the possession and settling of an area shared by two or more countries (p. 471)

Glossary

joint-stock company a company in which investors buy stock in the company in return for a share of its future profits (p. 93)

judicial branch the branch of government, including the federal court system, that interprets the nation's laws (p. 205)

judicial review the right of the Supreme Court to determine if a law violates the Constitution (pp. 225, 309)

***justify** having a good reason for choosing a particular side (p. 556)

L

***labor** to work for wages, such as in production of goods and services (p. 725)

laissez-faire policy that government should interfere as little as possible in the nation's economy (pp. 307, 460, 771)

land-grant college originally, an agricultural college established as a result of the 1862 Morrill Act that gave states large amounts of federal land that could be sold to raise money for education (p. 760)

landslide an overwhelming victory (p. 448)

legislative branch the branch of government that makes the nation's laws (p. 204)

***levy** an imposed tax required to pay off a country, region, or district's loan or debt (p. 194)

literacy test a method used to prevent African Americans from voting by requiring prospective voters to read and write at a specified level (p. 647)

lock in a canal, an enclosure with gates at each end used in raising or lowering boats as they pass from level to level (p. 392)

lode a mass or strip of ore sandwiched between layers of rock (p. 667)

Loyalists American colonists who remained loyal to Britain and opposed the war for independence (p. 153)

lynching putting to death a person by the illegal action of a mob (p. 648)

M

***maintain** to keep up (p. 286)

***major** to be great in size, number, or length (p. 105)

Manifest Destiny the idea popular in the United States during the 1800s that the country must expand its boundaries to the Pacific (p. 474)

***manual** done by hand (p. 399)

manumission the freeing of some enslaved persons (p. 196)

martyr a person who sacrifices his or her life for a principle or cause (p. 553)

mass production the production of large quantities of goods using machinery and often an assembly line (p. 717)

Mayflower Compact a formal document, written in 1620, that provided law and order to the Plymouth colony (p. 120)

mercantilism the theory that a state's or nation's power depended on its wealth (p. 94)

merger the combining of two or more businesses into one (p. 722)

***migrate** to move from one country to another (p. 329)

***military** armed forces (p. 124)

militia a group of civilians trained to fight in emergencies (p. 139)

***ministry** the office, duties or work of a minister (p. 413)

minutemen companies of civilian soldiers who boasted that they were ready to fight on a minute's notice (p. 140)

mission religious settlement (p. 88)

***modify** to make changes (p. 777)

***monitor** to observe for a special purpose (p. 227)

monopoly total control of a type of industry by one person or one company (p. 720)

mountain man a frontiersman living in the wilderness, as in the Rocky Mountains (p. 472)

muckraker a journalist who uncovers abuses and corruption in a society (p. 767)

mudslinging attempt to ruin an opponent's reputation with insults (p. 447)

N

national debt the amount of money a national government owes to other governments or its people (p. 281)

National Grange the first farmers' organization in the United States (p. 694)

nationalism loyalty to a nation and promotion of its interests above all others (pp. 321, 345)

nativist a person who favors those born in his country and is opposed to immigrants (pp. 401, 746)

naturalization to grant full citizenship to a foreigner (p. 236)

* **network** a system of connected parts (p. 711)

neutral taking no side in a conflict (p. 153)

neutral rights the right to sail the seas and not take sides in a war (p. 339)

neutrality a position of not taking sides in a conflict (p. 288)

* **nevertheless** despite what has just been said or referred to (p. 606)

nomadic moving from place to place with no permanent home (p. 686)

normal school a two-year school for training high school graduates as teachers (p. 405)

Northwest Passage water route to Asia through North America sought by European explorers (p. 88)

* **notion** an idea or concept (p. 529)

nullify to cancel or make ineffective (pp. 296, 450, 537)

* **obtain** to gain (p. 669)

* **obvious** easily found, seen or understood (p. 573)

* **occupy** to take possession of (pp. 157, 326)

* **occur** to happen (p. 603)

offensive position of attacking or the attack itself (p. 573)

oligopoly a market structure in which a few large companies control the prices of the industry (p. 766)

open range land not fenced or divided into lots (p. 673)

ordinance a law or regulation (p. 181)

ore a mineral mined for the valuable substance it contains, such as silver (p. 667)

* **outcome** result (p. 605)

override to overturn or defeat, as a bill proposed in Congress (p. 630)

overseer person who supervises a large operation or its workers (pp. 127, 430)

* **participate** to take part in something that others are doing (p. 194)

partisan favoring one side of an issue (p. 291)

patent a document that gives an inventor the sole legal right to an invention for a period of time (p. 384)

Patriots American colonists who were determined to fight the British until American independence was won (p. 153)

* **percent** one unit of 100 (p. 386)

* **period** length of time (p. 625)

persecute to treat someone harshly because of that person's beliefs or differences (p. 122)

petition a formal request (p. 150)

philanthropy charitable acts or gifts of money to benefit the community (p. 722)

philosophe French for "philosopher"; during the Enlightenment thinkers, such as writers, teachers, journalists, and observers of society (p. 105)

philosophy a set of beliefs or ideas related to a particular system of cultural values (p. 307)

planter large landowner (p. 326)

plurality largest single share (p. 447)

* **policy** a plan or course of action (p. 367)

political machine an organization linked to a political party that often controlled local government (p. 765)

poll tax a tax of a fixed amount per person that had to be paid before the person could vote (p. 647)

pool a group sharing in some activity, for example, among railroad barons who made secret agreements and set rates among themselves (p. 711)

popular sovereignty political theory that government is subject to the will of the people (pp. 179, 222); before the Civil War, the idea that people living in a territory had the right to decide by voting if slavery would be allowed there (p. 544)

Populist Party U.S. political party formed in 1892 representing mainly farmers, favoring free coinage of silver and government control of railroads and other monopolies (p. 695)

***pose** to put forth; to present (p. 504)

preamble the introduction to a formal document, especially the Constitution (pp. 152, 219)

precedent a tradition (p. 279)

***predominant** greater in importance, strength, influence, or authority (p. 424)

prejudice an unfair opinion not based on facts (p. 397)

presidio Spanish fort in the Americas built to protect mission settlements (p. 88)

***primary** the main or most important (p. 573); an election in which voters choose their party's candidate (p. 769)

***principle** a basic truth that other theories are based on (p. 130)

privateer armed private ship (p. 355)

***process** a continuing action or series of actions (p. 743)

***professional** engaging in a given activity as a source of support or as a career (p. 752)

***prohibit** to forbid (p. 633)

***promote** to encourage or contribute to the growth of an idea (p. 203)

proportional to be the same as or corresponding to (p. 199)

proprietary colony colony run by individuals or groups to whom land was granted (p. 130)

***prospect** the idea of something that will or might happen in the future (p. 580)

protective tariff tariff that raises the price of goods from other countries (p. 537)

***publication** printed material offered for distribution or sale (p. 530)

***publish** preparing printed material for public display or sale (p. 407)

pueblo home or community of homes built by Native Americans (p. 88)

***purchase** to buy (p. 429)

***pursue** strive to gain or accomplish a goal (p. 102)

R

radical extreme (p. 625)

ragtime a type of music with a strong rhythm and a lively melody with accented notes, which was popular in early 1900s (p. 762)

ranchero Mexican ranch owner (p. 492)

rancho huge properties for raising livestock set up by Mexican settlers in California (p. 492)

***range** series of mountain peaks (p. 501)

ratify to give official approval to (pp. 181, 206, 594)

realism an approach to literature, art, and theater that shows things as they really are (p. 761)

rebate discount or return of part of a payment (p. 710)

Rebel Confederate soldier, so called because of opposition to the established government (p. 574)

recall the right that enables voters to remove unsatisfactory elected officials from office (p. 769)

reconciliation settling by agreement or coming together again (p. 641)

Reconstruction the reorganization and rebuilding of the former Confederate states after the Civil War (p. 625)

referendum the practice of letting voters accept or reject measures proposed by the legislature (p. 769)

***region** an area, division, or district (p. 638)

regionalism in art or literature, the practice of focusing on a particular region of the country (p. 761)

***register** a written record or list of items (p. 743)

***regulate** to govern by rules or laws (p. 199)

***reinforce** to provide an army with more soldiers or weapons to make it stronger (p. 577)

***reject** to refuse to grant or consider (p. 776)

relocate to force a person or group of people to move (p. 453)

***reluctance** an unwillingness to act (p. 593)

***remove** take away or dismiss (p. 453)

Renaissance a period of intellectual and artistic creativity, c. 1300–1600 (p. 102)

rendezvous a meeting (p. 472)

repeal to cancel an act or law (p. 136)

republicanism favoring a republic, or representative democracy, as the best form of government (p. 222)

***require** to have a need for (p. 307)

reservation an area of public lands set aside for Native Americans (p. 687)

reserved powers powers retained by the states (p. 222)

resolution a formal expression of opinion (p. 139)

***resolve** to clear up any unsettled matters (p. 341)

***resource** a useful or valuable possession (p. 719)

***restrict** to place under limits (p. 550)

***reveal** to allow something to be seen that, until then, had been unknown or hidden (p. 544)

***revenue** incoming money (p. 284)

revival a series of meetings conducted by a preacher to arouse religious emotions (p. 403)

right of deposit Americans reached an agreement with Spain that would allow free navigation along the Mississippi River (p. 185)

***role** a function assigned or taken on (p. 447)

***route** an established course of travel (p. 472)

royal colony colony run by a governor and a council appointed by the king or queen (p. 130)

rule of law in ancient Roman law, everyone should be treated equally (p. 99)

S

scalawags name given by former Confederates to Southern whites who supported Republican Reconstruction of the South (p. 638)

scientific method an orderly way of collecting and analyzing evidence (p. 105)

secede to leave or withdraw (pp. 316, 450, 541)

secession withdrawal from the Union (p. 556)

sectionalism loyalty to a region (p. 536)

***secure** guarding from danger or loss (p. 155)

sedition activities aimed at weakening established government (p. 295)

segregation the separation or isolation of a race, class, or group (p. 648)

settlement house institution located in a poor neighborhood that provided numerous community services such as medical care, child care, libraries, and classes in English (p. 753)

sharecropping system of farming in which a farmer works land for an owner who provides equipment and seeds and receives a share of the crop (p. 639)

shareholder a person who invests in a corporation by buying stock and is a partial owner (p. 719)

***shift** to change from one place or position to another (p. 396)

***significant** having a major effect on something (p. 308)

***similar** having common qualities (p. 484)

slave code the laws passed in the Southern states that controlled and restricted enslaved people (p. 434)

slum poor, crowded, and run-down urban neighborhoods (p. 752)

smuggling trading illegally with other nations (p. 136)

sodbuster a name given to the Plains farmer (p. 678)

***sole** being the only one (p. 474)

sovereignty supreme power (p. 180)

speculator person who risks money in order to make a large profit (p. 282)

spiritual an African American religious folk song (p. 433)

spoils system practice of handing out government jobs to supporters; replacing government employees with the winning candidate's supporters (p. 449)

standard gauge the uniform width of 4 feet, 8.5 inches for railroad tracks, adopted during the 1880s (p. 709)

states' rights rights and powers independent of the federal government that are reserved for the states by the Constitution; the belief that states' rights supersede federal rights and law (pp. 296, 556)

***status** position or rank in relation to others (p. 482)

steerage cramped quarters on a ship's lower decks for passengers paying the lowest fares (p. 742)

stock shares of ownership a company sells in its business which often carry voting power (p. 719)

* **strategy** a careful plan or method of action (p. 341)

strike a stopping of work by workers to force an employer to meet demands (p. 397)

strikebreaker person hired to replace a striking worker in order to break up a strike (p. 727)

* **structure** an arrangement of parts (p. 279)

subsidy grant of money from the government to a person or a company for an action intended to benefit the public (p. 669)

subsistence farming farming in which only enough food to feed one's family is produced (p. 126)

* **substitute** a person or thing that takes the place of another (p. 602)

suburbs residential areas that sprang up close to or surrounding cities as a result of improvements in transportation (p. 752)

* **sufficient** enough to achieve a goal or fulfill a need (p. 573)

suffrage the right to vote (pp. 409, 449)

* **sum** describe or express briefly the important facts about something or someone (p. 425)

* **survive** to remain alive despite hardships and trauma (p. 119)

sweatshop a shop or factory where workers work long hours at low wages under unhealthy conditions (pp. 725, 744)

* **symbol** a letter, character, or sign used instead of words (p. 461)

tariff a tax on imports or exports (pp. 282, 450)

* **technique** the method or skill used in accomplishing a goal (p. 156)

* **technology** the application of scientific discoveries to practical use (pp. 82, 384, 710)

Tejano a Mexican who claims Texas as his home (p. 481)

temperance the use of little or no alcoholic drink (p. 403)

tenant farmer farmer who works land owned by another and pays rent either in cash or crops (p. 428)

tenement a building in which several families rent rooms or apartments, often with little sanitation or safety (p. 752)

theology the study of religion and religious beliefs (p. 101)

* **theory** an idea that is the starting point for argument or investigation (p. 556)

toleration the acceptance of different beliefs (p. 121)

* **topic** a subject that is discussed, written about, or studied (p. 552)

total war war on all aspects of the enemy's life (p. 609)

trade union organization of workers with the same trade or skill (pp. 397, 726)

transcendentalist any of a group of New England writers who stressed the relationship between human beings and nature, spiritual things over material things, and the importance of the individual conscience (p. 406)

transcontinental extending across a continent (p. 670)

* **transmit** transfer from one person or place to another (p. 713)

* **transport** carrying from one place to another (p. 286)

triangular trade a trade route that exchanged goods between the West Indies, the American colonies, and West Africa (p. 126)

tribute money paid for protection (p. 339)

trust a combination of firms or corporations formed by a legal agreement, especially to reduce competition (pp. 720, 766)

turnpike a road that one must pay to use; the money is used to pay for the road (p. 389)

* **ultimate** the final or extreme result (p. 279)

unconstitutional not agreeing or consistent with the Constitution (p. 282)

Underground Railroad a system that helped enslaved African Americans follow a network of escape routes out of the South to freedom in the North (p. 534)

* **underlie** to be the support or basis of (p. 767)

undertake take on as a duty (p. 389)

* **unify** to unite or bring together (p. 713)

Glossary

* **unique** being the only one of its kind (p. 325)

utopia community based on a vision of a perfect society sought by reformers (p. 403)

vaquero Hispanic ranch hand (p. 674)

vaudeville stage entertainment made up of various acts, such as dancing, singing, comedy, and magic shows (p. 763)

vertical integration the combining of companies that supply equipment and services needed for a particular industry (p. 721)

veto to reject a bill and prevent it from becoming a law (p. 459)

vigilantes people who take the law into their own hands (pp. 504, 668)

* **violate** to do harm or damage (p. 136)

* **vision** the intellectual ability to think or plan ahead (p. 505)

ward a person under the guardianship of the U.S. government (p. 782)

War Hawks Republicans during Madison's presidency who pressed for war with Britain (p. 343)

Yankee Union soldier (p. 574)

yellow journalism writing which exaggerates sensational, dramatic, and gruesome events to attract readers, named for stories that were popular during the late 1800s (p. 761)

yeoman Southern owner of a small farm who did not have enslaved people (p. 428)

Spanish Glossary

This glossary includes all the yellow highlighted and boldfaced vocabulary words from your text. Content vocabulary (those words highlighted in yellow in your text) are words that relate to history content. Academic vocabulary (those words **boldfaced** in your text) are words that will help you understand all of your school subjects. Academic vocabulary is shown with an asterisk (*).

A

***abandon / abandoner** renunciar o dejar un lugar o a una persona (p. 578)

abolitionist / abolicionista una persona que favorece firmemente suprimir la esclavitud (p. 529)

abstain / abstenerse no tomar parte de una actividad, como de votar (p. 542)

***access / acceso** modo de acercarse o entrada (p. 471)

***accommodate / acomodar** hacer ajustes o proporcionar ayuda (p. 743)

***accompany / acompañar** servir de acompañante (p. 296)

***achieve / lograr** alcanzar un objetivo o meta (p. 691)

***acquire / adquirir** obtener o tomar posesión de algo (p. 676)

***adapt / adaptar** ajustar a una nueva situación (p. 128)

***adequate / adecuado** lo suficiente para satisfacer un requisito en particular (p. 201)

***aid / ayudar** dar asistencia o socorrer (p. 626)

alien / extranjero una persona inmigrante que vive en un país en el cual no es ciudadano (p. 295)

amendment / enmienda una adición a un documento formal tal como la Constitución (p. 223)

amnesty / amnistía el otorgar perdón a un número grande de personas; la protección del proceso a causa de una acción ilegal (p. 625)

annex / anexar añadir un territorio a su propio territorio (p. 486)

***annual / anual** que sucede una vez al año (p. 472)

***anticipate / prever** esperar que algo suceda (p. 224)

Antifederalists / antifederalistas personas que estaban en contra de que se ratificara la Constitución (p. 206)

***approach / enfoque** método de resolver un asunto (p. 625)

appropriate / destinar apartar para un propósito en particular, dicho especialmente de fondos (p. 227)

***area / área** parte de un país (p. 594)

arsenal / arsenal un lugar para el almacenaje de armas y municiones (p. 553)

article / artículo una parte de un documento tal como la Constitución que trata de un solo tema (p. 204)

***aspect / aspecto** manera en que algo luce o en que se puede ver (p. 743)

***assemble / reunir** acumular en un sitio o agrupar (p. 354)

assembly line / línea de montaje un sistema de producción arreglado con máquinas y trabajadores para que cada persona haga vez tras vez su trabajo designado mientras el artículo pasa por en frente de él (p. 717)

***assign / asignar** dar un trabajo o responsabilidad en particular a alguien (p. 296)

assimilate / asimilar introducir a un grupo dentro de la cultura de una población más grande (p. 744)

***assist / asistir** dar ayuda (p. 91)

***assume / asumir** adoptar una cualidad especial o responsabilidad nueva (p. 231)

astrolabe / astrolabio un instrumento usado por los marineros para observar las posiciones de las estrellas (p. 83)

***authority / autoridad** poder o influencia sobre otras personas (p. 180)

***available / disponible** fácil o posible de conseguir (p. 322)

B

barrio / barrio una vecindad hispanoparlante de una ciudad, especialmente en el sudoeste de EE.UU. (p. 782)

***benefit / beneficio** algo que le hace el bien a alguien o algo (p. 759)

***bias / parcialidad** actitud que siempre favorece el mismo modo de pensar o actuar (p. 780)

bicameral / bicameral que consiste de dos cámaras, especialmente dicho en una legislatura (p. 179)

black codes / códigos negros leyes establecidas en el Sur al terminar la Guerra Civil para controlar a los libertos y permitir a los dueños de plantaciones la explotación de los trabajadores afroamericanos (p. 630)

blockade / bloqueo el cerrar un área por medio de tropas o de buques de guerra para prohibir el entrar y el salir de abastos y de personas; cerrar los puertos de un país (p. 573)

bond / bono una obligación hecha por el gobierno la cual promete pagar un préstamo con interés (p. 281)

boomtown / pueblo en bonanza una comunidad experimentando un auge repentino de comercio o población (pp. 503, 668)

border ruffians / rufianes fronterizos hombres de Missouri que viajaban en grupos armados a votar en la elección de Kansas a mediados de los años 1850 (p. 546)

border states / estados fronterizos los estados entre el Norte y el Sur que fueron divididos sobre el problema de quedarse en la Unión o de unirse a la Confederación (pp. 555, 571)

bounty / gratificación dinero dado como recompensa, como para animar el alistamiento en el ejército (p. 602)

boycott / boicotear rehusar comprar artículos de un país en particular (p. 136)

brand / marca a fuego un símbolo quemado en la piel de un animal para mostrar título de propiedad (p. 673)

***brief / breve** no muy largo (p. 636)

bullion / lingotes barras de oro o plata (p. 94)

bureaucracy / burocracia sistema en el cual oficiales no elegidos administran las leyes y políticas (p. 449)

burgesses / burgueses representantes elegidos para una asamblea (p. 119)

C

cabinet / gabinete un grupo de consejeros al presidente (p. 280)

Californios / californios mexicanos que vivían en California (p. 496)

canal / canal vía artificial de agua (p. 392)

capital / capital dinero para inversión (pp. 383, 424)

capitalism / capitalismo un sistema económico basado en la propiedad particular y la empresa libre (pp. 91, 383)

carpetbaggers / carpetbaggers nombre dado a los blancos norteños que se trasladaban al Sur después de la guerra y apoyaban a los republicanos (p. 638)

cash crop / cultivo comercial cosecha cultivada para vender por dinero (pp. 126, 646)

casualty / baja un miliciano muerto, herido, o capturado (p. 579)

caucus / junta electoral una reunión llevada a cabo por un partido político para escoger el candidato a la presidencia de su partido o para decidir políticas (pp. 293, 449)

cede / ceder abandonar por tratado (p. 497)

census / censo registro oficial de una población (p. 389)

***challenge / reto** desafío o tarea muy difícil (p. 154)

charter / carta de privilegio un documento que otorga los derechos de organizar establecimientos en una área (p. 119)

charter colony / colonia a carta colonia establecida por un grupo de colonizadores a quienes se les había dado un documento formal permitiéndoles colonizar (p. 130)

checks and balances / inspecciones y balances el sistema en el cual cada rama de gobierno refrena las otras dos ramas para que ninguna rama vuelva a ser demasiado poderosa (p. 205)

circumnavigate / circunnavegar navegar alrededor del mundo (p. 85)

citizen / ciudadano una persona que debe ser leal y tiene derecho a la protección de un estado o nación (p. 236)

civil war / guerra civil conflicto entre grupos opuestos de ciudadanos del mismo país (p. 547)

coeducation / coeducación la enseñanza conjunta de estudiantes hombres y mujeres (p. 410)

* **collapse / derrumbarse** caer o venirse abajo de pronto (p. 542)

collective bargaining / negociaciones colectivas discusión entre el empresario y los representantes sindicales de los trabajadores sobre salario, horas, y condiciones del taller (p. 727)

colony / colonia asentamiento de personas en un nuevo territorio controlado por su país nativo (p. 95)

Columbian Exchange / Cambio Colombiano el cambio de productos, ideas, y personas entre Europa y las Américas (p. 95)

commission / comisión un grupo de personas dirigidas a hacer algún deber (p. 643)

* **commit / cometer** llevar a cabo un acto (p. 648)

* **communicate / comunicar** transmitir información, pensamientos o sentimientos de manera que se entiendan y comprendan (p. 434)

* **community / comunidad** grupo de personas con intereses en común, especialmente cuando viven en la misma localidad (p. 501)

compromise / compromiso un acuerdo entre dos o más partidos en el cual cada partido abandona algo de lo que quiere (p. 199)

* **concentrate / concentrarse** fijar la atención en una idea central (p. 386)

* **concept / concepto** principio o idea (p. 491)

* **conclude / concluir** llegar a una decisión final (p. 345)

concurrent powers / poderes concurrentes poderes compartidos por los estados y el gobierno federal (p. 222)

* **conduct / conducir** dirigir o controlar las relaciones entre dos o más personas o grupos (p. 205)

Conestoga wagon / conestoga vehículo firme cubierto de lona blanca usado por los pioneros para moverse hacia el oeste (p. 313)

confederation / confederación asociación voluntaria de estados independientes (p. 180)

* **confirm / confirmar** apoyar o consentir (p. 280)

* **conflict / conflicto** desacuerdo o lucha (p. 329)

conquistador / conquistador explorador español en las Américas en los años 1500 (p. 86)

conservation / conservación la protección y preservación de recursos naturales (p. 771)

* **consist / consistir** estar compuesto de (p. 354)

consolidation / consolidación la práctica de juntar compañías particulares en una (p. 707)

* **constant / constante** que ocurre a menudo o todo el tiempo (p. 433)

constituents / constituyentes personas representadas por miembros del Congreso (p. 227)

constitution / constitución un plan formal de gobierno (p. 121)

* **contract / contrato** acuerdo entre personas (p. 103)

* **contrary / contrario** lo opuesto (p. 327)

* **contrast / contrastar** mostrar las diferencias entre dos cosas que se comparan (p. 292)

* **contribute / contribuir** ayudar a causar un suceso o situación (p. 460)

* **controversy / controversia** gran desacuerdo o discusión sobre algo, generalmente porque afecta o les importa a muchas personas (p. 537)

* **convert / convertir** cambiar una cosa en otra (p. 710)

* **convince / convencer** hacer que alguien crea algo por medio de razones o hechos (p. 136)

* **cooperate / cooperar** trabajar con otros para completar una tarea (p. 221)

cooperative / cooperativa una tienda donde los granjeros compraban productos uno al otro; una empresa poseída y operada por los que usan sus servicios (p. 694)

corporation / sociedad anónima un grupo autorizado por ley a montar una actividad pero con los derechos y deberes de una persona particular (p. 719)

* **correspond / corresponder** comunicarse por cartas (p. 137)

corruption / corrupción acciones deshonestas o ilegales (p. 638)

cotton gin / despepitadora de algodón una máquina que sacaba las semillas de las fibras de algodón (pp. 384, 423)

court-martial / formar un consejo de guerra ser enjuiciado por una corte militar (p. 365)

covenant / pacto acuerdo formal o promesa entre dos o más personas (p. 99)

***create / crear** hacer o producir (p. 638)

credit / crédito una forma de préstamo; la capacidad de comprar productos basada en pagos futuros (p. 429)

***culture / cultura** la manera de vivir de un grupo de personas que tienen en común sus creencias y costumbres (p. 81)

***currency / moneda** dinero (p. 194)

D

***debate / debate** discusión oral (p. 536)

debtor / deudor persona o país que debe dinero (p. 124)

***decline / decaer** perder valor (p. 695)

decree / decreto una orden o decisión dada por alguien de autoridad (p. 482)

demilitarize / desmilitarizar quitar las fuerzas armadas de un área (p. 363)

***demonstrate / demostrar** enseñar por medio de ejemplos (p. 365)

***deny / negar** no aceptar algo (p. 626)

depression / depresión un período de poca actividad económica y de desempleo extenso (pp. 194, 460)

***derive / derivarse** venir de algo, como una palabra que se ha formado de otra (p. 674)

***design / diseño** creación de un producto de acuerdo con un plan (p. 83)

***despite / a pesar de** sin tomar algo en cuenta o sin ser influido por algo (p. 686)

***device / dispositivo** invento o aparato (p. 713)

***devote / dedicar** usar un espacio, área o período de tiempo para un propósito (p. 492)

***diminish / disminuir** empequeñecer (p. 238)

disarmament / desarme eliminación de las armas (p. 363)

discrimination / discriminación trato injusto de un grupo; trato parcial a causa de la raza, la religión, los antecedentes étnicos, o lugar de nacimiento de alguién (pp. 397, 778)

dissenter / disidente persona que no esta de acuerdo con u opínese a opiniones establecidas (p. 121)

***distinct / bien diferenciados** totalmente distintos (p. 291)

***distribute / distribuir** dividir entre varios o muchos (p. 599)

diversity / diversidad variedad o diferencia (p. 123)

dividend / dividendo cheque que se paga a los accionistas, por lo general trimestralmente, representa una porción de las ganancias de la corporación (p. 719)

***document / documento** escrito importante (p. 103)

***dominate / dominar** tener gran influencia sobre todos los demás (p. 636)

draft / reclutamiento la selección de personas a servicio militar requirido (p. 602)

dry farming / agricultura seca una manera de cultivar tierra seca en la cual las semillas se plantan al fondo de la tierra donde hay un poco de humedad (p. 678)

due process of law / proceso justo de ley idea de que el gobierno debe de seguir los procesos establecidos por ley y garantizados por la Constitución (p. 235)

***dynamic / dinámico** tener mucho carácter y energía (p. 697)

E

***economy / economía** sistema monetario de un país, región o comunidad (p. 359)

***eliminate / eliminar** quitar o deshacerse de algo (p. 645)

emancipate / emancipar liberar de la esclavitud (p. 594)

embargo / embargo una orden que prohibe el comercio con otro país (p. 340)

emigrant / emigrante una persona que sale de un país o una región para vivir en otras partes (p. 474)

emigrate / emigrar dejar su patria para vivir en otras partes (p. 742)

***empresario* / empresario** una persona que arregló la coloización de tierra en Texas durante los años 1800 (p. 481)

***enable / posibilitar** hacer posible; permitir que algo suceda (p. 634)

***encomienda* / encomienda** sistema de recompensar a los conquistadores con extensiones de tierra y el derecho de recaudar impuestos y exigir mano de obra a los Nativos Americanos que vivían en la tierra (p. 88)

***encounter / encuentro casual** hallarse con otras personas inesperadamente (p. 580)

***enforce / hacer respetar** hacer que la gente obedezca la ley o que acepte una nueva situación (p. 641)

Enlightenment / Siglo de las Luces movimiento durante los años 1700 que propagaba la idea de que el conocimiento, la razón, y la ciencia podrían mejorar la sociedad (p. 203)

***enormous / enorme** muy grande (p. 313)

***ensure / asegurar** confirmar o cerciorarse de algo (p. 309)

entrenched / atrincherado que ocupa una fuerte posición defensiva (p. 605)

entrepreneur / empresario alguien que empieza su propio negocio (p. 93)

enumerated powers / poderes enumerados poderes que pertenecen solamente al gobierno federal (p. 222)

***environment / medio ambiente** combinación de suelo, clima y seres vivos que influyen en la habilidad para sobrevivir de una planta, animal o ser humano (p. 239)

***equip / equipar** proporcionar los materiales necesarios para hacer un trabajo (p. 390)

***establish / establecer** fundar, instalar o abrir (p. 363)

***ethnic / étnico** adjetivo relativo a un grupo grande de personas clasificadas según orígenes o antecedentes raciales, nacionales o culturales comunes (p. 761)

ethnic group / grupo étnico una minoría que habla un idioma diferente o que sigue costumbres diferentes que la mayoría de la gente de un país (p. 742)

***evaluate / evaluar** juzgar sobre la calidad o cantidad de algo (p. 580)

***eventual / mucho después** que sucede al pasar bastante tiempo o finalmente, en general después de mucho trabajo o muchos problemas (p. 555)

***exceed / exceder** sobrepasar los límites (p. 430)

executive branch / rama ejecutiva la rama de gobierno, dirigida por el presidente, que administra las leyes y la política de una nación (p. 205)

***expand / expandir** abrirse o ensancharse; aumentar en tamaño, número o cantidad (p. 386)

***exploit / explotar** usar de manera injusta para ventaja propia (p. 641)

***export / exportar** vender bienes en el extranjero (p. 95)

***extract / extraer** sacar (p. 667)

F

factory system / sistema de fábrica sistema que junta en un solo lugar las categorías de fabricación para aumentar la eficiencia (p. 385)

famine / hambre una escasez extrema de comida (p. 398)

favorite son / hijo favorito candidato que recibe el apoyo de su estado natal en lugar del partido nacional (p. 447)

***federal / federal** gobierno nacional (p. 453)

federalism / federalismo el compartir el poder entre el gobierno federal y los gobiernos estatales (pp. 204, 222)

Federalists / federalistas apoyadores de la Constitución (p. 206)

***finance / financiar** proporcionar fondos o capital (p. 91)

fixed costs / costos fijos gastos regulares tal como de vivienda o mantenimiento de equipo que se quedan casi iguales año tras año (p. 429)

***focus / concentrarse** fijar la atención y reflexionar sobre una idea central (p. 405)

forty-niners / forty-niners personas que fueron a California durante la fiebre del oro en 1849 (p. 501)

***found / fundar** establecer (p. 403)

free enterprise / libre comercio la libertad de empresas privadas para operarse competetivamente para ganancias con la mínima regulación gubernamental (p. 383)

free silver / plata libre la producción sin límite de monedas de plata (p. 696)

freedman / liberto una persona liberada de la esclavitud (p. 626)

frigate / fragata buque de guerra (p. 355)

fugitive / fugitivo evadido que trata de huir (p. 541)

Spanish Glossary

***function / funcionar** trabajar o servir para alcanzar una meta (p. 221)

***fund / fondo** cantidad de dinero ahorrada, colectada o proporcionada para algún propósito (p. 93)

***generation / generación** personas que nacen y viven durante los mismos años (p. 314)

Gilded Age / la Época Dorada el nombre asociado con América al final de los años 1800, referente a la gran riqueza de los tiempos y la terrible pobreza que estaba debajo (p. 752)

***goal / meta** objetivo o propósito (p. 413)

grandfather clause / cláusula de abuelo una cláusula que permitía votar a las personas que no aprobaron el examen de alfabetismo si sus padres o sus abuelos habían votado antes de que empezó la Reconstrucción; una excepción a una ley basada en circunstancias preexistentes (p. 648)

***grant / conceder** dar el consentimiento o permiso (p. 122)

***guarantee / garantía** compromiso que se va a cumplir una condición (p. 341)

guerrilla tactics / tácticas de guerrilla referente a ataques sorpresas o incursiones en lugar de la guerra organizada (p. 455)

guerrilla warfare / contienda a guerrilleros una técnica de tirar y darse a la huída usada en combates de guerra (p. 156)

habeas corpus / hábeas corpus una orden legal para una encuesta para determinar si una persona ha sido encarcelada legalmente (p. 600)

homestead / homestead adquirir una pieza de tierra pública de EE.UU. por medio de vivir en ella y cultivarla (p. 676)

horizontal integration / integración horizontal la asociación de firmas competitivas en una sociedad anónima (p. 720)

impeach / acusar acusación formal a un oficial público de mala conducta en la oficina (pp. 227, 633)

implied powers / poderes implícitos poderes no mencionados específicamente en la Constitución (pp. 224, 292)

import / importar comprar bienes de mercados extranjeros (p. 136)

impressment / requisición captura de marineros para forzarlos a servir en una marina extranjera (pp. 288, 339)

indentured servant / sirviente contratado trabajador que consiente trabajar sin pago durante un cierto período de tiempo a cambio del pasaje a América (p. 126)

Industrial Revolution / Revolución Industrial el cambio de una sociedad agraria en una basada en la industria que empezó en la Gran Bretaña y se promulgó a los Estados Unidos alrededor del año 1800 (p. 383)

***inevitable / inevitable** que no se puede impedir o escapar (p. 546)

inflation / inflación aumento contínuo del precio de productos y servicios (p. 603)

initiative / iniciativa el derecho de los ciudadanos de poner una medida o tema ante los votantes o la legislatura para aprobación (p. 769)

injunction / amonestación una orden judicial para terminar una acción, tal como una huelga (p. 729)

***inspect / inspeccionar** examinar con cuidado (p. 771)

integrate / integrar suprimir la segregación de las razas diferentes e introducir a membrecía igual y común en la sociedad (p. 638)

interchangeable parts / partes intercambiables piezas uniformes que pueden ser hechas en grandes cantidades para reemplazar otras piezas idénticas (p. 385)

***interpret / interpretar** explicar el significado (p. 179)

***intervene / intervenir** ponerse entre dos cosas (p. 229)

***invest / invertir** gastar dinero en un negocio para sacar ganancias (p. 719)

***involve / envolver** contener, involucrar o incluir (p. 236)

ironclad / acorazado buque armado (p. 578)

***isolate / aislar** separar o mantener separado de otros (p. 760)

***issue / tema** un tema que se disputa entre dos o más partidos (p. 450)

isthmus / istmo una faja estrecha de tierra que conecta dos áreas de tierra más grandes (p. 776)

***item / artículo** una mercancía o producto (p. 504)

***job / trabajo** deber o labor por la cual se recibe pago (p. 725)

joint occupation / ocupación en común la posesión y colonización de un área como esfuerzo compartido por dos o más países (p. 471)

joint-stock company / compañía por acciones una compañía en la cual los inversionistas compran acciones de la compañia a cambio de una porción de las ganancias en el futuro (p. 93)

judicial branch / rama judicial la rama de gobierno, incluyendo el sistema de tribunales federales, que interpreta las leyes de una nación (p. 205)

judicial review / repaso judicial el derecho del Tribunal Supremo para determinar si una ley viola la Constitución (pp. 225, 309)

***justify / justificar** tener buenas razones para escoger un bando (p. 556)

***labor / laborar** trabajar por un sueldo, como en la producción de bienes y servicios (p. 725)

laissez-faire / laissez-faire la creencia de que el gobierno no debe de involucrarse en los asuntos comerciales y económicos del país (pp. 307, 460, 771)

land-grant college / colegio de tierras donadas originalmente, un colegio agrícola establecido como resultado del Decreto Morrill de 1862 que dio a los estados, grandes cantidades de tierras federales que podrían ser vendidas para recaudar dinero para la educación (p. 760)

landslide / victoria arrolladora una victoria abrumadora (p. 448)

legislative branch / rama legislativa la rama de gobierno que redacta las leyes de una nación (p. 204)

***levy / gravamen** impuesto que un país, región o distrito cobra para pagar un préstamo o deuda (p. 194)

literacy test / examen de alfabetismo un método usado para prohibir a los afroamericanos a votar por requerir a presuntos votantes que pudieran leer y escribir a niveles especificados (p. 647)

lock / esclusa en un canal un recinto con puertas en cada extremo y usado para levantar y bajar los buques mientras pasan de un nivel al otro (p. 392)

lode / filón una faja o venero de mena intercalada entre estratos de piedra (p. 667)

Loyalists / lealistas colonizadores americanos que quedaron leales a la Bretaña y se opusieron a la guerra para la independencia (p. 153)

lynching / linchamiento matar a una persona a través de la acción ilegal de una muchedumbre airada (p. 648)

***maintain / mantener** continuar o sostener (p. 286)

***major / mayor** importancia que tiene gran tamaño, número o longitud (p. 105)

Manifest Destiny / Destino Manifiesto la idea popular en los Estados Unidos durante los años 1800 de que el país debería de extender sus fronteras hasta el Pacífico (p. 474)

***manual / manual** hecho a mano (p. 399)

manumission / manumisión el liberar a unas personas esclavizadas (p. 196)

martyr / mártir una persona que sacrifica su vida por un principio o una causa (p. 553)

mass production / fabricación en serie la producción de grandes cantidades de productos usando máquinas y muchas veces una línea de montaje (p. 717)

Mayflower Compact / Convenio del Mayflower un documento formal escrito en 1620 que proporcionó leyes para el mantenimiento del orden público en la colonia de Plymouth (p. 120)

mercantilism / mercantilismo idea de que el poder de una nación dependía de ampliar su comercio y aumentar sus reservas de oro (p. 94)

merger / fusión de empresas la asociación de dos o más negocios en uno (p. 722)

***migrate / migrar** mudarse de un país a otro (p. 329)

***military / militares** las fuerzas armadas (p. 124)

militia / milicia un grupo de civiles entrenados para luchar durante emergencias (p. 139)

Spanish Glossary

***ministry / clerecía** oficio, deberes y labores de un pastor (p. 413)

minutemen / *minutemen* compañías de soldados civiles que se jactaban de que podrían estar listos para tomar armas en sólo un minuto (p. 140)

mission / misión una comunidad religiosa (p. 88)

***modify / modificar** hacer cambios (p. 777)

***monitor / observar** seguir de cerca con un propósito en particular (p. 227)

monopoly / monopolio control total de una industria por una persona o una compañía (p. 720)

mountain man / hombre montañés colonizador que vivía en el monte, como en las Montañas Rocosas (p. 472)

muckraker / expositor de corrupción periodista que descubre abusos y corrupción en una sociedad (p. 767)

mudslinging / detractar intentar arruinar la reputación de un adversario con insultos (p. 447)

national debt / deuda nacional la cantidad de dinero que un gobierno debe a otros gobiernos o a su pueblo (p. 281)

National Grange / Granja Nacional la primera organización de granjeros de los Estados Unidos (p. 694)

nationalism / nacionalismo lealtad a una nación y promoción de sus intereses sobre todos los demás (pp. 321, 345)

nativist / nativista una persona que favorece a los nacidos en su patria y se opone a los inmigrantes (pp. 401, 746)

naturalization / naturalización el otorgar la plena ciudadanía a un extranjero (p. 236)

***network / red sistema** de partes conectadas (p. 711)

neutral / neutral que no toma partido a ninguna persona ni a ningún país en un conflicto (p. 153)

neutral rights / derechos neutrales el derecho para navegar en el mar sin tomar partido en una guerra (p. 339)

neutrality / neutralidad una posición de no tomar partido en un conflicto (p. 288)

***nevertheless / no obstante** sin embargo (p. 606)

nomadic / nómada que se mueve de un lugar a otro sin hogar permanente (p. 686)

normal school / escuela normal una escuela con programa de dos años para entrenar a los graduados de preparatoria para ser maestros (p. 405)

Northwest Passage / Paso Noroeste ruta acuática para Asia por América del Norte buscada por exploradores europeos (p. 88)

***notion / noción** idea o concepto (p. 529)

nullify / anular cancelar o hacer sin efecto (pp. 296, 450, 537)

***obtain / obtener** conseguir (p. 669)

***obvious / obvio** fácil de ver, comprender o hallar (p. 573)

***occupy / ocupar** tomar posesión de (pp. 157, 326)

***occur / ocurrir** suceder (p. 603)

offensive / ofensiva la posición de atacar o el mismo ataque (p. 573)

oligopoly / oligopolio mercado en que hay pocos productores y cada uno afecta pero no controla el mercado (p. 766)

open range / terreno abierto tierra sin cercas ni dividida en solares (p. 673)

ordinance / ordenanza una ley o regulación (p. 181)

ore / mena un mineral minado por la sustancia valorable que contiene, tal como plata (p. 667)

***outcome / resultado** efecto, consecuencias, o producto (p. 605)

override / vencer rechazar o derrotar, como un proyecto de ley propuesto en el Congreso (p. 630)

overseer / capataz persona que supervisa una operación grande o a sus trabajadores (pp. 127, 430)

***participate / participar** tomar parte en una actividad con otras personas (p. 194)

partisan / partidario a favor de una parte de un asunto (p. 291)

patent / patente un documento que da al inventor el derecho exclusivo legal de una invención durante un período de tiempo (p. 384)

Patriots / patriotas colonizadores americanos que estaban determinados para luchar en contra de los británicos hasta que se ganara la independencia americana (p. 153)

***percent / por ciento** una parte de 100 (p. 386)

***period / período** cantidad de tiempo (p. 625)

persecute / perseguir tratar cruelmente a alguien a causa de sus creencias o diferencias (p. 122)

petition / petición una solicitud formal (p. 150)

philanthropy / filantropía acciones caritativas o donaciones de dinero para beneficiar a la comunidad (p. 722)

philosophe / filósofo palabra francesa; durante el Siglo de las Luces, se aplicaba a intelectuales, como escritores, maestros, periodistas y observadores de la sociedad (p. 105)

philosophy / filosofía conjunto de creencias o ideas relacionadas con un sistema de valores culturales (p. 307)

planter / hacendado dueño de muchas tierras (p. 326)

plurality / pluralidad el mayor número de individuos (p. 447)

***policy / política** plan o instrucciones para lo que se va a hacer (p. 367)

political machine / máquina política una organización aliada con un partido político que muchas veces controlaba el gobierno local (p. 765)

poll tax / impuesto de capitación un impuesto de una cantidad fija por cada persona que tenía que ser pagada antes de que pudiera votar la persona (p. 647)

pool / consorcio un grupo compartiendo de una actividad, por ejemplo, entre barones ferrocarrileros que hacían acuerdos secretos y fijaban tipos entre ellos mismos (p. 711)

popular sovereignty / soberanía popular la teoría política de que el gobierno está sujeto a la voluntad del pueblo (pp. 179, 222); antes de la Guerra Civil, la idea de que la gente que vivía en un territorio tenía el derecho de decidir por votar si allí sería permitida la esclavitud (p. 544)

Populist Party / Partido Populista partido político de los EE.UU. formado en 1892 que representaba principalmente a los granjeros, que favorecía la acuñación libre de plata y el control gubernamental de ferrocarriles y otros monopolios (p. 695)

***pose / presentar** plantear; causar (p. 504)

preamble / preámbulo la introducción de un documento formal, especialmente la Constitución (pp. 152, 219)

precedent / precedente una tradición (p. 279)

***predominant / predominante** que tiene mayor importancia, fuerza, influencia o autoridad (p. 424)

prejudice / prejuicio una opinión injusta no basada en los hechos (p. 397)

presidio / presidio un fuerte español en las Américas construido para proteger las colonias misioneras (p. 88)

***primary / primario** el principal o más importante (p. 573); **elección preliminar** una elección en la cual los votantes escogen al candidato de su partido (p. 769)

***principle / principio** una verdad fundamental en que se basan otras teorías (p. 130)

privateer / buque corsario buque armado privado (p. 355)

***process / proceso** una acción continua o serie de acciones (p. 743)

***professional / profesional** que participa en una actividad para su manutención o como carrera (p. 752)

***prohibit / prohibir** vedar o no permitir (p. 633)

***promote / promover** alentar o contribuir a la diseminación de una idea (p. 203)

proportional / proporcional que son iguales o que corresponden (p. 199)

proprietary colony / colonia propietaria colonia dirigida por personas o grupos a quienes se les había otorgado la tierra (p. 130)

***prospect / perspectivas** posibilidad de que algo suceda en el futuro (p. 580)

protective tariff / arancel tarifa que sube el precio de productos de otros países (p. 537)

***publication / publicación** material impreso que se ofrece para distribución o venta (p. 530)

***publish / publicar** preparar materiales impresos para exhibición pública o venta (p. 407)

pueblo / pueblo una casa o una comunidad de casas cons-truidas por Nativos Americanos (p. 88)

* **purchase / comprar** obtener por dinero (p. 429)

* **pursue / afanarse** luchar para alcanzar una meta (p. 102)

radical / radical extremo (p. 625)

ragtime / ragtime una clase de música con un ritmo fuerte y una melodía animada con notas acentuadas que era popular al principio del siglo (p. 762)

ranchero / ranchero dueño de rancho mexicano (p. 492)

rancho / rancho propiedades grandísimas para producir ganado establecidas por colonizadores mexicanos en California (p. 492)

* **range / cordillera** serie de montañas (p. 501)

ratify / ratificar dar aprobación oficial para (pp. 181, 206, 594)

realism / realismo una perspectiva de literatura, arte, y teatro que representa las cosas tal como son (p. 761)

rebate / rebaja descuento o devolución de una porción de un pago (p. 710)

Rebel / rebelde soldado confederado, así nombrado a causa de su oposición al gobierno establecido (p. 574)

recall / elección de revocación el derecho que permite a los votantes que despidan de la oficina a los oficiales elegidos que son inadecuados (p. 769)

reconciliation / reconciliación arreglar por acuerdo o por reunirse de nuevo (p. 641)

Reconstruction / Reconstrucción la reorganización y la reconstrucción de los anteriores estados confederados después de la Guerra Civil (p. 625)

referendum / referéndum la práctica de permitir a los votantes que acepten o rechazen medidas propuestas por la legislatura (p. 769)

* **region / región** un área, división o distrito (p. 638)

regionalism / regionalismo en arte o literatura, la práctica de enfocar en una región en particular del país (p. 761)

* **register / registro** escrito con informes o datos; lista de datos (p. 743)

* **regulate / regular** gobernar de acuerdo con reglas o leyes (p. 199)

* **reinforce / reforzar** dar más soldados o armas a un ejército para hacerlo más fuerte (p. 577)

* **reject / rechazar** negarse a dar o a considerar (p. 776)

relocate / reubicar forzar a una persona o a un grupo de personas a trasladarse (p. 453)

* **reluctance / renuencia** desagrado o mala gana de hacer algo (p. 593)

* **remove / quitar** sacar, despedir, retirar (p. 453)

Renaissance / Renacimiento un período de creatividad intelectual y artística, alrededor de los años 1300–1600 (p. 102)

rendezvous / rendezvous una reunión (p. 472)

repeal / revocar cancelar un decreto o ley (p. 136)

republicanism / republicanismo que favorece una república, o sea una democracia representativa, como la mejor forma de gobierno (p. 222)

* **require / requerir** necesitar (p. 307)

reservation / reservación un área de tierra pública apartada para los Nativos Americanos (p. 687)

reserved powers / poderes reservados poderes retenidos por los estados (p. 222)

resolution / resolución una expresión formal de opinion (p. 139)

* **resolve / resolver** solucionar un asunto (p. 341)

* **resource / recurso** un bien muy útil o valioso (p. 719)

* **restrict / restringir** limitar (p. 550)

* **reveal / revelar** descubrir algo que hasta entonces estaba escondido o se desconocía (p. 544)

* **revenue / ingresos** entrada de dinero (p. 284)

revival / renacimiento religioso una serie de reuniones dirigidas por un predicador para animar emociones religiosas (p. 403)

right of deposit / derecho de depositar Estados Unidos llegó a un acuerdo con España que le permitía navegar libremente por el río Mississippi (p. 185)

* **role / papel** función dada a una persona o de la cual se hace cargo (p. 447)

* **route / ruta** camino establecido (p. 472)

Spanish Glossary

royal colony / colonia real colonia administrada por un gobernador y un consejo nombrados por el rey o reina (p. 130)

rule of law / imperio de la ley de acuerdo con la antigua ley romana, todos debían ser tratados con igualdad (p. 99)

scalawags / scalawags nombre dado por los confederados anteriores a los blancos sureños que apoyaban la Reconstrucción republicana del Sur (p. 638)

scientific method / método científico manera ordenada de recopilar y analizar pruebas (p. 105)

secede / separarse abandonar o retirar (pp. 316, 450, 541)

secession / secesión retiro de la Unión (p. 556)

sectionalism / regionalismo lealtad a una región (p. 536)

***secure / salvaguardar** proteger contra el peligro o la pérdida (p. 155)

sedition / sedición actividades con el propósito de debilitar un gobierno establecido (p. 295)

segregation / segregación la separación o aislamiento de una raza, una clase, o un grupo (p. 648)

settlement house / casa de beneficencia institución colocada en una vecindad pobre que proveía numerosos servicios a la comunidad tal como cuidado médico, cuidado de niños, bibliotecas, y clases de inglés (p. 753)

sharecropping / aparcería sistema de agricultura en el cual un granjero labra la tierra para un dueño que provee equipo y semillas y recibe una porción de la cosecha (p. 639)

shareholder / accionista una persona que invierte en una sociedad anónima por comprar acciones y que es un dueño parcial (p. 719)

***shift / mover** cambiar una cosa de lugar o posición (p. 396)

***significant / importante** significativo; que tiene un efecto profundo en algo (p. 308)

***similar / similar** semejante o parecido; con las mismas cualidades (p. 484)

slave code / código de esclavos las leyes aprobadas en los estados sureños que controlaban y restringían a la gente esclavizada (p. 434)

slum / barrio bajo vecindad pobre, superpoblada, y de de vecindades ruinosas (p. 752)

smuggling / contrabandear cambiar ilegalmente con otras naciones (p. 136)

sodbuster / rompedor de césped nombre dado al granjero de las Llanuras (p. 678)

***sole / solo** sin otra cosa o sin compañía (p. 474)

sovereignty / soberanía poder supremo (p. 180)

speculator / especulador persona que arriesga dinero para hacer una ganancia grande (p. 282)

spiritual / espiritual una canción popular religiosa afroamericana (p. 433)

spoils system / sistema de despojos la práctica de dar puestos gubernamentales a los partidarios; reemplazar a los empleados del gobierno con los partidarios del candidato victorioso (p. 449)

standard gauge / medida normal la anchura uniforme de 4 pies, 8.5 pulgadas de las vías ferroviarias, adoptada durante los años 1880 (p. 709)

states' rights / derechos estatales derechos y poderes independientes del gobierno federal que son reservados a los estados por la Constitución (pp. 296, 556)

***status / status** posición o categoría con relación a las demás personas (p. 482)

steerage / entrepuente los cuarteles apretados de las cubiertas bajas de un barco para los pasajeros que pagan los pasajes más bajos (p. 742)

stock / acciones valores de propiedad de comercio que vende una compañía que llevan muchas veces el poder de votar (p. 719)

***strategy / estrategia** plan detallado o método de proceder (p. 341)

strike / huelga un paro de trabajo por los trabajadores para forzar al empresario a satisfacer demandas (p. 397)

strikebreaker / esquirol una persona contratada para reemplazar a un huelguista para suprimir una huelga (p. 727)

***structure / estructura** disposición de las partes de algo (p. 279)

subsidy / subsidio donación de dinero del gobierno a una persona o una compañía para una acción con el propósito de beneficiar al público (p. 669)

subsistence farming / agricultura para subsistencia labranza que produce solamente la comida que se necesita para dar de comer a la familia del trabajador (p. 126)

***substitute / sustituto** persona o cosa que reemplaza a otra (p. 602)

suburbs / suburbios áreas residenciales que brotaron cerca de o alrededor de ciudades como resultado de mejoramientos de transportación (p. 752)

***sufficient / suficiente** bastante para alcanzar una meta o satisfacer una necesidad (p. 573)

suffrage / sufragio el derecho al voto (pp. 409, 449)

***sum / resumir** describir o expresar en breve los datos importantes sobre un tema (p. 425)

***survive / sobrevivir** mantenerse vivo a pesar de dificultades y traumas (p. 119)

sweatshop / fábrica-opresora un taller o fábrica donde se explota a los trabajadores, trabajándolos muchas horas por poco pago y en condiciones malsanas (pp. 725, 744)

***symbol / símbolo** letra, carácter o signo que se usa en vez de palabras (p. 461)

T

tariff / tarifa impuesto sobre productos importados o exportados (pp. 282, 450)

***technique / técnica** método o destreza que se usa para lograr una meta (p. 156)

***technology / tecnología** el uso de conocimientos científicos para propósitos prácticos (pp. 82, 384, 710)

***Tejano* / tejano** un mexicano que reclama Texas como su patria (p. 481)

temperance / templanza el uso de poca o de ninguna bebida alcohólica (p. 403)

tenant farmer / granjero arrendatario un granjero que labra la tierra de otro dueño y paga renta ya sea con la cosecha o al contado (p. 428)

tenement / casa de vecindad un edificio en el cual varias familias alquilan cuartos o apartamentos, a menudo con pocas medidas sanitarias o seguridad (p. 752)

theology / teología el estudio de la religión y las creencias religiosas (p.101)

***theory / teoría** idea que sirve de punto de partida para una discusión o investigación (p. 556)

toleration / tolerancia el aceptar creencias diferentes (p. 121)

***topic / tema** materia bajo estudio y discusión, y sobre la cual se escribe (p. 552)

total war / guerra total la guerra en todo aspecto de la vida del enemigo (p. 609)

trade union / gremio una organización de artesanos con el mismo oficio o destreza (pp. 397, 726)

transcendentalist / transcendentalista uno de un grupo de escritores de Nueva Inglaterra que acentuaban la relación entre los seres humanos y la naturaleza, asuntos espirituales sobre asuntos materiales, y la importancia de la conciencia particular (p. 406)

transcontinental / transcontinental que se extiende a través del continente (p. 670)

***transmit / transmitir** pasar de una persona o sitio a otro (p. 713)

***transport / transportar** llevar de un lugar a otro (p. 286)

triangular trade / trato triangular una ruta de comercio para cambiar productos entre las Antillas, las colonias americanas, y África del Oeste (p. 126)

tribute / tributo dinero pagado para protección (p. 339)

trust / cártel una combinación de firmas o sociedades anónimas formada por un acuerdo legal, especialmente para reducir la competición (pp. 720, 766)

turnpike / autopista una carretera que uno debe de pagar para usar; el dinero se usa para pagar el costo de la carretera (p. 389)

U

***ultimate / último** resultado final o supremo (p. 279)

unconstitutional / anticonstitucional no de acuerdo ni consistente con la Constitución (p. 282)

Underground Railroad / Ferrocarril Subterráneo un sistema que ayudó a los afroamericanos esclavizados a seguir una red de rutas de escape afuera del Sur hacia la libertad del Norte (p. 534)

underlie / subyacer estar por debajo, o servir de base o apoyo (p. 767)

undertake / emprender asumir una responsabilidad (p. 386)

***unify / unificar** unir o reunir (p. 713)

***unique / único** solo en su clase; sin igual (p. 325)

utopia / utopía una comunidad basada en una visión de la sociedad perfecta buscada por los reformistas (p. 403)

vaquero / vaquero trabajador ranchero hispánico (p. 674)

vaudeville / teatro de variedades entretenimiento compuesto de varios actos, tal como baile, canción, comedia, y espectáculos de mágica (p. 763)

vertical integration / integración vertical la asociación de compañías que abastecen con equipo y servicios necesarios para una industria particular (p. 721)

veto / vetar rechazar un proyecto de ley y prevenir que vuelva a ser una ley (p. 459)

vigilantes / vigilantes gente que toman la ley en sus propias manos (pp. 504, 668)

***violate / violar** romper la ley o hacer daño (p. 136)

***vision / visión** habilidad para pensar en el futuro y planear de antemano (p. 505)

ward / pupilo persona bajo la tutela del gobierno de Estados Unidos (p. 782)

War Hawks / halcones de guerra republicanos durante la presidencia de Madison que insistían en la guerra con la Bretaña (p. 343)

Yankee / yanqui soldado de la Unión (p. 574)

yellow journalism / periodismo amarillista escritura que exageraba acontecimientos sensacionales, dramáticos, y repulsivos para atraer a los lectores, citando historias que fueron populares durante los fines de los años 1800 (p. 761)

yeoman / terrateniente menor dueño sureño de una granja pequeña que no tenía esclavos (p. 428)

Gazetteer

A Gazetteer (GA • zuh • TIHR) *is a geographic index or dictionary. It shows latitude and longitude for cities and certain other places. Latitude and longitude are shown in this way: 48°N 2°E, or 48 degrees north latitude and two degrees east longitude. This Gazetteer lists most of the world's largest independent countries, their capitals, and several important geographic features. The page numbers tell where each entry can be found in this book.*

Abilene City in Kansas (39°N/97°W) 673

Africa Continent of the Eastern Hemisphere south of the Mediterranean Sea and adjoining Asia on its northeastern border 27, 87, 96, 100, 558, 776

Alabama State in the southeastern United States; 22nd state to enter the Union 31, 644

Alamo Texas mission captured by Mexican forces in 1836 (29°N/98°W) 483, 485

Alaska State in the United States, located in northwestern North America 26, 31, 32, 776

Albany Capital of New York State located in the Hudson Valley; site where Albany Congress proposed first formal plan to unite the 13 colonies (42°N/74°W) 390

Angel Island Island in San Francisco, California; served as an immigrant processing center (37°N/122°W) 743

Annapolis Capital city of Maryland (39°N/76°W) 31

Antietam Civil War battle site in western Maryland (40°N/78°W) 614

Appalachian Mountains Chief mountain system in eastern North America extending from Quebec and New Brunswick to central Alabama 33, 122, 135

Appomattox Court House Site in central Virginia where Confederate forces surrendered, ending the Civil War (37°N/78°W) 610

Argentina Country in South America 26

Arizona State in the southwestern United States; 48th state to enter the Union 30

Arkansas State in the south central U.S.; acquired as part of Louisiana Purchase 31, 558, 606, 632

Asia Continent of the Eastern Hemisphere forming a single landmass with Europe 26, 776

Asia Minor The peninsula forming western boundary of Asia between the Black Sea and Mediterranean Sea and bordering on the Aegean Sea to form the greater part of Turkey 100

Atlanta Capital of Georgia located in the northwest central part of the state (34°N/84°W) 33

Atlantic Ocean Ocean separating North and South America from Europe and Africa 26, 33, 87, 96, 119, 135, 156

Augusta Capital city of Maine (44°N/69°W) 31

Austin Capital city of Texas (30°N/97°W) 31

Australia Continent and country southeast of Asia 27, 776

Baltimore City on the Chesapeake Bay in central Maryland (39°N/76°W) 122

Barbary Coast North coast of Africa between Morocco and Tunisia 339

Baton Rouge Capital city of Louisiana (30°N/91°W) 31

Birmingham City in north central Alabama; scene of several civil rights protests (33°N/87°W) 721

Bismarck Capital city of North Dakota (47°N/101°W) 31

Black Hills Mountains in southwestern South Dakota; site of conflict between the Sioux and white settlers during 1870s 688

Boise Capital city of Idaho (43°N/116°W) 30

Boston Capital of Massachusetts located in the eastern part of the state; founded by English Puritans in 1630 (42°N/71°W) 122

Brazil Country in South America 26

Bull Run Site of two Civil War battles in northern Virginia; also called Manassas (39°N/77°W) 577

California State in the western United States; attracted thousands of miners during gold rush of 1849 30, 558, 644

Canada Country in northern North America 26, 31, 32–33

Cape of Good Hope Southern tip of Africa (34°S/18°E) 84

Caribbean Sea Tropical sea in the Western Hemisphere 29

Carson City Capital city of Nevada (39°N/120°W) 30

Caspian Sea Inland salt lake between Europe and Asia 100

Central America Area of North America between Mexico and South America (11°N/87°W) 29

Central Park A municipal park located on Manhattan Island in New York City; designed by Frederick Law Olmsted 755

Chancellorsville Virginia site of 1863 Confederate victory (38°N/78°W) 605, 606

Charleston (SC) City in South Carolina on the Atlantic coast; original name Charles Town (33°N/80°W) 122, 156

Charleston (WV) Capital city of West Virginia (38°N/81°W) 31

Chattanooga City in southwest Tennessee; grew into a center for trade in the South (35°N/85°W) 430

Cheyenne City in southeast Wyoming; became an important rail station for cattle drives (41°N/105°W) 673

Chile South American country (35°S/72°W) 26

China Country in eastern Asia; mainland (People's Republic of China) under Communist control since 1949 27, 776

Cincinnati City in southern Ohio on the Ohio River; grew as a result of increasing steamship traffic during the mid-1800s (39°N/84°W) 387, 390

Cleveland City in northern Ohio on Lake Erie (41°N/81°W) 533

Colombia Country in South America 26

Colorado State in the western United States 30, 644

Colorado River River that flows from the Colorado Rockies to the Gulf of California 32, 316

Columbia Capital of South Carolina; became a center for trade in the South (34°N/81°W) 430

Columbia River River flowing through southwest Canada and northwestern United States into the Pacific Ocean 32

Columbus Capital city of Ohio (40°N/83°W) 31

Concord (MA) Village northwest of Boston, Massachusetts; site of early battle of the American Revolution (42°N/71°W) 140

Concord (NH) Capital city of New Hampshire (43°N/71°W) 31

Connecticut State in the northeastern United States; one of the original 13 states 31, 121, 355, 558, 606

Cuba Country in the West Indies, North America 29, 775

Dakota Territory Included North and South Dakota, most of Wyoming and Montana; this land was created by Congress as Indian Territory 687

Delaware State in the northeastern United States; one of the original 13 states (38°N/75°W) 122, 355, 558, 606

Delaware River River flowing through eastern U.S.; empties into the Delaware Bay 390

Denver Capital city of Colorado (39°N/105°W) 31

Des Moines Capital city of Iowa (41°N/93°W) 31

Detroit City in southeastern Michigan; site of significant battles during the French and Indian War and the War of 1812 (42°N/83°W) 31, 355

Dodge City Kansas cattle town during the 19th century (37°N/100°W) 673

Dominican Republic Country in the West Indies on the eastern part of Hispaniola Island 29

Dover Capital city of Delaware (39°N/75°W) 31

Ellis Island Island in upper New York Bay; served as immigrant station from 1892–1954 (41°N/74°W) 743

England Division of the United Kingdom of Great Britain and Northern Ireland 87

Europe Continent of the northern part of the Eastern Hemisphere between Asia and the Atlantic Ocean 26, 87, 96, 776

Fallen Timbers Site in northwestern Ohio of General Anthony Wayne's victory over Native Americans in 1794 (42°N/84°W) 287

Florida State in the southeastern United States 31, 558

Fort Sumter Union fort during the Civil War located on island near Charleston, South Carolina; site of first military engagement of Civil War (33°N/80°W) 558

France Country in western Europe 30, 87

Frankfort Capital city of Kentucky (38°N/85°W) 31

Fredericksburg City and Civil War battle site in northeast Virginia (38°N/77°W) 605

Freeport City in northern Illinois; site of 1858 Lincoln-Douglas campaign debate (42°N/89°W) 552

Gadsden Purchase Portion of present-day Arizona and New Mexico; area purchased from Mexico in 1853 34, 497

Gaul Ancient country of Europe 100

Genoa Important seaport city in northwest Italy (44°N/10°E) 94

Georgia State in the southeastern United States 31, 119, 355, 558, 632

Gettysburg City and Civil War battle site in south central Pennsylvania; site where Lincoln delivered the Gettysburg Address (40°N/77°W) 605

Great Britain Kingdom in west Europe comprised of England, Scotland, and Wales 100

Great Lakes Chain of five lakes—Superior, Erie, Michigan, Ontario, and Huron—in central North America 33

Great Plains Flat grassland in the central United States 30

Great Salt Lake Lake in northern Utah with no outlet and strongly saline waters (41°N/112°W) 31, 506

Greece Country in southeastern Europe 100

Guam Unincorporated U.S. territory 775, 776

Guatemala Country in Central America, south of Mexico 29

Gulf of Mexico Gulf on the southeast coast of North America 33, 117

Haiti Country on Hispaniola Island in the West Indies 29

Harpers Ferry Town in northern West Virginia on the Potomac River (39°N/77°W) 553

Harrisburg Capital city of Pennsylvania (40°N/77°W) 31

Hartford Capital city of Connecticut (41°N/72°W) 31

Hawaii State in the United States located in the Pacific Ocean 31, 776

Hawaiian Islands Chain of volcanic and coral islands in north central Pacific Ocean; comprised of eight major islands and 114 minor islands 775, 776

Helena Capital city of Montana (46°N/112°W) 31

Hispaniola Island in the West Indies in North America (17°N/73°W) 29

Homestead City in southwest Pennsylvania; the location of Andrew Carnegie's steel plant where workers went on strike in 1892 (40°N/80°W) 729

Honolulu Capital city of Hawaii (21°N/158°W) 30

Hudson Bay Large bay in northern Canada (60°N/85°W) 29, 89, 135

Hudson River River flowing through New York State 390

Idaho State in the northwestern U.S.; ranks among top states in silver production 30

Illinois State in the north central United States; one of the states formed from the Northwest Territory 31, 558, 644

Indian Territory Land reserved by the United States government for Native Americans, now the state of Oklahoma 316, 454

Indiana State in the north central United States; one of the states formed from the Northwest Territory 31, 644

Indianapolis Capital city of Indiana (39°N/86°W) 31

Indonesia Country in Southeast Asia 27

Iowa State in the north central U.S. acquired as part of the Louisiana Purchase 31, 35, 558

Italy Country in southern Europe along the Mediterranean 26, 100

Jackson Capital city of Mississippi (32°N/90°W) 430

Jamestown First permanent English settlement in North America; located in southeastern Virginia (37°N/77°W) 122

Japan Island country in eastern Asia 27

Jefferson City Capital city of Missouri (38°N/92°W) 31

Judea The south division of Palestine under Persian, Greek, and Roman rule, succeeding the kingdom of Judah 100

Juneau Capital city of Alaska (58°N/134°W) 30

Kansas State in the central United States; fighting over slavery issue in 1850s gave territory the name "Bleeding Kansas" 31, 558, 644

Kentucky State in the south central United States; border state that sided with the Union during the Civil War 31, 558, 644

Lake Erie One of the five Great Lakes between Canada and the U.S. (42°N/81°W) 33, 355

Lake Huron One of the five Great Lakes between Canada and the U.S. (45°N/82°W) 33, 355

Lake Michigan One of the five Great Lakes between Canada and the U.S. (43°N/87°W) 33, 355

Lake Ontario The smallest of the five Great Lakes (43°N/79°W) 33, 355

Lake Superior The largest of the five Great Lakes (48°N/89°W) 33, 355

Latin America Central and South America; settled by Spain and Portugal 26

Lexington Revolutionary War battle site in eastern Massachusetts; site of first clash between colonists and British, April 19, 1775 (42°N/71°W) 140

Lincoln Capital city of Nebraska (41°N/97°W) 31

Little Bighorn River River south of Montana; where Sioux and Cheyenne warriors defeated the United States army 688

Little Rock Capital of Arkansas located in the center of the state; site of 1957 conflict over public school integration (35°N/92°W) 533

Los Angeles City along Pacific coast in southern California; industrial, financial, and trade center of western United States (34°N/118°W) 670

Louisiana State in the south central United States 31, 119, 606

Louisiana Territory Region of west central United States between the Mississippi River and the Rocky Mountains purchased from France in 1803 35, 135, 313, 316, 558, 606

Louisville City in north central Kentucky (38°N/86°W) 387

Lowell City in Massachusetts (43°N/71°W) 385

Maine State in the northeastern United States; 23rd state to enter the Union 31, 122, 558, 644

Mali Country in Western Africa 26

Manhattan Island Island at northeast end of New York Bay; part of New York City between Hudson and East rivers (44°N/76°W) 117

Maryland State in the eastern United States; one of the original 13 states 35, 122, 355, 387, 558, 606

Massachusetts State in the northeastern United States; one of the original 13 states 121, 122, 140, 558, 606

Mediterranean Sea Sea between Europe and Africa 27, 100

Memphis Tennessee city on the Mississippi River near the Mississippi border (37°N/90°W) 429

Mexican Cession Territory gained by the United States after war with Mexico in 1848 497

Mexico Country in North America south of the United States 26, 30–31, 32, 485, 495

Mexico City Capital and most populous city of Mexico (19°N/99°W) 26

Michigan State in the north central United States; one of the states formed in the Northwest Territory 31

Minnesota State in the north central United States; fur trade, good soil, and lumber attracted early settlers 31, 558, 644

Mississippi State in the southeastern United States; became English territory after French and Indian War 31, 558, 606, 644

Mississippi River River flowing through the United States from Minnesota to the Gulf of Mexico; explored by French in 1600s 33, 117

Missouri State in the south central U.S.; petition for statehood resulted in sectional conflict and the Missouri Compromise 31

Missouri River River flowing through the United States from the Rocky Mountains to the Mississippi River near St. Louis 31, 315, 316, 491

Mobile Commercial seaport in southwest Alabama; exported cotton, coal and agricultural products (31°N/88°W) 429

Mobile Bay Boundary of southwest Alabama and the Gulf of Mexico; the Union controlled this area in 1864 609

Montana State in the northwestern United States; cattle industry grew during 1850s 31, 644

Montgomery Capital of Alabama located in the central part of the state; site of 1955 bus boycott to protest segregation (32°N/86°W) 430

Nashville Capital of Tennessee located in the north central part of the state (36°N/87°W) 533

National Road Road from Baltimore, Maryland, to Vandalia, Illinois 389

Nebraska State in the central United States 31, 644

Netherlands Country in northwestern Europe 27, 87

Nevada State in the western United States 30, 644

New Amsterdam Town founded on Manhattan Island by Dutch settlers in 1625; renamed New York by British settlers (41°N/74°W) 117

New England Region in northeastern United States 33

New France French land claims stretching from Quebec to Louisiana 117, 119

New Hampshire State in the northeastern United States; one of the original 13 states 122, 558, 606

New Haven Coastal city in Connecticut; settled by Puritans in 1638 (41°N/73°W) 122

New Jersey State in the northeastern United States; one of the original 13 states 122, 355, 558, 606

New Mexico State in the southwestern United States; ceded to the United States by Mexico in 1848 31, 117

New Netherland Dutch Hudson River colony 117

New Orleans City in Louisiana in the Mississippi Delta (30°N/90°W) 289, 313, 316, 429

New Spain Part of Spain's empire in the Western Hemisphere 35, 119

New York State in the northeastern United States; one of the original 13 states 31, 117, 122, 387, 558, 606, 644

New York City City in southeastern New York State at the mouth of the Hudson River; first capital of nation (41°N/74°W) 117, 122

Newfoundland Province in eastern Canada (48°N/56°W) 29, 87, 119

Norfolk City in southeastern Virignia; Confederate forces seized a naval shipyard and rebuilt the *Merrimack* and renamed it *Virginia* (37°N/76°W) 578

North America Continent in the northern part of the Western Hemisphere between the Atlantic and Pacific oceans 26, 87, 96, 776

North Carolina State in the southeastern United States; one of the original 13 states 119, 122, 355, 558, 606, 632

North Dakota State in the north central U.S.; Congress created Dakota Territory in 1861 31

North Sea Arm of the Atlantic Ocean and east of Great Britain 100

Northwest Territory Territory north of the Ohio River and east of the Mississippi River 34, 183

O

Ohio State in the north central United States; first state in the Northwest Territory 31, 341, 389, 644

Ohio River River flowing from Allegheny and Monongahela rivers in western Pennsylvania into the Mississippi River 33, 355, 386

Oklahoma State in the south central United States; Five Civilized Tribes moved to territory in the period 1830–1842 31, 689

Oklahoma City Capital city of Oklahoma (35°N/98°W) 31

Olympia Capital city of Washington (47°N/123°W) 30

Omaha City in east Nebraska where the Populist Party held their presidential convention in 1892 (41°N/96°W) 696, 670

Oregon State in the northwestern United States; adopted woman suffrage in 1912 30, 558, 644

Oregon Country Area that is now Oregon, Idaho, Washington state, and parts of western Montana and Wyoming 363

Oregon Trail Pioneer trail from Independence, Missouri, to the Oregon Territory 474

Pacific Ocean World's largest ocean, located between Asia and the Americas 26–27, 31, 87, 119, 776

Panama Country in the southern part of Central America, occupying the Isthmus of Panama 29, 776

Panama Canal Canal built across the Isthmus of Panama through Panama to connect the Caribbean Sea and the Pacific Ocean (9°N/80°W) 776–777

Pawtucket City in north Rhode Island; location where Samuel Slater opened a cotton mill (42°N/71°W) 385

Pennsylvania State in the northeastern United States 31, 122, 558, 606, 644

Peru Country in South America, south of Ecuador and Colombia 26, 86

Petersburg City in southeastern Virginia; an important railroad city that the Union seized for nine months (37°N/78°W) 608

Philadelphia City in eastern Pennsylvania on the Delaware River; Declaration of Independence and the Constitution both adopted in city's Independence Hall (40°N/75°W) 122, 726

Philippines Island country in southeast Asia 27, 776

Phoenix Capital city of Arizona (33°N/112°W) 30

Pierre Capital city of South Dakota (44°N/100°W) 31

Pikes Peak Mountain in Rocky Mountains in central Colorado 316

Pittsburgh City in western Pennsylvania; one of the great steelmaking centers of the world (40°N/80°W) 387

Plymouth Town in eastern Massachusetts; first successful English colony in New England (42°N/71°W) 120, 122

Portsmouth Seaport city in southeast New Hampshire (43°N/71°W) 122

Portugal Country in southwestern Europe 26, 87

Potomac River River flowing from West Virginia into Chesapeake Bay 307, 390

Princeton City in west central New Jersey (40°N/75°W) 153

Promontory Summit Site where two sets of the transcontinental railroad connected 670

Providence Capital of Rhode Island; site of first English settlement in Rhode Island (42°N/71°W) 31, 122, 670

Puerto Rico United States commonwealth in the West Indies 29

Quebec City in Canada, capital of Quebec Province, on the St. Lawrence River; first settlement in New France (47°N/71°W) 117

Raleigh Capital city of North Carolina (36°N/79°W) 31

Rhode Island State in the northeastern United States; one of the original 13 states 31, 121, 355, 558, 606

Richmond Capital of Virginia located in the central part of the state; capital of the Confederacy during the Civil War (38°N/78°W) 31

Rio Grande River between the United States and Mexico in North America; forms the boundary between Texas and Mexico 32

Roanoke Island off the coast of present-day North Carolina that was site of early British colonizing efforts (36°N/77°W) 119

Rocky Mountains Mountain range in western United States and Canada in North America 32

Rome City in Italy; one of the most ancient of the European civilizations; developed a republic form of government 99

Russia Name of republic; former empire of eastern Europe and northern Asia coinciding with Soviet Union 27, 776

Sacramento Capital of California located in the north central part of the state (38°N/121°W) 670

Salem Capital city of Oregon (45°N/123°W) 30

Salt Lake City Capital of Utah located in the northern part of the state; founded by Mormons in 1847 (41°N/112°W) 474

San Antonio City in south central Texas (29°N/98°W) 483

San Diego City in southern California (33°N/117°W) 118

San Francisco City in northern California on the Pacific coast (38°N/122°W) 503

San Juan Capital city of Puerto Rico (18°N/66°W) 31

Santa Fe Capital of New Mexico located in the north central part of the state (36°N/106°W) 117, 491, 495

Santa Fe Trail Cattle trail from Independence, Missouri, to Santa Fe, New Mexico 491

Saratoga Revolutionary War battle site in the Hudson Valley of eastern New York State (43°N/74°W) 154

Savannah City in far eastern Georgia (32°N/81°W) 429

Scandinavia Region of north Europe encompassing Denmark, Norway, and Sweden 87

Seattle Washington city bordered by Puget Sound and Lake Washington (47°N/122°W) 30

Sedalia City in Missouri; the nearest trail point for Texas cattle ranchers (39°N/93°W) 673

Seneca Falls Town in New York State; site of women's rights convention in 1848 (43°N/77°W) 409

Shiloh Site of 1862 Union victory in Tennessee (35°N/88°W) 579

South America Continent in the southern part of the Western Hemisphere lying between the Atlantic and Pacific oceans 26, 119, 776

South Carolina State in the southeastern United States; one of the original 13 states 122, 355, 556, 558, 606, 632

South Dakota State in the north central United States; acquired through the Louisiana Purchase 31

Spain Country in southwestern Europe 26, 87, 100

Springfield Capital city of Illinois (40°N/90°W) 31

St. Augustine City in northeastern Florida on the Atlantic coast; oldest permanent existing European settlement in North America, founded in 1565 (30°N/81°W) 117

St. Louis City in Missouri; the invention of the steamboat played an important role in the growth of this city (39°N/90°W) 31, 390

St. Paul Capital city of Minnesota (45°N/93°W) 31

Switzerland European country in the Alps 27

Syria Ancient country in Asia at the eastern end of the Mediterranean Sea 100

Tallahassee Capital city of Florida (30°N/84°W) 31

Tennessee State in the south central United States; first state readmitted to the Union after the Civil War 31, 558, 606, 644

Tenochtitlán Aztec capital at the site of present-day Mexico City (19°N/99°W) 86

Texas State in the south central United States; Mexican colony that became a republic before joining the United States 31, 485, 495, 558, 606, 632

Topeka Capital city of Kansas (39°N/96°W) 31

Toronto City in Canada on Lake Ontario; capital of the province of Ontario (44°N/79°W) 26

Trenton Capital of New Jersey located on the Delaware River in the central part of the state; site of Revolutionary War battle in December 1776 (40°N/75°W) 153

Union of Soviet Socialist Republics See Soviet Union.

United States Country in central North America; fourth largest country in the world in both area and population 26, 495, 776

Utah State in the western United States; settled by Mormons in 1840s 30

Valley Forge Revolutionary War winter camp northwest of Philadelphia (40°N/75°W) 154

Vandalia City in south central Illinois; the National Road reached here (39°N/89°W) 389

Venezuela South American country on the Caribbean Sea 26

Venice Important seaport city in northeast Italy 94

Vermont State in the northeastern United States; 14th state to enter the Union 606

Vicksburg City and Civil War battle site in western Mississippi on the Mississippi River (32°N/91°W) 606

Virginia State in the eastern United States; colony of first permanent English settlement in the Americas 31, 120, 122, 340, 355, 558, 606, 632

Virginia City City in west Nevada; became a Comstock boomtown during the gold and silver strikes of 1859 (39°N/120°W) 668

Waltham City in northeast Massachusetts; Francis Cabot Lowell opened a textile plant in 1814 (42°N/71°W) 385

Washington State in the northwestern United States; territory reached by Lewis and Clark in 1805 30

Washington, D.C. Capital of the United States located on the Potomac River at its confluence with the Anacostia River, between Maryland and Virginia coinciding with the District of Columbia (39°N/77°W) 31, 282, 307

West Indies Islands in the Caribbean Sea, between North America and South America (19°N/79°W) 29

West Virginia State in the east central United States 31

Willamette Valley Valley of the Willamette River in western Oregon 474

Williamsburg City in southeastern Virginia (37°N/77°W) 122

Wisconsin State in the north central United States; passed first state unemployment compensation act, 1932 31, 558

Wounded Knee Site of massacre of Native Americans by soldiers in southern South Dakota in 1890 and of American Indian Movement protest in 1973 (43°N/102°W) 689, 692

Wyoming State in the western United States; territory provided women the right to vote, 1869 31

Yorktown Town in southeastern Virginia and site of final battle of Revolutionary War (37°N/76°W) 156

Index

Italicized page numbers refer to illustrations. The following abbreviations are used in the index: c = chart or graph, ctn = cartoon, m = map, p = photograph or picture, ptg = painting, q = quote.

Index

D

G

Index

Index

Index

One-Stop Internet Resources

This textbook contains one-stop Internet resources for teachers, students, and parents. Log on to ca.hss.glencoe.com for more information. Online study tools include Study Central, Chapter Overviews, ePuzzles and Games, Self-Check Quizzes, Vocabulary e-Flashcards, and Multi-Language Glossaries. Online research tools include Student Web Activities, Current Events, Beyond the Textbook Features, Web Resources, and State Resources. Especially for teachers, Glencoe offers an online Teacher Forum and Web Activity Lesson Plans. The interactive online student edition includes the complete Interactive Student Edition along with textbook updates.

Acknowledgements

Text

186 From *Second Daughter: The Story of a Slave Girl* by Mildred Pitts Walter. Copyright © 1996 by Mildred Pitts Walter. Reprinted by permission of Scholastic Inc. **346** Excerpt from *Crossing the Panther's Path* by Elizabeth Adler. Copyright © 2002 by Elizabeth Adler. Reprinted by permission of Farrar, Straus & Giroux, LLC. **507** From *Thunder on the Sierra*, by Kathy Balmes. Copyright © 2001 by Kathy Balmes. Reprinted by permission of Silver Moon Press, New York. **584** From *Rifles for Watie*, by Harold Keith. Text copyright © 1957 by Harold Keith. Used by permission of HarperCollins Publishers. **680** Excerpt from *A Lantern in Her Hand*, by Bess Streeter Aldrich. Copyright 1928 by D. Appleton & Company, renewed © 1956 by Mary Aldrich Beechner, Robert Streeter Beechner, Charles S. Aldrich, and James Whitson Aldrich. Used by permission of Penguin Group (USA) Inc.

Glencoe would like to acknowledge the artists and agencies who participated in illustrating this program: American Artists Rep., Inc.; The Artifact Group; John Brewster Creative Services; Mapping Specialists, Ltd.; Morgan-Cain & Associates; Studio Inklink; WildLife Art Ltd.

Photo Credits

vi Royalty-Free/CORBIS; **vii** (tl)Fort Ticonderoga Museum, (tr)Lexington Historical Society, Lexington, MA, (br)Copyright 1996, Virginia Historical Society, Lora Robins Collection of Virginia Art; **viii** (tr)Henry Groskinsky/Timepix, (br)Manassas National Battlefield Park/Larry Shere; **ix** Courtesy Ford Motor Company; **xi** (l)Stock Montage, (r)Chester County Historical Society, West Chester, PA; **xii** Fraunces Tavern Museum, New York City; **xiii** Jacob A. Riss Collection, Museum of the City of New York; **CA0–CA1** Royalty-Free/CORBIS; **CA2–CA3** Getty Images; **CA4–CA5 CA6–CA7** Royalty-Free/CORBIS; **CA8–CA9 CA10–CA11 CA12–CA13** Getty Images; **CA20** John Elk III./Lonely Planet Images, Inc.; **CA35** Royalty-Free/CORBIS; **38** Getty Images; **39** (bl)Rober Landau/CORBIS, Getty Images; **40** Getty Images; **48** (l)Comstock Images, (c)AP/Worldwide Photos, (r)Getty Images; **49** (t)Ron Sheridan/Ancient Art & Architecture Collection, (cl)Katie Deits/Index Stock Imagery, (b)Photo Researchers, Inc.; **50** (t)Scala/Art Resource, NY, (b) Nimatallah/Art Resource, NY; **51** (l)Michel Zabe/Museo Templo Mayor, (r)Kunsthistorisches Museum, Wien oder KHM, Wien; **52** (t)National Portrait Gallery, Smithsonian Institution/Art Resource, NY, (c)Henry Groskinsky, (bl)Mark Burnett, (br)Library of Congress; **54** NASA; **55** (l)Courtesy Denver Public Library Western History Department, (c)Huntington Library/SuperStock, (r)Henry Groskinsky; **56 59 60 62** Getty Images; **57** H. Armstrong Roberts; **60** (t)Will Hart/PhotoEdit, (bl)Massachusetts Historic Royal Palaces, (bc)The Shelburne Museum, (br)Charles & Josette Lenars/CORBIS; **61** (l)Bettmann/CORBIS, (r)Getty Images; **62** (t)Wenham Museum, (bl) Missouri Historical Society, St. Louis, (bc) Thomas Gilcrease Institute of American Art, Tulsa, OK, (br)Collection of David J. & Janice L. Frent; **63** Bettmann/CORBIS; **64** (l)St. Louis Art Museum, St. Louis, Missouri, USA/SuperStock, (r)Bettmann/CORBIS; **65** (l)Private Collection/Picture Research Consultants, (c)New York Historical Society, (r)The Saint Louis Art Museum. Gift of Bank of America; **66** (t)Richard A. Cooke/CORBIS, (b)The City of Plainfield, NJ; **68** (cw from top)Photograph Courtesy Peabody Essex Museum, SuperStock, H. ARMSTRONG ROBERTS, Pablo San Juan/CORBIS, Morgan-Cain, Tim Flach/Getty Images; **69** (cw from top)Dennis Brack/Black Star, Ted Spiegel/CORBIS, (cl)Fraunces Tavern Museum, (br)Stock Montage; **70** (cw from top)California State Library, Levi Strauss & Company, Bettmann/CORBIS, Larry Lee Photography/CORBIS, EyeWire Images; **71** (tl)Flip Schulke/Black Star, (tr)Collection of Cheekwood Museum of Art, (cl)Library of Congress, (cr)Picture Research Consultants, (bl)Bettmann/CORBIS, (br)Arthur Schatz/TimePix, Nashville, Tennessee; **72** (t)U.S. Architect of the Capitol, (bl)Scala/Art Resource, (br)Bettmann/CORBIS; **73** (bl)The Pilgrim Society, (bc)National Portrait Gallery, (br)Bettmann/CORBIS; **74** (t)Charles & Josette Lenars/CORBIS, (c)Giraudon/Art Resource, NY, (bl)Scala/Art Resource, NY, (bcl)National Portrait Gallery, (bcr)Historical Picture Collection/Stock Montage, (br)Mary Evans Picture Library; **74–75** (bkgd)Worldsat International Inc. 2004, All Rights Reserved; **75** (t)Jamestown Foundation, (c)Francis G. Mayer/CORBIS, (bl)Independence National Historical Park, (bcl)White House Historical Association, (br)Stock Montage, (bcr)National Portrait Gallery, Smithsonian Institution/Art Resource, NY; **76–77** William S. Helsel/Getty Images; **79** U.S. Architect of the Capitol; **81** (l)Hulton Archive, (r)The Bodleian Library, Oxford, Ms. Bodl. 264, fol.219R; **82** (l)National Museum of American History, Smithsonian Institution, Behring Center, (r)Photograph Courtesy Peabody Essex Museum; **83** (l)National Maritime Museum, (r)CORBIS; **84** Giraudon/Art Resource, NY; **85** Doug Martin; **88** Florida State Archives; **91** Bibliotheque Nationale, Paris; **92** Scala/Art Resource, NY; **93** Réunion des Musées Nationaux/Art Resource, NY; **94** Jack Fields/CORBIS; **99** The Jewish Museum, NY/Art Resource; **101** Archivo Iconografico, S.A./CORBIS; **102** SuperStock; **104** National Portrait Gallery, London, copyright Snark/Art Resource, NY; **106** Stock Montage; **108** The City of Plainfield, NJ; **109** 1997 Suzanne-Murphy-Larronde; **112–113** Owaki-Kulla/CORBIS; **115** Yale University Art Gallery, Bequest of Eugene Phelps Edwards; **117** Bettmann/CORBIS; **118** Robert Holmes/CORBIS; **123** Gibbes Museum of Art/Carolina Art Association; **125** (bl)National Museum of American History/Smithsonian Institution, (br)Bettmann/CORBIS; **127** file photo; **128** (bkgd)Getty, Yale University Art Gallery, Bequest of Eugene Phelps Edwards; **129** National Portrait Gallery, London/SuperStock; **130** Patrick Henry Before the Virginia House of Burgesses (1851) by Peter F. Rothermel. Red Hill, The Patrick Henry National Memorial, Brookneal, VA; **132** White House Historical Association; **133** Bettmann/CORBIS; **136** (tr)Courtesy of the Massachusetts Historical Society, (bl)file photo; **137** (bl)Library of Congress, (br)Kevin Fleming/CORBIS; **138** (tl)The Royal Collection © 2003 Her Majesty Queen Elizabeth II, (t)DAR Museum on loan from Boston Tea Party Chapter, (bl)Stock Montage, (br)Courtesy American Antiquarian Society; **139** Photograph Courtesy Peabody Essex Museum; **142** Museum of Fine Arts, Boston. Gift of Joseph W. Revere, William B. Revere, and Edward H.R. Revere; **148** (tl cl br)Doug Martin, (cr)file photo; **151** (tr)National Portrait Gallery, Smithsonian Institution/Art Resources, NY, (bl)Yale University Art Gallery; **152** Copyright 1996, Virginia Historical Society, Lora Robins Collection of Virginia Art; **153** Bettmann/CORBIS; **154** (tr)Bill Gentile/CORBIS, (bl)Fraunces Tavern Museum, New York City; **155** William T. Ranney, MARION CROSSING THE PEDEE, 1850, o/c, 1983.126; Amon Carter Museum, Fort Worth, Texas; **158 159 160** Bettmann/CORBIS; **161** Stapleton Collection/CORBIS; **165** Francis G. Mayer/CORBIS; **167** Bettmann/CORBIS; **168** (bl)Photograph Courtesy Peabody Essex Museum, (br)Courtesy Pilgrim Society, Plymouth, MA; **169** (c)Hulton-Deutsch Collection/CORBIS, (cr)Fort Ticonderoga Museum, (cl)Lexington Historical Society, Lexington, MA, (br)Bettmann/CORBIS; **170** (t)Library of Congress; **171** (tl)Bettmann/CORBIS, (tr)Charles E. Rotkin/CORBIS, (b)CORBIS; **172** (t)file photo, (c)Bettmann/CORBIS, (cr)Burstein Collection/CORBIS, (bl)Moorland Spingarn Research Center, Howard University, (bcl)Delaware Art Museum, Wilmington. Gift of Absalom Jones School, Wilmington, (br)Yale University Art Gallery, gift of Roger Sherman White, B.A. 1859; **172–173** (bkgd)Worldsat International Inc. 2004, All Rights Reserved; **173** (t)SuperStock, (tcr)Mary Evans Picture Library, (c)David R. Frazie, (bl)Bettmann/CORBIS, (bcl)Museum of Fine Arts, Boston; Bequest of Winslow Warren, (br)Getty Images; **174–175** SuperStock; **180** Picture Research Consultants; **181** (b)Minute Man National Historic Park/Rob Huntley for Chromographics; **184** Chicago Historical Society; **192** Doug Martin; **194** Bettmann/CORBIS; **195** Gallo Images/CORBIS; **196** (tr)Moorland Spingarn Research Center, Howard University, (bl)Delaware Art Museum, Wilmington. Gift of Absalom Jones School, Wilmington; **197** Independence National Historic Park; **198** Burstein Collection/CORBIS; **200** (l)Francis G. Mayer/CORBIS, (r)Joseph Sohm; Visions of America/CORBIS; **203** National Portrait Gallery, London, copyright Snark/Art Resource, NY; **204** Fred Maroon/Smithsonian Institution; **205** Richard Strauss, Smithsonian Institution/The Supreme Court Historical Society; **208** Stock Montage; **209** Bettmann/CORBIS; **210** Library of Congress/American Antiquarian Society; **211** Collection of The New York Historical Society; **214–215** Elliot Teel Photography; **217** Jeff Greenberg/Photo Edit; **218** (l) Bettmann/CORBIS, (r)White House Historical Association; **219** David Young-Wolff/Photo Edit; **220** Mary Evans Picture Library; **226** (l) Francis G. Mayer/CORBIS, (c) White House Historical Association (r)Getty Images; **227 229** Courtesy U.S. Congress; **231** Richard T. Nowitz/CORBIS; **232** Getty Images; **233** Carl Iwaski/TimePix/Getty Images; **234 235** White House Historical Association; **237** (l)North Wind/North Wind Picture Archives, (r) Jeff Greenberg/Photo Edit; **240** (t)Getty Images, (b) Bettmann/CORBIS; **241** Glenn Martin/Denver Post/Wide World Photos; **242** The Pierpont Morgan Library/Art Resource, NY; **243** (t)Burstein Collection/CORBIS, (b) Bettmann/CORBIS; **246** (t)Bettmann/CORBIS, (bl)Picture Research Consultant, (br)Courtesy U.S. Congress; **247** (t)Carl Iwaski/TimePix/Getty Images, (bl)Burstein Collection/CORBIS, (br)Mary Evans Picture Library; **248** (bkgd)Wes Thompson/The Stock Market/CORBIS, (l)Library of Congress; **250** White House Historical Association; **251** Courtesy U.S. Senate; **252** Bettmann/CORBIS; **254** Boltin Picture Library; **255** White House Historical Association; **262** Joseph Sohm; ChromoShom Inc./CORBIS; **266** Bettmann/CORBIS; **267** Nathan Benn/CORBIS; **268** TimePix; **269** Sandy Schaeffer/TimePix; **270** (t)Frank & Marie-Therese Wood Print Collection, Alexandria, VA, (bl)AKG London, (br)Giraudon/Art Resource, NY; **271** (t)North Wind Picture Archives, (bl)Michael T. Sedman/CORBIS, (br)Royalty Free/CORBIS; **272** (t)Chicago Historical Society, (c)North Wind Picture Archive, (bl)Archivo Iconografico, S.A./CORBIS, (bcl)White House Historical Association, (bcr)Bettmann/CORBIS, (br)E.S. Paxson,"Lewis and Clark at Three Forks," Courtesy of the Montana Historical Society, photograph by Don Beaty; **272–273** (bkgd)Worldsat International Inc. 2004, All Rights Reserved; **273** (t)Western American Prints, (c)Don Troiani, www.historicalartprints.com, (bl bcl)Bettmann/CORBIS, (br)Stock Montage, (bcr)Greenville County Museum of Art; **274–275** Royalty-

Free/CORBIS; 277 Stock Montage; 278 (l r)White House Historical Association, (c)Yale University Art Gallery; 279 Frank & Marie-Therese Wood Print Collection, Alexandria, VA; 280 (l)General Washington on a White Charger, Gift of Edgar William & Bernie Chrysler Garbisch, Image © 2004 Board of Trustees, National Gallery of Art, Washington D.C., (r)Fred Prouser/Reuters/CORBIS; 282 David R. Frazier; 283 Archivo Iconografico, S.A./CORBIS; 286 Courtesy Winterthur Museum; 287 Chicago Historical Society; 291 Museum of the City of New York/CORBIS; 292 Stock Montage; 294 (tr)Stock Montage, (bl)Bettmann/CORBIS; 296 Stock Montage; 298 Bettmann/CORBIS; 299 file photo; 302–303 Joe Sohm/Alamy Images; 305 Stock Montage; 306 (l)White House Historical Association, (r)Duke University Archives; 308 White House Historical Association; 310 Getty Images; 311 Museum of the City of New York/CORBIS; 312 Western American Prints; 314 Brown Brothers; 315 Bettmann/CORBIS; 318 Bates Littlehales, (t)From Curtis's Botanical Magazine, 1863, photo by Volkmar Wentzel, (bl)E.S. Paxson, "Lewis and Clark at Three Forks," Courtesy of the Montana Historical Society, photograph by Don Beaty; 319 (t)Western American Prints, (b)Kevin C. Chadwick; 321 Beinecke Rare Book and Manuscript Library, Yale University; 322 Old Dartmouth Historical Society/New Bedford Whaling Museum; 323 The Wadsworth Atheneum Museum of Art, Hartford, CT. Purchased from the Artist before 1850; 324 Bettmann/CORBIS; 325 Angelo Hornak, CORBIS; 326 327 Getty Images; 328 North Wind/North Wind Picture Archives; 330 Thomas Gilcrease Institute; 331 Missouri Historical Society, St. Louis; 334–335 Mark E. Gibson/CORBIS; 337 340 CORBIS; 342 (Tecumseh) Field Museum of Natural History; 343 Lorence Bjorklund; 344 (tr)Greenville County Museum of Art, (bl)New York Historical Society; 352 Doug Martin; 354 Library of Congress; 357 Stock Montage; 358 Don Troiani, www.historicalartprints.com; 360 (tr)Hulton Getty, (c)TIME Inc. Picture Collection, (bl)Bettmann/CORBIS; 361 (t)National Gallery of Art, (b)NY Public Library/TIME Picture Collection; 364 (l)Library of Congress, (r)Collection of the Boston Public Library, Print Division; 366 file photo; 368 Smithsonian Institution; 369 Brown Brothers; 372 (t)H. Armstrong Roberts, (bl)National Museum of American History, Smithsonian Institution, Behring Center, (br)Western American Prints; 373 (t)Missouri Historical Society, St. Louis, (r)(Tecumseh)Field Museum of Natural History, (b)Michael T. Sedman/CORBIS; 374 (t)New York Historical Society, (cl)Smithsonian Institution, (cr)HOLT-ATHERTON SPECIAL COLLECTIONS, UNIVERSITY OF THE PACIFIC LIBRARIES, (b)Bettmann/CORBIS; 375 (t)Chicago Historical Society, (c)California State Library, (b)Harper's Weekly/CORBIS; 376 (t)Joseph Sohm; Chromosohm Inc./CORBIS, (c)SuperStock, (bl)Bettmann/CORBIS, (bcl bcr)National Portrait Gallery, Smithsonian Institution/Art Resource, NY, (br)Stock Montage; 376–377 (bkgd)Worldsat International Inc. 2004, All Rights Reserved; 377 (t)Steve Vidler/SuperStock, (c)Robert Holmes/CORBIS, (bl)White House Historical Association, (bcl)Stock Montage, (bcr)Smithsonian American Art Museum, Washington, DC/Art Resource, NY, (br)file photo; 378–379 David Muench/CORBIS; 381 (l r)Bettmann/CORBIS; 382 (l)Bettmann/CORBIS, (r)Getty Images; 383 Bettmann/CORBIS; 384 Aaron Haupt; 385 Lewis Hine/Museum of Photography at George Eastman House; 388 (l)SuperStock, (c)Stock Montage; 391 Stock Montage; 392 Joseph Sohm; Chromosohm Inc./CORBIS; 395 Howard University; 396 Jack Naylor; 397 Museum of Fine Arts, Boston; Gift of Maxim Karolik 398 National Park Service Collection; 399 (bkgd)(Detail) The Bay and Harbor of New York c. 1953–1855 Samuel B. Waugh (1814–1885) Watercolor on canvas, 99 1/5 X 198 1/4 Gift of Mrs. Robert L. Littlejohn, Museum of the City of New York, 33.169, (inset)Courtesy of The Bostonian Society/Old State House; 400 United States Naval Academy Museum; 402 (c)CORBIS, (r)National Portrait Gallery, Smithsonian Institution/Art Resource, NY; 403 Bettmann/CORBIS; 404 (t)National Portrait Gallery, Smithsonian Institution, Washington, DC/Art Resource, (b)Time Life Pictures/Getty Images; 406 (bl)Brown Brothers, (br)FPG/Getty Images; 408 (r)Chicago Historical Society; 408 (l)Mount Holyoke College Art Museum, South Hadley,Massachusetts; 409 Bettmann/CORBIS; 410 (l)Chicago Historical Society, (r)Meserve-Kunhardt Collection, courtesy Picture History, Mt. Kisco, NY; 411 (tl)Courtesy of Maria Mitchell Association, (tr)National Archives of Canada, (bl)Bettmann/CORBIS, (bc)Hulton Archive, (br)Nebraska State Historical Society Photograph Collections; 412 Robert Jackson; 414 (t)Library of Congress, (b)Old Dartmouth Historical Society/New Bedford Whaling Museum; 418–419 Bob Krist/CORBIS; 421 The J. Paul Getty Museum; 422 Smithsonian Institution; 423 James Randklev/CORBIS; 424 Bettmann/CORBIS, (r)Smithsonian Institution; 428 Jan Butchofsky-Houser/CORBIS; 429 The J. Paul Getty Museum; 430 Bettmann/CORBIS; 432 (l)Picture Research Consultants, (r)Stock Montage; 434 Trustees of the Boston Public Library; 435 (bkgd)Photo Researchers, (tr)John Deere Museum, (c)Adam Woolfitt/CORBIS (bl)Courtesy of The Charleston Museum, Charleston, South Carolina, (br)Valentine Museum; 436 Stock Montage; 438 Bettmann/CORBIS; 439 Photo Researchers; 442–443 Peter Gridley/Getty Images; 442 (l)White House Historical Association, (c)SuperStock, (r)National Portrait Gallery, Smithsonian Institution/Art Resource, NY; 445 Bettmann/CORBIS; 446 White House Historical Association; 447 New York Historical Society; 448 Pat & Chuck Blackley; 449 Library Company of Philadelphia; 450 North Wind Picture Archive; 452 (l)Smithsonian American Art Museum, Washington, DC/Art Resource, NY, (r)SuperStock; 453 Stock Montage; 455 SuperStock; 456 Smithsonian American Art Museum, Washington, DC/Art Resource, NY; 457 Thomas Gilcrease Institute of American Art, Tulsa, OK; 458 (l)Bettmann/CORBIS, (r)National Portrait Gallery, Smithsonian Institution/Art Resource, NY; 459 Bettmann/CORBIS; 460 New York Historical Society; 462 CORBIS; 463 Archives and Manuscripts Division of the Oklahoma Historical Society; 466–467 Steve Vidler/SuperStock; 468 Hulton Archive/Getty Images; 470 (l)Mongerson-Wunderlich Gallery, Chicago, (r)White House Historical Association; 471 Hulton Archive/Getty Images; 472 (l)Joel W. Rogers/CORBIS, (r)Bettmann/CORBIS; 473 (t)Mongerson-Wunderlich Gallery, Chicago, (b)Henry Groskinsky/Timepix; 476 National Portrait Gallery, Smithsonian Institution/Art Resource, NY; 477 Library of Congress, Prints & Photographs Division; 478 (l)Brown Brothers, (r)Bettmann/CORBIS; 479 (br)Northwind Picture Archives, (r)Brown Brothers, (bl)Chicago Historical Society/Photo Researchers Inc.; 480 (l)Texas Department of Highways and Public Transportation, (r)Texas State Library and Archives Commission; 481 (l)Center for American History/Barker Collection/UT-Austin, (r)Texas State Library and Archives Commission; 482–483 (bkgd)Friends of the Governor's Mansion, Austin; 484 Susanna Dickinson by Harry Anthony DeYoung. Alamo Collection. Photograph courtesy the Daughters of the Republic of Texas Library. CT97.9.; 485 Texas State Library and Archives Commission; 486 (l)Texas State Library and Archives Commission, photo by Eric Beggs, (r)San Jacinto Museum History Association; 488 (tr)Jim Corwin/Index Stock Imagery, (bl)Royalty-Free/CORBIS; 489 CORBIS; 490 (l)Chicago Historical Society, (r)California State Library; 491 (tl)Robert Holmes/CORBIS; 492 Thomas Gilcrease Institute of American Art, Tulsa, OK; 493 Arte Publico Press Archives; 494 Courtesy The Bancroft Library, University of California, Berkeley; 496 (l)file photo, (r)California State Library; 498 (l)Gerald French/CORBIS, (r)In house file; 499 Alaska Division of Tourism; 500 (l)Courtesy Wells Fargo Bank, (r)California State Capitol; 501 Courtesy The Oakland Museum; 502 Courtesy The Bancroft Library University of California, Berkeley; 503 (l)Levi Strauss & Company, (r)Syracuse Newspapers/The Image Works; 504 (t)Royalty-Free/CORBIS, (l)Courtesy The Bancroft Library University of California, Berkeley, (r)Monterey Public Library, California History Room Archives; 505 Courtesy Museum of Art, Brigham Young University; 513 Doug Martin; 514 Courtesy Denver Public Library Western History Collection; 515 Bettmann/CORBIS; 518 (t)Henry Groskinsky, (bl)American Antiquarian Society, (br)Collection of David J. and Janice L. Frent; 519 (t)New York Historical Society, (c)Stock Montage, (b)Courtesy The Oakland Museum; 520 (tr)CORBIS, (br)Courtesy of the United States Naval Academy Museum; 521 (tl)Michigan Capitol Committee, photography by Peter Glendinning, (tr)Museum of the Confederacy, (c)CORBIS, (b)Image Select/Art Resource, NY; 522 (l)Bettmann/CORBIS, (c)Thad Samuels Abell II/Getty Images, (bl)Chester County Historical Society, West Chester, PA, (bcl)Collection of William Gladstone, (bcr)Missouri Historical Society, St. Louis, (br)Courtesy Chicago Historical Society; 522–533 (bkgd)Worldsat International Inc. 2004, All Rights Reserved; 523 (t)Joseph Sohm; ChromoSohm Inc./CORBIS, (c)Lee Snider/Photo Images/CORBIS, (bl)National Archives, (bcl)CORBIS, (bcr)FPG, (br)White House Historical Association; 524–525 William A. Bake/CORBIS; 527 Getty Images; 530 Peabody Essex Museum/Mark Sexton; 531 CORBIS; 532 Collection of William Gladstone; 536 New York Historical Society; 537 Bettmann/CORBIS; 538 file photo; 539 The Corcoran Gallery of Art/CORBIS; 540 Gianni Dagli Orti/CORBIS; 541 New York Public Library, print division.; 544 Bettmann/CORBIS; 545 Schlesinger Library, Radcliffe Institute, Harvard University; 548 (l)White House Historical Association, (c)Missouri Historical Society, St. Louis, (r)National Portrait Gallery, Smithsonian Institution; 550 (t)The Supreme Court of the United States Office of the Curator, #1991.402.2, (b)Library of Congress; 551 The Miriam Matthews Collection; 552 Courtesy Illinois State Historical Library; 555 Chicago Historical Society; 557 Bettmann/CORBIS; 560 561 CORBIS; 562 Massachusetts Historical Society/Picture Research Consultants; 563 Bettmann/CORBIS; 560 (cl)Doug Martin; 565–566 Thad Samuels Abell II/Getty Images; 566 (tl)Museum of the Confederacy, (bl)Michigan Capitol Committee, photography by Peter Glendinning, (r)Getty Images; 569 Museum of the Confederacy; 570 Seventh Regiment Fund, New York City; 572–573 (bkgd)Getty Images; 574 Kean E. Wilcox Collection; 575 Royalty Free/CORBIS; 577 Manassas National Battlefield Park/Larry Sherer; 578 Getty Images; 580 (l)Michigan Capitol Committee, photography by Peter Glendinning, (r)Museum of the Confederacy; 582 Medford Historical Society Collection/CORBIS; 590 Doug Martin; 591 (l)Getty Images, (r)McLellan Lincoln Collection, The John Hay Library, Brown University/John Miller; 592 593 Getty Images; 595 file photo; 597 Kean E. Wilcox Collection; 598 (bkgd)Getty Images, (t)Museum of the Confederacy; 599 Library of Congress; 601 Hulton Archive/Getty Images; 602 (l)Brown Brothers, (c)file photo, (r)CORBIS; **607** Lester Lefkowitz/CORBIS; **610** Northwind Picture Archives; **611** (tr)Washington & Lee University, Virginia, (bl)Bettmann/CORBIS; **612** National Archives; **616** Medford Historical Society Collection/CORBIS; **617** Museum of the Confederacy; **620** (tl)Time Life Books, from the series Civil War/Edward Owen, (bl)Illinois State Historical Library, (bc)Bettmann/CORBIS; **620–621** CORBIS; **623** Photographic History Collection, National Museum of American History, Smithsonian Institution, negative number 86-11374; **624** (l)National Museum of American History, Smithsonian Institution, Behring Center, (r)North Wind Picture Archive; **625** Thaddeus Stevens by Edward Dalton, The Library of the Union League of Philadelphia photo by Rick Echelmeyer; **627** Howard University; **629** White House Historical Association; **630** Chicago Historical Society; **631** Collection of Cheekwood Museum of Art, Nashville, Tennessee; **633** Bettmann/CORBIS; **635 636** CORBIS; **637** Chester County Historical Society, West Chester, PA; **639** Photographic History Collection, National Museum of American History, Smithsonian Institution, negative number 86-11374.; **640** White House Historical Association; **641** Stock Montage; **642** (c)file photo; **642–643** (bkgd)CORBIS; **643** (r)Bettmann/CORBIS; **646** Pembroke Herbert/Picture Research Consultants; **647** Amistad Foundation/Wadsworth Atheneum; **648** The Museum of American Political Life, University of Hartford; **649** Brown Brothers; **650** Bettmann/CORBIS; **651** Carl Iwaski/TimePix/Getty Images; **652** Cook Collection/Valentine Museum; **653** Library of Congress/CORBIS; **656** (tl tr)Museum of the Confederacy, (bl)Frank & Marie-Therese Wood Print Collection, Alexandria, VA, (br)Getty Images; **657** (t)Illinois State Historical Library, (c)Chicago Historical Society, (b)Getty Images; **658** (t)Stanford University Museum of Art, (c)Getty Images, (bl)Museo Civico Modigliana, Italy/Dagli Orti/Art Archive, (br)Mary Evans Picture Library; **659** (t)Library of Congress, (c)Ted Streshinsky/CORBIS, (b)Brown Brothers; **660** (t)Wolfgang Kaehler/CORBIS, (cl)Stock Montage, (cr)Worldsat International Inc. 2004, All Rights Reserved, (bl)National Anthropological Archives, Smithsonian Institution (neg. #2906), (bcl)CORBIS, (bcr)Bettmann/CORBIS, (br)Jane Addams Memorial Collection (JAMC neg. 1003), The University Library, University of Illinois at Chicago; **660–661** (bkgd)Worldsat International Inc. 2004, All Rights Reserved; **661** (t)CORBIS, (cl)Worldsat International Inc. 2004, All Rights Reserved, (cr)Bettmann/CORBIS, (bl)Oscar White/CORBIS, (bcl)Archive Photo, (bcr)Oscar B. Willis/The Schomburg Center for Research in Black Culture, New York Public Library, (br)The Schomburg Center for Research in Black Culture, New York Public Library; **662** (l)Library of Congress, (r)Collection of David J. & Janice L. Frent; **662–663** Wyoming Division of Cultural Resources; **665** Photograph from the book The Life and Adventures of Nat Love by himself/Rare Book and Manuscripts, Special Collections Library, Duke University, Durham, North Carolina; **667** CORBIS; **668** Colorado Historical Society; **669** (l)Brown Brothers, (r)L. Berger/SuperStock; **670** From the original painting by Mort Kunstler, The Race, Mort Kunstler, Inc.; **673** Photograph from the book The Life and Adventures of Nat Love by himself/Rare Book and Manuscripts, Special Collections Library, Duke University, Durham, North Carolina; **674** Thomas Gilcrease Institute of American Art, Tulsa, OK; **675** Yale Collection of Western Americana, Beinecke Rare Book & Manuscript Library; **677** United States Military Museum, West Point; **678** (l)Nebraska State Historical Society Photograph Collections, (r)Montana Historical Society, Helena; **684** Doug Martin; **686** Smithsonian American Art Museum, Washington, DC/Art Resource, NY; **687** Courtesy, National Museum of the American Indian, Smithsonian Institution (20/6563). Photo by Carmelo Guadagno.; **688** Denver Public Library, Western History Collection; **690** Bettmann/CORBIS; **691** National Portrait Gallery, Smithsonian Institution/Art Resource, NY; **693** (l)Collection of David J. & Janice L. Frent, (r)White House Historical Association; **694** New York Historical Society; **695** Kansas State Historical Society; **696** AP/Wide World Photos; **698** Amon Carter Museum, Fort Worth, Texas; **699** file photo; **702–703** Huntington Library/SuperStock; **702** (l)Courtesy Rockefeller Archive Center, (r)Photo by Dane Penland, National Air and Space Museum, Smithsonian Institution (SI 79-764); **705** Kansas Collection, Spencer Research Library, University of Kansas Libraries; **707** Michael Masslan Historic Photographs/CORBIS; **708** Getty Images; **712** (l)Electricity Collections, National Museum of American History, Smithsonian Institution, (r)Courtesy Ford Motor Company; **714–715** Brown Brothers; **716** (tl)Electricity Collections, National Museum of American History, Smithsonian Institution, (tc)Picture Research Consultants, (tr)The Queens Borough Public Library, Long Island Division, Latimer Family Papers, (bl)Picture Research Consultants, (br)Courtesy George Eastman House; **718** (l)Courtesy Rockefeller Archive Center, (r)National Portrait Gallery/Smithsonian Institution/Art Resource, NY; **720** Library of Congress; **721** (l)National Portrait Gallery/Smithsonian Institution/Art Resource, NY, (r)National Park Service; **722** Courtesy Rockefeller Archive Center; **724** (l)The George Meany Memorial Archives, (r)Library of Congress; **725** Library of Congress; **726** Fine Arts Museums of San Francisco, Gift of Mr. and Mrs. John D. Rockefeller 3rd 1979.7.4 zz; **728** Bettmann/CORBIS; **730** Time Life Pictures/Getty Images; **731** North Wind/North Wind Picture Archives; **732 733** CORBIS; **736–737** Charles O'Rear/CORBIS; **736** (l)Bettmann/CORBIS, (r)Brown Brothers; **738** CORBIS; **739** Picture Research Consultants; **741** Library of Congress; **743** Jacob A. Riis Collection, Museum of the City of New York; **744** (t)National Archives, (b)Brown Brothers; **745** Bettmann/CORBIS; **746** Picture Research Consultants; **748** Rykoff Collection/CORBIS; **749** Austrian Archives/CORBIS; **752** Orchard Films; **753** Jane Addams Memorial Collection (JAMC neg. 1003), The University Library, University of Illinois at Chicago; **754** Brown Brothers; **755** CORBIS; **757** (l)Doug Martin, (c)Courtesy, National Museum of the American Indian, Smithsonian Institution (N36122/3), (r)Harris Ewing; **758** Library of Congress; **759** (bc br)Bettmann/CORBIS, (others)Library of Congress; **760** (t)CORBIS, (bl)Courtesy, National Museum of the American Indian, Smithsonian Institution, (br)Courtesy, National Museum of the American Indian, Smithsonian Institution (N36122/3).; **762** Winslow Homer American, 1836–1910. Girls with Lobster, 1873. Watercolor and gouache over graphite, 24.2 X 32.9 cm. (c) The Cleveland Museum of Art, 2002. Purchase from the J. H. Wade Fund, 1943.660; **764** (l)White House Historical Association, (r)The Ida M. Tarbell Collection, Pelletier Library, Allegheny College; **765** Library of Congress; **766** CORBIS; **768** file photo; **769** Bettmann/CORBIS; **770** Collection of David J. & Janice L. Frent; **772** Daniel J. Cox/naturalexposures.com; **773** Robin Brandt; **777** (l)Leonard de Selva/CORBIS, (r)Private Collection/courtesy R.H. Love Galleries, Chicago; **779** (l)Bettmann/CORBIS, (r)Private Collection; **781** (t)Oscar White/CORBIS, (b)The Schomburg Center for Research in Black Culture, New York Public Library; **782** CORBIS; **784** (bl)Harris Ewing; **785** (tr)Schenectady Museum/Hall of Electrical History Foundation/CORBIS, (others)Bettmann/CORBIS; **786** Underwood & Underwood/CORBIS; **787** Library of Congress; **790** (t)Brown Brothers, (bl)Bob Mullenix, (br)Picture Research Consultants; **791** (t)Courtesy, National Museum of the American Indian, Smithsonian Institution (20/6563). Photo by Carmelo Guadagno., (c)National Portrait Gallery/Smithsonian Insitiution/Art Resource, NY, (b)Yale Collection of Western Americana, Beinecke Rare Book & Manuscript Library; **792** Underwood Archives/Index Stock Imagery; **793** Getty Images; **794** (t)Franklin D. Roosevelt Library, (b)Library of Congress; **795** (t)National Archives, (b)US Army; **796** (t)Robert Reiff/MagicLight Productions, (b)Flip Schulke/Black Star; **797** (t)Mike Segar/Reuters/TimePix, (b)Thomas E. Franklin/Bergen Record/SABA/CORBIS; **798** Bettmann/CORBIS; **799** Underwood & Underwood/CORBIS; **800** Library of Congress; **801** Charles Moore/Black Star; **802** (t)AP/Wide World Photos, (b)Collection of David J. & Janice L. Frent; **804** (t)CORBIS, (c)A.J. SISCO/CORBIS, (b)Bruce Kliewe/Index Stock; **806** (t)Library of Congress; **807** Detroit Publishing Company; **808** Rob Lewine/The Stock Market; **809** (t)Swim Ink/CORBIS, (b)US Air Force Museum; **810** (t)Bettmann/CORBIS, (b)Getty Images; **812** Christie's Images; **813** Getty Images; **814** Official Senate Photo/CNP/Getty Images; **816** (t)Schlesinger Library, Radcliffe Institute, Harvard University, (b)Joe Raedle/Newsmakers; **817** (l)Bob Daemmrich, (r)AP/Wide World Photos; **818** (t)Tony Freeman/PhotoEdit, (b)James Shaffer/PhotoEdit; **819** Royalty Free/CORBIS; **820** (tl)Picture Research Consultants, (tr)Peter Turnley/CORBIS, (tcr)file photo, (cl)SuperStock, (cr bcl)Getty (bcr)Brown Brothers, (br)Courtesy Smithsonian Institution, NMAH/Transportation; **823** MAK I; **824** Maritime Museum, Seville/Artephot/Oronoz; **826** file photo; **828** White House Historical Association; **830** National Archives; **831 832** Bettmann/CORBIS; **833** Geoffrey Clements/CORBIS; **834** Library of Congress; **835** US Army Military History Institute; **836** Choctaw Removal, 1966. Valjean McCarty Hessing, Choctaw, B. 1934. Watercolor on paper, Museum purchase, The Philbrook Museum of Art, Tulsa, Oklahoma., 1967.24; **837** The Museum of American Political Life, University of Hartford; **838** Tim Flach/Getty Images, (l)North Wind Picture Archives, (r)Electricity Collections, National Museum of American History, Smithsonian Institution; **840 841 842 843** White House Historical Association; **844** (br)Official White House Photo by Eric Draper, (bcr)White House Historical Association (White House Collection, 6196), (others)White House Historical Association; **845** (bkgd)Getty Images, (tl)CORBIS; **846** Missouri Historical Society, St. Louis; **847 848** Bettmann/CORBIS; **850** North Wind Picture Archive; **851 852** Bettmann/CORBIS; **853** (t)Bettmann/CORBIS, (b)Courtesy, National Museum of the American Indian, Smithsonian Institution (20/1843). Photo by Carmelo Guadagno.; **854** National Portrait Gallery, Smithsonian Institution/Art Resource, NY; **855** (t)National Portrait Gallery, Smithsonian Institution/Art Resource, NY, (b)Mark Burnett; **856** (l)file photo, (r)Mark Burnett; **857** (t)Denver Art Museum, (b)Bettmann/CORBIS; **859** UPI/Bettmann/CORBIS; **860** Bettmann/CORBIS; **861** Flip Schulke/Black Star.